T0202878

Lecture Notes in Computer Science   13832

Founding Editors

Gerhard Goos
Juris Hartmanis

Editorial Board Members

The series Lecture Notes in Computer Science (LNCS), including its subseries Lecture Notes in Artificial Intelligence (LNAI) and Lecture Notes in Bioinformatics (LNBI), has established itself as a medium for the publication of new developments in computer science and information technology research, teaching, and education.

LNCS enjoys close cooperation with the computer science R & D community, the series counts many renowned academics among its volume editors and paper authors, and collaborates with prestigious societies. Its mission is to serve this international community by providing an invaluable service, mainly focused on the publication of conference and workshop proceedings and postproceedings. LNCS commenced publication in 1973.

Alexander Meschtscherjakov · Cees Midden ·
Jaap Ham
Editors

Persuasive Technology

18th International Conference, PERSUASIVE 2023
Eindhoven, The Netherlands, April 19–21, 2023
Proceedings

 Springer

Editors
Alexander Meschtscherjakov 🆔
University of Salzburg
Salzburg, Austria

Cees Midden 🆔
Eindhoven University of Technology
Eindhoven, The Netherlands

Jaap Ham 🆔
Eindhoven University of Technology
Eindhoven, The Netherlands

ISSN 0302-9743   ISSN 1611-3349 (electronic)
Lecture Notes in Computer Science
ISBN 978-3-031-30932-8   ISBN 978-3-031-30933-5 (eBook)
https://doi.org/10.1007/978-3-031-30933-5

Preface

As technology continues to permeate people's daily lives, the ability to alter human behavior and attitudes through its use becomes critical in addressing societal and personal challenges. Therefore, investigating the potential for technology to influence human behavior, attitudes, and information processing is crucial.

The interdisciplinary research field of persuasive technology centers on designing, developing, and assessing technologies that seek to influence individuals' attitudes and behaviors through informed persuasion, without resorting to coercion or deception. Researchers aim to enhance people's lives in domains such as health, sustainability, education, and well-being by facilitating the setting and attainment of their self-determined goals, resulting in behavior change.

The PERSUASIVE conference series is the leading venue to meet and discuss cutting-edge theoretical, methodological, and technical perspectives and to present recent insights from research and development. The conference provides a venue for networking between researchers and practitioners from all corners of the world. These researchers have very diverse scientific backgrounds, ranging from engineering, computer science, human-computer interaction, design, psychology, ethics, communication, and many other specializations.

The 2023 conference was hosted by Eindhoven University of Technology. It was the first purely onsite conference after three editions of online conferences due to the COVID-19 pandemic. Previous editions of the conference have been successfully organized in Doha (2022, online due to COVID-19), Bournemouth (2021, online due to COVID-19), Aalborg (2020, online due to COVID-19), Limassol (2019), Waterloo (2018), Amsterdam (2017), Salzburg (2016), Chicago (2015), Padua (2014), Sydney (2013), Linköping (2012), Columbus (2011), Copenhagen (2010), Claremont (2009), Oulu (2008), Palo Alto (2007), and Eindhoven (2006). Thus, after 17 years it returned to its place of origin.

PERSUASIVE 2023 invited the following categories of papers:

- Technical papers that introduce novel persuasive technology approaches and solutions alongside evidence of their potential.
- Empirical studies which seek to provide evidence and explanation of methods, principles, and theories in persuasive systems.
- Conceptual-theoretical papers which primarily seek to contribute to the general understanding of the field's core themes and specificities.
- Other papers, e.g., literature reviews or experience reports.

In addition, submissions to the following special tracks were welcomed:

- Sensor-based Persuasive Technology – Future Wearable Technologies (promoted by Marwa Qaraqe and Qammer H. Abbasi).
- Persuasive Technologies and Virtual Reality (promoted by Isaac Wiafe and Jaap Ham).

- Persuasive Social Robots (promoted by Emilia Barakova, Goldie Nejat, JongSuk Choi, and Kazuhiro Nakadai).

This volume contains the accepted short and long papers presented during the main track of the conference. In total, 68 papers were submitted of which 57 were long papers (up to 12 pages) and 11 were short papers (up to 6 pages) by 197 authors from 25 countries around the globe. The top five countries with respect to authors were: The Netherlands (33), the USA (23), Austria (18), Canada (17), and Japan (15).

The submitted papers were reviewed by the Program Committee in a double-blind review process conducted in EasyChair. Overall, 78 reviewers (all experts in the field of Persuasive Technology) from 20 countries were assigned to review the papers. Reviewers were allowed to indicate their interest in specific (anonymized) papers in a bidding procedure. On the basis of these preferences, and using additional random assignment and excluding conflicts of interest, at least three reviewers evaluated each manuscript. The three detailed and constructive reviews provided the program chairs with significant insights concerning the individual submissions but also ensured that the authors were provided with high-quality feedback and recommendations for the final versions of their papers. Building on these detailed reviews and numerical rankings, the Program Committee chairs selected the papers to be presented at the conference, and to be published in this volume.

From the 68 submitted papers 26 were accepted, (24 long papers and 2 short papers), leading to an overall acceptance rate of 38,24%. Authors for these 26 papers came from 14 countries: The Netherlands, the USA, Austria, Canada, Japan, the UK, Italy, Australia, China, Switzerland, Ghana, Denmark, Qatar, and Israel.

The 18th International Conference on Persuasive Technology (PERSUASIVE 2023) was hosted by Eindhoven University of Technology, April 19-21, 2023.

During the conference a doctoral consortium and eight workshops took place:

- 11th International Workshop on Behavior Change Support Systems
- Personalizing Persuasive Technologies Workshop 2023
- Persuasive AI Workshop
- How can Persuasive Technologies be (Ethically) Repurposed for Digital Well-Being?
- Using Serious Games to Support Inclusivity and Accessibility in the Mobility Sector
- 2nd International Workshop on Digital Nudging and Digital Persuasion
- AI Methods for Health Behavior Change
- Visual Interfaces and Interactions for AI-based Persuasive Systems

The main program consisted of 26 papers presented in seven single-track sessions. Furthermore, the program included two keynotes, as well as a poster session and a panel session. The keynotes were given by:

- Luca Chittaro, Director of the Human-Computer Interaction Lab, Dept of Mathematics, Computer Science, and Physics; University of Udine, Italy: *"Designing Virtual Reality and Serious Game Experiences for a Safer World"*
- Astrid Rosenthal-von der Pütten, Director of Individual and Technology (iTec) Group, Dept of Society, Technology, and Human Factors; RWTH Aachen University, Germany: *"The Complexity of Social Influence by Artificial Agents – How Intended Social Influence Can Bring About Unintended Effects (… and new research ideas)"*

In addition to the papers presented in this volume, the conference also published adjunct proceedings, which include abstracts of the keynote talks, the abstracts of accepted poster submissions, the accepted position papers submitted to the doctoral consortium, as well as contributions to the workshops.

The success of this conference is attributable to the dedicated efforts of a vast number of individuals. We extend our heartfelt appreciation to the authors for submitting their exceptional work, the reviewers for their insightful and detailed feedback, and the scientific and organizational chairs for their hard work in making this conference a valuable contribution to scientific knowledge and the Persuasive Technology research and practice community.

March 2023   Alexander Meschtscherjakov
                                                      Cees Midden
                                                      Jaap Ham

Organization

General Chair

Jaap Ham   Eindhoven University of Technology,
The Netherlands

Program Chairs

Alexander Meschtscherjakov   Salzburg University, Austria
Cees Midden   Eindhoven University of Technology,
The Netherlands

Poster Track Chairs

Khin Than Win   University of Wollongong, Australia
Uwe Matzat   Eindhoven University of Technology,
The Netherlands

Workshops and Tutorial Chairs

Sandra Gram-Hansen   Aalborg University, Denmark
Nilufar Baghaei   University of Queensland, Australia

Local Chair

Peter Ruijten   Eindhoven University of Technology,
The Netherlands

Doctoral Consortium Chairs

Harri Oinas-Kukkonen   Oulu University, Finland
Lisette van Gemert   Twente University of Technology,
The Netherlands

Web and Publicity Chairs

Felix Koranteng   Eindhoven University of Technology,
                                    The Netherlands
Khansa Chemnad   Hamad Bin Khalifa University, Qatar

Volunteer Coordination Chair

Sherry Ma   Eindhoven University of Technology,
                                    The Netherlands

Steering Committee

Raian Ali   Hamad Bin Khalifa University, Qatar
Nilufar Baghaei   University of Queensland, Australia
Sandra Burri Gram-Hansen   Aalborg University, Denmark
Alexander Meschtscherjakov   University of Salzburg, Austria
Rita Orji   Dalhousie University, Canada
Lisette van Gemert-Pijnen   University of Twente, The Netherlands
Khin Than Win   University of Wollongong, Australia

Program Committee

Ifeoma Adaji   University of Saskatchewan, Canada
Eunice Eno Yaa F. Agyei   University of Oulu, Finland
Dena Al-Thani   Hamad Bin Khalifa University, Qatar
Aftab Alam   Hamad Bin Khalifa University, Qatar
Mona Alhasani   Dalhousie University, Canada
Raian Ali   Hamad Bin Khalifa University, Qatar
Mohamed Basel   Almourad Zayed University, UAE
Amen Alrobai   King Abdulaziz University, Saudi Arabia
Emily Arden-Close   Bournemouth University, UK
Santosh Basapur   IIT Institute of Design, USA
Andrea Bertolini   Sant'Anna School of Advanced Studies, Italy
Robert Biddle   Carleton University, Canada
Rachel Blagojevic   Massey University, New Zealand
Anne-Gwenn Bosser   Lab-STICC, ENIB, France
Dimitrios Buhalis   Bournemouth University, UK
Barbara Caci   University of Palermo, Italy

Kiemute Oyibo	University of Saskatchewan, Canada
Keith Phalp	Bournemouth University, UK
Daniel Playne	Massey University, New Zealand
Marwa Qaraqe	Hamad Bin Khalifa University, Qatar
Dennis Reidsma	University of Twente, The Netherlands
Andreas Riener	Ingolstadt University of Applied Sciences, Germany
Peter Ruijten	Eindhoven University of Technology, The Netherlands
Stefan Schiffer	RWTH Aachen, Germany
Johann Schrammel	Austrian Institute of Technology, Austria
Zubair Shah	Hamad Bin Khalifa University, Qatar
Hanne Spelt	Philips Research, The Netherlands
Nava Tintarev	University of Maastricht, The Netherlands
Thomas Tran	University of Ottawa, Canada
Manfred Tscheligi	University of Salzburg, Austria
Robby van Delden	University of Twente, The Netherlands
Lisette van Gemert-Pijnen	University of Twente, The Netherlands
Julita Vassileva	University of Saskatchewan, Canada
Isaac Wiafe	University of Ghana, Ghana
Khin Than Win	University of Wollongong, Australia
Burkhard Wuensche	University of Auckland, New Zealand
Affan Yasin	Tsinghua University, China
Kyung-Hyan Yoo	William Paterson University, USA
Leah Zhang-Kennedy	University of Waterloo, Canada
Jürgen Ziegler	University of Duisburg-Essen, Germany

Sponsors

Human Technology Interaction group at Eindhoven University of Technology

Eindhoven Artificial Intelligence Systems Institute

Contents

Persuasive Design and Applications

Methods for Tailoring and Personalization

Artificial Persuasive Agents

xviii   Contents

Persuasive Technologies in Virtual and Augmented Reality

Sharing Speaker Heart Rate with the Audience Elicits Empathy and Increases Persuasion

Prasanth Murali$^{(\boxtimes)}$ ⓘ and Timothy Bickmore ⓘ

Khoury College of Computer Sciences, Northeastern University, Boston, MA, USA
{murali.pr,t.bickmore}@northeastern.edu

Abstract. Persuasion is a primary goal of public speaking, and eliciting audience empathy increases persuasion. In this research, we explore sharing a speaker's heart rate as a social cue, to elicit empathy and increase persuasion in the audience. In particular, we developed two interfaces embedding the speaker's heart rate over a recorded presentation video - as an animated line graph (raw representation) and as a color coded channel (abstract representation). In a randomized, counter-balanced, within subjects study (n = 18), we evaluated the concept using the two interfaces along with a baseline no heart rate condition. We observed that heart rate sharing significantly increased persuasion for participants with normal baseline empathy levels and increased empathic accuracy for all participants. Our qualitative analysis showed that heart rate was a useful cue in highlighting the emotions of the speaker, making the participants empathize with the speaker and pay more attention to the talk during those times. Our findings lead to a discussion of using heart rate as a social signal in a persuasive context, with implications for future research.

Keywords: Heart Rate · Empathy · Persuasion · Social Biofeedback

1 Introduction

Public speaking is a necessity in most jobs including teaching [1], management [84], and sales [67,91], and a large component of it is persuasive - to get an audience to buy into the speaker's beliefs, thoughts, and intentions [15,33]. Speakers tend to use a variety of persuasive tactics such as humor in speech [12,82], relevant nonverbal behaviors and facial expressions [66,75], eye contact with the audience [11,25], and appropriate voice tone [75] in order to persuade their audience. In addition, eliciting empathy and emotional appeal from the audience is a core tenet of persuasive public speaking [12,88]. Studies on communication have identified that evoking empathy with the audience is a strong predictor of how persuasive the speaker's messaging can be [56,73,80]. Furthermore, researchers have identified that narrative styles that appeal to an audience's

J. Ham et al. (Eds.): PERSUASIVE 2023, LNCS 13832, pp. 3–21, 2023.
https://doi.org/10.1007/978-3-031-30933-5_1

emotions complemented by credible information can make presentations more compelling [4, 21]. Persuasive messages that evoke empathy have also been shown to be more successful not only in public speaking but in several other domains, such as health behavior change [7, 78, 79], politics [96], risk communication [14], and marketing [35, 56]. Within public speaking, eliciting audience empathy can not only lead to better persuasion and thus a more positive experience for the speaker, but also, empathic audiences tend to be more engaged and entertained, elevating their own experience as well [5, 37, 60, 61].

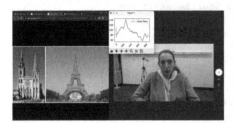 

Fig. 1. Embedded Heart Rate on the video recording of a presentation. We developed two versions, Heart Rate as a Line Graph (left) and as a Color Coded Channel (right).

In our work, we leverage research on social biofeedback systems to elicit audience empathy. Social biofeedback systems facilitate interpersonal communication, integrating biosignals such as heart rate into the communication context [68]. These *expressive biosignals* [58], augment human-human communication in a variety of contexts such as increasing intimacy among romantic couples [59, 81, 94], affinity towards strangers [28, 47, 76], and engagement towards sports participants [18, 47]. Furthermore, research also shows that social biofeedback is a viable design strategy that should be adopted to enhance technologically mediated empathy [13, 19, 53, 58, 59, 68, 95, 100]. Finally, social biofeedback is also framed as a form of emotional self-disclosure [52, 81, 87], which is found to mediate authenticity [26], liking [46, 57], and trust [78] in other humans - all key facets of persuasion. With that inspiration, we explored and evaluated the effects of embedding a speaker's heart rate on a recorded presentation and its impact on audience empathy and persuasion. While the overarching goal of the research is to support the elicitation of empathy and persuasion in synchronous speaker audience scenarios, we used an asynchronous (recorded) presentation video of the speaker to test the concept. Recorded settings that incorporate physiological signals such as heart rate offer reminders to be mindful of each other's emotional states without getting invested in the person's well-being [42, 62, 74, 77, 89], thereby offering an ideal platform to evaluate our concept. In our study, the speaker gave talks on France/Italy/Spain in order to convince an audience to take a trip to those countries. Thus, we measured persuasion as the willingness displayed by the audience to visit those countries [56], after listening to the speaker's talk. To the best of our knowledge, this is the first system to explore the sharing of speaker's heart rate to elicit empathy and improve persuasion of the audience in a presentation setting.

2 Related Work

Using Social Biofeedback to Elicit Empathy

One focus of our review was on identifying ways to elicit audience empathy towards the speaker. Recent works at the convergence of physiological, affective, and social computing research (*"social biofeedback"*) have used physiological signals as social cues about someone's emotional and/or cognitive states to augment human-human communication and promote empathy [58,68]. The design of these systems centers around sharing biosignals such as heart rate [2,36,38,45,95], breathing patterns [16], electrodermal activity ("EDA") [19], etc., to communicate the emotional experiences of one user to another. The Social Biofeedback Interactions framework categorizes these systems in terms of user group (primary/secondary), data flow (who has access to the feedback), data representation (collective/individual), temporal context (synchronous/asynchronous), and physical context (distributed/co-located) [68]. In relation to that framework, our work falls at the intersection of secondary user, uni-directional data flow, individual data representation, asynchronous temporal context, and distributed physical context dimensions. Within that niche, the authors of HeartChat [36] show that embedding heart rate in a text messaging platform supports empathy between people. In direct relevance to our work informing one of our conditions, they identify that abstracting heart rate as a color-coded signal helped infer the emotional state of the other person. In addition, our work is also informed by Curran et al. on mediating empathy [19] in digital contexts. In that research, the authors were successful in eliciting cognitive empathy (i.e., one's capacity to understand another's emotional state) towards someone else, as opposed to affective empathy (that relate to one's ability to respond to another's emotional state) [8,22,30,55] through EDA signal sharing. We contribute further to this growing body of work [19,36,53,58,59,95], by sharing speaker heart rate in the context of recorded presentations, with the goal of eliciting audience's cognitive empathy and consequently persuasion towards the speaker's message.

Designing a Persuasive System

Our review of the related work in the persuasive technology space focuses on strategies and best practices to design persuasive systems. Typical strategies draw from behavior change theories [34] in conjunction with Fogg's seminal work in this space [29], as best practices for developing persuasive technologies. Broadly, out of the 8 principles listed by Fogg, the following are directly relevant to our current study: (1)choose a familiar technology channel (video presentations), (2)imitate successful examples (recent developments on social biofeedback systems), (3)test and iterate quickly (prototype and evaluate), and (4)expand on success (share findings with the scientific community). While a common criticism of this model is the lack of description of direct software requirements [3], we looked into a follow up work by Oinas-Kukkonen et al. [72], who postulated seven key directions as a lens to view the design of persuasive systems. Of relevance to our work are that persuasive systems should be: (1)open, (2)unobtrusive, (3)useful, and (4)easy-to-use. These dimensions lend themselves to Weiser's notion of calm technologies [92,93] that technologies that minimize software attentional requirements lend to better usability. Our takeaway from the review so far was thus two fold: a) heart rate should be visualized in an easily interpretable form imposing less cognitive load on the audience. b) the placement of the heart rate within the interface should be unobtrusive to the primary goal of the audience, viz., listening to the speaker. Finally, we also reviewed Berdichevsky and Neuenschwander [6] as well as other recent work on introducing ethical guidelines for the design of modern day persuasive systems [43,48], to additionally contribute to this space by extracting design guidelines on facilitating heart rate sharing in persuasive scenarios. Through our findings, we highlight a need for privacy, disclosure, training, accuracy, and cognitive load for leveraging heart rate sharing as a persuasive technology.

3   System Design

For this formative study, we chose an animated line graph (raw representation + persistent) and a color coded channel (abstract representation + ephemeral) as two different representations of heart rate (Fig. 1). The "raw" representation of someone's heart rate in the form of a line graph [36,59] has been observed to help relate to emotional experience of other contextually over time due to its persistent nature, whereas an "abstract" heart rate representation is ephemeral, and has shown to provide a degree of ambiguity to make subjective interpretations, both concepts finding utility in different scenarios [19]. While we acknowledge that the design space of representing heart rate is vast, choosing effective proxies from prior work for formative acceptance studies is argued as a good method when prototyping a novel technology in HCI [40,50].

Heart Rate as an Animated Line Graph Condition: For generating the heart rate as an animated line graph ("Line Graph Condition") superimposed on the video, we adopted the same approach followed by Curran et al. [19], in their research. The heart rate was derived from the blood volume pulse data [85], and then resampled 1 Hz. We then used Matplotlib's[1] animation class to plot and overlay the heart rate graph on the frames of the recorded presentation video in the periphery, as shown in Fig. 1 - Left. The HR data then populates the graph in real-time as the video plays.

Heart Rate as a Color Coded Condition: The color coded representation ("Color Coded Condition") presents heart rate as an ambient circle, that continuously changes color 1 Hz using information from the heart rate file. We mapped

---

[1] https://matplotlib.org/.

the heart rate to the HSV^2 color space, in the green to red range, closely following previous research [36]. The color coding ranged from minimum to maximum heart rate of the person. We again used Matplotlib to generate the color coded plot, and overlayed this on the frames of the presentation video in the periphery, as shown in Fig. 1 - Right.

No Heart Rate Condition: This condition had no heart rate ("No HR") information embedded in the video.

4   Evaluation Study

To investigate the empathic and persuasive effects of sharing speaker heart rate with an audience, we conducted an evaluation study, closely matching the approach in [19]. The study was split into two phases. In the first phase, we gathered stimulus videos and synchronous heart rate data from a speaker (90 min session). In the second phase, we showed this stimulus to audience participants as they simultaneously completed an empathic accuracy task, followed by surveys, and semi-structured interviews (60 min session). The overall study protocol was approved by the institution's review board, and participants were compensated for their time. The participants for both phases of this study were recruited via online advertisements. They were required to be at least 18 years old, read and speak English, and have some experience presenting. Upon their scheduled visits to the lab, we first obtained informed consent from the participants and they completed the following surveys: baseline demographics and the Toronto Empathy Questionnaire ("TEQ") [83].

Phase 1: Collecting Speaker Stimulus Videos
After completing the baseline measures, the speaker was instructed to give three presentations with the aim of convincing their audience to take a trip to France, Italy, and Spain. To facilitate this, we provided a template of nine slides containing information on the geography, things to do, art and architecture, music and cinema, food, and travel costs to visit each of those countries for a week. The speaker was then given 10 min to prepare and 10 min to present an online talk in front of a neutral confederate audience, in line with other studies on assessing novel presentation technologies [69,70]. The presentation was videotaped. The speaker also wore the Empatica E4 sensor[3], to collect their heart rate during the talk. After the presentation, its recording was retrieved and subsequently played back for the speaker on a computer. While watching the playback, the speaker was asked to perform a retrospective review of the presentation ("recall task"), and record their affect levels, using a continuous affect rating application [31], in line with previous studies on affect data collection using retrospective review techniques [49,64,97]. Ratings were annotated every second on a scale

---

[2] https://en.wikipedia.org/wiki/HSL_and_HSV.
[3] https://www.empatica.com/research/e4/.

of -10 (Negative Affect) to 10 (Positive Affect). To get them accustomed to the interface, speakers completed a similar task on a 3-minute practice video, and were given a chance to clarify any questions. Next, the speaker rated the level of difficulty and their confidence in their retrospective review task using a two item seven point Likert scale [19]. The entire process was then repeated for the other two presentations.

Phase 2: Assessment of Stimulus Videos by the Audience
After completing the baseline measures, participants were briefed on the study. Every audience participant watched all three presentations on France, Spain, and Italy. For each of the participants, one of the presentations was randomly assigned to have the speaker heart rate as an animated line graph, the other had the speaker heart rate as a color coded channel, and the last presentation had no heart rate. The order of presentations was also randomized and counter balanced across all the subjects.

Next, participants were assigned to watch their first presentation and simultaneous review the affect of the speaker. Although the task requires the audience to both watch the video for the first time and parse the speaker's affect together, this methodology is consistent with other studies that seek to assess the empathic accuracy of an observer towards a target [19,101]. The task was similar to the recall task performed by the speaker. However, as opposed to rating their own affect, audience participants were asked to rate how they thought the speaker was feeling on the same -10 to 10 affect scale continuously throughout the video. Participants also received short verbal instructions describing the task. The description consisted of the topic (France/Spain/Italy), reminder of the affective rating task, heart rate (if present), and modality of heart rate (line graph/color coded). Next, audience participants did a practice task, to get familiar with the interface for affective rating. Following the completion of this empathic accuracy task while watching the presentation, audience participants were asked to complete surveys on the level of difficulty and their confidence in their rating task [19], and were additionally assessed on the following measures:

- *Persuasion*: Adapted from the Empathy, Persuasion, Travel Willingness, and Tourism Cognition constructs for an individual's overall impression or attitude towards traveling to a specific location [56], items shown in Table 3.
- *Affective benefits and costs of the presentation interface*: The survey measures the benefits and costs of interfaces from an affective standpoint on Emotion Expression, Engagement, Presence, Opportunity for Social Support, Unmet Expectations, Unwanted Obligations, and Threat to Privacy ("ABCCT"), as shown in Table 2 [98].
- *State Empathy*: two item seven point Likert scale about the ability to assess the audience empathy towards the speaker, shown in Table 1 [19,23].

Next, the audience were asked to participate in a semi-structured interview. Finally, the entire process was then repeated for the other two presentations (Fig. 2).

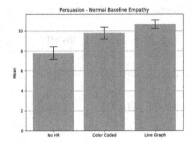

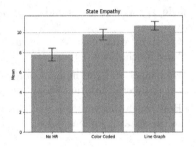

Fig. 2. Persuasion Scores for Individuals with Normal Baseline Empathy

Fig. 3. State Empathy Across Conditions

5 Results

To analyze the data, we followed a mixed-methods approach. The self-reports and affective ratings from the recall task were used as the data for quantitative analysis. The recorded semi-structured interviews across all subjects(3.5 h of audio data) were transcribed and the lead author of this submission open-coded the audience responses for qualitative analysis [9,39], using the NVivo 12 software[4].

Participants: We recruited one speaker ("S") and 18 audience ("A") participants for the study. The speaker was not intended to be representative of the population but rather an example to generate stimulus for our study. The speaker was 25 years old, identified as female, and expressed normal empathy levels (TEQ = 42). They had a suitable range in heart rate data (60 bpm–110 bpm) with meaningful variations and was hence an appropriate fit for the experiment. Among the audience, 10 participants identified as male and eight participants identified as a female. The participant group had a mean age of 29 years (min = 21, max = 40). Of the 18 participants, 14 displayed normal empathy levels (TEQ: 40–48) and four displayed high empathy levels (TEQ: 55+), based on a median split, as measured by the Toronto Empathy Scale [83]. Research has shown that the level of empathizing displayed by individuals may differ depending on their original trait empathy [71]. Thus, the inclusion of both normal and high empathy participants enabled us to disentangle the effects of prior empathy on our measures. Our participants also had varying presentation experience and backgrounds ranging from students of biology to software professionals.

---

[4] https://www.qsrinternational.com/nvivo-qualitative-data-analysis-software/home.

Table 1. Average and standard deviation for the items in State Empathy Survey

Question with anchors (Not at all - Very much, Scale 1 to 7)	Line Graph	Color Coded	No HR
How much did you imagine yourself in the speaker's situation today?	**5.57(0.2)**	5.33(0.28)	4.67(0.63)
How much did you feel as if you were in the speaker's shoes today?	**6.31(0.41)**	5.30(0.31)	4.67(0.67)

Table 2. Average and standard deviation for the ABCCT Measure

Question with anchors (Totally Disagree - Totally Agree, Scale 1 to 7)	Line Graph	Color Coded	No HR
The software helps me tell how the speaker is feeling.	**4.30(1.21)**	3.35(1.37)	2.93(1.38)
I am excited about using the software.	**3.78(0.81)**	**3.78(0.94)**	3.56(0.85)
I have fun while using the software.	**3.44(0.85)**	**3.56(0.85)**	3.33(1.08)
The software helps me feel closer to the speaker.	**3.22(0.85)**	3.19(0.81)	3.11(0.75)
I still keep thinking back to something the speaker shared using the software.	**3.67(1.08)**	3.11(1.23)	3.22(0.94)
The software helps me feel more connected to the speaker.	**3.78(1.26)**	**3.33(0.97)**	3.33(0.84)
I worry that I am violating the speaker's privacy when using the software	2.67(1.10)	**2.61(1.02)**	**2.11(1.23)**

Impact of Heart Rate Sharing on Audience Empathy: We used empathic accuracy (the ability to read others' emotions [41]), to assess how well the audience gauged the speaker's emotions. In order to assess the differences between the conditions (Line Graph vs Color Coded vs No HR) on empathic accuracy, we used the Pearson's Correlation Tests. The correlation was computed between the time series data of the speaker's retrospective review of their affect and the audience's review of the speaker's affect. The average correlation values across all the participants for the No HR condition was 0.34 ± 0.16 ($p < 0.05$), for Line Graph condition was 0.52 ± 0.23 ($p < 0.05$), and for the Color Coded condition was 0.55 ± 0.29 ($p < 0.05$). In addition, there were also significant differences among the three conditions on speaker-audience HR correlations assessed via a one-way ANOVA, $F(2, 51) = 5.71$, $p = 0.01$. Followup posthoc comparisons showed a significant difference between the Line Graph and No HR conditions $t(34) = 4.81, p = 0.03$, as well as Color Coded and No HR conditions $t(34) = 4.53$, $p = 0.04$. No significant difference on empathic accuracy was found between the Line Graph and Color Coded conditions $t(34) = 2.65$, $p = 0.16$. Further, our analysis of the composite state empathy data (Table 1) (Cronbach's $\alpha = 0.85$)

Table 3. Average and standard deviation for the items in Persuasion Measure

Question with anchors (Totally Disagree - Totally Agree, Scale 1 to 7)	Line Graph	Color Coded	No HR
The speaker was persuasive in convincing me to go to the place .	**5.33(1.28)**	5.00(0.68)	4.56(1.38)
I feel that the information conveyed about the place is true.	6.22(0.94)	**6.33(0.84)**	6.22(0.94)
I trust the information being conveyed about the place.	**6.22(0.64)**	6.11(0.75)	5.11(0.90)
I'd like to pay a visit to the place.	**6.22(0.64)**	6.11(1.23)	5.33(1.18)
I will prioritize the place as my next travel destination.	**5.33(1.08)**	4.89(1.49)	4.11(1.23)
Watching this presentation has affected my intention to visit the place in a positive way.	5.73(1.16)	**5.77(1.06)**	5.11(1.49)
The place has become a travel destination I would like to visit.	5.00(1.18)	**5.55(1.19)**	5.22(1.66)
If I have enough budget, I will visit the place	6.22(0.65)	**6.44(0.70)**	5.44(1.19)

using Paired Wilcoxon signed-rank tests showed that participants significantly rated the Line Graph and Color Coded conditions significantly higher (Fig. 3) than the No HR condition (Z = 2.40, p = 0.008; Z = 2.70, p = 0.006).

These findings were further supported by qualitative feedback, where audience participants reported that having access to the heart rate helped achieve *"empathic connection"*[A2] with the speaker. For instance, participant [A11] felt that they could *"put themselves in the shoes of the speaker"*, especially when the *"speaker's heart rate was rising"*, *"because I've [they have] certainly been in presentations where I've [they have] been nervous"*. Other participants mentioned that they can *"feel it [speaker's stress] themselves"* [A14], and that *"could relate to the speaker's emotions as she was presenting"*, whenever a *"noticeable change in heart rate occurred"* [A6]. On being asked to compare the two heart rate conditions, participants felt that the line graph *"helped contextualize and connect with the speaker emotion as a whole over time"* [A12], both when the *"speaker was displaying positive emotions such as excitement as well as negative emotions such as stress"* [A15]. On the other hand, the Color Coded condition *"was more impulsive and made them empathize with the speaker during moments of stress but they just moved on when the color changed to green [lower heart rate]"* [A7].

Impact of Heart Rate Sharing on Persuasion: Persuasion was measured as a composite score (Cronbach's $\alpha = 0.72$) of item ratings from Table 3. Since the core message of the presentation was to convince an audience to travel to France/Italy/Spain, we measured persuasion by the willingness displayed by the audience to visit those countries after listening to the speaker's talk. The measure was adapted from Li and Liu's work [56] on investigating the effects of empathic tourism videos on tourists' persuasion to travel. There was a significant interaction effect of condition (Line Graph vs Color Coded vs No HR) and baseline empathy levels (Normal vs High), on persuasion: $F(2,51) = 5.22$, $p = 0.02$. Consequently, we performed Paired Wilcoxon signed-rank tests with Bonferroni corrections to compare the pairs and observed that for participants with normal baseline empathy, significantly higher persuasion was reported (Fig. 3) for both the Line Graph and Color Coded video conditions as compared to the No HR video condition ($Z = -3.70, p = 0.03; Z = -3.56, p = 0.02$). No significant differences on persuasion was observed between the conditions for participants with high baseline empathy levels.

Our qualitative findings suggest that participants paid more attention to the presentation in the heart rate sharing conditions, possibly explaining the persuasion finding. For example, multiple participants reported that they *"paid more attention"*[A1] and *"stuck with the speaker"*[A9], even when the speaker did not say anything new. In addition, several participants mentioned that *"having an eye on the heart rate monitor like whenever it changes noticeably, made them put some extra focus on the talk"* [A13] and that *"they actively gathered information"* [A18], even when the speaker was disengaging.

System Perception and Use: Table 2 shows the average responses for the questions focused on the benefits and costs of each of the interfaces, as defined by ABCCT [98]. We conducted Paired Wilcoxon Signed-Rank tests on this composite data (Cronbach's $\alpha = 0.67$) with Bonferroni corrections, and observed that the Line Graph condition was rated significantly higher than both the Color Coded condition and No HR video ($Z = -3.52$, p = 0.02; Z = -3.46, p < 0.01) and the Color Coded condition was rated significantly higher than No HR video, on the question "the software helps me tell how the speaker is feeling" ($Z = 5.51$, p = 0.046). No other significant differences between the conditions were observed across for the other items.

In the qualitative interviews, participants described how representations of heart rate impacted their experience as the audience. Participants had a general idea of how heart rate could convey both excited and stressed emotional states, and *"used it with cautious effect"* during the empathic accuracy task. They also reported trusting the Line Graph condition more as compared to the Color Coded condition, because it helped them *"contextualize and interpret the meaning of heart rate in a more detailed manner"* and *"to reaffirm the understanding of the presenter's emotions."* Furthermore, this also translated in how they used the heart rate information for the empathic accuracy task: participants in the Line Graph condition used the heart rate *"in equal parts"*, *"keeping a close eye on when it spikes up or down"*, with other cues such as facial expressions and voice activity during the rating task. However, participants in the Color Coded condition mentioned using the heart rate as a *"secondary/supplementary signal"* to validate their original guess using the speaker's affect.

Furthermore, we identified several key considerations for the design and development of heart rate sharing in persuasive contexts.

Provide on Demand Control to Heart Rate: Participants were comfortable *"sharing their own heart rate in speaking scenarios"* [A8], but *"privacy concerns"* [A16] remain that could limit potential adoption of the technology. From a speaker's point of view, participants indicated that they wouldn't want the *"audience to be aware of their stress levels"* [A11], particularly *"in evaluative contexts"* [A3]. This also aligns with Goffman's work on self image [32] in everyday communication, which shows that adding heart rate as an additional social cue might create images of one self that is different than intended [81]. However, users ultimately tend to use the affordances offered by an interface to positively impact the receiver, finding a way around the concerns [90]. Thus, to best utilize the tool, we recommend providing both the speaker and audience with features to control sharing and accessing the heart rate information respectively, only on demand. This also lends itself to tackling the 'openness' dimension of Oinas-Kukkonen et al.'s [72] postulates as well as recent arguments for ethical deployment in affective [69] and persuasive systems [48].

Provide Training for Using the System: One way to further improve empathic accuracy would be to include a formal training where users learn the meaning of heart rate, it's relationship to affect, and how it applies to public speaking, prior to using the software. This was also echoed by a participant in that: *"If you have a really good understanding of how heart rate is correlated with how your neural thinking and your brain processing your information works, I feel it is a really good tool"* [A4]. This caters to Oinas-Kukkonen et al.'s [72] postulates of persuasive systems needing to be easy to use.

Design for Reducing Cognitive Load: While the two heart rate conditions shared similarities in other measures, a primary distinction was centered around the cognitive load imposed by them. Most participants agreed that the Color Coded Condition was *"mildly distracting"* [A5], and *"sometimes effortful to use"* [A11], whereas the attention for Line Graph Condition could be *"tuned in and out"* [A16]. Since heart rate data fluctuates sensitively and visualizing its changes in the form of a color can be quite distracting when watching a presentation, we recommend using general trends to represent it. This also makes the system unobstrusive, catering to another of Oinas-Kukkonen et al.'s [72] postulates while tapping into Weiser's notion of calm technologies [92,93].

6   Discussion

Firstly, our analysis showed that participants with normal baseline empathy levels reported significantly greater persuasion in the heart rate conditions. However, no effect on persuasion was found between the conditions for participants with high baseline empathy. We believe this can be explained by the multidimensional nature of empathic interventions, as has been previously demonstrated in research [20,44,95]. Similar to [17,63,71,86], we posit that participants with high baseline empathy were already sensitive to changes in the speaker's affect because of their close attention and focus on the speaker's facial expressions. Thus, the overall utilization of heart rate could have been low in this case. In contrast, participants with normal baseline empathy levels could have utilized the heart rate information more during the experiment. The higher utilization of heart rate by the participants with normal baseline empathy might explain our findings on persuasion for that group. For those participants that utilized the heart rate information, it is also possible to connect the findings on persuasion, in part, to self-disclosure effects. Heart rate sharing is a form of emotional self-disclosure [52,59,81,87], and studies have shown that self-disclosure mediates authenticity [26], liking [46,57], and trust [78], all constructs within our persuasion measure (Table 3), which could have increased the acceptance of the speaker's message by the audience in the heart rate conditions.

Secondly, participants in our study not only used heart rate for information about the speaker's emotions but also for connection with the speaker, similar to [81]. Research as also shown that self-disclosure can also increase feelings of connectedness with one another [45,52,54,59,99], potentially explaining our finding that heart rate sharing facilitated audience empathy towards the speaker. In addition, social sharing of heart rate has been observed to remind someone to consider and acknowledge both the presence and emotions of the other person [24,100]. Researchers have referred to this as "mind perception", and leveraged it to design systems that tune one's attention towards another's affective cues [19], shedding light on our findings around empathic accuracy.

Finally, our findings also indicated that participants used heart rate as a multidimensional construct to assess emotions - depending on the representation, the context where it occurred, and other cues such as facial expressions and voice tone. Changes in heart rate can have different meanings depending on any of these cues [10,27,51], and given its subjective nature, it is important to unpack the effects of these factors to aid design of future systems.

7   Limitations

Despite the positive results, there are several limitations to our study, beyond the small convenience samples used. We used just one speaker to generate the stimulus videos; different speakers have different emotional experiences that could be reflected by their heart rate, as well as persuasive capabilities unique to their style, which was not accounted for in the current experiment. We also had more participants with normal baseline empathy levels, which could have impacted our results. We also used an animated Line Graph as a proxy for the raw representation of heart rate and a color coded channel for the abstract representation of the heart rate, based on previous research. However, different designs of heart rate representation could yield different results, that need to be carefully examined and studied. We also used recorded, rather than live presentations, and the speaker and audience did not get to interact with each other as they would typically. We also used brief presentations on prepared topics and did not assess the longitudinal effects of viewing multiple presentations over time. Thus, our results may not generalize to real-world presentations.

8 Future Work

Future work should consider unpacking the various design dimensions that inform the development of a heart rate sharing application towards the goal of persuasion in presentation contexts. We also did not explore the audience having access to their own heart rate, in addition to the speaker's. Empathic accuracy in such symmetric systems might be higher since participants can contextualize a speaker's heart rate and their corresponding emotions by reflecting on their own heart rate and emotions. Furthermore, systems like CardioLens [65] demonstrate the potential of heart rate sharing in immersive Augmented Reality settings. Given the focus on immersive presentations in the recent times, embedding heart rate and seeing the effects on social-presence and co-presence of audience and the speaker in addition to empathy and persuasion presents another exciting opportunity for research. In addition, extending heart rate sharing to live online presentations could shed light on the synchronous interplay of emotions between a speaker and their audience. Moreover, it could also be interesting to observe the effects of heart rate sharing in other public speaking scenarios such as lectures and classes, where the focus might be more on the delivery of information than persuading an audience. The relationship between empathy and information retention in such scenarios could be interesting to investigate.

9 Conclusion

This work introduces the concept of sharing speaker heart rate with an audience in online presentations. Using two heart rate visualizations, in comparison to a baseline no heart rate video, we showed that heart rate sharing had potential benefits on eliciting audience empathy and persuasion. Our findings and design recommendations will help extend the possibilities of persuasive computer mediated interactions. Social biofeedback represents a promising approach for enhancing experiential outcomes for speakers and audiences in online presentations.

Acknowledgements. The authors would like to thank Hye Sun Yun, Teresa O'Leary, Vrindaa Somjit, and Yunus Terzioglu for providing initial feedback on the concept and reviewing the manuscript.

References

1. Ames, M.G., Go, J., Kaye, J., Spasojevic, M.: Making love in the network closet: the benefits and work of family videochat. In: Proceedings of the 2010 ACM Conference on Computer Supported Cooperative Work, pp. 145–154 (2010)

2. Aslan, I., Seiderer, A., Dang, C.T., Rädler, S., André, E.: Pihearts: resonating experiences of self and others enabled by a tangible somaesthetic design. In: Proceedings of the 2020 International Conference on Multimodal Interaction, pp. 433–441 (2020)
3. Atkinson, B.M.C.: Captology: a critical review. In: IJsselsteijn, W.A., de Kort, Y.A.W., Midden, C., Eggen, B., van den Hoven, E. (eds.) PERSUASIVE 2006. LNCS, vol. 3962, pp. 171–182. Springer, Heidelberg (2006). https://doi.org/10.1007/11755494_25
4. Baccarani, C., Bonfanti, A.: Effective public speaking: a conceptual framework in the corporate-communication field. Corp. Commun. Int. J. **20**(3), 375–390 (2015)
5. Bavelas, J.B., Black, A., Lemery, C.R., Mullett, J.: "i show how you feel": motor mimicry as a communicative act. J. Pers. Soc. Psychol. **50**(2), 322 (1986)
6. Berdichevsky, D., Neuenschwander, E.: Toward an ethics of persuasive technology. Commun. ACM **42**(5), 51–58 (1999)
7. Bickmore, T., Mauer, D., Crespo, F., Brown, T.: Persuasion, task interruption and health regimen adherence. In: de Kort, Y., IJsselsteijn, W., Midden, C., Eggen, B., Fogg, B.J. (eds.) PERSUASIVE 2007. LNCS, vol. 4744, pp. 1–11. Springer, Heidelberg (2007). https://doi.org/10.1007/978-3-540-77006-0_1
8. Borke, H.: Interpersonal perception of young children: egocentrism or empathy? Dev. Psychol. **5**(2), 263 (1971)
9. Braun, V., Clarke, V.: Using thematic analysis in psychology. Qual. Res. Psychol. **3**(2), 77–101 (2006)
10. Brosschot, J.F., Thayer, J.F.: Heart rate response is longer after negative emotions than after positive emotions. Int. J. Psychophysiol. **50**(3), 181–187 (2003)
11. Bull, R., Gibson-Robinson, E.: The influences of eye-gaze, style of dress, and locality on the amounts of money donated to a charity. Hum. Relat. **34**(10), 895–905 (1981)
12. Cacioppo, J.T., Petty, R.E.: The elaboration likelihood model of persuasion. ACR North American Advances (1984)
13. Calvo, R.A., Peters, D.: Positive Computing: Technology for Wellbeing and Human Potential. MIT press, Cambridge (2014)
14. Campbell, R.G., Babrow, A.S.: The role of empathy in responses to persuasive risk communication: overcoming resistance to hiv prevention messages. Health Commun. **16**(2), 159–182 (2004)
15. Carey, C.: Rhetorical means of persuasion. In: Persuasion: Greek Rhetoric in Action, pp. 38–57. Routledge (2002)
16. Cho, Y., Julier, S.J., Marquardt, N., Bianchi-Berthouze, N.: Robust tracking of respiratory rate in high-dynamic range scenes using mobile thermal imaging. Biomed. Optics Exp. **8**(10), 4480–4503 (2017)
17. Cowan, D.G., Vanman, E.J., Nielsen, M.: Motivated empathy: the mechanics of the empathic gaze. Cogn. Emot. **28**(8), 1522–1530 (2014)
18. Curmi, F., Ferrario, M.A., Southern, J., Whittle, J.: Heartlink: open broadcast of live biometric data to social networks. In: Proceedings of the SIGCHI Conference on Human Factors in Computing Systems, pp. 1749–1758 (2013)
19. Curran, M.T., Gordon, J.R., Lin, L., Sridhar, P.K., Chuang, J.: Understanding digitally-mediated empathy: an exploration of visual, narrative, and biosensory informational cues. In: Proceedings of the 2019 CHI Conference on Human Factors in Computing Systems, pp. 1–13 (2019)
20. Davis, M.H.: Empathy: A Social Psychological Approach. Routledge, Abingdon (2018)

21. Den Hartog, D.N., Verburg, R.M.: Charisma and rhetoric: communicative techniques of international business leaders. Leadersh. Q. **8**(4), 355–391 (1997)
22. Deutsch, F., Madle, R.A.: Empathy: historic and current conceptualizations, measurement, and a cognitive theoretical perspective. Human Dev. **18**(4), 267–287 (1975)
23. Devlin, H.C., Zaki, J., Ong, D.C., Gruber, J.: Not as good as you think? trait positive emotion is associated with increased self-reported empathy but decreased empathic performance. PloS One **9**(10), e110470 (2014)
24. Dey, A.K., de Guzman, E.: From awareness to connectedness: the design and deployment of presence displays. In: Proceedings of the SIGCHI Conference on Human Factors in Computing Systems, pp. 899–908 (2006)
25. Dillard, J.P., Pfau, M.: The Persuasion Handbook: Developments in Theory and Practice. Sage Publications, Thousand Oaks (2002)
26. Enli, G.: Mediated authenticity. Peter Lang Incorporated (2014)
27. Fairclough, S.H.: Fundamentals of physiological computing. Interact. Comput. **21**(1–2), 133–145 (2009)
28. Fajardo, N., Moere, A.V.: Externaleyes: evaluating the visual abstraction of human emotion on a public wearable display device. In: Proceedings of the 20th Australasian Conference on Computer-Human Interaction: Designing for Habitus and Habitat, pp. 247–250 (2008)
29. Fogg, B.J.: Creating persuasive technologies: an eight-step design process. In: Proceedings of the 4th International Conference on Persuasive Technology, pp. 1–6 (2009)
30. Gerdes, K.E., Segal, E.A., Lietz, C.A.: Conceptualising and measuring empathy. Brit. J. Social Work **40**(7), 2326–2343 (2010)
31. Girard, J.M.: Carma: software for continuous affect rating and media annotation. J. Open Res. Softw. **2**(1), e5 (2014)
32. Goffman, E.: The presentation of self in everyday life. Anchor (2021)
33. Haiman, F.S.: An experimental study of the effects of ethos in public speaking. Commun. Monogr. **16**(2), 190–202 (1949)
34. Harjumaa, M., Muuraiskangas, S.: Building persuasiveness into information systems. Electron. J. Inf. Syst. Eval. **17**(1), 23–35 (2014)
35. Harper, J.: Presentation skills. Industrial and Commercial Training (2004)
36. Hassib, M., Buschek, D., Wozniak, P.W., Alt, F.: Heartchat: heart rate augmented mobile chat to support empathy and awareness. In: Proceedings of the 2017 CHI Conference on Human Factors in Computing Systems, pp. 2239–2251 (2017)
37. Hatfield, E., Cacioppo, J.T., Rapson, R.L.: Emotional contagion. Curr. Direct. Psychol. Sci. **2**(3), 96–100 (1993)
38. Howell, N., Niemeyer, G., Ryokai, K.: Life-affirming biosensing in public: sounding heartbeats on a red bench. In: Proceedings of the 2019 CHI Conference on Human Factors in Computing Systems, pp. 1–16 (2019)
39. Hsieh, H.F., Shannon, S.E.: Three approaches to qualitative content analysis. Qual. Health Res. **15**(9), 1277–1288 (2005)
40. Hutchinson, H., et al.: Technology probes: inspiring design for and with families. In: Proceedings of the SIGCHI Conference on Human Factors in Computing Systems, pp. 17–24 (2003)
41. Ickes, W.J.: Empathic Accuracy. Guilford Press, New York (1997)
42. IJsselsteijn, W., van Baren, J., van Lanen, F.: Staying in touch: social presence and connectedness through synchronous and asynchronous communication media. Hum.-Comput. Interact.: Theory Pract. (Part II) **2**(924), e928 (2003)

43. Jalowski, M.: Using inspiration cards for designing persuasive technology to improve creative situations. In: Ali, R., Lugrin, B., Charles, F. (eds.) PERSUASIVE 2021. LNCS, vol. 12684, pp. 231–244. Springer, Cham (2021). https://doi.org/10.1007/978-3-030-79460-6_19

44. Janssen, J.H.: A three-component framework for empathic technologies to augment human interaction. J. Multimodal User Interfac. **6**(3), 143–161 (2012)

45. Janssen, J.H., Bailenson, J.N., Ijsselsteijn, W.A., Westerink, J.H.: Intimate heartbeats: opportunities for affective communication technology. IEEE Trans. Affect. Comput. **1**(2), 72–80 (2010)

46. Jiang, L.C., Bazarova, N.N., Hancock, J.T.: The disclosure-intimacy link in computer-mediated communication: an attributional extension of the hyperpersonal model. Human Commun. Res. **37**(1), 58–77 (2011)

47. Khot, R.A., Lee, J., Hjorth, L., Mueller, F.: Tastybeats: celebrating heart rate data with a drinkable spectacle. In: Proceedings of the Ninth International Conference on Tangible, Embedded, and Embodied Interaction, pp. 229–232 (2015)

48. Kight, R., Gram-Hansen, S.B.: Do ethics matter in persuasive technology? In: Oinas-Kukkonen, H., Win, K.T., Karapanos, E., Karppinen, P., Kyza, E. (eds.) PERSUASIVE 2019. LNCS, vol. 11433, pp. 143–155. Springer, Cham (2019). https://doi.org/10.1007/978-3-030-17287-9_12

49. Kimani, E., Bickmore, T., Picard, R., Goodwin, M., Jimison, H.: Real-time public speaking anxiety prediction model for oral presentations, pp. 30–35 (2022). https://doi.org/10.1145/3536220.3563686

50. Klasnja, P., Consolvo, S., Pratt, W.: How to evaluate technologies for health behavior change in hci research. In: Proceedings of the SIGCHI Conference on Human Factors in Computing Systems, pp. 3063–3072 (2011)

51. Kreibig, S.D.: Autonomic nervous system activity in emotion: a review. Biol. Psychol. **84**(3), 394–421 (2010)

52. Laurenceau, J.P., Rivera, L.M., Schaffer, A.R., Pietromonaco, P.R.: Intimacy as an interpersonal process: current status and future directions. In: Handbook of Closeness and Intimacy, pp. 71–88 (2004)

53. Lee, M., Kim, K., Rho, H., Kim, S.J.: Empa talk: a physiological data incorporated human-computer interactions. In: CHI 2014 Extended Abstracts on Human Factors in Computing Systems, pp. 1897–1902 (2014)

54. Lee, Y.C., Yamashita, N., Huang, Y., Fu, W.: "i hear you, i feel you": encouraging deep self-disclosure through a chatbot. In: Proceedings of the 2020 CHI Conference on Human Factors in Computing Systems, pp. 1–12 (2020)

55. Levenson, R.W., Ruef, A.M.: Empathy: a physiological substrate. J. Pers. Soc. Psychol. **63**(2), 234 (1992)

56. Li, C.H., Liu, C.C.: The effects of empathy and persuasion of storytelling via tourism micro-movies on travel willingness. Asia Pac. J. Tour. Res. **25**(4), 382–392 (2020)

57. Lin, R., Utz, S.: Self-disclosure on SNS: do disclosure intimacy and narrativity influence interpersonal closeness and social attraction? Comput. Human Behav. **70**, 426–436 (2017)

58. Liu, F., Kaufman, G., Dabbish, L.: The effect of expressive biosignals on empathy and closeness for a stigmatized group member. In: Proceedings of the ACM on Human-Computer Interaction, vol. 3, no. CSCW, pp. 1–17 (2019)

59. Liu, F., et al.: Significant otter: understanding the role of biosignals in communication. In: Proceedings of the 2021 CHI Conference on Human Factors in Computing Systems, pp. 1–15 (2021)

60. Lundqvist, L.O., Dimberg, U.: Facial expressions are contagious. J. Psychophysiol. **9**, 203–203 (1995)
61. MacDonald, A.: I feel your pain (and joy): new theories about empathy. Brain Work **13**(4), 1–3 (2003)
62. Madianou, M.: Ambient co-presence: transnational family practices in polymedia environments. Glob. Netw. **16**(2), 183–201 (2016)
63. Martínez-Velázquez, E.S., Ahuatzin González, A.L., Chamorro, Y., Sequeira, H.: The influence of empathy trait and gender on empathic responses. a study with dynamic emotional stimulus and eye movement recordings. Front. Psychol. **11**, 23 (2020)
64. Mauss, I.B., Levenson, R.W., McCarter, L., Wilhelm, F.H., Gross, J.J.: The tie that binds? coherence among emotion experience, behavior, and physiology. Emotion **5**(2), 175 (2005)
65. McDuff, D., Hurter, C.: Cardiolens: remote physiological monitoring in a mixed reality environment. In: ACM SIGGRAPH 2017 Emerging Technologies. ACM (2017). https://www.microsoft.com/en-us/research/publication/cardiolens-remote-physiological-monitoring-mixed-reality-environment/
66. Mehrabian, A., et al.: Silent messages, vol. 8, no. 152 (1971)
67. Miller, M.K., Mandryk, R.L., Birk, M.V., Depping, A.E., Patel, T.: Through the looking glass: the effects of feedback on self-awareness and conversational behaviour during video chat. In: Proceedings of the 2017 CHI Conference on Human Factors in Computing Systems, pp. 5271–5283 (2017)
68. Moge, C., Wang, K., Cho, Y.: Shared user interfaces of physiological data: systematic review of social biofeedback systems and contexts in hci. In: CHI Conference on Human Factors in Computing Systems, pp. 1–16 (2022)
69. Murali, P., Hernandez, J., McDuff, D., Rowan, K., Suh, J., Czerwinski, M.: Affectivespotlight: facilitating the communication of affective responses from audience members during online presentations. In: Proceedings of the 2021 CHI Conference on Human Factors in Computing Systems, pp. 1–13 (2021)
70. Murali, P., Trinh, H., Ring, L., Bickmore, T.: A friendly face in the crowd: reducing public speaking anxiety with an emotional support agent in the audience. In: Proceedings of the 21st ACM International Conference on Intelligent Virtual Agents, pp. 156–163 (2021)
71. Nebi, E., Altmann, T., Roth, M.: The influence of emotional salience on gaze behavior in low and high trait empathy: an exploratory eye-tracking study. J. Soc. Psychol. **162**(1), 109–127 (2022)
72. Oinas-Kukkonen, H., Harjumaa, M.: A systematic framework for designing and evaluating persuasive systems. In: Oinas-Kukkonen, H., Hasle, P., Harjumaa, M., Segerståhl, K., Øhrstrøm, P. (eds.) PERSUASIVE 2008. LNCS, vol. 5033, pp. 164–176. Springer, Heidelberg (2008). https://doi.org/10.1007/978-3-540-68504-3_15
73. Park, M.J., Lee, D.H.: Effects of storytelling in advertising on consumers empathy. Asia Mark. J. **15**(4), 5 (2014)
74. Peng, V.: Wigglears: wiggle your ears with your emotions. In: Extended Abstracts of the 2021 CHI Conference on Human Factors in Computing Systems, pp. 1–5 (2021)
75. Richmond, V.P., Gorham, J.S., McCroskey, J.C.: The relationship between selected immediacy behaviors and cognitive learning. Ann. Int. Commun. Assoc. **10**(1), 574–590 (1987)

76. Robinson, R., Rubin, Z., Segura, E.M., Isbister, K.: All the feels: designing a tool that reveals streamers' biometrics to spectators. In: Proceedings of the 12th International Conference on the Foundations of Digital Games, pp. 1–6 (2017)
77. Roseway, A., Lutchyn, Y., Johns, P., Mynatt, E., Czerwinski, M.: Biocrystal: an ambient tool for emotion and communication. Int. J. Mob. Human Comput. Interact. (IJMHCI) **7**(3), 20–41 (2015)
78. Schulman, D., Bickmore, T.: Persuading users through counseling dialogue with a conversational agent. In: Proceedings of the 4th International Conference on Persuasive Technology, pp. 1–8 (2009)
79. Shamekhi, A., Bickmore, T., Lestoquoy, A., Gardiner, P.: Augmenting group medical visits with conversational agents for stress management behavior change. In: de Vries, P.W., Oinas-Kukkonen, H., Siemons, L., Beerlage-de Jong, N., van Gemert-Pijnen, L. (eds.) PERSUASIVE 2017. LNCS, vol. 10171, pp. 55–67. Springer, Cham (2017). https://doi.org/10.1007/978-3-319-55134-0_5
80. Shelton, M.L., Rogers, R.W.: Fear-arousing and empathy-arousing appeals to help: the pathos of persuasion. J. Appl. Soc. Psychol. **11**(4), 366–378 (1981)
81. Slovák, P., Janssen, J., Fitzpatrick, G.: Understanding heart rate sharing: towards unpacking physiosocial space. In: Proceedings of the SIGCHI Conference on Human Factors in Computing Systems, pp. 859–868 (2012)
82. Spatharas, D.: Persuasive γελως: Public speaking and the use of laughter. Mnemosyne **59**(3), 374–387 (2006)
83. Spreng*, R.N., McKinnon*, M.C., Mar, R.A., Levine, B.: The toronto empathy questionnaire: scale development and initial validation of a factor-analytic solution to multiple empathy measures. J. Pers. Assess. **91**(1), 62–71 (2009)
84. Straus, S.G., Miles, J.A., Levesque, L.L.: The effects of videoconference, telephone, and face-to-face media on interviewer and applicant judgments in employment interviews. J. Manag. **27**(3), 363–381 (2001)
85. Stuyck, H., Dalla Costa, L., Cleeremans, A., Van den Bussche, E.: Validity of the empatica e4 wristband to estimate resting-state heart rate variability in a lab-based context. Int. J. Psychophysiol. **182**, 105–118 (2022)
86. Vaidya, A.R., Jin, C., Fellows, L.K.: Eye spy: the predictive value of fixation patterns in detecting subtle and extreme emotions from faces. Cognition **133**(2), 443–456 (2014)
87. Vetere, F., et al.: Mediating intimacy: designing technologies to support strong-tie relationships. In: Proceedings of the SIGCHI Conference on Human Factors in Computing Systems, pp. 471–480 (2005)
88. Wagner, B.C., Petty, R.E.: The elaboration likelihood model of persuasion: thoughtful and non-thoughtful social influence (2011)
89. Walmink, W., Wilde, D., Mueller, F.: Displaying heart rate data on a bicycle helmet to support social exertion experiences. In: Proceedings of the 8th International Conference on Tangible, Embedded and Embodied Interaction, pp. 97–104 (2014)
90. Walther, J.B.: Computer-mediated communication: impersonal, interpersonal, and hyperpersonal interaction. Commun. Res. **23**(1), 3–43 (1996)
91. Wegge, J.: Communication via videoconference: emotional and cognitive consequences of affective personality dispositions, seeing one's own picture, and disturbing events. Human-Comput. Interact. **21**(3), 273–318 (2006)
92. Weiser, M., Brown, J.S.: The coming age of calm technology. In: Beyond Calculation, pp. 75–85. Springer, Heidelberg (1997). https://doi.org/10.1007/978-1-4612-0685-9_6

93. Weiser, M., Gold, R., Brown, J.S.: The origins of ubiquitous computing research at parc in the late 1980s. IBM Syst. J. **38**(4), 693–696 (1999)

94. Werner, J., Wettach, R., Hornecker, E.: United-pulse: feeling your partner's pulse. In: Proceedings of the 10th International Conference on Human Computer Interaction with Mobile Devices and Services, pp. 535–538 (2008)

95. Winters, R.M., Walker, B.N., Leslie, G.: Can you hear my heartbeat?: hearing an expressive biosignal elicits empathy. In: Proceedings of the 2021 CHI Conference on Human Factors in Computing Systems, pp. 1–11 (2021)

96. Wittenberg, C., Tappin, B.M., Berinsky, A.J., Rand, D.G.: The (minimal) persuasive advantage of political video over text. Proc. Natl. Acad. Sci. **118**(47), e2114388118 (2021)

97. Yang, X., Ram, N., Lougheed, J.P., Molenaar, P., Hollenstein, T.: Adolescents' emotion system dynamics: network-based analysis of physiological and emotional experience. Dev. Psychol. **55**(9), 1982 (2019)

98. Yarosh, S., Markopoulos, P., Abowd, G.D.: Towards a questionnaire for measuring affective benefits and costs of communication technologies. In: Proceedings of the 17th ACM Conference on Computer Supported Cooperative Work & Social Computing, pp. 84–96 (2014)

99. Yu, Q., Nguyen, T., Prakkamakul, S., Salehi, N.: "i almost fell in love with a machine" speaking with computers affects self-disclosure. In: Extended Abstracts of the 2019 CHI Conference on Human Factors in Computing Systems, pp. 1–6 (2019)

100. Zaki, J.: Empathy: a motivated account. Psychol. Bull. **140**(6), 1608 (2014)

101. Zaki, J., Bolger, N., Ochsner, K.: Unpacking the informational bases of empathic accuracy. Emotion **9**(4), 478 (2009)

Sugarcoating a Bitter Pill - VR Against Police Ethnic Profiling

Peter W. de Vries[1]([✉]), Bas Böing[1,2,3], Els Mulder[4], and Jean-Louis van Gelder[5]

[1] Psychology of Conflict, Risk and Safety, University of Twente, Enschede, The Netherlands
{p.w.devries,b.s.boing}@utwente.nl, bas.boing@politie.nl
[2] Dutch National Police, The Hague, The Netherlands
[3] Police Academy, Apeldoorn, The Netherlands
[4] Veiligheidsregio IJsselland, Zwolle, The Netherlands
e.mulder@vrijsselland.nl
[5] Max Planck Institute for the Study of Crime, Security and Law, Freiburg, Germany
j.vangelder@csl.mpg.de

Abstract. Ethnic profiling is a growing concern for police organizations. However, attempts to reduce possible biases toward certain demographic groups have shown little effect, possibly because of the unpopularity of the topic. This study was set up to explore whether a dedicated VR training may contribute to officers' knowledge, attitude and willingness to communication about ethnic profiling. This was done by comparing effects of the VR training with that of the same training presented in 2D with a smart phone, and a control condition in which no training content was administered. Although no results were found for attitude and communication, the results do show some consistent results regarding knowledge in favour of VR. In addition, VR proved to result in higher ratings of presence, engagement, and enjoyment, indicating that in addition to providing more persuasive content, another strong advantage of VR as part of a training is the experience it affords.

Keywords: Virtual Reality · ethnic profiling

1 Introduction

Although ethnic profiling has been on the EU agenda for years now, EU Parliament reported being unsatisfied with the outcomes of a recent study proving (again) large numbers of migrants experiencing discrimination and racial profiling inside the EU [9]. The demonstrations against racial profiling throughout the EU, triggered by the death of George Floyd in May 2020 in the United States, reminded parliament members of the urgency of the matter, and led to the adoption of a resolution for intensifying measures to ensure human rights and strengthen training to prevent racial profiling [19].

Police officers engage in ethnic or racial profiling whenever they "use criteria, such as race, colour, language, religion, nationality or national or ethnic origin, in control, surveillance or investigation activities, without objective and reasonable justification"

J. Ham et al. (Eds.): PERSUASIVE 2023, LNCS 13832, pp. 22–35, 2023.
https://doi.org/10.1007/978-3-031-30933-5_2

[7]. This constitutes illegal discrimination in the EU, US, and in international law [20]. People who are frequently stopped for no other reason than their appearance are often embarrassed and humiliated, and may well lose trust in law enforcement. Eventually, this may damage relationships between the police and various communities, to the extent that cooperation with law enforcement decreases [20].

The potential damage to the police's reputation and information position has urged many law enforcement agencies to invest in means to prevent ethnic profiling. However, attempts to improve officers' knowledge and skills, so as to reduce possible biases toward certain demographic groups, have shown little effect [6, 15, 16]. Many researchers have discussed the factors that hinder adoption or limit the effectiveness of training programs targeting ethnic profiling [10, 13, 14, 16, 18, 22–25]. Chief among these is that police officers sometimes trivialize the issue and that accusations of being racially or ethnically biased is felt as a direct attack on their professional identity, craftsmanship, and integrity.

A prerequisite of professionalizing police work is that ethnic profiling is a topic that can be freely discussed in police teams. Officers should be willing to reflect on their own day-to-day work practices and those of their colleagues, as well as to place these practices under scrutiny and to discuss them. The sensitivity of the topic, however, largely prevents such healthy conversations from happening in practice. An important question would therefore be how police officers' motivation to take part in them could be stimulated. In this paper, we propose that the use of Virtual Reality (VR) holds part of the answer. Not only do VR applications appeal to many, research has also shown that content delivered through VR may be more persuasive than that delivered through other means [e.g., see 4, 30]. On the one hand, VR may be a means to expose police offers to content in a more persuasive way; on the other, the eagerness to engage in a VR experience may well prove stronger than the resistance to enter a training about ethnic profiling.

The question central to this research therefore is: To what extent does a 360°-VR training contribute to knowledge, attitude and communication regarding (prevention of) ethnic profiling?

2 Backgrounds

Virtual Reality (VR) is a medium that allows us not only to simulate reality, but also transcend the restrictions posed by reality. In VR people can be exposed to situations that in reality would be impossible or dangerous [26], such as walking on Mars, deep-ocean swimming without Scuba gear, or balancing on a plank between two skyscrapers. The latter situation typically results in feelings of stress and even fright, although partici-pants know full well that they are in fact in a perfectly safe physical environment [1]. Perhaps not surprisingly, VR has found widely varying fields of application, ranging from therapies to help people overcome phobias and post-traumatic stress to trainings in which athletes and soldiers can learn new skills [1, 5].

VR can also be used to change social behaviour by virtually placing them in the shoes of others. For instance, placing white people in the virtual body of a black person caused a decline in their implicit racial biases [21]. Other research not only replicated this finding, but also showed that the reduction in racial bias were still visible one week later [2]. Studies such as these suggest VR to be an effective means to let people take an alternative perspective so as to reduce discrimination [also see 27].

In its best-known guise VR environments consist of computer-generated virtual worlds in which the environment responds instantaneously to changes in viewing direction, movement, and eye level, allowing users to experience high freedom of movement and interactivity. 360° VR-film simulation, or 360° VR for short, is another frequently used format. In 360° VR, the user is exposed to environment based on 360°-video recordings from a limited number of camera positions. Although visually more realistic than computer-generated environments, 360° VR has a more limited interactivity: the environment does respond to changes in viewing direction, but not to movement and changes in eye level. Sometimes 360° VR allows the user to make a limited number of choices in order to proceed through an interactive scenario or to take another position in the virtual environment.

2.1 Benefits of Virtual Reality

Because of its highly immersive nature, use VR has been argued to be beneficial for the learning process [8, 17, 29]. Important in this respect are immersion and presence. Immersion is the degree to which users are enveloped in the virtual environment while stimuli from the real world are blocked; the use of VR headsets is particularly beneficial for immersion [5].

Presence, or the sense of 'being there', relates to how users actually experience immersion, i.e., the perception of the extent to which they perceive themselves to be in the virtual, rather than the real environment. Although presence is not restricted to VR, and can also be experienced when being engrossed in a book or movie, it has been particularly well studied in the context of VR because if its strong immersive nature. It has been shown, for instance, that immersion and presence have a positive effect on the learning process, as both increase motivation and commitment of the trainee [8, 29]. Presence has also been positively related to the effectiveness of virtual treatments and learning environments [8, 12, 17] and the persuasiveness of provided information [4, 30]. Based on these and other results, Cornet et al. [5] concluded VR to be especially suited for education and training involving target groups that are known to lack motivation to participate in more conventional programs. Reason for this is that VR is seen as enjoyable and something people would like to experience. It is a great way to address difficult issues like ethnic profiling, make issues like this more negotiable and learn from the experience in VR.

2.2 A 360°-VR Training Against Ethnic Profiling

A VR training was developed to stimulate dialogue about ethnic profiling amongst police officers, using scenarios closely matching day-to-day police work. To increase realism, the VR environment was based on 360° camera recordings (also known as "VR-film simulation"). The interactive scenario that was created allows users to take action, i.e. to engage in interaction with civilians as they see fit; the scenario requires them to repeatedly chose between two or more, either escalating of de-escalating, behavioural options. The behaviour of the civilians they choose to interact with is contingent upon these choices.

The training consists of two parts, the interactive, 360°-VR simulation simultaneously administered to small groups of police officers, followed by a group dialogue in which all officers take part (Fig. 1).

Fig. 1. Example of a choice during gameplay in which participants were given the choice between apprehending ("aanhouden") or dismissing ("deëscaleren") the character.

Specifically, the simulation puts participants in a 360° VR environment in the position of a police officer at the train station Amsterdam-Sloterdijk, a reasonably well-known location for most Dutch police officers. A virtual police officer in the game asks them whether they "see someone who is worth investigating". The participants then have two minutes to observe the people passing by. They can take action at their own discretion based on their observations. Although dozens of people can be seen in the simulation, the participants can only initiate an interaction with some of them (i.e., only the actors, not regular pedestrians).

Among the characters that can be selected for interaction is a party of four adolescent men, all with a supposed non-western background. Although they are laughing and making fun, they do nothing illegal. Still, they can draw the attention of police officers, particularly of those with negative experiences with similar-looking groups. As such, participants could miss another man seeking dialogues with random pedestrians, apparently, as turns out later in the game, to sell drugs. When having selected the party of four, participants can choose to check for their identification, to apprehend, or to dismiss them. Similar choices can be made when participants choose to interact with the drugs dealer. Illustration 1 presents an example of a dilemma during gameplay.

Once having selected someone, participants are presented with a number of questions on how to proceed. Each question comes with two or three answer options to choose from, including both escalating (i.e. identification check, search, fine, arrest), and deescalating options (i.e., to cease the interaction). With every presented question, participants have a maximum of five seconds to respond. The time window is deliberately short to stimulate more impulsive and fast decision-making. We consider this to be more 'honest', and in line with the operational decisions in real life. Police officers holding particular prejudices towards certain groups in society may be more focused on characters in the game who ostensibly belong to such groups. If this is indeed the case, they are at risk of missing the real culprit, who can be detected by deviant or criminal behaviour. Moreover, these officers may also be more motivated to choose for escalation (i.e. identification checks, searches, fines, arresting) rather than de-escalations (not searching cars, sending away).

Upon completion, participants receive a code, ranging from 'Alpha' to 'Juliet', representing the choices made during the simulation.

Subsequently, participants are encouraged to discuss their choices in the VR simulation in group dialogue sessions. Trained discussion leaders start with identifying officers who have made identical choices (as evidenced by identical codes), and inviting some of them to expand on the choice they made and the reasons they did so. Next, participants who have made different choices are invited to speak. The discussion leader frequently linked back to the code of practice ('handelingskaders proactief controleren') that is part of the Dutch National Police policy on proper conduct.

Exposure to others' choices differing from their own, participants may feel challenged, or uncertain about their choices. This may lead them to re-evaluate their initial point of view, causing them to engage in higher-level cognitive reasoning, and, ultimately, stimulate awareness of their own potential biases in day-to-day police activities. Part of this methodology is based on *constructive controversy* (Johnson et al. [11]).

2.3   The Present Study

To test the effectiveness of the 360°-VR training, an experiment was set up that compares effects of undergoing the VR training with that of undergoing the same training presented in 2D with a smart phone, and a control condition in which no training content was administered. Based on the literature discussed above, we expect the following:

H1: In the VR condition police officers will report having more knowledge about proper policing practice (H1a) and knowledge about ethnic profiling (H1b) than in the 2D and control conditions.

H2: In the VR condition police officers will have a more positive attitude towards ethnic profiling in their work than in the 2D and control conditions.

H3: In the VR condition police officers will report less reluctance to discuss ethnic profiling in their work than in the 2D and control conditions.

H4: In the VR condition presence (H3a), engagement (H3b), and enjoyment (H3c) will be rated higher than in the 2D condition.

The commissioning organization, the Dutch National Police, also liked to know if the effects of VR depended on participants' work experience. Therefore, this variable is incorporated here as well. As we do not have well-founded expectations as to such potential differences, this variable is treated here as a covariate.

3 Method

3.1 Participants and Design

One hundred and three police officers (29 females, 74 males) participated in this experiment, in groups of eight to 12, which had a one-factor, Presentation (VR versus 2D versus control) between-participants design knowledge about ethnic profiling, attitude towards (preventing) ethnic profiling, and perceived safety in communicating about ethnic profiling constituted the dependent variables.

3.2 Procedure

Groups of police officers were randomly assigned to the control, 2D and VR conditions. Those in the latter two conditions were informed that they would afterwards participate in a group dialogue session. In the 2D condition participants received a smart phone with a headphone to experience the simulation, and in the VR condition they received a VR headset with headphone. In the control condition no simulation was provided; participants in this condition received a questionnaire right away; in the 2D and VR conditions this was administered afterwards.

After the training, groups in the 2D and VR conditions were directed to a separate area, where the discussion leader was waiting to guide the group dialogue. The discussion leader was blind to the conditions participants had been in; participants were explicitly requested not to inform him about this.

In addition to the measures listed below, demographic variables as age, gender, and number of years work experience were measured as part of the questionnaire.

3.3 Measures

All items were measured on a five-point scale from 1 (strongly disagree) to 5 (strongly agree), unless indicated otherwise.

Knowledge. This was measured with various items, and breaks up in two aspects: self-reports on the grounds participants use to stop someone in daily practice (we regarded these as knowledge about proper conduct in practice) and more formal knowledge in relation to National Police policy and the action framework resulting from this policy.

Knowledge About Proper Policing Practices. This was measured using the following items: "Please indicate to what extent you use the aspects below to decide whether to check someone: a. Behaviour; b. Information; c. Appearance; d. Intuition; e. Previous experiences" [1. Never; 2. Rarely; 3. Sometimes; 4. Often; 5. Always].

This question was repeated, this time with more concrete items than the ones above: a. Availability of information specifically pointing to illegal conduct; b. Having a gut feeling upon seeing one or more individuals; c. Previous experience with similar situations; d. Overrepresentation of certain groups in crime statistics; e. Information suggesting that someone was at one time active in crime; f. Behaviour and circumstances unequivocally matching a modus operandi; g. Behaviour of civilians in response to police presence; h.

Seeing someone whose appearance (age, gender, clothing style, ethnicity, etc.) matches that of groups causing nuisance or engaged in crime; i. Seeing someone who based on appearance (age, gender, clothing style, ethnicity, etc.) does not belong at a location; j. Presence of civilians at certain ('criminal') locations at certain times. Aspects a. and f. are good grounds for a stop, whereas b., d, h., and i. carry a particularly high risk of causing ethnic profiling.

Knowledge About Ethnic Profiling. This was measured with the following questions: "I know what ethnic profiling entails according to National Police policy"; "This training makes me more knowledgeable about (preventing) ethnic profiling [2D and VR conditions only]". As it would be easy to answer these questions in a socially desirable manner, we also asked a more specific question: "Please indicate to what extent you believe the aspects below can be used to decide whether to check someone according to the code of practice [of the National Police]", followed by aspects a. to j. described above.

Attitude. This was measured with the following items: "I believe ethnic profiling is a problem", "This training makes me more motivated to prevent ethnic profiling" [2D and VR conditions only], and "Preventing ethnic profiling will improve the work of the police". The first and last item correlated, with $r = .47$, and were averaged to form one attitude construct to be incorporated in an analysis comparing all three Presentation conditions.

Communication. This was measured with two or three items: "I am often reluctant to discuss ethnic profiling when someone brings it up" and "This training helps me to talk about (preventing) ethnic profiling". Because of the low correlation, $r = .17$, these items were analyzed separately.

Experience. Experience-related measures targeted presence, engagement, and enjoyment; these were not administered in the control condition.

Presence. Three items were created to measure presence. 'During the simulation I often thought I was at station Amsterdam-Sloterdijk', 'During the simulation the situation at station Amsterdam-Sloterdijk felt realistic' and 'During the simulation the interaction with the other people felt realistic'. The Cronbach's α of this scale is .73.

Engagement. Two items were used to measure engagement: 'During the simulation I had the feeling that my choices influenced the course of the story' and 'During the simulation I felt involved in the story'. The correlation was $r = .65$.

Enjoyment. One item was used to measure enjoyment, 'I had a lot of fun during the simulation'.

3.4 Practical Limitations

It quickly became apparent that the time available to the participants was limited to just one hour. Because there was only one discussion leader, groups often had to wait for the group dialogue room to become available to them. Maintaining separate dialogue sessions for groups in the 2D and VR conditions was therefore not possible in practice, and we were forced to switch to sessions in with multiple groups form different conditions.

In addition, in hindsight the knowledge measures we adopted were conceptually more diverse than we had in mind when we formulated the hypothesis. It would therefore make little sense to be average them into constructs; instead we analyzed items separately in multivariate ANOVAs.

4 Results

In the following analyses, the demographic variable work experience is incorporated as a covariate. However, as its role is beyond the scope of this paper, only the multivariate effect of the covariate will be reported. In addition, the items used to measure attitude and communication did not differ between the conditions; for the sake of brevity, these will not be reported.

4.1 Knowledge

Knowledge About Proper Policing Practice (General). A multivariate ANOVA was conducted, with Presentation (control versus 2D versus VR) as independent variable, and the extent to which behaviour, information, appearance, intuition, and previous experience are used to decide whether to check someone as dependent variables, and work experience as covariate. This yielded a significant multivariate effect of Presentation, $F (10, 192) = 3.77, p < .001$, Wilk's Lambda $= .70$. Work experience also had a significant effect, $F (5, 95) = 2.48, p = .037$.

Subsequent univariate analyses showed the effect of Presentation to be present for behaviour (albeit only marginally so) and intuition ($F (2, 99) = 2.90, p = .060$ and $F (2, 99) = 9.68, p < .001$, respectively).

Behaviour. Subsequent contrast for behaviour showed higher ratings for behaviour as a ground for stops in the VR compared to the control condition ($p < .021$). No contrasts were found between VR and 2D ($p = .169$), and 2D and the control condition ($p = .256$). See Table 1a for means and standard deviations In the VR and 2D conditions, therefore, participants were more likely to use behaviour as a ground for policing action.

Intuition. For intuition as a ground for stops, contrasts showed higher ratings in the control condition than in both the VR ($p < .001$) and the 2D condition ($p < .001$); see Table 1a. The VR and 2D conditions did not differ ($p = .912$). In other words, participants in the 2D and VR conditions were less likely to use intuition as a ground for a stop than those in the control condition.

Table 1. Means and standard deviations as a function of Presentation; identical subscripts denote (marginally) significant contrasts, and grey shading indicates the most preferable rating(s) for each item.

	Presentation					
	Control		2D		VR	
a. Knowledge proper policing (general)	M	SD	M	SD	M	SD
Behaviour	3.77$_a$	0.78	3.92	0.78	4.18$_a$	0.66
Intuition	3.90$_{a,b}$	0.44	3.04$_b$	0.97	3.09$_a$	0.74
b. Knowledge proper policing (specific)						
Information pointing to illegal conduct	4.00	0.84	3.92$_a$	0.58	4.30$_a$	0.51
Gut feeling upon seeing individual(s)	3.48$_{a,b}$	0.75	2.82$_b$	0.77	2.91$_a$	0.68
Information that someone was at one time active in crime.	3.52$_a$	0.60	3.24$_b$	0.85	2.23$_{a,b}$	0,87
Someone who based on appearance does not belong at a location.	2.67$_a$	0.89	2.29$_a$	0.84	2.50	0.85
c. Knowledge action framework						
Gut feeling	3.52$_{a,b}$	0.75	2.27$_b$	0.93	2.55$_a$	0.83
Information that someone was at one time active in crime.	3.33$_{a,b}$	0.86	2.89$_b$	0.94	2.67$_a$	0.93

Knowledge About Proper Policing Practice (Specific). When analyzing the reported suitability of the set of more concrete behaviours, patterns congruent with the previous results emerge. Specifically, another multivariate ANOVA was conducted, with Presentation (control versus 2D versus VR) as independent variable, the extent to which participants will reportedly use the various aspects to decide whether to check someone as dependent variables, and work experience as covariate. A marginally significant multivariate covariate effect was found, $F (10, 90) = 1.77, p = .077$. Moreover, the multivariate effect of Presentation turned out significant $F (20, 180) = 2.41, p = .001$, Wilk's Lambda $= .62$. Subsequently, (marginally) significant univariate Presentation effects were found on "availability of information specifically pointing to illegal conduct" ($F (2, 99) = 2.59, p = .080$); "having a gut feeling upon seeing one or more individuals" ($F (2, 99) = 6.02, p = .003$); "information suggesting that someone was at one time active in crime" ($F (2, 99) = 4.25, p < .017$);"seeing someone who based on appearance (age, gender, clothing style, ethnicity, etc.) does not belong at a location" ($F (2, 99) = 2.38, p < .098$).

Information Pointing to Illegal Conduct. Contrasts showed that this was more likely to be used for participants in the VR condition than in the 2D condition ($p < .033$). However, both the 2D and VR conditions did not differ from the control condition ($p = .748$ and $p = .135$, respectively). See Table 1b for means and standard deviations.

Gut Feeling Upon Seeing Individual(S). As can be seen in Table 1b, this was less likely to be used as a ground for a stop in both the VR and 2D conditions as compared to the control condition ($p = .004$ and $p = .001$, respectively). The VR and 2D did not differ ($p = .561$).

Information that Someone was at One Time Active in Crime. This was least likely to be used in the VR condition, as evidence by (marginally) significant contrasts between VR and control condition ($p = .005$ and $p = .099$, respectively), and between the VR and 2D conditions (see Table 1b). The 2D condition did not differ from the control ($p = .167$).

Someone Who Based on Appearance does not Belong at a Location. No   differences were found between the VR and control conditions ($p = .272$), and the VR and 2D conditions ($p = .196$). However, participants in the 2D conditions were less likely to use this than those in the control condition ($p = .034$).

Knowledge About Ethnic Profiling. A univariate ANOVA was conducted, with Presentation (control versus 2D versus VR) as independent variable, and the extent to which participants knew what ethnic profiling entails according to National Police policy as dependent variables, and work experience as covariate. This yielded a non-significant effect of Presentation, $F (2, 99) = 0.65$, $p = .53$. Work experience had a significant effect, $F (1, 99) = 5.40$, $p = .022$.

Another univariate ANOVA, with Presentation (2D versus VR) as independent variable, the extent to which participants believed the training made them more knowledgeable about (preventing) ethnic profiling as dependent variable, and work experience as covariate, did not reveal a significant difference between the 2D and VR conditions either, $F (1, 79) = 0.36$, $p = .55$; the covariate was also not significant, $F (1, 79) = 0.26$, $p = .609$.

Finally, a multivariate ANOVA was conducted, with Presentation (control versus 2D versus VR) as independent variable, the extent to which participants believed the various aspects can be used according to the action framework of the National Police as dependent variables, and work experience as covariate. In addition to a significant multivariate covariate effect, $F (10, 87) = 2.53$, $p = .010$, a significant effect of Presentation was found $F (20, 174) = 2.00$, $p = .009$, Wilk's Lambda $= .66$. Significant univariate results were found for having a gut feeling as a ground for a decision permitted by the action framework, ($F (2, 96) = 14.54$, $p < .001$), and information suggesting that someone was at one time active in crime ($F (2, 96) = 3.53$, $p = .033$).

Gut Feeling. Subsequent contrasts showed that these were lower for VR ($M = 2.55$, $SD = 0.83$) and 2D conditions as compared to the control ($M = 3.52$, $SD = 0.75$, $p < .001$ and $p = .001$, respectively). The 2D ($M = 2.27$, $SD = 0.93$) and VR conditions, however, did not differ ($p = .201$). See Table 1c for means and standard deviations. In other words, participants in both in the VR and 2D conditions were more aware that the action framework does not permit gut feeling to be used in policing decisions.

Information that Someone was at One Time Active in Crime. Contrasts   showed   that ratings were significantly lower for VR as compared to the control condition ($p = .009$), but not compared to the 2D condition ($p = .372$). The ratings in the 2D condition were marginally significantly lower than in the control condition ($p = .070$). See Table 1c. Therefore, similar to the previous item, participants in the 2D, and particularly the 2D conditions believed more strongly that the action framework is critical on information suggesting that someone was at one time active in crime as a basis for policing decisions.

4.2 Experience

To test for differences between the 2D and VR conditions, a multivariate ANOVA was conducted, with Presentation (2D versus VR) as independent variable, and presence, engagement, and enjoyment as dependent variables, and work experience as covariate. This yielded a significant multivariate effect of Presentation, F (3, 77) = 9.49, $p < .001$. Work experience did not have a significant effect, F (3, 77) = 1.60, $p = .20$.

Subsequent univariate analyses showed VR to result in higher ratings of presence (M_{2D} = 2.99, SD_{2D} = 0.87 versus M_{VR} = 3.85, SD_{VR} = 0.60; F (1, 79) = 28.35, $p < .001$), engagement (M_{2D} = 3.34, SD_{2D} = 0.98 versus M_{VR} = 4.08, SD_{VR} = 0.52; F (1, 79) = 18.15, $p < .001$), and enjoyment (M_{2D} = 3.84, SD_{2D} = 0.79 versus M_{VR} = 4.30, SD_{VR} = 0.55; F (1, 79) = 11.39, $p < .001$) than the 2D condition.

5   Conclusion and Discussion

The sensitivity of the topic ethnic profiling prevents many police officers to reflect on their work and that of others, and to have healthy conversations about it on the work floor. In this paper, we have explored whether the Virtual Reality (VR) is a promising element in trainings against ethnic profiling. This was done by comparing effects of a training based on VR with that of the same training using 2D presentation of content with a smart phone, and a control condition in which no training content was administered.

Although we had envisioned the study to be of a strictly hypothesis-testing nature, the changes we made in relation to the knowledge measures meant we have changed tack to a more explorative path [cf. 28]. Multivariate analyses were used to curb the risk of Type 1 errors that is associated with exploratory research. Be that as it may, we would like to argue that our results provide at least minimal support for Hypotheses 1a and 1b: the training with VR performed slightly better than that with 2D presentation of content on a smartphone (and far better than the control in which no content was provided whatsoever). The knowledge items that responded to the VR, and to a lesser extent the 2D conditions, were rather consistent – whether general, specific, or policy-related, the knowledge items related to (information about) behaviour were more strongly favoured in VR, and, to a lesser extent in the 2D condition, as opposed to the control. Items related to intuition (or "gut feeling"), on the other hand, showed the reverse pattern.

Use of VR did not result in a more positive attitude towards (prevention of) ethnic profiling, and neither did it affect reluctance to discuss ethnic profiling on the work floor; Hypotheses 2 and 3, therefore, are rejected.

Finally, VR had a pronounced effect on participants' experience. The used of VR resulted in higher ratings of presence, engagement, and enjoyment than the use of a smartphone (2D); Hypotheses 4a, 4b, and 4c are therefore accepted.

With a sensitive topic as ethnic profiling, we cannot exclude the possibility that social desirability inspired at least some of the participants' responses. Indeed, they may well have been motivated to portray themselves more favourably by answering in a way that would correspond with the police organization's policy. However, we would like to point out that although social desirable response tendencies may have had an absolute effect, but not necessarily a relative effect. In other words, as the police organization's stance on ethnic profiling was likely to be (partly) known among participants in all conditions, a desire to respond in line with this stance may explain overall ratings, but not the differences between conditions.

Unfortunately, the setup of this study did not allow us to establish effects of the various trainings on actual behaviour, and neither did it allow us to study the robustness of the findings. Instead, we had to make do with self-reports measured immediately after the training. We feel it would be useful to know to what extent this training affects actual communication in police teams and interactions with civilians, and how these effects hold up over longer periods of time. Future research should therefore be directed to establishing the long- term effects of this VR training on knowledge, attitude, communication, and corresponding behaviour.

Our study aligns with previous work showing that content delivered through VR may be more persuasive than that delivered through other means, such as video clips and still slides [30]. In addition, engagement, and especially presence, have been argued and shown to increase motivation and commitment of trainees [8, 29], effectiveness of virtual treatments and learning environments [8, 12, 17]. Although we did not test for mediation, we have no reason to suspect that these findings would not apply to the current work.

In addition to relatively high ratings of presence and enjoyment in the VR condition, we also found high enjoyment ratings, underscoring the common idea that VR is enjoyable and holds considerable appeal to many people. We therefore cautiously agree with Cornet et al. [5] in that VR is especially suited for education and training involving target groups that are known to lack motivation to participate. Indeed, VR is a promising means to expose police offers to content about controversial topics such as ethnic profiling in a more persuasive way - after the eagerness to engage in a VR experience has proved stronger than the resistance to the topic.

References

1. Bailenson, J.: Experience on Demand: what virtual reality is, how it works, and what it can do. W.W. Norton & Company, New York (2018)
2. Banakou, D., Hanumanthu, P.D., Slater, M.: Virtual embodiment of white people in a black virtual body leads to a sustained reduction in their implicit racial bias. Front. Hum. Neurosci. 10, 1–12 (2016). https://doi.org/10.3389/fnhum.2016.00601
3. Barbot, B., Kaufman, J. C.: What makes immersive virtual reality the ultimate empathy machine? Discerning the underlying mechanisms of change. Comput. Human Behav. 111, 106431 (2020). https://doi.org/10.1016/j.chb.2020.106431
4. Chittaro, L., Zangrando, N.: The persuasive power of virtual reality: effects of simulated human distress on attitudes towards fire safety. In: Ploug, T., Hasle, P., Oinas-Kukkonen, H. (eds.) Persuasive Technology. Lecture Notes in Computer Science, vol. 6137, pp. 58–69. Springer, Heidelberg (2010). https://doi.org/10.1007/978-3-642-13226-1_8

5. Cornet, L., Den Besten, A., Van Gelder, J.-L.: Virtual reality en augmented reality in justitiële context. Universiteit Twente (2019). https://www.utwente.nl/en/bms/pcrv/research/research-projects/vrandar/

6. Engel, R.S., McManus, H.D., Isaza, G.T.: Moving beyond "best practice": experiences in police reform and a call for evidence to reduce officer-involved shootings. Annal. Am. Acad. Polit. Soc. Sci. **687**(1), 146–165 (2020). https://doi.org/10.1177/0002716219889328

7. ECRI, European Commission against Racism and Intolerance: General policy recommendation No 11 on combating racism and racial discrimination in policing (2007). https://ec.eur opa.eu/migrant-integration/sites/default/files/2010-01/docl_11725_686421442.pdf

8. Fox, J., Arena, D., Bailenson, J.N.: Virtual Reality: A survival guide for the social scientist. J. Media Psychol. **21**(3), 95–113 (2009)

9. FRA, European Union Agency for Fundamental Rights: Second European Union Minorities and Discrimination Survey Muslims – Selected findings. Luxembourg: Publications Office of the European Union (2017)

10. Hine, J.: Stop and Search: Exploring Disproportionality. De Montfort University Community and Criminal Justice Division, Leicestershire (2015)

11. Johnson, D.W., Johnson, R.T., Tjosvold, D.: Constructive controversy: the value of intellectual opposition. The Handbook of Conflict Resolution: Theory and Practice (2000)

12. Ke, F., Lee, S., Xu, X.: Teaching training in a mixed-reality integrated learning environment. Comput. Hum. Behav. **62**, 212–220 (2016)

13. Kleijer-Kool, L., Landman, W.: Boeven vangen. Een onderzoek naar proactief politieoptreden. Apeldoorn/Amersfoort: Politie & Wetenschap/Twynstra Gudde (2016)

14. Kuppens, J., Ferwerda, H.: De politieaanpak van etnisch profileren in Amsterdam: Een onderzoek naar effecten, criteria en meetbare indicatoren. Arnhem: Bureau Beke (2019)

15. Landman, W., Sollie, H.: Tegengaan van etnisch profileren. Apeldoorn/Amersfoort: Politie & Wetenschap/Twynstra Gudde (2018)

16. MacQueen, S., Bradford, B.: Where did it all go wrong? Implementation failure—and more—in a field experiment of procedural justice policing. J. Exp. Criminol. **13**(3), 321–345 (2016). https://doi.org/10.1007/s11292-016-9278-7

17. Martirosov, S., Kopecek, P.: Virtual reality and its influence on training and education-literature review. Annals of DAAAM and Proceedings of the International DAAAM Symposium, pp. 708–717 (2017). https://doi.org/10.2507/28th.daaam.proceedings.10

18. Miller, J., Gounev, P., Pap, A., Wagman, D.: Racism and Police Stops: Adapting US and British Debates to Continental Europe. European Journal for Criminology **5**(2), 161–191 (2008)

19. Narrillos, E.: Parliament condemns all forms of racism, hate and violence and calls for action. https://www.europarl.europa.eu/news/en/press-room/20200615IPR81223/parliament-con demns-all-forms-of-racism-hate-and-violence-and-calls-for-action (2020). Accessed 12 Dec 2022

20. OSF, Open Science Foundation: ethnic profiling: what it is and why it must end. https://www.opensocietyfoundations.org/explainers/ethnic-profiling-what-it-and-why-it-must-end (2022). Accessed 12 Dec 2022

21. Peck, T.C., Seinfeld, S., Aglioti, S.M., Slater, M.: Putting yourself in the skin of a black avatar reduces implicit racial bias. Conscious. Cogn. **22**, 779–787 (2013). https://doi.org/10.1016/j. concog.2013.04.016

22. Reiner, R.: The Politics of the Police, Oxford: Oxford University Press

23. Harris, D. (2012). Against Evidence: Why Law Enforcement Resists Science, New York: New York University Press (2010)

24. Shiner, M.: post-lawrence policing in england and wales: guilt, innocence and the defence of organizational ego. British J. Criminol. **50**(5), 935–953 (2010)

25. Skogan, W.G.: Why reform fails. Polic. Soc. **18**(1), 23–34 (2008)
26. Slater, M., Sanchez-Vives, M.V.: Enhancing our lives with immersive virtual reality. Front. Robot. AI, **3**(DEC), 1–47 (2016). https://doi.org/10.3389/frobt.2016.00074
27. Tassinari, M., Aulbach, M.B., Jasinskaja-Laht, I.: The use of virtual reality in studying prejudice and its reduction: a systematic review. PLoS ONE **17**(7), e0270748 (2022). https://doi.org/10.1371/journal.pone.0270748
28. Wigboldus, D.H.J., Dotsch, R.: Encourage playing with data and discourage questionable reporting practices. Psychometrika **81**(1), 27–32 (2015). https://doi.org/10.1007/s11336-015-9445-1
29. Witmer, B.G., Singer, M.J.: Measuring presence in virtual environments: a presence questionnaire. Presence: Teleoper. Virt. Environ. **7**(3), 225–240 (1998)
30. Zaalberg, R., Midden, C.: Enhancing human responses to climate change risks through simulated flooding experiences. In: Ploug, T., Hasle, P., Oinas-Kukkonen, H. (eds.) Persuasive Technology. Lecture Notes in Computer Science, vol. 6137, pp. 205–210. Springer, Heidelberg (2010). https://doi.org/10.1007/978-3-642-13226-1_21

Perception of Virtual Agents as Communicators in Virtual vs. Augmented Reality by a Male Sample

Marta Serafini[(⊠)] [iD] and Luca Chittaro [iD]

HCI Lab, Department of Mathematics, Computer Science and Physics, University of Udine, via delle Scienze 206, 33100 Udine, Italy
marta.serafini@uniud.it

Abstract. Virtual agents are often employed in persuasive applications, and different studies in the literature have shown that the gender of the agent may have an impact on how users perceive the agent as a communicator. This paper adds a new variable to this line of research, considering the possible effects of presenting the agent in Virtual Reality (VR) vs. Augmented Reality (AR). We measured attentional allocation, perceived affective understanding, speaker credibility and speaker strength. While attentional allocation was the same in all conditions, an interesting pattern emerged for the other variables. The transition from VR to AR apparently changed the perception of some communicator aspects to the advantage of the female virtual agent. We also found associations between participants' personality traits (in particular, extraversion) and perception of the agent. The paper describes and discusses these findings.

Keywords: Virtual Agent · Communicator · Virtual Reality · Augmented Reality

1 Introduction

Humanlike virtual agents have been widely used in a variety of fields, including education (e.g., [1, 2]), training (e.g., [3]), and healthcare (e.g., [4, 5]). Due to their capability to simulate social interaction, research is increasingly exploring how to use them in roles such as persuasive communicators (e.g., [6–9]) or learning facilitators (e.g., [10]), also studying the perception of the emotions they convey (e.g., [11, 12]). In this paper, we focused on the use of virtual agents as communicators that give hints about public speaking for job interviews.

Virtual agents should appear credible, trustworthy, confident and non-threatening in order to be effective and persuasive. A virtual agent might provide social presence, that is a subjective feeling of being there with a "real" person and having access to his or her thoughts and emotions [13]. Studies have shown that feeling socially present is linked to several effective communication outcomes, including attraction and persuasion (e.g., [14, 15]). It is thus important that a virtual agent conveys strong social presence.

The literature indicates that the gender of the virtual agent may have an impact on how the user perceives the agent as a communicator (e.g., [2, 16–23]). However, studies

J. Ham et al. (Eds.): PERSUASIVE 2023, LNCS 13832, pp. 36–49, 2023.
https://doi.org/10.1007/978-3-031-30933-5_3

on these effects have reported mixed results. Moreover, the role of virtual agents and how they are perceived has mainly been studied in immersive (e.g., [16, 21, 24, 25]) or non-immersive virtual reality (VR) (e.g., [1, 2, 17–20, 22, 26]), whereas studies in augmented reality (AR) are still rare [27–29]. In addition, to the best of our knowledge, there are no studies that contrast how the same virtual agents are perceived when displayed in VR vs. AR. To begin filling this gap, our research questions concern whether the perception of a virtual agent changes when shown in VR vs. AR and whether the possible change might depend on the gender of the agent. Specifically, this study aims to examine whether user's attentional allocation and perception of a male and a female agent's credibility, strength and affective understanding might differ in VR and AR.

2 Related Work

The literature reports mixed results regarding how the gender of virtual agents affects users. While some studies found that certain categories of users preferred virtual agents of the same gender as their own [20], other studies came to the opposite conclusion [16, 20] or have not found a gender preference of virtual agents by users [16, 17, 20, 21, 24]. Some studies have also focused on how users' perceptions of virtual agents might change based on agent behavior [18, 21, 24] and agent gender [18, 22].

Makransky et al. [16] compared learning outcomes of teenager students who learned laboratory safety rules from virtual agents in immersive VR. The virtual agents exhibited features intended to look more appealing to males (i.e., a sphere-shaped robot) or females (i.e., a young female scientist). Results concerning social presence felt by students revealed a nearly significant interaction between agent type and user's gender, with girls giving the same ratings to both agents and boys giving the female agent a higher social presence rating than the robot agent. However, this result cannot be generalized to a female vs. male agent comparison because the study compared a female agent with a non-anthropomorphic robot.

Bailenson and Yee [24] examined the effectiveness of virtual agent persuasiveness resulting from the chameleon effect (i.e., the tendency for mickers to gain social influence [30]) in immersive VR. The virtual agent, who was either male or female, mimicked the participant's head movements or reproduced those of another participant. The study organized participants into gender-balanced groups that experienced one of the two virtual agents performing one of the two behaviors. Measures included how much realistic and pleasant the virtual agents were perceived. Results showed that the virtual agent who mimicked participants' head movements was viewed as more persuasive and likable than the virtual agent who used recorded head movements. However, no effect was found for gender of the participants or agents on the perception of the virtual agents.

Guadagno et al. [21] investigated the interaction between agent gender and participants' gender using a male and a female agent with high or low behavioral realism. In the high behavioral realism condition, the agent maintained eye contact with the participant by moving the head, blinked the eyes and moved the lips in synch with speech. In the low behavioral realism condition, the agent did not move. The study organized the participants in groups that experienced one of the two virtual agents performing one of the two behaviors. The authors measured how much the agent looked like a real person to participants and whether social presence changed with agent's behavior. Greater social presence was found when agents displayed high behavioral realism, but there were no significant effects for gender of the participants or agents on this measure.

Gulz et al. [22] investigated how levels of visual femininity and masculinity of a virtual agent might influence user's perception of the agent, using four agents: two females (one feminine-looking, one slightly masculine-looking) and two males (one masculine-looking, one slightly feminine-looking). Participants were organized into four counterbalanced groups, each one experiencing one of the two male agents and one of the two female agents. Results showed that the feminine-looking female was perceived as more personal, warm and pleasant than the slightly masculine-looking female. On the contrary, there were no significant differences between the two male agents. Moreover, users perceived male and female agents as equally (or almost equally) warm, intelligent, emphatic, friendly, knowledgeable, personal, pleasant, and expert regardless of the levels of visual femininity and masculinity. Significant differences were instead found in objectiveness, decisiveness, and persuasiveness, with the female agents receiving higher scores.

Qui and Benbasat [17] studied if changing demographic characteristics of an agent might improve users' social interactions with it. The considered demographic factors were gender and ethnicity, and four virtual agents were used: a Caucasian female, a Caucasian male, an Asian female and an Asian male. Results revealed that participants gave better ratings to the agents with the same ethnicity as their own but there were no significant effects of the gender of participants or the gender of virtual agents.

Rosenberg-Kima et al. [20] also focused on ethnicity and gender, comparing four agents: two males (one White and one Black) and two females (one White and one Black). Participants were Black females who were organized into four groups, where each group experienced one of four agents trying to persuade participants of the value of engineering. The same experiment was also conducted on a sample of White females. Black females preferred the female among Black agents and the male among White agents. White females had no gender preferences instead.

Nunamaker et al. [18] manipulated agent gender and behavior, and investigated the perception of power, likeability, experience, and trustworthiness of the agents. The study used a male and a female agent that could maintain either a neutral or smiling facial expression as behavior. Participants experienced both virtual agents with both behaviors. Each virtual agent was in an almost authoritarian position and asked the participants the same questions about the contents of a bag. The results showed that the male agent was perceived to be more powerful, trustworthy, and experienced than the female agent, that was instead perceived to be more likeable. Moreover, smiling was viewed as more pleasant whereas neutral behavior was perceived as more powerful.

Studies of the perception of virtual agents have typically employed immersive [16, 21, 24] or non-immersive VR [17, 18, 20, 22]. On the contrary, available studies of humanlike virtual agents in AR are still rare [27–29] and, to the best of our knowledge, have not investigated possible effects of agent gender on user's perception. Furthermore, the few AR studies used see-through headsets with a limited field of view, which can make it difficult to perceive large virtual objects in their entirety.

In this paper, we study user's attentional allocation and perception of a male and a female agent's credibility, strength and affective understanding on a male sample using VR or AR. We also assessed possible relationships between participants' personality traits and perception of virtual agents.

3 Materials and Methods

3.1 Participants

Since participant's gender might influence perception of the agent, we focused this first study on a male sample of 67 participants. They were recruited among undergraduate Computer Science students of the University of Udine, and their age ranged from 20 to 28 (M = 21.82, SD = 0.20).

3.2 Virtual Environment

The virtual environment was developed in Unity version 2021.3.12f. In AR, the headset was used in see-through video mode so that participants saw the actual room where the experiment took place, and were able to see their own body. In VR, the headset was used in non-see-through mode so that participants were unable to see the real world, they saw instead a virtual reproduction of the same room, and they had a neutral human embodiment that moved accordingly to the tracking of their hands and head. The space in which the agent was positioned in VR and AR is depicted in Fig. 1.

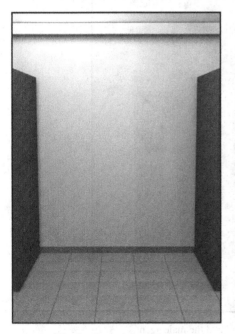

Fig. 1. Space in which the agent was positioned in VR (left) and AR (right).

3.3 Virtual Agents

The two virtual agents were chosen from the characters in the Microsoft Rocketbox library [31] and purposely modified to be similar except for gender. The specific characters were "Male_Adult_08" and "Female_Adult_01" in the library [31]. They had the same age and the same height (1.72 m). Moreover, we added a white tank top to the clothing of the female character and changed the color of the character's shirt to light blue, in order to make the clothing appear similar to the male character (Fig. 2). The voices of the two virtual agents were synthesized using Azure Cognitive Services text-to-speech: the male agent spoke with the "Benigno (Neural)" voice, and the female agent spoke with the "Fiamma (Neural)" voice. The voice of the male agent was slowed down by 9% to match the speech rate of the female agent. Both virtual agents delivered the same 138-s speech in which they offered advice on how to appropriately introduce oneself at a job interview.

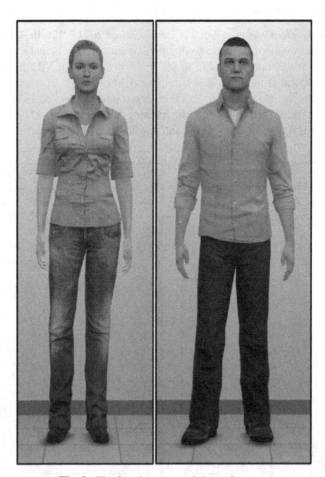

Fig. 2. The female agent and the male agent.

We made the agents blink their eyes and display similar facial expressions to emphasize the speech. Moreover, while speaking to the user, they maintained eye contact and performed a sequence of animations from the Microsoft Rocketbox library, following the order listed in Table 1. The animated gestures performed by the two agents were similar and followed Andre et al.'s [32] recommendations for developing a convincing virtual agent. Each animation was fully performed before moving on to the following animation. When the two-minute speech ended, the virtual agents switched from the animation they were performing (i.e., "m_gestic_talk_relaxed_02" for the male agent, "f_gestic_talk_relaxed_02" for the female agent) to the subsequent animation (idle) that was performed for three seconds, then the session ended.

Table 1. Chosen characters and animations in the Microsoft Rocketbox library [31].

Virtual agent name	Virtual agent gender	Animations
"Male_Adult_08"	Male	"m_gestic_talk_neutral_02"
		"m_gestic_talk_neutral_01"
		"m_gestic_talk_relaxed_01"
		"m_gestic_talk_relaxed_02"
		"m_idle_breathe_01"
"Female_Adult_01"	Female	"f_gestic_talk_neutral_01"
		"f_gestic_talk_neutral_02"
		"f_gestic_talk_neutral_03"
		"f_gestic_talk_relaxed_01"
		"f_gestic_talk_relaxed_02"
		"f_idle_breathe_01"

3.4 Task

Participants were told to listen to a virtual agent who would speak to them for about two minutes, offering advice on how to behave in a job interview.

3.5 Measures

Participants completed a demographic questionnaire before starting the session. Collected data were used to balance participants between groups. They were: gender (participants could choose among male, female, and non-binary), age, whether or not participants were regular VR or AR headset users, and the number of hours they have spent wearing such headsets.

Big Five Inventory-2 Extra-Short Form (BFI-2-XS). The BFI-2-XS was used to measure participants' personality [33]. It is a 15-item short version of the Big Five Inventory with responses measured in a Likert format ranging from 1 (disagree strongly) to 5 (agree strongly).

Attentional Allocation and Perceived Affective Understanding. Subscales from the Networked Mind Measure of Social Presence [34] were used to measure participants' social presence. Participants were asked to rate eight items on a 7-point Likert scale, ranging from 1 (Strongly disagree) to 7 (Strongly agree). We used two subscales, respectively measuring the two independent dimensions of "attentional allocation" (i.e., the amount of attention the user allocated to and perceived to receive from the agent) and "perceived affective understanding" (i.e., the perceived ability of the user to understand the agent's emotional and attitudinal states). The "attentional allocation" subscale included four items (i.e., "I remained focused on the agent the whole time", "The agent remained focused on me the whole time", "The agent did not receive my full attention", "I did not receive the agent's full attention"), Cronbach's alpha was 0.62. The "perceived affective understanding" subscale included four items (i.e., "I could tell how the agent felt", "The agent could tell how I felt", "The agent's emotions were not clear to me", "I could describe the agent's feelings accurately"), Cronbach's alpha was 0.74.

Speaker Credibility and Strength. We used subscales from the same questionnaire used in [35] to measure how participants perceived the speaker. Participants were asked to rate 11 items on a 7-point scale anchored by bi-polar adjectives. We used two subscales, respectively measuring seven dimensions of "speaker credibility" and four dimensions of "speaker strength". The "speaker credibility" subscale included seven items (i.e., dishonest-honest, uninformed-informed, untrustworthy-trustworthy, unintelligent-intelligent, evasive-straightforward, unqualified-qualified, sincere-insincere), Cronbach's alpha was 0.79. The "speaker strength" subscale included four items (i.e., unassertive-assertive, timid-bold, inactive-active, meek-forceful), Cronbach's alpha was 0.82.

3.6 Procedure

Written consent for participation in the study was obtained from participants. They were verbally briefed about the anonymity of the collected data. Then, they sat on a chair and filled the demographic and BFI-2-XS questionnaires. The demographic data were used to balance participants in the following four conditions: (1) male agent in VR (VR-M); (2) female agent in VR (VR-F); (3) male agent in AR (AR-M); (4) female agent in AR (AR-F). A Kruskal-Wallis test on regular use of headsets, and a one-way ANOVA on age and hours of headsets usage confirmed that there were no significant differences between the four groups. The experimenter asked participants to stand in a specific place in the room and listen to a virtual agent who would give them a two-minute speech with some tips on how to present oneself in a job interview. Then, the experimenter helped the participants wear a Varjo XR-3 (a mixed reality headset with a field of view of 115° in VR as well as AR) and over-ear headphones. The virtual agent delivered the speech at a 1-m distance from the participant. Once the agent finished the speech, a blank black screen filled the participants' view indicating the end of the session. At that time, the experimenter helped the participants remove the headset. Participants filled the questionnaires and were thanked for their participation.

4   Results

All the analyses were conducted using SPSS version 28.0.1.0. Results are graphically depicted in Fig. 3.

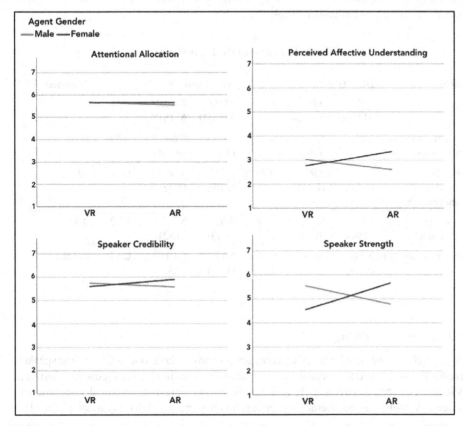

Fig. 3. Scores of attentional allocation, perceived affective understanding, speaker credibility, speaker strength.

4.1   Attentional Allocation

A 2x2 ANOVA was conducted with agent gender (male or female) and display mode (VR or AR) as factors, and attentional allocation score as dependent variable. There were no differences in attentional allocation between VR and AR, and between male and female agent. Moreover, there was no interaction between agent gender and display mode (Table 2).

4.2 Perceived Affective Understanding

A 2x2 ANOVA was conducted with agent gender and display mode as factors and perceived affective understanding score as dependent variable. The differences in perceived affective understanding between VR and AR, and between male and female agent, were not statistically significant. However, the interaction between agent gender and display mode was close to significance (Table 2).

Table 2. Results of the 2x2 ANOVAs.

Scale	Display mode			Agent gender			Interaction
	VR M (SD)	**AR** M (SD)	p	**Male** M (SD)	**Female** M (SD)	p	p
Attentional allocation	5.67 (0.97)	5.61 (0.94)	0.79	5.61 (1.05)	5.66 (0.86)	0.83	0.79
Perceived affective understanding	2.90 (1.14)	2.99 (1.21)	0.77	2.83 (1.09)	3.06 (1.23)	0.40	0.08
Speaker credibility	5.67 (0.94)	5.74 (0.99)	0.78	5.67 (1.09)	5.75 (0.82)	0.72	0.33
Speaker strength	5.04 (1.29)	5.23 (1.34)	0.56	5.17 (1.29)	5.10 (1.33)	0.84	0.003

4.3 Speaker Credibility

A 2x2 ANOVA was conducted with agent gender and display mode as factors and speaker credibility score as dependent variable. The differences in speaker credibility between VR and AR, and between male and female agent, were not statistically significant. Moreover, there was no interaction between agent gender and display mode (Table 2).

4.4 Speaker Strength

A 2x2 ANOVA was conducted with agent gender and display mode as factors and speaker strength score as dependent variable. No statistically significant effect of agent gender or display mode was found. However, as shown in Table 2, there was a significant interaction between agent gender and display mode, $F(1,63) = 9.63$, $p < 0.01$, $\eta_p^2 = 0.13$: the mean score of the male agent was worse in AR (M = 4.78, SD = 1.64) than VR (M = 5.54, SD = 0.72), whereas the score of the female agent was better in AR (M = 5.66, SD = 0.80) than VR (M = 4.54, SD = 1.53). As suggested in [36], we used Bonferroni correction for the analysis of simple effects of display mode separately at the two levels of the agent gender and the simple effect of the agent gender separately at the two levels of display mode. Results showed a significant increase in the score of the female agent between VR and AR ($p < 0.05$) and a significant difference between the score of the male and the female agent in both AR ($p < 0.05$) and VR ($p < 0.05$).

4.5 Participant's Personality Traits

A Pearson correlation was computed to assess possible relationships between the five personality traits (extraversion, agreeableness, conscientiousness, negative emotionality, open mindedness) and scores of attention allocation, perceived affective understanding, speaker credibility and speaker strength.

The following statistically significant correlations were found: (i) a moderate positive correlation between extraversion and attentional allocation in the AR-M condition ($r = 0.52$, $n = 16$, $p = 0.04$); (ii) a moderate positive correlation between conscientiousness and attentional allocation in the VR-F condition ($r = 0.56$, $n = 17$, $p = 0.02$); (iii) a moderate positive correlation between extraversion and perceived affective understanding in the VR-F condition ($r = 0.54$, $n = 17$, $p = 0.02$); (iv) a moderate negative correlation between extraversion and speaker credibility in the VR-M condition ($r = -0.57$, $n = 17$, $p = 0.02$).

5 Discussion

Results indicate that there were no changes in attentional allocation between AR and VR, and male and female agent, but results on perceived affective understanding, speaker credibility and speaker strength display an interesting pattern. In particular, the strength of the female agent was perceived to be significantly greater in AR than in VR, whereas the strength of the male agent decreased in AR with respect to VR. Furthermore, there were significant differences between the strengths of the virtual agents in AR as well as VR, with the female agent perceived as stronger than the male agent in AR, while the male was stronger in VR. Although the interaction was significant only for speaker strength, and close to significant for perceived affective understanding, it is interesting to note that results on all three variables (speaker strength, perceived affective understanding, and speaker credibility) were consistent with the same pattern: perceptions flipped when moving from VR to AR. In general, consistently with some studies in the literature, the perception of the two virtual agents in VR does not appear to differ [17, 21, 24] (except for the strength of the agent). Moving from VR to AR seems to enhance the perception of the female agent while negatively impacting the perception of the male agent. To the best of our knowledge, research on how the gender of the virtual agent influences its perception in AR is not yet available in the literature. Looking at the pattern in this study, we can hypothesize that closeness to reality obtained through AR in the virtual-real continuum (i.e., the continuous scale ranging between the completely virtual and the completely real [37]) might change the perception of the virtual agent. Since AR makes it possible to contextualize the experience in the real world, we could conjecture that this contextualization makes users' perceptions of the virtual agent in AR very close to those they would have in the real world. This would be consistent with studies of human communicators in the real world reporting that when a woman's communicative behavior is the same as a male speaker's, she is more likely to be perceived as more good-willed, more correct, and more experienced than the male communicator [38].

Regarding the positive correlation found between conscientiousness and attentional allocation, we can consider the fact that a conscientious person has a strong feeling of responsibility and is deeply concerned about finishing duties and doing them correctly.

As a result, participants with higher levels of the conscientious trait may have diligently followed the rules of the task in our study, which consisted of listening and paying attention to the virtual agent.

Extraversion emerged as the trait that obtained more associations with the results. Regarding the positive correlation found between extraversion and attentional allocation, we can consider the fact that an extravert individual is more likely to be interested in other people and social activities. In our case, the extravert participants might have thus consistently reacted to the presence of an anthropomorphic social agent. Moreover, earlier research has already shown that variation in extraversion is strongly associated with the extent to which a social stimulus evokes enhanced attentional allocation [39].

Regarding the positive correlation we found between extraversion and perceived affective understanding, we can consider the fact that extravert individuals have more experience in social settings than introverts; therefore, they can decode nonverbal cues in social interaction more accurately. Since more extravert participants are more confident in their capability of detecting social cues [40], in our case, they might have assumed that they correctly interpreted the emotional state of the virtual agent.

Regarding the negative correlation we found between extraversion and speaker credibility, we can consider the fact that extravert individuals are good at conversing with people in the real world and enjoy doing it. We could thus conjecture that in our case the absence of interpersonal interaction and the virtual nature of the agent led them to be less impressed by the agent than introvert participants.

6 Conclusions

This study compared user's perception of a male and a female virtual agent that gave tips about self-introduction in job interviews. Contrasting immersive VR with AR, the study assessed possible effects on user's attentional allocation and perception of agent's credibility, strength and affective understanding. To the best of our knowledge, this is the first comparison of this kind of AR vs VR. While attentional allocation was the same in all conditions, an interesting pattern emerged for the other three variables. As discussed in the paper, the transition from VR to AR seems to change the perception of some communicator aspects to the advantage of the female agent. These results motivate further investigation of the possible differences in the perception of virtual agents displayed in VR vs AR, also to identify possible implications on virtual agent design.

Two limitations of this study should be noted. First, the study used a limited size sample. In future studies, we will aim to assess these results with a larger sample. Second, the study was conducted on a male sample. Future studies should replicate the procedure on a female sample to assess the possible role of users' gender differences.

Finally, the virtual agent gave participants a brief speech about common sense tips which are typically recommended for job interviews. It would be interesting to repeat the study with a speech that deals instead with a divisive subject which could provoke disagreement with participants.

References

1. Johnson, A.M., DiDonato, M.D., Reisslein, M.: Animated agents in K-12 engineering outreach: Preferred agent characteristics across age levels. Comput. Hum. Behav. **29**(4), 1807–1815 (2013). https://doi.org/10.1016/j.chb.2013.02.023
2. Ashby Plant, E., Baylor, A. L., Doerr, C. E., Rosenberg-Kima, R. B.: Changing middle-school students' attitudes and performance regarding engineering with computer-based social models, Comput. Educ., 53(2), pp. 209–215 (2009) https://doi.org/10.1016/j.compedu.2009.01.013
3. Buttussi, F., Chittaro, L.: Humor and Fear Appeals in Animated Pedagogical Agents: An Evaluation in Aviation Safety Education. IEEE Trans. Learn. Technol. **13**(1), 63–76 (2020). https://doi.org/10.1109/TLT.2019.2902401
4. Tielman, M.L., Neerincx, M.A., Brinkman, W.-P.: Design and Evaluation of Personalized Motivational Messages by a Virtual Agent that Assists in Post-Traumatic Stress Disorder Therapy. J. Med. Internet Res. 21(3), e9240 (2019). https://doi.org/10.2196/jmir.9240
5. Parmar, D., Olafsson, S., Utami, D., Murali, P., Bickmore, T.: Designing empathic virtual agents: manipulating animation, voice, rendering, and empathy to create persuasive agents. Auton. Agents Multi-Agent Syst. **36**(1), 17 (2022). https://doi.org/10.1007/s10458-021-09539-1
6. Ruijten, P.A.M., Midden, C.J.H., Ham, J.: Lonely and Susceptible: The Influence of Social Exclusion and Gender on Persuasion by an Artificial Agent. Int. J. Human-Computer Interact. **31**(11), 832–842 (2015). https://doi.org/10.1080/10447318.2015.1067480
7. Verberne, F.M.F., Ham, J., Ponnada, A., Midden, C.J.H.: Trusting Digital Chameleons: The Effect of Mimicry by a Virtual Social Agent on User Trust. In: Berkovsky, S., Freyne, J. (eds.) PERSUASIVE 2013. LNCS, vol. 7822, pp. 234–245. Springer, Heidelberg (2013). https://doi.org/10.1007/978-3-642-37157-8_28
8. Roubroeks, M., Ham, J., Midden, C.: When Artificial Social Agents Try to Persuade People: The Role of Social Agency on the Occurrence of Psychological Reactance. Int. J. Soc. Robot. 3(2), 155–165 (2011). https://doi.org/10.1007/s12369-010-0088-1
9. Midden, C., Ham, J.: Using negative and positive social feedback from a robotic agent to save energy In: Proceedings of the 4th International Conference on Persuasive Technology, New York, NY, USA, (2009), pp. 1–6. https://doi.org/10.1145/1541948.1541966
10. Fountoukidou, S., Ham, J., Matzat, U., Midden, C.: Effects of an artificial agent as a behavioral model on motivational and learning outcomes. Comput. Hum. Behav. **97**, 84–93 (2019). https://doi.org/10.1016/j.chb.2019.03.013
11. Ruijten, P.A.M., Midden, C.J.H., Ham, J.: Ambiguous Agents: The Influence of Consistency of an Artificial Agent's Social Cues on Emotion Recognition, Recall, and Persuasiveness. Int. J. Human-Computer Interact. **32**(9), 734–744 (2016). https://doi.org/10.1080/10447318.2016.1193350
12. Ruijten, P.A.M., Midden, C.J.H., Ham, J.: I Didn't Know That Virtual Agent Was Angry at Me: Investigating Effects of Gaze Direction on Emotion Recognition and Evaluation. In: Berkovsky, S., Freyne, J. (eds.) PERSUASIVE 2013. LNCS, vol. 7822, pp. 192–197. Springer, Heidelberg (2013). https://doi.org/10.1007/978-3-642-37157-8_23
13. Biocca, F.: The Cyborg's Dilemma: Progressive Embodiment in Virtual Environments [1] J. Comput.-Mediat. Commun., 3 (2), p. JCMC324, (1997) https://doi.org/10.1111/j.1083-6101.1997.tb00070.x
14. Fogg, B. J., Tseng, H.: The elements of computer credibility," In: Proceedings of the SIGCHI conference on Human Factors in Computing Systems, New York, NY, USA, Maggio, pp. 80–87 (1999) https://doi.org/10.1145/302979.303001

15. Lee, K.M., Jung, Y., Kim, J., Kim, S.R.: Are physically embodied social agents better than disembodied social agents?: The effects of physical embodiment, tactile interaction, and people's loneliness in human–robot interaction. Int. J. Hum.-Comput. Stud. **64**(10), 962–973 (2006). https://doi.org/10.1016/j.ijhcs.2006.05.002

16. Makransky, G., Wismer, P., Mayer, R.E.: A gender matching effect in learning with pedagogical agents in an immersive virtual reality science simulation. J. Comput. Assist. Learn. **35**(3), 349–358 (2019). https://doi.org/10.1111/jcal.12335

17. Qiu, L., Benbasat, I.: A study of demographic embodiments of product recommendation agents in electronic commerce. Int. J. Hum.-Comput. Stud. **68**(10), 669–688 (2010). https://doi.org/10.1016/j.ijhcs.2010.05.005

18. Nunamaker, J.F., Derrick, D.C., Elkins, A.C., Burgoon, J.K., Patton, M.W.: Embodied Conversational Agent-Based Kiosk for Automated Interviewing. J. Manag. Inf. Syst. **28**(1), 17–48 (2011)

19. Ozogul, G., Johnson, A.M., Atkinson, R.K., Reisslein, M.: Investigating the impact of pedagogical agent gender matching and learner choice on learning outcomes and perceptions. Comput. Educ. **67**, 36–50 (2013). https://doi.org/10.1016/j.compedu.2013.02.006

20. Rosenberg-Kima, R.B., Plant, E.A., Doerr, C.E., Baylor, A.L.: The Influence of Computer-based Model's Race and Gender on Female Students' Attitudes and Beliefs Towards Engineering. J. Eng. Educ. **99**(1), 35–44 (2010). https://doi.org/10.1002/j.2168-9830.2010.tb01040.x

21. Guadagno, R., Blascovich, J., Bailenson, J., McCall, C.: Virtual Humans and Persuasion: The Effects of Agency and Behavioral Realism. Media Psychol. **10**, 1–22 (2007). https://doi.org/10.1080/15213260701300865

22. Gulz, A., Ahlner, F., Haake, M.: Visual Femininity and Masculinity in Synthetic Characters and Patterns of Affect. In: Paiva, A.C.R., Prada, R., Picard, R.W. (eds.) ACII 2007. LNCS, vol. 4738, pp. 654–665. Springer, Heidelberg (2007). https://doi.org/10.1007/978-3-540-74889-2_57

23. Ter Stal, S., Tabak, M., op den Akker, H., Beinema, T., Hermens, H.: Who Do You Prefer? The Effect of Age, Gender and Role on Users' First Impressions of Embodied Conversational Agents in eHealth. Int. J. Human–Computer Interact., 36(9), pp. 881–892 (2020) https://doi.org/10.1080/10447318.2019.1699744

24. Bailenson, J.N., Yee, N.: Digital Chameleons: Automatic Assimilation of Nonverbal Gestures in Immersive Virtual Environments. Psychol. Sci. **16**(10), 814–819 (2005). https://doi.org/10.1111/j.1467-9280.2005.01619.x

25. Casasanto, D., Casasanto, L.S., Gijssels, T., Hagoort, P.: The Reverse Chameleon Effect: Negative Social Consequences of Anatomical Mimicry. Front. Psychol. **11**, 1876 (2020). https://doi.org/10.3389/fpsyg.2020.01876

26. Stein, J.-P., Ohler, P.: Uncanny…But Convincing? Inconsistency Between a Virtual Agent's Facial Proportions and Vocal Realism Reduces Its Credibility and Attractiveness, but Not Its Persuasive Success. Interact. Comput. **30**(6), 480–491 (2018). https://doi.org/10.1093/iwc/iwy023

27. Wang, I., Smith, J., Ruiz, J.: Exploring Virtual Agents for Augmented Reality. In: Proceedings of the 2019 CHI Conference on Human Factors in Computing Systems, Glasgow Scotland Uk, pp. 1–12. (2019) https://doi.org/10.1145/3290605.3300511

28. Huang, A., Knierim, P., Chiossi, F., Chuang, L. L., Welsch, R.: Proxemics for Human-Agent Interaction in Augmented Reality In: CHI Conference on Human Factors in Computing Systems, New Orleans LA USA, pp. 1–13. (2022) https://doi.org/10.1145/3491102.3517593

29. Miller, M.R., Jun, H., Herrera, F., Villa, J.Y., Welch, G., Bailenson, J. N.: Social interaction in augmented reality, *PLOS ONE*, 14(5), p. e0216290 (2019) doi: https://doi.org/10.1371/journal.pone.0216290

30. Chartrand, T.L., Bargh, J.A.: The chameleon effect: The perception–behavior link and social interaction. J. Pers. Soc. Psychol. **76**, 893–910 (1999). https://doi.org/10.1037/0022-3514.76.6.893
31. Gonzalez-Franco, M., et al.: The Rocketbox Library and the Utility of Freely Available Rigged Avatars. Front. Virtual Real. **1**, 561558 (2020). https://doi.org/10.3389/frvir.2020.561558
32. Andre, E., et al.: Non-verbal Persuasion and Communication in an Affective Agent. In: Cognitive Technologies, pp. 585–608 (2011)https://doi.org/10.1007/978-3-642-15184-2_30
33. Soto, C.J., John, O.P.: Short and extra-short forms of the Big Five Inventory–2: The BFI-2-S and BFI-2-XS. J. Res. Personal. **68**, 69–81 (2017). https://doi.org/10.1016/j.jrp.2017.02.004
34. Harms, C., Biocca, F.: "Internal Consistency and Reliability of the Networked Minds Measure of Social Presence", presented at the Seventh annual international workshop: Presence. Valencia, Spain **2004**, 8 (2004)
35. Stern, S.E., Mullennix, J.W., Yaroslavsky, I.: Persuasion and social perception of human vs. synthetic voice across person as source and computer as source conditions. Int. J. Hum.-Comput. Stud. **64**(1), 43–52 (2006). https://doi.org/10.1016/j.ijhcs.2005.07.002
36. Cohen, B. H.: Explaining Psychological Statistics. John Wiley & Sons, (2008)
37. Milgram, P., Kishino, F.: A Taxonomy of Mixed Reality Visual Displays, IEICE Trans. Inf. Syst., E77-D, (12), pp. 1321–1329, (1994)
38. Kenton, S. B.: Speaker Credibility in Persuasive Business Communication: A Model Which Explains Gender Differences. J. Bus. Commun., 26(2), pp. 143–157, Spring 1989, https://doi.org/10.1177/002194368902600204
39. Fishman, I., Ng, R., Bellugi, U.: Do extraverts process social stimuli differently from introverts? Cogn. Neurosci. **2**(2), 67–73 (2011). https://doi.org/10.1080/17588928.2010.527434
40. Akert, R.M., Panter, A.T.: Extraversion and the ability to decode nonverbal communication. Personal. Individ. Differ. **9**(6), 965–972 (1988). https://doi.org/10.1016/0191-8869(88)90130-4

ReadAR, Playful Book Finding Through Peer Book Reviews for Multi-faceted Characters in AR

Lars Wintermans[1], Robby van Delden[2]([⊠]) [iD], and Dennis Reidsma[2] [iD]

[1] Creative Technology, University of Twente, Enschede, The Netherlands
l.j.wintermans@student.utwente.nl
[2] Human Media Interaction, University of Twente, Drienerlolaan 5, Enschede,
The Netherlands
{r.w.vandelden,d.reidsma}@utwente.nl

Abstract. One important element to provide reading enjoyment and to persuade children to read (more) is providing children with books that fit their interests. We structure filtering and recommendation of books in a playful way via animated 3D characters. These characters have an unusual mix of characteristics that can be related to categories of books, while at the same time aiming for overcoming a filter bubble effect. In our Augmented Reality application the characters playfully 'structure' the process of book review and searching. We tested the prototype during two within-subject sessions, testing reflecting on the book as well as searching for books, with respectively 18 and 15 participants. When comparing to a regular 'writing a book report'-approach, children indicated they would more likely want to use the app again for providing feedback about the book to peers as well as for finding books. Although they wanted to look again for the books and watch the accompanying localised video reviews from their peers, almost half did not want to record videos themselves again which points out a clear challenge for future improvements.

Keywords: kids · library · play · books · reading · AR

1 Introduction

Dutch primary and secondary school children have the lowest reading enjoyment level of all 79 countries participating in the Programme for International Student Assessment (PISA) 2018 research [8]. This is an alarming statistic, because reading enjoyment positively impacts the development of reading skills [22]. To make matters worse, there seems to be a negative trend, with reading enjoyment levels being lower than in the PISA 2009 [8]. This could be the result of decreasing skills which might be attributed to an increase of reading short texts (e.g., text messages) and a decrease in reading long texts (e.g., books) [8,23]. As the report of the Dutch council for culture and education summarizes: *'It is*

J. Ham et al. (Eds.): PERSUASIVE 2023, LNCS 13832, pp. 50–64, 2023.
https://doi.org/10.1007/978-3-031-30933-5_4

an important joint task to stimulate reading and make motivation for reading a spearhead' [23].

Merga [19] showed that finding the right engaging books is important to create reading enjoyment. Children in that study (aged 8 to 11) commented that they have difficulty finding books that suited their taste. Several primary school educators reiterated this problem when interviewed as part of our current study.

Adding pleasure to the process of visiting libraries and finding books is thus not surprisingly a recurring research topic. There are large scale interactive systems that facilitate browsing through a set of books, such as the camera-projection floor surface of the StorySurfer [7], audio playback and recording devices to leave –and listen to– reviews in public libraries [18], or interactive technologies such as new or free apps in school libraries (co-designed) by children [12]. The StorySurfer project emphasized the role of some physical movement within the browsing process [7], the BibPhone emphasized the link between digital and physical [18], and Itenge-Wheeler et al. emphasized the importance of school libraries. For our current project we combined the focus on in-school libraries with movement and location-based personalised interactions using smart devices.

In a typical library setting, the number of books is too large to scan through. Therefore, besides providing pleasure, a practical focus in this domain is often how to support browsing and dealing with (category-based) filtering in child-friendly ways to keep the number of books manageable for the child. For instance, the well-known participatory design work related to the International Children's Digital Library (ICDL) [10,11] details how they, together with children, came up with properties and categories such as reading age, colour, and length. This led to insights in how these can be integrated in screen- and child-friendly ways with various trade-offs. Whereas Hutchinson et al. focused on children actively browsing based on book properties, we instead facilitate exploring based on a few reader 'personas'. This is similar to the approach of stores like Amazon who base book recommendations on the preferences of "other people like you"; however, it is known that this approach may suffer from the filter bubble effect [21]. We show how we address this by making personas that are not too precisely constrained.

In our study we build on these starting points from related work. Similar to [29] who built their application from theories on play and child development [27], we are also targeting a playful experience and state of mind [1] building on the elements of the PLayful EXperiences (PLEX) framework [14,16]. Following standard HCI practices [15] we use interviews, surveys, and other feedback from children, teachers, and a library expert. After discussing context and related work, we will explain the ReadAR design rationale, and present the setup and results of our study comparing the ReadAR application to typical approaches currently used by the school, and end the paper with a discussion.

The main contribution of this paper is the context-informed concept of combining peer book reviews with multi-faceted animated characters as a possible direction for steering children towards finding books that fit their interests.

2   Background – Playful Experiences for Finding Books

We build on related systems that go beyond traditional screen-based search for finding books. We also used information obtained from experts and children, as will be discussed in the next section.

Fig. 1. The ReadAR app explained in three pictures. On the left, a (translated) screenshot of the application. In the review mode, the child picks a character that fits the book that was reviewed, and in the search mode they pick the character to search by. For this character visualisation we customised Mixamo's Mousey animated 3D model, assigning different looping animations and colours. In the middle, an example of using the tablet's camera while walking around, the child sees the selfie-based book review by a peer connected to the book of interest. On the right, a school library with books having the AR markers attached, to identify the books currently available in the system.

With *the StorySurfer* children search for books in the library [7]. It consists of one big floor surface that they can stand on, and a tabletop. Various book covers as well as search interfaces are projected on these surfaces. Children can use multiple themes to search by stepping on buttons and moving around. Based on the input, similar to a Venn diagram, books that fit several themes are in the overlapping part of a visualisation. By keeping the focus on one book for a longer time on the floor, the book is selected and 'sent' to the tabletop where they reveal new properties such as information about the author, a summary, and related books. The StorySurfer seemed to foster social interaction, partly because multiple users can use it at once. This created the opportunity for children to 'look over the shoulder' of others, potentially broadening their horizon.

With *the BibPhone* children can add audio annotations to books, which other children can listen to [18]. By scanning RFID tags a child can either listen to what was recorded onto the book or leave a message behind for someone else. Reviews were provided by school classes of children that were invited to the library. Evaluations showed that children liked listening to the recorded messages on the books. Recording messages themselves, however, was often found to be embarrassing by the children. This ties in with an important issue for user-generated content: such systems are only as interesting as the content on it.

The Department of Hidden Stories (DoHS) aims at storytelling and improved engagement in a public library [29]. Children can create information relating to books to be added onto the physical books via their barcodes. The concept revolves around triggering storytelling and includes *character cards*, suggestions to include a fortunate or unfortunate event, as well as instructions for content such as 'where does the story begin?'. The generated stories are related to the books the children find in the library. There are two modes, one to *create* stories and one to *discover* stories of other children. How the story is structured is left open but in their evaluation children showed many key points of stories.

With *the Search Wall*, children can physically create their search with a combination of tangibles [5]. For instance, rotating cubes with icons, rotating knobs, and placing physical puppets (animal characters) that represent a media type (e.g. comics [6]). On the central screen search results are shown in the order of their popularity, scroll-able via knobs.

The ReadAR application is different in the following ways: we make use of video and Augmented Reality, work in an in-school library, and have a different approach to finding books (described later). Similar to related work we deliberately include active movement and relation to the physical environment for exploring different books. We also include listening to another child's review, also with the aim to foster (mediated) social interactions. Similar to the approach of the BibPhone, we include recordings of a book review by fellow children, and similar to DoHS we do this by having a *search* and *book review* mode. To further increase chances to generate interesting content, similar to DoHS we included suggestions for content. For our case, as is also described in our context analysis, we build on the traditional written book report forms.

3   Context Analysis

During the project we were informed by three teachers of the primary school that participated in this research, each with more than 20 years of experience, and by an education coordinator of ten public libraries. These interviews were held online, as an unstructured interview. The interviews included discussing what children do when they are looking for a book, the motivations for choosing a book, and what problems the children experience when choosing books. Additionally, a survey was conducted among primary school students.

3.1   Teachers and Expert on 'Children Choosing Books'

The interviewees mentioned that most children primarily look at the cover of the book, and furthermore at font size and images inside. One teacher mentioned that children look at the number of pages, sometimes looking for the thinnest book possible. The blurb on the back is often ignored. These findings fit with Reuter's study on (digitally) choosing books with the ICDL [26] and other studies [9,10]. Out of seven dimensions analysed by Reuter, the one mentioned as the biggest influence on book choice was the metadata and physical entity of the book (e.g., title, cover and front matter) [26]. Literature does show differences exist between age groups, where these findings fit our target group of early elementary children whereas older children are expected to make more use of summaries and genres [9,10].

One teacher mentioned that some children have no systematic way of choosing books, but simply walk up to the shelf corresponding with reading level and choose a random book, putting it back when the cover does not appeal to them. Level of difficulty was also part of the second most prevalent decision factor in Reuter's study, the 'accessibility dimension' [26]. In the school library of the interviewees, bookshelves fit reading level, but were not sorted by theme.

Finally, a teacher remarked that children influence each other when choosing books. When his students spend more time in the library, they start conversations and recommend books to each other. This fits with older children indicating to rely more on their friend's than teacher's recommendations [9]. Our ReadAR application uses this by having other children suggest and give feedback about books. Our system also acknowledges the difficulties of children with lower reading levels, where we for instance link this to liking books with many pictures.

3.2 Teachers and Expert on 'Problems Experienced by Children When Choosing Books'

The teachers identified multiple problems that pupils experience in their decision-making process. One of these is choice overload, which might reduce the quality of the decision [4]. Libraries offer so many different choices that children often do not know where to start. Children furthermore often lack the verbal tools to describe which books they might like. They might *know*, but lack the tools to define their taste. A teacher or librarian could help them discover their literary taste, by asking questions and guiding them in finding a suitable book. However, several teachers stated that while they would love to help their students find a good book, they simply lack the time to do this for all students.

Teachers also stated that some children are *unmotivated* to make an informed decision on what book to read. The process of choosing a book is deemed unimportant. Children often do not examine the contents of the book, but instead focus on external things like the cover images and the size of the letters.

Finally, according to the library education coordinator, the typical setup of a library, with rows upon rows of book spines, makes it hard for children to see what is available and thus choose a book; they need more information. The library does try to address these things, for instance by placing some books with the cover towards the outside, but this is not sufficient.

3.3 Survey on Finding Books - Fun and Difficulty

We conducted a survey among pupils of the participating school, to get an idea of their experiences or attitude towards the library and towards choosing books. We focused on how easy and fun they consider the process to be. Similar to [3] who targeted 8-12-year-old children, we used Likert-scale questions. After obtaining approval from the CIS ethical committee of the EEMCS faculty under RP 2021-14, respondents were recruited via the participating school. The teachers of the students then distributed the survey to those children for whom we had written consent by their legal representative and approval for use of videos. Of the 40 participants, 25% were in the Dutch fifth grade (equivalent to US school system's third grade), 37,5% in the sixth grade, 20% in the seventh grade and 17.5% in the eighth grade.

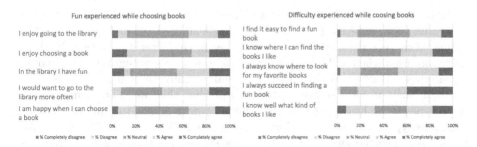

Fig. 2. Translated responses of the children (5th-8th grade) on a 5-point Likert scale about fun and difficulty while choosing and finding books (in any type of library).

Although we did not use a validated questionnaire, we did investigate reliability of both constructs. The first construct, the amount of fun experienced while choosing books, achieved acceptable reliability, with Cronbach's $\alpha = 0.896$. The second construct, the experienced difficulty of finding books, had a lower but still acceptable reliability, with $\alpha = 0.742$. Removing the statement 'I know well what kind of books I like' would result in an improved $\alpha = 0.761$.

Responses to the question 'Why is [this] your favourite book?' were all quite short. Children made two common arguments: a book being exciting/thrilling, and a book being funny, but not with strong reasons for why they liked a book. This fits with the expert interviews indicating it might be hard for a child to verbalize their taste. Many of the arguments focused on only one or two aspects of a book; whether it is funny, thrilling, has nice images, or is adventurous.

The results seem to indicate that the problems that children experience while looking for books are not that related to knowing what books they like, nor to a lack of enjoyment when looking for books. Rather it seems that there is some difficulty in finding fun books and some resistance to going to and enjoying the library. Elements we hope to address with the ReadAR application by providing and going through recommendations in an 'exploring' way.

4   ReadAR

ReadAR was designed building on the related work and expert input, taking PLEX elements [14,16] into account[1], as well as design input from one teacher.

---

[1] During our design iterations we primarily took into account captivation, completion, control, discovery, exploration, expression, fantasy, humor, and sympathy. For

This teacher also helped to inform us on the types of books to be included. ReadAR was made in Unity and runs on an Apple iPadAir (2019) due to availability and support for ARfoundation (i.e., ARkit for Apple devices). The ReadAR app consists of two modes: a *book review* and *search* mode, similar to [29].

4.1 Four 3D Characters

In ReadAR the children have to think about what type of person would enjoy a certain book, expressed by choosing from a limited set of four virtual 3D-animated characters (also see Fig. 1) with specific characteristics. The same characters are used when looking for a new book to read. We recognise that 'reading stereotypes' attached to the character could actually have negative effects on children, such as filter bubble effects. To prevent this, we choose the reading stereotypes to be broad yet specific, aiming to have all children finding a reading stereotype they can somewhat relate to, or at least relate a book to. We furthermore avoided visual attributes in the stereotypes that might alienate certain users on things other than reading preference. Striking a balance between having enough options to choose from and having enough books per character, four stereotypes were created in discussion with the teacher. In the app, the characters introduce themselves and which types of books they like, see Table 1.

Table 1. The four types of characters in the ReadAR app, targeted to not fall too much towards stereotypes but rather covering a wider range of books.

Name	Type of books	Description
Peep	Funny books, sports books	I don't love reading... I'd rather go outside to play! If I have to read anyways, I'd want a funny book, or a book about sports!
Fluff	Thrilling stories, fantasy books, history books	I like reading a lot! Especially thrilling stories. I also enjoy books about magic, and about the past
Pow	Realistic books, non-fiction books	I enjoy books that could really have happened. I also really like books with information!
Pika	Picture books, comics, books about animals, funny books	I think reading is quite hard... That's why I like when there are a lot of graphics in the book. I also really like books about animals!

instance, the characters' traits are intended to be relatable and triggering emotional feelings, similar to the suggestion in [14] that Sim characters might trigger sympathy.

4.2   Book Review Mode

The reviewing of a book upon is supposed to happen upon returning it, and consists of three main parts: taking a picture of the book to be returned, choosing a character to which the book fits, and making a video telling why this book belongs to this specific character. Similar to [29], these child-generated materials are then used in the search mode.

The app starts by showing the camera feed with the instruction: *'Create a picture of your book'* and a big red button to take the picture. The child can than navigate the four characters with two arrows, see Fig. 1. The third step consists of recording the video. The camera feed is put in selfie-mode, and the child needs to press and hold a red recording button to start recording the video, which is indicated with an instruction at the bottom. On the same screen, some cues on what to say were added: on top as main instruction *'Tell $<Name\ character>$ whytheyshouldfindthisafunbook'* and next to the selfie-feed *'What did you think about the book?'*, *'What is the book about?'*, and *'What type of book is it?'*. These are the same questions that are on the traditional book report that the children commonly used.

For recording and saving the picture of the book and the video, the NatCorder and NatShare APIs were used to record video and save it to a specific folder. [2] The photos and videos that were recorded were kept on device, with each video saved in a specific folder, representing the character the child has chosen. These videos were (for now still) manually added to the AR experience in the search mode based on markers and on basis of the book cover.

4.3   Search Mode

Finding (or: looking for) a book starts with the user choosing a character that fits them. This is essentially the same interface as when returning a book, with the descriptive text on the top of the screen changed to *'Choose a character to choose a book with'*. After this, the interface becomes a viewfinder. When the user hovers the tablet over one of the markers attached to the books that fits the character they are looking with, a video of their peer who created a book review on that book starts playing, see Fig. 1.

5   Method

To evaluate whether the prototype helped children choose books and made the process more fun, we tested the prototype during two within-subject sessions with respectively 18 and 15 participants.

Children were selected via a familiar teacher in the participating primary school, inviting two classes of this school (Dutch fifth and sixth grade). These were children from the age of 8 until 11 (same range as [19]), $\mu_{age} = 8.9$ with

---

[2] NatSuite "NatCorder AP", https://docs.natsuite.io/natcorder/ and NatSuite "Nat-Share", https://docs.natsuite.io/natshare/, accessed on 18th of June 2021.

$\sigma = 0.96$, including 7 boys and 11 girls. To provide more comfort for the children, the tests were done with two children present each session at the school's library. Legal representatives signed both the consent form and separately we asked for consent for use of the video recordings in the study, accessible only to the involved participants during the study and to the involved researchers for a minimum of 10 years. This study including expert interviews was approved by the ethical committee of our faculty.

In the first session we focused on the reflective part of the experience. Children were asked to review a book of their choice with the ReadAR prototype, and to fill in a book report[3]. The latter was seen as the baseline alternative, as this was currently in use in the primary school to make children reflect on book choices. In the second session children were asked to find a book using the ReadAR prototype and compare this to the current baseline of finding a book without the help of the prototype.

Measurements mainly built on the Fun Toolkit [24,25]. The first form consisted of four parts. An adapted *smiley-o-meter* [25] to measure fun (translated and with revamped visuals, analysed with Wilcoxon's signed-rank test based on non-parametric characteristic of visual rating). A place where children could give the activity a grade (based on their experience a 1-10 scale, using a t-test, assuming a reasonable continuous scale with meaningful equal distances). Finally, there were two open questions where they could write down what they found the most and least fun (first author coding recurring responses and providing counts). For the second session, a question was added concerning why they chose the book they did, and a Visual Analog Scale (5-point scale from very hard to very easy, using Wilcoxon's signed-rank test) for experienced difficulty when looking for a book. After exposure to both situations, another form was used to compare the two experiences. On this form, the participants had to pick their preferred situation. In addition, this form included an again-again table [25]. For each of the elements of the experience, children could state whether or not they wanted to do it again. For example, the elements in the again table for the first evaluation session were: choosing a mouse (character), recording a video, writing down what the book is about, giving the book a mark, using the iPad app, and filling in the book report.

While the children were using the ReadAR prototype they were observed, during which we paid special notice to playful behaviour. We made a draft observation scheme with anticipated playful elements. Unfortunately, details are outside the scope of this short paper (although we do briefly look at its potential in the discussion). In total the sessions took six hours spread over two mornings, during both mornings the sessions with two children directly following each other.

---

[3] We used an online randomizer to decide who started in which of the conditions. After each of the conditions they filled in the evaluation forms. In the second session, about finding books, three children could not make it to school due to sickness(-related) reasons.

6   Results

We did not observe a significant difference in the reported amount of fun experienced when comparing reflecting through a book report with reflecting through the ReadAR prototype (Wilcoxon's signed-rank test, $Z = -1.883, p = 0.060$). However, the participants (61.1%) did report that they experienced more fun using the prototype as compared to writing the book report. This fits with the again-again table where 12 (out of 18) wanted to use the app again, 6 maybe; whereas only 3 wanted to use the book report again 12 maybe and 3 not again. There was no significant difference found in the overall grade given to the experience ($\mu_{report} = 8.21, \mu_{app} = 8.94, T = 1.553, df = 18, p = 0.139$). Children enjoyed the characters that were included in the prototype, with 77.8% mentioning this as their favourite part of the application. The children disliked recording the video review, for 66.6% their least favourite part (besides mentioned as least fun in this open field, also in the again-again table 6x indicated as not again and only 1x again).

There was no significant difference in the experienced difficulty of finding a book when comparing finding a book with and without the prototype (Wilcoxon's signed-rank test, $Z = -1.633, p = 0.102$). More than half of the participants (53.3%) reported they found it easier to find a book using the ReadAR prototype. Looking at the types of reasons children gave why they chose a book: we could observe that children more frequently gave a very general motivation for their book choice when they chose a book without using the app. An example of an overly general motivation is 'it seems good'. With the ReadAR prototype instead (nine out of fifteen times) children mentioned an aspect that was featured either as a preference of one of the characters, or an aspect mentioned in one of the reviews.

Children did experience significantly more fun when looking for a book using the application, compared to finding a book without it, based on the Wilcoxon's signed-rank test ($Z = -3.219, p = 0.001$). The majority (86.6%) of the children reported to have experienced more fun when using the ReadAR prototype. This also fits with results of the again-again table, 13 indicated wanting to do it again using the app and 3 maybe; whereas for finding the book without the app only 3 again, 11 maybe, and 1 not again. The mean grade given for the experience is also significantly higher ($\mu_{app} = 9.51\ \sigma_{app} = .45$ vs $\mu_{without} = 7.76, \sigma_{without} = 1.52$) for finding a book using the application ($T = 4.571, df = 14, P < 0.001$).

Some of the favourite elements that were mentioned by the participants were choosing the characters (also 10x again), watching the videos (11x again), and looking for the videos (11x again). All children were able to pick a character that fit them, and many children even checked out multiple characters. Sometimes children got frustrated, because they thought there would be a video linked to the book, but not every character contained a review for every book.

7   Discussion and Future Work

From the evaluation with the primary school children, we see a significant increase in the reported amount of fun when using the ReadAR prototype to find a book. The children indicated to enjoy choosing the characters, looking for videos, and watching the videos. We did not record a significant improvement in the reported amount of fun when using the ReadAR prototype to reflect on a book. Children seemed to simply not enjoy recording the videos and were slightly uncomfortable when recording their review. Even though nowadays children are used to more regular video recordings (e.g., using Tiktok) this is still similar to the findings of fifteen years ago when recording audio with the Bibphone [18]. We were also unable to see an improvement in the reported difficulty of finding a book. We did get the impression that the book they chose using ReadAR was more well-considered, although we cannot substantiate this with clear data.

7.1   Limitations

To make the children more comfortable, the evaluation of the prototype was done in pairs of students. One student would start with using the prototype, the other student would start with the alternative. In several cases, this led to distraction for the student who had to do the alternative interaction, which was arguably less novel. This could have influenced how children experienced the interactions. Similar to studies with the BibPhone, for which the authors reported technical problems including range and database connections [18], we also had some usability issues. Several children did not understand that they had to hold the recording button to keep recording, which led to some frustration among them. In addition, for the first few students, the limit for the recording time was too short (30s), which was solved on the spot (120s). Finally, it was not that easy for children to switch characters as they had to close and reopen the app. In general students seemed to have no difficulty doing this, as they tried several characters. This difficulty might also be a potential strength, as it steers the user to really go through one perspective before proceeding to the next.

We did not yet analyse book choices in detail. For instance, did they manage to find a book that better fit them, and achieve the increase in pleasure of reading? We do tentatively see a possible effect that the children give a more elaborate argument for their book choice with the app. Although a different medium comparison (app vs writing) and content (reading rather than 'scientific method thinking') this seems to fit with Wijnen's et al. findings when comparing a learning task done with a robot instead of a tablet, that also indicated more elaboration of answers with the more elaborate medium (there: the robot) [28]. At the same time, we see they do not yet more easily find a book with ReadAR.

7.2   Future Work: Towards Playful Child-Driven Intelligence Suggestions

We see an interesting difference of our study and design with current apps popular among children, such as Tiktok. On the one hand, rather than have an

Artificial Intelligence (AI) system decide the content-suggestion based on view-ing/reading history, rather we have fellow children provide the content and fil-tering. We also view this approach fits with the recurring values seen in related work, such as 'focusing on children's sense of autonomy, agency, and empow-erment' [13, p205]. Unlike automatically learned reading profiles, the reading stereotypes were also not to be found in the real world. Together with the teacher we deliberately added elements that are a somewhat unnatural fit of an underly-ing stereotype, purposefully going outside characterizations of occurring profiles. This also has the practical use to get them into contact with other books than they would normally read.

On the other hand, we see a difference with the apparent fun that children can have in making and sharing videos for platforms such as Tiktok. We were fascinated to see this finding from the Bibphone still holds [18], and can only hypothesize to why this is. It is interesting to look for an alternative way of giving feedback and to retrieve why children disliked recording the video. Maybe, the children required more structure when talking about a book, or the opposite if they feel forced. Or perhaps, children feel vulnerable showing their face to others. One alternative to explore could be an avatar that repeats what the child is saying, something like the popular 'My Talking Tom Cat' app[4]. Another alternative is having an AR face filter to alter the face of the users to make recording a video less intrusive. This might also diminish an urge seen with Department of Hidden Stories to play 'the game' right, and a need 'to know they were doing the "right" thing' [29, p1891]. Which leaves us to still wonder how we can further the aimed-for playful attitude, rather than triggering a gameful mindset of following predetermined rules in such systems (cf. [17]).

Furthermore, even if we manage to trigger more playful elements, we also need to find suitable ways to measure this. Arrasvuori et al. suggest the use and creation of a questionnaire to investigate the experience [1]. Perhaps for children it might be worthwhile to instead employ observation schemes to see what kind of playful behaviours are elicited. Currently we only did this in an informal manner, with direct observations by the first author without proper checks for validity and reliability (cf. [15]). In other studies with interactive products for children, choosing the right training, schemes, and methods, authors managed to get reasonable levels of agreement, including observations of other play categories fitting interactive playgrounds [20] and Head-Up Games [2].

8 Conclusion

The ReadAR system with our participants clearly showed potential to truly change the experience of choosing a book for a child. However, some elements in the product should still be improved and need to be investigated on a longer and larger scale. We also learnt that children did not enjoy recording the videos, even though they appreciated those of others. We identified challenges and the

---

[4] See https://play.google.com/store/apps/details?id=com.outfit7.talkingtom&hl=en \&gl=US, accessed 26th of January 2021.

potential for impact of more playful ways to search books, and urge others to continue investigating similar directions.

Acknowledgements. Thanks to all the experts and especially Helma Bouman from the Z-O-U-T Library and Niels Bakker from Stichting Lezen, and also a big thanks to the children involved in particular those from the participating primary school.

References

1. Arrasvuori, J., Boberg, M., Holopainen, J., Korhonen, H., Lucero, A., Montola, M.: Applying the plex framework in designing for playfulness. In: Proceedings of the 2011 Conference on Designing Pleasurable Products and Interfaces. DPPI 2011, Association for Computing Machinery, New York, NY, USA (2011). https://doi.org/10.1145/2347504.2347531
2. Bakker, S., Markopoulos, P., de Kort, Y.: OPOS: an observation scheme for evaluating head-up play. In: Proceedings of the 5th Nordic Conference on Human-Computer Interaction: Building Bridges, pp. 33–42. NordiCHI 2008, Association for Computing Machinery, New York, NY, USA (2008). https://doi.org/10.1145/1463160.1463165
3. Bekker, T., Sturm, J., Eggen, B.: Designing playful interactions for social interaction and physical play. Personal Ubiquitous Comput. **14**(5), 385–396 (2010). https://doi.org/10.1007/s00779-009-0264-1
4. Besedeš, T., Deck, C., Sarangi, S., Shor, M.: Reducing choice overload without reducing choices. Rev. Econ. Stat. **97**(4), 793–802 (2015)
5. Detken, K., Martinez, C., Schrader, A.: The search wall: tangible information searching for children in public libraries. In: Proceedings of the 3rd International Conference on Tangible and Embedded Interaction, pp. 289–296. TEI 2009, Association for Computing Machinery, New York, NY, USA (2009).https://doi.org/10.1145/1517664.1517724
6. Detken, K., Schrader, A.: Tangible information interfaces for children in public libraries. In: Lucke, U., Kindsmüller, M.C., Fischer, S., Herczeg, M., Seehusen, S. (eds.) Workshop Proceedings der Tagungen Mensch & Computer 2008, DeLFI 2008 und Cognitive Design 2008, pp. 435–440. Logos Verlag, Berlin (2008)
7. Eriksson, E., Lykke-Olesen, A.: StorySurfer: a playful book browsing installation for children's libraries. In: Proceedings of the 6th International Conference on Interaction Design and Children, pp. 57–64. IDC 2007, Association for Computing Machinery, New York, NY, USA (2007). https://doi.org/10.1145/1297277.1297289
8. Gubbels, J., van Langen, A., Maassen, N., Meelissen, M.: Resultaten PISA-2018 in vogelvlucht. Univer. Twente (2019). https://doi.org/10.3990/1.9789036549226
9. Hawkins Wendelin, K., Zinck, R.: How students make book choices. Reading Horizons J. Literacy Lang. Arts **23**(2), 2 (1983)
10. Hutchinson, H., Druin, A., Bederson, B.B., Reuter, K., Rose, A., Weeks, A.C.: How do i find blue books about dogs? the errors and frustrations of young digital library users. Proceed. HCII **2005**, 22–27 (2005)
11. Hutchinson, H.B., Bederson, B.B., Druin, A.: The evolution of the international children's digital library searching and browsing interface. In: Proceedings of the 2006 Conference on Interaction Design and Children, pp. 105–112. IDC 2006, Association for Computing Machinery, New York, NY, USA (2006). https://doi.org/10.1145/1139073.1139101

12. Itenge-Wheeler, H., Winschiers-Theophilus, H., Soro, A., Brereton, M.: Child designers creating personas to diversify design perspectives and concepts for their own technology enhanced library. In: Proceedings of the 17th ACM Conference on Interaction Design and Children, pp. 381–388 (2018)
13. Kawas, S., et al.: Another decade of IDC research: Examining and reflecting on values and ethics. In: Proceedings of the Interaction Design and Children Conference, pp. 205–215. IDC 2020, Association for Computing Machinery, New York, NY, USA (2020). https://doi.org/10.1145/3392063.3394436
14. Korhonen, H., Montola, M., Arrasvuori, J.: Understanding playful user experience through digital games. In: International Conference on Designing Pleasurable Products and Interfaces, vol. 2009 (2009)
15. Lazar, J., Feng, J.H., Hochheiser, H.: Research methods in human-computer interaction. Morgan Kaufmann (2017)
16. Lucero, A., Arrasvuori, J.: Plex cards: a source of inspiration when designing for playfulness. In: Proceedings of the 3rd International Conference on Fun and Games, pp. 28–37. Fun and Games 2010, Association for Computing Machinery, New York, NY, USA (2010). https://doi.org/10.1145/1823818.1823821
17. Lucero, A., Karapanos, E., Arrasvuori, J., Korhonen, H.: Playful or gameful? creating delightful user experiences. Interactions 21(3), 34–39 (2014). https://doi.org/10.1145/2590973
18. Lykke-Olesen, A., Nielsen, J.: Bibphone: adding sound to the children's library. In: Proceedings of the 6th International Conference on Interaction Design and Children, pp. 145–148. IDC 2007, Association for Computing Machinery, New York, NY, USA (2007). https://doi.org/10.1145/1297277.1297307
19. Merga, M.K.: What would make children read for pleasure more frequently? Engl. Educ. 51(2), 207–223 (2017)
20. Moreno, A., van Delden, R., Reidsma, D., Poppe, R., Heylen, D.: An annotation scheme for social interaction in digital playgrounds. In: Herrlich, M., Malaka, R., Masuch, M. (eds.) ICEC 2012. LNCS, vol. 7522, pp. 85–99. Springer, Heidelberg (2012). https://doi.org/10.1007/978-3-642-33542-6_8
21. Pariser, E.: The filter bubble: what the Internet is hiding from you. Penguin Press, New York (2011)
22. Petscher, Y.: A meta-analysis of the relationship between student attitudes towards reading and achievement in reading. J. Res. Reading 33(4), 335–355 (2010)
23. Raad voor Cultuur, Onderwijsraad: Een oproep tot een leesoffensief-lees! (2019). https://www.rijksoverheid.nl/documenten/richtlijnen/2019/06/30/een-oproep-tot-een-leesoffensief-lees
24. Read, J.C.: Validating the fun toolkit: an instrument for measuring children's opinions of technology. Cogn. Technol. Work 10(2), 119–128 (2008)
25. Read, J.C., MacFarlane, S.: Using the fun toolkit and other survey methods to gather opinions in child computer interaction. In: Proceedings of the 2006 Conference on Interaction Design and Children, pp. 81–88. Association for Computing Machinery, New York, NY, USA (2006). https://doi.org/10.1145/1139073.1139096
26. Reuter, K.: Assessing aesthetic relevance: children's book selection in a digital library. J. Am. Soc. Inform. Sci. Technol. 58(12), 1745–1763 (2007)
27. Verenikina, I., Harris, P., Lysaght, P.: Child's play: computer games, theories of play and children's development. In: Proceedings of Young Children and Learning Technologies, pp. 99–106 (2003)
28. Wijnen, F.M., Davison, D.P., Reidsma, D., Meij, J.V.D., Charisi, V., Evers, V.: Now we're talking: Learning by explaining your reasoning to a social robot. J. Hum.-Robot Interact. 9(1), 3345508 (2019). https://doi.org/10.1145/3345508

29. Wood, G., et al.: The department of hidden stories: Playful digital storytelling for children in a public library. In: Proceedings of the SIGCHI Conference on Human Factors in Computing Systems, pp. 1885–1894. CHI 2014, Association for Computing Machinery, New York, NY, USA (2014). https://doi.org/10.1145/2556288.2557034

Persuasive Strategies

mRAPID Study: Effect of Micro-incentives and Daily Deadlines on Practice Behavior

Michael Sobolev[1]([⊠]) [ID], Fabian Okeke[1] [ID], and Ori Plonsky[2] [ID]

[1] Cornell Tech, New York, NY, USA
michael.sobolev@cornell.edu
[2] Technion - Israel Institute of Technology, Haifa, Israel

Abstract. Many goals people have, like getting into shape or getting good grades on important exams, require small daily deferrable efforts, like exercising or studying. To help people sustain these efforts over time, behavioral research explored the use of interventions like planning, reminders, commitment devices, and incentives. In an exploratory study, we tested the effectiveness of these interventions in a real-life setting, practicing exam questions, using four versions of a study app (mRAPID) over 30 days. The basic app allowed users to plan their next study time and get reminders for it. The other versions added either a commitment device (a practice deadline), a contingent micro-incentive, or both. The results of N = 58 participants suggested micro-incentives had a positive effect whereas the commitment device had a negative effect of deadlines on daily practice. We discuss the implications of these findings to behavior design and the use of technology in behavior change, with a focus on designing for behavior over time.

Keywords: behavior change · persuasive technology · habit formation · incentives · deadlines · reminders · planning

1 Introduction

Many goals people have, like physical health and academic success, require small and repeated daily efforts, like exercising or studying. In comparison with the benefits of the larger goal, the costs of these daily efforts are insignificant, yet because they can easily be deferred or put off "for later", these efforts are highly susceptible to procrastination amidst day-to-day distractions. To tackle this problem, support people's goals, and help them form good habits, behavioral research proposed a variety of potential behavior change interventions, ranging from incentives to nudges.

J. Ham et al. (Eds.): PERSUASIVE 2023, LNCS 13832, pp. 67–81, 2023.
https://doi.org/10.1007/978-3-031-30933-5_5

Nowadays, many behavior change techniques are implemented as part of the design of mobile apps and digital interventions [14,18]. Mobile devices and applications are ubiquitous, can objectively measure behavior [13,18] and are often designed to be persuasive and habit forming [9,10,16]. These aspects have led to proliferation of research on human-centered technologies for behavior change in computing [1,5,6,14,18]. As a result, mobile apps designed to help people become more physically active, eat healthier, reduce stress, and increase productivity, are currently used by millions around the world.

Despite this progress, a significant gap in behavior change research remains. Technology-mediated nudges, even if effective, often have only modest effects on behavior and usually do not persist over time [1]. Behavioral research still lacks sufficient understanding of the mechanisms behind and the unintended consequences of different incentive structures over time [8,11]. In particular, there is not enough evidence on the interaction between different nudges and the long-term effect of combining incentives and nudges on desired daily behaviors [11,25]. In behavior change technology, systematic experimentation and evaluation of behavioral components implemented in mobile apps is lacking. Using mobile devices, there is an opportunity to measure behavior in real time (e.g. physical activity, daily practice) and provide personalized and timely behavioral nudges and incentives [13,18,23].

The use of incentives for daily behavior became a popular research area with successes in domains such as physical activity promotion [2], medication adherence [12], and screen time reduction [19]. Incentives are generally effective in changing behavior but must be designed properly [11]. For example, small incentives can sometimes backfire and decrease motivation to perform the behavior [11]. Behavioral designers should ensure extrinsic incentives do not decrease the intrinsic motivation to perform a behavior [11] or increase the probability of regretting a specific action [8]. Additionally, to be scalable, incentives should be cost-effective and maintain effect on long-term behavior [11].

The nudging approach has provided behavior change designers a less costly set of tools, such as reminders and planning prompts [5,7,18,23]. Reminders are meant to help with the demands of daily life, to address procrastination and inertia, and are generally effective in encouraging desired behavior [4]. Reminders can be more effective when coupled with planning. In the context of daily behavior, reminders about previously made plans (i.e. plan reminders) were found to be effective for reinforcing healthy habits [21,24,26]. Extensive research exists on personalizing and optimizing the timing and content of reminders and notifications based on individual context and previous behavior [4,22,24].

An additional type of nudge involves the use of commitment devices: self-regulatory techniques designed to mitigate the gap between intention and behavior by clarifying timing, context, or the cost of future actions. Deadline is a form of a costly commitment device. In a famous study, Ariely and Wertenbroch [3] found that self-imposed deadlines can decrease procrastination and increase performance of students in class. There is evidence suggesting that people understand the limits of their self-control and therefore demand, and self-select into, costly commitment devices such as deadlines [3]. Yet deadlines do not always work as intended. For example, recent research indicates that longer deadlines can be more detrimental to goal pursuit than shorter deadlines [27].

The goal of our research is to design, implement, and evaluate a behavior change technology that implements micro-incentives and daily deadlines. We designed the mobile Reminders, Planning, Incentives, and Deadlines (mRAPID) app to promote easily procrastinated behaviors amidst day-to-day distractions. We evaluated the mRAPID mobile app and its behavioral components using a field experiment (the RAPID Study), in the context of daily practice for an important exam. The importance of the exam was highlighted for participants by the use of a large monetary incentive that was guaranteed to the top 50% of examinees in a post-study test. The goal was to increase the number of users' sessions of practice for the exam, as well as the daily regularity of practices across the 30 days of study.

In the design of the mRAPID app, we assumed that to promote exam practice, it was necessary that the app will allow planning of study sessions and that it will provide reminders when the time for a session is reached. Therefore, even in its most basic version, the app allowed users to plan their next-day study time and get reminders when it arrives (Control condition). We compared this basic version to three other versions that added either a daily deadline until which the practice session should be completed (Daily deadlines only condition), a small monetary incentive awarded for a successful completion of a practice session (Micro-incentives only condition), or both a micro-incentive and a daily deadline (Both condition). Our primary research question focuses on the relative effect of micro-incentives and daily deadlines on practice behavior over time.

This paper makes three main contributions. First, we provide empirical and experimental evidence for the effectiveness of micro-incentives and daily deadlines in a real-life setting and over time. Second, we reveal that the effects of the micro-incentives and daily deadlines are stronger in the long term than in the short term, highlighting an important dimension that behavioral interventions designed to impact behavior over time should consider. Third, we identify and discuss the implications of our findings to behavioral science research, behavioral design, and the use of technology in behavior change.

2 Method

2.1 Design of mRAPID App

Our research aims to explore the design and evaluation of behavior change technology for easily procrastinated daily behaviors such as exercising or studying. We first design and study this technology in the context of daily practice for important exams like the SAT, GRE, and GMAT. Our design process was informed by prior research in behavioral science, and behavior change technologies. We first identified common behavioral barriers to achieve the goal of daily physical exercising or studying such as procrastination, forgetfulness, and day-to-day distractions. Then, based on evidence from prior research in behavioral science and behavior change, we surveyed the pertinent behavioral interventions to change behavior in this context. Based on this process, we identified behavior tracking, ability to create plans, and timely reminders as necessary features in a study app designed to encourage behavior amid day-to-day distractions. We further discuss two features of the mRAPID app we experimentally test in our study: micro-incentives and daily deadlines.

1. *Micro-incentives:* Rewards are a central mechanism for behavior change technologies and habit-forming technologies. Micro-incentives are a class of monetary incentives that are small enough to be delivered daily and are contingent on objectively measured behavior.
2. *Daily deadlines:* Deadlines are a restrictive self-regulatory technique designed to mitigate the gap between intention and behavior. Deadlines must be seamlessly integrated with planning and reminders to increase motivation to engage with behavior without decreasing ability to perform behavior.

We developed mRAPID based on the guidelines above for both the iOS and Android platforms. To study the context of daily practice for an exam, we connected our app to a commercial external application (the publicly available "GMAT Question Bank" app by Veritas Prep) via an API to allow for tracking of practices. Practice always happened in the external GMAT app (that we had no control over) while behavior tracking, reminders, planning, micro-incentives, and daily deadlines were delivered via our mRAPID app. Figure 1 shows the main features of the study app: (1) tracking previous practices with feedback on duration, score, and timing compared to reminders set by the user; and (2) the ability to plan ahead and set practice reminders for the next day at the preferred time for the user. Reminders with and without daily deadlines are delivered via a push notification from the mRAPID app. A time for a reminder could only be set once per day, and only starting the next day (to avoid allowing users to set a reminder directly before practicing). After a reminder time was set, the app sent a reminder on that time daily (i.e. users did not have to reset the time daily unless they wanted to change the timing).

2.2 Participants

Participants were recruited to participate in a study that encouraged them to practice GMAT questions. We initially enrolled $N = 104$ participants, with $N = 26$ participants randomly allocated to each of four experimental conditions, as described below. Participants were mainly advanced undergraduate students, all from the same Israeli university. In a pre-survey, all but one of the participants indicated that they had never studied for the GMAT before. 84% indicated they did not plan to take the exam in the following six months. Of the 104 recruited, nine participants were removed from the study due to technical errors with their phones that did not allow proper functioning of the app. Of the remaining, we focus on a subgroup of $N = 58$ participants, who engaged with the app and completed at least one valid practice session (i.e. a session lasting at least 3 min

Fig. 1. Screenshot of the mRAPID App from an iPhone device

answering at least 3 GMAT questions; see below) over the 30 days of the study. We refer to this subgroup as the "active" participants. Notably, none of the "inactive" participants asked for their monetary compensation nor participated in the post-intervention mock exam (see below). Eventually, there were 11, 17, 17, and 13 active participants in the control, daily deadline only, micro-incentive only, and both conditions respectively.

Participants' compensation depended on the randomly assigned treatment: in the conditions without micro-incentives, participants were given the local currency equivalent of (approximately) 30 USD, independently of the number and nature of practice sessions they completed. In the micro-incentive conditions, participants were paid the local equivalent of (approximately) 1 USD for each day (of the 30 days) in which they completed at least one valid practice session. This procedure led to an average compensation of the equivalent of 24 USD per active participant. In addition, $N = 15$ participants were compensated (approximately) 65 USD for succeeding in a mock GMAT exam at the end of the study.

2.3 Procedure and Experimental Design

The study was approved by the Technion Social and Behavioral Sciences Institutional Review Board. To participate in the study, participants were asked to download two apps: the mRAPID study app we developed for the study and the free and publicly available "GMAT Question Bank" app from either the Apple App Store or the Google Play Store. The study ran for 30 consecutive days. All participants were told their goal was to practice at least once a day, answering a quiz of at least 3 questions. They were also told that answering a 3-question quiz in less than 3 min is extremely unlikely and therefore a valid practice session will only be one in which 3 questions were answered in a duration no smaller than 3 min. To motivate participants to practice, we announced that at the end of the study, we will hold a mock GMAT test using GMAT questions taken from the pool of questions in the Practice App, and participants who will be in the top 50% among all those who take the mock test will be compensated the local currency equivalent of (approximately) 65 USD. The mock exam consisted of 20 questions and was physically taken at the university lab.

All participants could use the basic features of the study app (track practices, plan ahead and set reminders) and they could also use the GMAT app to practice exam questions as many times as they liked during the duration of the study. Our 2X2 experimental design resulted in a control condition and three treatment conditions. Participants were randomized to one of four conditions: Control, Daily deadlines only, Micro-incentives only, and Both micro-incentives and daily deadlines. Detailed description of each experimental conditions is below:

1. *Control condition:* Participants are using the basic version of the mRAPID app and can practice GMAT questions as much as they like and at any time. They can set reminders and plan ahead as they like (though changing the timing of reminders was allowed only once per day) but no daily deadlines were set nor were micro-incentives given for practicing. Participants receive 30 USD for participation in the study.

2. *Daily deadlines only condition:* Participants are using the version of the mRAPID app with daily deadlines but without micro-incentives. A deadline for completing a practice session is set for no later than 15 min after the reminder time which is set in the system. Participants select the timing of the reminder (and hence of the deadline) for the next day using the app's planning and reminder mode. The reminder time remains fixed for all future days unless participants actively change it, which can be done only once per day (starting the next day). There are no monetary consequences for not completing the session within the set deadline. Participants receive 30 USD for participation in the study.

3. *Micro-incentives only condition:* Participants are using the version of the mRAPID app with micro-incentives but without daily deadlines. Participants earn the equivalent of 1 USD for the first completed valid practice of each day. Practicing more on the same day carries no incentive. Participants are free to set their own reminders, but the incentive is not contingent on the timing of the practice during the day. Participants are not compensated for participation in the study beyond the daily incentives that they earn.

4. *Both micro-incentives and daily deadlines condition:* Participants are using the version of the mRAPID app with incentives and with deadlines. This condition essentially combines the previous two conditions. Participants earn the equivalent of 1 USD for the first valid practice in each day that they complete within the deadline (i.e. practice within 15 min of reminders). Participants are

not compensated for participation in the study beyond the daily incentives that they earn.

Our study includes two main outcomes: (a) Practice Days: we recorded the number of days in which users had at least one valid practice session. This is a measure of the regularity of practices over 30 days. In each of 30 days, a user either practiced (at least once) or not. This is the main outcome in the study since we incentivized only one valid practice session per day. (b) Practices: we also recorded the total number of valid practice sessions since users could practice as many times as they wanted. We used total number of practices as a secondary outcome to measure habit formation and spillover effect of micro-incentives.

3 Results

Although we aimed for recruiting a larger sample we ended with too few participants per condition to perform confirmatory analysis so we treat this study as exploratory. Across the $N = 58$ active participants and all conditions, we observed a total of 1115 practices ($M = 19.2; Mdn = 18.5; Max = 70; Min = 1$), 897 practice days ($M = 15.5; Mdn = 16; Max = 30; Min = 1$), and 193 reminder times set ($M = 3.3; Mdn = 2; Max = 20; Min = 0$). The descriptive results per condition are presented in Table 1.

Table 1. Descriptive Results: Mean and Median number of practice days, valid practice sessions, and reminders across the four conditions: *control (N = 11), deadlines only (N = 17), incentives only (N = 17), and both incentives and deadlines (N = 13).*

	Practice Days	Practices	Reminders
Control	$M = 16.8, Mdn = 18$	$M = 22.6, Mdn = 23$	$M = 3.4, Mdn = 2$
Daily deadlines	$M = 9.4, Mdn = 5$	$M = 11.8, Mdn = 7$	$M = 2.7, Mdn = 2$
Micro-incentives	$M = 20.1, Mdn = 27$	$M = 24.9, Mdn = 30$	$M = 2.8, Mdn = 2$
Both	$M = 16.2, Mdn = 20$	$M = 18.7, Mdn = 24$	$M = 4.9, Mdn = 3$
All Conditions	$M = 19.2, Mdn = 18.5$	$M = 15.5, Mdn = 16$	$M = 3.3, Mdn = 2$

3.1 Association Between Planning and Reminders and Practicing

Our working hypothesis is that planning to practice and getting reminders for it increase the chances of practicing. Because all versions of the mRAPID app include a planning and reminders feature, we cannot validate this causal assumption. We nevertheless verified that there is a positive correlation ($r = .495, p < .001$) between the number of reminders a participant set and the number of days that same participant practiced. That is, as expected, those who planned ahead and set more reminders for the next day were also more likely to practice. The descriptive results show that participants in condition *Both* set slightly more reminders than others. This observation may reflect the fact that to get the daily incentive, participants in this condition had to practice within 15 min from the reminder time that they set. Hence, unlike participants in other conditions, those in condition *Both* were directly incentivized to plan ahead for practice time. Yet, the difference was far from being statistically significant, possibly due to lack of statistical power.

To test whether planning ahead was associated with the likelihood of practicing the next day, we used a mixed-effects logistic regression predicting whether a participant practiced on a specific day t using an indicator for setting a reminder time in day t-1 and including a random effect for participant (to control for correlated observations within participants; $SD = 2.45$). The results showed a positive and highly significant effect for setting a reminder on practicing the next day: $OR = 12.3, 95\%CI[5.8, 28.7], \chi^2(1) = 51.85, p < .001$. Hence, as expected, people who planned ahead for the next day and got a reminder in a desired time were far more likely to practice that day.

3.2   Effect of Micro-incentives and Daily Deadlines

We now turn to test our main effects of interest. The descriptive results per condition are presented in Table 1. Figures 2 and 3 present violin plots that demonstrate the difference between experimental conditions in the number of practice days and number of valid practice sessions. The results hint that micro-incentives tend to increase practice and the commitment device in the form of deadlines tend to decrease the tendency to practice, in general and per day.

Due to the small sample size, we use the non-parametric Mann-Whitney (Wilcoxon) test to estimate the effect of incentives and deadline factors independently. In line with our research questions, we use a one-sided confirmatory test to test if micro-incentives increase practice behaviors and a two-sided test to test how deadlines affect these behaviors. Number of practice days was greater with incentives ($Mdn = 23.5$) than without incentives ($Mdn = 8.5$), $U = 308.5$, $p = .042$, $r = .229$. Number of practice sessions was also greater with incentives ($Mdn = 28.5$) than without incentives ($Mdn = 9$), $U = 310$, $p = .044$, $r = .225$. Number of practice days was lower with deadlines ($Mdn = 9.5$) than without deadlines ($Mdn = 25.5$), $U = 276.5$, $p = .026$, $r = -.294$ Number of practice sessions was also lower with deadlines ($Mdn = 9.5$) than without deadlines ($Mdn = 27.5$), $U = 275$, $p = .024$, $r = -.297$. These results indicate a positive effect of incentives and a negative effect of deadlines serving as commitment devices on the number of practice days and on the total number of practice sessions during the study. We also do not observe differences between the control condition and the treatment condition with both incentives and deadlines in the number of practice days (Fig. 2) and practice sessions (Fig. 3). This results suggests that the effect of incentives and deadlines cancel each other out when combined in the same condition.

We also use several regression methods to check the robustness of our findings. For the effects of incentives and deadlines on the number of prac-

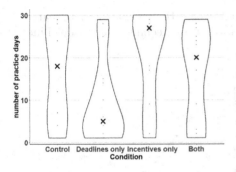 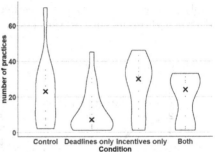

Fig. 2. Violin-plots of the number of practice days across the four conditions. The X's mark the medians. Dots mark individual participants

Fig. 3. Violin-plots of the number of valid practice sessions across the four conditions. The X's mark the medians. Dots mark individual participants

tice days, we used a mixed-effects binomial regression, as the dependent variable is binary. To control for the correlation between observations of the same participant, we introduced a random effect for participants ($SD =$ *2.31*). The results indicate that deadlines reduced the number of practice days by 77%, $OR = 0.23, 95\%CI[0.06, 0.83], \chi^2(1) = 4.97, p = .026$. However, the (directionally positive) effect of incentives was not significant, $OR = 2.86, 95\%CI[0.79, 10.5], \chi^2(1) = 2.61, p = .106$.

Next, we evaluated the impact of the deadlines and incentives on the number of valid practice sessions using a negative binomial regression, as the number of practices can be any natural number. Using this analysis, we estimate that deadlines decreased the number of practice sessions by 63%, $95\%CI[39, 101], p = .061$, a marginally significant effect, whereas incentives increased the number of practice sessions per participant by 33%, although this effect was insignificant $95\%CI$ for IRR $[0.82, 2.14], p = .244$. Note that each participant could only get an incentive for practicing once a day. Hence, it may not be surprising that the effect for incentives, insofar it exists, is stronger for the number of days practiced than for the number of total practice sessions. In addition, we checked for interaction effects using the above regressions, and found nothing in this regard. Complete code for the analysis can be found in the Open Science Framework (https://osf.io/vn73m/).

Effect Over Time. We now evaluate whether any effects of incentives and deadlines are a result of initial reaction to the experimental condition or experience with the intervention over time. To do so, we divided the 30 days of the experiment into three "blocks" of 10 days each. We analyzed the interaction between each factor (deadlines and incentives) and time (i.e., blocks). Figure 4 show that in all conditions, both the number of practice days and the number of valid practice sessions tended to decrease with time. However, the decrease appears to be sharper with deadlines than without. Moreover, when incentives for daily practices were provided, the decrease over time seems minimal, particularly when those incentives were not contingent on keeping a preset deadline.

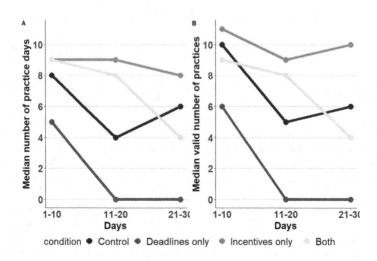

Fig. 4. Effects over time. (A) Median number of practice days over time across the four conditions. (B) Median number of valid practice sessions over time across the four conditions

To check these effects statistically, we implemented a mixed-effect binomial regression with fixed effects for deadlines, incentives, block, the two-way interactions of incentives and deadlines with block, and with random effect for participant ($SD = 2.63$), predicting daily practice. The results show no indication for an interaction of block with the other factors. Yet, the main effect for block was highly negative and significant, $OR = 0.31, 95\%CI[0.25, 0.38], \chi^2(1) = 148.7, p < .001$, suggesting that later in the experiment, participants were far less likely to complete daily practices.

We also implemented a mixed-effect negative binomial regression with fixed effects for deadlines, incentives, block, the two-way interactions of incentives and deadlines with block, and with random effect for participant ($SD = 1.02$), predicting number of practices. The results indicated that the positive effect of incentives increased over time (interaction between incentives and block), $OR = 1.22, 95\%CI[1.04, 1.42], \chi^2(1) = 6.28, p = .012$. That is, relative to participants who were not directly incentivized to practice, those who were given incentives had 22% more valid practice sessions for each additional block. In contrast, deadlines tended to decrease number of practice sessions more over time (interaction between deadlines and block), $OR = 0.86, 95\%CI[0.74, 1.00], \chi^2(1) = 3.89, p = .049$. That is, relative to participants who were not under deadlines for practicing, those who were under deadlines had 14% fewer valid practice sessions for each additional block.

3.3 Follow-Up Results

N=30 participants chose to take the final GMAT exam at the end of the study. Although all of the participants were eligible to participate in the final exam, our results show an obvious self-selection based on frequency of practices during the study. Participants who took the exam ($N = 30$) had a median of 27.5 of practice days while participants who did not take the exam ($N = 28$) had a median of 4 practice days. To validate our assumption that more practice sessions during the study are associated with higher chances of getting a high score in the exam, we tested and found a significant correlation between number of valid practice sessions and the final exam score ($r = .48, p = .007$). Notably, controlling for the number of practices, there were no significant associations between the condition a participant was assigned to and the exam score, suggesting the interventions only affected the scores through their influence on the number of practices. Moreover, the qualitative results reported above were also replicated for the subsample of participants who took the final exam, although there was clearly a severe lack of statistical power.

4 Discussion

The *mRAPID* study contributes to behavior change research and design of persuasive technologies. The findings from this preliminary field study generally indicate that both daily deadlines to perform the targeted behavior and direct micro-incentives provided for that behavior influence participants' practice behavior over a period of 30 days. However, while micro-incentives increased uptake of practice behavior, setting a deadline to perform the behavior generally decreased practice. The positive effect of daily micro-incentives was found in comparison to conditions in which participants were paid the maximal amount incentives for behavior could have provided. That is, the effect observed in our study is probably not due to the payment itself but due to the direct link between behavior and reward that was enabled by the design of *mRAPID* app. From a habit formation perspective, the largest effects of both micro-incentives and daily deadlines on behavior materialized in the last 10 days of the study, perhaps after participants' initial intrinsic motivation for behavior (that we assume was relatively high as they chose to volunteer into the study) waned. This observation implies that to sustain easily deferrable behavior over the long-term, providing micro-incentives contingent on the behavior may be a promising design option in behavior change technologies.

Our findings highlight a potentially crucial limitation in applying commitment devices (i.e. deadlines) to change daily behavior. Since commitment devices decrease the ability to perform behavior, these devices should be carefully designed to sufficiently increase the motivation to act. Our findings identify a negative effect of deadlines on daily behavior such as studying in contrast to mainstream behavioral research, which often finds a positive effect [3]. In our setting, the deadlines were applied on repeated daily behavior, as opposed to the more common single decision. In this setting, deadlines can potentially undermine habit formation. An interesting dimension to explore in future research could be the differential effect of daily commitment devices on maintaining good habits (e.g. studying, exercising) as opposed to breaking bad habits (e.g. smoking, digital distraction) [20].

There is an active debate in behavioral research on the effect of small and contingent incentives on behavior and performance. Previous research discovered that you often have "to pay enough or not pay at all" since in many cases no compensation was more effective than small compensation [11] with crowding out of intrinsic motivation as the usual explanation for such negative effects on performance [11]. It is also important to select the correct target for rewarding behavior. In an educational context, prior research discovered that rewarding student daily behavior such as school attendance is more effective than rewarding academic outputs such as exam scores [15]. Our research builds on this prior work by evaluating the effect of small incentives on daily academic input (i.e. daily practice). Our findings indicate a potential positive and even cost-beneficial effect of micro-incentives when applied in this context. This is a promising result that should facilitate further research on how micro-incentives can improve daily behavior and habit formation. This finding was obtained in the context of a mobile app with the ability to plan ahead and receive timely reminders, which allowed participants to maximize the effect of incentives on desired behavior. This is an important element of behavior change technology design [23].

Our analysis indicated that the positive effect of incentives and the negative effect of deadlines mostly emerge over time as a result of learning and experience. This highlights important implications for research on and design of behavioral interventions. To change behavior, experience should ideally amplify and not attenuate the initial effect of the behavioral intervention but too often, the opposite occurs in such studies. Examples include crowding out of intrinsic motivation due to incentives [11] and attrition due to excessive reminders or deadlines. To evaluate the effect of experience, technology should be designed to continuously and objectively measure the targeted behavior [13, 18].

Our study design allowed us to investigate the differential effects on days of practice, which were the proximal target of micro-incentives, and total number of practice sessions which were not rewarded beyond once a day. We find that that total number of practice sessions increased in the incentive conditions and over time, indicating a positive spillover effect. That is, our findings suggest that micro-incentives can help foster the habit of practicing, even when the incentive was no longer in place. This is a particularly attractive result to designers of incentive structures [11]. To achieve habit formation, the effect of an incentive should remain even after it has been removed, and there can be spillover to related positive behaviors that are not directly rewarded. Future research should continue examining how behavior change research might achieve this goal.

We acknowledge that our study has a number of limitations. Our experiment ($N = 58$) included a smaller sample compared to common practice in randomized controlled trials (RCT) of behavioral nudges or incentives (e.g., [2]) but a larger sample than usual in similar research on design of behavior change technologies in human-computer interaction (HCI) and related fields (e.g., [17]). In some domains, recruiting a large sample size in a trial of incentive is challenging due the high cost incurred. Due to the small sample, we therefore consider our findings preliminary with potential design implications. Despite these limitations, this study design allowed us to discover a strong negative effect of deadlines in the context of daily practice behavior. The generalizability of the negative effect of deadlines and other commitment devices that can be applied daily is currently unexplored and should be studied in greater detail in behavioral research.

Overall, our findings have unique implications to behavioral research and the design of behavior change technologies. In the context of daily practice behavior on a mobile app, micro-incentives have the potential to have a positive effect on desired behavior while daily deadlines have a negative effect. These effects arise over time as a result of experience of being in the study and using the app. Therefore, behavioral research should examine the long-term effects of micro-incentive and nudges and the experience mechanism that attenuate or amplify the effects of behavioral interventions over time.

Acknowledgments. This research has been supported by Technion-Cornell Tech Julia and Joshua Ruch Exchange Program 2016. The authors would like to thank Ido Erev and Deborah Estrin for their help in designing the study, Faisal Alquaddoomi for developing the app, and Zohar Gilad for collecting data.

References

1. Adams, A.T., Costa, J., Jung, M.F., Choudhury, T.: Mindless computing: designing technologies to subtly influence behavior. In: Proceedings of the 2015 ACM International Joint Conference on Pervasive and Ubiquitous Computing, pp. 719–730 (2015)
2. Adams, M.A., et al.: Adaptive goal setting and financial incentives: a 2×2 factorial randomized controlled trial to increase adults' physical activity. BMC Pub. Health **17**(1), 1–16 (2017)
3. Ariely, D., Wertenbroch, K.: Procrastination, deadlines, and performance: self-control by precommitment. Psychol. Sci. **13**(3), 219–224 (2002)
4. Bidargaddi, N., et al.: To prompt or not to prompt? a microrandomized trial of time-varying push notifications to increase proximal engagement with a mobile health app. JMIR Mhealth Uhealth **6**(11), e10123 (2018)
5. Caraban, A., Karapanos, E., Gonçalves, D., Campos, P.: 23 ways to nudge: a review of technology-mediated nudging in human-computer interaction. In: Proceedings of the 2019 CHI Conference on Human Factors in Computing Systems, pp. 1–15. CHI 2019, Association for Computing Machinery, New York, NY, USA (2019). https://doi.org/10.1145/3290605.3300733
6. Consolvo, S., McDonald, D.W., Landay, J.A.: Theory-driven design strategies for technologies that support behavior change in everyday life. In: Proceedings of the SIGCHI Conference on Human Factors in Computing Systems, pp. 405–414. CHI 2009, ACM, New York, NY, USA (2009). https://doi.org/10.1145/1518701.1518766

7. Cuadra, A., Bankole, O., Sobolev, M.: Planning habit: daily planning prompts with Alexa. In: Ali, R., Lugrin, B., Charles, F. (eds.) PERSUASIVE 2021. LNCS, vol. 12684, pp. 73–87. Springer, Cham (2021). https://doi.org/10.1007/978-3-030-79460-6_7

8. Erev, I., Roth, A.E.: Maximization, learning, and economic behavior. Proc. Natl. Acad. Sci. **111**(Supplement 3), 10818–10825 (2014)

9. Fogg, B.J.: Persuasive technology: using computers to change what we think and do. Ubiquity **2002**, 5:2 (2002). https://doi.org/10.1145/764008.763957

10. Fogg, B.: A behavior model for persuasive design. In: Proceedings of the 4th International Conference on Persuasive Technology, pp. 1–7. Persuasive 2009, ACM, New York, NY, USA (2009). https://doi.org/10.1145/1541948.1541999

11. Gneezy, U., Meier, S., Rey-Biel, P.: When and why incentives (don't) work to modify behavior. J. Econ. Perspect. **25**(4), 191–210 (2011)

12. Guinart, D., Sobolev, M., Patil, B., Walsh, M., Kane, J.M., et al.: A digital intervention using daily financial incentives to increase medication adherence in severe mental illness: Single-arm longitudinal pilot study. JMIR Mental Health **9**(10), e37184 (2022)

13. Harari, G.M., Lane, N.D., Wang, R., Crosier, B.S., Campbell, A.T., Gosling, S.D.: Using smartphones to collect behavioral data in psychological science: opportunities, practical considerations, and challenges. Perspect. Psychol. Sci. **11**(6), 838–854 (2016)

14. Hekler, E.B., Klasnja, P., Froehlich, J.E., Buman, M.P.: Mind the theoretical gap: interpreting, using, and developing behavioral theory in HCI research. In: Proceedings of the SIGCHI Conference on Human Factors in Computing Systems, pp. 3307–3316. CHI 2013, ACM, New York, NY, USA (2013). https://doi.org/10.1145/2470654.2466452

15. Levitt, S.D., List, J.A., Neckermann, S., Sadoff, S.: The behavioralist goes to school: leveraging behavioral economics to improve educational performance. Am. Econ. J. Econ. Pol. **8**(4), 183–219 (2016)

16. Oinas-Kukkonen, H., Harjumaa, M.: Persuasive systems design: key issues, process model, and system features. Commun. Assoc. Inf. Syst. **24**(1), 28 (2009)

17. Okeke, F., Sobolev, M., Dell, N., Estrin, D.: Good vibrations: can a digital nudge reduce digital overload? In: Proceedings of the 20th International Conference on Human-Computer Interaction with Mobile Devices and Services, pp. 1–12. MobileHCI 2018, ACM, New York, NY, USA (2018). https://doi.org/10.1145/3229434.3229463

18. Okeke, F., Sobolev, M., Estrin, D.: Towards a framework for mobile behavior change research. In: Proceedings of the Technology, Mind, and Society, pp. 1–6. TechMindSociety 2018, ACM, New York, NY, USA (2018). https://doi.org/10.1145/3183654.3183706

19. Park, J., Lee, H., Park, S., Chung, K.M., Lee, U.: GoldenTime: exploring system-driven timeboxing and micro-financial incentives for self-regulated phone use. In: Proceedings of the 2021 CHI Conference on Human Factors in Computing Systems, pp. 1–17 (2021)

20. Pinder, C., Vermeulen, J., Cowan, B.R., Beale, R.: Digital behaviour change interventions to break and form habits. ACM Trans. Comput.-Human Interact. **25**(3), 1–66 (2018). https://doi.org/10.1145/3196830

21. Prestwich, A., Perugini, M., Hurling, R.: Can the effects of implementation intentions on exercise be enhanced using text messages? Psychol. Health **24**(6), 677–687 (2009)

22. Rabbi, M., Aung, M.H., Zhang, M., Choudhury, T.: Mybehavior: automatic personalized health feedback from user behaviors and preferences using smartphones. In: Proceedings of the 2015 ACM International Joint Conference on Pervasive and Ubiquitous Computing, pp. 707–718 (2015)
23. Sobolev, M.: Digital nudging: using technology to nudge for good. Available at SSRN 3889831 (2021)
24. Stawarz, K., Cox, A.L., Blandford, A.: Beyond self-tracking and reminders: designing smartphone apps that support habit formation. In: Proceedings of the 33rd Annual ACM Conference on Human Factors in Computing Systems, pp. 2653–2662 (2015)
25. Volpp, K.G., et al.: Effect of electronic reminders, financial incentives, and social support on outcomes after myocardial infarction: the heartstrong randomized clinical trial. JAMA Intern. Med. **177**(8), 1093–1101 (2017)
26. Wicaksono, A., Hendley, R.J., Beale, R.: Using reinforced implementation intentions to support habit formation. In: Extended Abstracts of the 2019 CHI Conference on Human Factors in Computing Systems, pp. 1–6 (2019)
27. Zhu, M., Bagchi, R., Hock, S.J.: The mere deadline effect: why more time might sabotage goal pursuit. J. Consumer Res. **45**(5), 1068–1084 (2019)

What the Fork? The Impact of Social Norm Violation on User Behavior

Rosanna E. Guadagno[1]([⊠]) [iD], Nicole L. Muscanell[2] [iD], and Seth Gitter[3]

[1] University of Oulu, 90014 Oulu, Finland
Rosanna.Guadagno@oulu.fi
[2] EDUCAUSE, Washington, DC, USA
[3] Auburn University, Auburn, AL, USA

Abstract. Research indicates that exposure to swearing, an experience often perceived as a norm violation may affect individual and group behaviors. To further explore this, we examined whether personal and group norms for swearing influence the extent to which exposure to swearing spreads virally and affects group performance during an online group discussion. Participants engaged in an online group decision-making task that assesses group performance and opinion polarization. Results revealed that groups exposed to profanity and were permissive of swearing were more likely to demonstrate deviant behavior that spread beyond swearing (i.e., less task focus and less formal language) as compared to groups not exposed to profanity. Furthermore, exposure to swearing decreased the quality of group decisions and increased group polarization. These results have implications for social norms and user behavior and productivity in distributed teams.

Keywords: Social Norms · User Behavior · Virtual Groups · Norm Violation

1 Introduction

1.1 Literature Review

Recently, in an effort to prevent instances of cyberbullying, the US state Arizona passed a law deeming offensive language used in online settings, including profanity, to be a class 1 misdemeanor and punishable by up to 25 years in jail. This was significant as political groups have made much headway in encouraging legislation to regulate sexual and excretory acts in the media and online, but issues of free speech have generally made it difficult to restrict profane language. For example, the US Communications Decency Act (CDA) aimed at regulating pornographic and other profane material on the Internet was successfully passed in 1996. Nevertheless, free speech advocates successfully overturned portions of the bill aimed at regulating profane language just one year later. In further support of free speech, a judge in London ruled that people should not be punished for using profane language in public [1]. The judge argued that profanity is so common that it has lost its shock value and no longer causes people distress. It is clear that there is disagreement on whether or not such speech should be restricted. What is less clear is

J. Ham et al. (Eds.): PERSUASIVE 2023, LNCS 13832, pp. 82–89, 2023.
https://doi.org/10.1007/978-3-031-30933-5_6

whether restricted speech has the intended effect of making society more "decent," and what the implications of restricted speech actually are.

Many of the aforementioned concerns and legal clashes are predicated on the assumption that exposure to profanity negatively impacts behavior and might in some way be contagious, infecting today's youth and leading them to be more likely to use profanity [2]. Yet, little research has tested the assumption that being exposed to profanity has harmful effects.

1.2 Contagion of Indecent Behavior

Contagion of indecent behavior can be interpreted and understood within the framework of the theory of normative conduct [3]. Similar to social learning theory [4, 5], the theory of normative conduct proposes that we look to others' behavior to guide our own behavior. In general, if many other people are behaving a certain way, then we may behave similarly – this is known as The Cialdini Effect [3, 6]. More specifically, Cialdini and colleagues suggest we do this in order to understand the norms, or what is consider appropriate or inappropriate, are in a given situation. They further propose that there are two types of norms, injunctive and descriptive. Injunctive norms tell us what we ought to do in general, are less context specific, and result from a lifetime of experience, whereas descriptive norms tell us how others have behaved in a specific context and are more strongly influenced by the here and now. Importantly, descriptive norms can actually lead us to violate injunctive norms. For example, if one sees someone in the act of littering, this may suggest that littering is acceptable in that particular park because others are engaging in that behavior in that specific context (descriptive norm) despite strong injunctive norms discouraging littering. Injunctive norms may also be set by frequent exposure to normative information that is descriptive in nature. For example, if one frequents a park that is heavily littered (vs. not littered), this suggests that littering may be okay because others approve of it.

Research supports these assumptions. For example, people will litter more in contexts that already contain litter, particularly after seeing someone else litter [3, 7], or vandalize property that appears to be abandoned or uncared for [6, 8, 9]. That is, undesirable behaviors may occur because of the descriptive norms being conveyed, and when we see others performing a certain act, we will take their behavior as a cue to guide our own behavior. Furthermore, evidence suggests that being exposed to just one person's bad or unethical behavior can set the norm that bad behavior for others is acceptable [10, 11].

We suggest that the theory of normative conduct affects profanity, such that when a person uses profanity, observers may use it as a cue to guide their own behavior. Specifically, we argue that being exposed to profanity may provide descriptive normative information suggesting that other inappropriate behavior is acceptable. Supporting this, several previous studies suggest that exposure to profanity, which is often seen as indecent behavior, decreases motivation to engage in self-control [12]. Self-control can be broadly defined as the act of exerting effortful control over one's own thinking and behavior [13]. Generally, we engage in self-control (by effortfully refraining from engaging in negative behaviors and/or engaging in appropriate behaviors) in order to maximize rewards and minimize punishments or other unpleasant consequences. In effect, engaging in self-control means following the rules and norms set by society.

1.3 Online Disinhibition and Social Influence

Prior research on interpersonal interactions mediated by ICT suggests that there are four key differences between this form of mediated-communication relative to face-to-face interactions [10, 11]: 1) a temporal aspect; 2) the experience of relative/visual anonymity; 3) minimal importance of geographic location; 4) and a decreased focus on interactant's appearance. These differences have been shown to account for differences in interactions in contexts ranging from work settings [16] to online dating [17] and generally suggest that people interacting over ICT show more disinhibited behavior than they would if interacting in person. Furthermore, because the norms regarding behavior in online contexts is still evolving, people are often more sensitive to social norms created by the specific online context [18]. Generally, this literature documents a greater propensity for people to engage in disinhibited behavior, to disregard social cues associated with other interactants (e.g., expertise) and violations of social norms dictating appropriate behavior that exist in face-to-face interactions.

1.4 Overview of the Present Study

With the current study, we attempted to further examine whether personal and group norms influence user behavior after being exposed to profanity. Specifically, we exposed participants to swearing where group influence concerning the appropriateness of swearing was unclear. To do this, we examined group norms in digital interactions (group permissiveness of swearing) as a predictor deviant chat behavior – i.e., task focus, grammar, and language formality). Additionally, we examined whether or not being exposed to profane language would lead to actual contagion of profanity within a group discussion.

This study contributes to the literature by examining group norms – specifically group permissiveness of swearing -- in addition to personal norms and self-control after exposure to swearing. Furthermore, given attention to the regulation of profanity on the Internet, we sought to extend these findings to an online setting. Parents, media watchdog groups, and political figures have become increasingly concerned that the fabric of society is slipping into moral disarray owing to exposure to questionable content in the media. These concerns have ramped up as of late due to the ready availability of such content on the Internet. For instance, a recent report from Reppler, Facebook's monitoring service, reported that out of 30,000 Facebook profiles examined, 47% contained profanity [19]. In this study, individuals participated in an online group discussion, in which half of the groups were exposed to swearing. We predicted that being exposed to swearing would lead to more norm violation within online chat discussions. We also predicted that participants who were exposed to a confederate using profanity would be more likely to use profanity themselves and demonstrate other instances of decreased self-control. Finally, we predicted that group norms would moderate the effect of exposure to swearing on self-control, such that groups who are more permissive of swearing should demonstrate a reduction in self-control.

Additionally, the findings of [11] and normative conduct theory (the Cialdini Effect) present the possibility that swearing may also be contagious. If exposure to swearing can reduce an individual's self-control, and rule violating behavior (including swearing) is more likely to occur under situations in which people lack self-control [20], then exposure to swearing could lead to a contagion-like effect where exposure to swearing leads others to swear themselves. This study explores this possibility by examining a group discussion, in which some, but not all, groups were exposed to profanity in an online chat environment. Chat logs were coded by trained raters to observe the presence of swearing contagion as well as evidence of whether those exposed to swearing showed other signs of decreased self-control.

2 Method

2.1 Procedure

One hundred and twenty undergraduate students (22% male) enrolled in introductory psychology classes from a university in the Southeastern United States were recruited to complete an online questionnaire that included a variety of personality and individual difference measures. To assess perceived swearing norms, an adapted version of the Permissiveness Concerning Swearing Scale (PCSS; see [21]) was embedded within this questionnaire. The adapted version contained 3 new items including ("*I don't like music that contains swear words*", "*When other people swear, it offends me*", and "*It often bothers me when movies have swear words*"). Several weeks after completing the online questionnaire, participants were invited to the lab for an experiment on group discussions.

This study used a single factor (exposure to swearing vs. no exposure to swearing) between subjects design. All groups were randomly assigned to condition. Additionally, within all groups who were exposed to swearing, one participant was chosen by random selection to use profanity during the group chat. Participants arrived at the lab with 2 to 3 other participants (total group size 3 or 4), matched for gender, and were told that they would be participating in a study in which the purpose was to learn about how people get to know each other and work together in an online chat environment. They were then informed that to help facilitate their group discussion, the experimenter would ask them to complete a group task called the desert survival task. The desert survival task has previously been used in small group research [22], and requires group members to rank order 15 items in order of importance that they would like to have in a survival situation.

Participants were each seated individually in separate lab rooms and given several minutes to look over the survival task and items on their own and rank order them. At this point, within the swearing condition, the experimenter approached the randomly assigned swearer while they were alone in waiting for the Google Hangouts chat to begin. The experimenter filled the participant in on the true nature of the study, provided them with a list of suggested phrases involving profanity, and then asked the participant if they would be willing to use profanity 3 times (once every 5 min) during the group chat[1].

After completing their individual rankings, participants were informed that they would be discussing these 15 survival items in a group chat for 20 min. We asked them to discuss their individual rankings and to try to come to a group consensus on the order the

---

[1] Only one participant declined to use profanity and this group was excluded from the final analyses.

items should be ranked (from most to least important). Participants communicated from their individual lab rooms using Google Hangouts chat feature. After their discussion, participants rankings were re-assessed, then each participant was individually suspicion-probed, debriefed, thanked for their time, and dismissed.

3 Results

3.1 Chat Coding

Overall, there were a total of 33 groups (19 were exposed to swearing, 14 were not). None one in any of the groups reporting knowing the other participants in their groups. Two independent raters coded the online chat transcripts. Coding categories were generated by the researchers and included contagion (the number of times participants other than the assigned swearer used profanity), and several behaviors that we believed operationalized the extent to which the groups demonstrated loss of self-control. These included the number of times the chat went off topic (e.g., any time participants discussed something other than the desert survival task), the amount of laughter[2] that occurred within the chat (e.g., use of "lol" and "ha"), and the number of grammatical errors and slang use or text speak (e.g. OMG, thnx, u)[3] that occurred within the chat. We conducted correlation analyses to assess interrater reliability. The correlations between the coders were high, suggesting acceptable interrater reliability. The correlations were: perfect correlation for contagion, $p < .001$, number of times chat went off topic, $r = .97$, $p < .001$, amount of laughter within the chat, $r = .95$, $p < .001$, and amount of grammar errors/slang use, $r = .90$, $p < .001$. Because we had such high reliability, we used an average for each of the categories for the main analyses.

3.2 Main Effects

Next, we conducted a series of multiple regression analyses, using the [23] cross-centered method. In each model we included condition (swearing exposure vs. no swearing exposure), group acceptance of profanity, and the interaction term of these two variables as predictors of contagion and the coded self-control categories. Group acceptance of swearing was computed by averaging the group members' scores from the PCSS measured several weeks earlier. The PCSS yielded acceptable reliability ($M = 3.95$, $SD = .89$, $\alpha = .81$). There were no significant main effects of condition or group acceptance of profanity on contagion or the self-control measures[4].

---

[2] Given the serious nature of the discussion topic (a survival task), we argue that laughter was a good indicator of lowered self-control.

[3] "lol" was counted only as laughter and not as text speak for the analyses.

[4] Results did not vary based on the gender of the group (all groups were same-sex). Thus, analyses are collapsed across group gender.

3.3 Group Norms

We found several significant interaction effects between condition and group acceptance of profanity on contagion and the self-control measures. There was a significant interaction effect of condition and group acceptance of profanity on contagion, $b(29) = .93$, $t = 3.10$ $p = .004$. Simple effects tests demonstrated participants other than the assigned swearer used more profanity in groups who were exposed to profanity and who were also more permissive of profanity, $b(29) = .399$, $t = 3.77$, $p = .001$.

Additionally, there were significant interaction effects of condition and group acceptance of swearing on the self-control categories, including the number of times the discussion went off topic, $b(29) = 6.42$. $t = 1.07$, $p = .03$, the amount of laughter that occurred during the discussion $b(29) = 8.93$, $t = 2.01$, $p = .05$, and the amount of grammatical issues/use of slang that occurred during the discussion, $b(29) = 18.91$, $t = 2.29$, $p = .03$. Specifically, simple effects tests demonstrated that participants in groups exposed to profanity who were also more permissive of profanity, were more likely to go off topic in their discussion, $b(29) = 5.57$, $t = 2.62$, $p = .01$, to use laughter within the discussion, $b(29) = 11.13$, $t = 3.37$, $p = .002$, and use slang and make grammatical errors, $b(29) = 14.98$, $t = 2.44$, $p = .02$. No such effects were observed among those who reported disapproval of swearing on the PCSS.

Finally, in order to ensure that the confederate swearers did not significantly change their own chat behaviors after swearing and influence the nature of the conversation, we had two new independent raters, different than the raters mentioned above, code the online chat transcripts specifically for the swearers (confederates). We examined the categories mentioned above (number of swear words used, number of times the swearer went off topic, number of times the swearer laughed, and number of grammatical errors/slang for each swearer). We then subtracted the scores specific to the swearer from the overall group values, leaving us with a sum value for the group of unknowing participants. We then conducted a series of ANOVAs comparing the swearer to the unknowing participants on the main outcomes. In general, we found that the unknowing participants were more likely to change the topic $F(1, 36) = 5.04$, $p = .03, \eta_p^2 = .12$, use laughter within the chat topic, $F(1, 36) = 8.87$, $p = .005$, $\eta_p^2 = .20$, and also make grammatical errors and/or use slang, $F(1, 36) = 33.07$, $p < .001$, $\eta_p^2 = .27$ as compared to the swearers. In terms of the number of curse words used, all swearers used exactly 3 profanities as instructed, and any additional profanity was introduced to the conversation by the unknowing participants. These findings suggest any changes in the conversation after the introduction of swearing was likely due to the unknowing participants as opposed to the swearer.

3.4 Discussion

The results of this study demonstrated that profanity served as a cue to normative expectations for behavior in online chats. Consistent with predictions, we found that exposure to profanity was contagious and related to less self-control; however, this was moderated by attitudes towards profanity. Specifically, groups who were exposed to profanity and who were also more permissive of profanity, were more likely to engage in less controlled behavior (e.g., using more profanity, chatting off topic, laughing, using more slang).

Overall, this provides evidence of the Cialdini Effect in another context, one online rather than in an offline context, and suggests that when individuals who are accepting of swearing are exposed to profanity, they may consider the use of swear words as a signal that self-control exertion is not required within that context. Furthermore, these results were demonstrated in a context in which disinhibited behavior is often observed.

3.5 Limitations

These findings are not without their limitations. First, the data were collected using a convivence sample of college students rather than examined using a more diverse sample of adults. Furthermore, while we controlled for individual perceptions on the social acceptability of swearing, these norms may vary by the gender of the swearer, the gender composition of the group, and the social context surrounding the interaction. Because data were collected solely with same-sex groups, these results may not generalize to mixed-sex groups. Furthermore, because the majority of participants in the sample were women, these results may be more applicable to groups of women rather than groups of men. Future attempts at replication of these results should examine whether the results generalize beyond the sample characteristics reported in the present study.

3.6 Implications

Overall, it is likely the case that because of the rules and regulations pertaining to profanity, most individuals are aware that profanity is a norm violation, regardless of their tolerance of it. Thus, one implication of these findings is that strict rules prohibiting the use of profanity, making it anti-normative, may largely contribute to it being a cue to other deviant behavior, specifically to those who are already tolerant of profanity and might question these rules. This has implications for widely popular Internet sites such as Facebook, as can be seen in the example of Arizona's recently passed law deeming offensive language used in online settings to be a class 1 misdemeanor. However, while such campaigns on anti-cyberbullying are much needed [24], by creating strict regulations and punishments, this may actually serve to further bolster the relationship between profanity and deviant behavior. Future research should more closely determine how profanity affects those who are not tolerant of it, and importantly, how regulations on profanity directly influence cyber bullying and other deviant user behaviors.

References

1. Kelly, J.: Should swearing be against the law? Retrieved November 16, 2022 from (2011) http://www.bbc.co.uk/news/magazine-15816761
2. Kaye, B., Sapolsky, B.: Taboo or not taboo? That is the question: Offensive language and prime-time broadcast and cable programming. J. Broadcast. Electron. Media 53, 1–16 (2009)
3. Cialdini, R.B., Reno, R.R., Kallgren, C.A.: A focus theory of normative conduct: Recycling the concept of norms to reduce littering in public places. J. Pers. Soc. Psychol. 58, 1015–1026 (1990)
4. Bandura, A., Ross, D., Ross, S.A.: Transmission of aggression through imitation of aggressive models. J. Abnorm. Soc. Psychol. 63, 575–582 (1961)

5. Bandura, A., Ross, D., Ross, S.A.: Imitation of film-mediated aggressive models. J. Abnorm. Soc. Psychol. **66**, 3–11 (1963)
6. Keizer, K., Lindenberg, S., Steg, L.: The spreading of disorder. Science **322**, 1681–1685 (2008)
7. Cialdini, R.B.: Influence: Science and Practice. William Morrow, New York (2009)
8. Wilson, J.Q., Kelling, G.L.: Broken windows: The police and neighborhood safet. Atlantic **249**, 29–38 (1982)
9. Zimbardo, P.G.: A field experiment in auto shaping. In: Ward, C. (Ed.),Vandalism. The Architectural Press, London (1973)
10. Colman, A.M.: Game theory and experimental games. Pergamon Press, New York (1982)
11. Gino, F., Ayal, S., Ariely, D.: Contagion and differentiation in unethical behavior. Psychol. Sci. **20**(3), 393–398 (2009)
12. Gitter, S.A., Baumeister, R.F., Tice, D.M.: (under review). Profanity, Normative Influence, and Self-Control
13. Baumeister, R.F.: Ego depletion and self-control failure: An energy model of the self's executive function. Self Identity **1**, 129–136 (2002)
14. McKenna, K.Y.A., Bargh, J.A.: Plan 9 from cyberspace: The implications of the Internet for personality and social psychology. Pers. Soc. Psychol. Rev. **4**(1), 57–75 (2000)
15. Bargh, J.A., McKenna, K.Y.A.: The Internet and social life. Annu. Rev. Psychol. **55**, 573–590 (2004)
16. Cummings, J., Butler, B., Kraut, R.: The quality of online social relationships. Commun. ACM **45**(7), 103–108 (2002)
17. Guadagno, R.E., Okdie, B.M., Kruse, S.: Dating deception: Gender, online dating, and exaggerated self-presentation. Comput. Hum. Behav. **28**, 642–647 (2012)
18. Spears, R., Postmes, T., Lea, M., Wolbert, A.: The power of influence and the influence of power in virtual groups: A SIDE look at CMC and the Internet. J Soc Issues **58**, 91–108 (2002)
19. Golijan, R.: 47 percent of Facebook walls covered in profanity. Retrieved June 15, 2022 from msnbc news at May 24 2011 http://digitallife.today.msnbc.msn.com/_news/2011/05/24/670 7280-47-percent-of-facebook-walls-covered-in-profanity?lite
20. Gailliot, M.T., Gitter, S.A., Baker, M.D., Baumeister, R.F.: Breaking the rules: low trait or state self-control increases social norm violations. Psychology **3**(12), 1074–1083 (2012)
21. Gitter, S.A.: Shooting the shit: Profanity, self-control, and aggressive behavior. Florida State University Electronic Theses, Treatises and Dissertations. Paper 4261(2010).
22. Littlepage, G., Robison, W., Reddington, K.: Effects of task experience and group experience on group performance, member ability, and recognition of expertise. Organ. Behav. Hum. Decis. Process. **69**(2), 133–147 (1997)
23. Aiken, L.S., West, S.G.: Multiple regression: Testing and interpretinginteractions. Sage, Newbury Park, CA (1991)
24. Wingate, V.S., Minney, J.A., Guadagno, R.E.: Sticks and Stones May Break Your Bones, But Words Will Always Hurt You: A Review of Cyberbullying. Soc. Influ. **8**(2–3), 87–106 (2013). https://doi.org/10.1080/15534510.2012.730491

Evaluative Conditioning in Consumer Psychology: Can Affective Images of Climate Change Influence Sustainability Perception of Supermarket Products?

Nikki Leeuwis[1,2]([✉]) [iD], Tom van Bommel[2], and Maryam Alimardani[1] [iD]

[1] Tilburg University, 5037 AB Tilburg, The Netherlands
N.leeuwis@tilburguniversity.edu
[2] Unravel Research, 3581 KW Utrecht, The Netherlands

Abstract. Most individuals are aware of the wastefulness of plastic packaging but do not know what sustainable packaging exactly is or choose not to buy it. In an effort to educate consumers about the sustainability of their products, the current study employed an evaluative conditioning approach in which sustainable and unsustainable products were paired with affective images of climate change. We hypothesized that conditioning consumers with positive and negative images of nature would either reinforce or weaken their perception of the sustainability of the product. Sustainability Ratings revealed that consumers already had a strong opinion about (un)sustainability of the product packaging. Nevertheless, the information provided during the conditioning phase impacted their ratings such that sustainable products that were paired with a negative image were perceived less sustainable after conditioning. These results have implications for communication practitioners and pave the way for future research into evaluative conditioning as a technology to impact consumer attitude and behavior.

Keywords: Evaluative Conditioning · Affective Images · Sustainability · Behavior Change · Implicit Associations

1 Introduction

Pollution from fossil-based plastic waste may take up to thousand years to decompose completely [1] and thereby waste related to packaging affects the quality of air, soil, and water, accelerating the problem of climate change [2, 3]. While consumers have become increasingly aware of their environmental impact, excessive consumption patterns still exist [4]. Even for those consumers who wish to act sustainably, survey studies show that they could not correctly describe an ecological-friendly packaging or did not have a clear idea of what it looked like [5, 6]. In this way, the behaviors consumers (and thus all of us) perform on a daily basis have a longer-term effect on the health and well-being of their own, but also of other individuals and on society at large [7].

Although many consumers, when asked, express preference for green and sustainable products [8], they do not always purchase them [9]. This discrepancy between what

J. Ham et al. (Eds.): PERSUASIVE 2023, LNCS 13832, pp. 90–104, 2023.
https://doi.org/10.1007/978-3-031-30933-5_7

people say and what they do is labeled as the attitude-behavior gap [10], which is an often encountered problem for responsible consumer behavior. Recently, Leeuwis et al. [11] proposed a framework for the design of behavior change interventions that could promote pro-environmental attitude and behavior among consumers. In their review, Leeuwis et al. [11] specifically investigated evaluative conditioning (also known as affective or emotional conditioning) as a potential method that could change consumers' behavior toward more sustainable purchase decisions and therefore bridge their attitude-behavior gap.

Evaluative Conditioning (EC) is a type of learning that is facilitated by pairing a neutral stimulus to a stimulus that is already (dis-)liked until the previously neutral stimulus elicits the same affective response in the desired direction [12, 13]. EC has shown to be effective [14] on subjective attitude and behavioral measures [15] although some studies found EC effects only on attitude but not behavioral measures [16] or the other way around [17], and some reported no change at all [18]. In environmental research, EC has been adopted by presenting images or texts concerning positive or negative natural scenes when a subject grabbed a product in a virtual reality supermarket [19]. The study showed that an EC intervention of this kind could affect consumer attitudes and behavior until two weeks after the experiment [19].

Another EC study in the health domain paired images of snack foods with images of potential adverse health consequences in order to promote healthy eating [20]. They showed that the pairing of snacks with health risk information influenced food-choice behavior directly after the experiment towards healthier choices. Moreover, before and after the conditioning phase, implicit attitudes were assessed with the Implicit Association Test (IAT) [21], where fruit (healthy choice) and snacks (unhealthy choice) were coupled to words communicating pleasant and unpleasant attributes. They found that compared to a control group who received no health risk information (i.e., no conditioning), the intervention group showed significantly higher IAT scores after conditioning, indicating that unhealthy food was perceived less pleasant [20].

The IAT is a psychological test intended to detect automatic and subconscious preferences by measuring the time it takes an individual to classify a stimulus into two categories [21]. In some contexts, implicit attitudes are considered to be a more reliable predictor of behavior than explicitly expressed attitudes because they are less likely to be guided by social influences and desire to conform to peer group norms [22]. In previous environmental research, implicit tests provided different results on sustainability ratings than explicit surveys, showing low congruence between explicit and implicit sustainability orientations [23, 24].

There have been few investigations on consumers' perceptions towards sustainable packaging and the impact that evaluative conditioning can have on their attitudes toward products. The current study aims to fill this gap by exploring the potential of evaluative conditioning as a technique for development of future persuasive technologies in environmental research. We collected a dataset of climate change images including strongly-valenced (both positive and negative) nature sceneries. By pairing these images with either products in excessive plastic packaging or foods without any packaging, we

investigated how the perception of product packaging changed before and after exposure to climate change and nature images. We hypothesized that conditioning consumers
with negative images of climate change would weaken their perception of sustainability
for product packaging and conditioning with positive images of nature would reinforce
it. While EC is consciously perceived, it has an automatic or unintentional effect [12],
therefore we both measured attitude change using explicit sustainability ratings and
inferred attitude strength from the associative response latencies.

2 Methods

2.1 Participants

A total of 70 respondents (17 Male, 51 Female, 2 Non-binary; $M_{age} = 20.74$, $SD_{age} = 3.44$) were recruited to participate in an online experiment. They were all university
students and received course credit in return for their participation in the experiment. The
study was approved by the Research Ethics Committee of Tilburg School of Humanities
and Digital Sciences. Prior to the experiment, participants read an information letter and
singed an informed consent form. After preprocessing the data (see section Analysis for
the exclusion criteria), 4 respondents were removed, leaving 66 subjects in the analysis
(16 Male, 49 Female, 1 Non-binary; $M_{age} = 20.58$, $SD_{age} = 3.10$).

Before the experiment, a power analysis was conducted using g*power [25] to determine the number of required subjects in the study. We set the power at 0.95, the alpha
level at .05, and the effect size of the primary outcome at d = 0.5 (in line with a review
on evaluative conditioning [12] and used by Hollands et al. [20]). Concerning a paired
Wilcoxon rank test, the required sample size would be 57. This number was oversampled
to ensure that after data rejection the sample size would still be sufficient.

2.2 Stimuli

Product images were selected based on their appearance on a Dutch grocery retailer
website[1] and websites with open creative licenses such as Pexels.com. Images were
selected based on their packaging; they either contained no packaging, re-usable, recy-
clable packaging (including packaging that claimed to be better for the climate) or
products that were packed in (excessive) plastic. The images from the websites were
modified such that their background was white and the logos on all packages were made
unrecognizable.

In an initial test for stimuli validation, we explored the sustainability perception of
these products (n = 94) by asking 94 subjects to rate the sustainability of their packaging
on a 7-point Likert scale. Sustainability in this case was defined: "in the sense of packages
owning attributes aiming at reducing the product's environmental footprint. Think of the
materials of the package, recyclability and ecological footprint". The products were then
sorted based on this initial rating test and the top and bottom nine products were selected
to serve as stimuli in the main experiments. Products with the highest Sustainability
Ratings ($M = 6.57$, $SD = 0.03$) did not include any packaging, while products with the

---

[1] https://www.ah.nl/producten.

lowest Sustainability Ratings ($M = 1.93$, $SD = 0.15$) were all using unnecessary extra plastic (Fig. 1).

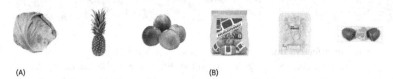

(A)   (B)

Fig. 1. Examples of product images included in the test. (A) Products whose packaging was rated most sustainable and (B) products which packages were rated most unsustainable.

The climate related images for the evaluative conditioning were selected based on another stimuli validation test. In this test, nature images promoting either positive or negative emotions were gathered from three sources: an openly available database of affective climate change images by Lehman et al. [26] where images were rated on relevance, arousal and valence; an openly available database of positive nature images by Dal Fabbro et al. [27] that were rated on arousal and valence; and images that were obtained from websites with creative licenses such as Pexels.com and Unsplash.com. When looking for images online, search terms such as 'waste' and 'pollution' were used to search for negative images. To keep the images in both negative and positive conditions as similar as possible, we tried to match their context. For instance, if the selected negative image showed a polluted ocean, we would search for 'ocean' and 'water' to find its positive counterparts in the same context. In this validation test, 125 respondents rated a random subset of 20 out of 35 images (11 negative, 10 neutral and 14 positive images) on their valence, arousal and relevance to climate change on a 9-point Likert scale. Afterwards, subjects performed a pairing task where negative images were presented together with four neutral or positive images which researchers thought might be visually or contextually resembling them. Subjects were instructed to choose one of the four images that they considered the most appropriate opposite of the shown negative image. Each subject rated 6 out of the 11 pairs that were included in the study.

From all climate related images, six pairs (positive vs. negative) were selected to be used in the conditioning experiment (Fig. 2). The selection was based on subjects' pairing and how large the difference in valence ratings were. The average difference in valence evoked by this selection of pairs was 3.60 ($SD = 0.53$), where the average valence rating for positive images was 6.34 ($SD = 0.60$) and for negative images was 2.93 ($SD = 0.14$) ($t(5) = -13.33$, $p < .001$). The arousal ($M = 4.66$, $SD = 0.31$) and relevance ($M = 5.52$, $SD = 0.64$) ratings for positive images were lower than the arousal ($M = 7.07$, $SD = 0.10$) and relevance ($M = 6.91$, $SD = 0.33$) for the negative images ($t(5) = 16.17$, $p < .001$; $W = 21$, $p = 0.03$). On average, the match between the selected pairs as perceived by the subjects was 48.40% ($SD = 10.78\%$), meaning that almost half of the subjects selected this positive image as being the best counterpart to the negative one presented (out of four choices).

Fig. 2. Example of affective images that were presented during the EC phase. The pairs were defined by the subjects, and were selected when the difference in their valence ratings was the greatest. The mean valence score is provided below each image (on a 9-point Likert scale).

2.3 Procedure

The experiment was administered online using Qualtrics and could only be taken on desktop. Subjects read the information letter and were only able to continue when they signed the informed consent (Fig. 3). First, subjects answered questions regarding demographics and plastic attitude, then New Environmental Paradigm (NEP; Dunlap et al. [28]), and Health Consciousness (HC; [29, 30]). After that, they conducted the Sustainability Association Task (see details below) on 18 product images. This was followed by Evaluative Conditioning (EC) phase where subjects received positive or negative information (affective images) about 6 sustainable and 6 unsustainable product images (note that 3 sustainable and 3 unsustainable products were not included in the conditioning phase in order to serve as control items). The EC phase was repeated three times to ensure associative learning. After that, the Sustainability Association Task was once again conducted to evaluate attitude change. Afterwards, subjects were debriefed that the presented combinations in this study were not real but rather served as experimental manipulation and subjects were thanked for their participation.

Information + Consent	Questionnaires	Pre-EC SAT	EC phase (3 repetitions)	Post-EC SAT	Debriefing
Subjects read information letter and sign informed consent before they continue	Demographics, New Environmental Paradigm (NEP), Health Consciousness (HC)	18 product images were evaluated with the Sustainability Association Task (SAT)	12 of these product images were coupled to positive or negative climate change information	The same 18 product images were evaluated with the SAT	Subjects were debriefed and thanked for their participation

Fig. 3. Overview of the procedure of this experiment.

2.4 Questionnaires

The demographical questions assessed the gender and age of the subjects as well as their responsibility for grocery shopping at least for most of their meals. Subjects' environmental belief was assessed with the New Environmental Paradigm (NEP; [28]) (including 15 items answered on a 5-point Likert-scale). Thereafter, Health Consciousness (HC) [29] was measured by 4 items on a 7-point Likert scale. Health is considered important for grocery purchase decisions [30]. A question about the consideration of the negative impact of plastic packaging was added according to [31] where subjects were asked

"To what extent do you think about the negative impact of plastic packaging on the environment?".

2.5 Sustainability Association Task (SAT)

The perception of sustainability and wastefulness of each product was assessed before and after the EC phase with the Sustainability Association Task (SAT). This task is based on the presumption that the strength of an association between an object (i.e., product) and an attribute (i.e., sustainability) is reflected in the subject's Response Latency: when stimuli are easy to process (which is the case for objects and evaluations that are perceived to be congruent) subjects respond faster to these stimuli [32]. Compared to Likert-scale, this may better represent the subjects' opinion or cognitive process [33]. These basic assessments of evaluative priming [32] provide the basis upon which the IAT has been developed [21, 34] and is preferred for the measurement of attitude accessibility [35]. The SAT consisted of the presentation of a product image with the words *Sustainable* or *Wasteful* (one at a time) underneath. Subjects answered whether they thought these words fit the product using E (*No*) and I (*Yes*) keys on the keyboard (see Fig. 4). Subjects had 5 s to answer each trial. The timer was shown on top of the screen as a blue bar that was filling up. If subjects could not answer on time, the test moved to the next trial. Before the task, there was a practice block where subjects could practice the task with two products and two association (four trials in total) that were not included in the analysis. After the practice round, subjects were once again presented with the task explanation and were granted 5 s to place their fingers on the keyboard. The same was true for the post-EC task.

| Yes | | No |
| press E | **Sustainable** | press I |

Fig. 4. Example trial of the Sustainability Association task. Nine sustainable and nine unsustainable products were presented with both words *Sustainable* and *Wasteful* (in total 36 trials). Subjects had to press E (*Yes*) or I (*No*) within the time limit of five seconds.

2.6 Evaluative Conditioning (EC)

The EC phase comprised of six conditions. From each group of highly sustainable (n = 9) and highly unsustainable (n = 9) products, three images were paired to a positively-valenced nature image, three were paired to negatively-valenced images and three products were not paired at all. In the group of sustainable products, this led to three products where sustainability was reinforced, three products where sustainability attributes were weakened, and three products that were not conditioned (i.e., sustainability perception should not be changed). Similarly, for three wasteful products the wasteful association was weakened, for three products the wastefulness attribute was reinforced and for three products no affective information was provided. Each product was shown for 1 s, followed by the climate image for 1 s. Then a fixation cross was shown with an inter-trial interval that varied between 800 and 1200 ms before the next combination was shown. All combinations were shown three times. In between every block, a grey circle was shown where the subject could choose to take a break and continue when they felt ready to do so.

2.7 Analysis

Responses were filtered when the response latency was below the lower boundary of 300 ms or above 5000 ms as in [36]. Subjects were removed from analysis completely if more than 10% of the SAT trials were filtered. Responses to trials with *Wasteful* association were re-coded such that *yes* meant unsustainable and *no* meant sustainable. Data was calculated per person and condition. This means that for every subject, their responses to each product group (sustainable vs. unsustainable; 3 products each) receiving one of the three affective conditioning options (either Positive, or Negative, or No Affect (NA)) were summarized as Sustainability Rating and Response Latency for that product group.

The explicit Sustainability Rating was calculated as the number of *yes* answers to *Sustainable* trials and *no* answers to *Wasteful* trials divided by the total number of included trials for that subject in that condition (maximum of six). Consequently, the Unsustainability Rating would be 1 minus the Sustainability Rating. Response Latencies were calculated as the average time it took each subject to respond to the six product-attribute combinations presented in each of the EC conditions.

Besides the Sustainability Ratings and the corresponding Response Latencies, Associative Strength was calculated that combined both measurements into one comprehensive value. The Associative Strength reflects both the Sustainability Rating and the strength of that rating by incorporating the Response Latency and is calculated according to Eq. 1. Here, %yes is the percentage of trials in which the subject answered *yes* when the word *Sustainable* was shown and *no* when the word *Wasteful* was shown (reversed for the %no), RT_{yes} and RT_{no} are the averaged reaction time corresponding to those trials, and RT_{mean} is the grand average of RTs over all trials in the pre- or post-EC tests together for a specific subject. This grand averaging was employed in the equation to normalize the RT values per participant and successfully reflect their variation between conditions and measurements, which is an important modulation in response latency research [34]. Reaction times (RT_{yes}, RT_{no}, and RT_{mean}) were reversed in the equation such that a shorter reaction time indicated a stronger association.

$$\frac{\left(\%_{yes} \times \frac{1}{RT_{yes}}\right) - \left(\%_{no} \times \frac{1}{RT_{no}}\right)}{\frac{1}{RT_{mean}}} \tag{1}$$

Consequently, the obtained Sustainability Ratings, Response Latencies and Associative Strengths from the pre-EC and post-EC SAT tests were compared using paired Wilcoxon Rank test due to non-normal distribution of all metrics. Since, there were multiple comparisons per product type and metric, the alpha level was adjusted to 0.016. In calculation of questionnaire scores, the odd questions of the NEP were reversed before the average score was calculated for each subject.

3 Results

3.1 Subject Demographics

The average Environmental Belief (NEP) in the sample was 3.58 ($SD = 0.44$; on a scale of 5). The average Health Consciousness (HC) score was 5.19 ($SD = 0.94$; on a scale of 7). In total, 68.18% of the sample was responsible for their own grocery shopping for the majority of the week. This distribution was similar between genders. There was also no difference in NEP or HC scores between genders. Most subjects indicated to think about the negative impact of plastic packaging but buying it anyway (36.92%) or not buying it sometimes (32.31%). A minority looked at alternatives (12.31%) or did not think about the impact at all (18.64%).

3.2 Sustainability Association Test

The results from the SAT are presented in the following paragraphs using three metrics that describe an explicit measurement (Sustainability Rating), the accessibility of the opinion (Response Latency) and the implicit Associative Strength Score, which reflects how strongly that product is associated with sustainability.

3.3 Sustainability Rating

The Sustainability Rating is the number of times the subject responded that a product is sustainable: either by answering *yes* when the attribute *Sustainable* was shown or *no* when the attribute *Wasteful* was presented. Figure 5 demonstrates the Sustainability Ratings for both product categories before and after EC in three directions (Positive, Negative, NA). As can be seen in this figure, for both product categories the pre-EC SAT test shows considerably strong opinions: the median is at 100% for most of the sustainable products and at 0% for most of the unsustainable products.

While these rather explicit measurements show small differences in the general outcome of the pre- and post-EC tests, the difference was significant for the Sustainable-Negative condition, where the sustainability perception of sustainable products was weakened after conditioning with negative climate images ($W = 653, p = .012$). Even though the medians of both pre- and post-EC tests are the same in this condition (*Mdn* $= 0.83$), this result is caused by the greater variation that was observed in the post-EC test compared to the pre-EC test.

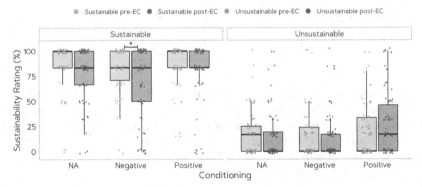

Fig. 5. Averaged Sustainability Ratings per subject for each condition in pre- and post-EC SAT tests (* p < .016).

3.4 Response Latency

The result of Response Latency is summarized in Fig. 6. There was no difference in average Response Latency per subject between the pre- and post-EC tests. Response Latency for sustainable products was in general faster in the pre-EC test ($Mdn = 1007$, $IQR = 370$) than the post-EC test ($Mdn = 1077$, $IQR = 532$), while for unsustainable products this was the other way around (pre-EC test: $Mdn = 1234$, $IQR = 512$; post-EC test: $Mdn = 1109$, $IQR = 483$).

When comparing pre-EC and post-EC SATs, unsustainable products showed significant decreases in Response Latency in all conditions. The products that were conditioned with positive affect were responded faster in post-EC test ($Mdn = 1107$, $IQR = 449$) than in pre-EC test ($Mdn = 1256$, $IQR = 507$) ($W = 1514$, $p = .009$). Similarly, unsustainable products that were reinforced with negative affect ($W = 1502$, $p = .011$) (pre-EC: $Mdn = 1201$, $IQR = 449$; post-EC: $Mdn = 1056$, $IQR = 431$) or not conditioned at all showed significantly faster response in post-EC test ($Mdn = 1107$, $IQR = 425$) than in pre-EC test ($Mdn = 1329$, $IQR = 607$) ($W = 1603$, $p = .001$).

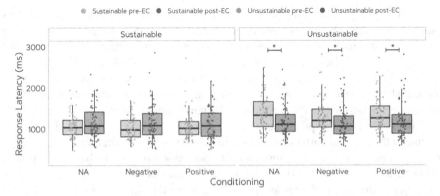

Fig. 6. Averaged Response Latencies (ms) per subject for each condition in pre- and post-EC SAT tests (* p < .016).

3.5 Associative Strength Scores

Associative Strength scores (Fig. 7) were lower after negative conditioning of unsustainable products ($W = 1448, p = .029$), although this result cannot be considered significant after correction of multiple comparisons. Nevertheless, it shows that negative affective images paired to unsustainable products could strengthen the unsustainable association subjects had.

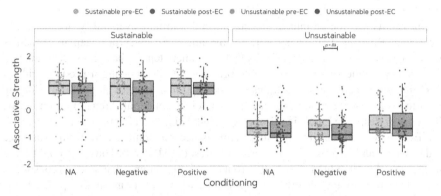

Fig. 7. Averaged Associative Strength per subject for each condition in pre- and post-EC SAT.

4 Discussion

This study aimed to establish the potential of evaluative conditioning as an intervention for changing consumers' perception of (un)sustainable packaging. Using images of (un)sustainable products that were paired with affective images of natural scenery, it was demonstrated that reinforcing information about a product's environmental impact did not significantly change subjects' perception of the product. That is, when sustainable products were conditioned with positive images of nature and unsustainable products were conditioned with negative images of climate change impact, Sustainability Ratings remained unchanged. However, when sustainable products were paired with incongruent affective images (i.e., negative images), we observed a significant weakening effect of conditioning on subjects' Sustainability Rating of the products. For unsustainable products, the Association Strength towards unsustainability was reinforced when paired with negative images.

The explicit Sustainability Ratings that were collected in pre-EC SAT test (see Fig. 3) revealed a ground truth in the selected product images: before conditioning, the sustainable products were perceived very sustainable and the unsustainable products were perceived very unsustainable. This implied however, that reinforcement conditioning could not really affect the perception of these products, as they were already rated very high or low on sustainability. However, we did observe that reversing the association by conditioning the products in the unexpected direction could change the Sustainability Ratings toward a weakened perception. Although this induced change was not large, there was more variability in the post-EC responses in that sustainable products were perceived slightly less sustainable and unsustainable products were rated slightly more sustainable. For future research, we would therefore suggest exerting the same conditioning paradigm but with products for which consumers are uncertain about its sustainability. Previous research already showed that repeatedly presenting an object paired with an affective stimulus seems to be effective in increasing attitude availability [37], for example four repetitions of an advertisement already increased the associative strength of the brand with the advertised attitude (although the direction of the attitude itself was not impacted by the ad) [38].

Our results provide an interesting insight in the attitude availability of consumers. The fact that Response Latencies before conditioning were lower for sustainable products than for unsustainable products, shows that consumers tend to have a faster evaluation of sustainable rather than unsustainable products. While showing a product without packaging might activate the sustainability perception at once, a product in packaging seems to require more cognitive processing to assess the material. After conditioning, the difference in Response Latencies disappeared, indicating that after the information phase (i.e., EC) the evaluation time for all conditions became similar. For all unsustainable products, this marked a significant decrease in Response Latency. Thus, one might argue that the mental availability for wasteful products is not pronounced: it requires consumers observable effort to appraise wasteful products, whereas for sustainable products the appraisement seems to require relatively less effort. The importance of fluent processing of sustainability is also underlined by [39] who highlighted that the pure existence of ecolabels on food packaging does not mean these labels are perceived or cognitively processed.

The combination of Sustainability Rating and Response Latency into one metric of Associative Strength provided additional information: here the results showed that negative conditioning had stronger effects on Associative Strength than positive conditioning. That is, the products that were paired with negative affective images showed the largest decrease in Associative Strength after the conditioning phase, while the products paired with positive affective images did not show a significant change in Associative Strength. This effect is known in the psychology field as the negativity bias [40]: negative news tends to activate individuals more than positive news [41].

In discussing these results, one should consider that the sample of this study was young, educated and primarily female. Previous studies have shown that gender, age and education can impact climate change engagement and concern [42–45], although it varies between countries whether young or old people are more concerned with climate change [46]. Besides, reaction time during association tasks can increase with age [47]. Another factor to note is participants' background and personal experience of climate change. Although this study was conducted in the Netherlands, the recruited sample consisted of university students with a large percentage of internationals. We did not collect participants' nationality, but it can be speculated that some of the affective images were of less or more relevance to these participants depending on their country of origin (e.g., Dutch participants might relate less to beaches with palm trees than a participant from Southeast Asia). All nature imagery employed in the study were first rated by another group of respondents in a stimuli validation test to minimize such effect. Nevertheless, it is advised that future studies incorporate more variety in their sample to reflect for these differences. Moreover, it would be useful to investigate the difference in the effect of evaluative conditioning on subjects with various education levels.

A challenge in this study was defining sustainability for a product. Given that various factors could influence a product's environmental impact (e.g., transport, deforestation, water and soil quality), we decided to direct participants' attention to only packaging of the product and not the product itself. However, it is possible that despite many reminders, some subjects forgot this criterion when evaluating the products. For example, for a product like "avocado", it is commonly known that this "green gold" requires a lot of water, deforestation and transportation emissions [48], whereas in our experiment this product was presented without packing and hence was categorized in the sustainable group (also by subjects in the prior stimulus validation task). In the same line, the healthiness of the content of the packaging can also have an effect: the healthiness perception of the product might elicit similar or even stronger effects than relating the product or packaging to environmental problems [19, 30]. In order to minimize this impact of such errors, we randomized the (un)sustainable products over all three conditioning conditions, and hence the risk of error caused by a specific product should have been equally distributed across conditions.

Since this study taps into real-life problems such as climate change, excessive consumption and plastic waste, the implications beyond academic literature should also be discussed. Our study showed that emotional conditioning on sustainability could be a key asset in moving consumers towards more pro-environmental behavior. Future research could further explore this emotional connection in other modalities as well. For example, in Virtual Reality supermarkets, environmental impact messages could pop up when the user makes a purchase decision. This could then be used as an educational tool to make consumers aware of the impact of their food choices and empower personal response efficacy beliefs, which may ultimately affect their environmental behavior [19]. Thus, future technological advancements could include evaluative conditioning as an interaction paradigm to persuade consumers towards more pro-environmental behavior.

References

1. Sumrin, S., Gupta, S., Asaad, Y., Wang, Y., Bhattacharya, S., Foroudi, P.: Eco-innovation for environment and waste prevention. J. Bus. Res. **122**, 627–639 (2021)
2. Boz, Z., Korhonen, V., Sand, C.K.: Consumer Considerations for the Implementation of Sustainable Packaging: a review. sustainability 12(2192), 12, (2020)
3. Phelan, A.A., Meissner, K., Humphrey, J., Ross, H.: Plastic pollution and packaging: Corporate commitments and actions from the food and beverage sector. J. Cleaner Prod., 331, (2022)
4. Stolz, J., Molina, H., Ramírez, J., Mohr, N.: Consumers' perception of the environmental performance in retail stores: an analysis of the German and the Spanish consumer. Int. J. Consum. Studies. **37**(4), 394–399 (2013)
5. Lindh, H., Olsson, A., Williams, H.: Consumer Perceptions of Food Packaging: Contributing to or Counteracting Environmentally Sustainable Development? Packag. Technol. Sci. **29**, 3–23 (2016)

6. Lindh, H., Williams, H., Olsson, A., Wikström, F.: Elucidating the Indirect Contributions of Packaging to Sustainable Development: a Terminology of Packaging Functions and Features. Packag. Technol. Sci. **29**, 225–246 (2016)

7. Fishbein, M., Ajzen, I. Predicting and changing behavior: The reasoned action approach. In: Psychology press; (2011)

8. Rokka, J., Uusitalo, L.: Preference for green packaging in consumer product choices–do consumers care? Int. J. Consum. Stud. **32**(5), 516–525 (2008)

9. Jerzyk, E.: Design and Communication of Ecological Content on Sustainable Packaging in Young Consumers' Opinions. J. Food Prod. Mark. **22**(6), 707–716 (2016)

10. Kennedy, E.H., Beckley, T.M., McFarlane, B.L., Nadeau, S.: Why we don't" walk the talk": Understanding the environmental values/behaviour gap in Canada. Hum. Ecol. Rev., 151–60 (2009)

11. Leeuwis, N., van Bommel, T., Alimardani, M.: A framework for application of consumer neuroscience in pro-environmental behavior change interventions. Front. Hum. Neurosci. **16**, 886600 (2022)

12. Hofmann, W., De Houwer, J., Perugini, M., Baeyens, F., Crombez, G.: Evaluative conditioning in humans: a meta-analysis. Psychol. Bull. **136**(3), 390 (2010)

13. Purves, D., Cabeza, R., Huettel, S.A., LaBar, K.S., Platt, M.L., Woldorff, M.G., et al. Principles of Cognitive neuroscience. In. 2 ed. Sunderland: Sinauer Associates, Inc; (2013)

14. Moran, T., Nudler, Y., Bar Anan, Y.: Evaluative Conditioning: Past, Present, and Future. Annual Review of Psychology. 74, (2022)

15. Houben, K., Schoenmakers, T.M., Wiers, R.W.: I didn't feel like drinking but I don't know why: The effects of evaluative conditioning on alcohol-related attitudes, craving and behavior. Addict. Behav. **35**(12), 1161–1163 (2010)

16. Geng, L., Liu, L., Xu, J., Zhou, K., Fang, Y.: Can evaluative conditioning change implicit attitudes towards recycling? Soc. Behav. Personal. Int. J. **41**(6), 947–955 (2013)

17. Ellis, E.M., Homish, G.G., Parks, K.A., Collins, R.L., Kiviniemi, M.T.: Increasing condom use by changing people's feelings about them: An experimental study. Health Psychol. **34**(9), 941 (2015)

18. Glashouwer, K.A., Neimeijer, R.A., de Koning, M.L., Vestjens, M., Martijn, C. Evaluative conditioning as a body image intervention for adolescents with eating disorders. In., vol 12. American Psychological Association; (2018)

19. Meijers, M.H.C., Smit, E.S., de Wildt, K., Karvonen, S.G., van der Plas, D., van der Laan, L.N.: Stimulating Sustainable Food Choices Using Virtual Reality: Taking an Environmental vs Health Communication Perspective on Enhancing Response Efficacy Beliefs. Environmental Communication, 1–22 (2021)

20. Hollands, G.J., Prestwich, A., Marteau, T.M.: Using aversive images to enhance healthy food choices and implicit attitudes: An experimental test of evaluative conditioning. Health Psychol. **30**(2), 195 (2011)

21. Greenwald, A.G., McGhee, D.E., Schwartz, J.L.: Measuring individual differences in implicit cognition: the implicit association test. J. pers. soc. psychol. **74**(6), 1464 (1998)

22. Govind, R., Singh, J.J., Garg, N., D'Silva, S.: Not walking the walk: How dual attitudes influence behavioral outcomes in ethical consumption. J. Bus. Ethics. **155**(4), 1195–1214 (2019)

23. Steiner, G., Geissler, B., Schreder, G., Zenk, L.: Living sustainability, or merely pretending? From explicit self-report measures to implicit cognition. Sustain. Sci. **13**(4), 1001–1015 (2018). https://doi.org/10.1007/s11625-018-0561-6

24. Panzone, L., Hilton, D., Sale, L., Cohen, D.: Socio-demographics, implicit attitudes, explicit attitudes, and sustainable consumption in supermarket shopping. J. Econ. Psychol. **55**, 77–95 (2016)

25. Faul, F., Erdfelder, E., Lang, A.-G., Buchner, A.: G Power 3: A flexible statistical power analysis program for the social, behavioral, and biomedical sciences. Behav. Res. Methods. **39**(2), 175–191 (2007)
26. Lehman, B., Thompson, J., Davis, S., Carlson, J.M.: Affective Images of Climate Change. Front. Psychol. 0,960 (2019)
27. Dal Fabbro, D., Catissi, G., Borba, G., Lima, L., Hingst-Zaher, E., Rosa, J., et al.: e-Nature Positive Emotions Photography Database (e-NatPOEM): affectively rated nature images promoting positive emotions. Sci. Rep. **11**(1), 1–15 (2021)
28. Dunlap, R.E., Van, K.D., Primen, L., Mertig, A.G., Jones, R.E.: Measuring Endorsement of the New Ecological Paradigm: A Revised NEP Scale. J. Soc. Issues. **56**(3), 425–442 (2000)
29. Mai, R., Hoffmann, S.: How to combat the unhealthy= tasty intuition: The influencing role of health consciousness. J. Pub. Policy Mark. **34**(1), 63–83 (2015)
30. Koenig-Lewis, N., Grazzini, L., Palmer, A.: Cakes in plastic: A study of implicit associations of compostable bio-based versus plastic food packaging. Resources, Conservation and Recycling. 178, 105977 (2022)
31. Weber Macena, M., Carvalho, R., Cruz-Lopes, L.P., Guiné, R.P.: Plastic food packaging: perceptions and attitudes of Portuguese consumers about environmental impact and recycling. Sustainability. **13**(17), 9953 (2021)
32. Fazio, R.H., Sanbonmatsu, D.M., Powell, M.C., Kardes, F.R.: On the automatic activation of attitudes. J. Pers. Soc. Psychol. **50**(2), 229 (1986)
33. Fazio, R.H.: A practical guide to the use of response latency in social psychological research. (1990)
34. Kardes, F.R., Escoe, B., Wu, R. Response latency methodology in consumer psychology. Handbook of research methods in consumer psychology. Routledge. pp. 132–42. (2019)
35. Fazio, R.H., Powell, M.C., Williams, C.J.: The role of attitude accessibility in the attitude-to-behavior process. Journal of consumer research. **16**(3), 280–288 (1989)
36. Nosek, B.A., Bar-Anan, Y., Sriram, N., Axt, J., Greenwald, A.G.: Understanding and using the brief implicit association test: Recommended scoring procedures. PLoS ONE **9**(12), e110938 (2014)
37. Powell, M.C., Fazio, R.H.: Attitude accessibility as a function of repeated attitudinal expression. Pers. Soc. Psychol. Bull. **10**(1), 139–148 (1984)
38. Berger, I.E., Mitchell, A.A.: The effect of advertising on attitude accessibility, attitude confidence, and the attitude-behavior relationship. Journal of consumer research. **16**(3), 269–279 (1989)
39. Grunert, K.G.: Sustainability in the food sector: A consumer behaviour perspective. International Journal on Food System Dynamics. **2**(3), 207–218 (2011)
40. Kanouse, D.E., Hanson Jr, L.R.: Negativity in evaluations. Journal, (Issue), (1987)
41. Soroka, S., Fournier, P., Nir, L.: Cross-national evidence of a negativity bias in psychophysiological reactions to news. Proc. Natl. Acad. Sci. **116**(38), 18888–18892 (2019)
42. Geiger, N., McLaughlin, B., Velez, J.: Not all boomers: temporal orientation explains inter- and intra-cultural variability in the link between age and climate engagement. Clim. Change **166**(1), 1–20 (2021)
43. Wolf, J., Moser, S.C.: Individual understandings, perceptions, and engagement with climate change: insights from in-depth studies across the world. Wiley Interdisciplinary Reviews: Climate Change. **2**(4), 547–569 (2011)
44. McMillan, M., Hoban, T.J., Clifford, W.B., Brant, M.R.: Social and demographic influences on environmental attitudes. Journal of Rural Social Sciences. **13**(1), 5 (1997)
45. Dias, N.M.O.C., Vidal, D.G., Sousa, H.F.P.e., Dinis, M.A.P., Leite, Â.: Exploring associations between attitudes towards climate change and motivational human values. Climate. 8(11), 135 (2020)

46. Lewis, G.B., Palm, R., Feng, B.: Cross-national variation in determinants of climate change concern. Environmental Politics. **28**(5), 793–821 (2019)
47. Woods, D.L., Wyma, J.M., Yund, E.W., Herron, T.J., Reed, B.: Factors influencing the latency of simple reaction time. Front. Hum. Neurosci. **9**, 131 (2015)
48. Denvir, A., Arima, E.Y., Gonzalez-Rodriguez, A., Young, K.R.: Ecological and human dimensions of avocado expansion in Mexico: towards supply-chain sustainability. Ambio **51**(1), 152–166 (2022)

System to Induce Accepting Unconsidered Information by Connecting Current Interests
Proof of Concept in Snack Purchasing Scenarios

Taku Tokunaga[1], Hiromu Motomatsu[1], Kenji Sugihara[2], Honoka Ozaki[2],
Mari Yasuda[2], Yugo Nakamura[1(✉)], and Yutaka Arakawa[1]

[1] Kyushu University, Fukuoka 819-0395, Japan
tokunaga.taku@arakawa-lab.com
[2] Sony Group Corporation, Tokyo 141-8610, Japan

Abstract. In this paper, we propose a purchasing support system for offline stores that can present information to users without being evasive by interactively presenting a small amount of product information according to their interest in the product as predicted by the system. We design and implement a proof-of-concept system for an actual use case scenario: a snack purchasing area in an office. We evaluated the effectiveness of the proposed system through a snack purchasing experiment with 11 participants. Experimental results suggest that the proposed method can induce user interest and encourage viewing and that some users may receive and consider the information presented while making a purchase.

Keywords: interactive display · purchasing support system

1 Introduction

People make decisions in various everyday situations, but they sometimes make decisions without examining each option in depth and without clear criteria for judgment. This human tendency may lead to the vicious circle of repeatedly making choices that are good in the short term but have bad consequences in the long term. For example, in purchasing lunch and snacks that occur every day, people often decide what to buy based on whether or not they like the taste or if it fits their mood. Continuing to make such decisions may make you happy in the short term because you can eat what you like. Still, long-term, it may lead to an unbalanced diet and cause lifestyle-related diseases such as obesity and diabetes due to nutritional imbalance.

Therefore, in such situations, it is ideal if the information system can support a convincing choice that considers not only taste and mood but also other information, including nutrients, that can lead to long-term benefits. Currently, many offline stores place displays near product shelves from which commercials are broadcast in a marketing-like effort to draw attention and interest to their products. Following this approach, presenting nutrient information from a display near the product shelf may affect attitudes and purchasing behavior at the time of purchase.

J. Ham et al. (Eds.): PERSUASIVE 2023, LNCS 13832, pp. 105–119, 2023.
https://doi.org/10.1007/978-3-031-30933-5_8

However, the one-way presentation of information from displays in offline stores can adversely affect the purchasing experience [5,6,16]. One of its adverse effects is advertising avoidance, defined as any behavior that the audience performs to reduce the level of contact with the advertisement [19]. There are three types of advertisement avoidance: "cognitive avoidance" (intentional disregard for information), "emotional avoidance" (negative feelings and emotional reactions to information), and "behavioral avoidance" (avoidance behaviors other than lack of attention) [18]. Therefore, in designing an information system to support behavior change at the time of purchase, it is important to consider information presentation methods that reduce these avoidance behaviors and increase the acceptability of the presented content.

In this study, we aim to design a purchasing support system for offline stores that can present information to users without being evasive by interactively presenting a small amount of product information according to their interest in the product as predicted by the system. Herein, we designed and implemented a proof-of-concept model of the system for an actual use case scenario: a snack purchasing area in an office. The design of the proposed system is based on the results of previous studies [15] that show that the quality and quantity of information people are receptive to vary depending on their interests. In this paper, we present our information presentation model and functional hypotheses, as well as clarify the design and implementation of the proposed system. We also evaluated the effectiveness of the proposed system based on our hypotheses through a purchasing experiment with 11 participants. Experimental results suggest that the proposed method can induce user interest and encourage viewing and that some users may receive and consider the information presented while making a purchase. Our research will contribute to providing new insights into the design of information presentation methods for offline stores and expanding the design space for interactive purchasing support systems.

2   Related Works

2.1   Interest Estimation Method

Several methods have been proposed to estimate internal mental states, such as interest and wondering during purchase. Li et al. used the camera of a smartphone to estimate eye gaze and compared the user's gaze on the Google Play Store screen with the areas of interest reported by the user [13]. The results showed that users looked significantly longer at areas in which they reported interest than at other areas. They also used features such as eye gaze information and the user's favorite categories to achieve a binary classification of interested or uninterested, resulting in an AUC score of more than 90%. Jacob et al. use a spectacle eye tracker to obtain gaze information and estimate which newspaper articles users are interested in [9]. In addition, Karolus et al. performed interest estimation for presented images using multiple gaze estimation and gazing information metrics, and found that they achieved better accuracy than random in all estimations [10]. Several studies of offline store purchases that investigate the relationship between the position of purchased products on the shelf and eye gaze [1,3] also suggest that eye gaze information at the time of purchase is a very important feature in expressing people's interest. Following the findings of these previous studies, we develop a method for estimating the level of interest in products displayed on snack shelves based on the user's gaze during offline purchases.

2.2 Interactive Display and Purchasing Support System

Previous studies have shown that presenting calorie information [4], changing the price of healthy products, suggesting healthy alternatives [2,8], presenting information on the purchase of healthy others to less healthy users [7], etc. have been suggested to influence users' food choices. However, these studies primarily focus on investigating analog approaches that do not use information systems and do not investigate whether users accept presentations via information systems when making offline purchases. This study focuses on how to put information such as nutrients into the buyer's consideration via interactive displays installed in offline stores.

Several interactive information presentation systems for the offline environment have been proposed. Schiavo et al. proposed a presentation method that calculates the level of interest in a public display based on the user's face and body orientation and position and changes the content step by step according to the level of interest [17]. In addition, Kim et al. proposed a method for switching detailed and comparative information about two products in an experimental environment according to the user's line of sight [11]. However, in an offline purchase with multiple candidate products displayed on shelves in front of them, it may not be easy to attract users simply by switching information according to their behavior. Therefore, designing an information system that can present information in a way acceptable to users is still considered a remaining challenge.

3 Proposed System

3.1 Design of an Information Presentation Model

This study aims to develop a presentation method that increases the likelihood that users will view information even if they are not interested in it and a system that changes their purchasing behavior. The model for determining whether a person will view information is considered to have much in common with the technology acceptance model (TAM) [14], which determines whether a person will use a system. Based on TAM, our study focused on the level of interest in information and the amount of information as parameters that can be sensed and estimated in the targeted purchasing scenario. They have the following characteristics: (1) People do not view information when their interest in the information is low, (2) If the amount of information is too large, people are less likely to view the information because of the burden. To get users to watch information, it is considered effective to make them interested in the information or to reduce the amount of information. Based on this, we thought that by presenting a small

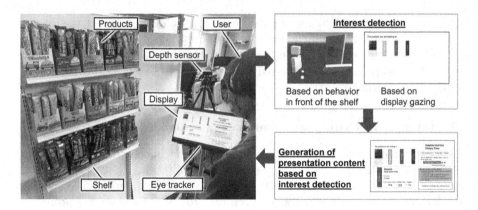

Fig. 1. System overview

amount of information related to the interest, which is easy to accept, and by strengthening the user's interest, we could make users accept more information outside of their interest, which is inherently difficult to accept.

In this study, we assume that the item of interest to users (hereafter referred to as Focused Item) is the product. During the purchasing behavior, the user obtains information as needed from products (hereafter referred to as Gazed Information). At this time, by presenting unseen information to users, for example, nutritional information on the back of the package, a change in behavior based on new decision criteria can be expected.

3.2 System Configuration

This system was designed for 1 person as a first step. The system consists of a computer (Windows10, Intel Core i9-11900K, 128 GB), a depth sensor (Azure Kinect DK), an eye tracker (Tobii Eye Tracker 5), a display (21.5-inch, 1920 × 1080 Pixels), and a shelf where products are placed (Fig. 1). The depth sensor captures users and calculates the three-dimensional posture. An eye tracker calculates the gaze of users looking at the display. The system that generates the display using the data sent from sensors was implemented using Unity. The size of the entire product area is H90cm * W74.5cm, and the size of each product is approximately H25cm*W14cm. Purchasing users look at the products in front of the shelf. While selecting items, users can view information on displays placed next to the shelf. In this scenario, 15 products are placed in boxes on the shelf.

3.3 Implemented Features

To confirm the effectiveness, we set the following 3 hypotheses.

H1 Interactive presenting a small amount of information related to their interests triggers the users' interest in the system and encourages them to look at the information.

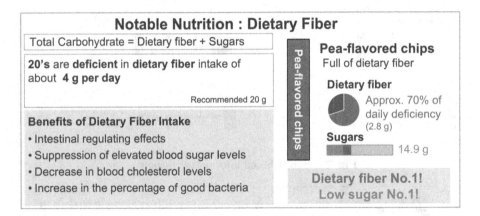

Fig. 2. Information to be presented to users (actual system is in Japanese, product images is actual package). In Japan, sugar refers to the value that also includes starch.

H2 By encouraging users to view, they receive and consider the information presented to them.

H3 User's consideration of the presented information changes the purchase outcome.

In this study, we chose commercial snacks that offer a variety of flavors and allow for uniformity in package size and price. The content of the presentation was determined based on a questionnaire to users conducted in advance. Based on the results of the questionnaire, "Pea-flavored chips" was applied to the uninteresting products, and "dietary fiber (hereafter referred to as fiber) information" and "Pea-flavored chips information" were applied to the uninteresting information. (Figure 2)

Two-stage Interest Detection. We implemented a two-stage interest detection method that stably acquires the head position and posture with the depth sensor and then narrows down the user's target of interest with the eye tracker and the display UI for stable detection.

Stage 1: Interest Detection Using Head Position/Posture from the Depth Sensor. The system calculates the user's head position and orientation vector from the skeletal information estimated using the depth sensor. It also calculates a vector from the head to the product position. By determining the angle between these two vectors and the distance from the user for each product, the interest level in the product is calculated in the range of 0.0–1.0. The smaller the angle and distance, the higher the interest level. The interest level calculation is performed with a guaranteed speed of 60 fps or higher.

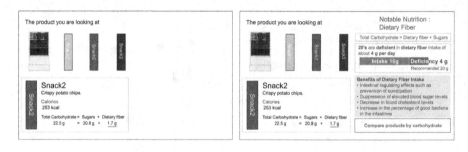

Fig. 3. Interest-based information display

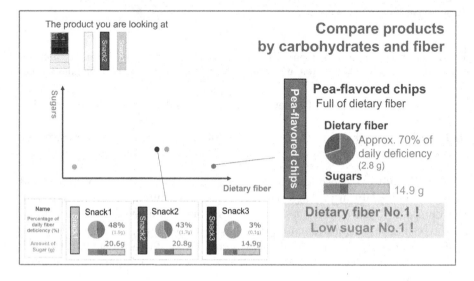

Fig. 4. Comparative information display

Stage 2: Narrowing Down Interests using the Eye Tracker and Display UI. Products that are within the top 3 interest levels and above the threshold are considered "Candidate Items". Candidate Items are presented on a display, and the products whose gazing is detected by the eye tracker are considered of "Focused Item." This method displays information at the timing when the user's interests are determined. The system updates the level of interest when a facial stillness decision or gaze stillness occurs. The system notifies users of this with a notification tone. This feature allows information to be presented interactively in response to non-explicit user input.

Presentation Content Design. The presentation content design based on the detection results is described below.

Presentation of Interest-Based Summary Information. The system displays nutritional information for that product as summary information when it determines Focused Item (Fig. 3 left). By displaying less information at the beginning of the presentation and displaying new information the more user views the content, the system achieves presentation with the amount of information corresponding to the user's level of interest in and acceptance of the information.

Presentation of Summary Information Outside of Interest. Even after the information on Focus Item is presented, other products set as Candidate Products continue to be presented on the display. When the user looks at these images, summary information on the products that are different from Focused Item is presented.

Presentation of Detailed Information Outside of Interest. Once gazing at the summary presentation is detected, the system presents additional detailed information about Focused Item (Fig. 3 right). This system presents "detailed dietary fiber information". After adding the effect of highlighting fiber data in the nutritional information, present detailed information on fiber. A button for transition is displayed in the lower right corner of the screen, and when gazing at this button is detected, the presentation proceeds to the next step.

Presentation of Comparative Information. The system uses the 2 axes of sugar and fiber to present information that encourages comparison between Focused Item and other products (Fig. 4). A product with low sugar and high fiber content ("Pea-flavored snack" in this case) was selected for comparison with the Focused Item.

4 Experiment

The purpose of this experiment is to find out how interaction with the proposed system leads to changes in users' attitudes and awareness during purchasing and to test the hypotheses described in the previous section. To achieve this goal, we conducted a simulated purchasing experiment in the snack purchasing area in an office. 11 students (10 males, 1 female, age: M = 22.5, SD = 0.934) participated in the experiment. None of the participants had any background information about the experiment prior to participating in the study.

4.1 Settings

We adopted a within-participants design and observed the experience of two conditions: presenting Fig. 2 from the display as the existing method and presenting Figs. 3 and 4 according to interest as the proposed method (The detailed process of the proposed method is described in the previous section). The experimental environment is shown on the left of the Fig. 1. A display is installed next to the snack shelf, and information is presented from the display. A depth sensor is placed behind the display and a eye tracker is placed on the display. These sensors are used to measure the participant's viewing time and estimate the

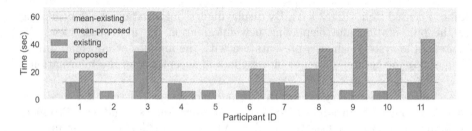

Fig. 5. Viewing time by participants

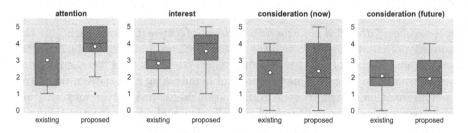

Fig. 6. Results of survey responses

degree of interest in snack shelf and displays. Participants were asked to select one of the 15 types of snacks displayed on the shelf they would like to buy. Here, participants didn't pay actually and received a snack as a reward. Participants experienced each condition once, in the order of the existing method and the proposed method. We set a one-week washout period to reduce the influence of order effects. Furthermore, the participants were instructed not to share the contents of the experiment with each other during the period. Before the experiment, we were told that some information would be presented from the display, and that there would be a questionnaire and an interview after the experiment. Additionally, a calibration was performed to improve the accuracy of the eye tracker. The experimental description and questionnaire are the same for the existing method and proposed method conditions. After each experiment, the participants were asked to complete a questionnaire about their buying experience and the system. The questionnaire included the following questions, which were answered by the five-case method:"Did you pay attention to the information presented in the display?", "Did you pay interest on the information presented in the display?", "Did you confirm or agree with the nutritional information before purchasing the product?", "Would you consider purchasing food with nutrients in mind in the future?". After all experiments, participants were interviewed about each purchasing experience.

4.2   Results

Results for Hypothesis 1. Figures 5 and 6 show the results of the display
viewing time and attention/interest questionnaires obtained from the system,
respectively. Figure 5 is a graph of viewing time on the vertical axis and each
participant's ID on the horizontal axis. The green bar and dotted line represent the participant's viewing time and its average for the existing method, and
the orange bar and dotted line represent the participant's viewing time and its
average for the proposed method. Figure 6 is a box plot with the results of each
questionnaire on the vertical axis and the methods on the horizontal axis. Blue
indicates the results of the existing method, orange the results of the proposed
method, and the white dots are the mean values. Here, each response is on a 5-
point Likert scale, with the addition of the option "did not see the presentation"
(corresponding to 0). Note that the vertical scale is a 6-point scale from 0 to 5.
The result of Fig. 5 shows that the average viewing time for the proposed method
was 25.3 (sec), while the average time for the existing method was 12.6 (sec),
indicating that the viewing time has increased. The attention and interest results
in Fig. 6 show that the distribution of responses is biased toward the upper side
of the graph, indicating an upward trend in responses for the proposed method.
These results suggest that our proposed method may tend to attract buyers'
attention and interest more than the existing method.

Results for Hypothesis 2. The results of consideration(now) and consider-
ation(future) in the Fig. 6 show that the proposed method does not show an
upward trend compared to the existing method. The distributions in the Fig. 6
show that the interquartile range is widening and the dispersion is increasing
in both cases. The results in the Fig. 5 show a large variation in viewing time
among participants, and the difference is particularly pronounced for the proposed method, indicating that the response results are expected to vary depending on viewing time. To investigate the relationship between viewing time and
responses, Fig. 7 shows a scatter plot of viewing time and responses. The results
in the figure show that the proposed method (orange) has a stronger correlation between viewing time and responses than the existing method (green). The
results suggest that longer viewing of the presentation based on our proposed

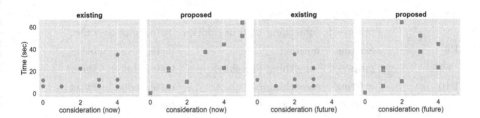

Fig. 7. Relationship between time and survey responses. From left to right, the correlation ratios are 0.37, 0.90, 0.20, and 0.58. (Color figure online)

114   T. Tokunaga et al.

method, compared to the existing method, may lead to decision making with
acceptance and conviction of the presented information. In Hypothesis 2, we
focus on users who viewed the system for more extended periods. Thus, we split
the participants into two groups, one that regarded the display more and the
other that did not, and examined the results of the group that viewed the display more. The results of the survey responses of the top 6 viewers in terms
of viewing time (6 persons) are shown in the Fig. 8. Here, the two results of
"consideration(now)" and "consideration(future)" show an upward trend in the
responses, indicating that the respondents are considering presented information when making decisions. In addition, the items of attention and interest also
showed an upward trend for these groups.

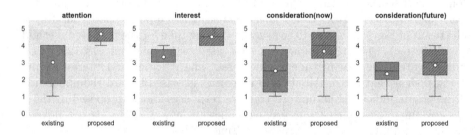

Fig. 8. Results of survey responses (top6)

Table 1. Participant's pre-purchase mood, reasons for purchase, and products purchased

Participant ID	System	Mood	Reason	Purchased product (target : Pea-flavored snack)
P3	existing	something sweet	fiber	other
	proposed	something sweet	taste, fiber	other
P6	existing	something salty	taste	other
	proposed	something sweet	taste	other
P8	existing	something sweet	taste	other
	proposed	something high in calories	taste, calories	other
P9	existing	nothing	taste	other
	proposed	something like chips	taste, fiber	target
P10	existing	something like chips	taste, mood	other
	proposed	something light	taste	other
P11	existing	something salty	taste	other
	proposed	something salty	taste	other

Results for Hypothesis 3. The top 6 viewers were surveyed to determine how the reasons for purchase and products purchased, obtained through questionnaires and interviews changed compared to their initial mood at the time of purchase. The results are shown in Table 1. The results show that the number of respondents who cited some nutrients as the reason for purchase was three in the proposed system, compared to one in the existing method. Regarding the behavioral change in the choice of snacks, only one person in the proposed method bought the snacks that were the target of the inducement. He revealed in an interview that he had initially wanted to try a different type of chips, but was persuaded by the system to opt for the pea-flavored chips. The other participants chose the one that conformed to their initial mood. The interviews revealed that a certain number of participants did not want to be conscious of nutrients when purchasing snacks in the first place. This suggests that purchasing snacks may have been a more difficult scenario to make people aware of nutrients than decisions such as meal menu choices. Since previous research [12] has clearly shown that it is challenging to design information systems that have enough impact on changing behavior in short-term decision-making, the fact that 1 out of 11 people changed can be viewed as a positive starting point. In addition, given the results of partial support for hypotheses 1 and 2, there may be a possibility that continued presentation over a long period could induce behavioral change. This underscores the need for further research.

5   Discussion

Acceptance Difficulty of Information. As shown in the experimental results, the total viewing time was longer for the presentation of the proposed method compared to the existing method. However, the proposed method did not increase the viewing time for all content, and it varied depending on the information category. For example, for the proposed method, the average viewing time for the product summary information was 7.1 s, while that for the fiber information was shorter, at 4 s on average, which was less likely to be viewed. In the interview, participants mentioned the category of information and the amount of information as reasons for not viewing the fiber information, such as not considering fiber when purchasing snacks and not wanting to read too much information. As these comments suggest, the summary information, which was viewed for a longer period of time, was indeed the type of information often used for selecting snacks, and the amount of information was about 1/4 of the fiber information in terms of the number of words. This suggests that the acceptability of certain information for a given product can be estimated from the amount of information and whether that information tends to be used in general when the product is purchased. Therefore, we define the difficulty of accepting certain information as a characteristic of that information, as "Acceptance difficulty of information", derived from the above two variables.

Using this acceptance difficulty, the experimental results can be explained as follows. In the proposed method, participant's level of interest was increased by viewing the information of the product of interest, and participants was willing to view the summary information. However, the level of interest may not have been high enough to make the participants willing to view the fiber information, which has a higher level of acceptance difficulty.

Level of Interest in Information Categories. On the other hand, in the experiment, there were individual differences in the amount of time the same information was viewed. For example, when presenting the fiber information in the proposed method, 4 participants watched for only 1 s or less, 5 participants watched for 34 s, 1 participant watched for 7.7 s, and the participant who watched the longest watched for 14.6 s. In the interview, the participant stated that the participant is usually health-conscious and was interested in fiber information. Another participant who watched the presentation for 8 s stated that the presentation triggered a fiber-conscious purchase. Thus, it can be considered that the level of interest in the information category also affects the viewing time, and this interest may be inherent in users, or it may be aroused by presentation. Combined with the model we described in Chap. 3, it can be considered that interest in information categories and products has similar characteristics and influences the user's information acceptance.

In the proposed system, by increasing the level of interest in products, we tried to increase the acceptability of various types of information outside of the interest, without distinction. From the above discussion, the model in Sect. 3 can be improved by considering the acceptance difficulty and the interest in the information category.

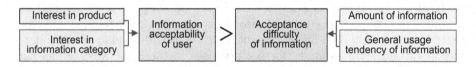

Fig. 9. Information acceptability model derived from the experimental results. It represents the conditions under which user can accept certain information. When the information acceptability of the user exceeds the acceptance difficulty of the information, the user can accept the information.

Information Acceptability Model. Based on the above discussion, the model in Chap. 3 is modified as follows, considering the acceptance difficulty of information and level of interest in the information category (Fig. 9). First, from the amount of information and the extent of how much the information tends to be used when the product is purchased (General usage tendency of information), the acceptance difficulty can be defined as a constant that is unique to each piece of information. On the other hand, the user's acceptability of information can be derived from the user's level of interest in the product and information category at that time. Those are variables that change from moment to moment depending on the user's internal state during purchase. When the information acceptability of user exceeds the acceptance difficulty of information, the information is accepted and viewed by the user.

If the model is reliable, it is possible to estimate the user's level of acceptability and acceptance difficulty for each piece of information, and to select information that is likely to be viewed. In addition, it is also possible to present information that increases the level of acceptance of other category of information, and to adjust the amount of information according to general usage tendency of information.

Limitations and Future Work. In this section, we discuss the limitations of this study. First, we have not been able to verify the validity and accuracy of the interest detection method. In the post-experiment interviews, many participants favorably received the information that products of their interest were presented, but there were a few comments that products of no interest were displayed. Therefore, the accuracy of the interest estimation method needs to be evaluated and improved. Furthermore, there were cases where the estimation of the interest have changed while the participants was comparing the shelf and the presented information, and the content of the presentation changed, confusing the participants. We need to discuss how to realize context-sensitive interest estimation.

Moreover, the effectiveness of the proposed presentation method was only verified in a single scenario, i.e., a one-time purchase of snacks. Although our experiment included a one-week washout period, it is possible that the order effect may not have been completely removed. In addition, since our experiment was a simulated purchase without payment, the behavior may be slightly different from the actual purchase. We plan to study the long-term impact of the proposed approach in actual purchasing situations, examining its effectiveness not only for low-cost, high-frequency purchases, but also for expensive, infrequent purchases.

In addition, the model proposed in the previous section only considers the parameters identified from the results of this experiment, and it is possible that a variety of other parameters are involved. We believe that by evaluating the validity of the model and improving it through further experiments, it may be possible to develop a presentation method that uses a small amount of interest-related information to increase the acceptance of information outside the user's interests, and a behavior change system that uses this method.

6 Conclusion

In this paper, we proposed a purchasing support system for offline stores that can present information to users without being evasive by interactively presenting a small amount of product information according to their interest in the product as predicted by the system in real-time. We designed and implemented a proof-of-concept system for an actual use case scenario: a snack purchasing area in an office. We evaluated the effectiveness of the proposed system based on our hypotheses through a purchasing experiment with 11 participants. The experimental results suggest that the proposed method can induce users' interest in the system and encourage them to watch the information, and that users may receive the information presented and make a purchase, even if partially considered.

References

1. Atalay, A.S., Bodur, H.O., Rasolofoarison, D.: Shining in the center: central gaze cascade effect on product choice. J. Consumer Res. **39**(4), 848–866 (2012)
2. Bianchi, F., Garnett, E., Dorsel, C., Aveyard, P., Jebb, S.A.: Restructuring physical micro-environments to reduce the demand for meat: a systematic review and qualitative comparative analysis. Lancet Planetary Health **2**(9), e384–e397 (2018)
3. Clement, J., Kristensen, T., Grønhaug, K.: Understanding consumers' in-store visual perception: the influence of package design features on visual attention. J. Retail. Consum. Serv. **20**(2), 234–239 (2013)
4. Crockett, R.A., et al.: Nutritional labelling for healthier food or non-alcoholic drink purchasing and consumption. Cochrane Database Syst. Rev. **2**, CD009315 (2018)
5. Eppler, M.J., Mengis, J.: The concept of information overload-a review of literature from organization science, accounting, marketing, mis, and related disciplines (2004). Kommunikationsmanagement im Wandel, pp. 271–305 (2008)
6. Gao, J., Zhang, C., Wang, K., Ba, S.: Understanding online purchase decision making: the effects of unconscious thought, information quality, and information quantity. Decis. Support Syst. **53**(4), 772–781 (2012)
7. Gonçalves, D., Coelho, P., Martinez, L.F., Monteiro, P.: Nudging consumers toward healthier food choices: a field study on the effect of social norms. Sustainability **13**(4), 1660 (2021)
8. Hartmann-Boyce, J., et al.: Grocery store interventions to change food purchasing behaviors: a systematic review of randomized controlled trials. Am. J. Clin. Nutr. **107**(6), 1004–1016 (2018)
9. Jacob, S., Ishimaru, S., Bukhari, S.S., Dengel, A.: Gaze-based interest detection on newspaper articles. In: Proceedings of the 7th Workshop on Pervasive Eye Tracking and Mobile Eye-Based Interaction. PETMEI 2018, Association for Computing Machinery, New York, NY, USA (2018). https://doi.org/10.1145/3208031.3208034
10. Karolus, J., Dabbert, P., Wozniak, P.W.: I know what you want: Using gaze metrics to predict personal interest. In: The 31st Annual ACM Symposium on User Interface Software and Technology Adjunct Proceedings, pp. 105–107. UIST 2018 Adjunct, Association for Computing Machinery, New York, NY, USA (2018). https://doi.org/10.1145/3266037.3266116
11. Kim, M., Lee, M.K., Dabbish, L.: Shop-i: Gaze based interaction in the physical world for in-store social shopping experience. In: Proceedings of the 33rd Annual ACM Conference Extended Abstracts on Human Factors in Computing Systems, pp. 1253–1258 (2015)
12. Klasnja, P., Consolvo, S., Pratt, W.: How to evaluate technologies for health behavior change in HCI research. In: Proceedings of the SIGCHI Conference on Human Factors in Computing Systems, pp. 3063–3072 (2011)

13. Li, Y., et al.: Towards measuring and inferring user interest from gaze. In: WWW, pp. 525–533 (2017)
14. Marangunić, N., Granić, A.: Technology acceptance model: a literature review from 1986 to 2013. Univ. Access Inf. Soc. **14**(1), 81–95 (2015)
15. Nakanishi, M., Takahashi, M.: Information design for purposeless information searching based on optimum stimulation level theory. In: Yamamoto, S., Mori, H. (eds.) HIMI 2018. LNCS, vol. 10905, pp. 132–143. Springer, Cham (2018). https://doi.org/10.1007/978-3-319-92046-7_12
16. Reutskaja, E., Hogarth, R.M.: Satisfaction in choice as a function of the number of alternatives: When "goods satiate". Psychol. Market. **26**(3), 197–203 (2009)
17. Schiavo, G., Mencarini, E., Vovard, K.B., Zancanaro, M.: Sensing and reacting to users' interest: an adaptive public display. In: CHI2013 Extended Abstracts on Human Factors in Computing Systems, pp. 1545–1550 (2013)
18. Seyedghorban, Z., Tahernejad, H., Matanda, M.J.: Reinquiry into advertising avoidance on the internet: a conceptual replication and extension. J. Advert. **45**(1), 120–129 (2016)
19. Speck, P.S., Elliott, M.T.: Predictors of advertising avoidance in print and broadcast media. J. Advert. **26**(3), 61–76 (1997)

Persuasive Design and Applications

Can We Re-design Social Media to Persuade People to Challenge Misinformation? An Exploratory Study

Selin Gurgun[1]([✉]), Emily Arden-Close[1], John McAlaney[1], Keith Phalp[1], and Raian Ali[2]

[1] Faculty of Science and Technology, Bournemouth University, Poole, UK
{sgurgun,eardenclose,jmcalaney,kphalp}@bournemouth.ac.uk
[2] College of Science and Engineering, Hamad Bin Khalifa University, Doha, Qatar
raali2@hbku.edu.qa

Abstract. Persuasive design techniques have often been presented where the desired behaviour is primarily within personal boundaries, e.g., one's own health and learning. Limited research has been conducted on behaviours that require exposure to others, including correcting, confronting mistakes and wrongdoing. Challenging misinformation in others' posts online is an example of such social behaviour. This study draws on the main persuasive system design models and principles to create interfaces on social media to motivate users to challenge misinformation. We conducted a questionnaire (with 250 participants from the UK) to test the influence of these interfaces on willingness to challenge and how age, gender, personality traits, perspective-taking and empathy affected their perception of the persuasiveness of the interfaces. Our proposed interfaces exemplify seven persuasive strategies: reduction, suggestion, self-monitoring, recognition, normative influence, tunneling and liking. Most participants thought existing social media did not provide enough techniques and tools to challenge misinformation. While predefined question stickers (suggestion), private commenting (reduction), and thinking face reactions (liking) were seen as effective ways to motivate users to challenge misinformation, sentence openers (tunneling) was seen as the least influential. Increasing age and perspective taking were associated with increased likelihood of perceived persuasiveness and increasing openness to experience was associated with a reduction in the likelihood of perceived persuasiveness for "predefined question stickers". Increasing openness to experience was associated with increased likelihood of perceived persuasiveness for "thinking face reaction", while increasing age was associated with a reduction in the likelihood of perceived persuasiveness for "private commenting".

Keywords: Persuasive system · misinformation · fake news · online social behaviour · social media design

1 Introduction

The growing proliferation of misinformation has raised interest in devising ways to combat it. Since social media plays a paramount role in disseminating misinformation [1,

© The Author(s), under exclusive license to Springer Nature Switzerland AG 2023
J. Ham et al. (Eds.): PERSUASIVE 2023, LNCS 13832, pp. 123–141, 2023.
https://doi.org/10.1007/978-3-031-30933-5_9

2], technology-based solutions to detect and mitigate misinformation are being proposed and used. Such solutions rely on artificial intelligence (AI) and machine learning [3, 4]. Despite offering promise, the existence of misinformation in recent events such as the COVID-19 pandemic [5] and Ukraine-Russia War [6] demonstrates that these techniques have limitations. In addition to algorithmic approaches provided by digital platforms and legislative measures taken by governments and social media platforms, individual attempts to correct misinformation have also been effective [7].

Although challenging misinformation is effective in reducing the spread of misinformation [7, 8], research shows that when people encounter misinformation in the online sphere, they tend to remain silent [9–12]. However, challenging others helps the poster correct or delete the shared information and helps others in the network adjust their perceptions about the content [13]. Therefore, users' silence contributes, albeit unintentionally, to the propagation of misinformation.

Studies on why people remain silent when they encounter misinformation indicate that users have interpersonal, intrapersonal and institutional concerns such as fear of being harassed, fear of conflict or lack of institutional support [10, 14]. Gurgun et al. [15] identified six reasons that might impact users' decisions to challenge others who post misinformation: self-oriented, relationship-oriented, others-oriented, content-oriented, individual characteristics, and technical factors. While it is necessary to overcome the barriers that hinder users from challenging misinformation, it is also worthwhile to design social media platforms that are more persuasive and encourage users to challenge misinformation.

In a digital environment, information systems may be designed to influence behaviour change [16]. Such systems are often referred to as persuasive systems [17] or persuasive technology [18]. These systems address behaviour change in areas where the intended behaviour is primarily within personal boundaries such as one's own wellbeing [19] and academic performance [20]. However, to the best of our knowledge, a few studies have addressed behaviours including interactions with other people. One study found that persuasive technology can promote acceptable workplace behaviour and etiquette [21]. As incorporating persuasive techniques into social media has been shown to lead to greater behaviour change and more engagement [22, 23] they could be applied to motivate users to challenge misinformation.

In this paper, we aim to develop an understanding of which persuasive techniques may aid users in challenging others in an environment where algorithms and a homogeneous network impede exposure to adverse opinions [24–26]. Given the lack of research on users' reluctance to challenge misinformation on social media, we aimed to provide a starting point and investigate potential solutions based on persuasive design principles, linking them to user characteristics such as personality traits, perspective-taking, and empathy. While we do not claim completeness in our coverage of design techniques and user characteristics, our choices were informed by theory. Personality traits have been shown to influence the willingness to participate in discussions, e.g. extroverts are typically more willing to do so [27]. In addition to that, evidence from the literature suggests that there is a significant relationship between persuasive strategies and personality traits [28, 29] To the best of our knowledge, no attempt has been made to examine the associations between perspective-taking, empathic concern and persuasive techniques.

Perspective-taking refers to the ability to adopt the perspective of other people [30]. According to research, perspective-taking influences attributional thinking and perceptions of others. For example, those who with a higher perspective-taking tendency made the same attributions to the target as they would have had they been in the same situation [31]. As giving negative feedback, disagreeing and confronting are related to the perception of others (e.g., whether they perceive it as futile or harmful to their relationship), we also examine whether perspective-taking has an association with the perception of the persuasiveness of the proposed interfaces. Empathic concern signifies the development of emotions of compassion and concern for those experiencing negative events [30]. Individuals with higher level of empathic concern are more likely to acquire positive attitudes toward being a decent and moral person and not to harm others [32]. Therefore, since empathy might be a useful component for challenging misinformation, we also investigated whether the interfaces we presented are associated with users' empathic concern. This insight may help for the future interface design to motivate users to challenge misinformation. In this paper, we aim to answer the following research questions:

RQ1: To what extent do users think that current social media design helps them to challenge misinformation?

RQ2: Can we increase users' willingness to challenge misinformation on social media through introducing persuasive interfaces?

RQ3: Do age, gender, personality traits, perspective-taking, and empathy have an impact on users' acceptance of these interfaces?

2 Method

Our work aims to investigate whether we can design new persuasive interfaces in social media to increase users' willingness to challenge misinformation. To achieve this goal, first, based on relevant literature, we explored effective persuasive tools that aid in increasing engagement or participation in the online social sphere. To stay within a manageable scope, we selected seven strategies (Table 1). Then, we created a high-fidelity prototype of a possible implementation of each strategy in the context of challenging misinformation. We then conducted a survey to assess users' perceptions of the influence of each prototype on their willingness to challenge misinformation.

2.1 Prototype Design

In order to create interfaces for challenging misinformation, we started with reviewing the pertinent literature regarding the tools and techniques that have a positive impact on motivating people to engage more in online discussion environments. We reviewed literature regarding the design recommendations suggested for promoting healthy discussions [33], strengthening engagement in discussions [34] and increasing participation in online communities [35]. We selected seven techniques based on their practicality and possibility to embed within social media design with no costly requirement. The interfaces have been deemed face valid through a combination of expert review and pilot testing with users. Descriptions of the techniques applied in this study, which were adapted from [36] are shown in Table 1 and prototypes are available on Open Science Framework (see https://osf.io/3x74c).

Table 1. Persuasive Strategies, corresponding descriptions and implementations

Strategy	Description	Our Implementation
Reduction	A strategy of reducing complex behaviour into simple tasks	**Private Commenting (PC):** This option makes private messaging easier. Instead of copying the link to the post in the private message section to refer to it, users can comment privately on the post directly by clicking the "send privately" button
Suggestion	A strategy that offers fitting suggestions	**Predefined Question Stickers (PQS):** A sticker set with pre-written questions for users to choose from when they want to challenge, e.g. stickers with labels like "what is your source"
Self-monitoring	A strategy that enables monitoring of one's own status or progress	**Tone Detector (TD):** An emotional scale mood indicator that enables users to visualise how their comments are likely to sound to someone reading them. As the user composes a comment, the indicator on the scale starts to move based on the word selections, writing style and punctuation, e.g., aggressive vs friendly
Recognition	A strategy that provides public acknowledgement for following certain behaviour	**"Fact Checker" Badge (FCB):** A badge that provides public recognition for users who correct misinformation occasionally
Normative influence	A strategy that displays norms regarding how most people behave and what behaviour they approve of	**Social Norm Message (SNM):** A pop-up prompt regarding other users' acceptance and positive disposition towards correcting misinformation on social media

(continued)

Table 1. (*continued*)

Strategy	Description	Our Implementation
Tunneling	A strategy that guides users or provides means to persuade	**Sentence openers (SO):** Pre-generated sentence openers to guide users to challenge misinformation, e.g. "My argument is…"
Liking	A strategy that highlights the persuasiveness of visually attractive	**Thinking Face Reaction (TFR):** A fun and appealing reaction that implies questioning the content

Recommended techniques were visualised to mimic Facebook's current user interface in the survey. The content displayed to participants was about an asteroid that will be possibly hitting Earth. This news was a misinformation article that appeared in CNN's iReport news hub in 2014[1] and was widely shared. We presented the interfaces to participants as a scenario. Before showing the interfaces, we informed the respondents about the scenario that the news is false, as this study was not to determine whether individuals can discern misinformation but rather to assess perceptions of the persuasive techniques. Additionally, care was taken not to include any political or social issues as these topics may influence users' decisions to challenge the misinformation regardless of the persuasive technique used [37, 38]. To make the scenario more realistic and prevent participants from perceiving the account as anonymous, we intentionally did not obscure the name and photo of the Facebook user sharing the content. The account holder was named Alex to avoid gender confounding as it is a gender-neutral name. Facebook was selected as the social network site for this study as it is the most used online social network worldwide with approximately 2.91 billion monthly active users [39] across all age groups [40]. The questions were about challenging an acquaintance, as previous research showed that it is more difficult to debate or challenge weak ties than strong ties [41]. Before presenting the interfaces we also explained that Alex is a contact who is known but not as close as a friend or family member, which also controlled for familiarity and personal ties.

Below, we explain each of the interfaces that we used and how they exemplify the persuasive design principles.

Private Commenting (Reduction). A private mode of communication such as direct messaging (DM) or private messaging (PM) can be preferred by users who hesitate to counteract misinformation due to fear of embarrassing the sharer [42]. Although Facebook provides private communication channels (e.g., Facebook Messenger), private commenting is proposed as it simplifies the challenging process. Private messaging requires effort. In contrast, private commenting allows users to engage with the content while scrolling through their feeds.

---

[1] https://www.cnet.com/science/cnn-posts-asteroid-to-hit-earth-article-people-take-it-seriously/.

Pre-defined Question Stickers (Suggestion). By suggesting to users some questions to challenge, we aimed to aid users who struggle with starting challenging misinformation. We developed three exemplar questions based on Toulmin's model of argumentation [43] which we implemented as stickers. As stickers are impersonal responses, they may alleviate the psychological and social costs associated with confronting, questioning and challenging by typing directly [44].

Tone Detector (Self-monitoring). Self-monitoring is one of the most popular persuasive strategies [45] and it helps people become more self-aware about their behavioural patterns [46] which also helps them to self-regulate [47]. One potential reason people do not challenge misinformation is that they want to avoid being viewed as aggressive [15]. A tone detector guides users to improve their self-awareness regarding how they sound to others, which would likely be helpful for those who are concerned about how their comments come across.

Fact Checker Badge (Recognition). In addition to providing public recognition, badges can function as incentives for people who challenge misinformation. SNS like Foursquare or StackOverflow have also used badges as a tool to encourage users to increase their level of engagement [48].

Social Norm Messages (Normative Influence). Normative social influence can be successfully used in persuasive technologies to alter existing behaviour [49, 50]. Social norms refer to the beliefs that individuals hold about others in a social group and what others in that social group do or think [51–53]. People are more likely to engage in a behaviour if they perceive it to be commonly accepted by others [54]. Taking that into account we proposed a hint prompt that provides information regarding injunctive norms (what most people approve of).

Sentence Openers (Tunneling). Tunneling is defined as guiding a user through a complex experience [36]. We used sentence openers to lead users to complete the sentences. In many cases, it is rhetoric rather than facts that causes contradictory opinions [55]. Sentence starters have been shown to facilitate expression of disagreement [56] and enhance the quality of online discussions [57] as they can steer thoughts and conversation in such a way that they keep conversations grounded [58].

Thinking Face Reaction (Liking). Facebook launched the "Like" button to enable users to show their affection for the content and introduced the "Reactions" feature to provide users with more ways to express their reactions to content in a fast and easy way [59]. The reactions feature has positively influenced engagement levels on Facebook [60]. As reactions are intended to be a way to express appreciation for the content with one-click, we used thinking face reactions to motivate users to challenge [61].

2.2 Data Collection

The survey was conducted online using Qualtrics, an online survey design platform. Before survey completion, participants were informed about the study objectives and asked to provide their consent to participate. They were provided with information regarding the confidentiality of the data, their freedom to participate and the right to withdraw from the study as well as their access to the study findings. Data was collected between 31st May and 7th July 2022 through Prolific™ (www.prolific.co), an established online participant recruitment platform for research studies.

2.3 Participants

250 adults living in the UK completed the survey and received payment (around £4). The following inclusion criteria were used to recruit potential participants: 1) aged 18 years or older; 2) using Facebook with an authentic identity 3) encountered misinformation on Facebook. Of those respondents who answered the demographic questions, 57.2% (143) were female, 41.6% (104) male, and 1.2% (3) non-binary. 17.8% (44) were aged 18 to 24 years, 37.2% (92) were between 25–34, 26.7% (66) between 35–44, and 18.2% (45) over 45 years. Most respondents (62.8%, 157) had at least a university degree, 22.8% (57) had completed secondary education and 14.4% (36) had not completed secondary education.

2.4 Measures

Demographic Characteristics
Participants answered questions about their age, gender and educational level.

Perceived Prevalence of Existing Tools to Challenge Misinformation
Participants were asked to rate the extent to which they think social media provides tools or ways for users to challenge misinformation on a seven-point scale (1 = None at all 7 = A great deal) (M = 3.37, SD = 1.6).

Perceived Persuasiveness on Willingness to Challenge
For this study, we developed seven prototypes informed by PSD and presented the participants eight high-fidelity prototypes including the standard comment box (SCB). Participants were asked how much each interface influenced their willingness to challenge misinformation on a seven-point scale (1 = Far too little 7 = Far too much). Prototypes were presented in random order for each respondent.

Personality Traits
The 10-item Big-Five inventory (BFI-10) [62] was used to assess the traits of extraversion, agreeableness, openness to experience, conscientiousness and neuroticism-stability. Each trait is measured by two items on a five-point Likert scale (1 = Strongly disagree to 5 = Strongly agree). Higher scores imply higher levels of each personality trait. The BFI-10 showed good reliability and validity [62].

Perspective-Taking and Empathic Concern
Perspective taking and empathic concern were assessed with the seven-item perspective-taking and seven-item empathy subscales from the Interpersonal Reactivity Index (IRI)

which assesses level of empathy and individuals' capacity to understand and feel the emotions of others [30]. It is widely used to examine the impact of empathy on various outcomes, including prosocial behaviour [63] and intergroup relations [64]. The perspective-taking subscale consisted of seven items ($\alpha = .78$) such as "I try to look at everybody's side of a disagreement before I make a decision"). Empathy subscale consisted of seven items ($\alpha = .81$) such as "When I see someone being taken advantage of, I feel kind of protective toward them."). The items are answered using a 5-point rating scale ranging from on a 0 (does not describe me well), to 4 (describes me very well). To get a single score for each participant for each construct, we averaged the answers to the items.

2.5 Data Analysis

Data were analysed using SPSS version 28. Descriptive statistics were used to report demographic information and the extent to which users think social media provides them with tools or techniques to counteract misinformation. As the data was not normally distributed, non-parametric tests were used. Spearman's rank-order correlation was used to analyse the association between continuous and ordinal data. A Wilcoxon signed-rank test was conducted to investigate differences in willingness to challenge misinformation between the status quo (standard comment box) and PSD-based interfaces. Interfaces were considered persuasive when users rated them as more influential than the standard comment box in motivating challenging misinformation. Binomial logistic regression analyses were performed to determine whether age, gender, personality traits, perspective-taking and empathy influence willingness to challenge misinformation.

3 Results

3.1 Social Media Tools to Challenge Misinformation

Most participants (58%) agreed that current social media platforms do not provide enough tools or ways to challenge misinformation. Only 26.8% believed that tools social media provides for challenging misinformation are prevalent. A Spearman's rank-order correlation was run to assess the relationship between age and evaluation of the tools on social media to challenge misinformation. Age was negatively correlated with agreement that social media offers tools to challenge r_s (248) = $-.153$, p < .05. Older participants were less likely to think that social media provide tools for challenging misinformation.

3.2 Comparing the Perceived Persuasiveness of Each Interface

A Wilcoxon signed-rank test asssessed the effect of the interfaces presented on users' willingness to challenge misinformation. As shown in Table 2, "predefined question stickers", "thinking face reaction" and "private commenting" elicited a statistically significant positive difference ($z = 2.43$, $p < .05$, $z = 5$, $p < .001$ and $z = 7.2$, $p < .001$ respectively) and "sentence openers" showed a statistically significant negative difference ($z = -2.7$, $p < .05$) in their influence on willingness to challenge misinformation compared to the standard comment box. Excepting sentence openers, most participants rated PSD-informed implementations as having more influence than the standard comment box.

Table 2. The influence on willingness to challenge for each presented interface versus standard comment box (N = 250)

Predefined Stickers (PQS)	N	Mean Ranks	Sum of Ranks	Z	P
Negative Ranks	80[a]	110.84	8867.50	-2.430^*	<.05
Positive Ranks	129[b]	101.38	13077.50		
Ties	41[c]				
Thinking Face Reaction (TFR)	N	Mean Ranks	Sum of Ranks	Z	P
Negative Ranks	65[d]	93.04	6047.50	-5.005^*	<.001
Positive Ranks	136[e]	104.81	14253.50		
Ties	49[f]				
Private Commenting (PC)	N	Mean Ranks	Sum of Ranks	Z	P
Negative Ranks	47[g]	99.67	4684.50	-7.239^*	<.001
Positive Ranks	162[h]	106.55	17260.50		
Ties	41[i]				
Sentence Openers (SO)	N	Mean Ranks	Sum of Ranks	Z	P
Negative Ranks	102[j]	96.22	9814.00	$-2.714^{¶}$	<.05
Positive Ranks	76[k]	80.49	6117.00		
Ties	72[l]				
Fact Checker Badge (FCB)	N	Mean Ranks	Sum of Ranks	Z	P
Negative Ranks	93[m]	102.62	9543.50	$-.139^*$	0.89
Positive Ranks	103[n]	94.78	9762.50		
Ties	54[o]				
Social Norm Message (SNM)	N	Mean Ranks	Sum of Ranks	Z	P
Negative Ranks	76[p]	111.68	8488.00	-1.821^*	0.06
Positive Ranks	123[q]	92.78	11412.00		
Ties	51[r]				
Tone Detector (TD)	N	Mean Ranks	Sum of Ranks	Z	P
Negative Ranks	91[s]	99.47	9051.50	-1.344^*	0.17
Positive Ranks	110[t]	102.27	11249.50		

(*continued*)

Table 2. (*continued*)

Predefined Stickers (PQS)	N	Mean Ranks	Sum of Ranks	Z	P
Ties	49^u				

a. PQS < SCB b. PQS > SCB c. PQS = SCB d. TFR < SCB e. TFR > SCB f. TFR = SCB
g. PC < SCB h. PC > SCB i. PC = SCB j. SO < SCB k. SO > SCB l. SO = SCB
m. FCB < SCB n. FCB > SCB o. FCB = SCB p. SNM < SCB q. SNM > SCB r. SNM = SCB
s. TD < SCB t. TD > SCB u. TD = SCB.
* Based on negative ranks.
¶ Based on positive ranks.

3.3 Effects of Age, Gender, Personality Traits Perspective Taking and Empathy

We investigated whether the positive impact of "predefined question stickers", "thinking face reaction", "private commenting" and the negative impact of "sentence openers" regarding perceived persuasiveness on willingness to challenge compared to the standard comment box were impacted by age, gender, Big Five personality traits, perspective-taking and empathy. We computed a difference score for each user and each interface by subtracting the level of the standard comment box reflected in users' ratings from the level of influence of presented interfaces. The difference score ranged from −6 to 6. Binomial logistic regression was performed using this score as a dependent variable to ascertain the effects of age, gender, personality traits, perspective taking and empathy on the likelihood that participants consider the presented interfaces to be more or less persuasive than the standard comment box. Positive difference scores were encoded as 1 which indicates that users found the presented interfaces more persuasive than the standard comment box. Any scores of zero or below were encoded as 0, which indicates either that there was no difference between the standard comment box and the interfaces or that users rated interfaces as less persuasive than the standard comment box.

A binomial logistic regression was performed to ascertain the effects of age, gender, personality traits, perspective taking and empathy on persuasiveness ratings. Linearity of the continuous variables with respect to the logit of the dependent variable was assessed via the Box-Tidwell [65] procedure. A Bonferroni correction was applied using all eight terms in the model resulting in statistical significance being accepted when p < 0.0027. Based on this assessment, all continuous independent variables were found to be linearly related to the logit of the dependent variable. The Hosmer and Lemeshow's tests suggest that the models for PQS, TFR, PC and SO provide good fit to the data. The result of the binary logistic regression estimates for each interface are presented in Table 3. Age and perspective taking were significantly positively associated with "predefined question stickers" ($b = 0.04$, p < .01 and $b = 0.08$, p < .05 respectively) such that increasing age and perspective-taking were associated with increased likelihood of positive influence of "predefined question stickers" relative to the standard comment box. However, increasing openness to experience was associated with a reduction in the likelihood of positive influence ($b = -0.21$, p < .01). Openness to experience was associated with belief in the persuasiveness of the "thinking face reaction" such that as it increased, the positive influence of "thinking face reaction" of 1.24. ($b = -0.24$, p <

.01). Age was significantly negatively associated with "private commenting," such that as age increased, belief in the persuasiveness of private commenting decreased ($b = -0.04$, $p < .01$).

Table 3. Binomial logistic regressions predicting the difference score between standard comment box and presented interfaces

Coefficients	PQS			TFR		
	B	SE	Exp(B)	B	SE	Exp(B)
Age	0.04*	0.01	1.04	−0.01	0.01	0.99
Gender (Female)	−0.38	0.31	0.68	−0.45	0.3	0.64
Extraversion	0.11	0.08	1.12	0.01	0.08	1.01
Agreeableness	−0.18	0.1	0.84	0.01	0.09	1.01
Conscientiousness	−0.12	0.1	0.89	0.06	0.1	1.07
Neuroticism	−0.02	0.08	0.98	0.03	0.08	1.03
Openness to experience	−0.21*	0.08	0.81	−0.24*	0.08	0.79
Empathy	−0.03	0.04	0.97	0.01	0.04	1.01
Perspective Taking	0.08**	0.04	1.08	−0.01	0.04	0.99
Constant	1.14	1.54	3.14	1.75	1.53	5.75
Modal summary						
Hosmer and Lemeshow X^2	5.28			9.87		
df	8			8		
p Value	.726			.27		
Nagelkerke R2	0.11			0.07		
Coefficients	PC			SO		
	B	S.E	Exp (B)	B	S.E	Exp (B)
Age	−0.04*	0.01	0.96	0	0.01	1
Gender (Female)	−0.15	0.31	0.86	−0.5	0.32	0.61
Extraversion	0.06	0.08	1.06	−0.06	0.09	0.94
Agreeableness	0.06	0.1	1.07	0.02	0.1	1.02
Conscientiousness	−0.09	0.1	0.91	−0.13	0.1	0.88
Neuroticism	0.01	0.08	1.01	−0.04	0.08	0.96
Openness to experience	−0.09	0.08	0.91	−0.14	0.08	0.87

(*continued*)

Table 3. (*continued*)

Coefficients	PC			SO		
	B	S.E	Exp (B)	B	S.E	Exp (B)
Empathy	0.04	0.04	1.04	0.02	0.05	1.02
Perspective Taking	0	0.04	1	0.04	0.04	1.04
Constant	2.06	1.6	7.83	0.66	1.62	1.93
Modal summary						
Hosmer and Lemeshow X^2	9.22			4.83		
df	8			8		
p Value	.32			.77		
Nagelkerke R2	0.1			0.05		

$*p < .01. * *p < .05.$

4   Discussion

4.1   Lack of Tools for Challenging Misinformation on Social Media

While social media platforms such as Facebook rely on persuasive tactics to increase engagement with the platform which is important for commercial success [66], they do not seem to encourage critical thinking or enabling questioning of the content. On the contrary, several features they provide such as "hide post" or "unfriend" are used as tactics to discourage users from voicing concerns through facilitating less confrontational, yet less constructive, alternatives [67] as users may more easily avoid, rather than confront content. Our results showed that the majority of participants thought social media did not provide enough tools or ways to challenge misinformation. Although some features such as "commenting" or "direct messaging" may be used as tools to challenge misinformation, it can be argued that users do not regard them as tools provided to challenge misinformation. This necessitates the development of more persuasive or engaging tools, and ones which users would also perceive to be explicitly available for such purposes.

In our study, age was significantly negatively associated with reported lack of tools, such older participants were less likely to believe that social media offered tools for challenging misinformation. This might be because younger people, who were raised in an environment with a wealth of digital possibilities are more receptive to different social media features than older people [68]. This difference is to be expected given that young people were raised in an environment with a wealth of digital possibilities, whereas older people learned about such digital opportunities as adults [69] This may also explain why older adults are less likely to report correcting others [70], though we recognise that there are other potential explanations here, such as different perceptions of acceptable behaviours (see below).

4.2 Influence of Social Media Interfaces on Challenging Misinformation

Social media interfaces may be considered as far more than just a means of providing access to information. They are also a way to alter users' attitudes and behaviours by creating opportunities for persuasive interaction [17]. Previous research investigated persuasive technologies to motivate users to change behaviours relating to themselves such as diet [71] and physical activity [72]. However, as challenging misinformation also includes interpersonal relationships in the online environment, the results may shed light on the influence of these persuasive techniques in interactive processes. Our results showed that "predefined question stickers" (suggestion), "thinking face reaction" (liking) and "private commenting" (reduction) influenced users the most and "sentence openers" (tunneling) influenced users the least to challenge misinformation. The suggestion technique was perceived as more persuasive than the standard comment box. In other words, people prefer the system to offer them prepared options to facilitate challenging misinformation, rather than having to write comments themselves. Along with providing suggestions to users, software-imposed interaction structures also make communication more impersonal [73], which may affect users' perceptions of information. The effectiveness of the "thinking face reaction" shows that liking as a technique positively impacted users' willingness to challenge misinformation relative to the standard comment box. In addition to being visually appealing, the thinking face also allows the user to provide an impersonal response by clicking a reaction, which may account for the positive influence. Our findings showed that people found "private commenting", which is a preferred way to challenge misinformation [42], more persuasive than the standard comment box. In addition to simplifying the process, doing so in a private way may also contribute to its positive impact. As much as a reduction technique implemented in the form of private commenting seems to be successful, the inability of others to view the interaction is a concern as research shows that observing corrections helps individuals change their own misperceptions [74].

Tunneling in the form of "sentence openers" was found to be less persuasive than the standard comment box. This might be because although participants are given the starters of the sentences, they still need to write their arguments which may require more effort on their side. Prior research identified the importance of perceived ease of use in users' acceptance of information technologies [75]. In this case, solely guiding the user does not seem to be an effective strategy to motivate users to challenge misinformation. However, future work could investigate whether it helps users create more constructive responses.

4.3 Effect of Age, Openness to Experience, and Perspective Taking on Influence of the Interfaces on Challenging Misinformation

Age, openness to experience, and perspective taking are moderated the effect of the interfaces that persuaded people more than the standard comment box. The positive association between age and "predefined question stickers" indicated that older adults found using prewritten statements more influential than the standard comment box. The negative association between age and "private commenting" shows that younger adults found it more influential to challenge misinformation in private. These findings suggest that as individuals age, concerns about self-presentation reduce and they feel more comfortable expressing themselves in public in line with previous research indicating that older adults tend to be less self-conscious and report fewer experiences of negative feelings such as shame, guilt and embarrassment relative to younger adults [76]. However, as people age, they choose to challenge misinformation in a more impersonal way, which may be an indication that they value their relationships with others. Perspective-taking is another predictor for "predefined question stickers". We found that users who have a greater tendency to consider events from the viewpoints, feelings, and reactions of others [77] find these stickers more persuasive than the standard comment box. As perspective-taking is related to make the same attributions to the target [31], it could be argued that participants are more likely to accept these stickers if they receive them as a response. Openness to experience negatively predicted both "predefined question stickers" and "thinking face reaction," such that users with higher levels of openness to experience did not feel that these two interfaces were more persuasive than the standard comment box. Individuals high in openness to experience, which refers to having an active imagination or artistic interests [62] may possess unique cognitive processes and thinking styles that enable them to challenge misinformation effectively in their own ways or using innovative methods. Therefore we anticipate they may not need any additional tools to challenge misinformation as they might already utilise their own methods of doing so.

4.4   Threats to Validity

This study had several threats to validity that could affect the quality and generalisability of our findings. Our sample consisted of users from the U.K only. Research has shown that in Western societies open discussions and direct confrontation are more socially acceptable [78, 79]. The measure we used to assess the influence of the interfaces on willingness to challenge misinformation was based on self-report meaning potential biases such as social desirability bias.

We chose Facebook as an example of a SNS to test our proposed persuasive techniques, but it is possible that the results may differ for other SNS platforms. User cultures, interface design and user experience may differ across social media platforms [80, 81].

We acknowledge that our explanation of the results reflect one possibility. Alternative explanations can also be plausible. Therefore, future research is required to fully understand the results.

5   Conclusion and Future Work

We conducted a survey with 250 participants to assess how users perceived the persuasiveness of seven PSD-informed design interfaces compared to the standard comment box on willingness to challenge misinformation. Our study provides novel contributions to Persuasive Technology by identifying which interfaces users consider to be most persuasive in motivating individuals to challenge others on social media. In addition, these results provide insights into techniques that can be utilised to persuade people who hesitate to confront the perpetrators in instances of racism, sexism or prejudice on social media. By demonstrating that particular techniques are perceived as persuasive in users' willingness to challenge we pave the way for future social network design features to motivate users to challenge when they encounter misinformation. We also noted that users' demographics and psychological factors impacted their evaluation of different techniques, with younger users tending to favour private messages more than their older counterparts.

One of the study limitations was the use of self-reporting to assess the influence of each interface on the willingness to challenge, though further work could experimentally assess changes in users' levels of challenge with varying design implementation. Similarly, although we selected just seven techniques from the PSD framework, future research could investigate whether other techniques influence willingness to challenge misinformation. Another area for future work would involve examining whether other variables such as self-efficacy or self-enhancement are associated with the use of PSD-informed techniques. Our results provide information regarding the level of influence of each technique, but future research may further explore the reasons, or at least require users to provide a rationale, for the ratings they provided, and factors influencing their acceptance of persuasive techniques. Many people who witness acts of racism or prejudice refrain from confronting the offenders [82]. Future research could investigate whether these techniques might influence willingness to confront such perpetrators.

References

1. Allcott, H., Gentzkow, M.: Social media and fake news in the 2016 election. J. Econ. Perspect. **31**, 211–236 (2017)
2. Allcott, H., Gentzkow, M., Yu, C.: Trends in the diffusion of misinformation on social media. Res. Polit. **6**, 2053168019848554 (2019)
3. Sharma, K., Qian, F., Jiang, H., Ruchansky, N., Zhang, M., Liu, Y.: Combating fake news: a survey on identification and mitigation techniques. ACM Trans. Intell. Syst. Technol. **10**, 1–42 (2019)
4. Bode, L.: User correction as a tool in the battle against social media misinformation. Georgetown Law Technol. Rev. **4**, 367 (2019)
5. Cinelli, M., et al.: The COVID-19 social media infodemic. Sci. Rep. **10**, 1–10 (2020)
6. Park, C.Y., Mendelsohn, J., Field, A., Tsvetkov, Y.: VoynaSlov: A Data Set of Russian Social Media Activity during the 2022 Ukraine-Russia War. arXiv preprint arXiv:2205.12382 (2022)
7. Bode, L., Vraga, E.K.: See something, say something: correction of global health misinformation on social media. Health Commun. 1131 (2018)
8. Walter, N., Brooks, J.J., Saucier, C.J., Suresh, S.: Evaluating the impact of attempts to correct health misinformation on social media: a meta-analysis. Health Commun. **36**, 1776–1784 (2021)
9. Chadwick, A., Vaccari, C.: News sharing on UK social media: Misinformation, disinformation, and correction (2019)
10. Chadwick, A., Vaccari, C., Hall, N.-A.: Covid vaccines and online personal messaging: the challenge of challenging everyday misinformation. Loughborough University (2022)
11. Tully, M., Bode, L., Vraga, E.K.: Mobilizing Users: Does Exposure to Misinformation and Its Correction Affect Users' Responses to a Health Misinformation Post? Social Media + Society 6, (2020)

12. Tandoc, E.C., Lim, D., Ling, R.: Diffusion of disinformation: How social media users respond to fake news and why. Journalism **21**, 381–398 (2020)
13. Vraga, E.K., Bode, L.: Using expert sources to correct health misinformation in social media. Sci. Commun. **39**, 621–645 (2017)
14. Bautista, J.R., Zhang, Y., Gwizdka, J.: US physicians' and nurses' motivations, barriers, and recommendations for correcting health misinformation on social media: Qualitative interview study. JMIR Public Health Surveill. **7**, e27715 (2021)
15. Gurgun, S., Arden-Close, E., Phalp, K.T., Ali, R.: Online silence: why do people not challenge others when posting misinformation? Internet Research (2022)
16. Oinas-Kukkonen, H.: A foundation for the study of behavior change support systems. Pers. Ubiquit. Comput. **17**, 1223–1235 (2013)
17. Oinas-Kukkonen, H., Harjumaa, M.: Towards deeper understanding of persuasion in software and information systems. In: ACHI 2008: Proceedings of the First International Conference on Advances in Computer-Human Interaction, pp. 200–205. IEEE (2008)
18. Fogg, B.J.: Creating persuasive technologies: an eight-step design process. In: Proceedings of the 4th International Conference on Persuasive Technology, pp. 1–6
19. Langrial, S., Lehto, T., Oinas-Kukkonen, H., Harjumaa, M., Karppinen, P.: Native mobile applications for personal well-being: a persuasive systems design evaluation. In: 16th Pacific Asia Conference On Information Systems (2012)
20. Widyasari, Y.D.L., Nugroho, L.E., Permanasari, A.E.: Persuasive technology for enhanced learning behavior in higher education. Int. J. Educ. Technol. High. Educ. **16**(1), 1–16 (2019). https://doi.org/10.1186/s41239-019-0142-5
21. Nkwo, M., Orji, R.: Personalized persuasion to promote positive work attitudes in public workplaces. In: UMAP 2019 Adjunct: Adjunct Publication of the 27th Conference on User Modeling, Adaptation and Personalization, pp. 185–190 (2019)
22. Wiafe, I., Koranteng, F.N., Owusu, E., Ekpezu, A.O., Gyamfi, S.A.: Persuasive social features that promote knowledge sharing among tertiary students on social networking sites: an empirical study. J. Comput. Assist. Learn. **36**, 636–645 (2020)
23. Elaheebocus, S.M.R.A., Weal, M., Morrison, L., Yardley, L.: Peer-based social media features in behavior change interventions: systematic review. J. Med. Internet Res. **20**, e8342 (2018)
24. Flaxman, S., Goel, S., Rao, J.M.: Filter bubbles, echo chambers, and online news consumption. Public Opin. Q. **80**, 298–320 (2016)
25. Pariser, E.: The Filter Bubble: What the Internet is Hiding from You. Penguin UK (2011)
26. Spohr, D.: Fake news and ideological polarization: filter bubbles and selective exposure on social media. Bus. Inf. Rev. **34**, 150–160 (2017)
27. Blau, I., Barak, A.: How do personality, synchronous media, and discussion topic affect participation? J. Educ. Technol. Soc. **15**, 12–24 (2012)
28. Alqahtani, F., Meier, S., Orji, R.: Personality-based approach for tailoring persuasive mental health applications. User Model. User-Adap. Inter. **32**, 253–295 (2021). https://doi.org/10.1007/s11257-021-09289-5
29. Halko, S., Kientz, J.A.: Personality and persuasive technology: an exploratory study on health-promoting mobile applications. In: Ploug, T., Hasle, P., Oinas-Kukkonen, H. (eds.) PERSUASIVE 2010. LNCS, vol. 6137, pp. 150–161. Springer, Heidelberg (2010). https://doi.org/10.1007/978-3-642-13226-1_16
30. Davis, M.H.: A multidimensional approach to individual differences in empathy. JSAS Catalogue Sel. Doc. Psychol. **10**, 85 (1980)
31. Davis, M.H., Conklin, L., Smith, A., Luce, C.: Effect of perspective taking on the cognitive representation of persons: a merging of self and other. J. Pers. Soc. Psychol. **70**, 713 (1996)
32. Wang, X.: To communicate or not to communicate: factors predicting passengers' intentions to ask a driver to stop text messaging while driving. Health Commun. **31**, 617–625 (2016)

33. Baughan, A., et al.: Someone is wrong on the internet: Having hard conversations in online spaces. In: Proceedings of the ACM on Human-Computer Interaction, vol. 5, pp. 1–22 (2021)
34. Dennen, V.P.: Pedagogical lurking: Student engagement in non-posting discussion behavior. Comput. Hum. Behav. **24**, 1624–1633 (2008)
35. Bishop, J.: Increasing participation in online communities: a framework for human–computer interaction. Comput. Hum. Behav. **23**, 1881–1893 (2007)
36. Oinas-Kukkonen, H., Harjumaa, M.: Persuasive systems design: key issues, process model, and system features. Commun. Assoc. Inf. Syst. **24**, 28 (2009)
37. Mascheroni, G., Murru, M.F.: "I can share politics but I don't discuss it": everyday practices of political talk on Facebook. Social Media+ Society 3, 2056305117747849 (2017)
38. Geiger, N., Swim, J.K.: Climate of silence: pluralistic ignorance as a barrier to climate change discussion. J. Environ. Psychol. **47**, 79–90 (2016)
39. Statista, Q.: Number of monthly active Facebook users worldwide as of 4th quarter 2015 (2016)
40. https://www.statista.com/statistics/376128/facebook-global-user-age-distribution/
41. Valenzuela, S., Kim, Y., Gil de Zúñiga, H.: Social networks that matter: exploring the role of political discussion for online political participation. Int. J. Public Opinion Res. **24**, 163–184 (2012)
42. Rohman, A.: Counteracting misinformation in quotidian settings. In: Toeppe, K., Yan, H., Chu, S.K.W. (eds.) iConference. LNCS, vol. 12646, pp. 141–155. Springer, Cham (2021). https://doi.org/10.1007/978-3-030-71305-8_11
43. Toulmin, S.E.: The Uses of Argument. Cambridge University Press (2003)
44. Tom Tong, S., Walther, J.B.: Just say "'no thanks'": romantic rejection in computer-mediated communication. J. Soc. Pers. Relat. **28**, 488–506 (2011)
45. Oyebode, O., Alqahtani, F., Orji, R.: Exploring for possible effect of persuasive strategy implementation choices: towards tailoring persuasive technologies. In: Baghaei, N., Vassileva, J., Ali, R., Oyibo, K. (eds.) PERSUASIVE 2022. LNCS, vol. 13213, pp. 145–163. Springer, Cham (2022). https://doi.org/10.1007/978-3-030-98438-0_12
46. Halttu, K., Oinas-Kukkonen, H.: need for cognition among users of self-monitoring systems for physical activity: survey study. JMIR Formative Res. **5**, e23968 (2021)
47. Bandura, A.: Social cognitive theory of self-regulation. Organ. Behav. Hum. Decis. Process. **50**, 248–287 (1991)
48. Anderson, A., Huttenlocher, D., Kleinberg, J., Leskovec, J.: Steering user behavior with badges. In: 22nd International Conference on World Wide Web, pp. 95–106 (Year)
49. Waardenburg, T., Winkel, R., Lamers, M.H.: Normative social influence in persuasive technology: intensity versus effectiveness. In: Bang, M., Ragnemalm, E.L. (eds.) PERSUASIVE 2012. LNCS, vol. 7284, pp. 145–156. Springer, Heidelberg (2012). https://doi.org/10.1007/978-3-642-31037-9_13
50. Stibe, A., Oinas-Kukkonen, H., Lehto, T.: Exploring social influence on customer engagement: a pilot study on the effects of social learning, social comparison, and normative influence. In: 2013 46th Hawaii International Conference on System Sciences, pp. 2735–2744. IEEE (2013)
51. Cialdini, R.B., Trost, M.R.: Social influence: Social norms, conformity and compliance. In: Gilbert, D.T., Fiske, S.T., Lindzey, G. (eds.) The Handbook of Social Psychology, pp. 151–192. McGraw-Hill, New Yor (1998)
52. Lapinski, M.K., Rimal, R.N.: An explication of social norms. Commun. Theory **15**, 127–147 (2005)
53. Chung, A., Rimal, R.N.: Social norms: a review. Review Commun. Res. (2016)
54. Perkins, H.W.: The emergence and evolution of the social norms approach to substance abuse prevention. The Social Norms Approach to Preventing School and College Age Substance Abuse: A Handbook for Educators, Counselors and Clinicians, pp. 3–17 (2003)

55. Wang, J.Z., Zhang, A.X., Karger, D.R.: Designing for engaging with news using moral framing towards bridging ideological divides. Proc. ACM Hum.-Comput. Interact. **6**, 1–23 (2022)
56. Albertson, B.P.: Promoting Japanese University students' participation in English classroom discussions: towards a culturally-informed bottom-up approach. J. Pan-Pacific Assoc. Appl. Linguist. **24**, 45–66 (2020)
57. Adler, M., Rougle, E.: Building Literacy Through Classroom Discussion: Research-Based Strategies for Developing Critical Readers and Thoughtful Writers in Middle School. Education Review (2007)
58. Herrmann, B., Gallo, J.R.: Facilitating discussion of theory and practice in education seminars. Networks: Online J. Teacher Res. **20**, 2 (2018)
59. https://www.facebook.com/brand/resources/facebookapp/reactions/
60. Yang, M., Ren, Y., Adomavicius, G.: Engagement by design: an empirical study of the "re-actions" feature on facebook business pages. ACM Trans. Comput.-Hum. Interact. (TOCHI) **27**, 1–35 (2020)
61. Cramer, H., De Juan, P., Tetreault, J.: Sender-intended functions of emojis in US messaging. In: Proceedings of the 18th International Conference on Human-Computer Interaction with Mobile Devices and Services, pp. 504–509 (Year)
62. Rammstedt, B., John, O.P.: Measuring personality in one minute or less: a 10-item short version of the Big Five Inventory in English and German. J. Res. Pers. **41**, 203–212 (2007)
63. Prot, S., et al.: Long-term relations among prosocial-media use, empathy, and prosocial behavior. Psychol. Sci. **25**, 358–368 (2014)
64. Dovidio, J.F., et al.: Empathy and intergroup relations. In: Mikulincer, M., Shaver, P.R. (eds.) Prosocial Motives, Emotions, and Behavior: The Better Angels of Our Nature. American Psychological Association (2010)
65. Box, G.E.P., Tidwell, P.W.: Transformation of the independent variables. Technometrics **4**, 531–550 (1962)
66. Fogg, B.J., Iizawa, D.: Online persuasion in Facebook and Mixi: a cross-cultural comparison. In: Oinas-Kukkonen, H., Hasle, P., Harjumaa, M., Segerståhl, K., Øhrstrøm, P. (eds.) PERSUASIVE 2008. LNCS, vol. 5033, pp. 35–46. Springer, Heidelberg (2008). https://doi.org/10.1007/978-3-540-68504-3_4
67. Zhu, Q., Skoric, M., Shen, F.: I shield myself from thee: selective avoidance on social media during political protests. Polit. Commun. **34**, 112–131 (2017)
68. Arli, D.: Does social media matter? Investigating the effect of social media features on consumer attitudes. J. Promot. Manag. **23**, 521–539 (2017)
69. Prensky, M.: Digital natives, digital immigrants. On the Horizon 9, (2001)
70. Bode, L., Vraga, E.K.: Correction experiences on social media during COVID-19. Social Media + Society 7 (2021)
71. Lee, M.K., Kiesler, S., Forlizzi, J.: Mining behavioral economics to design persuasive technology for healthy choices. In: CHI 2011: Proceedings of the SIGCHI Conference on Human Factors in Computing Systems, pp. 325–334 (2011)
72. Matthews, J., Win, K.T., Oinas-Kukkonen, H., Freeman, M.: Persuasive technology in mobile applications promoting physical activity: a systematic review. J. Med. Syst. **40**, 1–13 (2016)
73. Walther, J.B.: Computer-mediated communication: Impersonal, interpersonal, and hyperpersonal interaction. Commun. Res. **23**, 3–43 (1996)
74. Vraga, E.K., Bode, L.: I do not believe you: How providing a source corrects health misperceptions across social media platforms. Inf. Commun. Soc. **21**, 1337–1353 (2018)
75. Venkatesh, V.: Determinants of perceived ease of use: Integrating control, intrinsic motivation, and emotion into the technology acceptance model. Inf. Syst. Res. **11**, 342–365 (2000)
76. Henry, J.D., von Hippel, W., Nangle, M.R., Waters, M.: Age and the experience of strong self-conscious emotion. Aging Ment. Health **22**, 497–502 (2018)

77. Galinsky, A.D., Moskowitz, G.B.: Perspective-taking: decreasing stereotype expression, stereotype accessibility, and in-group favoritism. J. Pers. Soc. Psychol. **78**, 708 (2000)
78. Morris, M.W., et al.: Conflict management style: accounting for cross-national differences. J. Int. Bus. Stud. **29**, 729–747 (1998)
79. Friedman, R., Chi, S.-C., Liu, L.A.: An expectancy model of Chinese-American differences in conflict-avoiding. J. Int. Bus. Stud. **37**, 76–91 (2006)
80. Weller, K.: Trying to understand social media users and usage: the forgotten features of social media platforms. Online Inf. Rev. **40**, 256–264 (2016)
81. Dumbrell, D., Steele, R.: Social media technologies for achieving knowledge management amongst older adult communities. Procedia Soc. Behav. Sci. **147**, 229–236 (2014)
82. Dickter, C.L., Newton, V.A.: To confront or not to confront: non-targets' evaluations of and responses to racist comments. J. Appl. Soc. Psychol. **43**, E262–E275 (2013)

A Study of Women's Perceptions and Opinions of a Persuasive Breastfeeding mHealth App

Alaa Ali S. Almohanna[1]([✉]) [iD], Shahla Meedya[1,2] [iD], Elena Vlahu-Gjorgievska[1] [iD],
and Khin Than Win[1] [iD]

[1] University of Wollongong, Wollongong, NSW 2522, Australia
aaa933@uowmail.edu.au, {elenavg,win}@uow.edu.au
[2] Australian Catholic University, Blacktown, NSW 2148, Australia
shahla.meedya@acu.edu.au

Abstract. Women's perceptions of persuasive design principles implemented in a mHealth app to support breastfeeding have not been previously explored. This study aims to explore the persuasive features of a persuasive mHealth app (the Milky Way app) from the perspective of breastfeeding women to recognize design, functionality, and usability issues. The study used an online survey to gather women's perceptions of the persuasive design principles assimilated in the Milky Way mHealth app and explore their overall experience with the app. Quantitative responses were analyzed with descriptive analysis to explore women's perceptions of the implemented PSD features. A qualitative thematic analysis method was used to analyze participants' responses input to the online survey. A total of 168 women participated in the study survey. The results of the One-Sample T-Test showed that the perception scores of the various PSD features are statistically significant and higher than the neutral rating of 3 ($p < .001$). This indicates that participants perceived the features implementations as persuasive. A total of 96 women provided qualitative inputs, with an overall of 288 text inputs. Three themes emerged: Overall user experience, Opportunities for app improvements, and Technical aspects. The Milky Way app was perceived as an informative and credible app that is feasible for breastfeeding promotion and support. The results from this study strongly supported the use of the Milky way app for promoting breastfeeding, with particularly positive feedback received from breastfeeding mothers. Practical design recommendations for improving the app based on the findings are offered.

Keywords: Persuasive system design · mHealth · Breastfeeding · Persuasive system · behaviour

1 Introduction

1.1 Breastfeeding and mHealth

The establishment, practice and maintenance of breastfeeding are associated with improved maternal and child health. Despite the various benefits of breastfeeding and

J. Ham et al. (Eds.): PERSUASIVE 2023, LNCS 13832, pp. 142–157, 2023.
https://doi.org/10.1007/978-3-031-30933-5_10

targeted antenatal and postnatal support programs, rates of breastfeeding continuation and exclusivity remain low and fall short of the World Health Organization 2025 goals [1, 2] The low global prevalence of breastfeeding calls for the examination of new technologies and solutions. Mobile health (mHealth) technologies, such as mobile apps, can be a promising solution in supporting breastfeeding continuation [3]. Additionally, a major role of electronic health technology (e.g., mHealth) is to provide broader healthcare, and the importance of such mHealth-based breastfeeding support has increased significantly during the COVID-19 pandemic.

1.2 Persuasive System Design Model

Persuasive technologies are interactive information technology designed to motivate behavior change mainly through persuasion but, importantly, not through coercion [4]. Researchers, mHealth app designers and health practitioners have been interested in persuasive systems for health as tools for promoting healthy behavior. In persuasive technologies, it is suggested that the persuasive systems design (PSD) should aim to enhance motivation and promote active user participation [5].

The PSD model introduced by Oinas-Kukkonen and Harjumaa [6] offers a systematic method of understanding the persuasion context. The PSD model enlists persuasive design principles that comprise four principles, that is, (1) primary task support, (2) dialogue support, (3) system credibility support and (4) social support. The four PSD design principles provide an insightful understanding of the interaction between users and technologies [7]. Oinas-Kukkonen and Harjumaa's PSD framework encompasses various features to optimize human-computer interaction, influence users' attitudes, and ultimately support users in achieving their personal target behavior. Thus, incorporating the PSD model in the development and design approach may facilitate the implementation, acceptance, and effectiveness of mHealth applications [8]. For instance, Primary task support focuses on persuasive features that support carrying out the primary activities, that is, the tasks that lead to the attainment of the aims of the system, while Dialogue support refers to human-computer dialogue and techniques which aim to motivate users to use the system and achieve the goals. The system credibility support principles enhance users' perception towards the believability of the design and trustworthiness of the system. Lastly, social support principles focus on motivating system users through social influence to enhance their motivation and self-confidence in attaining their targeted behavior [6].

Existing systematic reviews have investigated the persuasive techniques and strategies most often used in mHealth technology. Win et al. [9] conducted a review to identify the persuasive system features most frequently used in computer-mediated physical activity technologies. Their results showed that the persuasive strategies most frequently utilized by the technologies were tailoring, tunnelling, reminders, trustworthiness, and expertise. Other reviews that investigated the most commonly applied persuasive strategies in health-related technologies found that self-monitoring, tailoring and personalization are among the most frequently applied persuasive principles in the examined technologies [10, 11].

Researchers are also using the PSD model to understand the influence of persuasive mHealth technology and to improve this influence and the uptake of mHealth technology

[12]. These technologies motivate user behavior through a variety of methods, such as providing relevant information, encouraging social and physical activities, and offering feedback [13]. However, the persuasion has to be intentional in the design of the technology for the purpose of guiding the user towards an attitude or behavior change for the technology to be truly called "persuasive" [14]. As a result, several persuasive mHealth apps have been developed for health promotion purposes. [9, 15–18].

Despite the increase in implementation and acceptance of persuasive mHealth apps, little is known about end-user perceptions and the opinions of each persuasive design feature [19]. For persuasion to be meaningful, mHealth apps must encourage positive user behavior and transform their ordinary experiences to be aesthetically pleasing [20]. Therefore, there is a need to explore users' perceptions of mHealth apps as they may influence users' engagement with health-promoting apps [21].

1.3   The Milky Way Breastfeeding mHealth App

Research has highlighted the feasibility of the PSD model in designing breastfeeding mHealth apps [22]. Despite the development of numerous apps aimed at assisting breastfeeding mothers [23], a recent study has identified a key challenge in the implementation of these mHealth apps [24]. This challenge lies in designing breastfeeding mHealth apps in a manner that not only attracts the interest of users, but also keeps them engaged to a sufficient degree that promotes behavior change [24]. This underscores the significance of considering user engagement and behavior change when designing breastfeeding mHealth apps and highlights the need for further research in this area. One promising approach for addressing this challenge is the use of the PSD model. Research has indicated that the PSD model is particularly well-suited for the design of breastfeeding mHealth apps, making it a valuable tool for addressing the identified challenge [25].

The Milky Way mHealth app is the first app based on the PSD model to support breastfeeding motivation and to improve mothers' access to support from early pregnancy to the postpartum period, with a focus on benefits and acknowledgement of challenges. The Milky way app involves nineteen PSD features, each represented in the app by different strategy implementation. Table 1 presents the main PSD features presented in the Milky Way. The app is publicly available as a free app in the major app stores (i.e., Apple App Store and Google Play). In a recent pilot-testing, the app was found to be effective in showing acceptability and usability [17].

Table 1. Main PSD features in the Milky Way app and the corresponding implementation

Persuasive design feature	How the feature is presented in the Milky Way app
Reduction	The app's layout was simplified into four sections: Home, Preparation, Milky Supply and FAQ
Tunnelling	The app lists the benefits of breastfeeding, and there is much information under the FAQ section used to provide opportunities to persuade women towards breastfeeding
Tailoring	The app was tailored for women with the intention of breastfeeding. The app has a section explicitly tailored to provide information to women who may have a perceived low milk supply
Simulation	Pictures showing mothers nursing happily advocate that breastfeeding is emotionally beneficial and can improve the mother-infant relationship
Suggestions	Suggestions were offered if women doubted their ability to breastfeed due to low milk supply
Similarity	The app has a variety of pictures of breastfeeding women from different cultural backgrounds to remind women that many other women breastfeed in the world. Sensitive topics, such as sore nipples, were proposed
Liking	The app has many family-friendly photos
Social role	The app has a link in the forum section that provides users with opportunities to connect with community members and support network
Trustworthiness	The app has referenced and linked national and international health and research authorities, e.g., World Health Organisation; National Health and Medical Research Council; Australian Breastfeeding Association
Expertise	The app offered a full disclaimer about the app information and the developers of the Milky Way app
Surface credibility	The logo of the University was located on the first page
Real-world feel	The app provides full information about the institution behind its content and information
Authority	The app refers to an authority such as the NSW child and family health centre and maternal and child health service
Third-party endorsements	The app is supported by the Local Health District
Verifiability	Answers in FAQ sections are supported by offering links to serval credible websites
Social learning	Links to the Australian Breastfeeding Association Facebook page can provide an opportunity to find out about other breastfeeding women

(continued)

Table 1. (*continued*)

Persuasive design feature	How the feature is presented in the Milky Way app
Social comparison	Users can compare and relate their experience with breastfeeding with other with other women's stories Users can share information related to their breastfeeding via social networking link
Normative influence	Connecting with the Australian Breastfeeding Association, Facebook may leverage normative influence or peer pressure
Cooperation	Provides a means to interact with others through online interaction so users feel that they are part of a community with a common interest

1.4 Aim

A number of researchers have focused on the implementation of the PSD features and functionalities in various mHealth apps, but there remains a need for a more detailed view of users' perceptions of the employed persuasive principles and how they interact with PSD features to help guide design processes. These facts prompted this study to investigate perceptions towards persuasive strategies. Therefore, this study aims to explore the persuasive features of an mHealth app (the Milky Way app) from the perspective of breastfeeding women.

2 Methods

Quantitative and qualitative data were obtained from the Milky Way app users through an online survey. Ethical approval was obtained for this study from the University of Wollongong, the Human Research Ethics Committee (Approval No. 2021/009). All participants were informed of the study, agreed to participate, and gave written consent.

This study used convenience and snowballing sampling methods. The study recruited the target participants anonymously using social media such as Facebook, Instagram, and WhatsApp. To participate in the study, the participants should be: (1) women who were pregnant or mothers who were breastfeeding or had experiences of breastfeeding, (2) being 18 years or older, (3) capable of reading and writing English, and (4) had an Apple/Android-based smartphone. All participants were required to download and explore the Milky Way app on their phones before completing the survey.

Descriptive statistics were computed for quantitative data derived from the survey. Nineteen survey items were asked, including 5-point Likert scale questions, with a score of one indicating total disagreement and five indicating total agreement with the proposed statements.

The survey was based on the assimilated PSD features in the Milky Way app. The survey items were developed in several stages following best practices of the instrument development [26]. First, an extensive literature review was conducted to identify relevant studies, and then a set of items were proposed and ensured each persuasive design principle employed in the Milky Way app was appropriately reflected in the item. Then, the items were further developed and validated by a modified Delphi technique incorporating the assessment of the Content Validity Index (CVI). The study result indicated that the research instrument demonstrated high content validity. The modified Delphi study is described in detail in a published study [27].

A qualitative thematic analysis method was used to analyze participants' responses input to the online survey supported by the Qualitative Research Data Analysis Software QSR NVivo 12 for the coding process. Initial codes were created by reading text inputs several times to produce a list of themes summarizing the data based on the issues discussed. Themes were defined to explore women's opinions and experiences.

3   Results

3.1   Participants Characteristics

A total of 168 women participated in this study. The demographics analyses (see Fig. 1) indicated that the study participants were predominantly aged between 30 and 39 (54.2%) and married (88.7%). The study participants varied in terms of educational backgrounds, although commonly educated to a tertiary degree (71.4%), while 39.3% had full-time employment.

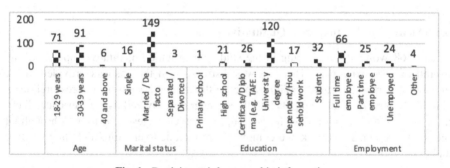

Fig. 1. Participants' demographic information

3.2   Analysis of the Quantitative Survey Results

User Perceptions of the Milky Way PSD Features. The average response score for each feature for analysis was calculated, and then a One-Sample t-test was used to measure the perception of each feature in comparison to the neutral score 3. The results indicated that the mean score (4.05 ± 65) was higher than the neutral score of 3, and thus, all the Milky Way app features were perceived in the app. The perceptions scores were statistically significantly higher than the neutral score, $t(167) = -21.7$, $p < .001$, and the p-value shows strong significance within the 95% Confidence Interval.

Presence of PSD Design Principles in the Milky Way app. Figure 2 shows the average scores of the perceived perception of each of the app's PSD features. Sixteen features were perceived to be the most perceived features, with an average of 4.2 each, while Reduction, Liking and Authority were perceived to be the least perceived features.

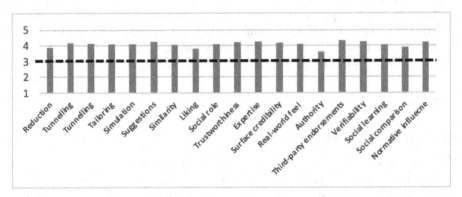

Fig. 2. The average scores of the perceptions of the persuasive features in the Milky Way app on a scale of 1 to 5 (The dotted vertical line represents the neutral rating of 3).

3.3 Analysis of Participants' Qualitative Data

Out of 168 women participating in the study, 96 provided qualitative inputs with an overall of 288 text inputs. The data was distilled from the answers provided in the qualitative part of the survey. With respect to the thematic analysis, the research team classified users' qualitative inputs into three categories: Overall user experience, Technical aspects, and Opportunities for app improvements suggested by users. Throughout the study, women's feedback and comments are included verbatim, including spelling and grammatical errors.

Theme 1. Overall user experience. Usability is an important aspect of the user experience of the Milky Way app. Findings from thematic analysis of qualitative comments showed that women perceived the app as **easy to use** and **functional**. Women reported that they like the app *"Visual information"* and *"Like the functionality of this APP"* as it is *"well organized and easy to use"*.

Women's perceptions of the Milky Way app **interface aesthetics** were positive. The app's visual appearance has been perceived as *"appealing"*. Women rated the app as **visually appealing** because it provided them with quick access to information and did not overwhelm them with the choice *"Easy to read information and not to much info so you don't feel overwhelmed"*. Visual design aims to improve the app's aesthetic appeal and usability. App visual attractiveness can be seen as an essential factor in the overall user experience of the app as users tend to perceive attractive apps as more usable, as evident in the following comment *"When I breastfed in the past, I was often stressed and* *sleep deprived in these early weeks and a clear and visually effective app is important. I need to be able to find the info I need quickly, which this is app has"*. Moreover, women appreciated the **simplicity** and **rationality** of the Milky Way app interface as women commented, *"The interface of The Milky Way is perfect and coincident with its logic."*.

Moving from one section to another in the app is an important task for app users as apps with easy navigation make it easy to accomplish any desired task. Most women reported that the Milky Way app is *"simple to navigate"* and *"easy to navigate"*. Women were **guided through the app process** by simplifying the homepage of the app, reducing the required user's tasks and providing efficient access to information*" I also like that there are lots of specific categories like Positions, Skin to Skin, so I can find what I need immediately."* and advice about professional healthcare services *"I like the page of websites and support services. It's clear and easy to see which link to click for support"*.

Several women pointed out that the Milky Way was **useful** as it was easier to use an app than websites, especially when using a smartphone to access the internet:*"That's it's right on hand to click through rather than flicking through a pamphlet or googling or waiting for an appointment with a healthcare provider."* The concept of convenience was highlighted as mothers need frequent access to breastfeeding information. The Milky Way app was found especially **convenient** for first-time mothers:*"I like how the Milky Way is convenient for the inexperienced baby mama"*. Users, who commend the app, highlighted its utility, demonstrating the usefulness of the Milky Way app. Based on the results, users strongly perceived the Milky Way app as **informative** as one woman said, *"I think the amount of information on each topic is concise and provides a good overview"*.

Being **informative** was the most commonly reported app feature that women perceived and appreciated. Women reported the usefulness of the app as an **educational** as it is *"helpful in learning to breastfeed"*. **Access to social/community support** and sharing mother breastfeeding stories normalizes the challenges of breastfeeding and encourages self-motivation. Facebook was embedded as the primary sharing platform, given its popularity and accessibility. Participants praised this feature; one woman reported she liked that the Milky Way app *"Connect more Mum together to share ideas"* and other women echoed that they liked the Milky Way app as: *"experienced breastfeeding mothers can share their experience"* and because: *"It shows experiences of others"*. To some extent, the Milky Way app adapts its elements and layout to the women's queries. The results indicated that the app provides a **tailored experience** to its users. *"I also like the 'Milk Supply' quiz like function - this provides good info."* Overall, women appreciated the fact that their most commonly faced milk supply issues could be explained and resolved through the tailored answers shown.

The **Milk supply section** was favoured by many women "There are a lot of articles on how to properly breastfeed and produce more milk" and other women agreed "I also like the 'Milk Supply' quiz like function - this provides good info". This section was seen by one woman as "The troubleshooting for suspected low supply" which points out that the Milk Supply section has the ability to **resolve breastfeeding issues** that may occur. Perceived low milk supply is regarded major barrier to breastfeeding and usually, women reach out for support to overcome this barrier. Thus, it was suggested to even add more information, for instance, about: "exclusive pumping and methods to increase your supply". The analysis indicated that women perceive the Milky Way app as **credible**. The credibility of the app and the information delivered by it was prominent in a number of women's inputs. **Trustworthiness** of the app was an aspect that women highly appreciated because it contains links to other **evidence-based** publications that support the evidence-based practice, as one woman described "The evidence based research links". Women indicated the value of having access to trustworthy and relevant sources they could trust and access when needed to"Uses reputable links, so information is at least reliable.". Women responded favourably to the fact that the information provided in the Milky Way app is backed up by generally accepted guidelines and scientific evidence "I like that the information is backed by studies and links to further reading of studies". Besides, women were **attracted to the app due to its logo**"The logo it very appealing". This indicates the value of the Milky Way app logo, which was purposefully designed to visually represents the identity of the app developers (the University of Wollongong).

Theme 2. Technical aspects. Women's feedback provided an overview of the issues faced when exploring the Milky Way app. **Technical design difficulties** faced by the Milky Way app users included the **app font colour on some of the pages**. One woman mentioned difficulties in reading text due to blurred background: *"When I tap on some pages of the app - there is white text over the blurred background photo which is also white in the upper right corner. This means that I cannot read most of the text. "*. Although this issue was raised by some women in their feedback, others pointed out that the font colour in some sections of the app **does not affect the positive impact** of the app: *"I wasn't a fan of the transparent background but that is only aesthetics and doesn't impact the effectiveness of the app. "* Furthermore, one women found the app to be a bit too basic*"Very simplistic"* and suggested that the simplicity of the app may not be of primary importance.

Women mentioned **accessibility features** as a potential approachability barrier to the app. Accessibility is a critical factor that enables users who have disabilities to access support and information. The results showed some possible accessibility issues in regard to users with visual disabilities:*" The app is not accessible to people with vision impairment. It does not work with Voice Over on iPhones. So it would not be able to help mothers who are blind and quite often given out of date information. "*.

Theme 3. Opportunities for app improvements. Women who participated in the study provided various ideas for app improvements. Modifications related only to the **aesthetic appeal** of the app were proposed, including changing the font colour and improving the use of images to improve the visibility of the app text: *"The font colour makes it difficult to read, I advise to change the font colour or the background colour in the app"*. Further **optimization suggestions** regarding the app design were to include more videos. The addition of more visual information was notable: *"As I mentioned above its need more visual and audio to improve the information delivery for those who prefer to watch and listen."*. **Supporting other languages** was recommended and seen as *"greater benefit"* as it will become easier for mothers based on their language to access the appropriate content for them; thus, the Milky Way app would reach a much wider audience. The **personalization** feature, which involves users in-app input or involvement, was highly suggested. For example, women suggested adding breastfeed tracker option would be beneficial *"Add a timer and diary option to add when you breast fed, for how long the feed was and from which side you fed"*. This suggestion would increase the interactivity of the app as women point out that *"Interactivity in the app would also be important - a place for women to track nursing sessions and nappy output perhaps.*

Various suggestions were proposed in regard to **adding specific breastfeeding-related information** into the app, such as allergies *"address issues such as allergies for example cows milk protein and soy"*, breast cancer *"there should also be ways in preventing cancer in the breast"* and the relation between breastfeeding infants and night sleep *"I couldn't see any information on breastfeeding and sleep"*, *"put some more specific information about the benefits of breastfeeding for example how do we know that formula feeding increases risk of obesity compared to breastfeeding, what were the actual outcomes of those studies"*.

Women believe that the addition of **more information would increase mothers' motivation** to continue breastfeeding: "I think that would motivate mothers to continue to try to breastfeed and they would be more informed about what their babies are going to be missing out on in they formula feed".

4 Discussion

Key factors that set the Milky Way breastfeeding app apart from many others are the use of PSD model principles, most obviously through the included features and functionalities. This paper set out to explore the Milky Way app that aims to promote and support breastfeeding. The study presents the results from an online survey exploring participants' perceptions of the assimilated persuasive features in the Milky Way app. Previous literature suggests it is fundamental to consider how persuasive principles are presented as design features, as this will impact the "potential persuasive effectiveness" of an app in influencing users' behavior and attitude [28]. The study identified several PSD features used in the Milky Way app that were perceived well. The online survey findings reported that all app features were perceived significantly above the median by the study participants. The study also provided a quantitative endorsement of the overall persuasive features. Tunneling, credibility, expertise and social support were perceived as rather valuable among participants. Moreover, the vast majority of the ninety-six participants who contributed qualitative inputs reported a positive experience and appreciation of the provided app features, yet only minor design-related issues were pointed out, such as (font colour, images quality and accessibility), and there were no negative comments regarding the core functionality of the app. The thematic analysis indicated that the first theme (Overall user experience) accounted for almost 60% of the input data, and only 24% and 14% accounted for Opportunities for app improvements and Technical aspects, respectively.

Following the One-Sample t-test, it can be concluded that all the implemented PSD features in the Milky Way app were almost equally perceived well. The fact that the PSD features are seen by and for all included participants in this study indicates that persuasion is present and could aid the desired change in attitude or behavior. This is further supported by participants' text inputs perceiving the app as informative, simple to use, appealing, and useful in supporting breastfeeding. Overall, the qualitative themes were related to app design and support needs. The themes highlight the importance of presenting the authenticity of the app. Participants noted the value of having well-known resources they could trust and that were easy to access when needed. In line with previous research, the credibility of the persuasive system is considered a key factor that affects users' continuance intentions to use the system [29]. One of the main features that were also noted by the participants included providing relevant information that is easy to access. The majority of the participants acknowledged the amount and quality of the information in the Milky Way app; nonetheless, participants expressed a strong desire for the app to have practical material that can support them in different situational contexts in order to motivate breastfeeding. This association between acquiring information and breastfeeding motivation is supported by a number of existing studies in the broader literature [30, 31]. Additionally, information that was to the point and concise was seen as highly appreciated; otherwise, participants implied they could feel overwhelmed and would be easily disengaged.

4.1 Emergent Themes and Theories

The qualitative data were further examined. The examination of the results of the thematic analysis showed that many of the participants' input data could be mapped to existing health behavior changes and the design of technology theories.

For instance, opportunities for app improvements are related to the Value Sensitive Design (VSD). This approach advocates for integrating human values into technologies throughout the design process [32]. The study participants indicated that the app is missing individual-specific meaningful breastfeeding information. Examples requested are integrating a feeding timer/tracker in the app, also requested targeted breastfeeding information, practical skills training and mother-and-baby feeding advantages. Assessing how technologies align with the norms and values of stakeholders is crucial to VSD. The VSD method would recognize the experiences of the stakeholders and their values. Thus, this study suggests that persuasive app design should respond to and align with the provided information and values of both direct and indirect stakeholders. This finding was consistent with a previous study by Davis [32], which emphasized the significance of user involvement in the design process and the application of VSD to persuasive technologies aimed at influencing behavior and attitudes.

Behavior could be explained as a combination of motivation, ability, and opportunity. The resultant themes are related to the constructs of the information-motivation-behavioural skills (IMB) model [33]. The IMB model can reflect the behavior change mechanisms and comprise three dimensions; accurate information to be translated to behavior performance, personal and social motivation to act on such information; and behavioral skills to effectively implement the health behavior. The participants pointed out that the app consisted of information delivered by the visual presentation and education (tips and advice), and motivation was provided by self-adjustments, goal attainment, feedback, and connection to social community support. Thus, the app aligns well with the IMB model.

Furthermore, reflecting on the participant's suggestions for improvements, a feeding tracker app component was commonly suggested. Although such an addition might provide convenience for mothers, their breastfeeding decisions most likely would not be influenced by this feature alone. As the IMB model specified, health-related information, motivation, and behavioural skills are the primary determinants of the performance of health behaviours. A recent investigation of feeding trackers indicated that mothers primarily need credible information to guide their breastfeeding decisions along with the tracker [34]. Therefore, utilizing the principles of VSD and incorporating the IMB model constructs that have a significant impact on behavioral changes, the addition of a breastfeeding tracker element to the Milky Way app, given it was perceived as informative and credible by the majority of participants, would be a valuable enhancement.

4.2 Mapping Themes to PSD Design Principles

The themes generated from the thematic analysis regarding users' perceptions and opinions of the Milky Way app were mapped to their corresponding persuasive strategies of the PSD framework.

Primary task support involves features that aid and motivate users, which in this study were to tailor the presented information, simulate pictures showing the benefits, guide users into the behavior change process, and enable behavior rehearsal. The findings of the study indicate that functionalities that employ primary task support features were highly perceived. However, though the Milky Way app provides app-tailored content to its users, the addition of a personalization feature was commonly requested. Oinas-Kukkonen [35] asserts the importance of understanding diverse user segments for designing successful persuasive systems and states that "specific target audiences may request very different kinds of software features". It has been pointed out that tailoring and personalizing mHealth apps enhance their effectiveness and thus increase their capability for persuasion [36]. Thus, this study recommends the addition of functionalities personalized to user characteristics along with offering adaptive, contextual suggestions as they would enhance users' perception of the persuasive features provided in the app.

Dialogue support principles such as suggestion, similarity, liking, and social role were reflected in the Milky Way app and perceived well. However, liking feature slightly differed from the overall perceptions. Oinas-Kukkonen and Harjumaa [6] offers describe Liking feature as it should be "a system that is visually attractive for its users is likely to be more persuasive.". Based on the findings, participants were doubtful about the visual attractiveness content as some appreciated the app's pleasant interface design while some criticized the simplicity of information display. Modifications suggestions related to aesthetics and functionality included unclear font color and some blurred images. Although participants indicated that, in their opinion, the app's effectiveness is not adversely affected by minor visual faults, aesthetics remains one of the main concepts that may affect user experience and technology behaviour [29]. Prior research has stated that visual aesthetics influence users' perception of dialogue support in persuasive systems [37, 38]. Thus, this study advises that app designers should modify the layout, graphics, and visual appeal experiences into aesthetically pleasing experiences. Moreover, it is useful to provide a help function in the app to accommodate different phones and provide enhanced accessibility settings.

Participants showed their appreciation of trustworthiness, expertise, and verifiability features which are an implementation example of **Credibility support principles**. The results demonstrated that participants' knowledge of the app's information sources (e.g., official government-recognized websites) and expertise (e.g., healthcare professionals) enhanced their credibility judgment of the app. This highlight one of the most noticeable insights from this study's results that information credibility positively mediates the relationship between digital-health technologies users and trust, as authenticity was frequently noted by the participants. Evidence already affirms that persuasive apps are particularly effective in persuading users to complete their target behavior when they implement trustworthiness, expertise, and authority strategies [39]. App designers must strive to establish trustworthiness and trust with the full user experience in mind so that trust can be imbued appropriately in the app [40]. It has been shown that users' visual judgments influence their perceptions of credibility [29]. Regardless of the credibility support capacity, this PSD principle is a noted gap in mobile apps [41]. Accordingly, the app should exhibit symbols of authority to clearly refer to people or organizations with authority, such as visible, e.g., official government websites and global health authorities and provide genuine information or details of the organization and/or people involved in providing the app's content. Therefore, this study recommends that persuasive health app designers should implement strategies in the system credibility category to motivate behavior change and increase engagement.

The features of the **Social support** principle leverage the power of social influence in motivating the users to perform a target behavior. Implementations include providing links to a community forum for peer support and opportunities for women to share experiences who have similar goals. Although the Milky Way app did not offer exclusive social/community support, participants still appreciated the provided platform for sharing their journey with others because sharing enables individuals to learn about others' abilities and performance and thus feel more motivated. Lehto et al. [42] found that social support was to be important in determining users' continuance intention to use the persuasive system. Therefore, this study suggests the inclusion of a community-sharing platform for app users, so they become immersed in their interactions with other individuals or groups via the app.

5 Conclusion

This paper explores women's perceptions of the employed persuasive design features in the Milky Way mHealth breastfeeding app. Feedback from women indicated that the app was designed well and positively embraced. The evidence-based information, educational materials, and credibility were appreciated. To optimize the user experience of the app, several design recommendations were proposed. The finding will inform the refinement of the next version of the app as a potential mediation for sustained behavior change. Insights derived will be helpful to other researchers and developers to inform future persuasive technology reaching out to breastfeeding women through persuasive information systems.

References

1. Matriano, M.G., Ivers, R., Meedya, S.: Factors that influence women's decision on infant feeding: an integrative review. Women and Birth. **35**, 430–439 (2022). https://doi.org/10.1016/j.wombi.2021.10.005
2. WHO/UNICEF: Global nutrition targets 2025: breastfeeding policy brief (WHO/NMH/NHD/14.7). World Health Organization (2014)
3. Almohanna, A.A., Win, K.T., Meedya, S.: Effectiveness of internet-based electronic technology interventions on breastfeeding outcomes: systematic review. J. Med. Internet Res. **22**, e17361 (2020). https://doi.org/10.2196/17361
4. Oinas-Kukkonen, H., Harjumaa, M.: Towards deeper understanding of persuasion in software and information systems. Proc. 1st Int. Conf. Adv. Comput. Interact. ACHI 2008. 200–205 (2008). https://doi.org/10.1109/ACHI.2008.31
5. Oyibo, K., Vassileva, J.: Investigation of persuasive system design predictors of competitive behavior in fitness application: a mixed-method approach. Digit. Heal. **5** (2019). https://doi.org/10.1177/2055207619878601
6. Oinas-Kukkonen, H., Harjumaa, M.: Persuasive systems design: Key issues, process model, and system features. Commun. Assoc. Inf. Syst. **24**, 485–500 (2009). https://doi.org/10.17705/1cais.02428
7. Lehto, T., Oinas-Kukkonen, H., Pätiälä, T., Saarelma, O.: Consumers' perceptions of a virtual health check: An empirical investigation. In: ECIS 2012 - Proceedings of the 20th European Conference on Information Systems (2012)
8. Langrial, S., Lehto, T., Oinas-Kukkonen, H., Harjumaa, M., Karppinen, P.: Native mobile applications for personal wellbeing: a persuasive systems design evaluation. In: Proceedings - Pacific Asia Conference on Information Systems. PACIS 2012. (2012)
9. Win, K.T., Roberts, M.R.H., Oinas-Kukkonen, H.: Persuasive system features in computer-mediated lifestyle modification interventions for physical activity. Informatics Heal. Soc. Care. **44**, 376–404 (2019). https://doi.org/10.1080/17538157.2018.1511565
10. Alhasani, M., Mulchandani, D., Oyebode, O., Orji, R.: A systematic review of persuasive strategies in stress management apps. In: CEUR Workshop Proceedings (2020)
11. Asbjørnsen, R.A., et al.: Persuasive system design principles and behavior change techniques to stimulate motivation and adherence in electronic health interventions to support weight loss maintenance: scoping review. J. Med. Internet Res. **21**, e14265 (2019). https://doi.org/10.2196/14265
12. van Gemert-Pijnen, L.J. E.W.C.., Kelders, S.M., Beerlage-de Jong, N., Oinas-Kukkonen, H.: Persuasive health technology. In: eHealth Research, Theory and Development, pp. 228–246. Routledge (2018)
13. Mukhtar, H., Ali, A., Belaid, D., Lee, S.: Persuasive healthcare self-management in intelligent environments. Proceedings - 8th International Conference on Intelligent Environments. IE 2012, pp. 190–197 (2012). https://doi.org/10.1109/IE.2012.51
14. Hamari, J., Koivisto, J., Pakkanen, T.: Do persuasive technologies persuade? - A review of empirical studies. In: Spagnolli, A., Chittaro, L., Gamberini, L. (eds.) PERSUASIVE 2014. LNCS, vol. 8462, pp. 118–136. Springer, Cham (2014). https://doi.org/10.1007/978-3-319-07127-5_11
15. Merz, M., Ackermann, L.: Design principles of persuasive systems - Review and discussion of the persuasive systems design model. In: 27th Annual Americas Conference on Information Systems. AMCIS 2021. 2021 (2021)
16. Win, K.T., Ramaprasad, A., Syn, T.: Ontological Review of Persuasion Support Systems (PSS) for health behavior change through physical activity. J. Med. Syst. **43**(3), 1–12 (2019). https://doi.org/10.1007/s10916-019-1159-y

17. Meedya, S., et al.: Developing and testing a mobile application for breastfeeding support: the Milky Way application. Women and Birth. **34**, e196–e203 (2021). https://doi.org/10.1016/j.wombi.2020.02.006

18. Orji, R., Moffatt, K.: Persuasive technology for health and wellness: State-of-the-art and emerging trends. Health Informatics J. **24**, 66–91 (2018). https://doi.org/10.1177/146045821 6650979

19. Liu, N., Yin, J., Tan, S.S.L., Ngiam, K.Y., Teo, H.H.: Mobile health applications for older adults: a systematic review of interface and persuasive feature design. J. Am. Med. Informatics Assoc. **28**, 2483–2501 (2021). https://doi.org/10.1093/jamia/ocab151

20. Oyibo, K., Vassileva, J.: HOMEX: persuasive technology acceptance model and the moderating effect of culture. Front. Comput. Sci. **2**, 1–17 (2020). https://doi.org/10.3389/fcomp.2020.00010

21. Bergevi, J., Andermo, S., Woldamanuel, Y., Johansson, U.B., Hagströmer, M., Rossen, J.: User perceptions of eHealth and mHealth services promoting physical activity and healthy diets: systematic review. JMIR Hum. Factors. **9** (2022). https://doi.org/10.2196/34278

22. Kuonanoja, L., Meedya, S., Win, K.T., Oinas-Kukkonen, H.: Ethical evaluation of a value sensitive persuasive system: Case milky way. In: Proceedings of the 22nd Pacific Asia Conference on Information System - Opportunities and Challenges for the Digitized Society: Are We Ready?, PACIS 2018, pp. 1–13 (2018)

23. Tang, K., Gerling, K., Geurts, L., Spiel, K.: Understanding the Role of Technology to Support Breastfeeding. In: Proceedings of the 2021 CHI Conference on Human Factors in Computing Systems, pp. 1–13. ACM, New York, NY, USA (2021)

24. Laws, R.A., et al.: Perinatal support for breastfeeding using mHealth: a mixed methods feasibility study of the My Baby Now app. Matern. Child Nutr. (2023). https://doi.org/10.1111/mcn.13482

25. Meedya, S., Sheikh, M.K., Win, K.T., Halcomb, E.: Evaluation of breastfeeding mobile health applications based on the persuasive system design model. In: Oinas-Kukkonen, H., Win, K.T., Karapanos, E., Karppinen, P., Kyza, E. (eds.) PERSUASIVE 2019. LNCS, vol. 11433, pp. 189–201. Springer, Cham (2019). https://doi.org/10.1007/978-3-030-17287-9_16

26. Boateng, G.O., Neilands, T.B., Frongillo, E.A., Melgar-Quiñonez, H.R., Young, S.L.: best practices for developing and validating scales for health, social, and behavioral research: a primer (2018). https://doi.org/10.3389/fpubh.2018.00149

27. Almohanna, A.A.S., Win, K., Meedya, S., Vlahu-Gjorgievska, E.: Design and content validation of an instrument measuring user perception of the persuasive design principles in a breastfeeding mHealth app: a modified Delphi study. Int. J. Med. Inform. **164**, 104789 (2022). https://doi.org/10.1016/j.ijmedinf.2022.104789

28. Thomson, C., Nash, J., Maeder, A.: Persuasive design for behaviour change apps: Issues for designers. ACM Int. Conf. Proceeding Ser. 26–28-Sept (2016). https://doi.org/10.1145/298 7491.2987535

29. Koranteng, F.N., Ham, J., Wiafe, I., Matzat, U.: The role of usability, aesthetics, usefulness and primary task support in predicting the perceived credibility of academic social networking sites. Behav. Inf. Technol. (2021). https://doi.org/10.1080/0144929X.2021.2009570

30. Kornides, M., Kitsantas, P.: Evaluation of breastfeeding promotion, support, and knowledge of benefits on breastfeeding outcomes. J. Child Heal. Care. **17**, 264–273 (2013). https://doi.org/10.1177/1367493512461460

31. Moon, H., Woo, K.: An integrative review on mothers' experiences of online breastfeeding peer support: Motivations, attributes and effects. Matern. Child Nutr. **17**, 1–21 (2021). https://doi.org/10.1111/mcn.13200

32. Davis, J.: Design methods for ethical persuasive computing. ACM Int. Conf. Proceeding Ser. 350 (2009). https://doi.org/10.1145/1541948.1541957

33. Fisher, J.D., Fisher, W.A., Amico, K.R., Harman, J.J.: An information-motivation-behavioral skills model of adherence to antiretroviral therapy. Heal. Psychol. **25**, 462–473 (2006). https://doi.org/10.1037/0278-6133.25.4.462

34. Dienelt, K., Moores, C.J., Miller, J., Mehta, K.: An investigation into the use of infant feeding tracker apps by breastfeeding mothers. Health Inform. J. **26**, 1672–1683 (2020). https://doi.org/10.1177/1460458219888402

35. Oinas-Kukkonen, H.: Behavior change support systems: a research model and agenda. In: Ploug, T., Hasle, P., Oinas-Kukkonen, H. (eds.) PERSUASIVE 2010. LNCS, vol. 6137, pp. 4–14. Springer, Heidelberg (2010). https://doi.org/10.1007/978-3-642-13226-1_3

36. McGowan, A., Sittig, S., Bourrie, D., Benton, R., Iyengar, S.: The Intersection of persuasive system design and personalization in mobile health: statistical evaluation. JMIR mHealth uHealth. **10**, e40576 (2022). https://doi.org/10.2196/40576

37. Lehto, T., Oinas-Kukkonen, H., Drozd, F.: Factors affecting perceived persuasiveness of a behavior change support system. Int. Conf. Inf. Syst. ICIS **2012**(3), 1926–1939 (2012)

38. Halttu, K., Oinas-Kukkonen, H.: Susceptibility to social influence strategies and persuasive system design: exploring the relationship. Behav. Inf. Technol. **41**, 2705–2726 (2022). https://doi.org/10.1080/0144929X.2021.1945685

39. Alhasani, M., Mulchandani, D., Oyebode, O., Baghaei, N., Orji, R.: A systematic and comparative review of behavior change strategies in stress management apps: opportunities for improvement. Front. Public Heal. **10**, 1–19 (2022). https://doi.org/10.3389/fpubh.2022.777567

40. Pintar, A., Erjavec, J.: A framework for designing behavioural change with the use of persuasive technology. Int. J. Manag. Knowl. Learn. **10** (2021). https://doi.org/10.53615/2232-5697.10.75-84

41. Coorey, G., Peiris, D., Usherwood, T., Neubeck, L., Mulley, J., Redfern, J.: Persuasive design features within a consumer-focused eHealth intervention integrated with the electronic health record: a mixed methods study of effectiveness and acceptability. PLoS ONE. **14** (2019). https://doi.org/10.1371/journal.pone.0218447

42. Lehto, T., Oinas-Kukkonen, H.: Explaining and predicting perceived effectiveness and use continuance intention of a behaviour change support system for weight loss. Behav. Inf. Technol. **34**, 176–189 (2015). https://doi.org/10.1080/0144929X.2013.866162

From Persuasive Applications to Persuasive Systems in Non-communicable Disease Care - A Systematic Literature Analysis

Dario Staehelin$^{(\boxtimes)}$ ⓘ, Karolin Franke ⓘ, Luca Huber ⓘ, and Gerhard Schwabe ⓘ

University of Zurich, Binzmühlestrasse 14, 8050 Zurich, Switzerland
staehelin@ifi.uzh.ch

Abstract. Non-communicable diseases (NCDs) are the leading cause of global deaths and an increasing economic burden. Adherence to treatment among NCD patients is generally low due to the demanding treatment plans (i.e., lifestyle changes). Persuasive systems are a promising approach to complement traditional NCD care to support patients in behavior change and increase long-term adherence. However, we ask ourselves: To what extent does current persuasive systems research address the need for continuous, comprehensive, and adaptive NCD care? And where are the blind spots that need to be addressed by developers and researchers of more comprehensive persuasive systems? To answer these questions, we analyzed 57 articles on persuasive systems for NCD care in a systematic literature review. Our results show clear gaps in research and design of persuasive systems. We conceptualize comprehensive persuasive systems in the Fogg-PDSA matrix combining social (e.g., medical professionals) and technical aspects (i.e., persuasive applications) of persuasion.

Keywords: Fogg behavior change model · persuasive systems · continuous care · non-communicable diseases · systematic review

1 Introduction

Non-communicable diseases (NCDs) such as diabetes and hypertension are the leading cause of global deaths [1]. NCDs require complex treatment (i.e., lifestyle changes) in close collaboration with medical professionals, frequently over the lifetime of a patient. However, NCD patients often do not adhere to treatment [2]. Do current persuasive applications contribute to better adhering to NCD treatment? At first sight, this is the case: There are tens of thousands of mobile health applications motivating and enabling NCD patients to change their behavior, and there is ample scientific literature on persuasive systems design [3]. However, at second sight, there are questions: NCDs require continuous, comprehensive, and adaptive care [4]. Do current persuasive applications provide that? Do they cover the whole medical cycle instantiated in the Plan-Do-Study-Act (PDSA) method? Prior work [3, 5, 6] questions that as they uncover challenges for persuasive systems in healthcare without conceptualizing the root cause for these challenges in detail. Consequently, we asked the following research question:

© The Author(s), under exclusive license to Springer Nature Switzerland AG 2023
J. Ham et al. (Eds.): PERSUASIVE 2023, LNCS 13832, pp. 158–172, 2023.
https://doi.org/10.1007/978-3-031-30933-5_11

To what extent does current persuasive systems research address the need for continuous, comprehensive, and adaptive NCD care (RQ1)? And where are the blind spots that need to be addressed by developers and researchers of more comprehensive persuasive systems (RQ2)?

We address this research question with a systematic literature review. First, we conceptualize our understanding of comprehensive, persuasive systems for NCD care in the Fogg-PDSA matrix. Second, we study the existing literature through this lens to elicit the extent to which existing knowledge addresses the needs for NCD care. For this, we analyze the coverage of the Fogg-PDSA matrix across all reviewed articles and the coverage of the PDSA cycle in each paper. The latter allows us to identify research potentially adopting a comprehensive approach for persuasive systems. Lastly, we analyzed a subset of 13 articles for their comprehensive persuasive system approach to gain in-depth insights into the current state of research. This study aims to open the door for future research on designing persuasive digital health systems moving beyond the current task-centricity. Such systems could assist in guiding users through the various opportunities for increasing adherence and improving their health outcomes.

2 Related Work

2.1 NCD Care

Non-communicable diseases (NCDs) are responsible for 41 million, which is equivalent to 74% of deaths globally every year [1] and responsible for most healthcare costs in the European Union [7]. Most NCDs, such as diabetes or hypertension, require continuous treatment due to their chronic nature. NCD treatment often includes a combination of medication and lifestyle changes to alleviate symptoms of chronic conditions [4]. Such treatment plans often target comprehensive changes in physical activity and nutritional behavior, as the current lifestyle is often the root cause of NCDs [8]. Lifestyle changes are demanding as they require patients to break habitual behaviors formed over decades of sedentariness and malnutrition to achieve sustainable health outcomes [9]. Medical professionals (e.g., doctors or dietitians) and patients engage in a continuous and close collaboration to adapt the treatment plan to the patient's needs and context. Despite those efforts, adherence to the treatment of NCDs is persistently low because due to the required continuity, comprehensiveness, and adaptivity. While adherence to simple treatments involving medication intake is generally high (91%), only 19% of the patients follow prescribed lifestyle interventions (i.e., exercise plans) [2].

Medical research has recently adopted quality improvement methods to break down long-term care for medical conditions such as NCDs into iterative cycles. Such closed-loop control systems are a promising approach to ensure comprehensive care [10]. The Plan-Do-Study-Act (PDSA) method is a widely accepted quality improvement method in healthcare and digital health applications [11]. The control loop of a PDSA cycle aims to improve therapy adherence by, firstly, expediting adjustments of interventions impending to fail and, secondly, by taking the patient's preferences and limitations into account for adaptation to personal needs. A PDSA cycle in the medical context consists of four phases: In the plan-phase, medical professionals and patients define objectives and develop a therapy plan. In the do-phase, patients execute the plans (i.e., taking medication, exercising, or other lifestyle adoptions) and document their progression. Data is analyzed individually and collaboratively in the study-phase to finally identify adjustments for the upcoming cycles in the act-phase. The PDSA cycle starts anew by integrating the adjustments into the therapy plan [11]. The comprehensiveness and wide acceptance in healthcare make the PDSA cycle a suitable lens for analyzing digital health applications as it resonates with NCD care's longitudinal and iterative characteristics.

2.2 Persuasive Technology in Healthcare

Persuasive Systems are a complementary approach to the PDSA method as they are more easily scalable and usually come at a lower cost than solely relying on humans [12, 13]. Since 2001, research on persuasive systems has become an emerging trend, growing exponentially after the introduction of smartphones in 2009 [3]. Unsurprisingly, persuasive systems have long found their way into the healthcare sector due to their potential to address key NCD care challenges. There is ample evidence of the potential to increase adherence with persuasive systems [14].

Despite its popularity, the term "persuasive systems" appears to need further clarification in the context of NCD care. Persuasive systems are "computerized software or information systems designed to reinforce, change or shape attitudes or behaviors or both without using coercion or deception" [15]. Behavior change is achieved as the outcome of the co-existence of three factors: sufficient (1) motivation and (2) ability of a user to perform a behavior, and (3) a trigger initiating the behavior [16]. Research on persuasive systems has produced a vast number of persuasive strategies and design frameworks based on this fundamental understanding of behavior change [15, 17]. The persuasive system design (PSD) model is one of the most popular frameworks, providing designers with actionable advice for designing and evaluating persuasive systems [18]. The definition mentioned above and the PSD model strongly focus on the interaction between a user and an application designed to persuade the user to perform a specific task. However, systems usually span further as they include more social aspects, such as other stakeholders and structures, besides the technical aspects (i.e., technology and task) [19].

In this study, the definition mentioned above by Oinas-Kukkonen and Harjuma [15] better describes our understanding of *persuasive applications* as they focus on a specific task. We adopt a more comprehensive perspective on *persuasive systems* as they are embedded in a specific health situation, including persuasive applications, traditional applications such as patient health records, the user, and other social aspects paramount in NCD care (e.g., medical professionals). Thus, we aim to understand how the existing research and design of persuasive systems address the need for continuous, comprehensive, and adaptive NCD care.

Seven recent studies reviewed the state of persuasive systems research in healthcare. Three of these studies focus on actual digital health applications available to the public [20–22]. The four remaining studies review the available scientific literature [3, 5, 6, 23]. Despite the promising prospects and the popularity of persuasive systems, all studies report mixed results and identify three challenges for persuasive systems in healthcare.

First, researchers and designers currently have an imbalance in their focus. Many reviews report a strong focus on a few persuasive strategies [5, 20, 21]. Geuens et al.

[21] report an average of 5.8 persuasive strategies across 28 apps for chronic arthritis with a strong focus on system credibility support and task support, neglecting dialogue (0.5 principles per app) and social support (0.01 principles per app). Existing persuasive systems appear to only focus on specific parts of the PSD and Fogg behavior models.

Second, we lack an understanding of the effects of individual and groups of persuasive strategies. Oyebode et al. [20] could not find a correlation between the number of persuasive strategies employed in 80 apps and their effectiveness. Asbjørnsen et al. [5] remain inconclusive on the ideal combination of persuasive strategies for long-term behavior change. Finally, the literature often fails to explain why specific strategies are less frequently used or are seemingly less effective [6]. While the variance in adherence can partly be explained by choice of the intervention style and the instantiated design of the persuasive strategies [23], there is a need to evaluate the engagement of real users with specific persuasive strategies to determine which strategies and combinations work best in real life [22].

Third, existing research often does not provide insights into the sustainability of persuasiveness. Asbjørnsen et al. [5] identify a gap in research on supporting to maintain weight loss (i.e., the changed behavior) with digital health. Geirhos et al. [22] draw similar conclusions and further criticize the lack of anchoring of such apps in scientific evidence (available for only 8% of 120 apps). Taj et al. [3] also identify a lack of theory-grounded persuasive systems. They call for closer cooperation between behavioral scientists and designers and more comprehensive research on how their knowledge can be combined in real-world digital health applications.

In summary, the current work strongly focuses on the effectiveness of persuasive application designs guided by the PSD model and other frameworks. The existing literature reviews identify three main challenges resulting from this task-centric perspective: (1) an imbalance in research and design focus only partially covering all design areas, (2) unclear effects of individual persuasive strategies and their interrelations with each other, and (3) a lack of focus on sustaining behavior change. While the studies call for more research to resolve these challenges, they do not question whether the current trajectory in research and design helps provide the comprehensive support needed for NCD care. This raises the question if the existing literature on persuasive systems addresses the need for continuous, comprehensive, and adaptive NCD care. We are missing a systematic approach to connecting behavior change theories, persuasive strategies, and insights from clinical practice. In this study, we adopt a comprehensive understanding of persuasive systems to assess the current state of research.

3 Methodology

To address our research aim, we performed a systematic literature review following the approach proposed by vom Brocke et al. [24]. The categorization of persuasive strategies in the Fogg-PDSA matrix allowed us to assess if the existing persuasive systems research comprehensively covers the requirements for continuous NCD care *(RQ1)*. We could further identify and review a subset of articles indicating to address all phases of the Fogg-PDSA matrix to elicit blind spots that need to be addressed by designers and researchers in future work to increase persuasiveness in continuous NCD care *(RQ2)*. In the following sections, we outline our approach along the five phases of the methodology: (1) definition of review scope, (2) conceptualization of topic, (3) literature search, (4) literature analysis and synthesis, and (5) results.

3.1 Definition of Review Scope and Conceptualization

We first familiarized ourselves with the existing literature on persuasive systems in healthcare to define the review scope (see Sect. 2). Then, we reviewed meta-analyses on behavior change with digital health for NCDs by searching PubMed and Cochrane library. We analyzed 5 meta-analyses to conceptualize our research topic [8, 12, 13, 25, 26]. As a result, we extracted a list of 57 persuasive strategies and behavior change techniques applied in digital health. This list served as the foundation of our coding schema in our analysis. Furthermore, the meta-analyses informed the definition of the search query for the literature search. As a result of this phase, we conceptualize the Fogg-PDSA matrix as our understanding of comprehensive, persuasive systems and the lens through which we study the current state of persuasive systems in NCD care.

3.2 Literature Search

In this phase, we collected the literature by searching the Scopus database. After iterative discussions in the author group, the following final search query was used:

	ALL ("digital health") OR ALL (ehealth) OR ALL (mhealth) OR ALL ("patient portal") OR ALL ("electronic medical record") OR ALL (emr) OR ALL (wearables) OR ALL ("personal health record") OR ALL (phr) OR ALL ("mobile app") OR ALL ("digital therapeutics") OR ALL ("electronic health record") OR ALL (ehr)
AND	(ALL ("behavior change") OR ALL ("lifestyle change"))
AND	(ALL ("non-communicable disease") OR ALL ("chronic disease") OR ALL (overweight) OR ALL (obesity))

We limited our search to the subject area of computer science, including human-computer interaction, information systems, and medical informatics. Additionally, we only considered publications from 2018 or later due to the fast technological advances. Finally, we only included literature published in outlets with a better or equal C rating. The ratings were taken from Serenko et al. [27] and The German Academic Association of Business Research [28].

In the following, we screened the title and abstract of each article to assess their fit for our study. Borderline cases were discussed in the author group, and uncertainties were resolved before screening the full texts of each article. Further exclusions were made if the full texts did not cover persuasive strategies or behavior change techniques.

3.3 Literature Analysis and Synthesis

In three steps, we analyzed the remaining articles using the qualitative data analysis software MAXQDA. First, we coded the articles using the persuasive strategies identified in Sect. 3.1. This analysis gave us a profound understanding of the persuasive strategies employed and their instantiated designs. After coding of approx. 20% of the articles, the coding schema was refined iteratively in discussion between the authors. For example, the initial code "feedback" was one of the most found strategies in the meta-analyses. We decided to adjust our coding as it was considered too broad. We assigned all code segments initially coded with feedback to different strategies that have feedback characteristics but are more specific. We found 36 from the initial 57 strategies in the literature. Second, we applied our conceptualization of the Fogg-PDSA matrix to the coding schema. Three researchers assigned each strategy to one of the dimensions of the Fogg behavior model (i.e., ability, motivation, trigger, and goals; we defined target behavior as goals in this study). We discussed differences in assignments and resolved any differences. We repeated the same process to assign the strategies to the PDSA cycle. All strategies except three could be assigned to one field in the Fogg-PDSA matrix. Third, we reviewed our coding before synthesizing the data.

Our synthesis included three steps: First, we created the Fogg-PDSA matrix to illustrate how many papers covered each field. Each study could potentially cover every field. However, a study would only be counted once per field if it employs more the one strategy. This illustration highlights focus areas and gaps across the reviewed literature. Second, we analyzed the coverage of the different phases of the PDSA cycle and their transitions within the individual papers. We define transitions as the coverage of subsequent phases. An example of a transition could be from plan to do to study (P-D-S) if all these phases are covered in a single paper. This step allowed us to understand the focus of individual studies and identify a subset that promises to cover all PDSA phases. Third, we analyzed this subset in more detail. We created a Fogg-PDSA matrix for this set of articles and aggregated the employed strategies in a separate table. Furthermore, we searched for explicit mention of any continuity or improvement method and analyzed whether any medical professionals were involved in the systems. Finally, we looked at those papers' aims and goals. We consolidated the data and documented our findings.

4   Results

The search in Scopus yielded 780 results. 134 papers met our selection criteria, and 108 were considered relevant after an initial review of the title and abstract. After screening the full text of the remaining 108 studies, 57 were included in our literature review. In the following, we first present the results across all reviewed articles in Sect. 4.1. Figure 1 highlights the focus areas and gaps in the Fogg-PDSA matrix, and Fig. 2 illustrates the coverage of the PDSA phases in individual papers. These results allow us to answer our first research question by assessing the extent to which current persuasive systems research addresses the need for continuous, comprehensive, and adaptive NCD care. We then present our in-depth analysis of articles promising to cover the complete PDSA cycle in Sect. 4.2. This detailed analysis answers our second research question as it uncovers blind spots that need to be addressed by developers and researchers of more comprehensive persuasive systems.

4.1 The Fogg-PDSA Matrix

Figure 1 shows the coverage of the Fogg-PDSA matrix, indicating the number of studies employing persuasive strategies in each field. The matrix uncovers an imbalance
in the reviewed literature: Most articles emphasize the do-phase (47.5%) and neglect
the act-phase (13.4%) of the PDSA dimension. A similar observation can be made for
the Fogg dimensions, where motivation (38.6%) and ability (35.1%) receive the most
attention from research, while goals (10.9%) are rarely covered. Furthermore, when
looking at individual fields, motivation (32), ability (33), and triggers (31) in the do-
phase are the only fields covered by more than half of the reviewed publications. The
fields study-ability (21), act-motivation (18), and study-motivation (17) are addressed
by approximately a third of the publications leaving the remaining fields below 25%
coverage. Our analysis further shows four fields not covered by the reviewed literature.
Goals do not appear in the do-phase, which can be explained by the PDSA cycle: Persuasive systems aims at motivating and enabling users after the goals are defined. The
do-phase is not intended to review or adjust goals, as this is done in the following phases.
However, the reviewed literature rarely discusses goals in the study- (2) and act-phase
(7).

Furthermore, triggers are only covered in the do-phase, leaving the other three phases
empty. This is due to our coding schema that consisted of triggers that only fit the do-
phase. Finally, the areas study-goals (2), act-goals (7), and act-ability (2) are rarely
addressed by the reviewed publications without an obvious explanation similar to the
do-goals area.

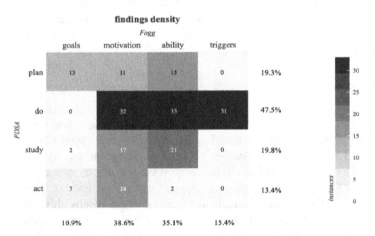

Fig. 1. Fogg-PDSA Matrix covering all reviewed articles

In our analysis, we further categorized individual articles into the covered PDSA
phases to identify studies adopting a comprehensive approach (see Fig. 2). For example,
we analyzed if an article employs persuasive strategies in adjacent phases (e.g., *plan-*
and *do*-phase) and categorized them accordingly (e.g., P-D). Except for the *do*-phase
(18), only a few articles focus on a single PDSA phase (4). Eleven studies employed

persuasive strategies in two PDSA phases with an almost exclusive focus on P-D (5) and D-S (5), neglecting S-A (1) and A-P (0). Most of the eleven studies covering three PDSA phases focus on P-D-S, like the other studies covering one or two phases. Furthermore, 13 out of 57 papers employ strategies in all PDSA phases. Overall, 35 out of 57 articles do not address the *act*-phase at all.

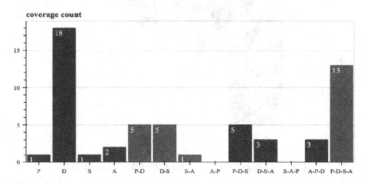

Fig. 2. Coverage of PDSA phases (phase + transition) for individual articles

4.2   In-Depth Analysis of Articles Covering the Complete PDSA Cycle

We further analyzed the 13 articles covering all PDSA phases in-depth regarding the employed strategies and their linkage, the evaluation method, and the involvement of medical professionals as part of the PDSA cycle.

We created another Fogg-PDSA matrix to illustrate some interesting insights into the 13 selected articles (see Fig. 3). While the do-phase (35.5%) still receives the most attention, the phases are much more evenly distributed across these articles leaving act (17.2%) only closely behind plan (24.7%) and study (22.6%). In addition, motivation (43%) appears to be at the center of attention in these articles. Compared to all reviewed literature, goals (15.1%) are studied more closely, making triggers (10.7%) the least attended dimension.

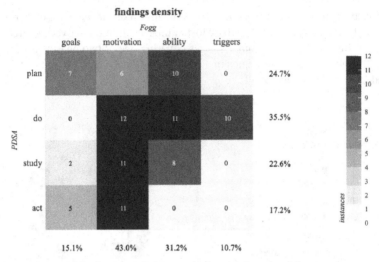

Fig. 3. Fogg-PDSA matrix for 13 selected articles

Furthermore, we identified the five most applied persuasive strategies for each PDSA phase (see Table 1). The list contains eight motivation strategies with social support being applied the most (8), five ability strategies with suggestion as the most used (9), two triggers (i.e., reminders (8) and prompts/cues (7)), and one goal strategy (i.e., goal setting (7)).

Table 1. Five most common strategies per phase (We only found four strategies for *study* and *act* in the articles), M = motivation, A = ability, T = trigger, G = goal

Plan	#	Do	#	Study	#	Act	#
goal setting (G)	7	suggestions (A)	9	self-monitoring (A)	8	reward (M)	7
action planning (A)	5	social support (M)	8	visualizing progress (M)	8	adaptive goals (A)	5
social learning (M)	4	reminder (T)	8	social comparison (M)	6	praise (M)	4
assist in setting optimal challenge (A)	3	prompts/cues (T)	7	review behavior goals (G)	2	vicarious consequences (M)	1
reduction (A)	2	social competition (M)	4				

Despite the promising insights from the matrix above (see Fig. 3), our in-depth analysis of the articles raised multiple concerns. First, none of the studies explicitly address any form of continuous care or quality improvement approach. As a result, only Noorbergen et al. [29] seem to explicitly address the need to connect individual persuasive strategies while also failing to attend to the continuity required in NCD care. Second, the aims of the studies vary between acceptance and persuasiveness [30–33] and medical outcomes [34, 35]. Third, the studies employed different evaluation approaches. About half of the studies, mainly focusing on acceptance and persuasiveness, adopted approaches such as (online) surveys [20, 30, 36], think-aloud sessions [33], or a combination of literature review and expert interviews [37]. Only a few studies draw their data from extended usage in experimental or real-world settings [31, 32, 34, 35]. Lastly, only one study explicitly involves medical professionals in their system to provide user feedback and context-dependent resources [29]. However, this study remains only theoretical and is not yet implemented in an actual application.

5 Discussion and Conclusion

In this systematic literature review, we aimed to understand if the existing persuasive systems research comprehensively covers the requirements for NCD care. We conceptualize persuasive systems for NCD care in the Fogg-PDSA matrix combining Fogg's behavior change model and NCD care approaches. This lens uncovers the extent to which current persuasive systems research addresses the need for continuous, comprehensive, and adaptive NCD care. We identify blind spots that need to be addressed by developers and researchers of more comprehensive persuasive systems. Our study offers profound insights into potential reasons for the persisting challenges in persuasive systems design. Thereby, we provide guidance in three areas:

First, we observe an imbalance in research efforts as most reviewed papers focus on the do-Phase (see Fig. 1). This existing research contributed to our in-depth design knowledge of motivating and enabling users to achieve their goals. However, designers of persuasive technology appear to have a task-oriented view of persuasion. The widely adopted PSD model advises designers to analyze the persuasion context (i.e., intent, event, strategy) before designing a persuasive system [15]. This approach offers valuable guidance for designers; however, it limits the scope to three aspects: the user, the persuasive technology, and the task. This view is also evident in the Fogg behavior model, where behavior change is reduced to one exact point in time. By strictly following this guidance and the resulting strong focus on a small number of persuasive strategies, researchers and designers seem to be caught in a self-confirmation trap. In this trap, the instantiation of persuasion strategies varies across studies, but the strategies are not questioned. Compared to the do-Phase, the other three phases of the PDSA cycle are mostly under-researched. The studies rather focus on confirmatory instead of exploratory studies that create new knowledge on persuasive digital health. As a result, the persuasive strategies are instantiated in a new context (i.e., NCDs) with limited knowledge of transferability, potentially explaining part of the challenges.

While the task-oriented perspective is acceptable for most persuasive technology, it does not account for the characteristics of NCD care (i.e., continuity, comprehensiveness, adaptivity). This study complements our understanding of behavior change through persuasive technology with the PDSA cycle to factor in the dynamics of NCD care. This matrix allows us to identify gaps in our knowledge and provides guidance for future research to successfully design persuasive technology for NCD care.

Second, our analysis of the coverage of the PDSA phases uncovers neglect of the transitions between the phases. A core principle of the PDSA cycle is the interconnection of each phase. For example, a user reviews their progress (do) towards their goal (plan) in the study-phase and adjusts according to this (act). We found that the transition from study to act to plan hardly receives attention from research (see Fig. 2), and only 13 papers in our review address each phase of the PDSA cycle with at least one strategy. Yet, none of these studies explicitly anchored their design in any improvement method, and we found little to no linkage between the phases. For example, the current designs focus on sending motivational messages such as "You can do this" or aim at improving ability by suggesting immediate measures to achieve the goal (e.g., "If you take a 5-min walk now, you are likely to reach your daily step goal") instead of linking the interventions to the plan-phase [33]. This limitation is even more evident when looking at the study-act transition. Most studies animate the users to reflect on their behavior by offering an overview of goal attendance for a set time (e.g., weekly); however, they almost entirely neglect the need for actionable measures to improve goal attendance. This resonates with Asbjørnsen et al. [5], who found unclear effects of strategies and their interrelations as a critical challenge in sustaining the effectiveness of persuasive technology. This uni-dimensional focus could be caused by the task-oriented perspective and partially explain the mixed outcomes as it shapes the designers' mental model of persuasion. Researchers and designers emphasize the do-phase as this is where they think persuasion happens and thereby risk losing their users as they miss to satisfy the need for continuous care. However, suppose persuasive systems support the user throughout the PDSA cycle by better linking the phases (cf. [38]). In that case, they could further personalize the user experience and reduce discontinued use caused by non-contextualized goals and the resulting difficulties in reaching those goals.

Evidence from medical research suggests that adherence to the principles of the PDSA method and the completion of a complete cycle significantly influence patients' health outcomes [4, 11]. To better support their users in achieving their goals, persuasive digital health must support users to act following the review of their progress toward their goals (study). Repeatedly completing these cycles personalizes the user's goals and plans and allows persuasive systems to deeply understand their users and their preferences. Consequently, we call for research to investigate the potential of this broadened view on persuasive digital health to sustain long-term behavior change. We invite researchers and designers to question our current understanding of persuasive strategies and design knowledge. The Fogg-PDSA matrix suggests that comprehensive NCD care requires an innovative rethinking of existing and potentially developing new strategies to interlink all four phases.

Third, we only found one study out of the 13 papers covering the PDSA cycle that considered the involvement of medical professionals in their design while remaining conceptual [29]. Still, this study addresses a central aspect of NCD care: The collaboration between medical professionals (e.g., doctors or dietitians) and patients are integral to successful NCD care [9]. The experts provide patients with a helping hand and support in breaking down the complexity of the subject matter into actionable pieces. This transition from abstract Furthermore, the personal relationship could increase a sense of accountability for the patients, as a person behind the persuasive technology is kept in the loop. Finally, medical professionals can offer patients tailored advice that is more likely to be adopted. For example, they can suggest low-impact activities instead of 10'000 steps per day to an overweight person with a walking disability. Persuasive technology might not be able to determine a user's readiness for a specific activity. We invite future research to explore ways of including medical professionals in the persuasive PDSA cycle and, thereby, the potential to increase persuasiveness and long-term adoption. One approach could be the integration of persuasive technology into the workflow of medical professionals. For example, the dietary plan provided by a dietitian could be shared with the application, that is supporting the user in adhering to this plan and providing feedback to both sides for further review in the subsequent encounter. Another approach could be to explore emerging technologies as they possess the potential to increase long-term adherence [14]. Technologies like conversational agents (e.g., chatbots) could provide the user with a sense of personal interaction, thereby extending the medical professionals' reach. This, in turn, could increase therapy effectiveness and reduce treatment costs as digital interventions are easily scalable [12, 13]. As a result, patients would be supported by a persuasive system that contains complementing social and technical subsystems.

In conclusion, the Fogg-PDSA matrix uncovered imbalances and gaps in our knowledge that hamper the success of persuasive systems in NCD care: imbalanced focus of persuasive strategies and the *do*-phase, missing transitions between the PDSA phases, and task-centricity of persuasive applications. The Fogg-PDSA matrix can help researchers and designers move from this task-centric perspective on persuasiveness to a more comprehensive understanding of persuasive systems by looking at the specific health situation. It creates room for other parties involved in NCD care, such as medical professionals. This involvement creates a persuasive system with complementing and interconnected social and technical subsystems. This complementation could combine the strength of each subsystem: involved medical professionals assist in moving from abstract goals (e.g., losing weight) to personalized and actionable interventions (e.g., walking your dog daily for one hour). Persuasive systems would take up these personalized interventions and support patients in adhering to them. With this study, we aim to invite future research to explore innovative rethinking of existing persuasive strategies and to challenge the current knowledge to advance our understanding of long-term behavior and further change through persuasive digital health systems. Future studies could address the limitations of this study: 1) we focused on NCD and obesity/overweight instead of behavioral risk factors such as alcohol abuse. Focusing on behavioral risk factors could provide further insights. 2) this study only hints at potential solutions. Future research by design should explore the validity of our assumptions and advance our understanding.

References

1. World Health Organization: Noncommunicable diseases: progress monitor 2022. World Health Organization, Geneva (2022)
2. Kravitz, R.L., et al.: Recall of recommendations and adherence to advice among patients with chronic medical conditions. Arch. Intern. Med. **153**, 1869–1878 (1993)

3. Taj, F., Klein, M.C.A., van Halteren, A.: Digital health behavior change technology: bibliometric and scoping review of two decades of research. JMIR mHealth and uHealth 21 (2019)
4. Hunter, D.J., Reddy, K.S.: Noncommunicable diseases. N. Engl. J. Med. **369**, 1336–1343 (2013)
5. Asbjørnsen, R.A., et al.: Persuasive system design principles and behavior change techniques to stimulate motivation and adherence in electronic health interventions to support weight loss maintenance: scoping review. J. Med. Internet Res. **21**, e14265 (2019). https://doi.org/10.2196/14265
6. Matthews, J., Win, K.T., Oinas-Kukkonen, H., Freeman, M.: Persuasive technology in mobile applications promoting physical activity: a systematic review. J. Med. Syst. **40**(3), 1–13 (2016). https://doi.org/10.1007/s10916-015-0425-x
7. Vandenberghe, D., Albrecht, J.: The financial burden of non-communicable diseases in the European Union: a systematic review. Eur. J. Pub. Health **30**, 833–839 (2020)
8. Carraça, E., et al.: Effective behavior change techniques to promote physical activity in adults with overweight or obesity: a systematic review and meta-analysis. Obes. Rev. **22**, e13258 (2021)
9. Nuño, R., Coleman, K., Bengoa, R., Sauto, R.: Integrated care for chronic conditions: the contribution of the ICCC Framework. Health Policy **105**, 55–64 (2012)
10. Hekler, E.B., et al.: Tutorial for Using Control Systems Engineering to Optimize Adaptive Mobile Health Interventions. J. Med. Internet Res. **20**, e214 (2018). https://doi.org/10.2196/jmir.8622
11. Taylor, M.J., McNicholas, C., Nicolay, C., Darzi, A., Bell, D., Reed, J.E.: Systematic review of the application of the plan–do–study–act method to improve quality in healthcare. BMJ Qual Saf. **23**, 290–298 (2014). https://doi.org/10.1136/bmjqs-2013-001862
12. Beleigoli, A.M., Andrade, A.Q., Cançado, A.G., Paulo, M.N., Diniz, M.D.F.H., Ribeiro, A.L.: Web-based digital health interventions for weight loss and lifestyle habit changes in overweight and obese adults: systematic review and meta-analysis. J. Med. Internet Res. **21**, e298 (2019). https://doi.org/10.2196/jmir.9609
13. Berry, R., Kassavou, A., Sutton, S.: Does self-monitoring diet and physical activity behaviors using digital technology support adults with obesity or overweight to lose weight? A systematic literature review with meta-analysis. Obes. Rev. **22**, e13306 (2021). https://doi.org/10.1111/obr.13306
14. Wang, Y., et al.: Effects of continuous care for patients with type 2 diabetes using mobile health application: a randomised controlled trial. Int. J. Health Plann. Manage. **34**, 1025–1035 (2019)
15. Oinas-Kukkonen, H., Harjumaa, M.: A systematic framework for designing and evaluating persuasive systems. In: Oinas-Kukkonen, H., Hasle, P., Harjumaa, M., Segerståhl, K., Øhrstrøm, P. (eds.) PERSUASIVE 2008. LNCS, vol. 5033, pp. 164–176. Springer, Heidelberg (2008). https://doi.org/10.1007/978-3-540-68504-3_15
16. Fogg, B.: A behavior model for persuasive design. In: Proceedings of the 4th International Conference on Persuasive Technology - Persuasive 2009, p. 1. ACM Press, Claremont, California (2009). https://doi.org/10.1145/1541948.1541999
17. Abraham, C., Michie, S.: A taxonomy of behavior change techniques used in interventions. Health Psychol. **27**, 379–387 (2008). https://doi.org/10.1037/0278-6133.27.3.379
18. Oinas-Kukkonen, H., Harjumaa, M.: Persuasive systems design: Key issues, process model, and system features. Communications of the association for Information Systems. 24, 28 (2009)
19. Sarker, S., Chatterjee, S., Xiao, X., Elbanna, A.: The sociotechnical axis of cohesion for the IS discipline: Its historical legacy and its continued relevance. MIS Q. **43**, 695–720 (2019)

20. Oyebode, O., Ndulue, C., Alhasani, M., Orji, R.: Persuasive mobile apps for health and wellness: a comparative systematic review. In: Gram-Hansen, S.B., Jonasen, T.S., Midden, C. (eds.) PERSUASIVE 2020. LNCS, vol. 12064, pp. 163–181. Springer, Cham (2020). https://doi.org/10.1007/978-3-030-45712-9_13

21. Geuens, J., Swinnen, T.W., Westhovens, R., de Vlam, K., Geurts, L., VandenAbeele, V.: A review of persuasive principles in mobile apps for chronic arthritis patients: opportunities for improvement. JMIR Mhealth Uhealth. 4, e118 (2016). https://doi.org/10.2196/mhealth.6286

22. Geirhos, A., et al.: Standardized evaluation of the quality and persuasiveness of mobile health applications for diabetes management. Sci. Rep. 12, 3639 (2022). https://doi.org/10.1038/s41 598-022-07544-2

23. Kelders, S.M., Kok, R.N., Ossebaard, H.C., Van Gemert-Pijnen, J.E.: persuasive system design does matter: a systematic review of adherence to web-based interventions. J. Med. Internet Res. 14, e152 (2012). https://doi.org/10.2196/jmir.2104

24. Brocke, J. vom, Simons, A., Niehaves, B., Riemer, K., Plattfaut, R., Cleven, A.: Reconstructing the Giant: On the Importance of Rigour in Documenting the Literature Search Process, 10 June 2009. Presented at the http://www.alexandria.unisg.ch/Publikationen/67910

25. Hu, R., van Velthoven, M.H., Meinert, E.: Perspectives of people who are overweight and obese on using wearable technology for weight management: systematic review. JMIR Mhealth Uhealth 8, e12651 (2020)

26. Hutchesson, M.J., et al.: eH ealth interventions for the prevention and treatment of overweight and obesity in adults: a systematic review with meta-analysis. Obes. Rev. 16, 376–392 (2015)

27. Serenko, A., Dohan, M.S., Tan, J.: Global Ranking of Management- and Clinical- centered E-health Journals. Commun. Assoc. Inf. Syst. 41, 198–215 (2017). https://doi.org/10.17705/1CAIS.04109

28. Verband der Hochschullehrer für Betriebswirtschaft: VHB-JOURQUAL3: Wirtschaftsinformatik (2015). https://vhbonline.org/fileadmin/user_upload/JQ3_WI.pdf

29. Noorbergen, T.J., Adam, M.T., Attia, J.R., Cornforth, D.J., Minichiello, M.: Exploring the design of mHealth systems for health behavior change using mobile biosensors. Commun. Assoc. Inf. Syst. 44, 44 (2019)

30. Alhasani, M., Orji, R.: SortOut: persuasive stress management mobile application for higher education students. In: Baghaei, N., Vassileva, J., Ali, R., Oyibo, K. (eds.) PERSUASIVE 2022. LNCS, vol. 13213, pp. 16–27. Springer, Cham (2022). https://doi.org/10.1007/978-3-030-98438-0_2

31. Cherubini, M., Villalobos-Zuniga, G., Boldi, M.-O., Bonazzi, R.: The unexpected downside of paying or sending messages to people to make them walk: Comparing tangible rewards and motivational messages to improve physical activity. ACM Trans. Comput.-Hum. Interact. (TOCHI). 27, 1–44 (2020)

32. Hoffmann, A., FaustChristmann, C.A., Zolynski, G., Bleser, G.: Gamification of a stress management app: results of a user study. In: Marcus, A., Wang, W. (eds.) HCII 2019. LNCS, vol. 11585, pp. 303–313. Springer, Cham (2019). https://doi.org/10.1007/978-3-030-23538-3_23

33. Ladwa, S., Grønli, T.-M., Ghinea, G.: Towards encouraging a healthier lifestyle and increased physical activity – an app incorporating persuasive design principles. In: Kurosu, Masaaki (ed.) HCI 2018. LNCS, vol. 10902, pp. 158–172. Springer, Cham (2018). https://doi.org/10.1007/978-3-319-91244-8_13

34. Karppinen, P., et al.: Opportunities and challenges of behavior change support systems for enhancing habit formation: a qualitative study. J. Biomed. Inform. 84, 82–92 (2018)

35. Sengupta, A., Bhattacherjee, A., Dutta, K.: Information technology interventions in cardiac rehabilitation: a theory driven approach (2020)

36. Wais-Zechmann, B., Gattol, V., Neureiter, K., Orji, R., Tscheligi, M.: Persuasive technology to support chronic health conditions: investigating the optimal persuasive strategies for persons with COPD. In: Ham, J., Karapanos, E., Morita, P.P., Burns, C.M. (eds.) PERSUASIVE 2018. LNCS, vol. 10809, pp. 255–266. Springer, Cham (2018). https://doi.org/10.1007/978-3-319-78978-1_21

37. Vemuri, A., Decker, K., Saponaro, M., Dominick, G.: Multi agent architecture for automated health coaching. J. Med. Syst. **45**, 1–7 (2021)

38. De Vries, R.A., Truong, K.P., Kwint, S., Drossaert, C.H., Evers, V.: Crowd-designed motivation: Motivational messages for exercise adherence based on behavior change theory. In: Proceedings of the 2016 CHI Conference on Human Factors in Computing Systems, pp. 297–308 (2016)

Methods for Tailoring
and Personalization

Comparing Psychometric and Behavioral Predictors of Compliance During Human-AI Interactions

Nikolos Gurney[1]([✉])[iD], David V. Pynadath[1,2][iD], and Ning Wang[1,2]

[1] Institute for Creative Technologies, Los Angeles, USA
{gurney,pynadath,nwang}@ict.usc.edu
[2] Viterbi School of Engineering, Computer Science Department, University of Southern California, Los Angeles, CA, USA

Abstract. Optimization of human-AI teams hinges on the AI's ability to tailor its interaction to individual human teammates. A common hypothesis in adaptive AI research is that minor differences in people's predisposition to trust can significantly impact their likelihood of complying with recommendations from the AI. Predisposition to trust is often measured with self-report inventories that are administered before interactions. We benchmark a popular measure of this kind against behavioral predictors of compliance. We find that the inventory is a less effective predictor of compliance than the behavioral measures in datasets taken from three previous research projects. This suggests a general property that individual differences in initial behavior are more predictive than differences in self-reported trust attitudes. This result also shows a potential for easily accessible behavioral measures to provide an AI with more accurate models without the use of (often costly) survey instruments.

Keywords: human-robot interaction · human-computer interaction · compliance · trust · intervention · decision making

1 Introduction

The capability to accurately model the attitudes that people will have towards an AI, such as trust, is critically important to the design of successful human-AI interactions. Lee and See [21] argue in their seminal work on trust in automation that minor differences between people in their predispositions to trust can result in significantly different interactions with an autonomous system. For example,

Part of the effort behind this work was sponsored by the Defense Advanced Research Projects Agency (DARPA) under contract number W911NF2010011. The content of the information does not necessarily reflect the position or the policy of the U.S. Government or the Defense Advanced Research Projects Agency, and no official endorsements should be inferred.

J. Ham et al. (Eds.): PERSUASIVE 2023, LNCS 13832, pp. 175–197, 2023.
https://doi.org/10.1007/978-3-031-30933-5_12

a person with a high predisposition to trust may take a chance and comply with the system's recommendation, while someone not so predisposed would not. The hypothesis goes that, if this autonomous system is sufficiently reliable, then the compliant teammate will most likely experience a positive outcome and, given the assumption that positive outcomes are predictive of increased trust, such an experience should in turn lead to more compliance, thus the act of complying will initiate a feedback loop in which trust begets trust. A person low in predisposition to trust, however, will be less likely to comply and subsequently less likely to enter the positive feedback loop.

Adaptive AI with the capability of modeling and integrating a person's predispositions, trust or otherwise, into its decision making may be able to avoid the negative effects of miscalibrated attitudes that people hold towards it. In the example of the non-compliant teammate, such an AI may attach a more in-depth explanation and justification with its recommendation, aimed at overcoming this person's deficient predisposition to trust. Such personalization of the recommendation necessitates continuous measuring and modeling of the trust-compliance relationship. Although Lee and See provide a model of the trust implications of a human and automated system team, they do not offer a measurement method.

Researchers have committed significant resources to study Lee and See's hypothesized relationship between predisposition to trust and trust in automation, including how to measure and adapt accordingly [17]. A common practice is to measure a person's predisposition to trust using a general-purpose scale and then correlate that measure with human behavior in an interaction with an automated system. A popular example of such a scale is the 12-item *Disposition to Trust* inventory (DTI) [23]. This measure attempts to capture a person's general likelihood of depending on others and is hypothesized to influence beliefs and intentions towards not only people but also other systems that are subject to a person's trust. There is evidence of this measure having (e.g. [2,33]) and not having (e.g. [34,44]) predictive value in interactions with both virtual and physical robots.

Understanding how individual characteristics, like predisposition to trust, impact compliance is more critical now than ever. Researchers, technologists, and funding agencies are increasingly pursuing automated systems capable of rich interactions with humans (e.g. [4,13,37,38]). Despite these efforts, AI agents will continue to make mistakes due to the complexity and inherent uncertainty of the environments in which they operate [4]. One solution for mitigating the damage done by these mistakes, which can lead to better-calibrated trust, is for an agent to ensure that its reasoning is communicated in a way to meet the varying information needs and preferences of its human teammates. Sufficient transparency in communication will allow people to know when they should comply with an AI's recommendation and when they should not, i.e. develop better-calibrated trust, which is an important precursor to good compliance behavior in human-AI interactions [2,8,21,33,44].

On the other hand, if an agent is *insensitive* to people's different predispositions to trust, it will use the same communication strategy for all of them. Given the ubiquity of individual differences, this one-size-fits-all strategy is sure to lead to unwarranted misuse or disuse of the agent [30]. This makes predicting trust as early as possible—perhaps even as a trait, as DTI aims to do—all the more important. If, for example, a robot can form a model of a new human teammate's predisposition to trust before an interaction even begins, it can get a head start on personalizing its communication to maximize transparency, trust calibration, and appropriate compliance. This reality points to an acute need for compliance prediction benchmarks that are not only accurate but which agents can acquire as early as possible without sacrificing predictive value.

We benchmark DTI against a set of four simple behavioral measures: whether or not a person follows a robot's first recommendation, its recommendation immediately after its first mistake, all its recommendations through that mistake, and its recommendations during the course of an early mission. We compare these measures in terms of their ability to predict objective (behavioral) outcomes, using data from three separate experiments collected to study human-robot interactions. DTI explains less variance in (and thus has less predictive power of) the performance of the human-AI teams than the behavioral measures across all three datasets, and contrary to the hypothesized effect of [23], does not predict initial or overall compliance. In two of the three datasets, DTI does not even manage to explain a significant amount of variance in the models, meaning that it does not have predictive value as modeled. In the third dataset, it is inversely correlated with compliance. That is, whereas higher DTI scores are hypothesized to predict more compliance, they actually predict the opposite. Given that administering a survey like DTI is impractical (and sometimes impossible) in many human-AI interaction domains, it is encouraging that these early behavioral measures (which are typically readily observable by the agent) can provide such predictive power. In fact, assuming that the hypothesized relationship between compliance and trust is accurate, they appear to be more accurate reflections of a person's true predisposition to trust than a measure like DTI, which is based on self-report.

We believe that this relatively simple finding will provide valuable input to models across a diverse set of human-AI interaction domains. There are, admittedly, many existing subjective measures of trust intended for predicting compliance—but administering said measures is often burdensome and they are not always as predictive as anticipated. Likewise, there are many computational models of trust used for predicting compliance, but they are mostly domain specific and almost always challenging to implement. On the other hand, our behavioral method is simple to assess, easy to implement, and, most importantly, predictive of compliance. Moreover, it holds the potential to aid in developing more robust predictors of compliance, identify when compliance interventions may be necessary, and serve as a prototype for other similar benchmarks. We argue that identifying and developing easy-to-assess measures, such as the behavioral measures of trust presented here, are critical steps toward developing robust, adaptive AI that are capable of personalized interventions.

2   Related Work

"Trust" is often used as an umbrella term that covers a variety of human factors that influence compliance (see [16] for a meta-analysis that catalogs such factors). Measuring and modeling some of these specific trust factors is a common practice in AI research. Beyond the aforementioned DTI, researchers have developed or adapted many other instruments in service of understanding them, typically in isolation from one another. The adoption of these instruments by AI researchers generally reflects the nuances of each target factor. Researchers can use these broad measures to establish a hypothetical baseline for each person, while a more specific measure may be adopted for other purposes, just as researchers can use DTI to provide a baseline on a particular person's predisposition to trust. It is beyond the scope of this investigation to examine all of these factors and instruments, so we focus on those related to a person's a priori inclination to trust in an autonomous system.

Whereas DTI seeks to identify human teammates' inherent levels of trust, the *propensity to trust inventory* seeks to identify whether they are inclined to trust [6]. The hypotheses related to its implementation are similar: people with a greater propensity to trust will be more likely to comply with recommendations from an automated system than those with a lower one. Researchers have deployed this measure as a means of controlling for individual variance in responses to social engineering by a robot [3,5] or to understand the relationship between attention control and trust [42].

The context of an interaction may alter how a person responds to an automated system. With this in mind, researchers have developed and adopted trust measures for numerous use cases. At one level of abstraction are scales developed for assessing trust in particular types of automation, like the human-robot interaction trust scale, which (as its name suggests) is for assessing the level of trust a person has in robots [49] or the human-robot trust scale which was developed to assess changes in a person's trust in a robot [35]. Researchers have further refined scales such as this, DTI, and others for specific use cases. The Social Service Robot Interaction Trust scale, for example, was designed with a specific focus on the service context of human-robot interactions [11].

Finally, there are computational methods to track the evolution of trust during extended interactions with robots. These methods, such as the probabilistic model developed in [48] or the Markovian model introduced in [32], allow a robot to dynamically adapt its representation of the trust that a person places in it. Typically, such methods are seeded with something like the results of a trust inventory like the human-robot trust scale but obviate the need for repeated measures.

3   Measuring Disposition to Trust

McKnight et al. [23] developed DTI (presented in Appendix A as Fig. 1) as part of a larger construct, specifically aimed at e-commerce, for predicting the outcome of an initial interaction with a vendor. It has four sub-measures of its own: benevolence, integrity, competence, and trusting stance (each has three items, ordered respectively). Typically, the assessment asks people to indicate how much they agree with each statement using a response scale. These responses are averaged and correlated with the outcome measure of interest, such as compliance. The basic assumption is that if a person scores high on DTI, then they will be more likely to trust (share private information with, make a purchase from, take advice from, etc.) a given vendor which will result in them complying with a request.

The tacit assumption in adapting a measure of trust, such as DTI, to human-AI interactions or similar settings is that it remains reliable and that the construct validity observed in the development of the measure will hold in the new domain. At the time of writing, the article introducing this measure had over 6000 citations including numerous applications in human-AI interactions (e.g. [2,3,22,31,33,34,41,44–46]). No publications were found that validated the scale for use in human-AI interactions settings.

Additionally, it is worth noting that the original authors did not validate DTI against actual trusting behavior. As they point out, common trust-related behaviors observed in e-commerce are sharing personal information, making a purchase, or acting on information provided via a website. None of these were utilized by the authors to validate their measure because of cost. Instead, study participants were asked to indicate their likelihood of performing different trusting behaviors, which the authors justified from prior research that suggested responses to such measures do not differ meaningfully from actual behavior (e.g. [43]). Summarily, this inventory was designed to study purchase intentions in e-commerce settings, not compliance potential in human-AI interactions.

These two details, that the measure was developed for a different setting and as a means of predicting intentions rather than behaviors, suggest that the scale may be a poor fit for building a model for human-AI interactions compliance. There are other measures available, like the propensity to trust measure used by [44] and measures recently developed for predicting trust in automation [18,24], but their adoption is limited and, again, they were not designed specifically for human-AI interactions settings either. There are still others developed for specific types of attitudes, like the negative attitudes towards robots scale [28], but, again, they are not designed specifically for predicting compliance. This all points to the need for other means of informing a model capable of predicting compliance behavior in human-AI interactions.

4   A Behavioral Predictor of Compliance

"The best predictor of future behavior is past behavior."   - ~~Walter Mischel~~
                                                                  - ~~B.F. Skinner~~
                                                                  - ~~Mark Twain~~

As the strikeouts suggest, this maxim has been floating around in the study of human behavior for a significant amount of time. Despite its resiliency, the maxim is still subject to the same critique as all maxims, does it *really* generalize? The answer appears to be yes, given a small set of caveats: a short time horizon, similarity in the decision scenario, and stability in the decision maker [26]. We posit that the past behavior maxim applies to human-AI interactions and that the best way to judge future compliance with recommendations from an AI counterpart is to observe one (or a small number of) interaction and extrapolate.

Past behavior is more than a simple measure of habit. It reflects a suite of factors that weigh on decision making in a reliable fashion. This drives the decision-maker toward self-consistency and is, at least in part, what gives past behavior its predictive power [1,29]. It also suggests that when past behavior is able to explain residual error left by a theoretical construct that the construct is not capturing some important predictive factor(s). Simply put, the construct is insufficient. This alone does not mean that the construct lacks explanatory value. It is possible (likely) that trust, for example, is only a small part of compliance and past behavior is predictive of future compliance because it captures some heretofore unidentified factors.

We do not believe that this is the case with measures of trust used to predict future compliance in many human-AI interaction experiments. This is because these trust measures, like DTI, fail to account for a significant amount of variance in regression models. In other words, they do not have predictive power. Moreover, our alternative predictor, prior behavior, does. It is also possible to test whether DTI or past behavior can account for variance in the data that the other did not. Testing whether past behavior can explain away residual error left by DTI in the datasets is straightforward: simply add a control for past behavior to a statistical model that includes DTI and observe whether residual error significantly goes down. Moreover, the same basic concept can be applied for determining if DTI explains a meaningful amount of variance in behavioral data by comparing two models, one with DTI as a regressor and one without (that is, with just the experimental treatment controls).

5   Empirical Strategy

We analyzed three datasets, described in Appendix B, to test whether DTI and past behavior are capable of predicting compliance, i.e. future behavior (FB), in human-AI interactions. We introduce four different measures of past behavior. The simplest measure of past behavior is the participants' first compliance choice (FC) to follow or ignore a robot's recommendations during an experimental session. Studies 1 and 2 were comprised of multiple missions (three and eight, respectively). For these two data sets, we compute participants' mission 1 compliance (M1C) as an extended measure of past behavior. The third study only consisted of one long mission, however, every participant in this study followed the same trajectory with the robot making the same set of mistakes. Thus, we use participants' compliance on the choice after the first mistake (AFM) made by the robot and average compliance through AFM (AC-AFM). Future behavior, the dependent variable for the various models, is the percentage of times in the remaining interactions that a participant complied with the robot's recommendations. Thus, the models with FC as an independent variable and the models presented for comparing them use a different dependent variable (average compliance for buildings 2:n) than the models with M1C (average compliance after mission 1) or AFM, and AC-AFM (average compliance for buildings *mistake*+2:n) as independent variables. Note that two of the data sets included multiple missions, meaning that there was a break between sets of buildings. Our analyses ignore this fact and treat all buildings the same.[1] We describe the data and models in full detail in Appendix B.

6   Results

As noted, we rely on regression analyses to model the data. Each regression model that we report for a given use case is presented as a column in a table in the appendix. In the tables that report regression models, the first column is always the reference (null) model. These are models that do not include DTI or prior behavior measures, simply experimental treatment controls. We do not report values for the treatment conditions as these are reported in the original papers. Coefficients for continuous variables, such as a participant's averaged DTI response, should be interpreted as the expected change in the dependent variable, all else being equal, if the variable in question increased by one. For indicator variables, such as whether a participant complied during their first interaction with the robot, the coefficient value indicates the average change, all else being equal, in the dependent variable when the independent variable goes from zero to one.

6.1   Study 1

The disposition to trust measure failed to explain a meaningful amount of variance in the data from Study 1. When predicting the compliance percentage for buildings 2:24, the penalty of having an additional regressor in the model meant that the adjusted R^2 was no better than that of the reference model (see columns (1) and (2) of Table 1; all tables are in Appendix C). Unsurprisingly, the F-test comparing these two models rejects the alternative hypothesis ($F = 0.832$, $p = 0.363$). However, adding the FC measure (see column (3) of Table 1) did result in a model that accounted for more variance than the reference model ($F = 11.032$, $p = 0.001$). The complete model with both measures is better than the DTI ($F = 10.575$, $p = 0.001$) model but not the FC ($F = 0.449$, $p = 0.504$).

Shifting from using one interaction to predict the next 23 to using the entirety of mission one compliance decisions to predict those of the next two missions (16 interactions) resulted in generally better model fits. In effect, this is a sanity check because we are using more of a given participant's past behavior to predict less of their future behavior. The resulting models, reported in Table 3 and compared in Table 4, reflect those for the FC measure. The M1C measure explained a meaningful amount of variance but DTI did not. Together, these results support the hypothesis that prior behavior was a better predictor of future compliance than DTI for study 1.

---

[1] Controlling for mission did not meaningfully change the interpretation of the results.

6.2   Study 2

The results for the FC measure from Study 2 replicated those of Study 1, as reported in Table 5; however, it should be noted that the model fits were generally poor (see the R^2 values in Table 5). The DTI model (2) was no better than (1) while (3) managed to explain significantly more variance in the parameters. Adding the DTI measure to (3), again, did not improve the model's performance. This means we can draw the same conclusion from Study 2 as we did from Study 1: FC explains variance in compliance behavior not captured by DTI. The M1C models were also generally poor fits (see the R^2 values in Table 7). Moreover, they did not replicate the findings of the M1C models from Study 1. It is unclear if this is an artifact of the difference in study designs, the low n, or actually reflective of the quality or generalizability of the measure. Although we cannot conclusively state that prior behavior predicted future behavior during study 2, the data do suggest that prior behavior was a better predictor than DTI.

6.3   Study 3

Study 3 offers more intriguing results than the two earlier experiments. DTI did predict future behavior, however, it was negatively correlated. In other words, participants that scored higher on DTI were less likely to comply with the robot's recommendations over the course of the experiment (see column (2) in Tables 9, 11, and 13). The model fits suggest that a 1 unit higher score on the DTI measure would predict about 5% *less* compliance, roughly the same as ignoring the robot's advice for two buildings more than the average participant. This effect reverberates in the F test: Model (2) accounts for significantly more variance than Model (1), thus we reject the null hypothesis when predicting compliance for buildings 2:45 ($F = 8.885$, $p = 0.003$) as well as the shorter horizon 9:45 ($F = 9.732$, $p = 0.002$).

The models also suggest that the FC, AFM, and AC-AFM measures were effective means of predicting future compliance behavior. Participants who complied during the first interaction complied nearly 12% more for the remaining missions (column (3) of Table 9). A similar effect was observed when using the first compliance decision after the robot's first mistake (AFM, in which case compliant participants were nearly 19% more compliant during remaining missions; column (3) of Table 11) and when using the average compliance through the first compliance decision after the robot's first mistake (AC-AFM, in which case the model suggests a roughly 31% difference in future compliance between participants that were perfectly non-compliant versus perfectly compliant; column (3) of Table 13).

In the case of the models including both DTI and past behavioral measures, for Study 3, we actually reject the null hypothesis that including DTI does not contribute to the models with just behavioral measures (AF: $F = 8.985$, $p = 0.003$, AFM:$F = 8.267$, $p = 0.005$, AC-AFM: $F = 9.046$, $p = 0.003$). Importantly, the predicted effect of DTI remains negatively correlated with compliance and with about the same impact. Summarily, the models we present over these three studies offer two insights: First, past compliance behavior, even in its simplest form, is a more reliable, consistent predictor of future compliance, and second, DTI is not as reliable and may even hold an inverse correlation from what is hypothesized in the literature.

6.4 An Alternative Explanation

McKnight et al. [23] specifically state that DTI should be positively correlated with early compliance, not necessarily overall compliance. It is possible that DTI does actually predict a participant's first compliance choice (FC). This means that, rather than comparing FC and DTI, DTI should be employed to predict FC. We tested this hypothesis using multiple linear regression for each study and report the results in Table 15. We also included treatment condition controls in each model; as in the other tables, their presence is indicated by the checkmarks and the associated coefficient values and intercepts are redacted as a simplification. Summarily, DTI did not significantly predict participants' first compliance choice in any of the studies. We interpret this as strong evidence in support of the null hypothesis that DTI is not correlated with early compliance choices. We also expanded the definition of early compliance to include the first five compliance choices; however, the result persisted so we did not include the results as an additional table.

7 Discussion

Our review and empirical evaluation of past research that employed the Disposition to Trust Inventory led us to conclude that DTI is not an accurate predictor of compliance in human-AI interactions. Data from three prior experiments support this conclusion. Additionally, the basic method that we employ can serve as a prototype for evaluating other instruments.

Across the studies from which we drew data, the robots did significantly better than chance at predicting when protective gear is needed (e.g., even the low-ability robot is 80% reliable). This means that compliance was highly correlated with mission success. Just as early compliance behavior predicts later compliance, the data also suggest that it can predict success. Drawing conclusions from this, of course, is problematic because it is an artifact of the correlation. We believe that a more robust study of early behavior and its relationship to later compliance is warranted. A deep understanding of this relationship may prove useful in the design of compliance interventions, even if it is not applicable in every situation (one-shot interactions, obviously, cannot benefit from early behavior insights).

Had DTI accounted for more significant variance in the models, we could have tested whether it captured variance explained by the future behavior measures and vice versa. Unfortunately, the datasets at our disposal simply did not allow for such analyses. Larger datasets, possibly from different settings in which DTI has more predictive value, may allow researchers to differentiate the factors captured by each measure that weigh on compliance.

It is worth acknowledging that trust and compliance are not perfectly aligned concepts. In the HCI and HRI spaces, it is common to reference Lee and See's definition of trust: *the attitude that an agent will help achieve an individual's goals in a situation characterized by uncertainty and vulnerability* (p. 51 [21]). This simple definition belies a very complex phenomenon of human cognition: the attitudes that people form about subjects and their properties. On the other hand, compliance is relatively simple: did a person (appropriately) follow the advice given by an automated system? The hypothesis present in much of the literature on trust and compliance is that humans maintain a specific, identifiable, attitude (trust) that has broad applications, including predicting compliance, with respect to automated systems and their myriad properties. Moreover, the hypothesis posits that this attitude is easily measured using short batteries of questions, such as DTI. Generally speaking, the attitudes that humans maintain are notoriously hard to study—we argue that this feature of attitudes leaves such approaches prone to failure, particularly when the behavior of interest is not directly linked to a given measure.

In the experiments from which we drew data, the robot is the assumed subject, and its reliability in predicting dangers is the implied property of interest. In order for the standard hypothesis to find support, the following items, minimally, need to hold:

- The disposition to trust hypothesis that, to some measurable degree, trust is a trait-like aspect of cognition.
- Disposition to trust is accurately measured via an inventory such as DTI.
- Disposition to trust universally maps to subjects and their properties, i.e. there are no exceptional cases or variables that mediate or moderate the relationship.
- Compliance is positively correlated with disposition to trust.

If any of these do not hold, we would expect DTI to underperform or even fail as a predictor of compliance, which is exactly what we observed. Unfortunately, the available data do not allow us to further investigate in what sense we reject the standard hypothesis.

Lee and See point out that trust is a multidimensional construct and even state that, "There does not seem to be a reliable relationship between global and specific trust...Developing a high degree of functional specificity in the trust of automation may require specific information for each level of detail of the automation." (p. 58 [21]). This insight alone, which is supported by extensive research in cognitive science, seems to undermine the first, second, and third items above. These three items are further eroded with the acknowledgment that the thoughts and attitudes which people maintain towards different subjects have long been topics of scientific inquiry that are known for their recalcitrance to consensus. Notable philosophical efforts to tame them dot history. From Aristotle's efforts in *On Interpretation* [39] to Daniel Dennett's *The Intentional Stance* [12] and Ruth Millikan's biosemantics [25] there are many laudable attempts. Nevertheless, open questions remain about what it means to have an attitude toward a subject. Modern psychology is similarly plagued: although Brentano, who heavily influence the German tradition of empirical psychology from Sigmund Freud on through Bertrand Russell, attempted to corral the subject with his work on intentionality [9], it is still a hotly debated matter [10].

The last item, that compliance is positively correlated with trust, is similarly fraught. The recent pandemic serves as a convenient case study: Trusting stances were found to have a significant positive correlation with European citizens' compliance with government policies during the early pandemic [7], however, in Singapore, despite general trust in the government, compliance was poor even with efforts from the government to change citizens' risk perceptions [47]. Together, these findings call into question the reliability of compliance's correlation with trust. Summarily, with the addition of our analyses, we believe that the standard hypothesis fails on multiple fronts: it is simultaneously too broad given its reliance on a trust-like trait, and too specific in its ignorance of important confounds.

Nevertheless, there may still be value in measures such as DTI, particularly when they are shown to have predictive value (no matter the directionality of the correlation). If a measure reliably accounts for variance in human behavior, it has value in developing automated systems since explaining variance is core to predicting choices. As far as we are aware, our analyses do not refute the findings of any human-AI interaction paper. Our key takeaway is that we should not only vet our measures with thorough literature reviews but also validate them for the specific modeling that is required for human-AI interaction domains.

Our overall recommendations for the community are:

- **Validate psychometric measures adopted from other disciplines for your specific model and outcome measure.** Additionally, as pointed out by [36], using a single item (or some subset of items) from a Likert scale undermines its original reliability and validation.
- **Consider alternative, simple measures that may already exist in your data.** These measures do not necessarily need to replace others but can serve as valuable companions and provide more robust inference.
- **Evaluate the usefulness of new measures against alternatives.** The statistical work put into understanding the ways in which different measures account for variance in data not only ensures a more rigorous examination of these alternate causes but also can produce new insights and drive new modeling formulations.

It would be uncanny if the effects that we observed in the data are unique to DTI, trust, and compliance. It seems highly probable that similar effects exist for other mental states that humans maintain towards automated systems, such as anger, belief, fear, hope, etc., and their affiliated outcomes. For example, extensive research suggests that negative attitudes towards robots can be highly predictive of interactions and outcomes [27, 28]. We would hypothesize that, just as early compliance is a better predictor of later compliance than DTI, there are behavioral measures that can outperform and/or are less intrusive than the negative attitudes towards robots instruments. Identifying, testing, and validating such measures, we believe, will prove a critical step towards improving relationships between humans and all types of automated systems, from recommender to robot.

8   Conclusion

Inventories measuring different psychological constructs are popular for informing models in human-AI interaction and are frequently misused [36]. In this
paper, we evaluated the usage of one such measure. This measure was used in
prior research in hopes that it would predict important human behaviors, like
compliance, and overall outcomes, like task performance. The measure failed in
two experiments and had the opposite correlation predicted by the measures'
creators in a third. We found that a simple behavioral measure was a better
predictor of future compliance and would thus be a more informative input to a
model of compliance reasoning. The methodology used here to evaluate the two
measures is a straightforward prototype for other researchers to use in evaluating
alternate measures that can serve as input into models in human-AI interaction.

Appendix A   Figures

Benevolence
1. In general, people really do care about the well-being of others.
2. The typical person is sincerely concerned about the problems of others.
3. Most of the time, people care enough to try to be helpful, rather than
   just looking out
   for themselves.

Integrity
1. In general, most folks keep their promises.
2. I think people generally try to back up their words with their actions.
3. Most people are honest in their dealings with others.

Competence
1. I believe that most professional people do a very good job at their
   work.
2. Most professionals are very knowledgeable in their chosen field.
3. A large majority of professional people are competent in their area of
   expertise.

Trusting Stance
1. I usually trust people until they give me a reason not to trust them.
2. I generally give people the benefit of the doubt when I first meet them.
3. My typical approach is to trust new acquaintances until they prove I
   should not trust them.

Fig. 1. Disposition to Trust Inventory Items

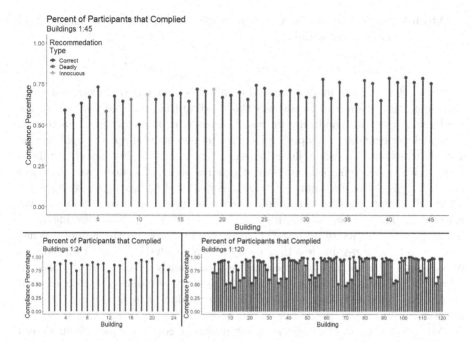

Fig. 2. The robot only communicated differently in study 3—it always made the same mistakes, in the same order. These features mean that the data lend themselves to concise, straightforward visual representation, which we present in the top panel. Note that the colors in this panel indicate the robot's recommendation type. Specifically, the robot made two deadly and three innocuous mistakes which are highlighted above. Overall, there is a trend of increasing compliance. The figures for studies 1 and 2, which are respectively the bottom left and right panels, only indicate compliance percentage, not the type of recommendations made by the robot.

Appendix B   Data and Models

B.1   Models

We used linear regression to model and test the predictive value of the various behavioral measures. The basic approach is to fit a reference model (**Model 1**) in which the outcome measure, future behavior, is predicted by the treatment conditions alone, such as:

$$Y_{iFB} = \beta_0 + \beta_{\text{Treat}} X_{\text{iTreat}} + \epsilon_i \tag{1}$$

We use this general form for the reference (null) model across the experiments. Note that there are different *FB* measures; which one is used in a given set of models depends on the independent variable in question. A given reference and test model, however, always use the same dependent variable.

Model 2: The first category of test models incorporate participants' DTI score as an independent variable:

$$Y_{iFB} = \beta_0 + \beta_{\text{Treat}} X_{i\text{Treat}} + \beta_{\text{DTI}} X_{i\text{DTI}} + \epsilon_i \tag{2}$$

Note that the reference model is nested within this model. In other words, Eq. (2) represents the alternative hypothesis that adding the predictor variable to the model will result in accounting for more variance, or a significant improvement in model performance. Comparing the two models is as simple as applying an F-test, which in this case tells us whether the more complex model results in a statistically different residual sum of squares value. If it does, we can reject the null hypothesis, i.e. that the reference model is sufficient, in favor of the alternative hypothesis, or that adding the additional predictor variable(s) was warranted. The F-test, in this instance, can be thought of as allowing us to investigate the utility of adding DTI or other measures to the model.[2] When this test returns a p-value less than 0.05, we can conclude that the residual sum of squares values for the two models are significantly different at the level of $\alpha = 0.05$, or in other words, the new explanatory variable is warranted as it significantly increases the amount of variance explained in the model (i.e. RSS is lower).

Model 3: The next category of test models incorporate participants' past behavior as independent variables, for example, the model:

$$Y_{iFB} = \beta_0 + \beta_{\text{Treat}} X_{i\text{Treat}} + \beta_{\text{FC}} X_{i\text{FC}} + \epsilon_i \tag{3}$$

This uses participants' first choice to predict their compliance for all of the remaining choices that they faced. Again, this has the reference model embedded in it, and a simple F-test will reveal the utility of the FC predictor. We construct similar models for M1C, AFM, and AC-AFM (but using appropriate FB measures).

Model 4: Since it is likely that DTI and the past behavior measures are accounting for different variance in the models, directly comparing equations (2) and (3) via R^2 is not entirely informative. Thus, we introduce a third category of test models in which both DTI and a past behavior measure are included. In the case of FC, the model is:

$$Y_{iFB} = \beta_0 + \beta_{\text{Treat}} X_{i\text{Treat}} + \beta_{\text{DTI}} X_{i\text{DTI}} + \beta_{\text{FC}} X_{i\text{FC}} + \epsilon_i \tag{4}$$

These models facilitate assessing whether the added complexity of including both DTI and the past behavior measure is warranted, again using F-tests. Finally, for readability, we refer to relevant statistics within the text of the manuscript but place regression and other tables for each set of models and their associated tests in the appendix. These tables include, in the same order as above, models that facilitate comparing DTI and the behavioral measures. Each regression table is followed by a table presenting the results of the relevant F-tests.

---

[2] A likelihood ratio test is another method of comparing such models and will produce similar insights.

B.2   Data

We used data from experiments conducted as part of a long-term research project on explainability and AI. Participants of these experiments team with a simulated robot during reconnaissance missions. The missions involve entering buildings to determine whether threats are present. The robot goes first and is equipped with a camera, microphone, and sensors for nuclear, biological, and chemical threats. These sensors are not perfectly reliable. Based on the data that it collects using its sensors, the robot makes a recommendation to the participant about putting on protective gear. The participant then makes a choice about wearing the gear, i.e., whether or not to comply with the robot's recommendation. When participants wear the gear, it always neutralizes any threat. If they do not wear it and encounter a threat, they die in the virtual world, but in reality, incur a prohibitive time penalty. Finally, participants incur a slight time delay (much smaller than that for death in the virtual world) when equipping the gear.

In all three studies, the robot based its recommendations on the noisy sensor readings as input to a policy computed through either Partially Observable Markov Decision Processes (POMDPs) [19] or model-free reinforcement learning (RL) [20,40] using the reward signal of the time cost and deaths incurred. The robot performed significantly better than chance across the studies. This means that compliance from the participants was highly correlated with making the normative choice, i.e., wearing protective equipment at the right time.

Participants of all three studies completed the 12-item DTI before starting their assigned mission(s). Gross experimental details and the results of these conditions are reported in the original publications. As such, we do not replicate those findings here for brevity's sake. Do note, however, that the n's we report may vary from the original papers because of incomplete observations (some participants chose to not complete the DTI).

Study 1 participants ($n = 198$, Amazon Mechanical Turk) completed three missions, each with eight buildings [44]. They were randomly paired with one of two POMDP-based robot types: a high-ability robot that was never wrong or a low-ability robot that made mistakes 20% of the time (or was 80% reliable). Both types of robots were crossed with four different recommendation explanation conditions: none, confidence level, sensor readings version 1, and sensor readings version 2. This experiment was fully between subjects, meaning that each participant interacted with only one robot type and received only one type of explanation throughout the missions. The coefficient β_{Treat} in the models for Study 1 captures which information condition participants experienced. First compliance choice (FC) takes 1 if participants heeded the robot's recommendation for the first building and 0 if not. Mission 1 compliance (M1C), on the other hand, is the fraction of times that a participant complied with the robot's recommendations during the first mission. The compliance future behavior (FB) measure associated with FC for study one is thus the fraction of times a participant complied for the remaining 23 buildings. Similarly, for M1C it is the fraction of times that a participant complied with the robot's advice during missions two and three. It should be noted that participants were not told whether they were interacting with the same robot across missions; instead, the robot started each mission as if it had not previously interacted with a participant.

Study 2 participants ($n = 53$, cadets at West Point Academy) completed eight missions, each with a different POMDP-based robot [46]. In each mission, the human-robot team carried out a reconnaissance task of 15 buildings. The mission order was fixed (i.e., always searched the buildings in the same order and across missions), but the robot order was randomized. The $2 \times 2 \times 2$ design crossed robot acknowledgment of mistakes (none/acknowledge), recommendation explanation (none/confidence), and embodiment (robot-like/doglike). Unlike Study 1, participants interacted with different robots during each mission. Nevertheless, to demonstrate the robustness of the simple behavioral measures, we rely on the same first compliance choice (FC) as Study 1 and a similar mission 1 compliance (M1C). The compliance measures, obviously, cover a longer horizon: 119 missions and 105 missions, respectively. The β_{Treat} of the models for Study 2 data captures the robot type of *the first mission*. It is possible that ordering of robot advisors mattered; however, the data are insufficient to specify a hierarchical model that would uncover such a feature.

Study 3 participants ($n = 148$, Amazon Mechanical Turk) completed one mission that covered 45 buildings with an RL-based (RL: reinforcement learning) robot in a fully between design [14,15,31]. The treatment conditions held the robot's ability constant but varied how it explained its recommendations: no explanation, explanation of decision, explanation of decision and learning. Again, the first compliance choice (FC) is the same as the previous two studies and the FC outcome measure is the compliance fraction for the remaining 44 buildings. Mission 1 compliance (M1C) is not applicable given that the entire experiment consisted of a single mission. Given that building order and robot performance were fixed across treatment conditions, however, the two additional compliance measures, choice after the first mistake (AFM) and average compliance through the first mistake (AC-AFM), become meaningful. The first mistake occurred during building six, thus participants' decision for building seven is the AFM measure and the fraction of times they complied during the first seven buildings is AC-AFM. Relatedly, the dependent variable is the fraction of times that a given participant complied during the remaining 38 buildings.

Appendix C   Tables

Table 1. Study 1 FC Models

	(1)	(2)	(3)	(4)
	Dependent variable: Compliance Percentage Buildings 2:24			
	Regression Models			
DTI		0.007		0.005
		(0.008)		(0.008)
FC			0.086**	0.084**
			(0.026)	(0.026)
Treatment Controls	✓	✓	✓	✓
Constant	0.762***	0.724***	0.687***	0.661***
	(0.032)	(0.052)	(0.038)	(0.054)
Observations	198	198	198	198
R^2	0.420	0.422	0.452	0.453
Adjusted R^2	0.398	0.398	0.429	0.427
Residual Std. Error	0.152 (df = 190)	0.152 (df = 189)	0.148 (df = 189)	0.148 (df = 188)
F Statistic	19.639*** (df = 7; 190)	17.273*** (df = 8; 189)	19.471*** (df = 8; 189)	17.307*** (df = 9; 188)

Note: $^*p<0.05$; $^{**}p<0.01$; $^{***}p<0.001$

Table 2. Study 1 FC Model Comparisons

Statistic	(1) Vs. (2)	(1) Vs. (3)	(2) Vs. (4)	(3) Vs. (4)
Sum of Sq	0.019	0.242	0.232	0.010
F	0.832	11.032	10.575	0.449
Pr(>F)	0.363	0.001	0.001	0.504

Table 3. Study 1 M1C Models

	(1)	(2)	(3)	(4)
	Dependent variable: Compliance Percentage Buildings 9:24			
	Regression Models			
DTI		0.003		−0.0004
		(0.009)		(0.008)
M1C			0.242***	0.243***
			(0.052)	(0.052)
Treatment Controls	✓	✓	✓	✓
Constant	0.770***	0.754***	0.587***	0.589***
	(0.035)	(0.058)	(0.052)	(0.066)
Observations	198	198	198	198
R^2	0.451	0.451	0.508	0.508
Adjusted R^2	0.431	0.428	0.487	0.484
Residual Std. Error	0.170 (df = 190)	0.170 (df = 189)	0.161 (df = 189)	0.161 (df = 188)
F Statistic	22.282*** (df = 7; 190)	19.421*** (df = 8; 189)	24.384*** (df = 8; 189)	21.561*** (df = 9; 188)

Note: $^*p<0.05$; $^{**}p<0.01$; $^{***}p<0.001$

Table 4. Study 1 M1C Model Comparisons

Statistic	(1) Vs. (2)	(1) Vs. (3)	(2) Vs. (4)	(3) Vs. (4)
Sum of Sq	0.003	0.568	0.565	<0.001
F	0.119	21.923	21.677	0.002
Pr(>F)	0.731	<0.001	<0.001	0.965

Table 5. Study 2 FC Models

	Dependent variable: Compliance Percentage Buildings 2:120			
	Regression Models			
	(1)	(2)	(3)	(4)
DTI		0.004		0.004
		(0.011)		(0.011)
FC			0.043*	0.043*
			(0.018)	(0.018)
Treatment Controls	✓	✓	✓	✓
Observations	49	49	49	49
R^2	0.047	0.050	0.163	0.165
Adjusted R^2	−0.016	−0.037	0.087	0.068
Residual Std. Error	0.053 (df = 45)	0.053 (df = 44)	0.050 (df = 44)	0.051 (df = 43)
F Statistic	0.742 (df = 3; 45)	0.574 (df = 4; 44)	2.137 (df = 4; 44)	1.704 (df = 5; 43)
Note:				*p<0.05; **p<0.01; ***p<0.001

Table 6. Study 2 FC Model Comparison

Statistic	(1) Vs. (2)	(1) Vs. (3)	(2) Vs. (4)	(3) Vs. (4)
Sum of Sq	<0.001	0.015	0.015	<0.001
F	0.112	6.071	5.964	0.137
Pr(> F)	0.739	0.017	0.019	0.713

Table 7. Study 2 M1C Models

	Dependent variable: Compliance Percentage Buildings 16:120			
	Regression Models			
	(1)	(2)	(3)	(4)
DTI		0.003		0.004
		(0.012)		(0.013)
M1C			−0.015	−0.016
			(0.067)	(0.068)
Treatment Controls	✓	✓	✓	✓
Observations	49	49	49	49
R^2	0.041	0.042	0.042	0.043
Adjusted R^2	−0.023	−0.045	−0.045	−0.068
Residual Std. Error	0.059 (df = 45)	0.060 (df = 44)	0.060 (df = 44)	0.060 (df = 43)
F Statistic	0.634 (df = 3; 45)	0.485 (df = 4; 44)	0.478 (df = 4; 44)	0.390 (df = 5; 43)
Note:				*p<0.05; **p<0.01; ***p<0.001

Table 8. Study 2 M1C Model Comparison

Statistic	(1) Vs. (2)	(1) Vs. (3)	(2) Vs. (4)	(3) Vs. (4)
Sum of Sq	<0.001	<0.001	<0.001	<0.001
F	0.076	0.051	0.054	0.078
Pr(> F)	0.785	0.822	0.818	0.782

Table 9. Study 3 FC Models

| | Dependent variable: Compliance Percentage Buildings 2:45 | | | |
| | | Regression Models | | |
	(1)	(2)	(3)	(4)
DTI		−0.052**		−0.050**
		(0.017)		(0.017)
FC			0.115***	0.112***
			(0.031)	(0.030)
Treatment Controls	✓	✓	✓	✓
Observations	148	148	148	148
R^2	0.040	0.096	0.125	0.177
Adjusted R^2	0.027	0.077	0.107	0.154
Residual Std. Error	0.193 (df = 145)	0.188 (df = 144)	0.185 (df = 144)	0.180 (df = 143)
F Statistic	3.011 (df = 2; 145)	5.078** (df = 3; 144)	6.850*** (df = 3; 144)	7.669*** (df = 4; 143)

Note: $^*p<0.05; ^{**}p<0.01; ^{***}p<0.001$

Table 10. Study 3 FC Model Comparison

Statistic	(1) Vs. (2)	(1) Vs. (3)	(2) Vs. (4)	(3) Vs. (4)
Sum of Sq	0.313	0.477	0.454	0.290
F	8.885	12.988	14.058	8.985
Pr(> F)	0.003	<0.001	<0.001	0.003

Table 11. Study 3 AFM Models

| | Dependent variable: Compliance Percentage Buildings 8:45 | | | |
| | | Regression Models | | |
	(1)	(2)	(3)	(4)
DTI		−0.056**		−0.047**
		(0.018)		(0.016)
AFM			0.187***	0.179***
			(0.032)	(0.032)
Treatment Controls	✓	✓	✓	✓
Observations	148	148	148	148
R^2	0.037	0.098	0.220	0.263
Adjusted R^2	0.024	0.080	0.204	0.242
Residual Std.Error	0.200 (df = 145)	0.194 (df = 144)	0.181 (df = 144)	0.176 (df = 143)
F Statistic	2.822 (df = 2; 145)	5.238** (df = 3; 144)	13.577*** (df = 3; 144)	12.763*** (df = 4; 143)

Note: $^*p<0.05; ^{**}p<0.01; ^{***}p<0.001$

Table 12. Study 3 AFM Model Comparison

Statistic	(1) Vs. (2)	(1) Vs. (3)	(2) Vs. (4)	(3) Vs. (4)
Sum of Sq	0.367	1.103	0.991	0.256
F	9.732	33.811	31.960	8.267
Pr(> F)	0.002	<0.001	<0.001	0.005

Table 13. Study 3 AC-AFM Models

	Dependent variable: Compliance Percentage Buildings 8:45			
		Regression Models		
	(1)	(2)	(3)	(4)
DTI		−0.056**		−0.049**
		(0.018)		(0.016)
AC-AFM			0.313***	0.301***
			(0.053)	(0.052)
Treatment Controls	✓	✓	✓	✓
Observations	148	148	148	148
R^2	0.037	0.098	0.223	0.269
Adjusted R^2	0.024	0.080	0.207	0.249
Residual Std. Error	0.200 (df = 145)	0.194 (df = 144)	0.180 (df = 144)	0.175 (df = 143)
F Statistic	2.822 (df = 2; 145)	5.238** (df = 3; 144)	13.767*** (df = 3; 144)	13.164*** (df = 4; 143)

Note: $^{*}p<0.05;$ $^{**}p<0.01;$ $^{***}p<0.001$

Table 14. Study 3 AC-AFM Model Comparison

Statistic	(1) Vs. (2)	(1) Vs. (3)	(2) Vs. (4)	(3) Vs. (4)
Sum of Sq	0.367	1.116	1.028	0.278
F	9.732	34.359	33.403	9.046
Pr(> F)	0.002	<0.001	<0.001	0.003

Table 15. DTI as a Predictor of First Compliance Choice

	Dependent variable: First Choice		
	Regression Models		
	Study 1	Study 2	Study3
DTI	0.024	0.002	−0.017
	(0.021)	(0.092)	(0.047)
Controls	✓	✓	✓
Observations	198	48	148
R^2	0.062	0.145	0.003
Adjusted R^2	0.022	0.065	−0.018
Residual Std. Error	0.415	0.434	0.499
	(df = 189)	(df = 43)	(df = 144)
F Statistic	1.562	1.820	0.141
	(df = 8; 189)	(df = 4; 43)	(df = 3; 144)

Note: $^{*}p<0.1;$ $^{**}p<0.05;$ $^{***}p<0.01$

References

1. Ajzen, I.: The theory of planned behavior. Organ. Behav. Hum. Decis. Process. **50**(2), 179–211 (1991)
2. Aliasghari, P., Ghafurian, M., Nehaniv, C.L., Dautenhahn, K.: Effect of domestic trainee robots' errors on human teachers' trust. In: Proceedings of the IEEE International Conference on Robot & Human Interactive Communication (RO-MAN), pp. 81–88. IEEE (2021)
3. Aliasghari, P., Ghafurian, M., Nehaniv, C.L., Dautenhahn, K.: How do different modes of verbal expressiveness of a student robot making errors impact human teachers' intention to use the robot? In: Proceedings of the 9th International Conference on Human-Agent Interaction, pp. 21–30 (2021)
4. Amershi, S., et al.: Guidelines for human-AI interaction. In: Proceedings of the 2019 CHI Conference on Human Factors in Computing Systems, pp. 1–13 (2019)
5. Aroyo, A.M., Rea, F., Sandini, G., Sciutti, A.: Trust and social engineering in human robot interaction: will a robot make you disclose sensitive information, conform to its recommendations or gamble? IEEE Robot. Autom. Lett. **3**(4), 3701–3708 (2018)
6. Ashleigh, M.J., Higgs, M., Dulewicz, V.: A new propensity to trust scale and its relationship with individual well-being: implications for HRM policies and practices. Hum. Resour. Manage. J. **22**(4), 360–376 (2012)
7. Bargain, O., Aminjonov, U.: Trust and compliance to public health policies in times of covid-19. J. Publ. Econ. **192**, 104316 (2020)
8. Barnes, M.J., Wang, N., Pynadath, D.V., Chen, J.Y.: Human-agent bidirectional transparency. In: Trust in Human-Robot Interaction, pp. 209–232. Elsevier (2021)
9. Brentano, F.: Psychology from an Empirical Standpoint. Routledge, Milton Park (2012)
10. Chater, N., Zeitoun, H., Melkonyan, T.: The paradox of social interaction: shared intentionality, we-reasoning, and virtual bargaining. Psychol. Rev. **129**(3), 415 (2022)
11. Chi, O.H., Jia, S., Li, Y., Gursoy, D.: Developing a formative scale to measure consumers' trust toward interaction with artificially intelligent (AI) social robots in service delivery. Comput. Hum. Behav. **118**, 106700 (2021)
12. Dennett, D.C.: The Intentional Stance. MIT press, Cambridge (1987)
13. Elliot, J.: Artificial social intelligence for successful teams (ASIST) (2021). www.darpa.mil/program/artificial-social-intelligence-for-successful-teams
14. Gurney, N., Pynadath, D., Wang, N.: My actions speak louder than your words: when user behavior predicts their beliefs about agents' attributes. arXiv preprint arXiv:2301.09011 (2023)
15. Gurney, N., Pynadath, D.V., Wang, N.: Measuring and predicting human trust in recommendations from an AI teammate. In: International Conference on Human-Computer Interaction, pp. 22–34. Springer (2022). https://doi.org/10.1007/978-3-031-05643-7_2
16. Hancock, P.A., Billings, D.R., Schaefer, K.E., Chen, J.Y., De Visser, E.J., Parasuraman, R.: A meta-analysis of factors affecting trust in human-robot interaction. Hum. Factors **53**(5), 517–527 (2011)
17. Hoff, K.A., Bashir, M.: Trust in automation: integrating empirical evidence on factors that influence trust. Hum. Factors **57**(3), 407–434 (2015)
18. Jessup, S.A., Schneider, T.R., Alarcon, G.M., Ryan, T.J., Capiola, A.: The measurement of the propensity to trust automation. In: Chen, J.Y.C., Fragomeni, G.

(eds.) HCII 2019. LNCS, vol. 11575, pp. 476–489. Springer, Cham (2019). https://doi.org/10.1007/978-3-030-21565-1_32

19. Kaelbling, L.P., Littman, M.L., Cassandra, A.R.: Planning and acting in partially observable stochastic domains. Artif. Intell. **101**(1), 99–134 (1998)

20. Kaelbling, L.P., Littman, M.L., Moore, A.W.: Reinforcement learning: a survey. J. Artif. Intell. Res. **4**, 237–285 (1996)

21. Lee, J.D., See, K.A.: Trust in automation: designing for appropriate reliance. Hum. Factors **46**(1), 50–80 (2004)

22. Lutz, C., Tamó-Larrieux, A.: The robot privacy paradox: understanding how privacy concerns shape intentions to use social robots. Hum. Mach. Commun. **1**, 87–111 (2020)

23. McKnight, D.H., Choudhury, V., Kacmar, C.: Developing and validating trust measures for e-commerce: an integrative typology. Inf. Syst. Res. **13**(3), 334–359 (2002)

24. Merritt, S.M., Huber, K., LaChapell-Unnerstall, J., Lee, D.: Continuous Calibration of Trust in Automated Systems. MISSOURI UNIV-ST LOUIS, Tech. rep. (2014)

25. Millikan, R.G.: Biosemantics. J. Philos. **86**(6), 281–297 (1989)

26. Mischel, W.: Personality and Assessment. Psychology Press, London (2013)

27. Nomura, T., Kanda, T., Suzuki, T.: Experimental investigation into influence of negative attitudes toward robots on human-robot interaction. AI Soc. **20**(2), 138–150 (2006)

28. Nomura, T., Suzuki, T., Kanda, T., Kato, K.: Measurement of negative attitudes toward robots. Interact. Stud. **7**(3), 437–454 (2006)

29. Ouellette, J.A., Wood, W.: Habit and intention in everyday life: the multiple processes by which past behavior predicts future behavior. Psychol. Bull. **124**(1), 54 (1998)

30. Parasuraman, R., Riley, V.: Humans and automation: use, misuse, disuse, abuse. Hum. Factors **39**(2), 230–253 (1997)

31. Pynadath, D.V., Gurney, N., Wang, N.: Explainable reinforcement learning in human-robot teams: the impact of decision-tree explanations on transparency. In: 2022 31st IEEE International Conference on Robot and Human Interactive Communication (RO-MAN), pp. 749–756. IEEE (2022)

32. Pynadath, D.V., Wang, N., Kamireddy, S.: A markovian method for predicting trust behavior in human-agent interaction. In: Proceedings of the 7th International Conference on Human-Agent Interaction, pp. 171–178 (2019)

33. Rossi, A., Dautenhahn, K., Koay, K.L., Walters, M.L.: The impact of peoples' personal dispositions and personalities on their trust of robots in an emergency scenario. Paladyn J. Behav. Robot. **9**(1), 137–154 (2018)

34. Rossi, A., Dautenhahn, K., Koay, K.L., Walters, M.L., Holthaus, P.: Evaluating people's perceptions of trust in a robot in a repeated interactions study. In: Wagner, A.R. (ed.) ICSR 2020. LNCS (LNAI), vol. 12483, pp. 453–465. Springer, Cham (2020). https://doi.org/10.1007/978-3-030-62056-1_38

35. Schaefer, K.: The perception and measurement of human-robot trust (2013). stars.library.ucf.edu/etd/2688

36. Schrum, M.L., Johnson, M., Ghuy, M., Gombolay, M.C.: Four years in review: statistical practices of likert scales in human-robot interaction studies. In: Companion of the 2020 ACM/IEEE International Conference on Human-Robot Interaction, pp. 43–52 (2020)

37. Seeber, I., et al.: Machines as teammates: a research agenda on AI in team collaboration. Inf. Manage. **57**(2), 103174 (2020)

38. Shneiderman, B.: Human-centered artificial intelligence: reliable, safe & trustworthy. Int. J. Hum. Comput. Interact. **36**(6), 495–504 (2020)
39. Stevenson, D.C.: The internet classics archive: on interpretation by aristotle (2009). https://classics.mit.edu/Aristotle/interpretation. htmlclassics.mit.edu/Aristotle/interpretation.html
40. Sutton, R.S., Barto, A.G.: Reinforcement Learning: An Introduction. MIT press, Cambridge (2018)
41. Tauchert, C., Mesbah, N., et al.: Following the robot? Investigating users' utilization of advice from robo-advisors. In: Proceedings of the International Conference on Information Systems (2019)
42. Textor, C., Pak, R.: Paying attention to trust: Exploring the relationship between attention control and trust in automation. In: Proceedings of the Human Factors and Ergonomics Society Annual Meeting. vol. 65 no. 1, pp. 817–821. SAGE Publications Sage CA: Los Angeles, CA (2021)
43. Venkatesh, V.: Determinants of perceived ease of use: integrating control, intrinsic motivation, and emotion into the technology acceptance model. Inf. Syst. Res. **11**(4), 342–365 (2000)
44. Wang, N., Pynadath, D.V., Hill, S.G.: The impact of POMDP-generated explanations on trust and performance in human-robot teams. In: Proceedings of the 2016 International Conference on Autonomous Agents & Multiagent Systems, pp. 997–1005 (2016)
45. Wang, N., Pynadath, D.V., Hill, S.G.: Trust calibration within a human-robot team: Comparing automatically generated explanations. In: 2016 11th ACM/IEEE International Conference on Human-Robot Interaction (HRI), pp. 109–116. IEEE (2016)
46. Wang, N., Pynadath, D.V., Rovira, E., Barnes, M.J., Hill, S.G.: Is It My Looks? Or Something I Said? The impact of explanations, embodiment, and expectations on trust and performance in human-robot teams. In: Ham, J., Karapanos, E., Morita, P.P., Burns, C.M. (eds.) PERSUASIVE 2018. LNCS, vol. 10809, pp. 56–69. Springer, Cham (2018). https://doi.org/10.1007/978-3-319-78978-1_5
47. Wong, C.M.L., Jensen, O.: The paradox of trust: perceived risk and public compliance during the COVID-19 pandemic in Singapore. J. Risk Res. **23**(7–8), 1021–1030 (2020)
48. Xu, A., Dudek, G.: OPTIMo: online probabilistic trust inference model for asymmetric human-robot collaborations. In: 2015 10th ACM/IEEE International Conference on Human-Robot Interaction (HRI), pp. 221–228. IEEE (2015)
49. Yagoda, R.E., Gillan, D.J.: You want me to trust a robot? The development of a human-robot interaction trust scale. Int. J. Soc. Robot. **4**(3), 235–248 (2012)

Kindness Makes You Happy and Happiness Makes You Healthy: Actual Persuasiveness and Personalisation of Persuasive Messages in a Behaviour Change Intervention for Wellbeing

Ana Ciocarlan[1]([✉]) [iD], Judith Masthoff[2] [iD], and Nir Oren[1] [iD]

[1] University of Aberdeen, Aberdeen, UK
{a.ciocarlan,n.oren}@abdn.ac.uk
[2] Utrecht University, Utrecht, The Netherlands
j.f.m.masthoff@uu.nl

Abstract. Happiness, or subjective wellbeing, brings lasting positive effects to individuals, communities, and societies. Intentional engagement in kind behaviours can have a significant effect on increasing and sustaining subjective wellbeing in humans. In this paper we investigate the effectiveness of a behaviour change intervention for kindness and subjective wellbeing. Using decision tree learning and training data on personality and susceptibility to Cialdini's persuasive principles, we developed a machine learning model to predict the most effective persuasive principle for an individual. We conducted a randomised controlled experiment to evaluate two interventions (personalised and non-personalised) to motivate kind behaviours. The results indicate that personalised persuasive messages are more effective at stimulating kind behaviours. However, both interventions were effective at improving behavioural intention and subjective wellbeing. These findings have implications for future work on personalisation and design of adaptive behaviour change interventions.

Keywords: persuasive technology · behaviour change · personalisation · adaptation · decision tree learning · wellbeing · kindness

1 Introduction

Happiness has intrigued researchers for millennia. Evidence in the literature shows that happiness brings lasting positive effects to individuals and the societies they live in [40], spanning across a multitude of life dimensions, including mental and physical health [6,15,18,23,32], work productivity and performance [17,25,48,53], social relationships [35,44], and life expectancy [9].

J. Ham et al. (Eds.): PERSUASIVE 2023, LNCS 13832, pp. 198–214, 2023.
https://doi.org/10.1007/978-3-031-30933-5_13

Experiencing positive affect may support humans to broaden their skills and resources, by inspiring exploratory thinking and responses, whilst experiencing negative affect prompts survival-oriented behaviours [22]. As a result, happy people are more likely to engage in healthy behaviours, which, in turn, influence their mental and physical health. They are more likely to respond positively to exercise and have healthier diets (e.g. [5,54]), and they have a lower risk of heart disease and are less susceptible to viral infections [15,18]. In addition, happy individuals engage in more social activities and build stronger friendships [35,44], which helps them handle challenging situations better [2]. They use positive strategies in times of adversity and develop psychological resilience [56].

The wide range of benefits associated with increased subjective wellbeing motivates research of interventions that contribute to increasing and sustaining happiness [35,55]. Recently, multiple studies have shown a strong relation between happiness and intentional engagement in kind activities [7,59]. In this paper we investigate and compare the effectiveness of two behaviour change interventions (personalised and non-personalised) to encourage kind behaviours, improve behavioural intention, and increase subjective wellbeing. To personalise persuasive messages, we used decision tree learning and training data on personality and susceptibility to Cialdini's persuasive principles [10,11] to develop a machine learning model that predicts the most effective persuasive principle for an individual. The findings have implications for future work on personalisation of behaviour change interventions for wellbeing. Our methodology can be applied to other domains to develop effective personalised interventions based on personality traits and susceptibility to persuasive principles.

2 Related Work

Persuasive technologies and behaviour change interventions can encourage, shape, and reinforce beneficial behaviours and attitudes [20]. Numerous persuasive interventions have been developed in recent years. Some of the targeted behaviours include motivating physical activity [30,41], nutrition and healthy eating [26,45,62,63], encouraging safe driving habits [8], or promoting sustainable travel behaviours [1,21]. There is growing evidence showing that interventions that encourage intentional engagement in kind activities such as writing letters of gratitude [34], practicing optimism [31], or performing acts of kindness and generosity [19,37,51], can significantly increase subjective wellbeing [7,59]. Behaviour change interventions for kindness and subjective wellbeing may have a greater impact than the sole provision of activities.

Gaining an understanding of the actual persuasiveness of different persuasive principles strategies is essential in optimising behaviour change. A large number of studies have focused on measuring *perceived* persuasiveness [47,50,60,65]. Several scales for perceived persuasiveness have been developed and validated (e.g. [27,61]). However, a study across 151 message pairs showed that there was no relation between how messages ranked when measuring perceived persuasiveness and actual persuasiveness [43]. People may not be able to distinguish the influence different factors have on behaviour due to their existing beliefs and theories which offer credible alternative justifications [42]. Measuring perceived persuasiveness can be reliable for predicting actual persuasiveness only when individuals have accurate conceptions of persuasion theories, so pre-testing for actual effectiveness is recommended [43].

However, measuring actual persuasiveness is a challenging endeavour and only a limited number of studies investigate actual persuasiveness (e.g. [8,14,29, 64]). For example, an intervention that encourages healthy eating habits may require comprehensive food and drink intake diaries. This task is intensively time consuming and has sometimes proved to be unreliable [16]. It may also be difficult to recruit a large number of participants from a target population (e.g. interventions which encourage help-seeking among people with depression [58], or persuasive reminders for skin cancer patients [60]). In addition, the number of strategies that need to be evaluated could be too large [4]. Other circumstantial or environmental factors may also contribute to the increased challenge (e.g. the effectiveness of interventions for sustainable mobility may be influenced by weather conditions or seasons [1]). Therefore, further investigation into actual persuasiveness is required to support the design of effective interventions.

In addition, personalisation contributes to increased overall effectiveness of interventions and adherence [3,27,28,38]. Many persuasive technologies use a general design, applying the same behaviour change techniques for everyone. However, this increases the risk of creating strong adverse responses if unsuitable strategies are applied [45]. Several efforts have been directed towards researching personalised interventions across a multitude of domains. Researchers have investigated perceived persuasiveness in different cultural communities [46,49] and studied the effect of age, gender, and personality [47,50,64,66]. However, further investigation is required to optimise personalisation and predict susceptibility to persuasive strategies given different individual or group characteristics.

3   Research Design and Methods

We conducted a randomised controlled experiment to evaluate two digital behaviour change interventions (personalised and non-personalised) that used persuasive messages to encourage kind behaviours. Participants were assigned 15 kind activities and asked to complete as many activities as possible within one day. The messages used Cialdini's principles to encourage participants to complete all the activities. In the personalised condition, participants received a personalised message using the persuasive principle predicted to be the most effective for them. In the non-personalised condition participants received a message using a randomly selected persuasive principle (excluding the one predicted to be the most effective for them). Participants completed a pre-questionnaire and a post-questionnaire one week after taking part in the intervention. This enabled us to evaluate changes in behavioural intention and subjective wellbeing.

3.1 Research Questions

The study was guided by the following research questions:

1. How effective are the persuasive messages in motivating kind behaviours?
2. What is the effect of the interventions on behavioural intention?
3. What is the effect of the interventions on subjective wellbeing?

3.2 Materials

We designed and developed *Be Kind*, a digital behaviour change intervention for kindness. The design was based on related work described in [13]. However, we made adjustments to allow for personalisation and address limitations, such as changing the duration of the study, increasing the number and variety of assigned kind activities, and randomising activity order. The intervention asked participants to complete kind activities which promote subjective wellbeing. The activities were derived from a corpus of kind activities [12], validated to belong to one of five categories. Participants were assigned 15 kind activities to complete within one day: three activities belonging to each of the five categories. The order in which activities were displayed was randomised and participants were informed that they may complete activities in any order. The complete list of kind activities used in this study, grouped by category, is shown in Table 1.

The number of activities might seem very high, given participants had to incorporate these activities in their existing schedules. However, we wanted to ensure that participants are assigned a variety of activities to minimise any effects of a poor fit between individuals and activities. It is difficult to determine the optimal number of activities to assign, as this will depend both on individual and activity characteristics. The study described in [37] showed that individuals who complete 5 kind activities on one day show a higher increase in subjective wellbeing than those who spread the activities throughout the week. Evidence in the literature also indicates that people who complete varied kind activities each week show a higher increase in subjective wellbeing, compared to those who complete the same kind activities [57].

For personalisation, we developed a machine learning model to predict the most effective principle for individuals, given their personality traits. The resulting model was used during the account creation process to predict the most effective principle of persuasion for each participant in the study. The training data set used to build the model was sourced from related work described in [14], and consisted of 130 entries. The attributes were represented by continuous values for the scores of the Five Factor Model (FFM) personality traits [39]. The target value was represented by the most effective persuasive principle for each individual, as identified in the study. The findings in [14] indicated that actual persuasiveness is influenced by personality, and people's susceptibility to persuasive principles remains consistent over time. Gender and age were not included as attributes, since these were shown to be weak predictors of susceptibility.

Table 1. Kind activities used in the Be Kind study, grouped by activity categories

Category	Activities
Positivity	(1) Write an encouraging comment addressed to all the other participants of this study
	(2) Write a comment describing the positive qualities of the last person you encountered today
	(3) Hide a positive message in a public space for someone else to find. Write a comment to tell us about it.
Generosity	(1) Volunteer to help someone you know with a simple task. Write a comment about your experience
	(2) Learn to say "Have a beautiful day!" in a new language and teach someone else how to say it too. Write a comment to tell us which language you chose
	(3) Draw a simple portrait of a friend and gift them the drawing. Write a comment to share their reaction.
Gratitude	(1) Write a comment reflecting on 3 things you feel very grateful for today
	(2) Write a comment with an appreciation message for someone who has made a positive impact in your life
	(3) Say thank you to a friend who has been kind to you. Write a comment to tell us how you feel.
Friendliness	(FR1) Make plans to meet a friend and do a fun activity together in the next month. Write a comment to tell us your plan
	(2) Make an honest compliment to one of your friends. Write a comment to tell us about their reaction
	(3) Start a friendly conversation with someone you have not talked to recently. Write a comment to tell us about your interaction.
Self-Kindness	(1) Write a comment with a compliment for yourself. You deserve it!
	(2) Take a deep breath, stretch and relax for 5 min. Write a comment to let everyone know how you feel after!
	(3) Go on a short walk outside and notice everything that is beautiful around you. Write a comment to share your experience

We used the *decisiontree* 0.5.0 Ruby library[1] to implement the ID3 algorithm for decision tree learning [52]. This uses a top-down greedy approach to build a binary decision tree, partitioned by thresholds. The tree is trained with two thirds of the training data, resulting in a set of rules which are then pruned with the remaining third of the data. To avoid overfitting and reduce variance, the

---

[1] Source: https://rubygems.org/gems/decisiontree/versions/0.5.0.

algorithm uses a bagging-based trainer class, generating ten training sets before choosing the best output for predictions. The resulting model consisted of 76 rules to predict persuasive principles, given personality trait scores as input. We created messages which reflected Cialdini's seven persuasive principles. Participants in the personalised condition received the message predicted to be the most effective for them, given the scores of their personality traits. We predicted the most effective persuasive principle for participants in the random condition as well, and then excluded it as a possible message that could be assigned to them. Therefore, the participants in the random condition were assigned a random message from the remaining 6 messages. While some persuasive principles are more effective than others overall, we tried to minimise any possible influence of this by distributing messages that were randomly assigned in even proportions. The list of messages used in the study is shown in Table 2.

Table 2. Messages created using Cialdini's principles of persuasion

Principle	Message
Reciprocity	Hey, *current user*! We analysed your data and we picked these kind activities for you! Will you complete all the kind activities assigned to you?
Liking	Hey, *current user*! Analysing your data, you seem to be a very kind person and we really like you! Will you complete all the kind activities assigned to you?
Social Proof	Did you know that the majority of participants in this study complete ALL the kind activities? Will you complete all the kind activities assigned to you too?
Commitment	You are already performing a kind activity by helping the researchers with this study! Will you complete all the kind activities assigned to you?
Authority	Did you know that health experts recommend engaging in kind activities to improve wellebing? Will you complete all the kind activities assigned to you?
Scarcity	Today is your only chance to engage with the kind activities and other participants. Will you complete all the kind activities assigned to you?
Unity	Hey, *current user*! You are part of the group of participants who completed the most kind activities! Will you complete all the kind activities assigned to you?

3.3   Procedure

Ethical consent was obtained from the Physical Sciences and Engineering ethics board of University of Aberdeen. We provided participants with information and requested that they complete a consent form before they can take part in the study. Participants were informed that their participation is voluntary and that they may withdraw from the study at any given time, for any reason. All the materials and data were anonymised and stored securely.

Participants completed a brief demographics questionnaire. The Subjective Happiness Scale (SHS) [36] was used to measure the subjective wellbeing of the participants, while the TIPI [24] was used to determine their scores for the FFM personality traits. Participants were also asked to complete a behavioural intention questionnaire.

Participants were shown the randomised list of kind activities. After completing an activity, participants rated it, indicating how happy it made them feel, as well as how enjoyable, meaningful, and motivating they found it. This allowed us to measure the appreciation for each completed activity. In addition, participants could create comments and interact with others. A persuasive message was displayed for the duration of the study. Participants were not aware that they might see a different message than others. The intervention, as seen from an administrator view (i.e. excluding a personalised or randomly selected persuasive message), is shown in Fig. 1. After one week participants were invited to complete a follow-up questionnaire. To make observations regarding changes in subjective wellbeing and behavioural intention, participants were required to complete the SHS [36] and the behavioural intention scale again. In addition, participants were asked to provide qualitative comments on what motivated them to engage in kind activities and what their intentions are for engaging in future kind behaviours.

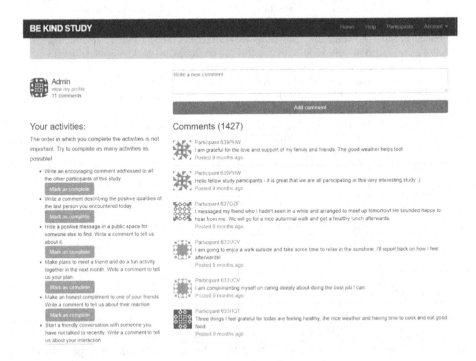

Fig. 1. Interface of the Be Kind behaviour change intervention

3.4   Participants

We recruited 234 unique participants, (140 females and 93 males, ages between 18 and 60 years old). Participants' geographical territories of origin were Europe (193 participants), Asia and Pacific (14 participants), Africa south of the Sahara (7 participants), the Middle East and North Africa (7 participants), North America (10 participants) and South America, Central America and the Caribbean (3 participants). A total of 89 additional participants created accounts, but never accessed the intervention. We excluded their data from the analysis, as they did not interact with the intervention. Out of the 234 participants, 67 returned after one week to complete the post-questionnaire. Participants were assigned randomly generated alphanumeric usernames to preserve anonymity. Participants were automatically assigned to, either the personalised condition (N = 124), or the non-personalised condition (N = 110), but they were not aware of this.

4   Results, Discussion, and Limitations

Participants completed a total of 1326 activities during the study and created 1121 comments, sharing their experiences, or writing encouragement and appreciation messages. This allowed us to observe behaviour directly, in addition to self-reporting. On average, participants completed 5.67 (std. dev. = 4.12) activities. While the average completion rate was only a third of the total activities assigned, this result is consequential, given participants only had one day to complete all of the activities and had to incorporate them into their existing schedule. The time and effort required for the activities was subjective. For example, a friendly conversation may require only a few minutes for certain individuals, but this time might increase considerably for others. Some participants indicated in their comments that they could not complete more activities due to time restrictions (e.g. Participant 676DJV: *"It took more time than I thought to do some activities"*). However, the average completion rate is higher than 5 activities in one day, which indicates there may be an influence on subjective wellbeing [37].

4.1   Influence of Persuasive Messages

Overall, the results indicate that personalised persuasive messages are more effective at encouraging kind behaviour than non-personalised messages. Participants in the personalised condition generally completed more kind activities than those in the random condition. An independent t-test was used on the data with a 95% confidence interval (CI) for the mean difference. We found a significant difference between the number of activities ($t(232) = 3.802$, $p<0.001$) with a mean difference of 2.00 (95% CI, 0.96 to 3.03). We found that the number of completed activities for the personalised condition (6.60 ± 4.16) was significantly higher than the number of activities completed by the participants in the random condition (4.61 ± 3.82). Figure 2 shows the percentage of activities completed out of the total activities assigned to participants for each persuasive principle in the two conditions. Participants in the personalised condition completed a higher percentage of activities, independent of the persuasive principle, than those in the random condition. This suggests that personalisation of persuasive principles plays a key role in the design of effective behaviour change interventions.

Comments in the post-questionnaire reflected the predictions made by model. For example, Reciprocity was predicted to be the most effective principle for Participant 586DZY and Participant 666HMP. When asked about future intentions, Participant 586DZY said: *"Next time someone is short on change (e.g., for a bus) I want to pay it forward because someone else paid my bus for me when I was traveling."*, while Participant 666HMP said: *"I wanted to give back for all the kindness I receive."*. The personalisation algorithm predicted the Commitment principle would be the most effective for Participant 726FKZ, who said: *"I wanted to complete the activities once I started the study"*. Similarly, the Social Proof principle was predicted for Participant 763LIA, who said: *"The spirit of those around me motivated to complete the activities"*.

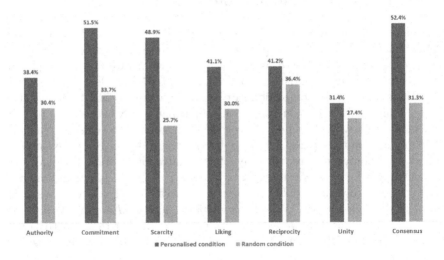

Fig. 2. Percentages of activities completed for each persuasive principle in the personalised and random conditions

4.2   Impact on Behavioural Intention

A paired samples t-test showed that behavioural post-intention was on average .653 higher than behavioural pre-intention (95% CI, .27 to 1.03). There was a significant difference between post-intention and pre-intention scores ($t(66) = 3.424$, $p<0.001$). Figure 3 shows the means of pre-intention and post-intention to perform kind activities in the personalised and random conditions. A pair comparison showed a significant difference in both conditions. However, calculating pair differences and using a t-test showed no significant difference between the personalised and random conditions. Behavioural intention increased regardless of the condition. In addition, we did not find a significant correlation between the total number of activities completed and post behavioural intention. This suggests that even completing a small number of kind activities may lead to increased behavioural intention. Taking part in the intervention and observing others engage in kind activities may act as a prompt or trigger for the participants, leading to changes in behaviour and intention. The results are shown in Table 3.

Table 3. Paired Samples test for behavioural pre-intention and post-intention in the personalised and random conditions

Condition	Mean (std. dev.)	t(df)	p	95%CI of difference
Personalised condition	.616 (±1.62)	t(36) = 2.309	<0.5	.07 to 1.15
Random condition	.700 (±1.51)	t(29) = 2.536	<0.05	.14 to 1.27

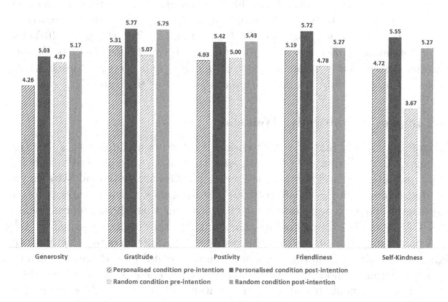

Fig. 3. Average pre-intention and post-intention in the personalised and random conditions

In the post-questionnaire participants wrote comments about their engagement in kind behaviours. Overall, participants enjoyed completing kind activities (e.g. Participant 666HMP: *"Thank you for this study. It made me gain hope."*; Participant 566WOG: *"This study was inspiring."*; Participant 705TVH: *"I thought it was a good motivator to make me reflect and act more on a few things.")*. Participants appreciated seeing others interact within the intervention (e.g. Participant 654VBA: *"I realised that I am surrounded by good people and I should appreciate them more."*; Participant 610WYU: *"I saw everyone posting comments, it felt like a little community")*. Participants indicated that they intend to continue engaging in kind behaviours in the future (e.g. Participant 569CSF: *"I will try to be a kinder person. It makes other people happy I hope, and it makes me happy too."*; Participant 602EIC: *"I want to perform acts of kindness every time I have the opportunity."*; Participant 633HQT: *"I would like to volunteer more and learn to observe and enjoy the good things around me."*; Participant 569SMZ: *"The world should be a little bit kinder, so I will do my best.")*. Participants expressed their intentions to be kinder towards those around them by being generous and supportive (e.g. Participant 598YSN: *"I'll try and be more attentive to my close friends and family."*; Participant 569HUD: *"I'll try and be more generous towards those around me.")*. Taking part in the intervention reminded participants to engage in kind behaviours, acting as a prompt for many who already had high motivation and ability (e.g. Participant 573WPQ: *"Sometimes it's easy to put kindness aside. It's good to be reminded."*; Participant 586DZY: *"Thanks for reminding me to be kinder.")*. Some participants expressed that they would have liked to complete more activities than they did (e.g. Participant 694EGP: *"I found the tasks very motivating. I wanted to complete more tasks, but didn't get to it unfortunately."*; Participant 646WON: *"I did not complete as many acts of kindness as I would have liked and this has made me aware that I focus too much of my time and energy on work, at the expense of those around me, some of whom I might be neglecting.")*.

4.3   Impact on Subjective Wellbeing

The results suggest that the intervention is effective at improving subjective wellbeing. A paired samples t-test was used to evaluate the subjective wellbeing before and after the intervention. A significant difference was found between the reported scores ($t(66) = 4.545$, $p<0.001$). Subjective wellbeing scores reported after the intervention were on average 0.526 higher than those reported before (95% CI, .29 to .76). These findings are similar to the results presented in [13].

A pair comparison showed that subjective wellbeing scores were significantly higher after taking part in the intervention in both conditions. However, calculating pair differences and using a t-test analysis showed no significant differences in between the personalised and random conditions. Participant subjective wellbeing improved, regardless of which condition they were assigned to. Nevertheless, participants in the personalised condition may have felt increased positive affect because they completed more kind activities than those in the random condition. A future study could investigate whether there is an effect of personalisation after a longer intervention which allows for habit formation. Table 4 shows the results.

Participants appreciated taking part in the intervention (e.g. Participant 586DZY: *"It made me happy and less focused on stressful things.")*. Some participants indicated that they intend to focus on their own wellbeing (e.g. Partic-

Table 4. Paired Samples test for subjective wellbeing before and after the intervention in the personalised and random conditions

Condition	Mean (std. dev.)	t(df)	p	95%CI of difference
Personalised condition	.405 (±.91)	t(36) = 2.699	<0.5	.10 to .70
Random condition	.675 (±.98)	t(29) = 3.761	<0.001	.30 to 1.04

ipant 661XNF: *"I'll pay more attention to myself also, I don't think I am getting enough rest."*; Participant 583FOA: *"Besides helping out people who are in need (because it's part of my work), I am willing and patient enough to listen to those who come to me with other non-work-related problems (whether I know something about it or to direct them to someone else). Paradoxically, helping myself always seems the hardest thing to do, and I realise it's important to do this in order to help others out, but I still don't find the motivation to do it easily. Hopefully, after getting on with some of the things from the study, I'll find it easier to pick up on that. Thank you."*).

4.4   Limitations

Observation of other participants may have had an effect on behaviour (e.g. Participant 683XNC: *"Seeing everyone so involved was very motivating."*). Environmental constraints may have also had an influence. For example, some participants might have been feeling less happy than usual (Participant 638CYX: *"I like the idea of being kind to everyone, in all circumstances. I think this is something we all should practice across spheres of life. I wish I could have had more time to perform all the activities that the study required, however I was going through a personally very challenging time."*). We found a weak positive correlation between subjective wellbeing measured before the intervention and the total activities participants completed (r = .139*, p <0.05, n = 234). Happy people actively seek rewarding situations [33], so they may engage in more activities

Using randomly assigned persuasive principles for the baseline may have also had an effect. Participants in the random condition (N = 110) completed an average of 4.61 ± 3.82 activities. Reciprocity might have provided a better non-personalised baseline, as this was the most common persuasive principle.[2] Participants in the random condition who were assigned Reciprocity (N = 15) completed an average of 5.47 ± 4.18 activities. However, participants in the personalised condition (N = 124) still performed better, completing an average of 6.6 ± 4.16 kind activities.

Finally, the model used to predict the most effective persuasive principle had 76 rules learnt from 130 entries. There may be too many minor rules that overfit the data and prevent good generalisation. It is possible that this is due to the training data on personality being very noisy. This leads to the creation of a

---

[2] No post-hoc statistical analysis was performed given the small sample (N = 15). This would need to be confirmed statistically in a future study.

complex model that tries to fit noisy instances from the training data. A future study will use a training data set with reduced noise to build the decision tree.

5   Conclusions and Future Work

Our findings indicate that messages which use personalised persuasive principles are more effective at stimulating kind behaviour than non-personalised messages. There is a consensus in the literature that personalised interventions and messages are more effective. However, most studies in the literature used perceived persuasiveness for personalisation. In this study we analysed the effect of personalisation based on actual persuasiveness and showed that providing personalised messages in an intervention motivates behaviour change. In addition to self-reporting for completed activities, we were able to observe actual behaviour and ensure participants actually engaged in kind behaviours through the numerous comments they wrote on the intervention message board. In addition, we showed that the Be Kind intervention is effective at improving participant behavioural intention and subjective wellbeing. These findings have implications for future work on personalisation and design of adaptive behaviour change interventions.

References

1. Anagnostopoulou, E., Bothos, E., Magoutas, B., Schrammel, J., Mentzas, G.: Persuasive technologies for sustainable mobility: state of the art and emerging trends. Sustainability 10(7) (2018). https://doi.org/10.3390/su10072128
2. Armenta, C., Ruberton, P., Lyubomirsky, S.: Subjective wellbeing, psychology of. International Encyclopedia of the Social & Behavioral Sciences 23 (12 2015). https://doi.org/10.1016/B978-0-08-097086-8.25039-3
3. Berkovsky, S., Freyne, J., Oinas-Kukkonen, H.: Influencing individually: fusing personalization and persuasion. ACM Trans. Interactive Intell. Syst. (TiiS) 2, June 2012. https://doi.org/10.1145/2209310.2209312
4. Bigsby, E., Cappella, J.N., Seitz, H.H.: Efficiently and effectively evaluating public service announcements: additional evidence for the utility of perceived effectiveness. Commun. Monogr. 80(1), 1–23 (2013)
5. Blanchflower, D., Oswald, A., Stewart-Brown, S.: Is psychological well-being linked to the consumption of fruit and vegetables? Soc. Indicators Res. 114, October 2012. https://doi.org/10.1007/s11205-012-0173-y
6. Boehm, J., Kubzansky, L.: The heart's content: the association between positive psychological well-being and cardiovascular health. Psychological Bull. 138, 655–91 (2012). https://doi.org/10.1037/a0027448
7. Bolier, L., Haverman, M., Westerhof, G., Riper, H., Smit, H., Bohlmeijer, E.: Positive psychology interventions: a meta-analysis of randomized controlled studies. BMC Public Health 13 (2013). https://doi.org/10.1186/1471-2458-13-119
8. Braun, D., Reiter, E., Siddharthan, A.: Saferdrive: an nlg-based behaviour change support system for drivers. Nat. Lang. Eng. 24(4), 551–588 (2018). https://doi.org/10.1017/S1351324918000050
9. Chida, Y., Steptoe, A.: Positive psychological well-being and mortality: a quantitative review of prospective observational studies. Psychosomatic Med. 70, 741–56 (2008). https://doi.org/10.1097/PSY.0b013e31818105ba

10. Cialdini, R.: The Psychology of Influence and Persuasion. NY Quill, NY (1991)
11. Cialdini, R.: Pre-Suasion: A Revolutionary Way to Influence and Persuade. Simon & Schuster, NY (2016)
12. Ciocarlan, A.: Be Kind: Adaptive Persuasive Technology for Wellbeing. Ph.D. thesis, July 2020
13. Ciocarlan, A., Masthoff, J., Oren, N.: Kindness is contagious: study into exploring engagement and adapting persuasive games for wellbeing. In: Proceedings of the 26th Conference on User Modeling, Adaptation and Personalization, UMAP 2018, pp. 311–319. ACM, New York (2018). https://doi.org/10.1145/3209219.3209233
14. Ciocarlan, A., Masthoff, J., Oren, N.: Actual persuasiveness: impact of personality, age and gender on message type susceptibility. In: Oinas-Kukkonen, H., Win, K.T., Karapanos, E., Karppinen, P., Kyza, E. (eds.) PERSUASIVE 2019. LNCS, vol. 11433, pp. 283–294. Springer, Cham (2019). https://doi.org/10.1007/978-3-030-17287-9_23
15. Cohen, S., Doyle, W., Turner, R., Alper, C., Skoner, D.: Emotional style and susceptibility to the common cold. Psychosomatic Med. **65**, 652–7 (2003). https://doi.org/10.1097/01.PSY.0000077508.57784.DA
16. Cook, A., Pryer, J., Shetty, P.: The problem of accuracy in dietary surveys. analysis of the over 65 uk national diet and nutrition survey. J. Epidemiology Commun. Health **54**, 611–6 (2000). https://doi.org/10.1136/jech.54.8.611
17. Cropanzano, R., Wright, T.: A 5-year study of change in the relationship between well-being and job performance. Consulting Psychol. J. Pract. Res. **51**, 252–265 (1999). https://doi.org/10.1037/1061-4087.51.4.252
18. Davidson, K.W., Mostofsky, E., Whang, W.: Don't worry, be happy: positive affect and reduced 10-year incident coronary heart disease: the Canadian Nova Scotia Health Survey. Eur. Heart J. **31**(9), 1065–1070 (2010). https://doi.org/10.1093/eurheartj/ehp603
19. Dunn, E., Aknin, L., Norton, M.: Spending money on others promotes happiness. Science **319**, 1687–1688 (2008)
20. Fogg, B.J.: Persuasive Technology: Using Computers to Change What we Think and Do. Morgan Kaufmann, San Francisco (2003)
21. Forbes, P., Wells, S., Masthoff, J., Nguyen, H.: Superhub: integrating behaviour change theories into a sustainable urban-mobility platform, September 2012. https://doi.org/10.14236/ewic/HCI2012.99
22. Fredrickson, B.L.: What good are positive emotions? Rev. Gen. Psychol. **2**(3), 300–319 (1998). https://doi.org/10.1037/1089-2680.2.3.300
23. Fredrickson, B.L., Mancuso, R.A., Branigan, C., Tugade, M.M.: The undoing effect of positive emotions. Motiv. Emot. **24**(24), 237–258 (2000)
24. Gosling, S.D., Rentfrow, P.J., Swann, W.B., Jr.: A very brief measure of the big-five personality domains. J. Res. Pers. **37**(6), 504–528 (2003)
25. Graham, C., Eggers, A., Sukhtankar, S.: Does happiness pay? an exploration based on panel data from russia. J. Econ. Behav. Organ. **55**, 319–342 (2004). https://doi.org/10.1016/j.jebo.2003.09.002
26. Grasso, F., Cawsey, A., Jones, R.: Dialectical argumentation to solve conflicts in advice giving: a case study in the promotion of healthy nutrition. Int. J. Hum.-Comput. Stud. **53**, 1077–1115 (2001). https://doi.org/10.1006/ijhc.2000.0429
27. Kaptein, M., De Ruyter, B., Markopoulos, P., Aarts, E.: Adaptive persuasive systems: a study of tailored persuasive text messages to reduce snacking. ACM Trans. Interact. Intell. Syst. **2**(2), June 2012. https://doi.org/10.1145/2209310.2209313

212   A. Ciocarlan et al.

28. Kaptein, M., Markopoulos, P., De Ruyter, B., Aarts, E.: Personalizing persuasive technologies: explicit and implicit personalization using persuasion profiles. Int. J. Hum. Comput. Stud. **77**, 38–51 (2015)
29. Kaptein, M., Markopoulos, P., de Ruyter, B., Aarts, E.: Can you be persuaded? individual differences in susceptibility to persuasion. In: Gross, T., Gulliksen, J., Kotzé, P., Oestreicher, L., Palanque, P., Prates, R.O., Winckler, M. (eds.) INTER-ACT 2009. LNCS, vol. 5726, pp. 115–118. Springer, Heidelberg (2009). https://doi.org/10.1007/978-3-642-03655-2_13
30. Kato, P.M., Cole, S.W., Bradlyn, A.S., Pollock, B.H.: A video game improves behavioral outcomes in adolescents and young adults with cancer: a randomized trial. Pediatrics **122**(2), e305–e317 (2008)
31. King, L.: The health benefits of writing about life goals. Pers. Soc. Psychol. Bull. **27**, 798–807 (2001)
32. Koivumaa-Honkanen, H., Kosekenvuo, M., Honkanen, R.J., Viinamaki, H., Heikkila, K., Kaprio, J.: Life dissatisfaction and subsequent work disability in an 11-year follow-up. Psychol. Med. **34**(2), 221–228 (2004). https://doi.org/10.1017/S0033291703001089
33. Luhmann, M., Lucas, R., Eid, M., Diener, E.: The prospective effect of life satisfaction on life events. Soc. Psycholgical Personality Sci. **4**, 39–45 (2013). https://doi.org/10.1177/1948550612440105
34. Lyubomirsky, S., Dickerhoof, R., Boehm, J., Sheldon, K.: Becoming happier takes both a will and a proper way: an experimental longitudinal intervention to boost well-being. Emotion **11**, 391–402 (2011)
35. Lyubomirsky, S., King, L., Diener, E.: The benefits of frequent positive affect: Does hapiness lead to sucess? Psychol. Bull. **131**, 803–55 (2005). https://doi.org/10.1037/0033-2909.131.6.803
36. Lyubomirsky, S., Lepper, H.: A measure of subjective happiness: preliminary reliability and construct validation. Soc. Indic. Res. **46**, 137–155 (1999)
37. Lyubomirsky, S., Sheldon, K., Schkade, D.: Pursuing happiness: the architecture of sustainable change. Rev. Gen. Psychol. **9**(2), 111–131 (2005)
38. Masthoff, J., Grasso, F., Ham, J.: Preface to the special issue on personalization and behavior change. UMUAI **24**(5), 345–350 (2014)
39. McCrae, R.R., Costa Jr, P.T.: The five-factor theory of personality (2008)
40. Neve, J.E., Diener, E., Tay, L., Xuereb, C.: The Objective Benefits of Subjective Well-Being, January 2013
41. Nguyen, H., Masthoff, J.: Mary: a personalised virtual health trainer. In: Bohnert, F., Quiroga, L. (eds.) Adjunct Proceedings of the 18th International Conference on User Modeling, Adaptation, and Personalization, pp. 58–60 (2010)
42. Nolan, J., Schultz, P., Cialdini, R., Goldstein, N., Griskevicius, V.: Normative social influence is underdetected. Personality Soc. Psychol. Bull. **34**, 913–23 (2008). https://doi.org/10.1177/0146167208316691
43. O'Keefe, D.J.: Message pretesting using assessments of expected or perceived persuasiveness: evidence about diagnosticity of relative actual persuasiveness. J. Commun. **68**(1), 120–142 (2018). https://doi.org/10.1093/joc/jqx009
44. Okun, M.A., Stock, W.A., Haring, M.J., Witter, R.A.: The social activity/subjective well-being relation: a quantitative synthesis. Res. Aging **6**(1), 45–65 (1984). https://doi.org/10.1177/0164027584006001003
45. Orji, R.: Design for behaviour change: a model-driven approach for tailoring persuasive technologies. Ph.D. thesis, Univ. of Saskatchewan, Canada (2014)
46. Orji, R.: Persuasion and culture: Individualism-collectivism and susceptibility to influence strategies. In: PPT@ PERSUASIVE, pp. 30–39 (2016)

47. Orji, R., Mandryk, R.L., Vassileva, J.: Gender, age, and responsiveness to cialdini's persuasion strategies. In: MacTavish, T., Basapur, S. (eds.) PERSUASIVE 2015. LNCS, vol. 9072, pp. 147–159. Springer, Cham (2015). https://doi.org/10.1007/978-3-319-20306-5_14
48. Oswald, A.J., Proto, E., Sgroi, D.: Happiness and productivity. J. Law Econ. **33**(4), 789–822 (2015). https://doi.org/10.1086/681096
49. Oyibo, K., Adaji, I., Orji, R., Olabenjo, B., Vassileva, J.: Susceptibility to persuasive strategies: a comparative analysis of Nigerians vs. Canadians. In: Proceedings of the 26th Conference on User Modeling, Adaptation and Personalization, pp. 229–238 (2018)
50. Oyibo, K., Orji, R., Vassileva, J.: Investigation of the influence of personality traits on cialdini's persuasive strategies. In: PPT@PERSUASIVE (2017)
51. Park, S.Q., Kahnt, T., Dogan, A., Strang, S., Fehr, E., Tobler, P.N.: A neural link between generosity and happiness. Nature Commun. **8**(15964) (2017)
52. Quinlan, J.R.: Induction of decision trees. Mach. Learn. **1**(1), 81–106 (1986)
53. Roberts, B., Caspi, A., Moffitt, T.: Work experiences and personality development in young adulthood. J. Personality Soc. Psychol. **84**, 582–93 (2003). https://doi.org/10.1037//0022-3514.84.3.582
54. Schneider, M., Graham, D., Grant, A., King, P., Cooper, D.: Regional brain activation and affective response to physical activity among healthy adolescents. Biol. Psychol. **82**, 246–252 (2009)
55. Seligman, M.E.P.: Authentic happiness: using the new positive psychology to realize your potential for lasting fulfillment, New York, NY (2002)
56. Seligman, M.E.P., Csikszentmihalyi, M.: Positive psychology. an introduction. Am. Psychol. **55**(1), 5–14 (2000)
57. Sheldon, K.M., Boehm, J., Lyubomirsky, S.: Variety is the spice of happiness: the hedonic adaptation prevention model. The Oxford handbook of happiness, pp. 901–914 (2013)
58. Siegel, J., Lienemann, B., Rosenberg, B.: Resistance, reactance, and misinterpretation: Highlighting the challenge of persuading people with depression to seek help. Soc. Personality Psychol. Compass **11**, e12322 (2017). https://doi.org/10.1111/spc3.12322
59. Sin, N.L., Lyubomirsky, S.: Enhancing well-being and alleviating depressive symptoms with positive psychology interventions: a practice-friendly meta-analysis. J. Clin. Psychol. **65**, 467–487 (2009)
60. Smith, K.A., Dennis, M., Masthoff, J.: Personalizing reminders to personality for melanoma self-checking. In: Proceedings of the 2016 Conference on User Modeling Adaptation and Personalization, pp. 85–93. ACM (2016)
61. Thomas, R.J., Masthoff, J., Oren, N.: Can i influence you? development of a scale to measure perceived persuasiveness and two studies showing the use of the scale. Front. Artif. Intell. **2**, 24 (2019)
62. Josekutty Thomas, R., Masthoff, J., Oren, N.: Adapting healthy eating messages to personality. In: de Vries, P.W., Oinas-Kukkonen, H., Siemons, L., Beerlage-de Jong, N., van Gemert-Pijnen, L. (eds.) PERSUASIVE 2017. LNCS, vol. 10171, pp. 119–132. Springer, Cham (2017). https://doi.org/10.1007/978-3-319-55134-0_10
63. Thompson, D., Baranowski, T., Buday, R., et al.: Serious video games for health how behavioral science guided the development of a serious video game. Simul. Gaming **41**(4), 587–606 (2010)
64. Vargheese, J., Collinson, M., Masthoff, J.: Exploring susceptibility measures to persuasion. In: Gram-Hansen, S., Svarre, T., Midden, C. (eds.) Persuasive 2020.

214   A. Ciocarlan et al.

Lecture Notes in Computer Science, Springer (Feb 2020), persuasive 2020: 15th
International Conference on Persuasive Technology; Conference date: 20-04-2020
Through 23-04-2020
65. Vargheese, J., Sripada, G., Masthoff, J., Oren, N.: Persuasive strategies for encouraging social interaction for older adults. Int. J. Hum.-Comput. Inter. **32**(3), 190–
214 (2016). https://doi.org/10.1080/10447318.2016.1136176
66. Wall, H.J., Campbell, C.C., Kaye, L.K., Levy, A., Bhullar, N.: Personality profiles
and persuasion: an exploratory study investigating the role of the big-5, type d
personality and the dark triad on susceptibility to persuasion. Personality Individ.
Differ. **139**, 69–76 (2019)

Persuasive Strategies and Emotional States: Towards Emotion-Adaptive Persuasive Technologies Design

Oladapo Oyebode(✉) 🆔, Darren Steeves, and Rita Orji🆔

Faculty of Computer Science, Dalhousie University, Halifax, NS B3H 4R2, Canada
oladapo.oyebode@dal.ca

Abstract. Technologies have been shown to alter how people feel and create outlets for expressing positive and/or negative emotions. This indicates that persuasive systems, which rely on persuasive strategies (PS) to motivate behaviour change, have the potential to elicit emotions in users. However, there is no empirical evidence on whether or not PS evoke emotions and how to tailor PS based on emotional states. Therefore, we conduct a large-scale study of 660 participants to investigate *if* and *how* individuals respond emotionally to various PS and *why*. Our results show that some PS (such as Reward, Reduction, and Rehearsal) evoke positive emotion only, while others (such as Self-monitoring, Reminder, and Suggestion) evoke both positive and negative emotions at varying degrees and for different reasons. Our research links emotion theory with behaviour change models to develop practical guidelines for designing emotion-adaptive persuasive systems that employ appropriate PS to motivate behaviour change while regulating users' emotion.

Keywords: Persuasive strategies · Emotional states · Emotion regulation · Persuasive systems · Behaviour change · Adaptivity · Tailoring · Design recommendations

1 Introduction

Persuasive systems employ persuasive strategies to motivate behaviour change across diverse domains including health, education [1, 2], and sustainable environment [3, 4]. For instance, persuasive systems for health use PS to promote healthy behaviours (such as healthy eating [5, 6], physical activity [7, 8], quality sleep [9, 10], and medication adherence [11, 12]) and discourage risky behaviours (e.g., excessive alcohol use [13] and smoking [14]). Yet, technologies can alter how people feel and create outlets for expressing positive and/or negative emotions [15]. Emotional states have been shown to influence physical and mental well-being [16, 17]. For example, negative emotional states (e.g., anger, fear, and sadness) create unhealthy patterns of physiological functioning, cause psychological disorders, and reduce quality of life [17–20]. Individuals exhibiting negative emotions are also at increased risk of immune relapse, illness, and mortality [17, 21]. On the other hand, positive emotional states (such as happiness) improve overall

© The Author(s), under exclusive license to Springer Nature Switzerland AG 2023
J. Ham et al. (Eds.): PERSUASIVE 2023, LNCS 13832, pp. 215–233, 2023.
https://doi.org/10.1007/978-3-031-30933-5_14

health and wellness including cardiovascular health, cognition, and resilience [22–26]. This highlights the need to regulate users' emotions (i.e., reducing negative emotions and promoting positive ones [27]) as they engage with technologies, specifically persuasive systems. To achieve this, it is imperative to determine which emotions are evoked by persuasive strategies in order to select and operationalize appropriate strategies that motivate desired behaviour change while reinforcing positive emotions. However, there is no empirical research in this area to date.

To contribute to this area, we conducted a large-scale empirical study of 660 participants to investigate *if* and *how* individuals respond emotionally to eleven (11) persuasive strategies operationalized in a system and *why*. We achieved our goal using three well-established theoretical frameworks: Ekman's emotion model [28–30], Persuasive Systems Design (PSD) model [31], and the App Behaviour Change Scale (ABACUS) [32]. The Ekman's emotion model comprises six basic emotional states out of which five are universal (i.e., emotions that all humans have in common) [30], namely *anger, fear, happiness, sadness*, and *disgust*. The model has been widely applied in the literature over the years, including in human-computer interaction (HCI) research [33–35]. The PSD model consists of twenty-eight persuasive strategies for designing and evaluating persuasive or behaviour change systems and has enjoyed widespread use in persuasive technology research including [36–40]. Similarly, the ABACUS framework comprises twenty-one persuasive strategies for assessing the behaviour change potential of smartphone-based applications or systems. Our choice of persuasive strategies was inspired by a recent study in which PSD and ABACUS strategies were harmonized and then ranked in terms of behaviour change score (BCS) which is a measure of the extent to which each strategy is implemented in applications [41]. The eleven strategies selected for this work include those with high BCS (such as *self-monitoring, reminders, reduction, rehearsal*, and *goal setting*) and those with moderate to low BCS (e.g., *suggestion, reward, expertise, opportunity to plan for barriers, distraction or avoidance*, and *recognition*) since rarely implemented strategies could also be effective [41].

To collect data from participants, we iteratively created and presented prototypes operationalizing each strategy within the mental health domain of resilience building (which involves developing the mental ability to bounce back or cope with adversities such as everyday stressors and traumatic life events [42]), followed by questionnaires measuring perceived persuasiveness [43] of each strategy and the emotion(s) evoked by that strategy. Next, we created models showing the relationship between individual strategies and the five universal emotional states (i.e., *anger, fear, happiness, sadness*, and *disgust*) using the structural equation modeling technique [44, 45] to uncover the emotion(s) evoked by each strategy. Lastly, we conducted thematic analysis of participants' qualitative comments to understand *why* a strategy evokes specific emotion(s) in participants.

Our work offers four main contributions in the area of emotion-adaptive persuasive systems design. First, we underpin the significance of people's emotional responses to persuasive strategies and establish that emotional states are important dimensions for tailoring persuasive strategies to improve the overall effectiveness of persuasive systems. Second, we provide empirical insights into the perceived persuasiveness of individual strategies, as well as the emotions evoked by the strategies using three well-established theoretical frameworks. Third, we offer qualitative insights to explain why each strategy evokes specific emotion(s) based on participants' comments. Finally, we reflect on our findings to offer practical guidelines for designing emotion-adaptive persuasive systems that use appropriate PS to motivate behaviour change while reinforcing positive emotions.

2 Background and Related Work

In this section, we reviewed literature on emotion theories, as well as persuasion frameworks and persuasive strategies. We also explored how emotion has been used to influence persuasion.

2.1 Emotion Theories

Emotion theories, which can be discrete or dimensional, define how emotions are represented in applications or systems. Discrete emotion theories including Ekman's emotion theory [28–30], Plutchik's theory of emotion [46, 47], OCC (Orthony, Clore, and Collins) emotion theory [48] and Parrot emotion theory [49] place emotion into distinct states or categories. Ekman's theory posits that there exist six basic and distinct emotional states: *happiness, sadness, anger, fear, disgust,* and *surprise.* Five of these emotions, excluding surprise, are considered *"five Universal Emotions: emotions that all humans, no matter where or how they are raised, have in common"* [30]. Other discrete theories are based on the Ekman's emotion theory. For instance, Plutchik's theory of emotion extends Ekman's basic emotions by including two additional emotional states: *trust* and *anticipation.* The OCC theory discretized emotion into twenty-two categories including the six basic emotional states. Parrot emotion theory generates one hundred secondary emotions (arranged in a tree structure) from Ekman's basic or "primary" emotions. Conversely, dimensional emotion theories such as Circumplex Model of Affect (CMA) [50, 51] project emotions on a dimensional space that shows how emotions are related, as well as their intensities or degree of occurrence. The CMA depicts emotion as a linear combination (or as varying degrees) of two dimensions: *valence* which is a pleasure-displeasure continuum and *arousal* which reflects whether an event is exciting or calm. A third dimension called *dominance* refers to the degree to which individuals have control over their emotion [52]. Compared to the dimensional theories, the discrete emotion theories have enjoyed widespread use in emotion-based HCI research including [33–35, 53]. We utilize Ekman's five universal emotional states – *happiness, sadness, anger, fear, disgust* – in this work.

2.2 Persuasion Frameworks and Persuasive Strategies

Persuasive systems operationalize various persuasive strategies to motivate behaviour change and have been shown to be effective [54, 55]. Persuasive technology researchers have proposed several persuasion frameworks offering various persuasive strategies that could bring about behaviour change. Popular frameworks include Persuasive Technology Tools [56], Cialdini's Principles of Persuasion [57], and Persuasive Systems Design

(PSD) model [31]. The PSD model, which comprises twenty-eight persuasive strategies, is grounded in psychological and behavioural theories, extends the other two frameworks, and facilitates the development and evaluation of persuasive or behaviour change systems. Another persuasion framework is the App Behaviour Change Scale (ABACUS) consisting of twenty-one strategies for assessing the behaviour change potential of mobile applications [32]. In a study by Alslaity et al. [41], both PSD and ABACUS strategies were combined to comprehensively assess the persuasiveness of mobile health applications. In particular, the strategies were ranked based on behaviour change score (BCS) which is a measure of the extent to which a strategy is implemented in applications. This study informed our choice of eleven (11) strategies used in this work (see Table 1). Specifically, we considered not only strategies with high BCS (such as *self-monitoring, reminders, reduction, rehearsal,* and *goal setting*) but also those with moderate to low BCS (e.g., *suggestion, reward, expertise, opportunity to plan for barriers, distraction or avoidance,* and *recognition*) since rarely implemented strategies could also be effective [41].

Table 1. Persuasive strategies and corresponding descriptions.

Strategy	Description
Self-monitoring	Provides means for users to track their own progress or performance towards their target behaviour or goal
Reminder	Reminds or notifies users of their target behaviour during system use
Reduction	Reduces efforts required to perform the target behaviour
Rehearsal	Provides means of rehearsing or practicing the target behaviour
Goal setting	Allows users to set a goal that can be achieved during system use
Suggestion	Provides tailored suggestions or tips for achieving the desired behaviour during system use
Reward	Incentivizes users for achieving specific milestones using virtual rewards such as badges, points, etc
Expertise	Provides content showing knowledge, experience, and competence
Opportunities to plan for barriers	Encourages users to think about potential barriers and identify ways of overcoming them
Distraction or Avoidance	Gives suggestions and advice on how users can avoid situations or distract themselves when trying to reach their goal
Recognition	Provides public recognition for users who perform the target behaviour

2.3 Emotion and Persuasion

Emotion has been found to influence persuasion and different emotions result in different persuasion outcomes [58, 59]. Majority of research in this area involves inducing certain emotions into communications to enhance their persuasiveness. For instance, loss-framed messages induce negative emotions such as *fear* while gain-framed messages induce positive emotions (e.g., *happiness*) to convince target audience to perform specific behaviours [60]. In the health domain, loss-framed messaging was used to influence people's intention to engage in healthy behaviour, such as consuming less salt or receiving vaccinations against diseases [60, 61]. However, *fear* induction in public health campaigns could lead to weaker intentions to adopt the target behaviour [60, 62], in line with evidence that loss-framed messages trigger defensive responses in people thereby reducing persuasion [60]. In contrast, positively-valenced or gain-framed health messages like those promoting healthy eating and physical activity were found to evoke positive attitude and improve self-efficacy [63]. A study in the domain of sustainable environment also found that negative emotions including *sadness* are significant barriers to people's willingness to make financial donations to environmental non-governmental organisations but inducing *happiness, pride*, or *empathy* influences users to give donations [64, 65].

2.4 Research Objective

Although emotions have been used to influence persuasive outcomes (see Sect. 2.3), this approach could be coercive or deceptive since the intent is to elicit emotions that could force or manipulate people to perform the target behaviour (such as using *fear* to drive product sales or *empathy* to boost donations). Besides, persuasion using negative emotions tend to trigger defensive responses, however, researchers have used positive emotions as countermeasures (e.g., [66]). Given the non-coercive and non-deceptive role of persuasive strategies (PS) for effective behaviour change and the vital role of positive emotional states in physical and mental well-being, we conducted a large-scale empirical study to uncover the relation between PS and emotional states. To the best of our knowledge, our work is the first to link emotion theory with behaviour change models to develop practical guidelines for designing emotion-adaptive persuasive systems that use appropriate PS to motivate behaviour change while reinforcing positive emotions.

3 Methodology

To achieve our research objective, we followed the methodological steps below:

1. We selected universal emotional states from the Ekman's emotion model (i.e., *happiness, sadness, anger, fear, disgust*) and eleven (11) persuasive strategies from the PSD and ABACUS persuasion frameworks (see Table 1), as described in Sects. 2.1 and 2.2.
2. We created prototypes illustrating each strategy contextualized in the mental health domain of resilience building.

3. We conducted a large-scale online study to assess the perceived persuasiveness or effectiveness of individual strategies and to determine emotional states that each strategy elicited in participants.
4. We analyzed the quantitative and qualitative data collected using well-established analytical methods and tools, and then discussed our findings.

We discuss the details of our methodology including study design and data analysis in subsequent sections.

3.1 Study Design

To collect data for our online study, we followed established methodologies employed in many HCI research including [38, 39, 67, 68], as described below.

Prototype Development. To assess the perceived persuasiveness of the strategies (i.e., *self-monitoring, reminder, reduction, rehearsal, goal setting, suggestion, reward, expertise, opportunities to plan for barriers, distraction or avoidance,* and *recognition*), we created a prototype that depicts each strategy as a persuasive feature in a mobile health (mHealth) application for building human resilience. Prior to designing the prototypes, we identified various resilience building mechanisms from the literature [69–72] that can be delivered using the strategies. We contextualized the prototypes within the mental health domain of resilience building (which involves developing the mental ability to bounce back or cope with adversities such as everyday stressors and traumatic life events [42]). Furthermore, the prototypes (one per strategy) were evaluated two times by ten mental health and persuasive technology (PT) researchers. We refined the prototypes each time based on the evaluators' feedback to arrive at the final designs. The prototypes were designed in such a way that they are easily understood by target audience from various backgrounds. Figure 1 shows the prototype illustrating the Reward strategy.

Fig. 1. Prototype illustrating the *Reward* strategy

Experimental Design. Our within-subject online study is in five phases: first, we asked participants to complete demographic-related questionnaire by indicating their age group, gender, marital status, education level, and profession. Second, we asked participants to watch a short (less than one minute) neutral video before examining each prototype to avoid bias or carryover effect while reporting their emotional states. Similar approach has also been used in HCI affective experiments including [73]. The neutral video clips utilized in this study were chosen at random from Stanford Psychophysiology Laboratory's film library for affective scientists [74]. Third, we presented prototype illustrating each strategy to participants as a set of images in a logical flow depicting user interaction. Participants see one prototype (or strategy) at a time and then respond to the perceived persuasiveness questionnaire (PPQ) adapted from [43] and used in many PT research including [7, 38, 39, 68, 75]. To prevent possible prototypes ordering bias, we used the randomization feature of the survey tool [76] to change the order of the prototypes for each participant. The PPQ comprises five items measured using a 7-point Likert scale which ranges from "1 – Strongly Disagree" to "7 – Strongly Agree": (a) *This application would influence me to be resilient*, (b) *This application would convince me to be resilient*, (c) *This application would be personally relevant for me*, (d) *This application would make me to reconsider my resilience level*, and (e) *The strategy would make or motivate me to use the application*. Next, we asked participants to report their emotional response while examining each application prototype. Participants rated their emotional response in terms of Ekman's five universal emotional states [30] – *happiness, sadness, anger, fear*, and *disgust* – on a 5-point Likert scale, an approach used in emotion-based HCI research including [77]. Lastly, we asked participants to justify their ratings by providing qualitative comments.

To ensure that participants were actively considering their responses, we included attention-check questions. Prior to the main study, we conducted two pilot studies with 20 randomly selected university students for the first pilot study and 40 MTurk (Amazon Mechanical Turk) participants for the second pilot study to test the validity of our study instruments.

Participants. To recruit participants for our large-scale online study, we used a variety of methods including email, social media, snowball sampling, SONA, and MTurk. SONA is a widely used experimental participation system that allows university students to participate in ongoing research and earn credit points [78]. MTurk is an established and reliable method of recruiting large and diverse participants and has been used in many HCI and PT studies including [38, 39, 67, 79, 80]. In compliance with research ethics approval, our inclusion criteria require that participants be adults (18 years or older) and proficient in English language. We included a total of 660 valid responses in our analysis, after removing incomplete responses and those containing inaccurate answers to attention-based questions. Table 2 summarizes our participants' demographic information.

Table 2. Participants' demographic information.

Number of Participants = 660	
Age	18–25 (42%), 26–35 (30%), 36–45 (17%), Over 45 (11%)
Gender	Male (39%), Female (60%), Other (1%)
Marital Status	Single (42%), Married (52%), Widowed (0%), Divorced (2%), Separated (1%), Registered Partnership (1%), Other (2%)

3.2 Data Analysis

We employed well-known analytical techniques and tools to analyze the data collected, as summarized below:

1. To assess the suitability of our data for factor analysis, we used the Kaiser-Meyer-Olkin (KMO) Measure of Sampling Adequacy and Bartlett Test of Sphericity (BTS) methods [81]. Our results showed that the KMO value was 0.969 (well above the recommended value of 0.6 [81]) and BTS was statistically significant ($\chi^2(7260)$ = 89249.635, $p < .0001$), thereby confirming that our dataset is suited for factor analysis.
2. We computed the persuasiveness score (average rating) for each strategy, and then conducted a One-Sample t-test to determine the persuasiveness of individual strategies using neutral rating of 4 as the test value in a 7-point scale. To examine and compare the strategies' persuasiveness, we performed a Repeated-Measure Analysis of Variance (RM-ANOVA) analysis using strategy type as within subject factor after checking for ANOVA assumptions, followed by Bonferroni pairwise comparison.
3. Next, we modeled the relationship between the persuasiveness of individual strategies and the five emotional states using partial least square structural equation modeling (PLS-SEM) method. PLS-SEM is highly suitable for creating complex models [82] and has been widely used in estimating relationships between latent and observed variables in many HCI research studies including [38, 83–85], making it a superior choice to other approaches (such as covariant-based). We used the Smart-PLS3 tool [86] to create the models, one strategy at a time. We validated the measurement models by establishing indicator reliability (Cronbach's alpha and composite reliability values were above recommended value of 0.7 [45, 87]), convergent reliability (Average Variance Extracted (AVE) values were above recommended value of 0.5 [45, 87]), and discriminant validity (heterotrait-monotrait (HTMT) ratio of correlations was below the recommended limit of 0.9 [45, 88] for all constructs). We also explored for differences between the structural models by calculating path coefficients (β) – which measure the influence of a variable on another – and their corresponding significant level (p).
4. Finally, we applied thematic analysis method to analyze participants' qualitative comments to justify their quantitative ratings.

4 Results

In this section, we present comparative analysis of the overall persuasiveness of the strategies and results of the relationship between individual strategies and the five emotional states.

4.1 Comparing the Overall Persuasiveness of the Strategies

Results of the One-Sample t-test show that the persuasiveness scores of the eleven strategies are significantly higher than the neutral rating of 4 ($p < .001$). This indicates that participants perceived the strategies as effective (at varying degrees) in terms of their capacity to motivate behaviour change (see Fig. 2). *Goal setting* strategy is perceived as the most persuasive (Mean = 5.519, SD = 1.155), closely followed by *reminder* (Mean = 5.436, SD = 1.050), *reduction* (Mean = 5.407, SD = 1.060), and *self-monitoring* (Mean = 5.392, SD = 0.983). *Opportunity to plan for barriers* (Mean = 5.315, SD = 1.242), *rehearsal* (Mean = 5.306, SD = 1.280), *reward* (Mean = 5.272, SD = 1.350), *suggestion* (Mean = 5.253, SD = 1.315), *expertise* (Mean = 5.249, SD = 1.216), and *distraction or avoidance* (Mean = 5.213, SD = 1.380) strategies are in the middle, while *recognition* strategy (Mean = 4.771, SD = 1.718) is perceived as the least persuasive overall.

Next, we explore for significant differences in persuasiveness of the strategies. The results of the RM-ANOVA analysis show significant main effects of strategy type on persuasiveness ($F_{7.090, 4672.573} = 31.578, p < .001$). This means that there is significant difference between the strategies with respect to their persuasiveness overall. Specifically, Bonferroni-corrected pairwise comparisons show that *goal setting* is the most persuasive, significantly different from *expertise* ($p < .001$), *rehearsal* ($p < .001$), *suggestion* ($p < .001$), *reward* ($p < .001$), *recognition* ($p < .001$), *distraction or avoidance*

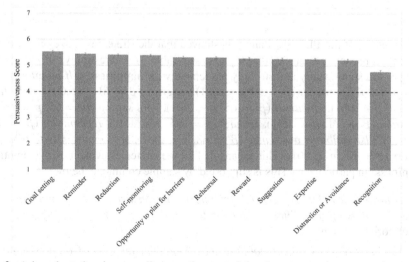

Fig. 2. A bar chart showing overall persuasiveness of the eleven strategies on a scale ranging from 1 to 7. The horizontal line indicates the neutral rating of 4.

($p < .001$), and *opportunity to plan for barriers* ($p < .001$). *Reminder* is the second most persuasive, significantly different from *expertise* ($p = .002$), *suggestion* ($p = .003$), *reward* ($p = .047$), *recognition* ($p < .001$), and *distraction or avoidance* ($p < .001$). *Recognition* is significantly less persuasive than all the other strategies ($p < .001$).

4.2   Relationship Between Persuasive Strategies and Emotional States

Table 3. Standard path coefficients (β) and significance level (p) of the relation between the persuasive strategies and the five emotional states. Bolded coefficients have significance level of $p < .001$, while unbolded coefficients have significance level of $p < .05$. "–" represents non-significant coefficients.

Strategy	ANGER	DISGUST	FEAR	HAPPINESS	SADNESS
Self-monitoring	.11	.11	**.18**	**.48**	**.13**
Reminder	−.11	–	.11	**.59**	–
Expertise	–	.08	.11	**.61**	–
Reduction	–	–	–	**.57**	–
Rehearsal	–	–	–	**.65**	–
Goal setting	−.10	–	–	**.65**	–
Suggestion	–	–	.14	**.71**	–
Reward	–	–	–	**.65**	–
Recognition	−.14	–	.13	**.75**	–
Distraction or Avoidance	–	–	.13	**.68**	.08
Opportunity to plan for barriers	–	–	–	**.65**	–

The results of our PLS-SEM analysis showed that the strategies evoke one or more emotions in participants at varying degrees (see Table 3). Interestingly, all the eleven strategies are significantly and strongly associated with **happiness**: *self-monitoring* ($\beta = .48, p < .001$), *reminder* ($\beta = .59, p < .001$), *expertise* ($\beta = .61, p < .001$), *reduction* ($\beta = .57, p < .001$), *rehearsal* ($\beta = .65, p < .001$), *goal setting* ($\beta = .65, p < .001$), *suggestion* ($\beta = .71, p < .001$), *reward* ($\beta = .65, p < .001$), *recognition* ($\beta = .75, p < .001$), *distraction or avoidance* ($\beta = .68, p < .001$), and *opportunity to plan for barriers* ($\beta = .65, p < .001$). This means that all the strategies evoke positive emotion (**happiness**) in participants. This is supported by sample comments below:

> *"I **enjoy** the idea of tracking moods, monitoring my resilience battery, and breaking my habits up into different sections to really examine them."* [P25] – Self-monitoring strategy

> *"'Wow' this rewards system would definitely motivate me to work on myself, do my tasks, set and achieve my goals, including being resilient. This made me feel **very happy**..."* [P97] – Reward strategy

"This is definitely one I ***don't want to miss out on*** *as it will help me carryout necessary activities back-to-back to help me get used to them."* [P390] – Rehearsal strategy

Yet, seven of the strategies could also evoke negative emotions. Specifically, *self-monitoring* strategy is significantly associated with **anger** ($\beta = .11, p < .05$), **disgust** ($\beta = .11, p < .05$), **fear** ($\beta = .18, p < .001$), and **sadness** ($\beta = .13, p < .001$). Below is a participant's comment to support this finding:

"I feel like by seeing how much I have not accomplished in the day could make me feel ***a bit sad****, but once I have completed those I will feel happy."* [P4]

Reminder strategy is significantly associated with **fear** ($\beta = .11, p < .05$) but negatively associated with **anger** ($\beta = -.11, p < .05$). The negative relation between *reminder* and **anger** indicates that the strategy reduces the degree of **anger**. In other words, participants focused more on the perceived benefits of reminders despite its likely challenges (e.g., timing of reminders). Sample comment below supports this finding:

"I find notifications ***useful and helpful*** *for reminder purposes. Even if I might not do it in the moment, it is a little reminder to do it within the day"* [P541]

Furthermore, *expertise* strategy is significantly associated with **disgust** ($\beta = .08, p < .05$) and **fear** ($\beta = .11, p < .05$), while the *goal setting* strategy is significantly negatively associated with **anger** ($\beta = -.10, p < .05$). *Suggestion* strategy is significantly associated with **fear** ($\beta = .14, p < .001$), while *recognition* strategy has a significant association with **fear** ($\beta = .13, p < .001$) but negative association with **anger** ($\beta = -.14, p < .001$). Lastly, *distraction or avoidance* strategy is significantly associated with both **fear** ($\beta = .13, p < .001$) and **sadness** ($\beta = .08, p < .05$).

5 Discussion

Our findings showed that the eleven persuasive strategies evoke positive and/or negative emotional states in participants (see Table 3). In subsequent sections, we discuss strategies that promote positive emotions, as well as guidelines or recommendations that could inform emotion-adaptive persuasive systems design.

5.1 Persuasive Strategies and Positive Emotional States

All strategies are associated with happiness (see Table 3) which is unsurprising since they are perceived as persuasive or effective by participants (see Fig. 2). Moreover, only four of the strategies – Reduction, Rehearsal, Reward, and Opportunity to plan for barriers (OPB) – are not associated with any of the negative emotional states (i.e., fear, anger, sadness, and disgust). This is due to the following reasons (after conducting thematic analysis of participants' qualitative comments):

- Reduction strategy presents interventions in a *"less overwhelming"* or *"simple"* manner and offers *"quick access"* to activities which in turn *"lessens cognitive load"* and *"improves productivity"*.
- Rehearsal strategy provides *"walkthrough and practical way of learning"* that ensures goals are *"accomplished in the right way"*.
- Reward strategy elicits *"feelings of personal accomplishment"*, provides *"incentives that increase the urge to achieve more goals"*, offers *"gamified experience"*, and provides means of *"unlocking additional contents with the rewards already earned"*.
- OPB strategy *"raises awareness of obstacles that could hinder goal achievement"* and by *"offering concrete steps for overcoming those obstacles"* serves as a *"useful problem-solving approach to challenges in daily lives"*.

Our findings imply that the four strategies above have strong potential to promote and reinforce positive emotion in persuasive systems users while also motivating behaviour change.

5.2 Design Recommendations

We offer four key recommendations that could guide persuasive systems designers in selecting and operationalizing persuasive strategies that reinforce positive emotion:

Recommendation 1: Employing *Reduction, Rehearsal, Reward*, and *Opportunity to plan for barriers* strategies to promote positive emotion. As discussed in the previous section, these four strategies are strongly and significantly associated with positive emotion (happiness) without any significant association with negative emotions. Therefore, to elicit positive emotion in users, designers should operationalize these strategies in persuasive systems.

Recommendation 2: Allowing individuals to set goals, with reminders to help them stay on track. Goal-setting strategy – which is the most persuasive (see Fig. 2) – could also reinforce positive emotion since it is strongly associated with happiness and only has a negative association with anger which indicates its ability to reduce it. This is because the strategy fosters *"setting and organizing daily tangible goals or tasks"* that can be *"measured and tailored to present needs"*, and promotes *"self-competition and accountability"* which in turn *"drive motivation and user engagement"*. To sustain positive emotion, reminders may be required as it would help individuals to keep track of their goals and accomplish them. The following comment supports the need for reminders in addition to goal setting: *"I find that this would require a lot more self-motivation and planning to get the tasks done as there is no reminder..."* [P15].

Recommendation 3: Presenting self-monitoring with complementary strategies to motivate and encourage people even when it appears they are lagging behind. In addition to fear and anger, Self-monitoring evokes disgust and sadness (see Table 3) which reflect participants' negative reactions when they fail to complete their daily tasks or goals. In line with research evidence, Self-monitoring could be boring and tedious because of the daunting nature of self-tracking, hence there is always a need for a complementary strategy (such as Reward) to be used alongside Self-monitoring to incentivize users and reduce the negative effect of self-tracking [89]. Moreover, concerns about coping with task completion could be addressed by allowing users to set reminders, as revealed in the following participant's comment: *"I have a hard time sticking to things but with reminders I may be able to improve my daily resilience…"* [P621].

Recommendation 4: Enabling customization of reminders, and making reminders adaptive to individuals' context. Reminder strategy, which is the second most persuasive, evokes fear but less anger in individuals (see Table 3). However, "flexible", "non-intrusive", and "less frequent" reminders would allay people's fears and bring about positive emotion, as revealed in the following comments: *"…Overall, I think reminders are beneficial but should not be excessive"* [P216] and *"I am not a person who likes notifications that interrupt my thoughts…The ability to choose the notifications' timing may make that better"* [P84].

6 Conclusion and Future Work

We conducted a large-scale study of 660 participants to investigate *if* and *how* individuals respond emotionally to eleven persuasive strategies (PS). Our work advances persuasive technology and HCI research by underpinning the importance of people's emotional reactions to PS operationalized in applications and established that emotional states are important dimensions for adapting persuasive systems by choosing PS that not only motivate behaviour change but also regulate users' emotional state by reinforcing positive emotion. As a secondary objective, we offered qualitative insights to explain *why* the PS evoke specific emotions based on participants' comments. Our findings showed that some PS (such as Reward, Reduction, and Rehearsal) evoke positive emotion only, while others (e.g., Self-monitoring, Reminder, and Suggestion) evoke both positive and negative emotions for different reasons. For example, the Reward strategy evokes *happiness* emotion because it elicits feelings of personal accomplishment, offers gamified experience, and increases the urge to achieve more goals. Based on our findings, we offer practical design recommendations.

Future work will apply findings and design recommendations from this work in developing an emotion-adaptive persuasive mobile application for delivering health interventions which in turn will be evaluated in real-world settings. Further studies will also be conducted to determine if our findings would be applicable in other domains besides health. Finally, we will investigate if emotional response and perceived persuasiveness of strategies are affected by user characteristics such as age, gender, and personality traits.

Acknowledgement. This research was undertaken, in part, thanks to funding from the Canada Research Chairs Program. We acknowledge the support of the Natural Sciences and Engineering Research Council of Canada (NSERC) through the Discovery Grant.

References

1. Kljun, M., Krulec, R., Pucihar, K.C., Solina, F.: Persuasive technologies in m-learning for training professionals: how to keep learners engaged with adaptive triggering. IEEE Trans. Learn. Technol. **12**, 370–383 (2019). https://doi.org/10.1109/TLT.2018.2840716
2. Widyasari, Y.D.L., Nugroho, L.E., Permanasari, A.E.: Persuasive technology for enhanced learning behavior in higher education. Int. J. Educ. Technol. High. Educ. **16**, 1–16 (2019). https://doi.org/10.1186/S41239-019-0142-5/FIGURES/7
3. Oppong-Tawiah, D., Webster, J., Staples, S., Cameron, A.F., Ortiz de Guinea, A., Hung, T.Y.: Developing a gamified mobile application to encourage sustainable energy use in the office. J Bus Res **106**, 388–405 (2020). https://doi.org/10.1016/J.JBUSRES.2018.10.051
4. Suruliraj, B., Nkwo, M., Orji, R.: Persuasive mobile apps for sustainable waste management: a systematic review. In: Gram-Hansen, S.B., Jonasen, T.S., Midden, C. (eds.) PERSUASIVE 2020. LNCS, vol. 12064, pp. 182–194. Springer, Cham (2020). https://doi.org/10.1007/978-3-030-45712-9_14
5. Liu, X., Ren, X., Pan, S.: Persuasive design for healthy eating: a scoping review. In: Streitz, N.A., Konomi, S. (eds.) Distributed, Ambient and Pervasive Interactions. Smart Living, Learning, Well-being and Health, Art and Creativity. HCII 2022. LNCS, vol. 13326, pp. 292–303. Springer, Cham (2022). https://doi.org/10.1007/978-3-031-05431-0_20
6. Hsu, A., Yang, J., Yilmaz, Y., Haque, M.S., Can, C., Blandford, A.: Persuasive technology for overcoming food cravings and improving snack choices. In: Proceedings of the SIGCHI Conference on Human Factors in Computing Systems, Toronto, Ontario, Canada, pp. 3403–3412. Association for Computing Machinery (2014)
7. Oyebode, O., Ganesh, A., Orji, R.: TreeCare: development and evaluation of a persuasive mobile game for promoting physical activity. In: 2021 IEEE Conference on Games (CoG), pp. 1–8. IEEE (2021)
8. Saksono, H., Castaneda-Sceppa, C., Hoffman, J., Morris, V., Seif El-Nasr, M., Parker, A.G.: Storywell: designing for family fitness app motivation by using social rewards and reflection. In: Conference on Human Factors in Computing Systems – Proceedings, pp. 1–13. Association for Computing Machinery (2020)
9. Oyebode, O., Alhasani, M., Mulchandani, D., Olagunju, T., Orji, R.: SleepFit: a persuasive mobile app for improving sleep habits in young adults. In: SeGAH 2021 - 2021 IEEE 9th International Conference on Serious Games and Applications for Health, pp. 1–8 (2021). https://doi.org/10.1109/SEGAH52098.2021.9551907
10. Wilson, E.V., Djamasbi, S., Strong, D., Ruiz, C.: Using a Key Informant Focus Group, Formative User Testing, and Theory to Guide Design of a Sleep Health BCSS. In: Hawaii International Conference on System Sciences 2017 (HICSS-50), pp. 3336–3345 (2017)
11. Suni Lopez, F., Condori-Fernandez, N.: Design of an adaptive persuasive mobile application for stimulating the medication adherence. In: Poppe, R., Meyer, J.-J., Veltkamp, R., Dastani, M. (eds.) INTETAIN 2016 2016. LNICSSITE, vol. 178, pp. 99–105. Springer, Cham (2017). https://doi.org/10.1007/978-3-319-49616-0_9
12. Win, K.T., Mullan, J., Howard, S., Oinas-Kukkonen, H.: Persuasive systems design features in promoting medication management for consumers. In: Hawaii International Conference on System Sciences 2017 (HICSS-50), pp. 3326–3335 (2017)
13. Puddephatt, J.-A., et al.: A qualitative evaluation of the acceptability of a tailored smartphone alcohol intervention for a military population: information about drinking for ex-serving personnel (InDEx) app. JMIR Mhealth Uhealth **7**, e12267 (2019). https://doi.org/10.2196/12267
14. Klein, P., Lawn, S., Tsourtos, G., van Agteren, J.: Tailoring of a smartphone smoking cessation app (kick.it) for serious mental illness populations: qualitative study. JMIR Hum. Factors **6**, e14023 (2019). https://doi.org/10.2196/14023

15. Shank, D.B.: Technology and emotions. In: Stets, J.E., Turner, J.H. (eds.) Handbook of the Sociology of Emotions: Volume II. HSSR, pp. 511–528. Springer, Dordrecht (2014). https://doi.org/10.1007/978-94-017-9130-4_24

16. Gross, J.J., Muñoz, R.F.: Emotion regulation and mental health. Clin. Psychol. Sci. Pract. 2, 151–164 (1995). https://doi.org/10.1111/J.1468-2850.1995.TB00036.X

17. Salovey, P., Rothman, A.J., Detweiler, J.B., Steward, W.T.: Emotional states and physical health. Am. Psychol. 55, 110–121 (2000). https://doi.org/10.1037/0003-066X.55.1.110

18. de Berardis, D., Fornaro, M., Orsolini, L., Ventriglio, A., Vellante, F., di Giannantonio, M.: Emotional dysregulation in adolescents: implications for the development of severe psychiatric disorders, substance abuse, and suicidal ideation and behaviors. Brain Sci 10, 591 (2020). https://doi.org/10.3390/BRAINSCI10090591

19. Miranda, J., Gross, J.J., Persons, J.B., Hahn, J.: Mood matters: negative mood induction activates dysfunctional attitudes in women vulnerable to depression. Cogn. Therapy Res. 22(4), 363–376 (1998). https://doi.org/10.1023/A:1018709212986

20. Kuppens, P., Realo, A., Diener, E.: The role of positive and negative emotions in life satisfaction judgment across nations. J. Pers. Soc. Psychol. 95, 66–75 (2008). https://doi.org/10.1037/0022-3514.95.1.66

21. Natt och Dag, Y., Mehlig, K., Rosengren, A., Lissner, L., Rosvall, M.: Negative emotional states and negative life events: Consequences for cardiovascular health in a general population. J. Psychosom. Res. 129:109888 (2020). https://doi.org/10.1016/J.JPSYCHORES.2019.109888

22. Boehm, J.K., et al.: Positive emotions and favorable cardiovascular health: a 20-year longitudinal study. Prev Med (Baltim) 136, 106103 (2020). https://doi.org/10.1016/J.YPMED.2020.106103

23. Alexander, R., et al.: The neuroscience of positive emotions and affect: implications for cultivating happiness and wellbeing. Neurosci. Biobehav. Rev. 121, 220–249 (2021). https://doi.org/10.1016/J.NEUBIOREV.2020.12.002

24. Ching, C.L., Chan, V.L.: Positive emotions, positive feelings and health: a life philosophy. Linguist. Cult. Rev. 4, 1–14 (2020). https://doi.org/10.21744/LINGCURE.V4N1.16

25. Fredrickson, B.L., Joiner, T.: Positive emotions trigger upward spirals toward emotional wellbeing. Psychol. Sci. 13, 172–175 (2002). https://doi.org/10.1111/1467-9280.00431

26. Gloria, C.T., Steinhardt, M.A.: Relationships among positive emotions, coping, resilience and mental health. Stress. Health 32, 145–156 (2016). https://doi.org/10.1002/SMI.2589

27. Gross JJ, Richards JM, John OP (2006) Emotion Regulation in Everyday Life. In: Snyder DK, Simpson J, Hughes JN (eds) Emotion regulation in couples and families: Pathways to dysfunction and health. American Psychological Association, pp 13–35

28. Ekman, P.: Basic emotions. Handbook Cogn. Emot. 98, 16 (1999)

29. Ekman, P.: An argument for basic emotions. Cogn. Emot. 6, 169–200 (1992). https://doi.org/10.1080/02699939208411068

30. Ekman, P., Ekman, E.: Atlas of Emotions (2016). http://atlasofemotions.org/#continents. Accessed 5 Sept 2022

31. Oinas-Kukkonen, H., Harjumaa, M.: Persuasive systems design: key issues, process model, and system features. Commun. Assoc. Inf. Syst. 24, 96 (2009)

32. McKay, F.H., Slykerman, S., Dunn, M.: The app behavior change scale: creation of a scale to assess the potential of apps to promote behavior change. JMIR Mhealth Uhealth 7, e11130 (2019). https://doi.org/10.2196/11130

33. Elgarf mahaeg, M., et al.: Reward seeking or loss aversion? Impact of regulatory focus theory on emotional induction in children and their behavior towards a social robot. In: Proceedings of the 2021 CHI Conference on Human Factors in Computing Systems, New York, NY, USA, pp. 1–11. ACM (2021)

34. Krekhov, A., Emmerich, K., Fuchs, J., Krueger, J.H.: Interpolating happiness: understanding the intensity gradations of face emojis across cultures. In: CHI Conference on Human Factors in Computing Systems - Proceedings. Association for Computing Machinery, pp. 1–17 (2022)

35. Zhang, X., Li, W., Chen, X., Lu, S.: MoodExplorer: towards compound emotion detection via smartphone sensing. Proc. ACM Interact. Mob. Wearable Ubiquitous Technol. **1**, 1–30 (2018). https://doi.org/10.1145/3161414

36. Ganesh, A., Ndulue, C., Orji, R.: PERMARUN- a persuasive game to improve user awareness and self-efficacy towards secure smartphone behaviour. In: CHI EA 2021: Extended Abstracts of the 2021 CHI Conference on Human Factors in Computing Systems, pp. 1–7. Association for Computing Machinery (2021)

37. Oduor, M., Oinas-Kukkonen, H.: Committing to change: a persuasive systems design analysis of user commitments for a behaviour change support system. Behav. Inf. Technol. **40**, 20–38 (2019). https://doi.org/10.1080/0144929X.2019.1598495

38. Oyebode, O., Ndulue, C., Mulchandani, D., Zamil Adib, A., Alhasani, M., Orji, R.: Tailoring persuasive and behaviour change systems based on stages of change and motivation. In: Proceedings of the 2021 CHI Conference on Human Factors in Computing Systems, New York, NY, USA, pp. 1–19. Association for Computing Machinery (2021)

39. Oyebode, O., Alqahtani, F., Orji, R.: Exploring for possible effect of persuasive strategy implementation choices: towards tailoring persuasive technologies. In: Baghaei, N., Vassileva, J., Ali, R., Oyibo, K. (eds.) PERSUASIVE 2022. LNCS, vol. 13213, pp. 145–163. Springer, Cham (2022). https://doi.org/10.1007/978-3-030-98438-0_12

40. Portz, J.D., Miller, A., Foster, B., Laudeman, L.: Persuasive features in health information technology interventions for older adults with chronic diseases: a systematic review. Heal. Technol. **6**(2), 89–99 (2016). https://doi.org/10.1007/s12553-016-0130-x

41. Alslaity, A., et al.: Mobile applications for health and wellness: a systematic review. Proc. ACM Hum. Comput. Interact. **6**, 1–29 (2022). https://doi.org/10.1145/3534525

42. VanMeter, F., Cicchetti, D.: Resilience. Handb. Clin. Neurol. **173**, 67–73 (2020). https://doi.org/10.1016/B978-0-444-64150-2.00008-3

43. Thomas, R.J., Masthoff, J., Oren, N.: Can i influence you? development of a scale to measure perceived persuasiveness and two studies showing the use of the scale. Front. Artif. Intell. **2**, 1–14 (2019). https://doi.org/10.3389/FRAI.2019.00024

44. Hair, J.F., Ringle, C.M., Sarstedt, M.: PLS-SEM: Indeed a silver bullet. J. Market. Theory Pract. **19**, 139–152 (2011). https://doi.org/10.2753/MTP1069-6679190202

45. Hair, J.F., Hult, G.T.M., Ringle, C.M., Sarstedt, M.: A Primer on Partial Least Squares Structural Equation Modeling (PLS-SEM), 2nd edn. (2017)

46. Plutchik, R.: A General Psychoevolutionary Theory of Emotion. In: Theories of Emotion, pp. 3–33. Academic Press (1980)

47. Plutchik, R.: A psychoevolutionary theory of emotions. Soc. Sci. Inf. **21**, 529–553 (1982). https://doi.org/10.1177/053901882021004003

48. Ortony, A., Clore, G.L., Collins, A.: The Cognitive Structure Of Emotions. Cambridge University Press, Cambridge (1990)

49. Parrott, W.G.: Emotions in Social Psychology: Essential Readings. Psychology Press (2001)

50. Posner, J., Russell, J.A., Peterson, B.S.: The circumplex model of affect: an integrative approach to affective neuroscience, cognitive development, and psychopathology. Dev. Psychopathol. **17**, 715 (2005). https://doi.org/10.1017/S0954579405050340

51. Russell, J.A.: A circumplex model of affect. J Pers. Soc. Psychol. **39**, 1161–1178 (1980). https://doi.org/10.1037/H0077714

52. Russell, J.A., Mehrabian, A.: Evidence for a three-factor theory of emotions. J. Res. Pers. **11**, 273–294 (1977). https://doi.org/10.1016/0092-6566(77)90037-X

53. Wagener, N., Niess, J., Rogers, Y., Schöning, J.: Mood worlds: a virtual environment for autonomous emotional expression. In: Proceedings of the 2022 CHI Conference on Human Factors in Computing Systems, pp 1–16. Association for Computing Machinery (2022)
54. Hamari, J., Koivisto, J., Pakkanen, T.: Do persuasive technologies persuade? - a review of empirical studies. In: Spagnolli, A., Chittaro, L., Gamberini, L. (eds.) PERSUASIVE 2014. LNCS, vol. 8462, pp. 118–136. Springer, Cham (2014). https://doi.org/10.1007/978-3-319-07127-5_11
55. Orji, R., Moffatt, K.: Persuasive technology for health and wellness: state-of-the-art and emerging trends. Health Inform. J. 24, 66–91 (2018). https://doi.org/10.1177/146045821665 0979
56. Fogg, B.J., Fogg, G.E.: Persuasive Technology: Using Computers to Change What We Think and Do. Morgan Kaufmann, San Francisco (2003)
57. Cialdini, R.B.: Harnessing the science of persuasion. Harv. Bus. Rev. 79, 72–81 (2001)
58. Hamby, A., Jones, N.: The effect of affect: an appraisal theory perspective on emotional engagement in narrative persuasion. J Advert 51, 116–131 (2022). https://doi.org/10.1080/00913367.2021.1981498/SUPPL_FILE/UJOA_A_1981498_SM2149.DOCX
59. Dillard, J.P., Seo, K.: Affect and persuasion. In: The SAGE Handbook of Persuasion: Developments in Theory and Practice, pp 150–166. SAGE Publications Inc. (2012)
60. van 'T Riet, J., Ruiter, R.A.C., Werrij, M.Q., Candel, M.J.J.M., de Vries, H.: Distinct pathways to persuasion: The role of affect in message-framing effects. Eur. J. Soc. Psychol. 40, 1261–1276 (2010). https://doi.org/10.1002/EJSP.722
61. Ye, W., Li, Q., Yu, S.: Persuasive effects of message framing and narrative format on promoting COVID-19 vaccination: a study on Chinese college students. Int. J. Environ. Res. Public Health 18, 9485 (2021). https://doi.org/10.3390/IJERPH18189485
62. Cho, H., Salmon, C.T.: Fear appeals for individuals in different stages of change: intended and unintended effects and implications on public health campaigns. Health Commun. 20, 91–99 (2006). https://doi.org/10.1207/S15327027HC2001_9
63. Ort, A., Siegenthaler, P., Fahr, A.: How positively valenced health messages can foster information selection: evidence from two experiments. Front. Commun. (Lausanne) 6, 16 (2021). https://doi.org/10.3389/FCOMM.2021.534496/XML/NLM
64. Ibanez, L., Roussel, S.: The effects of induced emotions on environmental preferences and behavior: An experimental study. PLoS ONE 16, e0258045 (2021). https://doi.org/10.1371/JOURNAL.PONE.0258045
65. Samad, A.M., Mishra, K., Firdaus, M., Ekbal, A.: Empathetic persuasion: reinforcing empathy and persuasiveness in dialogue systems. In: Findings of the Association for Computational Linguistics: NAACL 2022, United States, pp. 844–856. Seattle (2022)
66. Mukherjee, A., Dubé, L.: Mixing emotions: the use of humor in fear advertising. J. Consum. Behav. 11, 147–161 (2012). https://doi.org/10.1002/CB.389
67. Jia, Y., Xu, B., Karanam, Y., Voida, S.: Personality-targeted gamification: a survey study on personality traits and motivational affordances. In: Proceedings of the 2016 CHI Conference on Human Factors in Computing Systems, San Jose, California, USA, pp 2001–2013. Association for Computing Machinery (2016)
68. Wais-Zechmann, B., Gattol, V., Neureiter, K., Orji, R., Tscheligi, M.: Persuasive technology to support chronic health conditions: investigating the optimal persuasive strategies for persons with COPD. In: Ham, J., Karapanos, E., Morita, P.P., Burns, C.M. (eds.) PERSUASIVE 2018. LNCS, vol. 10809, pp. 255–266. Springer, Cham (2018). https://doi.org/10.1007/978-3-319-78978-1_21
69. Schiraldi, G.R.: The Resilience Workbook: Essential Skills to Recover from Stress, Trauma, and Adversity. New Harbinger Publications (2017)

70. Joyce, S., Shand, F., Tighe, J., Laurent, S.J., Bryant, R.A., Harvey, S.B.: Road to resilience: a systematic review and meta-analysis of resilience training programmes and interventions. BMJ Open **8**, e017858 (2018). https://doi.org/10.1136/BMJOPEN-2017-017858

71. Stanley, E.A.: Mindfulness-based mind fitness training: an approach for enhancing performance and building resilience in high-stress contexts. Wiley Blackwell Handbook Mindfulness **1–2**, 964–985 (2014). https://doi.org/10.1002/9781118294895.CH50

72. Neenan, M.: Developing Resilience : A Cognitive-Behavioural Approach. Routledge (2017)

73. Soleymani, M., Pantic, M., Pun, T.: Multimodal emotion recognition in response to videos. IEEE Trans. Affect. Comput. **3**, 211–223 (2012). https://doi.org/10.1109/T-AFFC.2011.37

74. Samson, A.C., Kreibig, S.D., Soderstrom, B., Wade, A.A., Gross, J.J.: Eliciting positive, negative and mixed emotional states: a film library for affective scientists. Cogn. Emot. **30**, 827–856 (2016). https://doi.org/10.1080/02699931.2015.1031089/SUPPL_FILE/PCEM_A_1031089_SM0547.ZIP

75. Orji, R., Tondello, G.F., Nacke, L.E.: Personalizing persuasive strategies in gameful systems to gamification user types. In: Proceedings of the 2018 CHI Conference on Human Factors in Computing Systems - CHI 2018, pp 1–14 (2018)

76. ObjectPlanet Inc. Conduct Online Surveys using Opinio. http://www.objectplanet.com/opinio/. Accessed 3 Jan 2020

77. Wilberz, A., Leschtschow, D., Trepkowski, C., Maiero, J., Kruijff, E., Riecke, B.: FaceHaptics: robot arm based versatile facial haptics for immersive environments. In: Conference on Human Factors in Computing Systems - Proceedings, pp. 1–14. Association for Computing Machinery (2020)

78. Sona Systems Ltd SONA: Cloud-based Subject Pool Software for Universities. https://www.sona-systems.com/default.aspx. Accessed 5 Sep 2022

79. Hasan, R., Bertenthal, B.I., Hugenberg, K., Kapadia, A.: Your photo is so funny that I don't mind violating your privacy by sharing it: effects of individual humor styles on online photo-sharing behaviors. In: Conference on Human Factors in Computing Systems - Proceedings (2021). https://doi.org/10.1145/3411764.3445258

80. Koshy, V., Park, J.S.: We just use what they give us: understanding passenger user perspectives in smart homes. In: Conference on Human Factors in Computing Systems - Proceedings (2021). https://doi.org/10.1145/3411764.3445598

81. Kaiser, H.F.: A second generation little jiffy. Psychometrika **35**, 401–415 (1970)

82. Kupek, E.: Beyond logistic regression: Structural equations modelling for binary variables and its application to investigating unobserved confounders. BMC Med. Res. Methodol. **6**, 1 (2006). https://doi.org/10.1186/1471-2288-6-13

83. Jicol, C., et al.: Effects of emotion and agency on presence in virtual reality, pp 1–13. In: Proceedings of the 2021 CHI Conference on Human Factors in Computing Systems. Association for Computing Machinery (2021)

84. Machuletz, D., Laube, S., Böhme, R.: Webcam covering as planned behavior. In: Proceedings of the 2018 CHI Conference on Human Factors in Computing Systems, New York, NY, USA, pp. 1–13. ACM (2018)

85. Wang, G., Suh, A., Kong, H.: Disorder or driver?: The effects of nomophobia on work-related outcomes in organizations. In: Proceedings of the 2018 CHI Conference on Human Factors in Computing Systems, New York, NY, USA, pp. 1–12. ACM (2018)

86. Sarstedt, M., Cheah, J.-H.: Partial least squares structural equation modeling using SmartPLS: a software review. J. Mark. Analyt. **7**, 196–202 (2019). https://doi.org/10.1057/s41270-019-00058-3

87. Chin, W.W.: The partial least squares approach to structural equation modeling. Modern Meth. Bus. Res. **295**, 295–336 (1998)

88. Henseler, J., Ringle, C.M., Sarstedt, M.: A new criterion for assessing discriminant validity in variance-based structural equation modeling. J. Acad. Mark. Sci. **43**(1), 115–135 (2014). https://doi.org/10.1007/s11747-014-0403-8
89. Orji, R., Lomotey, R., Oyibo, K., Orji, F., Blustein, J., Shahid, S.: Tracking feels oppressive and 'punishy': exploring the costs and benefits of self-monitoring for health and wellness. Digit. Health **4**, 205520761879755 (2018). https://doi.org/10.1177/2055207618797554

Tailoring Persuasive Health Messages to the Predominant Ego State of Patients

Xinying Zhao[1,2(✉)] ⬥, Mengzhe Tao[1] ⬥, Yingting Chen[3], Bin Yin[1] ⬥,
and Panos Markopoulos[2] ⬥

[1] Philips Research, Shanghai, China
{xinying.zhao_1,mengzhe.tao,bin.yin}@philips.com
[2] Eindhoven University of Technology, Eindhoven, The Netherlands
P.Markopoulos@tue.nl
[3] Philips Design, Shanghai, China
yingting.chen@philips.com

Abstract. Lack of patient engagement has long been a problem in healthcare for chronic disease management. We report a study that explored the feasibility of applying Transactional Analysis theory to tailor health messages to the patient's predominant ego state, assuming that messages with a complementary communication approach will be better comprehended and efficacious in triggering the targeted health behaviours. These personalized health messages were constructed by field experts in co-creation workshops and tested by chronic disease patients with various predominant ego states via interviews and a survey. Our experiment did not support the hypothesized superiority of complementary communication but revealed a general patient preference for supportive and professional communication styles. Future studies should explore the long-term efficacy of complementary communication considering also situational and cultural factors.

Keywords: Patient engagement · Chronic disease management · Personalized health messages · Transactional analysis

1 Introduction

Chronic diseases, such as cardiovascular diseases, diabetes, and respiratory diseases, are the leading cause of death in the aging world, accounting for 71% of deaths globally in 2016 [1]. These diseases are usually not curable and require long-term treatment, demanding patient engagement in completing routine health tasks. However, following through with repeated health tasks can be challenging for patients, while prompts and feedback for their self-management behaviours are not always sufficiently effective. Therefore, it is necessary to investigate how to design health messages that can enhance patient self-management and patient engagement in chronic disease management.

This study investigated the feasibility and performance of applying a personality and counseling theory called Transactional Analysis (TA) [2] to personalize health messages. TA has been shown to be practical in promoting effective communication in healthcare

J. Ham et al. (Eds.): PERSUASIVE 2023, LNCS 13832, pp. 234–247, 2023.
https://doi.org/10.1007/978-3-031-30933-5_15

settings, i.e., improving communication and empathy skills [3, 4] as well as building trusting physician-patient relationships [5]. In TA theory, it assumes that messages communicated according to the recipient's key personality characteristics (predominant ego state) would help produce complementary transactions, which could be efficacious in triggering the target health behaviors when applied in tailored health communication. With the context of transformation in digital health, we set the test of the personalized health messages in a specialized dialogue module of a digital telecare solution. A virtual avatar was expected to send the message to a patient. Three virtual avatar figures were designed to represent the key personality characteristics of three ego states respectively to facilitate the complementary transactions with patients with various personality profiles. Consequently, we assumed that, comparing to a generic message that contains only the essential information, receiving a persuasive health message that attempted to tailor the communication would generally make the patients more engaged in the health tasks mentioned in the message. Specifically, as TA implies, these health messages personalized according to their predominant ego state would also outperform those messages that not intended for their predominant ego states. Additionally, although TA theory is commonly used in face-to-face conversations in mental health and clinical settings, it is not yet clear how to apply TA theory in constructing and delivering text messages via a virtual avatar to increase patient engagement.

In the following sections, we report on our design of this theoretically driven personalization approach and its empirical evaluation. Specifically, we examined the feasibility of tailoring health messages based on TA by generating personalized health messages in co-creation workshops with healthcare professionals and psychologists, considering typical scenarios in chronic disease management, and addressing a patient's unique needs in health communication based on their predominant ego state. After preliminary evaluation and modification by the researchers, these messages were then evaluated by chronic disease patients with various predominant ego states via in-depth interviews and were tested by a larger chronic disease population via a survey. The workshop and interviews resulted in a framework for understanding the structure and personalization approach contained in these persuasive health messages, which could also be utilized for further message generation. The survey results did not support the superiority of complementary transactions but revealed a general patient preference for supportive and professional communication styles, regardless of their predominant ego state.

2   Related Work

There has been a large body of work that concerns the tailoring of persuasive messages to an individual's personality profile. For example, by measuring individuals' personality profiles via the Big-Five Aspect Scale, arguments could be adapted to each personality dimension and the persuasive effectiveness of such messages has been shown to match the targeted personality dimensions [6]. Subsequent studies have found a link between the Big-Five Personality and persuasive strategies or features on mobile applications [7–9], which offer a potential way to personalize information based on personality characteristics. One relevant study also investigated the relationship among health threat communication, Big-Five Personality traits and patients' personal model of diabetes

[10], suggesting that personality traits can allow practitioners to frame health messages accordingly. However, there has been less work regarding the practice of tailoring and evaluating the Big-Five Personality Model in personalized health communication. Some individual personality traits have been brought to this research topic together with cultural or contextual factors. Dutta-Bergman [11] explored the self-monitor as a personality index interacting with idiocentrism in message appeal construction in terms of functional, social and sensory appeal types. York, Brannon, and Miller [12] introduced schema matching and context matching (topic and values) in evaluating the effectiveness of messages to promote responsible undergraduate drinking. These studies have highlighted the effects of both personality traits and social influences, though they focused on a single personality trait and did not provide guidance for how to personalize messages based on the full set of traits from a personality theory.

Research into persuasion profiling has examined the tailoring of persuasive messages to different recipients to match their susceptibility to different social influence strategies [13, 14]. This method of tailoring has been found efficacious in improving adherence regarding snacking behaviours and physical activity, which involves cues to persuasive messages that, while not elaborated cognitively, can serve to enhance compliance. A potential disadvantage of this approach is that, while it can help design individual or even repeated reminders, it does not provide an overall organizing principle for designing communication with the patient. And as is well understood from the elaboration likelihood model, the effectiveness of the method for a sustained period and when messages are also elaborated cognitively is likely to be limited [15].

To provide a general strategy for tailoring communication, instead of the Big-Five personality theory, we apply TA. As a theory connecting knowledge between personality and communication, it provides a powerful handle for tailoring health communication. TA theory holds that in order to achieve effective communication, the communicator should adapt their way of speaking toward the recipient's need to build a complementary transaction instead of a crossed one. The transaction here is a unit of social action, which contains a transactional stimulus from a particular ego state in an agent plus a transactional response from a particular ego state in the respondent [16]. In a complementary transaction, the responses given match with the question or stimulus intended according to the agent's ego state. In this case, the conversation will go smoothly and be sustained. Otherwise, if the responses given are not the question or stimulus intended, communication tends to breakdown and be short-lived [17].

In TA theory, it is believed that an individual's personality is manifested in three ego states, namely Parent (P), Adult (A), and Child (C) ego states [2, 18]. The ego state is a coherent system of thoughts and feelings manifested by corresponding patterns of behaviours [18]. The one dominating an individual's feelings and behaviours is called the predominant ego state, which could be measured to capture their unique needs in health communication, thus allowing tailoring the corresponding content and delivery mechanism. Theoretically, the Parent ego state mainly originates from internalizing one's parent's or guardian's words and behaviours in their first five years of life. In contrast, the Child ego state is derived from one's recordings of feelings and responses in childhood, which can be spontaneous, irrational, carefree, and creative. Individuals in either of these two ego states may easily perceive the world deviated from the fact, leading to irrational reactions to the current situation. Still, an Adult ego state will succeed because it is characterized by logical reasoning and rational thinking toward current problems, as a result of their reasonable perceptions of the objective reality [19]. Moreover, we can explain ego states from a more descriptive perspective. The Parent ego state can be further divided into Nurturing Parent (NP, care for others, kindness, warmness) and Critical Parent (CP, unsupportive, critical) ego state. Similarly, the Child ego state can be split into Free Child (FC, spontaneous, carefree) and Adapted Child (AC, obey the rules or authority) ego state. The Adult (A, rational) ego state stays the same. The NP, A, and FC ego states have been estimated as the top three predominant ego states in Chinese chronic disease patients, which were found to cover around 70% of the sample [20]. Therefore, as our study was situated in China, we chose to create corresponding personalized health messages, covering all nine types of transactions (NP-NP, NP-A, NP-FC, A-NP, A-A, A-FC, FC-NP, FC-A, FC-FC) among these three ego states. The complementary transactions were defined as the transactions that are intended for the patient's predominant ego state, e.g., NP-NP, A-NP, FC-NP for NP patients. The crossed transactions are represented by the mismatching pairs that not intended for the recipient's predominant ego state, e.g., NP-A, NP-FC, A-A, A-FC, FC-A, and FC-FC for NP patients.

3 Method

We ran nine co-creation sessions with field experts and six in-depth interview sessions as well as a survey with 165 chronic disease patients, to explore and evaluate the feasibility of applying TA in personalized health messages for increasing patient engagement in chronic disease management.

3.1 Co-creation Workshop with Field Experts

The co-creation workshop with experts in clinical or psychotherapy background was aimed at generating a pool of personalized health messages and discussing how each of these messages could trigger patient engagement. The targeted message samples were designed to cover all nine types of transactions between an avatar and a patient under typical chronic disease management scenarios, including medication reminders, uploading test results, and reading health education materials.

A total of 18 participants joined this co-creation workshop, nine health care professionals and nine psychological counselors. One of each were assigned into nine pairs that each studied one of the nine transaction types mentioned above.

Three personas, representing the most common ego states (NP, A, and FC) in the Chinese population, were created based on the researcher's prior knowledge of chronic disease patients. Each persona described a patient with the targeted ego state. These descriptions included a patient's demographic profile, daily life, health condition, attitude and behaviours toward chronic disease management, etc. Similarly, three virtual avatars were designed in line with the three targeted ego states, namely Uncle Fei with NP, Expert Fei with A, and Xiao Fei with FC (see Fig. 1). Their key personality characteristics were defined according to the ego state they represented.

Uncle Fei	Expert Fei	Xiao Fei
Kind and gentle;	Listening;	Spontaneous;
Caring;	Rational;	Self-centered;
Willing to help;	Equal;	Emotional;
Willing to share	Responsible	Curious

Fig. 1. Three avatars and their key personality characteristics

Example messages between an avatar and a patient persona were provided in each transaction type separately for each session, to give an intuitive impression of the expected outcome and to inspire the participants. Generic messages containing the essential information under each scenario (e.g., It is time for your medication. Please take it on time) were also given as the starting point of personalization.

The nine workshop sessions were held online via teleconference software (Microsoft Teams) due to COVID-19-related restrictions on social contact. For each scenario, the participants were required to draft at least three messages in the role of their assigned ego state to ensure sufficient diversity of the raw message pool. They were given 5 min to generate the three messages for each scenario. We invited the participants to share their thoughts behind each message they composed, trying to capture the rationale of these messages. Moreover, we also generally discussed which are the suitable and unsuitable tones in drafting patient-friendly and motivated health messages.

All the discussions during the workshop sessions were recorded by taking notes. At the end of each session, we collected the drafted messages to build the raw message pool. These messages were evaluated by two researchers (with psychological background) in terms of their transaction type and congruence, motivation intensity, and readability [21]. We ranked them to identify the messages with both high performance and inter-rater agreement. Then we collaborated on the refinement to finalize the personalized health messages for each transaction type plus each scenario. 27 persuasive health messages (9 transaction types * 3 scenarios) were selected for the subsequent evaluation with chronic disease patients via interviews and a survey, respectively.

3.2   In-Depth Interviews with Chronic Disease Patients

We interviewed six chronic disease patients from the target population to investigate how they would react to these theory-driven persuasive health messages. The inclusion criteria of the interview were that: 1) patients who have been diagnosed with at least one of the target diseases, i.e., coronary disease, hypertension, atrial fibrillation, heart failure, chronic obstructive pulmonary disease, and sleep apnea syndrome; 2) their predominant ego states should be one of NP, A and FC (measured by the adapted and abbreviated version of ego state personality test, which includes 15 items measuring their preferences in daily activities [20]). The participants were assigned to one of the three target scenarios with nine messages to review. The interview started by getting to know how the participant usually acts to stay healthy in the assigned scenario. Then the moderator would introduce the concept of a dialogue system in a chronic disease management platform. Persuasive health messages sent by three virtue avatars for helping the patient complete the relevant health task were shown on a chat box interface, see Fig. 2. The participants were asked about their feedback of the persuasive health messages. The key interview questions in the example of the first three messages from Uncle Fei were:

1. Among these three messages, which one motivated you the most? Why?
2. Which one is speaking in a tone that you are comfortable with? Why?
3. Which one do you think is not good enough or should be further modified? Why? If possible, please indicate how you would like to refine it.

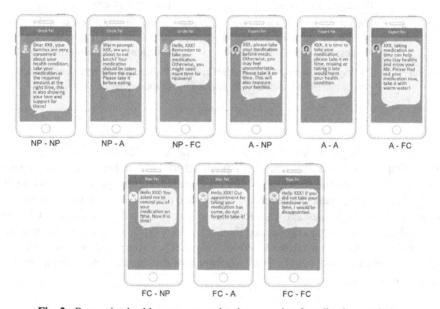

Fig. 2. Persuasive health messages under the scenario of medication reminder

The same discussion was repeated for the other six messages from Expert Fei and Xiao Fei under the same scenario, respectively. We also asked participants to choose their most preferable message and explain their reasons.

3.3 A Survey Among a Larger Chronic Disease Population

We launched a survey to evaluate the persuasive health messages with a larger chronic disease patient population, so as to test our hypotheses of the outperformance of persuasive health messages in general and the superiority of the personalized health messages (complementary transactions). The estimated sample size was 165, as calculated by the G-power software to achieve adequate power ($\alpha = 0.05$) and reasonable effect size (set as 0.15, [22–24]). The survey respondents were 81 females and 84 males, aged between 21–60, and diagnosed with at least one of the six aforementioned chronic diseases. We intentionally screened and recruited these participants to represent the target population. They were found to have a single predominant ego state of either NP (N = 51), A (N = 58), or FC (N = 56) and were pseudo-randomly assigned into one of the three scenarios according to their predominant ego state, to balance the number of participants in each condition.

Table 1. The three sections of the survey

Survey	Contents	Purpose
Section 1	The adapted and abbreviated version of the ego state personality test	To determine the participant's predominant ego state
Section 2	Evaluation of the ten messages under one of the three scenarios in terms of comfort, likeness, and motivation intensity	To test the effectiveness of the persuasive health messages and complementary transaction
Section 3	Participants' demographic profile: age group, gender, education level, chronic diseases	To describe the representativeness of the sample

The survey contains three sections, as shown in Table 1. After the ego state personality test, participants were asked to rate on a 7-point Likert scale on their level of agreement in terms of three items (listed below, [6]) for the effectiveness ratings of each message. In each scenario, nine persuasive health messages were displayed as sent by our designed avatars and one generic message was presented as sent by a health assistant with a default avatar. These ten messages represented the ten message types in the following analysis of the effectiveness of persuasive health messages. They were randomly presented to participants to avoid sequential effects. Examples of the three testing items under the medication reminder scenario are:

1. This message is phrased in a tone that I am comfortable with.
2. I would like to receive such a message to remind me of my medication under this specific context.
3. I feel very motivated to take my medication after reading this message.

4 Results

4.1 Personalization of the Health Messages Based on TA Theory

The core content of the messages was based on an analysis of the adherence challenges according to the COM-B model, which describes capability (physical and psychological), opportunity (social and physical), and motivation (reflective and automatic) [25]. Here we further explain the personalization framework derived from the analysis of field experts and chronic disease patients' views on the three different communication styles suggested by TA theory, distinguishing three aspects, the communication style toward the Nurturing Parent, Adult and Free Child patients, respectively, see Table 2.

Table 2. The personalization framework for generating personalized health messages

Category	Toward NP patients	Toward A patients	Toward FC patients
Greetings	Dear XXX Care for the wellbeing of patient	Hello XXX Remind patient of health task with facts	Hey XXX Remind patient of health task by stating purpose
Tone	Be kind, gentle, caring and supportive Informal and varied	Be equal and professional Not tendentious	Be human-like and customized Avoid formulaic/impersonal written language
Psychological capability	Supplementary health knowledge Soft reminders to raise awareness of health demands	Professional health knowledge Objective reminders of health requirements	Accessible health knowledge Supportive prompts of health tasks for increasing self-efficacy
Physical capability	Briefly refer to the target health task	Objective instructions for actions to take	Step-by-step guides
Automatic motivation	Bring self-value for enabling health management experience sharing with others Trigger the desire to keep healthy	Bring responsibility for providing full autonomy in health management Bring self-value for self-control in long-term health management	Evoke curiosity for innovative health management solutions Convey a sense of fighting against the disease together with other patients Trigger desire to keep healthy
Reflective motivation	Facilitate preparations by reminding health tasks in advance Facilitate the evaluation by stating the purpose, importance, or benefits of completing this health task	Provide feedback on progress in health management and indicate a corresponding coping strategy Explain the mechanism or rationale behind the task Analyze the cost/benefits of completing the task	Arrange upcoming health tasks in advance for patients Provide customized service adapting to a patient's unique needs in healthcare State benefits of completing health task

(continued)

Table 2. (*continued*)

Category	Toward NP patients	Toward A patients	Toward FC patients
Social opportunity	Refer family members' caring and support in health management Express expectations or provide positive feedback from the perspective of the doctor Invite the patient to join a health task together with the virtual avatar Generally express care for the well-being of the patients	Invite the patient to commit to completing the health task Express expectations or provide objective feedback from the perspective of the doctor Briefly restate the analytical contents sent previously, and relate it to real-life practice	Express specific concern and caring continuously according to a patient's health condition Indicate that other patients are all insisting on excellent adherence State what the virtual avatar has done for the patient to trigger target behaviour via reciprocity
Physical opportunity	A kind reminder of physical resources, timing, or locations needed	Objectively stating the physical resources, timing, or locations needed	Specifying the physical resources, timing, or locations needed

4.2 The Performance of Persuasive Health Messages

We removed two cases from the survey results because their answers in section 2 were the same for more than 90% of the testing items, leaving 163 cases for further analysis. The dependent variable was defined as the average effective ratings of the three testing items for each message, as we found they are highly correlated with each other ($r_{\text{item1 \& item2}}$ = .81, $r_{\text{item1 \& item3}}$ = .79, $r_{\text{item2 \& item3}}$ = .82).

The General Outperformance of Persuasive Health Messages. To evaluate the performance of the persuasive health messages compared with the generic messages, we compared the average effective ratings of all ten message types with reference to the participant's predominant ego state.

The scores of each message type violated the assumption of normality (Shapiro-Wilk's $ps < .05$), so we instead ran an Aligned Rank Transform ANOVA to compare their performance [26]. A significant main effect of the message type was found (F (9, 1440) = 27.86, $p < .001$, $\eta_p^2 = .15$). We found no significant effect of the participant's predominant ego state (F (2, 160) = 1.76, $p = 0.18$) nor interactions between them (F (18, 1440) = 0.81, $p = 0.69$). Pairwise comparisons showed that messages in all nine transaction types received higher effective ratings than the generic message (all $ps < .05$), suggesting that all persuasive health messages outperform generic messages. Consequently, we excluded the generic messages from further analysis.

The Engaging Tactics Beyond Complementary Transaction. We tested the assumption of whether the complementary transactions would be more effective in communication than crossed transactions as suggested by TA theory. The data fit the normal distribution (Shapiro-Wilk's $ps > .05$), so a Repeated ANOVA was performed to compare the effectiveness of complementary transactions with the crossed transaction based on the participant's predominant ego state [27]. The results revealed that, neither the main effect of the transaction (F (1, 160) $= .53$, $p = .47$) nor the main effect of the participant's predominant ego state (F (2, 160) $= 2.94$, $p = .06$) was significant.

Interestingly, an interaction effect was found between them (F (2, 160) $= 11.67$, $p < .001$, $\eta_p^2 = .13$). As shown in Fig. 3, chronic disease patients with an A ego state (A patients) were found to prefer the complementary transaction more than the crossed ones ($p = 0.02$), whereas patients with an NP ego state (NP patients) showed no obvious preference of complementary transaction or crossed transaction, ($p = 0.52$). On the contrary, patients with the Free Child ego state (FC patients) reported a preference for crossed transactions over complementary transactions ($p < .001$). The latter was inconsistent with the theoretical assumption, suggesting that further investigation is needed to interpret these findings.

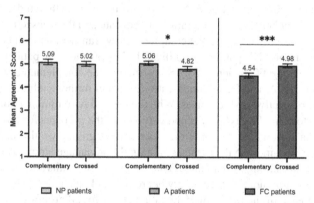

Fig. 3. Complementary versus Crossed Transactions of Different Patient Groups, the error bar stands for standard error (SE), * $p < .05$; ** $p < .01$; *** $p < .001$.

The General Preference of NP and A Communication Styles. To explore these theoretically inconsistent results, we considered separating the complementary and crossed transactions into NP, A, and FC communication styles toward patients. Together with the participant's predominant ego state, we compared the average effective ratings to interpret the above findings. The average effective ratings generally fit the assumption of normality, so we ran a Repeated ANOVA to compare their performance [27].

The results revealed that, only the main effect of the communication style was significant, F (2, 320) $= 21.15$, $p < .001$, $\eta_p^2 = .12$. Neither the main effect of the predominant ego state (F (2, 160) $= 1.49$) nor their interaction effect (F (4, 320) $= .45$) was significant, all $ps > .05$. The following pairwise comparisons suggested that the effective ratings of the communication style toward NP ($M = 4.99$, $SD = .80$) and A patients ($M = 5.11$, $SD = .74$) were both remarkably higher than the communication style toward FC patients ($M = 4.70$, $SD = .87$), all $ps < 0.001$. Also, the effective ratings of the A communication style were slightly higher than the NP style, with a marginal significance of $p =$

.06 < .10. This evidence suggests that the theoretically inconsistent performance may result from the collapsed means across the three communication styles when defining complementary and crossed transactions in each predominant ego state group.

5 Discussion

Our design and evaluation study explored the potential of tailoring the communication style in persuasive health reminders based on the TA theory. The effectiveness of persuasive health messages is generally promising compared to their generic form. Nevertheless, contrary to our expectations, the superiority of complementary transactions seems to exist only among patients with an Adult predominant ego state. The overall results demonstrate a common preference for health messages. Patients, regardless of their predominant ego states, tend to prefer the communication styles toward NP and A patients, leaving the FC style as the least favorable choice.

With these unexpected results, the question arising is why the theoretically advocating complementary communication fails to reveal its potential in this study. Confusingly, the interaction effect between the predominant ego state and the transaction shows contradictory results when comparing the complementary transactions with crossed transactions, closely among NP patients, significantly better among A patients, and unexpectedly worse among FC patients. By deconstructing the complementary and crossed transactions into NP, A, and FC communication styles in further analysis, we were able to observe their respective performances. With the NP and A communication styles consistently outperforming FC styles, it is understood that the averages for complementary and crossed transactions for the three different patient groups would finally result in flattening the effects among NP patients, retaining the advantage among A patients, and increasing contrasts among FC patients. Thus, the observed results seem to be irrelevant to whether transactions are complementary or crossed and rather, derive from the overall performance of each of the three communication styles for all groups of patients.

The remarkable performance of the communication style toward A patients is consistent with the TA theory, which favours Adult communication style in counseling [4, 28]. A possible explanation is that as the conversations start from an Adult ego state, the chance is assumingly greater for triggering the recipient's ego state adjustment toward an Adult, guiding patients to be more responsible for their health and meanwhile achieving effective health communication [28]. Additionally, the positive performance of the communication style toward NP patients might benefit from its caring and experienced nature, which is consistent with the patient's expectation of an experienced healthcare assistant. On the contrary, the communication style toward FC patients comes across as less competent for all three patient groups, possibly due to some perceived inappropriateness under the scenarios of chronic disease management and cultural preference of authority in health communication in China [29].

That the results did not confirm the hypothesis may also reflect limitations in the implementation of the theory in the design of the messages. For example, the content quality of the persuasive health messages was not well balanced across the three communication styles, perhaps confounding the impact of content quality and communication style. Given that, future research is needed to introduce the content quality as a covariate variable in the analysis to rule out its impact. In addition, only two researchers with psychological background participated in the examination of the representative messages applied in this study, so chances of bias may exist in their choices. Another potential explanation for these results is that participants were classified into three ego states (NP, A and FC) based on their preferences regarding daily activities rather than self-care behaviours. Furthermore, the effectiveness of persuasive health messages was evaluated based on participants' self-reported agreement level rather than their behavioural responses. Also, tailoring in our experiment was applied only to unidirectional communication in terms of reminders, thus weakening the extent to which aligning to TA theory can help build a trusting relationship between a patient and a virtue avatar. This therapeutic alliance is a significant predictor of outcomes in many areas of healthcare, including chronic disease management [30]. Even limited interactive communication with empathy is critical in promoting positive health outcomes, as this setting facilitates the construct of trusting rapport between the virtual avatar and the patient [31, 32]. Additionally, existing evidence of the TA theory concentrated on improving communication skills and building trusting relationships [3–5]. We have not yet found any motivational or behavioural proof in empirical research supporting the superiority of complementary transactions. It is possible that consistent use of complementary transactions would eventually lead to effective communication through improved communication and trusting relationship, but assessing its impact would require long-term observations of dynamically learning of complementary communication. Finally, the applicability of this personalized persuasive approach may also be confounded by other factors, such as patients having dual predominant ego states. One way to solve this problem is to introduce machine learning in the message delivery mechanism with reference to patients' behavioural responses, so as to build a personalized persuasive profile for any individual.

Conclusively, future research will need to consider the complexity of the dual predominant ego states and continuous conversations, measure the separate effectiveness of communication styles in long-term observations, and examine the impact of clinical settings and cultural influences in personality-driven tailored health communication.

6 Conclusion

This study explored the way to adopt personalized health messages to promote patient engagement in chronic disease management. By co-creating with field experts and discussing with chronic disease patients, a framework for generating personalized health messages was built based on TA theory. Persuasive health messages outperformed generic messages. However, contrary to our expectations, our results did not confirm that communications should be tailored to the TA ego state of the patient. Rather, all patients preferred supportive and professional communication styles. Future research is needed to overcome the limitations and observe the performance of complementary transactions in longitudinal and cross-cultural studies in healthcare settings.

Acknowledgments. The research leading to these results has received funding from the Zhejiang University-Philips-Eindhoven University of Technology Brain Bridge Program sponsored by Philips Research.

References

1. World Health Organization: Noncommunicable diseases country profile 2018 (2018). https://apps.who.int/iris/handle/10665/274512
2. Berne, E.: Transactional analysis in psychotherapy: A systematic individual and social psychiatry. Grove Press (1961)
3. Lawrence, L.: Applying transactional analysis and personality assessment to improve patient counseling and communication skills. Am. J. Pharm. Educ. **71**, 1–5 (2007). https://doi.org/10.5688/aj710481
4. Whitley-Hunter, B.L.: Validity of transactional analysis and emotional intelligence in training nursing students. J. Adv. Med. Educ. Prof. **2**, 138–145 (2014)
5. Fisher, Y.: Physician-Patient Communication: Building a Better Relationship to Improve Medication Adherence. https://digitalcommons.calpoly.edu/joursp/116/ (2016)
6. Hirsh, J.B., Kang, S.K., Bodenhausen, G.V.: Personalized persuasion: tailoring persuasive appeals to recipients' personality traits. Psychol. Sci. **23**, 578–581 (2012). https://doi.org/10.1177/0956797611436349
7. Anagnostopoulou, E., Magoutas, B., Bothos, E., Schrammel, J., Orji, R., Mentzas, G.: Exploring the links between persuasion, personality and mobility types in personalized mobility applications. In: de Vries, P.W., Oinas-Kukkonen, H., Siemons, L., Beerlage-de Jong, N., van Gemert-Pijnen, L. (eds.) Persuasive Technology: Development and Implementation of Personalized Technologies to Change Attitudes and Behaviors, pp. 107–118. Springer, Cham (2017). https://doi.org/10.1007/978-3-319-55134-0
8. Halko, S., Kientz, J.A.: Personality and persuasive technology: an exploratory study on health-promoting mobile applications. In: Ploug, T., Hasle, P., Oinas-Kukkonen, H. (eds.) Persuasive Technology, pp. 150–161. Springer, Berlin Heidelberg, Berlin, Heidelberg (2010)
9. Alqahtani, F., Meier, S., Orji, R.: Personality-based approach for tailoring persuasive mental health applications (2022). https://doi.org/10.1007/s11257-021-09289-5
10. Lawson, V.L., Bundy, C., Harvey, J.N.: The influence of health threat communication and personality traits on personal models of diabetes in newly diagnosed diabetic patients. Diabet. Med. **24**, 883–891 (2007). https://doi.org/10.1111/j.1464-5491.2007.02155.x
11. Dutta-Bergman, M.J.: The linear interaction model of personality effects in health communication. Health Commun. **15**, 101–116 (2003). https://doi.org/10.1207/s15327027hc1501_5
12. York, V.K., Brannon, L.A., Miller, M.M.: Increasing the effectiveness of messages promoting responsible undergraduate drinking: tailoring to personality and matching to context. Health Commun. **27**, 302–309 (2012). https://doi.org/10.1080/10410236.2011.585450
13. Kaptein, M., De Ruyter, B., Markopoulos, P., Aarts, E.: Adaptive persuasive systems: a study of tailored persuasive text messages to reduce snacking. ACM Trans. Interact. Intell. Syst. **2** (2012). https://doi.org/10.1145/2209310.2209313
14. Kaptein, M., Markopoulos, P., De Ruyter, B., Aarts, E.: Personalizing persuasive technologies: explicit and implicit personalization using persuasion profiles. Int. J. Hum. Comput. Stud. **77**, 38–51 (2015). https://doi.org/10.1016/j.ijhcs.2015.01.004
15. Petty, R.E., Cacioppo, J.T.: The elaboration likelihood model of persuasion. Adv. Exp. Soc. Psychol. **19**, 123–205 (1986). https://doi.org/10.1016/S0065-2601(08)60214-2
16. Berne, E.: What Do You Say After You Say Hello? The Psychology of Human Destiny. Grove Press (1972)
17. Hough, M.: Counselling Skills and Theory 4th Edition. Hodder Education (2014)
18. Stewart, I., Joines, V.: TA Today: A New Introduction to Transactional Analysis. Lifespace (1987). https://doi.org/10.5964/ejop.v3i1.390

19. Harris: I'm OK – You're OK: A Practical Guide to Transactional Analysis. HarperCollins (2004)
20. Tao, M., Xie, X., Fang, Y., Zhao, X., Yin, B.: Ego-state focused patient profiling approach: validating the adapted and abbreviated version of ego state personality test. Philips Research China, Shanghai (2019). Unpublished internal company document
21. Updegraffa, J.A., Shermanb, D.K., Luystera, F.S., Mannc, T.L.: The effects of message quality and congruency on perceptions of tailored health communications. J. Exp. Soc. Psychol. **43**, 249–257 (2007). https://doi.org/10.1016/j.jesp.2006.01.007
22. Cohen, J.: Statistical Power Analysis for the Behavioral Sciences. Lawrence Erlbaum Associates, New York (1988)
23. Faul, F., Erdfelder, E., Buchner, A.-G.L.A.A.: G*Power 3: a flexible statistical power analysis program for the social, behavioral, and biomedical sciences. Behav. Res. Methods **39**, 175–191 (2007). https://doi.org/10.3758/bf03193146
24. Rains, S.A., Levine, T.R., Weber, R.: Sixty years of quantitative communication research summarized: lessons from 149 meta-analyses. Ann. Int. Commun. Assoc. **42**, 105–124 (2018). https://doi.org/10.1080/23808985.2018.1446350
25. Michie, S., van Stralen, M.M., West, R.: The behaviour change wheel: a new method for characterising and designing behaviour change interventions. Implement. Sci. **6**, 42 (2011). https://doi.org/10.1186/1748-5908-6-42
26. Wobbrock, J.O., Findlater, L., Gergle, D., Higgins, J.J.: The aligned rank transform for nonparametric factorial analyses using only ANOVA procedures. In: Proceedings of the SIGCHI Conference on Human Factors in Computing Systems, pp. 143–146. Association for Computing Machinery (2011). https://doi.org/10.1145/1978942.1978963
27. IBM Corp.: IBM SPSS Statistics for Windows, Version 25.0 (2017)
28. Booth, L.: Observations and reflections of communication in health care - could transactional analysis be used as an effective approach? Radiography **13**, 135–141 (2007). https://doi.org/10.1016/j.radi.2006.01.010
29. Fu, P.P., Yukl, G.: Perceived effectiveness of influence tactics in the united states and china. Leadersh. Q. **11**, 251–266 (2000). https://doi.org/10.1016/S1048-9843(00)00039-4
30. Attale, C., et al.: Therapeutic alliance and glycaemic control in type 1 diabetes: a pilot study. Diabetes Metab. **36**, 499–502 (2010). https://doi.org/10.1016/j.diabet.2010.08.003
31. Watson, D., Clark, L.A., Tellegen, A.: Development and validation of brief measures of positive and negative affect: the PANAS scales. J. Pers. Soc. Psychol. **54**, 1063–1070 (1988). https://doi.org/10.1037//0022-3514.54.6.1063
32. Bickmore, T., Schulman, D.: Practical Approaches to Comforting. In: Proceedings of ACM CHI 2007 Conference Human Factors Computing System, pp. 2291–2296 (2007)

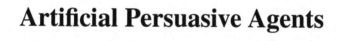

Artificial Persuasive Agents

Persuasive Robots in the Field

Rosalyn M. Langedijk$^{(\boxtimes)}$ ⓘ and Kerstin Fischer ⓘ

University of Southern Denmark, Alsion 2, 6400 Sonderborg, Denmark
{rla,kerstin}@sdu.dk

Abstract. In this paper, we investigate the effectiveness of a persuasive social robot in the field. The service robot drives around a public space and offers water to people using a persuasive message. The persuasive utterances used evoke either scientific expertise (e.g. "Research shows that it is important to drink enough water during the day") or a reference to other people's choices ("Most people/men/women actually do take something to drink"), hence exploring the principle of social proof. Our study makes three contributions: First, we show how persuasive utterances that are successful in the lab are not necessarily persuasive in the field. Second, we show that context factors influence the effectiveness of a persuasive message, as well as the sequential placement of the persuasive message. Lastly, the extent to which people construe the human-robot interaction situation as social influences the effectiveness of the robot as a persuasive technology in general.

Keywords: Robots in the wild · Persuasive utterances · Persuasive robots · Social robots

1 Introduction

Much recent work has shown that social robots can be effective persuasive agents (e.g. [18, 21]). Most of these findings have been achieved in controlled lab studies that ensure that the effects found are really due to the respective intervention. At the same time, much recent work in human-robot interaction has shown that field trials yield very different kinds of interactions than controlled lab studies (e.g. [24, 29, 30]). The current paper therefore addresses a possible mismatch between results from lab and field studies by testing the persuasiveness of persuasive utterances, whose effectiveness has been documented in previous lab studies, in the field. *The first contribution of this paper is thus the empirical analysis of the effects of persuasive messages when used by a social robot in the field.*

The robot we are using is a drink-serving service robot with several anthropomorphic design features (see Fig. 1). Specifically, it has eyes that blink, and it uses speech for interactive communication [26]. In our application, it carries glasses of water on a tray on the back. The robot is thus a service robot with some social characteristics, including

This research was partially supported by the Danish Innovations fonden in the framework of the Smooth project.

© The Author(s), under exclusive license to Springer Nature Switzerland AG 2023
J. Ham et al. (Eds.): PERSUASIVE 2023, LNCS 13832, pp. 251–264, 2023.
https://doi.org/10.1007/978-3-031-30933-5_16

human-aware navigation. However, for safety reasons, the robot is teleoperated even though it is generally able to navigate autonomously. Because the design of the robot is only moderately social – compared to robots like Sophia from Hanson Robotics, for instance – people in the field may or may not recognize the robot as a social actor and interact with it in social ways [8, 11, 37]. The construal of the robot as social may have an impact on the persuasiveness of the robot and on the effectiveness of the persuasive messages it uses. *The second contribution of this paper is therefore a better understanding of the role of the construction of the service robot as social on its effectiveness as a persuasive technology.*

The third contribution of this paper is to analyze the context factors that influence to what extent a persuasive message is persuasive in interaction. For instance, Liu et al. [31] find that context and robot interactivity matter. In the same vein, yet using a discourse analytical approach, we investigate what situation contexts are favorable to the persuasive message being successful, such as the sequential context (what happened before?) and what other preconditions are met (e.g. do people have something to drink already? Are they idle or in a hurry?).

The investigation presented is thus both exploratory and qualitative, yet using a large corpus of almost two hundred interactions.

2 Related Work

Related work concerns, on the one hand, studies that show that field research yields different results than lab studies, and work on robot persuasiveness in more controlled environments on the other.

2.1 Robots in the Field

Recently, increasingly more field studies in HRI are being carried out (e.g. [6, 10, 46]), and more field studies have been asked for (e.g. [3, 24, 35]) since field studies have shown that the results achieved in the lab cannot always be replicated in the field (e.g. [1]) and that field studies face very different challenges than lab studies (e.g. [29]), especially in elderly care (e.g. [4, 32, 44]). For example, several field studies have recorded interactions with robots that were not intended; for instance, Forlizzi [16] finds that the families in her study were using a vacuum cleaning robot in unexpected ways. Mutlu and Forlizzi [33] report that the way the logistics robots in a hospital were dealt with was influenced by the amount of space available, the degree of stress, as well as the patients' and staff's attitudes towards robots – which in turn was influenced by the kind of work done in the different wards (e.g. oncology versus maternity ward).

To sum up, field studies report unexpected, more messy situations, which may impact the persuasiveness of persuasive robots.

2.2 Persuasive Social Robots

The field of persuasive social robots addresses many aspects of persuasion. Robot persuasion can be achieved through different strategies, like through persuasive messages (e.g. [19, 47]), robot behavior like speech or gaze [13, 14] or a combination of several strategies (e.g. [18, 20, 21]). Specifically, previous studies have shown that a robot's nonverbal behavior influences its persuasiveness (e.g. [5, 21, 40]). The gender of the robot also plays a role in the success to persuade people (e.g. [18, 43, 45]). Only a few studies look at the persistence of persuasive messages over time (e.g. [22, 34]).

In this study, we focus on verbal persuasion by the robot, similar to, for instance, Winkle et al. [47], and explore what factors influence the robot's persuasiveness; specifically, we investigate how the persuasive messages influence people's behavior in interaction in the field with participants who do not expect to encounter a robot, who may not have seen a robot before in their lives, and who enter the space alone or in groups with very different intentions and agendas than when they are invited to the lab.

The persuasive utterances we use in this study were designed based on two of the six strategies of influence outlined by Cialdini [7], namely social proof and authority. The strategy of social proof relies on the fact that, in case of uncertainty, people look at what others do to plan their own behavior. Thus, the persuasive message consists in references to other people's decisions, and it has been found in more controlled research studies that personalized messages of social proof can be very effective (e.g. [17, 19, 25]). This is even true of human-robot interactions: Salomons et al. [39] show that people change their belief if a group of robots hold another belief than the participant, i.e. when several others say/do something else, people are more inclined to change their own view or behavior. In our case, the robot addresses the people using the more general term "*Most people actually do take something to drink*" or their specific gender for personalizing the social proof by saying "*Most men/women actually do take something to drink*".

The other principle by Cialdini [7] that we make use of is authority. Authority can be addressed in different ways, for instance by indicating expertise by means of a white lab coat, by using a speaking style that indicates expertise [2], or by referring to professional identity [47].

In our case, the robot addresses expertise by referring to scientific evidence, by saying '*Research shows that it is important to drink enough water during the day*' or '*Studies indicate that dehydration can cause fatigue, headache and dizziness you know*', which does not put the robot in an authoritative role but rather makes it a messenger of a scientific message.

Both persuasive utterances have previously been tested in the lab [27, 28], and both yielded increased water consumption in the participants. In these studies, the respective persuasive utterance was played when participants picked up a glass, i.e. about three minutes before they got the opportunity to drink. Still, participants were found to drink significantly more water at the end of the experiment when they had previously heard the persuasive utterance.

Thus, robots can be persuasive, but it is open what happens when they are deployed in the field; to our knowledge persuasive robots have not been tested in the field to investigate potential misalignments with the results from lab studies. Our investigation is therefore an exploratory study in which we identify those factors that may influence the robots' persuasiveness in the field.

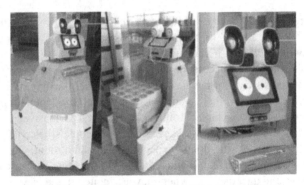

Fig. 1. The Drink-Serving Robot with the Tray of Water

3 Method

In the current study, we placed a drink-serving robot that uses persuasive dialog into a field scenario.

3.1 Procedure and Participants

We carried out experiments in the entrance hall and canteen area at our university, which also serves as the gathering space for people attending public events at the concert hall. We collected data over a period of four days, amounting to a total of 7 sessions of 1.5 h each: Friday (lunch and evening), Saturday (during the day), Monday (lunch and evening), and Tuesday (lunch and evening). During lunch time, the robot drove around and offered water to students and university staff, as well as to a few visitors. In line with the official language used at the international campus, these interactions were in English. During the evening events and on Saturday afternoon, the robot offered water to people from the general public who were gathering to attend a concert, a movie presentation or a body building convention. The interactions with the robot were held in Danish and took place right before people entered the concert hall.

3.2 Robot and Wizards

The robot (see Fig. 1) is a service robot developed to help caregivers with routine tasks in elderly care facilities, like transportation of laundry and garbage, guiding and serving beverages [26]. The robot's head includes a microphone, speakers, cameras and two touchscreens (one in the back and one in the front). The front touchscreen displays simulated eyes. The robot carries its load on the back, which is a disadvantage for the drink-serving task [15] - we will show some examples of this later in the paper.

The robot can navigate autonomously and is equipped with dialog capabilities. However, for safety reasons, two wizards controlled the robot: one for navigation and one for the dialog. They were on a deck above the experiment site so that people would not notice them. To minimize the wizards' contributions, all utterances were scripted and presynthesized so that the dialog wizard only had to choose between utterances that expressed the same dialog act; the navigation wizard was not specifically restricted, but tried to cause as little disturbance and threat as possible (cf. [36]) (Fig. 2).

Fig. 2. Wizards working from the deck

3.3 Utterance Design

Since the robot navigated in a crowded space and with many people around (i.e. 'over-hearers'), we created a set of different, comparable utterances so that people did not hear the same utterances several times. We created seven utterance categories (both in English and in Danish):

- greetings (e.g. *hi, hello, hi there, helloj*[1], *sorry to bother you, but..., and sorry to disturb you, but...*),
- utterances to offer some water (e.g. *How about some water?, Would you like something to drink?, I wonder if you would like something to drink*),
- persuasive messages (*Research shows that it is important to drink enough water during the day* or *Most women/men do actually take something to drink*),
- wordplay, jokes (e.g. *What did the ice cube say to the water? I was water before it was cool*) and event-specific utterances (e.g. *Did you know that muscles mainly consist of water? It is important to drink enough water even if one doesn't have big muscles -* played at the body-building convention),
- a request to take the water (*Take your drink please*),
- a toasting utterance (*Cheers*), and
- closings (e.g. *Bye bye, Enjoy your drink, Goodbye, It was nice meeting you, Have a lovely day*).

During the interactions, the dialog wizard chose utterances from each category based on when they had been played last.

3.4 Data Analysis

A total of 197 interactions was elicited, yet for the purpose of this paper, we focus on the interactions that comprise a persuasive message, i.e. either a cue to scientific Expertise

---

[1] An informal Danish greeting.

"Research shows that it is important to drink enough water during the day" or to Social Proof utterances *Most people/men/women actually do take something to drink*. The thus selected 47 interactions provide us with a starting point for the investigation, but we also draw on the larger corpus, for instance, regarding our observations concerning people's constructions of the human-robot interaction as social.

We exclude three interactions from our detailed analysis; these are two interactions in which children are playing with the robot, and one in which we know for sure that the woman did not hear the robot because she was wearing headphones. This leaves us with a subset of 44 interactions.

These data were analyzed using a discourse-analytical approach [23] and drawing on work in ethnomethodological conversation analysis [38]. We proceeded by analyzing and classifying the different kinds of behaviors people produced in response to the robot's persuasive messages, including aspects of the situational and the sequential context.

4 Results

In line with our three main research questions, we present our results in three steps; first, we compare the effects of persuasive utterances in the lab and in the field. Next, we investigate what actually happens in the field by analyzing the situational contexts in which the persuasive utterance occurs and its sequential placement, as well as how these factors influence the robot's persuasiveness. Finally, we suggest that the construal of the robot as social actor constitutes a precondition for the effectiveness of persuasive messages used by the robot.

4.1 Persuasive Utterances in the Lab and in the Field

Similar to the effects of the two kinds of persuasive messages identified in the lab studies by Langedijk et al. [28] and Langedijk and Fischer [27], there are interactions[2] in which these messages lead to increased water intake; for instance, the example below illustrates the persuasive effect of the authority-based message:

Two people are standing and looking at the robot (W and M), none of whom have something to drink:

- W: Hi (directed at robot and then she looks up to M)
- R: Hello
- W: How are you (looks excited for an answer, M laughs)
- R: Sorry to bother you but (W looks disappointed)
- W: Okay
- R: Can I offer you some water Overhearers discuss something *inaudible*
- W: No thank you
- M: I want some (laughs)

---

[2] Abbreviations in the transcripts: R = robot/W = woman The Danish interactions are translated into English.

– R: Research shows that it is important to drink enough water during the day
     Two men passing by, they look at the robot
– W: Why
– R: Did you know (W laughs) that drinking water can increase your productivity –
– W: How
– R: Drinking water is important whether you are planning on being productive or not
– W: Okay, I want water now
– R: (turns around) Take your drink please (W looks at M and they laugh)
– M: Awesome (he takes something, W moves around the robot while the robot turns
     back)
     An experimenter enters the interaction to ask for consent to use the video footage.
– R: Cheers (M makes cheers-gesture towards robot and he drinks)

However, we also observe that persuasive utterances that work in the lab do not always work in the field in the same way; for instance, in the following example, the person addressed responds to the persuasive message that uses social proof as a persuasive strategy by drinking from his own bottle:

A man is sitting and eating his lunch. He has a water bottle in front of him and is looking at his phone. When the robot approaches him, he looks up:

– R: Hi there - how about some water
– M: No thank you
– R: Most men actually do take something to drink
     M tries to open his bottle with one hand
– M: Okay, I'll take then (while still trying to open his bottle)
– R: Take your drink please (robot turns slightly, M smiles)
     Robot turns back and M drinks from his own bottle
– R: You can lead a horse to water but you can't make it drink. Are you sure you don't
     want something after all
– M: (puts his bottle down) Yes I'm sure
– R: It was nice meeting you (robot turns away)

Thus, in the field, many factors may influence the persuasiveness of persuasive messages, so that the persuasiveness of social robots in the field is highly context-dependent. In the following, we analyze some of these factors in more detail.

4.2 Situational Context: What Happens in the Field

We found both the situational context in which the interactions take place (e.g. whether participants have their own drink or not, as in the example above) and the sequential placement of the persuasive message to affect the persuasiveness of the persuasive messages.

As we have seen above, whether people have their own drinks (actually 47.7% do have something already) influences the persuasiveness of the robot; then they often exhibit those drinks to justify their declining of the robot's offer:

The robot approaches a man from behind who is sitting and eating his lunch (he has a water bottle). He turns around because he hears the robot approaching, the robot turns slightly more towards him:

- R: Sorry to bother you but - can I offer you some water
- M: No thanks (he looks at robot for several seconds and then continues to eat)
- R: Most men actually do take something to drink (M takes his bottle, turns around to show the robot that he has a bottle
- R: It was nice meeting you (M drinks while the robot moves backwards)

Thus, whether or not people have their own drinks has an influence on the interaction, even though the persuasive messages can be considered successful after all since they do result in people drinking whatever drink they have.

Given the multi-party, dynamic situational context, the persuasive messages may also be received by others than the intended interaction partner. For instance, in four interactions, we observe that, when the robot makes a turn when offering something to drink (because the water is on its back), not all interaction partners understand that the robot is turning to make the drink more accessible to them, but rather understand the robot to disengage. Some walk around it to remain in front of it; at the same time, new interaction partners may happen to come into view from the turn, who then believe they are interacted with since the robot gazes at them directly. An example of this is the interaction in the following example; when the robot utters "please take your drink," another person B2 assumes that the offer is addressed to him and takes a glass of water:

The robot stands in a hallway full of people. Close to the robot stand a man (M1) and a woman (W1), none of whom has something to drink. The woman is walking up to the robot:

- W1: (she steps forward) Don't you not have beer? (steps back)
- R: Hello (moves forward to the woman)
- W1: (repeats herself) Don't you have a beer (leaning down and looking at the robot)
- R: Research shows (W1 steps back and looks at M1 laughing, M1 looks at the robot) that it is important to drink enough water during the day.
     W1 walks away, and the man steps forward and leans down to the robot
- M1: And how do you know that (he laughs)
     M1 takes a step back and turns away from the robot
- R: Can I offer you something to drink (M1 turns around and looks at the robot)
     M1 laughs while looking at someone behind the robot. The robot turns around to expose its tray to M1, so that it is facing two boys (B1, B2).
     M1 says something *inaudible*
- R: Take your water please
- B2: Okay (steps forward to take water)

In addition to the situational context, also the sequential placement of the persuasive message matters. Here, we can distinguish between sequential contexts after an accept and after a decline.

When the persuasive message comes after people accepted the initial offer, the persuasive message works as affirmation that the participant has made a good choice:

The robot drives towards two men (M1 and M2) who are sitting separately without anything to drink; the robot moves closer to M1 who sits the closest:

- R: Hi there (M1 takes out his earplugs)
- R: Hi there - sorry to bother you but
- R: How about some water
- M1: Yeah sure
- R: Take your drink please (turns around, M1 gets up, takes his drink and sits down again, he drinks)
- R: Research shows that it is important to drink enough water during the day (M2 comes closer)
- M1: (nods and smiles) Yeah (drinks again)
- R: Have a lovely day (M1 nods)

While the robot is successful in this situation, the success is not due to the persuasive utterance, since the persuasive message is played after the person has already taken the glass of water. Thus, in order for a persuasive message to function as a persuasive message, rather than as an informing or affirmation, like in this example, its sequential placement plays a crucial role.

After rejections, as the following example shows, people often repeat their rejection (in line with the principle of commitment and consistency outlined by Cialdini [7]):

Three women standing with their lunch and something to drink:

- R: Hi there (there is no one in the vision of the robot)
- Robot turns around to three women, W1 tries to get out of the robot's sight by moving, the others laugh
- R: Sorry to bother you but - can I offer you some water
- W2: No thank you (shakes her head a little, the others smile and they all continue to look at the robot)
- W1 goes away
- R: Most women actually do take something to drink (W3 looks at W2 while the utterance is played, they all laugh)
- W2: Wow but I don't want water (they continue to laugh/smile)
- R: What did the ice cube say to the water
- W2: I don't know – what did it say (W1 comes back into the vision)
- R: I was water before it was cool
- W2: Ha ha ha (W3 takes a picture of/filming the robot) – that's so funny
- R: How does the ocean say hello
- W2: He waves (while making a waving-gesture)
- R: It waves
- All: Ohhh
- R: It was nice meeting you

– W2: Nice meeting you too (nodding) – bye bye (with waving-gesture)

This example shows that the interactants are very interested in engaging with the robot, as evidenced by their politeness markers, encouraging questions and contingent responses, just do not want any water and cannot be persuaded to take some anyway.

While persuasive messages are mostly unsuccessful once people have rejected the robot's offer some can be convinced, as we have seen in the first example above.

4.3   Perceived Sociality

In our analysis, it also became apparent that the persuasiveness of the robot may be influenced by its perceived sociality, i.e. the extent to which people are willing to interact socially with the robot [8, 12].

The examples above are in many respects similar to interactions between humans; they were characterized by successful and smooth adjacency pairs, like summons - answer, offer - acceptance, provision - acquisition, information - acknowledgement, and farewell - acknowledgement sequences (cf. [41, 42]). The interactions discussed so far exhibited many features of smooth interactions between humans and a high degree of social coupling; at the same time, the human participants attended to the social organization of interaction not only by producing the socially expectable second pair parts of the respective adjacency pairs, but also by using social signals, like nodding, laughing and smiling.

In our subset of 44 interactions, only seven interactions seem to be construed as non-social such that people do not enter into a dialog with the robot and rather treat is as a machine [12]. In two of these interactions, people leave during the interaction. In further two interactions, people talk *about* the robot without talking *to* it.

In another situation, only one of the participants is looking at the robot while the rest of her group do not want to talk to it, and so she ends up taking water from the back of the robot without interacting with it. In another interaction, the robot receives a dismissive 'ja ja' (*yeah yeah*). The example below is the only interaction in our subcorpus in which no one responds to the robot at all:

Two women are lying on two sofas, looking at their phones. The robot moves close to W1's feet. Neither of the women takes notice of the robot:

– R: I don't want to disturb you, but you look thirsty, would you like something to drink?
     W1 lying on the closest sofa turns around to look at the robot. She then turns back and continues to look at her phone.
– R: Most women actually do take something to drink.
– R: Do you know how to get a fish to laugh? You put it in spring water no response from W1 or W2
     R drives backwards

As these interactions illustrate, if people do not interact with the robot in social ways, the persuasive message is also not going to be effective. Thus, the perception of social robots as social is a precondition for their effectiveness as a persuasive technology.

5 Discussion

Our analysis has shown that in our field study, things were much messier than what is known from more controlled studies; however, the messiness observed is in fact informative regarding the conditions under which a social robot becomes a persuasive technology.

Our results show clearly that the robot is only effective in persuading people if people regard the human-robot interaction situation as social. While it was known that there are interindividual differences in regarding robots as social actors (e.g. [9, 11, 12]), few in-the-wild studies have documented these differences, and it was open to what extent the construal of the robot as social can influence whether it is persuasive or not. The detailed analysis of our sub-corpus has shown that responding to the robot in non-social ways is not very common (though it has been observed more often in the whole corpus (cf. [8]), and people who try to avoid the robot would also not show in our videos, which were recorded by the camera mounted on the robot), but has a large impact on whether people interact with the robot and how.

Furthermore, our results reveal many contextual factors that influence the effectiveness of persuasive messages. For instance, whether participants already have something to drink is of some influence, even though the persuasive message can also be regarded successful when people who already have a drink wave it at the robot or ostensively drink from it.

An important feature of the context is also whether participants had already rejected the robot's offer when it used the persuasive messages. In line with the principle of commitment and consistency [7], people who have declined the robot's offer prior to the persuasive message are not likely to quickly change their minds. This is the case in many of our interactions, in contrast to the sequential context in which the persuasive utterance was used in the lab studies reported by [28] and [27], which may have contributed to the different findings.

In addition, it became clear that much of the robot's success as a persuasive technology may be due to its novelty; people commented positively on the robot and were excited to interact with it because it was novel, which is likely to have influenced the persuasiveness of the robot. From this perspective, we need to restrict our conclusions about social robots as persuasive technology to a time frame in which robots are still novel and exciting; what will happen once they are more common is not yet known.

6 Conclusion

In this paper, we present a field study with a persuasive social robot that offers water to people in a public space. We used previously successful persuasive utterances from the lab and took them into the field to study their effects. Our results reveal that the robot can be persuasive, but different contextual factors influence its persuasiveness. Of considerable impact on the robot's persuasiveness is the sequential placement of the persuasive message, as well as the robot's construal as a social actor. If the robot is not perceived as social, it will not be persuasive.

Acknowledgements. We would like to thank the colleagues who have helped us during these experiments: Eduardo Ruiz Ramirez, Lotte Damsgaard Nissen, Matous Jelinek, Selina Eisenberger and Oskar Palinko.

References

1. Andriella, A., Torras, C., Alenya, G.: Short-term human–robot interaction adaptability in real-world environments. Int. J. Soc. Robot. **12**(3), 639–657 (2020)
2. Andrist, S., Spannan, E., Mutlu, B.: Rhetorical robots: making robots more effective speakers using linguistic cues of expertise. In: 2013 8th ACM/IEEE International Conference on Human-Robot Interaction (HRI). pp. 341–348. IEEE (2013)
3. Belpaeme, T.: Advice to new human-robot interaction researchers. In: Human-Robot Interaction. pp. 355–369. Springer (2020)
4. Broadbent, E., et al.: Benefits and problems of health-care robots in aged care settings: a comparison trial. Australas. J. Ageing **35**(1), 23–29 (2016)
5. Chidambaram, V., Chiang, Y.H., Mutlu, B.: Designing persuasive robots: how robots might persuade people using vocal and nonverbal cues. In: Proceedings of the Seventh Annual ACM/IEEE International Conference on Human-Robot Interaction, pp. 293–300 (2012)
6. Chun, B., Knight, H.: The robot makers: an ethnography of anthropomorphism at a robotics company. ACM Trans. Human-Robot Inter. (THRI) **9**(3), 1–36 (2020)
7. Cialdini, R.B.: Influence, vol. 3. A. Michel Port Harcourt (1987)
8. Clark, H.H., Fischer, K.: Social robots as depictions of social agents. Behavioral and Brain Sciences, pp. 1–33 (2022)
9. Epley, N., Waytz, A., Cacioppo, J.T.: On seeing human: a three-factor theory of anthropomorphism. Psychol. Rev. **114**(4), 864 (2007)
10. Feng, Y., Perugia, G., Yu, S., Barakova, E.I., Hu, J., Rauterberg, G.: Context- enhanced human-robot interaction: Exploring the role of system interactivity and multimodal stimuli on the engagement of people with dementia. Int. J. Soc. Robot. **14**(3), 807–826 (2022)
11. Fischer, K.: Interpersonal variation in understanding robots as social actors. In: 2011 6th ACM/IEEE International Conference on Human-Robot Interaction (HRI), pp. 53–60. IEEE (2011)
12. Fischer, K.: Tracking anthropomorphizing behavior in human-robot interaction. ACM Trans. Hum.-Robot Inter. (THRI) **11**(1), 1–28 (2021)
13. Fischer, K., Langedijk, R.M., Nissen, L.D., Ramirez, E.R., Palinko, O.: Gaze-speech coordination influences the persuasiveness of human-robot dialog in the wild. In: International Conference on Social Robotics, pp. 157–169. Springer, Cham (2020). Doi: https://doi.org/10.1007/978-3-030-62056-1_14
14. Fischer, K., Niebuhr, O., Jensen, L.C., Bodenhagen, L.: Speech melody matters—how robots profit from using charismatic speech. ACM Trans. Hum.-Robot Inter. (THRI) **9**(1), 1–21 (2019)
15. Fischer, K., et al.: Integrative social robotics hands-on. Interaction Studies **21**(1), 145–185 (2020)
16. Forlizzi, J.: How robotic products become social products: an ethnographic study of cleaning in the home. In: 2007 2nd ACM/IEEE International Conference on Human-Robot Interaction (HRI), pp. 129–136. IEEE (2007)
17. Fountoukidou, S., Ham, J., Matzat, U., Midden, C.: Persuasive design principles and user models for people with motor disabilities. In: Signal Processing to Drive Human-Computer Interaction: EEG and eye-controlled interfaces, pp. 49–79. Institution of Engineering and Technology (IET) (2020)

18. Ghazali, A.S., Ham, J., Barakova, E.I., Markopoulos, P.: Effects of robot facial characteristics and gender in persuasive human-robot interaction. Front. Robot. AI **5**, 73 (2018)
19. Goldstein, N.J., Cialdini, R.B., Griskevicius, V.: A room with a viewpoint: using social norms to motivate environmental conservation in hotels. J. Consumer Res. **35**(3), 472–482 (2008)
20. Ham, J., Bokhorst, R., Cuijpers, R., Pol, D.v.d., Cabibihan, J.J.: Making robots persuasive: the influence of combining persuasive strategies (gazing and gestures) by a storytelling robot on its persuasive power. In: International conference on social robotics, pp. 71–83. Springer (2011)
21. Ham, J., Cuijpers, R.H., Cabibihan, J.J.: Combining robotic persuasive strategies: the persuasive power of a storytelling robot that uses gazing and gestures. Int. J. Soc. Robot. **7**(4), 479–487 (2015)
22. Hashemian, M., Couto, M., Mascarenhas, S., Paiva, A., Santos, P.A., Prada, R.: Persuasive social robot using reward power over repeated instances of persuasion. In: International Conference on Persuasive Technology, pp. 63–70. Springer, Cham (2021). Doi: https://doi.org/10.1007/978-3-030-79460-6_6
23. Johnstone, B.: Discourse Analysis. John Wiley & Sons (2017)
24. Jung, M., Hinds, P.: Robots in the wild: A time for more robust theories of human- robot interaction (2018)
25. Kaptein, M., Markopoulos, P., De Ruyter, B., Aarts, E.: Personalizing persuasive technologies: Explicit and implicit personalization using persuasion profiles. Int. J. Hum Comput Stud. **77**, 38–51 (2015)
26. Kru¨ger, N., et al.: The smooth-robot: a modular, interactive service robot. Front. Robot. AI **8** (2021)
27. Langedijk, R.M., Fischer, K.: Appeals to expertise make robots persuasive in human-robot healthcare interaction. In: Manipulation, Influence, and Deception: The Changing Landscape of Persuasive Language. Cambridge University Press (submitted)
28. Langedijk, R.M., Jensen, L.C., Fischer, K.: Persuasive effects of social proof in human-robot interactive dialog. Int. J. Soc. Robot. (Submitted)
29. Langedijk, R.M., Odabasi, C., Fischer, K., Graf, B.: Studying drink-serving service robots in the real world. In: 2020 29th IEEE International Conference on Robot and Human Interactive Communication (RO-MAN), pp. 788–793. IEEE (2020)
30. Lee, H.R., Cheon, E., Lim, C., Fischer, K.: Configuring humans: what roles humans play in hri research. In: 2022 17th ACM/IEEE International Conference on Human-Robot Interaction (HRI), pp. 478–492. IEEE (2022)
31. Liu, B., Tetteroo, D., Markopoulos, P.: A systematic review of experimental work on persuasive social robots. International J. Soc. Robot., 1–40 (2022)
32. Melkas, H., Hennala, L., Pekkarinen, S., Kyrki, V.: Impacts of robot implementation on care personnel and clients in elderly-care institutions. Int. J. Med. Informatics **134**, 104041 (2020)
33. Mutlu, B., Forlizzi, J.: Robots in organizations: the role of workflow, social, and environmental factors in human-robot interaction. In: 2008 3rd ACM/IEEE International Conference on Human-Robot Interaction (HRI), pp. 287–294. IEEE (2008)
34. Okafuji, Y., Baba, J., Nakanishi, J., Amada, J., Yoshikawa, Y., Ishiguro, H.: Persuasion strategies for social robot to keep humans accepting daily different recommendations. In: 2021 IEEE/RSJ International Conference on Intelligent Robots and Systems (IROS), pp. 1950–1957. IEEE (2021)
35. Park, C.H., Ros, R., Kwak, S.S., Huang, C.M., Lemaignan, S.: Towards real world impacts: design, development, and deployment of social robots in the wild (2020)
36. Riek, L.D.: Wizard of oz studies in hri: a systematic review and new reporting guidelines. J. Hum.-Robot Interact. **1**(1), 119–136 (2012)

37. Rudaz, D., Tatarian, K., Stower, R., Licoppe, C.: From inanimate object to agent: impact of pre-beginnings on the emergence of greetings with a robot (2023). https://doi.org/10.1145/3575806

38. Sacks, H., Schegloff, E.A., Jefferson, G.: A simplest systematics for the organization of turn taking for conversation. In: Studies in the Organization of Conversational Interaction, pp. 7–55. Elsevier (1978)

39. Salomons, N., Van Der Linden, M., Strohkorb Sebo, S., Scassellati, B.: Humans conform to robots: Disambiguating trust, truth, and conformity. In: Proceedings of the 2018 ACM/IEEE International Conference on Human-Robot Interaction, pp. 187–195 (2018)

40. Saunderson, S., Nejat, G.: How robots influence humans: a survey of nonverbal communication in social human–robot interaction. Int. J. Soc. Robot. 11(4), 575–608 (2019)

41. Schegloff, E.A.: Sequence organization in interaction: a primer in conversation analysis I, vol. 1. Cambridge University Press (2007)

42. Schegloff, E.A.: Opening sequencing. Perpetual contact: mobile communication, private talk, public performance, pp. 326–385 (2002)

43. Siegel, M., Breazeal, C., Norton, M.I.: Persuasive robotics: the influence of robot gender on human behavior. In: 2009 IEEE/RSJ International Conference on Intelligent Robots and Systems, pp. 2563–2568. IEEE (2009)

44. Sung, J., Grinter, R.E., Christensen, H.I.: "Pimp my roomba" designing for personalization. In: Proceedings of the SIGCHI Conference on Human Factors in Computing Systems, pp. 193–196 (2009)

45. Thellman, S., et al.: He is not more persuasive than her: no gender biases toward robots giving speeches. In: Proceedings of the 18th International Conference on Intelligent Virtual Agents, pp. 327–328 (2018)

46. Weiss, A., Spiel, K.: Robots beyond science fiction: mutual learning in human– robot interaction on the way to participatory approaches. AI Soc. 37(2), 501–515 (2022)

47. Winkle, K., Lemaignan, S., Caleb-Solly, P., Leonards, U., Turton, A., Bremner, P.: Effective persuasion strategies for socially assistive robots. In: 2019 14th ACM/IEEE International Conference on Human-Robot Interaction (HRI), pp. 277–285. IEEE (2019)

Attitudes Toward a Virtual Smoking Cessation Coach: Relationship and Willingness to Continue

Nele Albers[1]([✉]) [ID], Mark A. Neerincx[1,2] [ID], Nadyne L. Aretz[1] [ID], Mahira Ali[1] [ID], Arsen Ekinci[1] [ID], and Willem-Paul Brinkman[1] [ID]

[1] Delft University of Technology, Delft, The Netherlands
{n.albers,m.a.neerincx,w.p.brinkman}@tudelft.nl,
m.ali-10@student.tudelft.nl
[2] TNO, Soesterberg, The Netherlands

Abstract. Virtual coaches have the potential to address the low adherence common to eHealth applications for behavior change by, for example, providing motivational support. However, given the multitude of factors affecting users' attitudes toward virtual coaches, more insights are needed on how such virtual coaches can be designed to affect these attitudes in a specific use context positively. Especially valuable are insights that are based on users interacting with such a virtual coach for longer. We thus conducted a study in which more than 500 smokers interacted with the text-based virtual coach Sam in five sessions. In each session, Sam assigned smokers a new preparatory activity for quitting smoking and provided motivational support for doing the activity. Based on a mixed-methods analysis of users' willingness to continue working and their relationship with Sam, we obtained eight themes for users' attitudes toward Sam. These themes relate to whether Sam is seen as human or artificial, specific characteristics of Sam (e.g., caring character), the interaction with Sam, and the relationship with Sam. We used these themes to formulate literature-based recommendations to guide designers of virtual coaches for behavior change. For example, letting the virtual coach get to know users and disclose more information about itself may improve its relationship with users.

Keywords: Conversational agent · Behavior change · eHealth

1 Introduction

Eating too few vegetables, working out too little, going to bed too late, ... - there are many health behaviors people wish to change. Numerous eHealth applications exist to support them, which have several potential benefits such as fostering user empowerment, providing all-time support, and being scalable [10, 29]. Behavior change support could thus become more widely available and effective.

© The Author(s) 2023
J. Ham et al. (Eds.): PERSUASIVE 2023, LNCS 13832, pp. 265–274, 2023.
https://doi.org/10.1007/978-3-031-30933-5_17

This is useful for behaviors such as smoking, where most people try to change without support [13] and often do not succeed [18]. Nevertheless, eHealth applications suffer from low adherence [22,27]. Virtual coaches have the potential to combat this by increasing engagement and forming a connection with users [34]. However, it is not yet well understood how such virtual coaches can be designed so that users have a positive attitude toward them.

Previous work on smoking cessation has identified several aspects of a virtual coach that contribute to such a positive attitude. This includes the caring character of and positive feedback from an embodied virtual coach for veterans [1], practical tips and the feeling of being supported by the StopCoach Suzanne [33], and the nonjudgmental, supportive, and caring character of the embodied virtual coach Jen [25]. Yet, not only characteristics of the virtual coach play a role, but also ones of users and their environment [21]. Meijer et al. [33], for example, saw that the StopCoach may be harder to use for older people and that its support may be especially beneficial for people with little support from their social environment. Given the multitude of factors that can affect users' attitudes toward a virtual coach, more insights are needed. Due to the novelty effect [19,37], insights that are based on users interacting with a virtual coach for a longer period of time are especially welcome.

We thus conducted a study with more than 500 smokers interacting with the virtual coach Sam in five conversational sessions spread over at least nine days. In each session, Sam assigned users a new preparatory activity for quitting smoking, such as noting and ranking reasons for quitting. As becoming more physically active may make it easier to quit smoking [23,35], half of the activities addressed becoming more physically active. In the next session, Sam asked users about their effort spent on and experience with the activity. After the five sessions, users were asked about their relationship and willingness to continue working with Sam. Based on a mixed-methods analysis of users' responses about their relationship and willingness to continue working with Sam, their characteristics, and findings from the literature, we identified eight themes describing users' attitudes toward Sam. We used these themes to formulate literature-based recommendations to guide designers of virtual coaches for behavior change.

2   Materials and Methods

We conducted a study from 20 May 2021 until 30 June 2021 on the online crowdsourcing platform Prolific. The study was approved by the Human Research Ethics Committee of Delft University of Technology (Letter of Approval number: 1523) and preregistered in the Open Science Framework (OSF) [3]. The dataset [5] and analysis code [4] are available online.

Virtual coach. We implemented the text-based virtual coach Sam [2] that introduced itself as wanting to help people prepare to quit smoking and become more physically active, with the latter possibly aiding the former. In each session, Sam proposed one of 24 preparatory activities and provided motivational support for doing the activity [6]. This included motivating people to do their next activity based on the persuasive strategies of commitment, consensus, and authority by Cialdini [16] and action planning [24], as well as giving compliments for spending much effort on activities and responding empathetically otherwise. To facilitate the interaction, users primarily communicated by clicking on buttons with answer options. To avoid repetitiveness of utterances [14], there were different formulations that Sam randomly chose from.

Measures. Instead of asking participants about their general attitude toward Sam, we asked two specific questions that would allow people to reflect on concrete elements of interacting with Sam and allow us to identify underlying concerns. Specifically, using an adaptation of the acceptance questions by Provoost et al. [36] similar to Albers et al. [8], we measured participants' willingness to continue working and their relationship with Sam. For both of these, participants provided a rating on a scale from -5 to 5, with 0 being neutral, as well as a free-text response to the question "Why do you think so?"

To explore the relationship between user variables and attitudes toward Sam, we measured participants' quitter self-identity with three items (e.g., "I see myself as someone who quits smoking") based on Meijer et al. [32] as well as participants' ease of and motivation to do preparatory activities with two items each (e.g., "It was easy to do the assigned activities.").

Participants. Eligible were people who reported smoking tobacco products at least once per day[1], being contemplating or preparing to quit smoking [20], being fluent in English, and not being part of another intervention to quit smoking. Participants further had an approval rate of at least 90% and at least one previous submission on Prolific and provided informed consent. 1406 people started the study, and 500 people successfully answered all attitude questions. Of these 500 participants, 247 were female (49.4%), 244 were male (48.8%), and 9 (1.8%) provided other or no data on their gender. Moreover, 397 (79.4%) participants indicated having previously at least once quit smoking for at least 24 h. The age of participants ranged from 18 to 74, with 43.8% of participants being between 18 and 30 years old. Participants who successfully completed a study component were paid based on the minimum payment rules on Prolific (i.e., five pound sterling per hour).

Procedure. After completing a prescreening and a pre-questionnaire, users interacted with Sam in five sessions, which lasted about five to eight minutes and were about two to five days apart. Two days after completing the last session, users were invited to a post-questionnaire in which they answered questions about their attitudes toward Sam.

Analysis strategies. We took a mixed-methods approach with four steps to analyze the data. These were the thematic analysis steps by Braun and Clarke [15], supplemented with triangulation based on quantitative data and literature. We now describe the four analysis steps in detail.

Step 1: Preparation of coding scheme. We created two separate coding schemes, one for the question on "willingness to continue" and one for the ques-

---

[1] People had to have indicated smoking tobacco products at least once per day on their Prolific profile and confirm this in an online questionnaire.

tion on "relationship". More precisely, after familiarizing themselves with the data, NLA and MA created draft coding schemes for the free-text responses on "willingness to continue" and "relationship", respectively. The codes were generated both inductively and deductively based on literature. More information on this process can be found in the reports by Aretz [11] and Ali [9]. The final coding schemes are available online [4].

Step 2: Coding of responses. Using the resulting coding schemes, NLA and MA coded all responses for their respective question. We assessed the reliability of the coding schemes through double coding. A second coder, AE for "willingness to continue" and NLA for "relationship", was trained on between 20 and 30 responses before independently coding the remaining responses. We obtained an average Cohen's κ of 0.59 for "willingness to continue" and 0.62 for "relationship", which indicates moderate to substantial agreement [28]. The two coders of a question then resolved all disagreements by means of discussion.

Step 3: Triangulation with literature and quantitative results. As we gained insights from the qualitative data, we turned to the literature and our quantitative data to triangulate our results. Our quantitative analysis included calculating the mean rating and 95% Highest Density Interval (HDI) per attitude question, as well as computing correlations between user variables and attitude ratings. We used the rethinking [31] and BayesianFirstAid [12] R-packages for this.

Step 4: Search, review, and definition of themes, as well as production of the report. Lastly, we examined the results to identify overarching themes and selected participant responses to illustrate these themes.

3   Results

Participants' attitudes toward Sam were overall positive, with a mean score of 2.42 (95%-HDI = [2.18, 2.65]) for "willingness to continue" and one of 0.46 (95%-HDI = [0.24, 0.67]) for "relationship" based on scales from -5 to 5. From our mixed-methods analysis we found eight themes, three for people's willingness to continue working and five for their relationship with Sam. To facilitate their discussion, we grouped these themes into the four topics that we now describe.

Human vs. AI. When describing their willingness to continue working with Sam, several participants referred to a lack of authenticity in their interactions with Sam ($N = 82$). This included the mere fact that Sam was artificial and not a human (e.g., P354, P378, P448), as well as specific consequences such as repetitiveness (e.g., P310, P410), lack of emotion (e.g., P341), and inability to respond to free-text responses from users (e.g., P465). Some participants also mentioned how they felt when interacting with an artificial agent: "Felt silly talking to a computer plus it did not help me because I knew it was not real" (P441).

With regard to participants' relationships, the perception of Sam as either human or artificial also played a role ($N = 325$). While some participants referred to Sam as a "he", "guy", "someone", somebody with a "character", or even a "friend" (e.g., P185, P196, P214), others regarded Sam as artificial. Terms used to refer to Sam's artificial nature included "machine" (e.g., P223), "computer" (e.g., P218), "agent" (e.g., P197), "artificial intelligence" (P62), "communication tool" (e.g., P234) and "bot" (e.g., P217): "I found him a nice "person" but also I think about the fact it's not a real person, it is artificial intelligence working" (P62). Interestingly, one participant mentioned that Sam asking them about their mood at the start of each conversation was pleasant even though they knew that Sam was artificial: "I was well aware that I wasn't talking to a real person ... However, I still appreciated the effort in asking me about my day and so on, it made the whole thing feel more realistic and the conversation more pleasant" (P218). Something participants appreciated about Sam's artificial nature was the resulting anonymity: "i loved the anonymity of it, that no one i know would know what i'd said so i could be totally open and honest ..." (P227).

Characteristics of the virtual coach. The second theme in participants' responses about their willingness to continue working with Sam is Sam's caring character ($N = 352$). Participants described Sam as motivating (e.g., P478, P485, P494), friendly (e.g., P47, P98, P107), comforting (e.g., P202, P227, P345), supporting (e.g., P65, P158, P370), understanding (e.g., P198, P227, P253), and unbiased (e.g., P38, P289, P311): "... being in contact with Sam gave a feeling of support it helped a great deal towards the motivation to carry on" (P161).

Also regarding their relationship with Sam did participants refer to Sam's positive characteristics ($N = 153$). Sam was seen as friendly (e.g., P297, P301), guiding (e.g., P336, P356), trustworthy (e.g., P201, P227, P453), warm (e.g., P68, P241, P341), caring (e.g., P73, P83, P140), welcoming (e.g., P120, P272, P380), and unprejudiced (e.g., P158, P201, P226), amongst others: "Friendly and just nice. You have a problem, Sam suggests activities to help you overcome it" (P403).

Interaction. The third theme concerning participants' willingness to continue working with Sam is the content of the interactions ($N = 183$). Participants found the interactions helpful (e.g., P178, P189, P191) and interesting (e.g., P228, P291, P303). Moreover, some participants specifically mentioned that Sam proposed good ideas or activities (e.g., P336, P405, P414) and provided clear explanations: "Sam explains clearly its minds, the activities and the final goals ..." (P256). The relationship between the activities Sam proposed and participants' willingness to continue is also confirmed by our quantitative analysis. Specifically, we found moderate correlations of 0.33 (95%-HDI = [0.25, 0.41]) and 0.48 (95%-HDI = [0.40, 0.54]), respectively, between participants' willingness to continue and their ease of and motivation to do the activities. The less than small [17] correlation between quitter self-identity and "willingness to continue" (Mean = 0.09, 95%-HDI = [0, 0.19]) could possibly be explained by the interaction content being seen as somewhat more useful by participants with a higher motivation to change.

Similarly, participants referred to characteristics of the chat when describing their relationship with Sam ($N = 83$). Participants with a positive opinion about the chat mentioned that Sam responded well (e.g., P76, P438), such as by being polite (e.g., P472) or showing an understanding of what the user wrote (e.g., P70). Several participants also pointed out that they felt like chatting with a friend (e.g., P121, P484): "It felt like talking with a friend, since at first he asks how you are, it feels like he cares about you" (P130). Several participants did, however, also voice objections to the chat. For example, some participants noted that the answer options provided as buttons were too limited (e.g., P320, P434), the options' language did not fit how they speak (P400), and the use of buttons was limiting compared to entering free text (e.g., P370, P398): "Having the pre selected options to answer Sam meant that I couldn't really respond as I would really ..." (P63). Furthermore, Sam's responses appeared automated and generic to some participants (e.g., P327, P334, P444). And looking at conversations as a whole, these were sometimes perceived as repetitive or monotonous (e.g., P28, P162): "... all our chats followed the same pattern ..." (P219).

Relationship. Participants' descriptions of their relations with Sam can be regarded as either positive, neutral, or negative ($N = 194$). Positive relations included ones where Sam was referred to as a "good relation" (P35), "friend" (P233), "more than just a stranger"(P287), or somebody they felt like knowing for a long time (P232). Participants with neutral or negative relations, on the other hand, regarded Sam as a "professional worker" (P186), "neither a stranger or close friend" (P340), or "not a close friend" (P40). Moreover, some participants pointed out that it was not necessary to be friends with Sam (P48) and that it was not possible to "create a relation with a robot" (P277).

Another theme related to participants' relationships with Sam is that Sam was sometimes experienced as not personal enough or lacking personality ($N = 53$). Participants mentioned that they had "no personal connection" with Sam (P470) or did not "know Sam personally" (P338). Reasons for this feeling of not knowing Sam were that Sam "shows no emotion nor can show empathy" (P160), that they did not "know his voice or how he looks" (P448), and that Sam is a "non-thinking individual" (P326) with a different "level of consciousness" (P489). Furthermore, participants pointed out that Sam did not know them (e.g., P12, P15): "I didn't feel like it was someone who knew me or wanted to get to know me and I think it would be good to develop something a little more personalised" (P20).

4   Conclusion and Recommendations

Based on a mixed-methods analysis of users' willingness to continue working and their relationship with a virtual coach that provides motivational support in the context of preparing to quit smoking, we identified eight themes describing users' underlying attitudes. We now use these themes to formulate literature-based recommendations to help designers of virtual behavior change coaches.

Given participants' views on interacting with Sam, we recommend reducing the repetitiveness of the utterances and the conversation structure, which can increase engagement, enjoyment, and motivation to engage in proposed behaviors [14, 19]. Comprehensive answer options should further be provided for closed questions, as also found by Issom et al. [26]. Moreover, in line with theories on technology acceptance [39] and our previous findings based on people's experiences with preparatory activities and views on interaction scenarios for a virtual coach [7], participants who found the content more useful were more willing to continue using the virtual coach. So it is important that interaction content is perceived as useful by users.

To help users feel like they and the virtual coach know each other, it might be beneficial to let the virtual coach disclose more about itself and ask more personal questions to users so they can also self-disclose. Self-disclosure is an important element of relationship formation in that disclosure of more intimate information has a positive effect on the quality of relationships [38]. Yet, user privacy needs to be protected [40]. Responding empathetically also to free-text utterances may further help to form and maintain a relationship [14,19,26].

Lastly, given participants' perception of Sam as either human or artificial, it may be helpful to make the conversations more human-like, although human skills such as learning from past conversations are still open challenges [19]. For example, asking users how they were doing was appreciated. Yet, users need to know that they are communicating with a virtual coach and not a human [30]. Explaining to users that and how the virtual coach is aiming to build a relationship to increase the intervention's effectiveness may further foster credibility and transparency.

Acknowledgments. This work is part of the Perfect Fit project, which is supported by several funders organized by the Netherlands Organization for Scientific Research (NWO) with project number 628.011.211. The analysis is based on the publicly available Bachelor's theses by Aretz [11] and Ali [9]. The authors thank Mitchell Kesteloo for his help in hosting the virtual coach on a server and the three anonymous reviewers for their helpful suggestions.

References

1. Abdullah, A.S., Gaehde, S., Bickmore, T.: A tablet based embodied conversational agent to promote smoking cessation among veterans: a feasibility study. J. Epidemiol. Global Health **8**(3–4), 225 (2018)
2. Albers, N.: Reinforcement learning-based persuasion for a conversational agent to support behavior change: code (2022). https://doi.org/10.5281/zenodo.6319356
3. Albers, N., Brinkman, W.P.: Perfect fit - experiment to gather data for and test a reinforcement learning-approach for motivating people. https://osf.io/k2uac (May 2021). https://doi.org/10.17605/OSF.IO/K2UAC
4. Albers, N., Neerincx, M.A., Aretz, N.L., Ali, M., Ekinci, A., Brinkman, W.P.: Attitudes toward a virtual smoking cessation coach: analysis code (2 2023). https://doi.org/10.4121/22015748.v2
5. Albers, N., Neerincx, M.A., Brinkman, W.P.: Acceptance of a virtual coach for quitting smoking and becoming physically active: dataset (5 2022). https://doi.org/10.4121/19934783.v1

6. Albers, N., Neerincx, M.A., Brinkman, W.P.: Addressing people's current and future states in a reinforcement learning algorithm for persuading to quit smoking and to be physically active. PLoS ONE **17**(12), e0277295 (2022)
7. Albers, N., Neerincx, M.A., Penfornis, K.M., Brinkman, W.P.: Users' needs for a digital smoking cessation application and how to address them: a mixed-methods study. PeerJ **10**, e13824 (2022). https://doi.org/10.7717/peerj.13824
8. Albers, N., Hizli, B., Scheltinga, B.L., Meijer, E., Brinkman, W.P.: Setting physical activity goals with a virtual coach: vicarious experiences, personalization and acceptance. J. Med. Syst. **47**(1), 15 (2023). https://doi.org/10.1007/s10916-022-01899-9
9. Ali, M.: Acceptance of a virtual coach for quitting smoking and becoming more physically active: a thematic analysis: traits for a virtual coach to be a "friend". Bachelor's thesis (2022)
10. Alpay, L.L., Henkemans, O.B., Otten, W., Rövekamp, T.A., Dumay, A.C.: E-health applications and services for patient empowerment: directions for best practices in the netherlands. Telemedicine e-Health **16**(7), 787–791 (2010)
11. Aretz, N.: Reasons to continue or stop using a virtual coach for quitting smoking and increasing physical activity: a mixed-methods analysis. Bachelor's thesis (2022)
12. Bååth, R.: Bayesian first aid: a package that implements Bayesian alternatives to the classical *.test functions in R. In: UseR! 2014 - the International R User Conference (2014)
13. Babb, S., Malarcher, A., Schauer, G., Asman, K., Jamal, A.: Quitting smoking among adults-united states, 2000–2015. Morb. Mortal. Wkly Rep. **65**(52), 1457–1464 (2017)
14. Bickmore, T.W., Caruso, L., Clough-Gorr, K., Heeren, T.: It's just like you talk to a friend relational agents for older adults. Interact. Comput. **17**(6), 711–735 (2005)
15. Braun, V., Clarke, V.: Using thematic analysis in psychology. Qual. Res. Psychol. **3**(2), 77–101 (2006)
16. Cialdini, R.B.: Influence: The Psychology of Persuasion, revised Harper Business, New York, USA (2006)
17. Cohen, J.: A power primer. Psychol. Bull. **112**(1), 155 (1992)
18. Cooper, J., et al.: To what extent do smokers make spontaneous quit attempts and what are the implications for smoking cessation maintenance? findings from the international tobacco control four country survey. Nicotine & Tobacco Research 12 (suppl_1), S51–S57 (2010)
19. Croes, E.A., Antheunis, M.L.: Can we be friends with mitsuku? a longitudinal study on the process of relationship formation between humans and a social chatbot. J. Soc. Pers. Relat. **38**(1), 279–300 (2021)
20. DiClemente, C.C., Prochaska, J.O., Fairhurst, S.K., Velicer, W.F., Velasquez, M.M., Rossi, J.S.: The process of smoking cessation: an analysis of precontemplation, contemplation, and preparation stages of change. J. Consult. Clin. Psychol. **59**(2), 295 (1991)
21. van Gemert-Pijnen, J.E., et al.: A holistic framework to improve the uptake and impact of ehealth technologies. J. Med. Internet Res. **13**(4), e1672 (2011)
22. Greenhalgh, T., et al.: Beyond adoption: a new framework for theorizing and evaluating nonadoption, abandonment, and challenges to the scale-up, spread, and sustainability of health and care technologies. J. Med. Internet Res. **19**(11), e8775 (2017)
23. Haasova, M., et al.: The acute effects of physical activity on cigarette cravings: systematic review and meta-analysis with individual participant data. Addiction **108**(1), 26–37 (2013)

24. Hagger, M.S., Luszczynska, A.: Implementation intention and action planning interventions in health contexts: state of the research and proposals for the way forward. Appl. Psychol.: Health Well-Being **6**(1), 1–47 (2014)
25. Heffner, J.L., et al.: An avatar-led digital smoking cessation program for sexual and gender minority young adults: intervention development and results of a single-arm pilot trial. JMIR Formative Res. **5**(7), e30241 (2021)
26. Issom, D.Z., Hardy-Dessources, M.D., Romana, M., Hartvigsen, G., Lovis, C.: Toward a conversational agent to support the self-management of adults and young adults with sickle cell disease: Usability and usefulness study. Front. Digit. Health **3**, 1 (2021)
27. Kelders, S.M., Van Zyl, L.E., Ludden, G.D.: The concept and components of engagement in different domains applied to ehealth: a systematic scoping review. Front. Psychol. **11**, 926 (2020)
28. Landis, J.R., Koch, G.G.: The measurement of observer agreement for categorical data. Biometrics, pp. 159–174 (1977)
29. Liao, Y., Wu, Q., Tang, J., Zhang, F., Wang, X., Qi, C., He, H., Long, J., Kelly, B.C., Cohen, J.: The efficacy of mobile phone-based text message interventions ('happy quit') for smoking cessation in china. BMC Public Health **16**(1), 1–11 (2016)
30. Madiega, T.: Eu guidelines on ethics in artificial intelligence: context and implementation. European Parliamentary Research Service, pp. 1–13 (2019)
31. McElreath, R.: Statistical rethinking: a Bayesian course with examples in R and Stan. Chapman and Hall/CRC (2020)
32. Meijer, E., Gebhardt, W.A., Van Laar, C., Kawous, R., Beijk, S.C.: Socio-economic status in relation to smoking: the role of (expected and desired) social support and quitter identity. Soc. Sci. Med. **162**, 41–49 (2016)
33. Meijer, E., et al.: "at least someone thinks i'm doing well": a real-world evaluation of the quit-smoking app stopcoach for lower socio-economic status smokers. Addict. Sci. Clin. Pract. **16**(1), 1–14 (2021)
34. Montenegro, J.L.Z., da Costa, C.A., da Rosa Righi, R.: Survey of conversational agents in health. Expert Syst. Appl. **129**, 56–67 (2019)
35. Priebe, C.S., Atkinson, J., Faulkner, G.: Run to quit: an evaluation of a scalable physical activity-based smoking cessation intervention. Mental Health Phys. Activity **13**, 15–21 (2017)
36. Provoost, S., et al.: Improving adherence to an online intervention for low mood with a virtual coach: study protocol of a pilot randomized controlled trial. Trials **21**(1), 1–12 (2020)
37. Sadeghi, S., Gupta, S., Gramatovici, S., Ai, H., Lu, J., Zhang, R.: Novelty and primacy: a long-term estimator for online experiments. Technometrics, pp. 1–26 (2022)
38. Valkenburg, P.M., Peter, J.: The effects of instant messaging on the quality of adolescents' existing friendships: a longitudinal study. J. Commun. **59**(1), 79–97 (2009)
39. Venkatesh, V., Morris, M.G., Davis, G.B., Davis, F.D.: User acceptance of information technology: toward a unified view. MIS Q. **27**(3), 425–478 (2003)
40. Zhang, J., Oh, Y.J., Lange, P., Yu, Z., Fukuoka, Y.: Artificial intelligence chatbot behavior change model for designing artificial intelligence chatbots to promote physical activity and a healthy diet. J. Med. Internet Res. **22**(9), e22845 (2020)

Persuasion-Building Fundamental Premises and Implications for Conversational Agents: A Conceptual Model in Captology

Pinkie Anggia[1]($\boxtimes$)(iD) and Kaoru Sumi[2](iD)

[1] Graduate School of Systems Information Science, Future University Hakodate, Hakodate, Japan
pinkie.anggia@outlook.jp
[2] Department of Media Architecture, Future University Hakodate, Hakodate, Hokkaido 041-0803, Japan
kaoru.sumi@acm.org
https://www.fun.ac.jp/en

Abstract. In the area of captology, computers as persuasive technology, conversational agent or dialogue system represent an interactive computing product as a key to changing people's viewpoints. Our former original experimental research addressed that a virtual agent's positive facial expressions and near-distance camera angle successfully influence participants' thoughts during an experiment. However, fragmentation in this growing topic led to theoretical confusion. To move the field forward, this paper uncovers the evidence-based elements as the standard compliance for designing the persuasive conversational agent. First, the fundamental premises, implications, constructs, and indicators from our previous original research were generated. Second, a theory synthesis from related articles on the interaction between virtual agents to humans, with the aim of persuading, was analyzed. Thus, it derives twelve fundamental premises, two implications, three main constructs, and fifteen indicators. Third, a model elaborates on the relationships between these constructs and indicators was developed. Its foundation is based on the three related concepts of the Persuasion Knowledge Model, Stimulus-Organism-Response Theory, Fogg's Captology Framework, and one measurement model of Partial Least Square Structural Equation Modeling. Hence, the theory synthesis provides the basis for inventing the proposed conceptual model, called the Agent-Subject Persuasion Model (ASPM), which emphasizes the originality of this research.

Keywords: Persuasive technology · Information science · Captology · Conversational agent · Human-agent interaction · Conceptual model

1 Introduction

Artificial agents have been going through continuous development over the years. Realizing natural, humane, and social way of interaction through SIAs (Socially

Interactive Agents) has been the goal all along [32]. Depending on the problem at hand, the attributes required differ greatly. The required attributes can be reactivity, autonomy, collaborative behavior, knowledge level, inferential capability, temporal continuity, personality, adaptivity, and mobility [11,17]. Due to the necessity of categorizing the agent's attributes, a well-known categorization was proposed by [37]. An interested reader is encouraged to read more in this chapter [8].

A trusting collaborative relationship between the agent and the user was found to be the foundational brick in persuasiveness even more than the appropriateness of the decision-making. A higher skill in social communication with the user was found to be closely correlated with the persuasive effectiveness of the agent [30]. Persuasive interactive agents were found to be influential in many industries, ranging from healthcare to coaching, marketing, etc.

Interactive agents are designed for many purposes and goals. For instance, an Embodied Conversational Agent (ECA) named Rachel can elicit social conversational behavior in autistic children [35]. An interactive agent can act like a travel agent too as shown in [42], where the agent acts as a route advice system that uses the driver's preferences in order to find a satisfactory route. Furthermore, an agent can be trained to assist the teacher in advising the student through knowledge that was acquired from a reinforcement learning framework where interactive teaching strategies are investigated [3].

Certainly, many studies are fragmented through many fields that can benefit from interactive agents. Thus, we realized the strong need to specifically address a solid basis for requirements to build an agent with the aim of persuasion.

To fill the gaps founded on previous research, this article will give an account to build a solid conceptual approach to highlight a clear research design, so the generated theories can be further measured in future studies.

This paper is organized in the following way. First, the persuasive system is defined. Section 2 reviews the related study. In Sect. 3, the research methodology is presented. Section 4 highlights the analysis results of proposed constructs, indicators, fundamental premises, implications, and conceptual model. Section 5 determines the theoretical contributions, limitations, and implications for future research. The whole paper concluded in Sect. 6.

2   Related Study

This section discusses related research in Artificial Intelligence (AI), particularly any interactive systems designed to convince people. A conversational agent or dialogue system is one of the examples of AI-based computer applications that will be covered in more detail. The proposed analytical statistic measuring approach will then be further described using a few related models as the first fundamental steps. Hence, it will connect the fragmented theories from artificial intelligence, persuasive technology, conversational agent, and theoretical models.

2.1 Artificial Intelligence and Persuasive Technology

The term Artificial Intelligence (AI) was first used in the 1950s to describe the straightforward theory that machines potentially demonstrate humans' intelligence [6]. AI seeks to create a machine that can think like humans, including learning, reasoning, and self-correction [28]. According to [15], humans or subjects will react to any computer program in accordance with accepted social standards, which has major implications for persuasion in the field of persuasive technology. To market particular products in the modern environment, a smart system can provide a variety of social cues that evoke social responses from human users.

2.2 Conversational Agent or Dialougue System

A conversational Agent (CA) or dialogue system is a computer program that interacts with humans using communication attributes, such as text, speech, facial expressions, and body gestures. Developing an agent depends highly on the goal in mind that the agent is supposed to accomplish. The goals of agents vary massively depending on the environment, setup, or culture. An example was shown in an intelligent friendly agent named iParrot, whose goal was to influence family members to conserve energy at their homes [1]. Designing an effective agent can be achieved by following the best practices from former research. Persuasive techniques were implemented by automated interactive agents and the persuasion quality was improved by the effectiveness of the persuasive dialogue. The personality of the system can be perceived as a trait of the interactive agent that affects the persuasion quality directly [4]. There is a correlation between human-like traits or the anthropomorphic look of agents with the system's use [41]. Scholars can also create animation since utilizing its expressive nature can enhance intuitive understanding as it involves direct movement [44]. Additionally, evaluating the user's impression of the agent was also studied comprehensively across 96 patterns of content from emotional scenarios, facial expressions, and words [45]. Thus, a *smart agent* is one that can learn and cooperate autonomously.

2.3 Theoretical Models

Persuasion Knowledge Model (PKM) [18] is presented in Fig. 1, which has many applications in persuasion contexts. The term *Agent* refers to the entity responsible for the implementation of the persuasion attempt (e.g., a company or a salesperson). The *Agent* is who the *Target* identifies as the one responsible for the persuasion attempt as the *Target* is the one who will experience the *Persuasion Attempt* as intended. Thus, this model considers the target's perception of the agent's behavior and goal. A persuasion attempt can be an ad or a sales presentation that is designed to influence the target. The observable part of the agent's attempt is called the *Persuasion Episode*, which is perceived by the target as any message delivered with the aim of persuading and influencing.

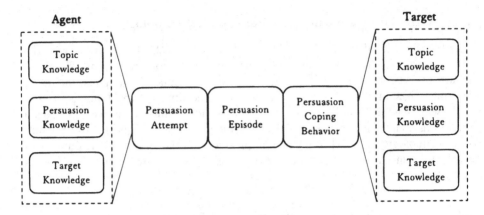

Fig. 1. Persuasion Knowledge Model (PKM) [18].

In response to the agent's persuasion attempts, the targets strive to achieve their own goals, which is modeled as *Persuasion Coping Behavior*. In [9], PKM has been used as a framework in investigating how personalized and formality affect the customer's perception, attitude, and behavior. In [46], PKM was used in investigating consumer resistance against covert selling, thus highlighting the negative ramifications of tactical deception in covert marketing communications.

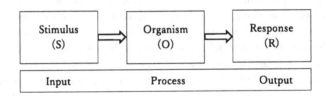

Fig. 2. Stimulus-Organism-Response (SOR) Framework [27].

Stimulus-organism-response (SOR) theory is represented in a framework shown in Fig. 2. SOR studies the individual's reaction to the surrounding environment. The individual's reaction could be either an approach behavior (positively acting) or an averting behavior (not positively acting). Several research was done to develop the theory through different approaches. The development range from considering the emotional quality of the environment as an aesthetic incitement to diversifying the SOR theory to the application of services capes by incorporating cognition and physiology. SOR model can predict the visual and vocal impact on motivation as an incitement, thus deriving a relationship between the intent and the actual action (e.g., tourists [40], hotel guests [23]).

As computers became distributed and increasingly ubiquitous, an interest in understanding and developing CHI started to arise. BJ Fogg proposed a new terminology, *Captology* [13], which refers to studying and utilizing computers in order to be used as effective persuasive technologies. BJ Fogg's model [14]

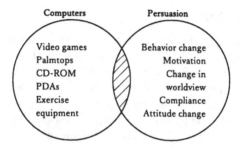

Fig. 3. Fogg's Captology Framework [14]: Captology [13] describes the shaded area where computing technology and persuasion overlap.

is shown in Fig. 3, thus studying captology can enrich HCI and lead to more effective interactive technologies, which will aid with the task of persuasion. BJ Fogg's captology framework was used in analyzing the persuasive and manipulative power of Emotionally Intelligent Conversational Agents (EICAs) in [29]. Thus highlighting some real upcoming issues that need to be regulated. A reflection on Fogg's captology framework was utilized in nudging users into projecting the male gender onto the technology when a company is developing a smart assistant that acts as a mechanic, thus investigating the premises that the male gender is commonly associated with higher degrees of authority, competence, and trustworthiness than the female gender [16]. Furthermore, Fogg's best practices for designing persuasive technology [12] were used in developing a CA that achieves some desired behavioral and clinical outcomes for patients suffering from chronic diseases especially Heart Failure, thus improving their self-care [34].

3 Research Design

3.1 Approach

This study applies a mixed-approach research design in a conceptual-theoretical paper: theory synthesis and model, which are adopted from [22]. Theory synthesis focuses on summarizing the current understanding of a phenomenon and structuring the fragmented field. The model focuses on the identification of variables, the prediction of relationships between them, the creation of new theoretical prepositions that introduce new variables and their relationships, as well as the justification of why a series of events lead to specific results.

3.2 Objectives

This study aims to (1) to develop a conceptual model that emphasizes the novel contribution of a general understanding of the field's core themes and specificities, (2) to test a theoretical model from a prediction perspective, (3) to test large sample size, and (4) to propose a theory development in exploratory research.

3.3   Measurement Method

There are many ways to measure the validity of a proposed theory, and it depends on whether the study has an intersection with other fields. Research on information science and persuasive technology studies the correlation in the fragments of fields in psychology, behavior change, and design. Most previous research [5,20,47] applied and proposed Structural Equation Modeling (SEM) as a method to measure the proposed conceptual model. As a considerably new technique in the early 1990s, SEM offers enhancement of benefits over traditional methods, which includes flexibility, controls over measurement error, allows straightforward evaluation, emphasizes theory testing, benefits large samples of data, and evaluates the relationship of variables from a prediction perspective [7].

Table 1. Measurement Methods.

	Exploratory Research	Confirmatory Research
First Generation (1900–1990)	Exploratory Factor Analysis Cluster Analysis Multidimensional Scaling	ANOVA Logistic Regression Multiple Regression
Second Generation (1990-present)	Variance-Based SEM: Partial Least Squares (with SmartPLS software)	Covariance-Based SEM, Confirmatory Factor Analysis (with AMOS/LISREL software)

Table 1 shows the measurement methods according to the types of research design. According to the aforementioned studies [5,7,20,47], PLS-SEM aims to generate results from a prediction perspective, while CB-SEM confirms an existing theory. Hence, PLS-SEM [19] is the model-fit method selected in this paper, and our proposed conceptual model ASPM follows its standards.

3.4   Procedures

Initially, the fundamental premises, implications, constructs, and indicators from our previous original research were generated. Second, a theory synthesis from related articles on the interaction between virtual agents to humans, with the aim of persuading, was analyzed. Then, it derives novel components of twelve fundamental premises and two implications, three main constructs, and fifteen indicators. This synthesis strengthens the basis for inventing the proposed conceptual model, named Agent-Subject Persuasion Model (ASPM).

ASPM's foundation derives from (1) the construct and indicators of our former experiment [39] and related studies (e.g., PKM, SOR Theory, Fogg's Captology Framework), (2) the prediction of relationships between these constructs and indicators in fundamental premises and implications, and (3) a method of a measurement model that fits with the case being investigated as a way to test the proposed theory.

4   Results

4.1   Evaluations from Our Previous Experimental Research

Fig. 4. 3D Real-Time Conversational Virtual Agents System: Do Facial Expressions and Camera Angles Persuade Human? [39].

Formerly, [39] presented in Fig. 4 aims to evaluate whether persuasion differs depending on the video setting. Developed with Unreal Engine MetaHuman 4.27, the experiment shows the interaction between 6 virtual agents and 37 subjects.

A quantitative numerical confirmatory analysis, ANOVA test (single-factor and two-factor without replication) under six measuring criteria, showed that the virtual agents' positive facial expressions and near-distance camera angle successfully influence predominantly extroverted participants' opinions during an experiment (*Alpha-level* = 0.05). These results correlate with [45] where virtual agents with good impressions were effective in persuasion.

Premise 1.1: The facial expressions of agents influence the change in worldview of subjects.

Premise 1.2: The video settings influence the change in worldview of subjects.
The number of agents plays an important role in being more persuasive to the subject as in [25], where a multiple-agent setting was shown to be more persuasive than a single-agent.

Premise 1.3a: The number of agents influences the change in worldview of subjects.
The use of animation utilizing its expressive nature can enhance the intuitive understanding as it involves direct movement was also investigated previously [44]. Moreover, the attractiveness of the agent was proven to be an important factor in how persuasive the agent can be and the amount of behavioral change was very noticeable [26].

Premise 1.3b: The agents' attractiveness influences the change in worldview of subjects.

The elements of facial expressions, camera angles, as well as positive and negative narratives, were investigated. These positive and negative narratives were used to evaluate the degree of persuasion to the subjects.

Premise 1.4: The agents' narrative influences the change in worldview of subjects.

Besides that, participants were asked in the research instrument prior to and after the interaction with the agents about the topic presented by the agents.

Premise 1.5: The agents' knowledge influences the change in worldview of subjects.

Implications of Premise 1 for Future Research: We found many proven components needed to develop a more interactive conversational agent. It is supported by [43] that an agent with a social dialogue is shown to be more effective than a text-based one. Moreover, the attractiveness of the agent was proven to be an important factor in how persuasive the agent can be and the amount of behavioral change was very noticeable [26]. Therefore, it is necessary that developers and narrative designers of persuasive conversational agent adopt the cutting-edge understanding offered in this study and ground persuasive conversational agent on a more nuanced conceptual understanding of experience.

The subjects who participated in this study were in a neutral and happy emotional state. Thus, affecting the coherence results that agents with smiling facial expressions are persuasive.

Premise 2.1: The emotions of subjects influence the change in worldview by virtual agents.

In the age group from 18 to 24 years old, Japanese subjects interact with Japanese-speaking agents through a synthesized voice recording.

Premise 2.2a: The subjects' age influences the change in the worldview by virtual agents.

Premise 2.2b: The subjects' ethnicity influences the change in worldview by virtual agents.

The purposive sampling method was chosen to target preferred participants.

Premise 2.3: The sampling methods to select the subjects influence the change in worldview by virtual agents.

The Big Five theory [14,15] was adopted to investigate the relationship between a subject's personality and how it can affect them being persuaded by the virtual agents. Additionally, the subjects were asked about their knowledge of the topics prior to the interaction with the agents.

Premise 2.4: The subjects' personalities influence the persuasion (e.g., change in worldview and emotional appeal) by virtual agents.

Premise 2.5: The subjects' knowledge influences the change in worldview by virtual agents.

Implications of Premise 2 for Future Research: We found that predominantly, our participants have extroverted personalities. People who score highly in extroversion tend to be triggered by a desire for excitement and social rewards and will find words (e.g., strong, outgoing, active, excitement, attention) more persuasive. It is proved by [21] that extroverted individuals are likely to engage more in online purchasing activities because online customers can share their shopping experience and information on the online platform. Thus, it is essential for developers, designers, and marketers to create a persuasive conversational agent where the content can give social rewards to the subjects.

4.2   Proposed Conceptual Model: Agent-Subject Persuasion Model (ASPM)

Insights across research practices have been analyzed, which reveal two constructs and ten indicators in Table 2, while one construct and five indicators are presented in Table 3. An ASPM conceptual model developed in this research covers the big picture of what a persuasive conversational agent is, what influences its effectiveness in persuading humans, its keys of contingencies, and the role other fields can play in it.

Figure 5 illustrates the correlations between variables based on the multivariate statistical method used in the PLS-SEM assessment for exploratory research. This method seeks to support the suggested theory. Any AI and persuasive technology-related experiments that are not only static but also dynamic, intelligent, and able to learn from the subjects can use this blueprint. The shift in subjects' worldviews is influenced by the facial expressions of agents, as stated in premise 1.1. Agents who convey a positive attitude and smiling [39, 45] are influential. This idea can be used in the future to determine how persuasive a system is already through studies that collect facial expression data from participants or detect their emotions using sensors.

5   Discussion

5.1   Theoretical Contributions

This research undertakes the specific criteria on compliance for a persuasive conversational agent, presented in fundamental premises, implications, constructs,

Table 2. Construct: Conversational Agent (CA) and Subjects (SU).

Code	Indicators from CA Construct	Sub-components	References
CA1	Agent's Facial Expressions	Joy, Fright, Sadness, Antipathy, Anger, Surprise	[39,45]
CA2	Video Settings	Near, Far, and Normal-distance Camera Angles	[39]
CA3	Design Compliance	NLU Capability, Voice Synthesis, Number of Agents, Agent's Attractiveness	[13,25,26,39,41,44]
CA4	Agent's Narrative	Positive, Negative	[39]
CA5	Agent's Knowledge	Topic Knowledge, Persuasion Knowledge, Knowledge about Targeted Subjects	[18,39]
Code	Indicators from SU Construct	Sub-components	References
SU1	Subject's Emotions	Joy, Fright, Sadness, Antipathy, Anger, Surprise	[39,45]
SU2	Demography	Gender, Age, Ethnicity	[39]
SU3	Sampling Method	Sample Size (n), Methods of Data Collection and Analysis	[24,39]
SU4	Subject's Personality	Openness, Conscientiousness, Extroversion, Agreeableness, Neuroticism	[36,39]
SU5	Subject's Knowledge	Topic Knowledge, Persuasion Knowledge, Knowledge about Targeted Subjects	[18,39]

Table 3. Construct: Persuasion in Conversational Agent (PCA).

Code	Indicators from PCA Construct	References
PCA1	Behavior Change	[13,18]
PCA2	Change in Worldview	[13,39]
PCA3	Motivation	[13,47]
PCA4	Adaptation	[13]
PCA5	Emotional Appeal	[2,10,15,31,39,47]

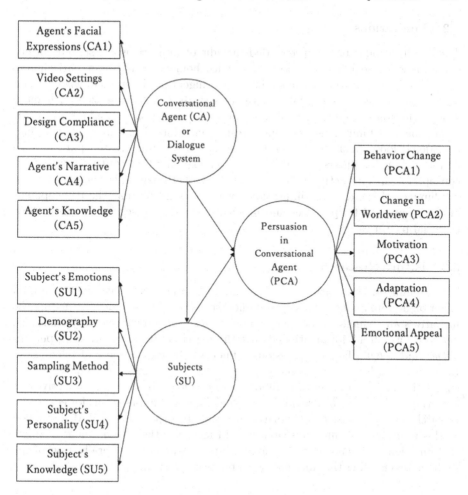

Fig. 5. Agent-Subject Persuasion Model (ASPM) provides a state-of-the-art persuasive conversational agent, which emphasizes the originality of this research.

and indicators in a conceptual model of ASPM that can advance future research. First, this study elaborates on concepts of a persuasive conversational agent and different approaches of the theoretical models (Fig. 1, Fig. 2, Fig. 3, Table 2, Table 3). Second, we incorporate the literature, illustrate relationships among entities, and generate a synthesis that accommodates this knowledge [33]. Third, the proposed fundamental premises demonstrate the concept, structure the related theories founded in fragmented fields, extend the research domain, and resolve ambiguities [38].

5.2   Limitations

The results should be comprehended in light of limitations. First, our former experimental research undertook solely with homogeneous target participants (e.g., Japanese students in a similar age range that interacted with virtual agents). To derive more reliable data, this study can be analyzed with more samples in non-homogeneous subjects. Second, the decision to adopt strict criteria generates limited results. These results may have been different if we had considered looser inclusion criteria. However, ASPM was created purposely to be focused on computers as persuasive technology and the input-process-output concept for an interactive dialogue system, with the specific goal of persuading humans. Despite these limitations, we are confident that the development of these fundamental premises and implications will help scholars address these essential priorities.

5.3   Future Research

We recommend that future research should ground persuasive conversational agent on a more nuanced conceptual understanding of experience. Adjusting the narratives and agents' chosen facial expressions to the preferred subjects is also necessary as [39,44,45] mentioned that the matching between subjects' personalities and agents' facial expressions influences the effectiveness of persuasion. In the next studies, solving some shortages (e.g., non-homogeneous data, sample size, strict inclusion criteria, redundant terminology to reach the objectives) is essential. ASPM (Fig. 5) provides clear guidelines and implications for continued research on a persuasive conversational agent. Incorporating ASPM developed in this study in continued research should facilitate the advancement of information science, persuasive technology, captology, and the generalization of the findings by enabling the different fields to speak the same language.

6   Conclusion

This study proposes a blueprint or conceptual model for AI and persuasive technology in which the correlations between variables were implied with a multivariate statistical method. It focuses on a specific novel idea to advance and present viewpoints on a particular research problem. It contributes to theorized links between variables.

This investigation gathers data from our former experiment and comparative studies to be statistically evaluated for use in future research. It derives twelve fundamental premises, fifteen indicators, three fundamental constructs, and two implications presented in an ASPM conceptual model. The relationships between constructs and indicators strengthen with the use of the PLS-SEM measurement.

Conclusively, ASPM can be applied to any AI and persuasive technology-related experiments that are dynamic, intelligent, and could learn from the subjects. The cutting-edge understanding offered in this study is the required step toward a more unified persuasive system theory.

References

1. Al Mahmud, A., Dadlani, P., Mubin, O., Shahid, S., Midden, C., Moran, O.: iParrot: towards designing a persuasive agent for energy conservation. In: de Kort, Y., IJsselsteijn, W., Midden, C., Eggen, B., Fogg, B.J. (eds.) PERSUASIVE 2007. LNCS, vol. 4744, pp. 64–67. Springer, Heidelberg (2007). https://doi.org/10.1007/978-3-540-77006-0_8
2. Albaina, I.M., Visser, T., Van Der Mast, C.A., Vastenburg, M.H.: Flowie: a persuasive virtual coach to motivate elderly individuals to walk. In: 2009 3rd International Conference on Pervasive Computing Technologies for Healthcare, pp. 1–7. IEEE (2009)
3. Amir, O., Kamar, E., Kolobov, A., Grosz, B.: Interactive teaching strategies for agent training. In: Proceedings of IJCAI 2016 (2016)
4. Andrews, P.Y.: System personality and persuasion in human-computer dialogue. ACM Trans. Interact. Intell. Syst. 2(2) (2012). https://doi.org/10.1145/2209310.2209315
5. Anggia, P., Sensuse, D.I., Sucahyo, Y.G., Rohajawati, S.: Identifying critical success factors for knowledge management implementation in organization: a survey paper. In: 2013 International Conference on Advanced Computer Science and Information Systems (ICACSIS), pp. 83–88. IEEE (2013)
6. Bini, S.A.: Artificial intelligence, machine learning, deep learning, and cognitive computing: what do these terms mean and how will they impact health care? J. Arthroplasty 33(8), 2358–2361 (2018)
7. Blanthorne, C., Jones-Farmer, L.A., Almer, E.D.: Why you should consider sem: a guide to getting started. In: Advances in Accounting Behavioral Research. Emerald Group Publishing Limited (2006)
8. Bradshaw, J.M.: An introduction to software agents. Softw. Agents 4, 3–46 (1997)
9. Decock, S., De Clerck, B., Lybaert, C., Plevoets, K.: Testing the various guises of conversational human voice: the impact of formality and personalization on customer outcomes in online complaint management. J. Internet Comm. 20(1), 1–24 (2021)
10. Dörmann, C.: Designing electronic shops, persuading consumers to buy. In: Proceedings of the 26th Euromicro Conference. EUROMICRO 2000. Informatics: Inventing the Future, vol. 2, pp. 140–147. IEEE (2000)
11. Etzioni, O., Weld, D.S.: Intelligent agents on the internet: fact, fiction, and forecast. IEEE Expert 10(4), 44–49 (1995)
12. Fogg, B.J.: Creating persuasive technologies: an eight-step design process. In: Proceedings of the 4th International Conference on Persuasive Technology, pp. 1–6 (2009)
13. Fogg, B.J.: Captology: the study of computers as persuasive technologies. In: CHI 98 Conference Summary on Human Factors in Computing Systems, p. 385 (1998)
14. Fogg, B.J.: Persuasive computers: perspectives and research directions. In: Proceedings of the SIGCHI Conference on Human Factors in Computing Systems, pp. 225–232 (1998)
15. Fogg, B.J.: Persuasive technology: using computers to change what we think and do. Ubiquity 2002(December), 2 (2002)
16. Fossa, F., Sucameli, I.: Gender bias and conversational agents: an ethical perspective on social robotics. Sci. Eng. Ethics 28(3), 1–23 (2022)

17. Franklin, S., Graesser, A.: Is it an agent, or just a program?: a taxonomy for autonomous agents. In: International Workshop on Agent Theories, Architectures, and Languages, pp. 21–35. Springer, Heidelberg (1996). https://doi.org/10.1007/bfb0013570
18. Friestad, M., Wright, P.: The persuasion knowledge model: how people cope with persuasion attempts. J. Cons. Res. **21**(1), 1–31 (1994)
19. Hair Jr, J.F., Hult, G.T.M., Ringle, C.M., Sarstedt, M., Danks, N.P., Ray, S.: Partial least squares structural equation modeling (pls-sem) using r: a workbook (2021)
20. Hidayanto, A.N., Ovirza, M., Anggia, P., Budi, N.F.A., Phusavat, K.: The roles of electronic word of mouth and information searching in the promotion of a new e-commerce strategy: a case of online group buying in Indonesia. J. Theor. Appl. Electron. Commer. Res. **12**(3), 69–85 (2017)
21. Hui, C.: Personality's influence on the relationship between online word-of-mouth and consumers' trust in shopping website. J. Softw. **6**(2), 265–272 (2011)
22. Jaakkola, E.: Designing conceptual articles: four approaches. AMS Rev. **10**(1–2), 18–26 (2020)
23. Jani, D., Han, H.: Influence of environmental stimuli on hotel customer emotional loyalty response: testing the moderating effect of the big five personality factors. Int. J. Hosp. Manag. **44**, 48–57 (2015)
24. Johnson, M., Ghuman, P.: Blindsight: The (Mostly) Hidden Ways Marketing Reshapes Our Brains. BenBella Books (2020)
25. Kantharaju, R.B., De Franco, D., Pease, A., Pelachaud, C.: Is two better than one? effects of multiple agents on user persuasion. In: Proceedings of the 18th International Conference on Intelligent Virtual Agents, pp. 255–262 (2018)
26. Khan, R.F., Sutcliffe, A.: Attractive agents are more persuasive. Int. J. Hum.-Comput. Interact. **30**(2), 142–150 (2014)
27. Kim, M.J., Lee, C.K., Jung, T.: Exploring consumer behavior in virtual reality tourism using an extended stimulus-organism-response model. J. Travel Res. **59**(1), 69–89 (2020)
28. Kok, J.N., Boers, E.J., Kosters, W.A., Van der Putten, P., Poel, M.: Artificial intelligence: definition, trends, techniques, and cases. Artif. Intell. **1**, 270–299 (2009)
29. Kuss, P., Leenes, R.: The ghost in the machine-emotionally intelligent conversational agents and the failure to regulate 'deception by design'. SCRIPTed **17**, 320 (2020)
30. Liu, S., Helfenstein, S., Wahlstedt, A.: Social psychology of persuasion applied to human agent interaction. Hum. Technol. Interdisc. J. Hum. ICT Environ. (2008)
31. Looije, R., Neerincx, M.A., Cnossen, F.: Persuasive robotic assistant for health self-management of older adults: design and evaluation of social behaviors. Int. J. Hum.-Comput. Stud. **68**(6), 386–397 (2010)
32. Lugrin, B.: Introduction to Socially Interactive Agents, 1 edn, p. 1–20. Association for Computing Machinery, New York (2021). https://doi.org/10.1145/3477322.3477324
33. MacInnis, D.J.: A framework for conceptual contributions in marketing. J. Mark. **75**(4), 136–154 (2011)
34. Moulik, S.: DIL-A Conversational Agent for Heart Failure Patients. Ph.D. thesis, The Claremont Graduate University (2019)
35. Mower, E., Black, M.P., Flores, E., Williams, M., Narayanan, S.: Rachel: design of an emotionally targeted interactive agent for children with autism. In: 2011 IEEE International Conference on Multimedia and Expo, pp. 1–6. IEEE (2011)

36. Norman, W.T.: Toward an adequate taxonomy of personality attributes: replicated factor structure in peer nomination personality ratings. J. Abnorm. Soc. Psychol. **66**(6), 574 (1963)
37. Nwana, H.S.: Software agents: an overview. Knowl. Eng. Rev. **11**(3), 205–244 (1996)
38. Palmatier, R.W., Houston, M.B., Hulland, J.: Review articles: Purpose, process, and structure (2018)
39. Pinkie, A., Kaoru, S.: 3d real-time conversational virtual agents system: do facial expressions and camera angles persuade human? In: The 2023 International Conference on Artificial Life and Robotics (2023)
40. Rajaguru, R.: Motion picture-induced visual, vocal and celebrity effects on tourism motivation: stimulus organism response model. Asia Pac. J. Tour. Res. **19**(4), 375–388 (2014)
41. Rheu, M., Shin, J.Y., Peng, W., Huh-Yoo, J.: Systematic review: trust-building factors and implications for conversational agent design. Int. J. Hum.-Comput. Interact. **37**(1), 81–96 (2021)
42. Rogers, S., Fiechter, C.N., Langley, P.: An adaptive interactive agent for route advice. In: Proceedings of the third annual conference on Autonomous Agents, pp. 198–205 (1999)
43. Schulman, D., Bickmore, T.: Persuading users through counseling dialogue with a conversational agent. In: Proceedings of the 4th International Conference on Persuasive Technology, pp. 1–8 (2009)
44. Sumi, K.: Learning story marketing through practical experience of story creation system. In: Aylett, R., Lim, M.Y., Louchart, S., Petta, P., Riedl, M. (eds.) ICIDS 2010. LNCS, vol. 6432, pp. 98–110. Springer, Heidelberg (2010). https://doi.org/10.1007/978-3-642-16638-9_13
45. Sumi, K., Nagata, M.: Evaluating a virtual agent as persuasive technology. In: Csapó, J., Magyar, A. (eds.) Psychology of Persuasion (2010)
46. Xie, G.X., Boush, D.M., Liu, R.R.: Tactical deception in covert selling: a persuasion knowledge perspective. J. Mark. Commun. **21**(3), 224–240 (2015)
47. Zulkifli, A.N., Noor, N.M., Bakar, J.A.A., Mat, R.C., Ahmad, M.: A conceptual model of interactive persuasive learning system for elderly to encourage computer-based learning process. In: 2013 International Conference on Informatics and Creative Multimedia, pp. 7–12. IEEE (2013)

On Further Reflection... Moral Reflections Enhance Robotic Moral Persuasive Capability

Ruchen Wen[1(✉)] , Boyoung Kim[2] , Elizabeth Phillips[2] , Qin Zhu[3] ,
and Tom Williams[1]

[1] Colorado School of Mines, Golden, CO, USA
{rwen,twilliams}@mines.edu
[2] George Mason University, Fairfax, VA, USA
{bkim55,ephill3}@gmu.edu
[3] Virginia Tech, Blacksburg, VA, USA
qinzhu@vt.edu

Abstract. To enable robots to exert positive moral influence, we need to understand the impacts of robots' moral communications, the ways robots can phrase their moral language to be most clear and persuasive, and the ways that these factors interact. Previous work has suggested, for example, that for certain types of robot moral interventions to be successful (i.e., moral interventions grounded in particular ethical frameworks), those interventions may need to be followed by opportunities for moral reflection, during which humans can critically engage with not only the contents of the robot's moral language, but also with the way that moral language connects with their social-relational ontology and broader moral ecosystem. We conceptually replicate this prior work ($N = 119$) using a design that more precisely manipulates moral reflection. Our results confirm that opportunities for moral reflection are indeed critical to the success of robotic moral interventions—regardless of the ethical framework in which those interventions are grounded.

Keywords: human-robot communication · role ethics · moral influence

1 Introduction

Research has shown that language-capable robots hold unique persuasive capability over human interactants. Robots can use their language not only to encourage human compliance with requests and commands [3,4,7,24,31], but also (intentionally or unintentionally [15,16]) to influence human systems of moral and social norms [28,35,41]. Critically, robots are not only able to influence the behaviors of those they directly interact with, but also may influence others indirectly. That is, robots may influence the behaviors their human interactants choose to perform around other humans [35]. These "ripple effects" thus have the potential to more broadly affect interactants' social and moral ecosystems, above and beyond their immediate interactions with robots. It is thus critical to understand how best to steer robots' potential for moral influence.

J. Ham et al. (Eds.): PERSUASIVE 2023, LNCS 13832, pp. 290–304, 2023.
https://doi.org/10.1007/978-3-031-30933-5_19

Steering Robots' Potential for Moral Influence

To prevent robots from exerting negative moral influence, language-capable robots must avoid violating moral norms or causing moral harm, and be able to explicitly communicate moral conceptions and values. For example, robots must be able to reject unethical commands given by interlocutors, and explain or justify the reason(s) for their non-compliance by highlighting how such commands violate moral principles [33, 42].

Moreover, given robots' unique persuasive power, they must be able to leverage their persuasive capability to exert *positive* moral influence. By demonstrating positive moral tendencies, robots might serve as "moral mediators" that inspire human interactants to cultivate their own moral tendencies. By issuing blame-laden moral rebukes, robots might emphasize the importance of key moral norms, and encourage their adherence by interactants [46]. And just as negative moral influence may cause negative "ripple effects", we must also consider the opportunities for robots to exert *positive influence*, and for this positive influence to similarly result in positive "ripple effects [28]."

A social-relational approach would suggest that robots can encourage, emphasize, and reinforce moral norms within communal contexts by leveraging the power resulting from the normative influences on human-robot relationships. This relational approach can be understood through the lens of a Confucian ethical framework, in which people cultivate self-reflections and virtuous tendencies through daily interaction with others [2], and in which people's moral self-reflection can often be initiated or influenced by other's words and actions [46]. Through their use of moral language, robots may help interactants cultivate their moral selves and contribute to a flourishing moral ecology for human-robot interaction that allows humans to grow.

To best leverage robots' persuasive capability to exert positive moral influence, we need to understand different forms of moral language, and the acute impacts of those different forms. But critically, as we will discuss in the next section, previous work argues that the effectiveness of different types of moral language could be mediated by the structure of the interactions in which they are embedded.

The Structure of Moral Interventions

The impacts of a robot's moral language are mediated by a host of contextual factors. One such contextual factor is the structure of the interaction that surrounds a robot's moral intervention. Previous work from [40], for example, suggested that for certain types of robot moral interventions to be successful, those interventions may need to be followed by opportunities for moral reflection, in which interactants can take their time to examine and digest the information they receive from the robot, and thus more deeply engage with the content of the robot's moral language. If this were the case, it would have significant impacts on the design of the broader interaction structure of robotic moral interventions. This suggestion by [40], however, was based on an emergent observation from an experiment not explicitly designed to test for the effect of moral reflection. This creates an obvious need to formally verify this suggestion.

In this work, we thus present a conceptual replication and extension of [40] ($N = 119$), following the same study procedures, but designed to systematically investigate the impacts of moral reflection on the effectiveness of robots' moral language on human behavior. Our results indicate that opportunities for moral reflection are indeed critical to the success of robots' moral interventions and their associated perlocutionary goals—regardless of the ethical framework in which those interventions are grounded.

2   Related Work

2.1   Persuasive Robots and Robotic Moral Influence

Human-Robot Interaction (HRI) researchers have demonstrated that interactive robots, especially language-capable robots, have unique potential to influence humans in a variety of ways [3,4,6,7,12,24,30–32]. Not only are robots able to exert influence over human behaviors, but also researchers have shown that they can exert moral influence, by weakening humans perceptions of certain moral norms [16]. This moral persuasive influence may be especially strong for language-capable robots, due to the uniquely high social agency [19] and moral agency [9] that may be evoked by natural language capabilities [18]. Critically, this exertion of negative moral influence can be unintentional [16], meaning it needs to be watched for and addressed even in contexts where persuasion is not the robot's perlocutionary goal [20]. Moreover, this potential for negative moral influence is particularly concerning due to previous observations that robots can mediate human–human interaction dynamics [10,11,36] and create ripple effects [28,35,38] in which robots influence over humans carries over into human–human interactions in which the robot is no longer involved.

Yet with this challenge of avoiding negative moral influence comes an opportunity for promoting positive moral influence and helping cultivate moral ecosystems. Research has shown a variety of ways that robots can engage in moral communication, including rejecting inappropriate commands [5,14,17,21,38,39], calling out norm violations [23,43,43], justifying necessary norm violations [33], and giving moral advice [25,26,34,40]. Although these types of approaches are often motivated by robots' obligation to avoid performing negative moral actions, or to avoid exerting negative moral influence, all of these activities, especially giving moral advice, may also be used to intentionally exert *positive* moral influence. Critically, just as the risks of unintentional exertion of negative moral influence are exacerbated by the possibility for negative ripple effects, we argue that the benefits of intentional exertion of positive moral influence can be accentuated by the possibility for positive ripple effects. Although positive moral influence could be exerted through a variety of moral communicative means, the most obvious and direct way of doing so may be through the use of moral advice that explicitly conveys particular moral principles.

2.2   Confucian Ethics and Moral Reflection

A number of scholars have begun to incorporate Confucian ethics into the philosophical and empirical studies of human–robot interaction, especially as they relate to calls for increased attention to non-Western ethical theories [42] and for ethical pluralism [47]. Self-reflection is of critical importance to moral development in Confucian ethics. It is also worth noting that moral reflection in the Confucian tradition is rarely done by people themselves. Rather, it is an interactive process in concert with others [44]. Such a relational approach can occur in various settings including: (1) observing and reflecting on how others (especially moral exemplars) make decisions in moral situations and how we can improve ourselves by incorporating our reflective thinking into future situations; and (2) exercising and developing moral sympathy toward others in moral thought experiments [45].

2.3   Confucian Ethics for Robot Moral Communication

As part of the recent effort to integrate Confucian ethics into human–robot interaction, some scholars have recently investigated how robotic moral interventions grounded in different moral frameworks might have different moral effects. [42] explored different ways that Confucian ethics could be used to guide the design of language capable robots. [38] explored the ways that Confucian ethics could guide the design and use of knowledge representations for generating robot norm violation responses. [25, 26] investigated the use of role-based, identity-based, and norm-based language in encouraging participant honesty. And most relevant to our work, [40] compared the use of role-based and norm-based language for encouraging interactants to adhere to community-relevant role norms. In that work, [40] used a Theory of Planned Behavior (TPB) [1] questionnaire to measure potential changes to the strength of these role-norms, and systematically varied the timing of this measure to control for potential ordering effects. Curiously, [40] found that role-based moral interventions led to greater observed adherence to the role-norms under investigation, but *only* when immediately preceded by the TPB questionnaire. [40] suggested that this observation may have been due to the TPB questionnaire serving as an opportunity for moral reflection, the importance of which would be well justified from a Confucian ethical perspective, as described above.

If this suggestion were to be accepted, it would mean that robots' use of role-based moral language is uniquely impactful for encouraging adherence to community-relevant role-norms, but only if the robot's moral language were followed by an opportunity for reflection on that language. We argue, however, that this suggestion cannot be accepted by the results of [40]'s study alone. First, their study was not explicitly designed to interrogate the role of reflection. Second, while the TPB may indeed have served some reflective role in their study, an intentionally designed reflective exercise would be needed to justify [40]'s suggestion. Finally, it is possible that the TPB questionnaire used by [40] may have overly primed people towards role-oriented modes of reflection, which could explain the localization of their observed effects to their role-based moral language condition. In this work, we thus conducted a conceptual replication of [40]'s experiment that manipulated the opportunity for reflection in a more controlled, explicit, and intentional manner. This work aims to test the two following experimental hypotheses:

Hypothesis H1 When a robotic moral language intervention is followed by an opportunity for moral reflection, it will lead to greater moral influence, as demonstrated by greater adherence to the moral principles encouraged by that moral intervention.

Hypothesis H2 The increases to moral influence facilitated by opportunities for reflection will be greater when following role-based moral language interventions than when following norm-based moral language interventions.

3 Method

3.1 Experimental Design

To evaluate our hypotheses, we conducted an IRB-approved human-subjects experiment with a mixed factorial design, similar to that used by [40]. This experiment used a 2 (Moral language) ×2 (Reflection) ×2 (Experimental Task), mixed between-within subjects design with two between-subjects factors and one within-subjects factor. Specifically, participants completed two experimental tasks (order counterbalanced) and were randomly assigned to receive either a *Norm-Based* or a *Role-based* moral language intervention immediately after completing the first experimental performance task. Half of participants then completed a moral reflection exercise after receiving their moral language intervention, and the other half did not complete the moral reflection exercise. After receiving the moral language intervention and/or moral reflection exercise, all participants then completed the experimental task for a second time to allow us to compute pre-intervention to post-intervention performance differences.

3.2 Experimental Task

We chose the experimental tasks used by [40] in order to expand and conceptually replicate the prior study's suggestion that a (certain type of) reflective exercise may have increased the efficacy of (a certain type of) moral language provided by a robot. As in [40]'s study, the experimental task asked participants to count the frequency of three articles ("a", "an", and "the") appearing in book pages.

3.3 Experimental Conditions

Moral Language Interventions. We also chose to replicate the two moral language interventions from [40]'s study, and then add an opportunity for reflection to address limitations of the original study and the interpretation of its results.

Thus, for the moral intervention conditions, we used the same two videos which consisted of a norm-based moral language intervention delivered by a Nao robot, and a role-based moral language intervention delivered by a Nao robot. All videos of NAO speaking used NAO's default 'voice' and were coupled with closed captioning located at the bottom center of each video. These videos can be found in this paper's OSF Repository. Participants were first introduced to the study and the task with a video of a NAO robot serving as the experimenter in the study. Participants then completed their first article counting task, and once complete, received either a norm-based moral intervention where the Nao robot said:

"As a reminder, you are obligated to provide high quality data if you are to accept payment for this task. Therefore, you should find all the articles in the text."

Or, participants received a role-based moral intervention:

"As a reminder, you are a paid research participant, and a good paid research participant helps researchers by providing high quality data. Therefore, your responsibility is to find all the articles in the text."

These two videos thus represent two possible robotic moral language interventions which use different moral frameworks (role-based vs. norm based). The effectiveness of these moral language interventions are then measured by assessing the difference in task performance before and after receiving the moral language intervention.

Reflection Exercises. The claims of Wen [40] regarding the role of moral reflection were made on the basis of the placement of a Theory of Planned Behavior (TPB) questionnaire they used as a dependent measure. Wen's findings suggested that the act of completing the TPB questionnaire immediately after receiving a moral language intervention may have inadvertently served as an opportunity for moral reflection. Although the TPB may have encouraged reflection, it was not explicitly designed for this purpose. Moreover, [40] identified several items within the TPB questionnaire whose wording may have heightened participants' sensitivity to reflect specifically on the role-based moral language.

We thus developed a two-stage reflection exercise for this experiment. In the first stage, participants were asked to think about the language that the robot used in their moral language intervention (i.e., either the norm-based intervention or the role-based intervention), and write down in a free response text box, what they thought about what the robot said. In the second stage, and immediately after completing their responses to the first stage, participants were then asked to indicate how convincing they found the robot's speech. Participants were also asked to explain why they felt that way.

To ensure that participants considered each stage of the exercise carefully, we required a minimum of three minutes to be spent on each stage, and a minimum of 300 characters to be typed for each free response.

3.4   Experimental Procedures

After completing an audio/video check to ensure that participants could see and hear the videos of the NAO robot, and providing informed consent, participants completed a demographic survey. Participants were then shown the video in which a NAO robot introduced itself and explained the experimental task. Next, participants performed the first article counting task, with a video of the robot continuing to play on the left-hand side of the screen as shown in Fig. 1. Once participants completed the first article counting task, they were shown a video in which the NAO robot either gave a norm-based language intervention or a role-based language intervention based on their assigned *Intervention* condition. After watching the intervention video, half of participants completed the reflection exercise and then completed the second experimental task. The other half of participants immediately completed the second experimental task with no opportunity for moral reflection. Finally, participants were paid.

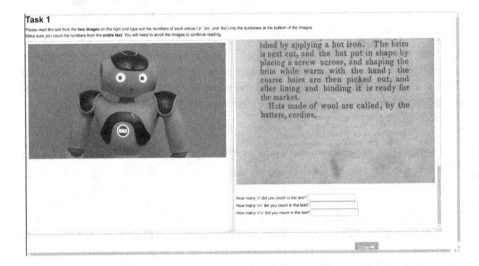

Fig. 1. Screenshot of the experimental task page.

3.5   Dependent Measures

Our key dependent variable in this experiment was *improvement of performance* between article counting experimental task one and article counting task two, which reflected changes in role-norm adherence. Performance was calculated by the difference between the reported counts and the actual counts for all three types of articles. To gain a deeper understanding of how the effectiveness of robots' moral interventions may have been mediated by reflection, we collected the text participants produced for the reflection exercise. We performed an exploratory content analysis of this text, with respect to: the amount of text participants wrote in their reflection exercises, participants' use of reflection-related verbs and role-related and norm-related words.

3.6 Participants

One hundred and nineteen participants (58F, 60M, 1NB) were recruited from Prolific (www.prolific.co). All participants passed "bot check" procedures. Participants' ages ranged from 19 to 71 years old ($M = 32.80$, $SD = 10.03$).

4 Performance Analysis

4.1 Analysis

We analyzed our data through a Bayesian analysis framework [37], using version 0.16.3 of the JASP statistical software [22]. Within this framework, we conducted a Bayesian Analyses of Variance (ANOVA) with Bayes Factor Analysis to assess (1) the impacts of the moral reflection exercise, (2) the impacts of the type of moral language intervention, and (3) the potential interaction between these two factors. Bayes Factors are odds ratios representing the relative strengths of evidence for and against hypotheses. A Bayes Factor BF_{10} represents the relative likelihood of the collected data under hypothesis H_1 versus hypothesis H_0. We specifically calculated Bayes Inclusion Factors across matched Models [13,29], which represent, for each candidate main effect and interaction effect, the relative likelihood of models containing that effect versus models not containing that effect, thus providing a measure of the strength of evidence in favor of that effect. Bayes Factors were then interpreted using community standards [27]. All data and analysis scripts can be found in this paper's OSF Repository.

4.2 Results

Our analysis provided very strong evidence in favor of an effect of the reflection exercise (BF 34.783), but moderate evidence against both an effect of intervention type (BF 0.193) and an interaction effect between the reflection exercise and the intervention type (BF 0.255). As shown in Fig. 2, participants who received an opportunity for reflection had greater improvement of performance in the second article counting task (M = −3.639, SD = 6.718) than did participant who received no such opportunity (M = −0.241, SD = 3.461).

5 Content Analysis

We will now discuss the exploratory content analysis that followed our hypothesis-driven statistical analysis.

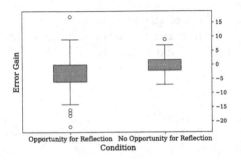

Fig. 2. Error Gain between tasks (errors made post-intervention minus errors made pre-intervention), by experimental condition. Lower numbers indicate better performance on the second task (post-intervention) relative to the first task (pre-intervention).

5.1 Analysis

After screening out one participant whose responses demonstrated a lack of understanding of the task, sixty participants remained who had been completed the reflection exercise. Two authors coded about half of these remaining responses each, looking for keywords that demonstrated either attention to roles, attention to norms, or direct evidence of reflection. After discussion, the two authors agreed on a final set of keywords in each of these three categories.

After defining the norm keywords, role keywords, and reflection verb categories, the two authors each coded a shared set of 20 responses, counting the frequency of words belonging to each of the three categories. We then computed interclass correlation coefficients to assess inter-rater agreement between the two coders, which showed good agreement for all categories (ICCs between 0.8 and 0.89). We thus proceeded to count the frequency of each keyword for each of the three categories for all responses. Analysis on the coded data set was conducted only for participants ($N = 60$) given the opportunity to engage in reflection after the robot's moral intervention. We also computed the total number of words used by each participant in their reflection.

Finally, we conducted a Bayesian repeated measures ANOVA (RM-ANOVA) with Inclusion Bayes Factor Analysis (with moral intervention type as a between-subjects factor and type of vocabulary assessed as a repeated measures factor) to explore differences between norm and role based vocabulary use in each of the two moral interventions, and conducted t-tests with Bayes Factor Analysis to explore the differences in reflection verb use, as well as total number of words typed (as a measure of reflection extensiveness), in each of the two conditions.

5.2 Results

Evidence of General Reflection. A t-test revealed anecdotal evidence in favor of an effect of moral intervention type on reflection verb use (BF 1.730) While there was probably no difference in reflection verb use, participants may have used more reflection verbs after norm-based moral interventions (M = 2.000,

SD = 1.789) than after role-based moral interventions (M = 1.172, SD = 1.104), A t-test revealed moderate evidence in favor of an effect on reflection as measured by character count (BF 5.907). Participants typed more characters after a norm-based moral intervention (M = 375.484, SD = 102.355) than after a role-based moral intervention (M = 309.414, SD = 80.231).

Moral Language Use. An RM-ANOVA revealed anecdotal evidence against an effect of robot's moral language intervention type on moral language use in the reflections (BF 0.747) suggesting that there is probably no effect, but participants may have generally used more morally relevant language in their reflection after a role-based moral intervention (M = 1.47, SD = 1.77) than after a norm-based moral intervention (M = 0.97, SD = 1.16). This analysis also revealed moderate evidence against an effect of type of moral language, suggesting that overall, norm-based and role-based moral language were used with relatively equal frequency across reflections (BF 0.297). Finally, this analysis revealed extreme evidence of an interaction between type of robot's moral language intervention and type of moral language use in reflections (BF 348.179), as visualized in Fig. 3.

Post-hoc t-tests provided moderate evidence (BF 3.469) that after the norm-based intervention, norm-based moral language (M = 1.323, SD = 1.249) was used more frequently than role-based moral language (M = 0.613, SD = 0.955), and moderate evidence that after the role-based moral intervention, role-based moral language was used even more frequently (M = 2.103, SD = 2.110) than norm-based moral language (M = 0.828, SD = 1.037), with very strong evidence (BF 39.871) that role based language was much more strongly encouraged after role-based moral interventions than after norm-based interventions.

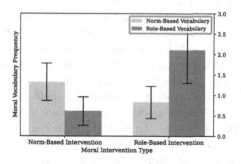

Fig. 3. Vocabulary Use in Moral Reflections by Type of Moral Intervention and Type of Moral Language. Error bars represent 95% Credible Intervals.

These results suggest that although the norm-based intervention may have been more effective at promoting general reflection, both interventions were effective at promoting their specific types of *moral* reflection, with the role-based intervention especially effective in this regard.

6   Discussion

We contribute to the growing body of research demonstrating the potential for positive moral influence of language capable robots. Specifically, we investigated the positive impact of robots' moral language, as mediated both by different moral frameworks and by the opportunity for reflection. Our work serves as a successful conceptual replication of [40]'s work, validating their suggestion that opportunities for people to reflect on ethics could increase the effectiveness of role-based moral language delivered by a robot, while building on and providing nuance to this suggestion.

A main contribution of this work was to address the limitations of their study, in which questionnaire placement may have inadvertently acted as an opportunity for moral reflection and potentially for only one type of moral language.

Building on [40]'s work, our first hypothesis was that when a robotic moral intervention was followed by an opportunity for moral reflection, it would lead to a greater moral influence, as demonstrated by greater adherence to the moral principles encouraged by that moral intervention. In this study, the adherence to the moral principles was reflected in the improvement in performance of a citizen science task. Our behavioral data support this hypothesis, with participant error rates decreasing only when provided with opportunities for reflection, regardless of which type of moral language was used to encourage their performance improvement. Thus, Hypothesis H1 was supported.

Our second hypothesis was that the increases to moral influence facilitated by reflection would be greater after role-based moral interventions than after norm-based moral interventions. This hypothesis (H2) was not supported. However, our exploratory content analysis provided preliminary insights that role-based moral interventions were slightly more successful at *encouraging moral reflection*, even if this moral reflection did not directly lead to increased norm adherence as we had expected. Together, these findings support the conclusion that role-based interventions can lead to moral reflection, and that reflection can serve as a means to influence human behavior, but that reflection's positive influence on human behavior is sufficiently strong that it is observed regardless of the ethical framework used to guide a robot's moral language.

Moreover, while our results suggest potential benefits of both types of moral language (especially role-based moral language) they also demonstrate a need to broaden consideration beyond the ethical grounding of robots' moral interventions, as the interaction context in which a moral intervention is embedded may be much more important than the nuances of the moral intervention itself. In our case, the structuring of an intervention to allow for moral reflection was more important than the norm-based or role-based grounding of our moral interventions. Future work should explore other ways that the context surrounding a moral intervention might be structured to best support intervention efficacy, and other ways that reflection exercises can be intentionally structured to facilitate or reduce the invasiveness of reflection.

7   Limitations and Future Work

Our work has several limitations that motivate future work. First, in conditions where participants were given the reflection opportunity, we required participants to reflect for a minimum amount of time and provide a minimum amount of content. It is possible that different types of reflection exercises, or ones people select themselves, would have different effects or different moderating effects on their behavior. Moreover, while we carefully controlled our reflection exercise, it is possible that reflection exercises that are specifically targeted to different moral frameworks could be beneficial, especially if they are shorter or less invasive. Second, this experiment operated on a brief timescale. As one of the tenets of Confucian ethical principles is that cultivating the moral self requires continued practice over time, change in behavior may require repeated moral reflection or repeated interventions over longer time scales. Third, future work should replicate our study in a context with increased ecological validity. This experiment was conducted using video stimuli of robots as a result of the COVID-19 pandemic [8]. In-person experiments would allow for increased ecological validity and richer qualitative analysis. Finally, just as our work helped to provide more formal basis for [40]'s suggestion through rigorous conceptual replication, so too should the results of our exploratory content analysis be replicated.

8   Conclusion

Robots stand to wield significant positive and pro-social impact through their unique capability for positive moral persuasion. By doing so, robots might help interactants to cultivate their moral selves, and moreover, might cause positive ripple effects that positively effect interactants' broader moral ecosystems. In this work, we explored the ways that robots' moral interventions – and moreover, the contexts into which they are embedded – can be structured to best wield this positive persuasive power. To do so, we conceptually replicated [40]'s prior work, justifying their intuitions that providing opportunities for moral reflection on robot-delivered moral language could be the key to unlocking robots' persuasive capabilities when giving moral advice. Moreover, our work simultaneously sheds light on the unique benefits of role-based moral interventions, while also encouraging HRI researchers to move beyond specific choices of phrasing and focus more attention on the interaction structures that will support such interventions. Our work thus provides substantial nuance to the understanding of this research landscape that was enabled by prior work [40], while opening up promising new directions to further explore that landscape in future work.

Acknowledgements. This work was supported in part by NSF grant IIS-1909847 and in part by Air Force Office of Scientific Research Grant 16RT0881f.

References

1. Ajzen, I.: The theory of planned behavior. Organ. Behav. Hum. Decis. Process. **50**(2), 179–211 (1991)
2. Ames, R.T.: Confucian role ethics: a vocabulary (2011)
3. Baroni, I., Nalin, M., Zelati, M.C., Oleari, E., Sanna, A.: Designing motivational robot: how robots might motivate children to eat fruits and vegetables. In: International Symposium on Robot and Human Interactive Communication (2014)
4. Bartneck, C., Bleeker, T., Bun, J., Fens, P., Riet, L.: The influence of robot anthropomorphism on the feelings of embarrassment when interacting with robots. Paladyn, J. Behav. Robot. **1**(2), 109–115 (2010)
5. Briggs, G., Williams, T., Jackson, R.B., Scheutz, M.: Why and how robots should say 'No'. Int. J. Soc. Robot. **14**(2), 323–339 (2021). https://doi.org/10.1007/s12369-021-00780-y
6. Chidambaram, V., Chiang, Y.H., Mutlu, B.: Designing persuasive robots: how robots might persuade people using vocal and nonverbal cues. In: International conference on Human-Robot Interaction (HRI). ACM (2012)
7. Cormier, D., Newman, G., Nakane, M., Young, J.E., Durocher, S.: Would you do as a robot commands? an obedience study for human-robot interaction. In: International Conference on Human-Agent Interaction (2013)
8. Feil-Seifer, D., Haring, K.S., Rossi, S., Wagner, A.R., Williams, T.: Where to next? the impact of covid-19 on human-robot interaction research (2020)
9. Floridi, L., Sanders, J.W.: On the morality of artificial agents. Mind. Mach. **14**(3), 349–379 (2004)
10. Gillet, S., van den Bos, W., Leite, I.: A social robot mediator to foster collaboration and inclusion among children. In: Robotics: Science and Systems (2020)
11. Gillet, S., Cumbal, R., Pereira, A., Lopes, J., Engwall, O., Leite, I.: Robot gaze can mediate participation imbalance in groups with different skill levels. In: Proceedings of the 2021 ACM/IEEE International Conference on Human-Robot Interaction, pp. 303–311 (2021)
12. Ham, J., Bokhorst, R., Cuijpers, R., van der Pol, D., Cabibihan, J.-J.: Making robots persuasive: the influence of combining persuasive strategies (gazing and gestures) by a storytelling robot on its persuasive power. In: Mutlu, B., Bartneck, C., Ham, J., Evers, V., Kanda, T. (eds.) ICSR 2011. LNCS (LNAI), vol. 7072, pp. 71–83. Springer, Heidelberg (2011). https://doi.org/10.1007/978-3-642-25504-5_8
13. Hinne, M., Gronau, Q.F., van den Bergh, D., Wagenmakers, E.J.: A conceptual introduction to Bayesian model averaging. Adv. Methods Pract. Psychol. Sci. **3**(2), 200–215 (2020)
14. Jackson, R.B., Wen, R., Williams, T.: Tact in noncompliance: the need for pragmatically apt responses to unethical commands. In: Proceedings of the 2019 AAAI/ACM Conference on AI, Ethics, and Society, pp. 499–505 (2019)
15. Jackson, R.B., Williams, T.: Robot: Asker of questions and changer of norms? In: Proceedings of ICRES (2018)
16. Jackson, R.B., Williams, T.: Language-capable robots may inadvertently weaken human moral norms. In: Companion of the 14th ACM/IEEE International Conference on Human-Robot Interaction (alt.HRI), pp. 401–410. IEEE (2019)
17. Jackson, R.B., Williams, T.: Language-capable robots may inadvertently weaken human moral norms. In: 2019 14th ACM/IEEE International Conference on Human-Robot Interaction (HRI), pp. 401–410. IEEE (2019)

18. Jackson, R.B., Williams, T.: On perceived social and moral agency in natural language capable robots. In: 2019 HRI workshop on the dark side of human-robot interaction. Jackson, RB, and Williams, pp. 401–410 (2019)
19. Jackson, R.B., Williams, T.: A theory of social agency for human-robot interaction. Front. Robot. AI **8**, 267 (2021)
20. Jackson, R.B., Williams, T.: Enabling morally sensitive robotic clarification requests. ACM Trans. Hum.-Robot Interact. (THRI) **11**(2), 1–18 (2022)
21. Jackson, R.B., Williams, T., Smith, N.: Exploring the role of gender in perceptions of robotic noncompliance. In: Proceedings of the 2020 ACM/IEEE International Conference on Human-Robot Interaction, pp. 559–567 (2020)
22. JASP Team, et al.: Jasp. Version 0.8. 0.0. software (2016)
23. Jung, M.F., Martelaro, N., Hinds, P.J.: Using robots to moderate team conflict: the case of repairing violations. In: Proceedings of the Tenth Annual ACM/IEEE International Conference on Human-Robot Interaction, pp. 229–236 (2015)
24. Kennedy, J., Baxter, P., Belpaeme, T.: Children comply with a robot's indirect requests. In: Proceedings of the 2014 ACM/IEEE International Conference on Human-Robot Interaction (HRI), pp. 198–199 (2014)
25. Kim, B., Wen, R., de Visser, E.J., Zhu, Q., Williams, T., Phillips, E.: Investigating robot moral advice to deter cheating behavior. In: TSAR Workshop at ROMAN 2021 (2021)
26. Kim, B., Wen, R., Zhu, Q., Williams, T., Phillips, E.: Robots as moral advisors: the effects of deontological, virtue, and confucian role ethics on encouraging honest behavior. In: Companion of the 2021 ACM/IEEE International Conference on Human-Robot Interaction, pp. 10–18 (2021)
27. Lee, M.D., Wagenmakers, E.J.: Bayesian Cognitive Modeling: A Practical Course. Cambridge University Press, Cambridge (2014)
28. Lee, M.K., Kiesler, S., Forlizzi, J., Rybski, P.: Ripple effects of an embedded social agent: a field study of a social robot in the workplace. In: Proceedings of the SIGCHI Conference on Human Factors in Computing Systems, pp. 695–704 (2012)
29. Mathôt, S.: Bayes like a BAWS: interpreting Bayesian repeated measures in jasp. Cognit. Sci. More (2017). www.cogsci.nl/blog/interpreting-bayesian-repeated-measures-in-jasp
30. Paradeda, R.B., Ferreira, M.J., Dias, J., Paiva, A.: How robots persuasion based on personality traits may affect human decisions. In: Proceedings of the Companion of the 2017 ACM/IEEE International Conference on Human-Robot Interaction, pp. 251–252. ACM (2017)
31. Rea, D.J., Geiskkovitch, D., Young, J.E.: Wizard of AWWWS: exploring psychological impact on the researchers in social hri experiments. In: Proceedings of the Companion of the 2017 ACM/IEEE International Conference on Human-Robot Interaction, pp. 21–29 (2017)
32. Robinette, P., Li, W., Allen, R., Howard, A.M., Wagner, A.R.: Overtrust of robots in emergency evacuation scenarios. In: The Eleventh ACM/IEEE International Conference on Human Robot Interaction, pp. 101–108 (2016)
33. Scheutz, M., Malle, B.F.: May machines take lives to save lives? human perceptions of autonomous robots (with the capacity to kill). Lethal autonomous weapons: re-examining the law and ethics of robotic warfare (2021)
34. Strait, M., Canning, C., Scheutz, M.: Let me tell you! investigating the effects of robot communication strategies in advice-giving situations based on robot appearance, interaction modality and distance. In: Proceedings of the 2014 ACM/IEEE International Conference on Human-Robot Interaction (HRI) (2014)

35. Strohkorb Sebo, S., Traeger, M., Jung, M., Scassellati, B.: The ripple effects of vulnerability: the effects of a robot's vulnerable behavior on trust in human-robot teams. In: Proceedings of the 2018 ACM/IEEE International Conference on Human-Robot Interaction, pp. 178–186 (2018)
36. Tennent, H., Shen, S., Jung, M.: MICBOT: a peripheral robotic object to shape conversational dynamics and team performance. In: 2019 14th ACM/IEEE International Conference on Human-Robot Interaction (HRI), pp. 133–142. IEEE (2019)
37. Wagenmakers, E.J., et al.: Bayesian inference for psychology. Part I: theoretical advantages and practical ramifications. Psychon. Bull. Rev. **25**(1), 35–57 (2018)
38. Wen, R., Han, Z., Williams, T.: Teacher, teammate, subordinate, friend: generating norm violation responses grounded in role-based relational norms. In: HRI, pp. 353–362 (2022)
39. Wen, R., Jackson, R.B., Williams, T., Zhu, Q.: Towards a role ethics approach to command rejection. In: HRI Workshop on the Dark Side of Human-Robot Interaction (2019)
40. Wen, R., Kim, B., Phillips, E., Zhu, Q., Williams, T.: Comparing norm-based and role-based strategies for robot communication of role-grounded moral norms. ACM Trans. Hum.-Robot Interact. (T-HRI) (2022)
41. Williams, T., Jackson, R.B., Lockshin, J.: A Bayesian analysis of moral norm malleability during clarification dialogues. In: Proceedings of the Annual Meeting of the Cognitive Science Society (COGSCI). Cognitive Science Society, Madison, WI (2018)
42. Williams, T., Zhu, Q., Wen, R., de Visser, E.J.: The Confucian matador: three defenses against the mechanical bull. In: Companion of the 2020 ACM/IEEE International Conference on Human-Robot Interaction (alt.HRI), pp. 25–33 (2020)
43. Winkle, K., Melsión, G.I., McMillan, D., Leite, I.: Boosting robot credibility and challenging gender norms in responding to abusive behaviour: a case for feminist robots. In: Companion of the 2021 ACM/IEEE International Conference on Human-Robot Interaction, pp. 29–37 (2021)
44. Wong, D.B.: Cultivating the self in concert with others. In: Olberding, A. (ed.) Dao companion to the Analects, pp. 171–197. Springer, Dordrecht (2014). https://doi.org/10.1007/978-94-007-7113-0_10
45. Zhu, Q.: Confucian moral imagination and ethics education in engineering. Front. Philos. China **15**(1), 36–52 (2020)
46. Zhu, Q., Williams, T., Jackson, B., Wen, R.: Blame-laden moral rebukes and the morally competent robot: a confucian ethical perspective. Sci. Eng. Ethics **26**, 2511–2526 (2020)
47. Zhu, Q., Williams, T., Wen, R.: Role-based morality, ethical pluralism, and morally capable robots. J. Contemp. East. Asia **20**(1), 134–150 (2021)

Gamification

Gamified Medication Adherence Applications for Chronic Health Conditions: Scoping Review

Saleh A. Altuwayrib[1,2](✉) ⓘ, Khin Than Win[1] ⓘ, and Mark Freeman[1] ⓘ

[1] School of Computing and Information Technology, University of Wollongongs, Wollongong, Australia
sasa948@uowmail.edu.au
[2] College of Public Health and Health Informatics, University of Hail, Hail, Saudi Arabia

Abstract. This scoping review aims to identify the gamification mechanics used in designing gamified mobile health applications to support medication adherence behaviour among people living with chronic conditions. The process of Arksey and O'Malley's framework was used in conducting this scoping review. Five databases were searched for eligible studies, including PubMed, Scopus, Science Direct, Web of Science, and ACM. Data charting characteristics included author, year, country, chronic health condition, application name, research method, data collection instruments, health behaviour change models, gamification elements and mobile health features. Seven studies were examined in this review. In addition to gamification mechanics, health behaviour change and motivation theories were used to design the interventions for chronic disease patients. Interventions reported positive impacts on medication adherence rates, mobile app usage, and patient motivation. All included studies used progression, goal setting, feedback and rewards mechanics incorporated with medication adherence features. Seven gamification mechanics were identified that could be used for medication adherence and health education. This review's findings suggest that medication adherence applications using gamification elements improve adherence levels for different chronic health conditions.

Keywords: Gamification · Mobile Health Applications · Medication Adherence · Scoping Review

1 Introduction

Chronic disease patients need to modify unhealthy behaviours and adopt healthy habits to help manage their disease and improve their quality of life [1]. Medication non-adherence is a common challenge among people living with chronic diseases and can negatively impact the treatment's effectiveness and patients' health outcomes if not managed effectively. Patient education and engagement are critical in supporting medication adherence behaviour. Patients must understand the importance of treatment and how their medications will help control chronic conditions. This can be supported by providing chronic disease patients with novel technologies designed to empower patients to support medication adherence behaviour [2, 3].

© The Author(s), under exclusive license to Springer Nature Switzerland AG 2023
J. Ham et al. (Eds.): PERSUASIVE 2023, LNCS 13832, pp. 307–321, 2023.
https://doi.org/10.1007/978-3-031-30933-5_20

Mobile health applications (m-health apps) have been successfully used to improve medication adherence and enhance the accessibility of healthcare services leading to optimal health outcomes [4–6]. The applicability of the persuasive systems design features in medication management applications has been studied in [7] and identified that reminders, tailoring and monitoring features had been the most cited features. In addition to these features, gamification design is used in medication adherence applications to motivate users and support health behaviour change [8]. The persuasive architecture of gamification in health applications depends on the game elements that make the process more engaging and enjoyable [9]. Game elements are activities, behaviours, and mechanisms designers incorporate into a specific context to create a gameful experience [10–12]. Using game design elements positively impacts individual adherence across different fields [13]. In addition, it improved the persuasiveness of m-health apps in various health disciplines and enhanced the user's competence in managing chronic health conditions [8, 9, 11, 14]. Cugelman [9] found seven gamification elements linked to proven health behaviour change techniques used to design gamified health systems, including goal setting, challenges, feedback, rewards, progression, social interaction, and fun. De Croon et al. [13] identify points, feedback, leader boards and social interaction as the most frequently used game elements for adherence across multidisciplinary applications.

Ahmed et al. [8] conducted an app review and found that only 1% of medication apps in Apple and Google stores have used gamification design; there is a need to investigate medication apps designed for specific diseases (e.g., chronic illnesses). The gamified medication adherence application design that positively impacts chronic disease patients needs to explore game elements and mobile app features and how they can support patient adherence [15, 16]. Different studies suggest gamification design frameworks for m-health applications targeting chronic health conditions; however, they do not focus on how the gamified apps can improve patients' adherence [17, 18]. Therefore, there is a need to explore how gamification elements are designed for medication adherence to support chronic disease patients. This review aims to identify the game elements and mobile health features used in designing gamified medication adherence applications for different chronic health conditions. The seven game-design elements proposed by Cugelman [9] are used in this review to extract the game-design elements and how these elements were incorporated with medication adherence features.

2   Methodology

2.1   Study Design

This scoping review aimed to identify the main concepts and knowledge gaps in using gamification design in medication adherence mobile applications. The scoping review can provide a researcher with an overview of how previous studies have designed and evaluated gamified apps for chronic health conditions in the context of medication adherence support. The research team followed the five steps to conduct scoping review described by Arksey and O'Malley [19], which include: finding the research question;

identifying relevant evidence; selecting relevant studies; extracting the data; and collating, summarising, and reporting the findings. The preferred reporting items for systematic reviews and meta-analysis (PRISMA) extension for scoping review were followed in reporting the results [20]. The study focused on identifying game elements and mobile health features used to design gamified medication adherence applications for people with chronic diseases. Hence, the research question was: *What are game elements used in designing medication adherence applications to support chronic health conditions?*

2.2 Identifying Relevant Studies

The team designed the search strategy to be comprehensive and include studies relevant to gamification design in medication adherence apps for chronic health conditions. Five databases, including PubMed, Scopus, Science Direct, Web of Science, and ACM, were searched to identify eligible studies. The search included studies published in English between 1 January 2010 and 15 August 2021, as gamified e-health applications began in 2010 [11]. The keywords used during the searches were: ("Gamification" OR Gamiful OR Gamifi* OR "Gamified" OR "Playful" OR "Game design" OR "Gameful") AND ("mobile health" OR "eHealth" OR "digital health" OR "smartphone" OR "mobile app" OR "mobile applications" OR "mHealth" OR "smartphones") AND ("Medication adherence" OR "Medication compliance" OR "Pharmacological adherence" OR "Adherence" OR medications).

2.3 Inclusion and Exclusion Criteria

A Population, Concept, and Context (PCC) [21] framework was used to determine the selection criteria. **Population::** individuals with chronic health conditions. **Concept**: all gamified applications are designed to enhance medication adherence behaviour. **Context**: m-health apps. Any study that met the following criteria was included: (i) Design and development of gamified medication adherence applications for chronic health conditions, (ii) Evaluation of gamified medication adherence applications for chronic health conditions. Exclusion criteria included: (i) Reviews, study protocols, opinion papers, books, and reports, (ii) Studies related to video games, exergames, and gamification in other fields, (iii) Studies not for chronic health conditions or did not use m-health applications and (iv) Studies that were not in English.

2.4 Charting the Data and Analysis

After removing the duplicate articles, two reviewers (Author 1 and Author 3) independently screened the titles and abstracts of the articles, and if there is any disagreement will be discussed with the third reviewer (Author 2) to reach a consensus. All reviewers come from academic backgrounds and are familiar with persuasive technology design in m-health applications. The characteristics of included studies were extracted, and each study was categorised based on author, year, country, health condition, research method, data source (e.g., survey, interview, etc.), participants' information, game elements and mobile health features (see Table A1 in the appendix). The reviewers summarised and synthesised the available data. The game design elements and m-health features were mapped to understand how m-health features were gamified to support patient adherence.

3 Results

3.1 Selection of Included Studies

The results of the search in the selected databases were imported into Endnote. Initially, 1072 articles were retrieved from the database searches. In total, 658 papers remained after removing duplicates and filtering articles based on eligibility criteria. After screening titles and abstracts, 581 articles were excluded that did not meet the criteria, and 77 articles were selected for full-text assessment. Finally, nine (9) studies met the study criteria and were selected for analysis (see Fig. 1).

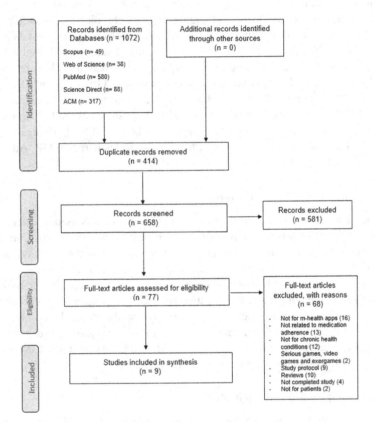

Fig. 1. PRISMA flow diagram

3.2 Study Characteristics

Table 1 presents information about the characteristics of the included studies, which investigated gamified medication adherence applications in Human Immunodeficiency Virus (HIV), asthma, diabetes, gastrointestinal diseases (GI), and one application for multi-morbid chronic health conditions [22–30]. Most of the studies were conducted in the United States of America (USA) [22–24, 27, 29] and other studies from different countries, including Portugal [28], Austria [30], Australia [26], and Canada [25]. Five studies adopted a mixed methods research approach to design and develop gamified medication adherence applications, and one study used qualitative data to build the gamified medication adherence app [22–25, 28, 29]. Three studies evaluated the effectiveness of gamified medication adherence solutions to assess the effect of using gamified medication adherence applications on clinical outcomes and medication adherence rates. The evaluation duration was one to six months with the quantitative research studies [26, 27, 30].

Table 1. Studies characteristics.

App name	Year	Condition	Theory	Method	Instrument	Participants age
Epic Allies [24]	2016	HIV	IMB	Mixed method	Focus groups, surveys	20–28
AllyQuest [23]	2018	HIV	SCT; FBM	Mixed method	Focus groups, Surveys, Interviews, Usage data	16–24
InspirerMundi [28]	2021	Asthma	FBM	Mixed method	Interviews, observational study, Surveys	17–40
AsthmaHero [22]	2016	Asthma	FBM	Mixed method	Focus group, Usage data, and Surveys	11–19
MySugr [30]	2019	Diabetes	N/A	Quantitative	Usage data and Surveys	N/A
MedVenture [29]	2021	GI	SDT	Qualitative	--	12–18
Bant [25]	2012	Diabetes	N/A	Mixed method	Surveys and Usage data	12–16
DiaSocial [27]	2018	Diabetes	Regulatory mode theory	Quantitative	Surveys, Usage data and Clinical out-comes	Average: 67
Perx Health [26]	2020	chronic diseases	SDT	Quantitative	Usage data	Average: 43–45

Six studies discussed the design and development of gamified medication adherence applications. Health behaviour change theories guide the design process of gamified medication adherence support applications. Then the design team employed prototyping with users involved in the app assessment [22–25, 29, 31]. Other studies started by applying users from the beginning to specify the requirements, and the outcomes of the user research were used in building the app prototypes, and then the app was evaluated by users [25, 29, 31]. User involvement and iterative design were necessary to create the best-gamified medication adherence application that was useful, engaging, and satisfied users' needs [23, 24, 28, 29]. Four studies involved healthcare professionals in the development process to ensure the application's trustworthiness [24, 25, 29, 31]. The Epic Allies application used The Information-Motivation-Behaviour model (IMB), and the AllyQuest app employed two theories, including the Social Cognitive Theory (SCT) and Fogg Behaviour Model (FBM) for persuasive technology and narrative communication theory [23, 24]. The FBM is the most health behaviour change model employed, which aims to improve skills and motivations and provide triggers that could drive positive health behaviour change [22, 23, 28]. MedVenture employed Self-Determination Theory (SDT) to design the gamified medication adherence application that could satisfy the three psychological needs: autonomy, competence and relatedness [29]. The regulatory mode theory was used to evaluate gamified applications and explore the different personality types of diabetic patients who used DiaSocial to improve adherence behaviours and health outcomes [27]. The evaluation studies assessed the apps using experiments, feasibility, acceptability, and usability evaluations; it was observed that studies began the app evaluation with a small number of participants before evaluating the efficacy of the intervention with a large number of patients [22–25, 28].

3.3 Gamification Elements and Mobile Health Features

All identified studies used the medication adherence features of reminders and medication trackers for doses to support chronic disease patients and empower self-care (see Table 2). The use of reminders could prevent unintentional nonadherence behaviour. Still, some younger chronic disease patients considered unnecessary reminders disturbing and could demotivate them from continuing to use the application [22, 24]. Health educational features are incorporated with game elements to support health behaviour change and enhance patient knowledge and skills [23, 24, 26, 30]. Gamified medication adherence apps were connected with medical devices to simplify self-monitoring activities, especially for diabetes and asthma patients [22, 25, 26, 32].

Table 2. Mobile health features

Category	Features	References
Medication management	Medication schedules	[26, 28–30]
	Medication image	[26, 28]
	Medication history/ trackers	[22–30]
	Reminders	[22–30]
	Refill alerts	[23]

(*continued*)

Table 2. (*continued*)

Category	Features	References
	Drug-to-drug interaction	[23]
	Tailored adherence strategies	[23, 28, 29]
Self-monitoring	Track symptoms	[22–30]
	Food intake	[30]
	Physical activity	[30]
	Visualize health measurements	[23–30]
	Health assessment tools	[28]
Health education	Informational modules	[23, 24, 26, 30]
Social support	Medical social network	[25, 27, 29]
	Peer support	[23, 28, 29]
	Share information	[22, 28–30, 32]
	Communicate with health professionals	[27, 28, 30]
General	Connected with other devices	[22, 25, 26, 32]
	Multiple languages	[27, 28, 30]
	App tutorial	[24]

In medication adherence applications, gamification elements were employed to support health behaviour change and patient motivation and improve user engagement. It was noted that medication adherence features were gamified by setting goals related to medication management, health monitoring or health education. Based on the user progression, the apps provide the user with feedback and rewards for successful behaviour. Our results demonstrated that most studies use the following combination of elements: progression, rewards, feedback, and goal setting (Table 3). The selected studies used several mobile health features that focus on different dimensions, including medication management, health monitoring, health education, connectivity and other general features. Table 4 shows the seven gamification elements and how they were combined with each medication adherence feature.

Progression. Gamified medication adherence apps provide users with a profile that represents the user identity and shows their progression towards health goals. Different methods were used to record and track the user progression, including: points, progress bars, level-ups and leaderboards [26, 28, 31]. Avatars were used to show user identity within the app, and personalised avatars were preferred by chronic disease patients [22–24]. Chronic disease patients preferred visualisation and quantification features to measure and show their adherence over time [22]. Users could earn points when they learn new facts about the disease or medication use [26]. Diabetic patients earned points for performing blood glucose tests three times or more per day and were allowed to level up when they achieved a certain number of points [25]. Moreover, they can learn from

Table 3. Gamification elements

Application name	Progression	Feedback	Rewards	Goal setting	Challenges	Social interaction	Fun
Epic Allies [24]	X	X	X	X	X	X	X
AsthmaHero [22]	X	X	X	X			X
AllyQuest [23]	X	X	X	X	X	X	X
Perx Health [26]	X	X	X	X	X	X	X
MySugr [30]	X	X	X	X	X		X
Bant [25]	X	X	X	X		X	
DiaSocial [27]	X	X	X	X	X	X	
InspirerMundi [28]	X	X	X	X	X	X	X
MedVenture [29]	X	X			X	X	X

their previous experiences through the historical adherence data and glucose levels on each occasion, which could support the patient's decisions [30].

Feedback. Personalised feedback based on regular health assessments could support health behaviour change and make the application activities more relevant [23, 24]. Providing users with positive feedback about their success in health monitoring activities improved adherence self-efficacy, the user engagement and helped users identify their adherence difficulties [24, 32]. The MySugr app was designed to be visually attractive and offer positive feedback based on successful behaviour [30]. The MySugr app enabled users to share data with their physicians and communicate with qualified healthcare providers for assistance when needed [32]. Asthma patients preferred the application messages to be personalised and to consider the patient's lifestyle [22].

Goal Setting. Daily goals enabled users to engage with the application and adhere to their medication requirements [28, 30]. System designers provided users with various goals to improve medication adherence, self-care, social interaction and health education [22–28, 30]. The Allyquest app enables HIV patients to learn and develop new skills related to routine self-management activities to improve their competence in managing and adhering to medications [23]. In gamified medication adherence applications, goals should be manageable and challenging, motivating users to increase their medication adherence levels [26]. Gamified apps enable users to connect with mobile health sensors or other devices to simplify the data entry for health goal monitoring [22, 25, 26, 28, 30].

Rewards. Different gamified medication adherence applications incentivise users to encourage the use and enhance medication adherence behaviour [22–26, 28]. Users were provided with daily routine tasks related to medication management and users were rewarded when they completed these tasks [26]. Asthma patients were rewarded with points when they performed different tasks such as: adding new medicines, updating the medication schedule, learning about the disease or the medication use, completing the health assessment questions and notifying other users to take their medication [28]. Rewards in the Bant app were associated with increasing self-monitoring activities for diabetes patients, which could elicit healthy behaviour change [25]. Badges were used as an internal reward for completing goals or encouraging other users to improve adherence behaviour [28]. Lottery-based rewards were used to improve medication adherence behaviour by providing users with non-predictable rewards for taking medications on time [26].

Challenges. Provide users with challenges related to self-management, physical activity, nutrition, and maintaining the app's use. Some apps challenged users to perform daily health measurements, and users will be rewarded for completing the task. Users were also rewarded for maintaining their blood glucose levels in the normal range over certain days [30]. Users could cooperate with other users to complete difficult challenges within the app games [24].

Social Interaction. HIV patients considered social support components vital as they were motivated to adhere to medications and accept HIV care. This could be because the patients felt less lonely knowing that other patients took the same medication(s) [23, 24]. Social support could positively impact patient motivation to adhere to prescribed medications [24]. Users could share their achievements via social media networks and share the medication schedule with friends, family or other app community members to support medication adherence [28].

Fun. Mini-games were incorporated with gamified applications as an easy, fun way to encourage users to complete tasks and improve the user experience [24, 28, 29, 31]. Mini-games for health education use narratives and challenges to engage users with the game story and assess the user's knowledge with simple questions. [28, 31]. Virtual characters were employed in the gamified apps to give users a tour and introduce the app features and storyline, which could help them learn more about the app use [24, 28]. Role modelling was used with storytelling to elicit health behaviour change [23].

3.4 Gamified Medication Adherence Applications Outcome

Most studies reported positive outcomes in different aspects, such as high user satisfaction, increased medication adherence rates, increased patient motivation and the use of m-health apps.

Medication Adherence Rates. Three studies found that gamified apps improved adherence rates. Perx Health app showed a high adherence rate for different chronic disease patients, averaging over 85% across the study period. According to the study, adherence

Table 4. Game elements and medication adherence features

Features	Progression	Challenges	Rewards	Feedback	Goal setting	Social interaction	Fun
Medication management	X		X	X	X	X	
Self-monitoring	X		X	X	X		
Health education	X	X	X	X	X	X	X
Social support	X	X	X	X		X	X
General	X				X		X

rates remained optimal over time, but a slight decline was not statistically significant [26]. For asthma patients, the adherence level for inhalers was 75%, whereas, for other medications, it was 82% [28]. Users who collected a large number of points within the gamified application showed better health outcomes [27].

The Use of m-health Apps. The frequency of health data measurements in the Bant app for diabetes patients increased by 50%, and users were interested in continuing to use the app [25]. AllyQuest App found that the high use of the application positively affects self-management outcomes, patient knowledge and ability to manage medications [23].

The User Experience. Reminders, points, adherence graphs, and rewards in asthma management applications improved the experience of medication taking and disease management [22, 28]. Some gameful m-health apps offer chronic disease patients with virtual coaching features. This feature helps users to learn more about the condition and make informed health decisions that could improve patient empowerment and healthcare quality and reduce healthcare costs [32].

User Satisfaction. The use of the MySugr App positively impacted user satisfaction and ability to control their blood glucose. It was noticed that the app affected the group of patients with less glucose control [30]. User satisfaction was high for diabetic patients in the Bant application, and users were interested in continuing to use the application [25]. Gamified medication adherence applications supported intrinsic and extrinsic motivation by reminding the users to complete self-management or monitoring tasks and rewarding them based on their adherence behaviour [25, 26, 32]. Using rewards and praise immediately following medication intake could motivate users to maintain optimal adherence and continue taking the medications as prescribed [26]. HIV participants were satisfied with the gamified application and interested in using the system again and recommending the application to friends if they needed it [23].

4 Discussion

The results suggested that gamification elements in m-health apps are used to reduce nonadherence rates, improve user experience and satisfaction, and motivate users to continue using medication adherence applications. Motivation is a significant factor in supporting medication adherence behaviour, and m-health apps could support user motivation through gamification elements that have a positive effect and meet user needs [33, 34].

4.1 Main Findings

The findings of this paper showed that most studies employed the combination of progression, feedback, goal setting and rewards to motivate and engage users with gamified applications and improve adherence levels. Gamification elements could support intentional nonadherence (especially feedback and progression), whereas mobile health features can help users with unintentional non-adherence. Gamified apps that provide relevant health information and enable users to set health goals have improved patients' capability and competence in managing medications [13, 39]. Health education features with gamification elements should motivate users to learn about safe medication use and access credible content that shows the importance of a healthy lifestyle and medication adherence in disease management. This could help patients to realise the importance of adherence and improve their competency in medication management. The features of medication management and health education combined with health behaviour change techniques reduced nonadherence behaviour for individuals with chronic health conditions [26]. The app content needs to be educational, cover all medication management tasks, and be enjoyable to engage the users by showing their progression in learning, challenging them to learn or adopt new healthy habits related to medication management and a healthy lifestyle. Gamification elements should be tied to informative content and the persuasion context of the system [11, 14]. Reward the users with different rewards when they complete health education tasks. Empower users to learn from others by interacting with other users that have a similar condition or treatment plan. As presented in the MySugr app, chronic disease patients should have easy access to health coaches who can provide users with the information and training required in treatment management. These efforts could decrease intentional nonadherence and ensure that patients are aware of the risks associated with nonadherence behaviour. Self-monitoring features can be gamified by providing users with goals that are designed to improve medication adherence and health behaviour changes. Users should feel a sense of progression and receive feedback that encourages users to continue performing healthy behaviours. Personalisation, visualisation and quantification are critical features in gamified applications that make the use of applications more useful and relevant. Personalised features are significant and should be considered to meet the needs of different users [35]. This review showed that most development studies are guided by health behaviour change models to design gamified medication adherence apps. The Fogg Behaviour Model (FBM) of persuasive technology was used in designing gamified applications and supporting medication adherence for different chronic health conditions, such as asthma and HIV apps [22, 23, 28]. Persuasive design in gamified medication adherence apps aims to simplify the medication management process and provide chronic disease people with a sense of belonging. Moreover, offer prompts to promote health behaviour change and habit formation, praises user progression, and rewards successful behaviours.

4.2 Design Recommendations

The gamification design process should focus on the context of use and involve interdisciplinary stakeholders to improve motivation and persuasion [14, 36]. User-centred game design can support intrinsic motivation and create a sustainable engagement by satisfying user needs [11, 26]. Most studies have involved young patients in the development studies, while older patients were only involved in the evaluation studies. Gamification elements are not one size fits all; as a result, the designer should consider the different personalities of users and understand their preferences to select appropriate elements that motivate users to adhere to the treatment [27, 30]. Most gamified medication adherence applications were designed in developed countries, which is consistent with previous studies in gamified e-health literature [11]. Future gamified medication adherence support applications should provide users with more goals, challenges and levels to support health behaviour change [27]. Challenges in gamified medication adherence apps help users to collaborate with others to achieve their health goals, whereas in gamified physical activity help users to compete with each other. Not all game elements that are used in other gamified health apps can be used in apps that designed to support medication adherence. Different chronic health conditions can be investigated to make using m-health apps for medication-taking enjoyable and rewarding.

4.3 Limitations

The scope of this study is limited to studies published in academic journals, and grey literature is not included in this review. Gamification elements and mobile health features are extracted from the identified manuscripts rather than the actual app. Not all identified studies provide detailed information about the development process and only mention the used game elements and how they were evaluated.

5 Conclusion

Medication management is an ongoing process for chronic disease patients, and gamification design makes the process enjoyable, rewarding, and a source of motivation and knowledge. Gamification elements incorporated with medication management, health education, and self-monitoring could support medication adherence behaviour for different chronic health conditions. Users should have the choice and feel a sense of progression in their health goals and obtain instantaneous and personalised feedback during the application use. Health behaviour change models help gamification designers to focus on supporting the user's capability, motivation, knowledge, and socialisation. Designers should understand chronic disease patients' needs and nonadherence factors for the given disease population.

Appendix 1

(See Table 1)

Table A1. Data charting table.

Authors	Year	Country	Health condition	Application name	Study aim	Theory	Study method	Data source	Participants age	Game elements	Category of mobile features
Bull et al	2016	USA	HIV	Epic Allies	App development and evaluation	IMB	Mixed method	Focus groups, surveys	20-28	progression, feedback, rewards, goal setting, challenges, social interaction, fun	Medication Management, Self-Monitoring, Health Education and General Features
Cushing et al	2016	USA	asthma	Asthma Hero	evaluation	FBM	Mixed method	Focus group, Usage data, and Surveys	11 – 19	progression, feedback, rewards, goal setting, fun	Medication Management, Self-Monitoring, Social Support and General Features
Schnall et al	2018	USA,	HIV	AllyQuest	App development and pilot evaluation	SCT; FBM	Mixed method	Focus groups, Surveys, Interviews, Usage data	16-24	progression, feedback, rewards, goal setting, challenges, social interaction, fun	Medication management, Self-monitoring, Health Education, Social Support
Wiecek et al.,	2020	Australia	different chronic diseases	Perx Health	retrospective (evaluation)	SDT	Quantitative	usage data	43-45	progression, feedback, rewards, goal setting, challenges, social interaction, fun	Medication Management, Self-Monitoring, Health Education and General Features
Fredrick Debong et al.	2019	Austria	Diabetes	MySugr	retrospective (evaluation)	N/A	Quantitative	Usage data and Surveys	N/A	progression, feedback, rewards, goal setting, challenges, fun	Medication Management, Self-Monitoring, Health Education, Social Support and General Features
Cafazzo	2012	Canada	Diabetes	Bant	App development and evaluation	UCD	Mixed method	Surveys and Usage data	12-16	progression, feedback, rewards, goal setting, social interaction	Medication Management, Self-Monitoring, Social Support and General Features
Michelle Dugas	2018	USA	Diabetes	DiaSocial	evaluation	Regulatory mode theory	Quantitative	Surveys, Usage data and Clinical out-comes.	65-67	progression, feedback, rewards, goal setting, challenges, social interaction	Medication Management, Self-Monitoring, Social Support and General Features
Jácome, Almeida	2021	Portugal	asthma	InspirerMundi	evaluation	FBM	Mixed method	Interviews, observation al study, Surveys	17-40	progression, feedback, rewards, goal setting, challenges, social interaction, fun	Medication Management, Self-Monitoring, Social Support and General Features
Mehta, Moore [36]	2021	USA	Gastrointestinal disease	MedVenture	app development	SDT	Qualitative	Semi-Structured Interviews	12-18	progression, feedback, challenges, social interaction, fun	Medication Management, Self-Monitoring, Social Support

References

1. Newson, J.T., et al.: Health behaviour changes after diagnosis of chronic illness among Canadians aged 50 or older. Health Rep **23**, 49–53 (2012)
2. Iuga, A.O., McGuire, M.J.: Adherence and health care costs. Risk Manag Healthc Policy 7, 35–44 (2014)
3. Neiman, A.B., et al.: CDC grand rounds: improving medication adherence for chronic disease management - innovations and opportunities. MMWR Morb Mortal Wkly Rep **66**, 1248–1251 (2017)
4. Free, C., Phillips, G., Felix, L., Galli, L., Patel, V., Edwards, P.: The effectiveness of M-health technologies for improving health and health services: a systematic review protocol. BMC. Res. Notes **3**, 250 (2010)
5. Pérez-Jover, V., Sala-González, M., Guilabert, M., Mira, J.J.: Mobile apps for increasing treatment adherence: systematic review. J. Med. Internet Res. **21**, e12505 (2019)
6. Armitage, L.C., Kassavou, A., Sutton, S.: Do mobile device apps designed to support medication adherence demonstrate efficacy? A systematic review of randomised controlled trials, with meta-analysis. BMJ Open **10**, e032045 (2020)
7. Win, K.T., Mullan, J., Howard, S., Oinas-Kukkonen, H.: Persuasive Systems Design features in Promoting Medication Management for consumers. In: Proceedings of the 50th Hawaii International Conference on System Sciences (2017)
8. Ahmed, I., et al.: Medication Adherence Apps: Review and Content Analysis. JMIR Mhealth Uhealth **6**, e62 (2018)
9. Cugelman, B.: Gamification: What It Is and Why It Matters to Digital Health Behavior Change Developers. JMIR Serious Games 1, (2013)
10. Dayer, L.E., et al.: Assessing the medication adherence app marketplace from the health professional and consumer vantage points. JMIR Mhealth Uhealth **5**, e45 (2017)
11. Sardi, L., Idri, A., Fernández-Alemán, J.L.: A systematic review of gamification in e-Health. J. Biomed. Inf. **71**, 31–48 (2017)
12. Pereira, P., Duarte, E., Rebelo, F., Noriega, P.: A review of gamification for health-related contexts, pp. 742–753. Springer, Cham (2014)
13. De Croon, R., Geuens, J., Verbert, K., Vanden Abeele, V.: A systematic review of the effect of gamification on adherence across disciplines. In: Fang, X. (ed.) HCII 2021. LNCS, vol. 12789, pp. 168–184. Springer, Cham (2021). https://doi.org/10.1007/978-3-030-77277-2_14
14. Alahäivälä, T., Oinas-Kukkonen, H.: Understanding persuasion contexts in health gamification: A systematic analysis of gamified health behavior change support systems literature. Int. J. Med. Inf. **96**, 62–70 (2016)
15. Miller, A.S., Cafazzo, J.A., Seto, E.: A game plan: gamification design principles in mHealth applications for chronic disease management. Health Informatics J. **22**, 184–193 (2016)
16. Tran, S., Smith, L., El-Den, S., Carter, S.: The Use of Gamification and Incentives in Mobile Health Apps to Improve Medication Adherence: Scoping Review. JMIR Mhealth Uhealth **10**, e30671 (2022)
17. Abdul Rahim, M.I., Thomas, R.H.: Gamification of Medication Adherence in Epilepsy. Seizure **52**, 11–14 (2017)
18. AlMarshedi, A., Wills, G., Ranchhod, A.: Guidelines for the gamification of self-management of chronic illnesses: multimethod study. JMIR Serious Games **5**, e12 (2017)
19. Arksey, H., O'Malley, L.: Scoping studies: towards a methodological framework. Int. J. Soc. Res. Methodol. **8**, 19–32 (2005)
20. Tricco, A.C., et al.: PRISMA extension for scoping reviews (PRISMA-ScR): checklist and explanation. Ann. Intern. Med. **169**, 467–473 (2018)

21. Peters, M., Godfrey, C., McInerney, P., Soares, C., Khalil, H., Parker, D.: The Joanna Briggs Institute reviewers' manual 2015: methodology for JBI scoping reviews (2015)
22. Cushing, A., Manice, M.P., Ting, A., Parides, M.K.: Feasibility of a novel mHealth management system to capture and improve medication adherence among adolescents with asthma. Patient Prefer Adherence 10, 2271–2275 (2016)
23. Hightow-Weidman, L., et al.: A Gamified smartphone app to support engagement in care and medication adherence for HIV-positive young men who have sex with men (AllyQuest): development and pilot study. JMIR Public Health Surveill 4, e34 (2018)
24. LeGrand, S., et al.: Epic allies: development of a gaming app to improve antiretroviral therapy adherence among young HIV-positive men who have sex with men. JMIR Serious Games 4, e6 (2016)
25. Cafazzo, J.A., Casselman, M., Hamming, N., Katzman, D.K., Palmert, M.R.: Design of an mHealth App for the Self-management of Adolescent Type 1 Diabetes: A Pilot Study. J. Med. Internet Res. 14, e70 (2012)
26. Wiecek, E., Torres-Robles, A., Cutler, R.L., Benrimoj, S.I., Garcia-Cardenas, V.: Impact of a multicomponent digital therapeutic mobile app on medication adherence in patients with chronic conditions: retrospective analysis. J. Med. Internet Res. 22, e17834 (2020)
27. Su, J., Dugas, M., Guo, X., Gao, G.G.: Influence of Personality on mHealth Use in Patients with Diabetes: Prospective Pilot Study. JMIR Mhealth Uhealth 8, e17709 (2020)
28. Jácome, C., et al.: Feasibility and acceptability of an asthma app to monitor medication adherence: mixed methods study. JMIR Mhealth Uhealth 9, e26442 (2021)
29. Mehta, P., Moore, S.L., Bull, S., Kwan, B.M.: Building MedVenture – a mobile health application to improve adolescent medication adherence – using a multidisciplinary approach and academic–industry collaboration. Digital Health 7, 20552076211019876 (2021)
30. Debong, F., Mayer, H., Kober, J.: Real-world assessments of mySugr mobile health app. Diabetes Technol. Therapeutics 21, S2-35-S32-40 (2019)
31. Jácome, C., et al.: Inspirers: an app to measure and improve adherence to inhaled treatment. In: Proceedings of the International Conference on E-Health, EH 2017 - Part of the Multi Conference on Computer Science and Information Systems 2017, pp. 135–139. (2017)
32. Neumann, C.J., Kolak, T., Auschra, C.: Strategies to digitalize inert health practices: The gamification of glucose monitoring. It-Information Technology 61, 231–241 (2019)
33. Williams, G.C., Rodin, G.C., Ryan, R.M., Grolnick, W.S., Deci, E.L.: Autonomous regulation and long-term medication adherence in adult outpatients. Health Psychol. 17, 269 (1998)
34. Ryan, R., Rigby, C., Przybylski, A.: The motivational pull of video games: a self-determination theory approach. Motiv. Emot. 30, 344–360 (2006)
35. Guo, Y., Yuan, T., Yue, S.: Designing personalized persuasive game elements for older adults in health apps. Appl. Sci. 12, 6271 (2022)
36. Richards, C., Thompson, C.W., Graham, N.: Beyond designing for motivation: the importance of context in gamification. In: Proceedings of the first ACM SIGCHI Annual Symposium on Computer-Human Interaction in Play, pp. 217–226 (2014)

Relatedness for Moral Courage: Game Experience Dimensions as Persuasive Strategies for Moral Courage in Contrast to Other Facets of Altruistic Behavior

Julia Himmelsbach[1]([✉]) [iD], Wolfgang Hochleitner[2] [iD], Anke Schneider[1] [iD], Stephanie Schwarz[1] [iD], David Sellitsch[1] [iD], and Manfred Tscheligi[1,3] [iD]

[1] Center for Technology Experience, AIT Austrian Institute of Technology, Giefinggasse 2, 1210 Vienna, Austria
julia.himmelsbach@ait.ac.at
[2] Playful Interactive Environments, University of Applied Sciences Upper Austria, Softwarepark 11, 4232 Hagenberg im Mühlkreis, Austria
[3] Center for Human-Computer Interaction, University of Salzburg, Jakob-Haringer-Straße 8, 5020 Salzburg, Austria

Abstract. Moral courage has rarely been the focus of persuasive technologies. So far, few insights on persuasive strategies for moral courage exist, which mainly target a social psychological perspective but do not address game-based specifics. Against this background, we conducted an experimental study to identify game-related persuasive strategies. We show that the players' experience of relatedness, i.e., social belonging and interactions with fictitious characters or other players, is key for enabling courageous altruistic behavior change, namely moral and civil courage, but not other forms of altruistic behavior, such as help-giving. We present large to medium effect sizes with an increase in the relationship between moral courage and relatedness over time. We conclude that persuasive technologies for moral courage require specific persuasion strategies. By addressing relatedness, users can negotiate social norms in a reciprocal relationship with the technology, and future persuasive games could contribute to increased moral courage and, thus, social justice.

Keywords: Moral courage · Persuasive games · Relatedness · Pesuasive strategies

1 Introduction

Dealing with some of the biggest challenges contemporary societies are facing requires committed and courageous behavior that benefits not only the actors themselves but, more importantly, society. This action often has negative consequences for the individuals in question, at least in the short term: fighting

J. Ham et al. (Eds.): PERSUASIVE 2023, LNCS 13832, pp. 322–336, 2023.
https://doi.org/10.1007/978-3-031-30933-5_21

climate change involves not only the effort of changing behavior but sometimes also foregoing convenience; standing up for democratic values takes not only time but, in some situations also civil disobedience; standing up against social injustice can involve the loss of one's privileges; speaking out against discrimination and violent attacks can involve the risk of being attacked oneself. Such situations require moral courage, i.e., pursuing moral values despite high costs, and civil courage, i.e., advocating democratic values and human rights at high costs [8,32,37]. This behavior is important because it negotiates social norms at the micro level, which can support greater change and negotiate what kind of society we want to live in.

Especially when it comes to behavior change, whose general importance is evident but which is difficult to (un)learn, persuasive technology has a high potential. Current research and development of persuasive technologies foremost focus on individual behavior with more direct benefits for the user, such as better well-being and health (e.g., [3,16,31]). However, moral courage takes a special status among socially desirable behavior because it has only indirect advantages for the person (see e.g., [7,32]). Additionally, people need to act immediately and require action competencies that enable effective interventions while protecting their own safety. Games have the potential to stimulate motivation and depict scenarios interactively. By that, ways of behavior can be tested and learned, and awareness can be raised through persuasive strategies.

So far, research has rarely considered persuasive strategies for moral courage. When moral courage has been examined, researchers focused on a social psychological or social science perspective regarding social influential factors for moral courage in general (e.g., [34]). Up to now, the research did not consider technology-related strategies. Against this background, we formulated the following research question:

To what extent do game experience dimensions influence the effectiveness of persuasive games designed to promote moral courage?

By answering our research question, we aim to identify game-related persuasive strategies to account for the specifics of technology-mediated, game-based fostering of moral courage. By game-related persuasive strategy, we define approaches to persuasive technology design that address dimensions of the player's game experience, such as relatedness, player autonomy, and competencies development [37], to promote the desired behavior and persuasive goal, i.e., moral courage. Such strategies are game-immanent and typically realized by game mechanics. Hence, this study does not aim to prove the persuasive effects but identify relevant strategies that enable such effects.

To this end, we conducted an experimental study with 46 participants who played different persuasive games, namely a virtual reality (VR) game, an urban game, and a hybrid card game, to draw conclusions across game modes. We collected altruistic behaviors, including moral courage, at three measurement time points: before the game as a control variable, immediately after the game to analyze short-term correlations, and one week later to look at medium-term correlations.

By that, we contribute to the understanding of persuasion for moral courage, especially regarding game-related aspects and in distinction to other forms of altruistic behavior, such as help-giving. We aim to enable more effective persuasive game design and, by that, increase moral courage in the long term. Finally, we aim to set the foundation for understanding how the persuasive potential of moral courage games is leveraged and mediated and how users negotiate this behavior with games by understanding the game-related experience.

2 Related Work

Moral courage training is usually conducted in the form of workshops. The training aims to promote awareness and perceptual sensitivity, intervention competencies, and behavioral routines [10,32] and usually refers to motivational or process models [12,32]. Such models specify the steps necessary for moral courage: To act with moral courage, individuals have to perceive an incident, recognize it as an emergency, affirm their personal responsibility, recognize the capacity and skills to intervene, and decide to provide moral courage [32].

Increasing interest in fostering prosocial behavior in the context of technology interaction strives for a better understanding of influential factors that can mediate a bystander's behavior when confronted with a situation involving help-seeking others. As such, factors of personality, attitudes, and social norms, as well as situational aspects, are to be considered. Available research has been done for different social technology-mediated settings, such as Kinnunen et al. [21] in the context of willingness to help in online social networks. With their aim to foster affective and attitude change, specific persuasive mechanics in video games have been developed and investigated regarding their effects on prosocial behavior. Examples are games designed to ease affective learning and modulate attitudes towards homeless people [35] or attempts to increase empathy for refugees and willingness to help [33]. In a meta-analysis, Kolek et al. show that narrative games can change players' attitudes towards a depicted topic [22]. This is supported by the comparative review of 21 years of games for behavior change, presented in [28]. The authors report that over 75% of the analyzed studies showed a positive outcome regarding the desired behavior change.

However, few studies specifically explore the effects of persuasive games on prosocial behavior in high-cost situations and morally courageous behavior, respectively, which has to be regarded differently from other prosocial behaviors [32]. In contrast to help-giving, a morally courageous action not only happens at the risk of facing negative social consequences [20] but underlies a particular motivation i.e. to restore a violated moral standard [14]. Moral courage is influenced by various factors, including anger [14], social responsibility, and openness [20]. Being sensitive to injustice, holding a moral mandate, showing civil disobedience, or being resistant to group pressure, as well as feeling anger, have been identified as predictors for morally courageous behavior [14,20]. In a meta-analysis, Röderer et al. [34] sought to gain a more comprehensive overview of the main influential factors on moral courage toward elaborating promising strategies in terms of persuasive design. They highlighted social responsibility, altruistic moral reasoning, attention and emergency awareness, attitudes toward civil disobedience, intervention skills, resistance to group pressure as well as empathy as the most important factors. To foster moral courage, factors such as social responsibility as a personal norm might be promising [6].

With the emergence of social impact games, some strategies for fostering prosocial behavior have been implemented. The amount of applications using gamification to improve social interactions between different actors remains very limited. From 308 screened papers about gamification applications, 7% dealt with social behavior change [19]. Only a few strategies for fostering prosocial behavior have been implemented. In [13], playing a prosocial (relative to a neutral), video game showed increased prosocial behavior in terms of intervening for a person against their perpetrator. However, their work did not address specific persuasive aspects in the provided games nor other relevant factors that can influence moral courage. Lastly, persuasive design factors that can be used to foster moral courage in a social impact game remain underresearched. Referring to the recommendations of [34], more attention should be given to the factors of social responsibility as a personal norm [6] as well as altruistic moral reasoning, reflecting abstract and internalized (high order) reasoning regarding solving moral dilemmas involving another persons' needs [27].

Thus, altruistic behavior, in general, and moral courage, in particular, have received little attention in the design of persuasive technologies. First insights give indications for persuasive strategies from a social psychological perspective and the potential of persuasive technology to support altruistic behavior change. Up to now, research did not deal with persuasive strategies which are targeting technology-mediated, game-based specifics.

3 Methodology

To answer our research question of to what extent game experience dimensions influence the effectiveness of persuasive moral courage games , we implemented an experimental study. To this end, study participants with different social identities, who were more or less likely to have been affected by discrimination and therefore had different levels of experience with benefiting from moral courage, were invited to play the moral courage games on a one-time basis. This chapter presents the methodology of the study. We provide an overview of the study's procedure, introduce the persuasive games, and go into more detail about the operationalization of game experience and altruistic behavior.

3.1 Procedure of the Study

The study is structured in several phases: first, pre-questionnaires were used to collect data for the sampling and control variables on altruistic behavior; next, the games were played, and questionnaires on the game experience as well as altruistic behavior were asked again to determine short-term effects; finally, after one week, the survey on altruistic behavior was conducted again to determine medium-term effects.

In detail, participants were asked to first complete a screening questionnaire with initial information about their social identity, detailing age, categorical gender (female, male, non-binary, or a self-selected open-ended description), ethnicity, subjective social status [2] and their own as well as their parents' education. This questionnaire aimed to facilitate a sample as diverse as possible.

Next, we asked the participants to fill in a pre-questionnaire on their moral courage and related altruistic behavior [37] as well as their attitude on social responsibility [7]. In addition, we also assessed attitudes towards poverty [11] and experience with discrimination (BIAS-TS-Short Form [36]). These variables served as control variables to account for individual differences based on past practices and attitudes in the effects.

After completing the questionnaires, the participants received instructions on how to play the respective game independently. We developed a virtual reality game, an urban game, and a hybrid card game (see Sect. 3.2). The VR study was conducted with subjects who own a VR headset, and the urban game was played independently in public spaces. Subjects played the hybrid game in their homes in natural groups after receiving the materials by mail.

Immediately after playing, we again surveyed altruistic behavior and social responsibility to measure short-term effects (see Sect. 3.3). In addition, we also asked open-ended questions about the impression of the game and the emotional experience (SAM [9]). The measurement was repeated after one week to assess medium-term effects. Additionally, we further raised aspects of gender identity (applying the items of [18] for femininity and masculinity separately).

3.2 Moral Courage Games

We developed three games that allow us to examine game experience dimensions across game modes and thus arrive at more generalized results. Table 1 gives an overview of the games' differences and similarities.

All games follow the primary goal of raising awareness and introducing a number of intervention options to expand the user's available repertoire of moral courage actions. Thus, the designs mainly build on *primary task support* as defined by [29]. This strategy is in line with the finding of [34] on the relevance of *intervention skills* and *emergency awareness* for moral courage behavior change. We aimed at *reduction* and *tunneling* by providing concrete means of interventions and establishing a readily available repertoire of actions in emergencies. All games are based on a narrative story about moral courage situations which were *tailored* to real incidents, circumstances, and social issues. For instance, we involved a self-advocacy group of homeless people, the NGO SOS-Menschenrechte which promotes human rights, and moral courage trainers to incorporate realistic and meaningful game scenarios which relate to potential incidences the player experience in their everyday life. Further, the games allow *simulation* and *rehearsal* to different degrees.

The *virtual reality game* (see Fig. 1) allows for virtual immersion in a scenario where moral courage is required. The interface of the VR experience uses a

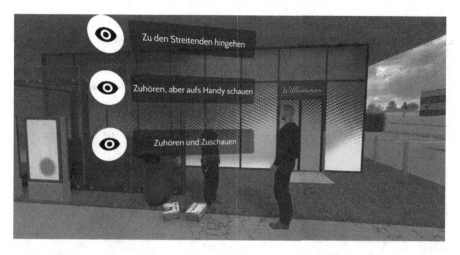

Fig. 1. The VR experience offers multiple ways to act in a situation. Here, the player can either walk towards the two people, listen while looking at their mobile phone or keep watching from a distance.

Table 1. Comparison of the three games based on different aspects

Aspect/Game	VR Game	Urban Game	Hybrid Game
Single-player/ Multi-player	single-player	single-player	multi-player with 2–8 players
Main Gameplay Loop	Players observe the virtual environment and select from predefined actions and dialog options	Players observe the real world environment while listening to dialogues on their phone and select from predefined dialog options	Players cooperatively agree on actions before playing action cards while trying to balance resource costs
Presentation	Immersive virtual environment via VR headset	voice output narrates the story	Printed cards to be used together with a companion smartphone app
Story	Branching story with multiple endings	Branching story with multiple endings	Initial narration; narrative situations arise through discussions and random events; positive or negative ending
Interaction	Exploring the environment and selecting options via gaze	Calling a phone number; voice output (story); options selection via number keys	Action cards are played and logged in the app

combination of gaze interaction and hand gestures. The scenario tells the story of a newspaper saleswoman who is accosted in a classist way by a man in front of a supermarket. The game presents several dialog options, including ignoring the situation and different forms of interventions; each interaction unlocks a new branch of possibilities. Playing the experience multiple times allows for behavior rehearsal and experimenting with different moral courage choices in a safe environment.

For the *urban game*, an audio game with an automated telephone system was developed. It prompted players to interact with their physical environment (public space) and make decisions within a fictional science-fiction story. The game transforms real-world environments into game locations, allowing players to explore aspects of moral courage in context. The concept focused on repeatability and trying out decisions in moral courage scenarios. Players called a phone number and were greeted by two aliens who wrapped them in a story in which they must make decisions about moral courage situations, interacting by a button press on their cell phones. In the story, aliens want to destroy planet Earth. By their standards, they can only destroy planets populated by antisocial, vicious, and unjust species. Humanity, therefore, seems ideal. However, the aliens need to statistically prove their assumptions about humans and conduct a covert experiment in form of a game, which the player learns over time.

Fig. 2. Players play cooperatively in the hybrid card game. By selecting the right cards, they can earn courage points and master the situation.

The *hybrid game* (see Fig. 2) is a haptic card game extended by an app. When starting, the app provides the player with a game scenario, again of a newspaper saleswoman facing classist assaults by a stranger. The game thus emphasizes the multitude of behavioral options and conveys how to choose from them in an emergency. The goal is to de-escalate the situation by cooperating with other players and using action cards. Thus, arguments are discussed in natural peer groups and also social support persuasive strategies as definied by [29] are implemented as social facilitation and cooperation are core parts of the game. Played cards are recorded and processed by the app to allow the players to focus on the game. Each playing card requires action points representing the needed courage for respective behavior. The players must therefore play together and find a balance between weighty actions and available action points. The app presents the development of the narrative according to the scores.

3.3 Operationalization of Game Experience and Moral Courage Related Behavior

To measure the game experience, we used the *Ubisoft Perceived Experience Questionnaire* (UPEQ) [4], which builds on self-determination theory and includes subscales on relatedness, autonomy, and competencies. This questionnaire is particularly suitable for the research aim because, on the one hand, it is specifically designed to capture game-related experiences and, on the other hand, it also addresses the sociality of these game experiences and thus fits the concept of moral courage as a form of social action [17]. The construct of *relatedness* refers to social belonging and interactions with fictitious characters or other players, fostering autonomy or competencies in the case of games. The construct of *autonomy* describes aspects of volition through choices. The agency over types of activities, how they are performed, and the game's emancipating support for these decisions are considered aspects. *Competence* encompasses aspects of capability and improvement through challenges.

To assess moral courage-related effects, we aimed for a broad concept of altruistic behavior to enable the exploration of moral courage specifics in comparison to other forms of courageous behavior, non-costly altruistic behavior, and related attitudes that are known to be closely associated with moral courage. We applied the *Constructing the Facets of Altruistic Behaviors* (FAB) scale [37], one of the few validated scales to assess altruism as a behavioral trait beyond help-giving. The scale comprises three behaviors: *Help-giving* (HG) refers to resource sharing, *peer punishment* (PP) refers to defending social norms of fairness, and *moral courage* (MC) refers to defending moral norms. In contrast to *peer punishment*, moral courage also challenges the norms of a social group, whereas *peer punishment* aims at protecting the norms of a reference group.

Further, we applied the *Civil Courage Scale* (CC) [37], capturing the behavior of defending civil-democratic values and human rights. The CC overlaps with moral courage also covering the behavior of defending values within a reference group if needed but it is more specific because it focuses on democratic values in line with humanitarian ideals. As shown by a meta-analysis on influencing factors on moral courage [34], social responsibility plays a key role with the largest effect size. Thus, we also decided to include the short version [7] of the *Social Responsibility Scale* (SRS) [5,6], a widely used scale for capturing social responsibility as a norm.

Table 2 summarizes the main scales and survey phases:

Table 2. Survey time, operationalizations, and purpose of the data collection

Time	Applied scales	Purpose
Before playing the game	FAB, CC, SRS	Control variables
Immediately after playing the game	FAB, CC, SRS, UPEQ	Short term effects
One week after playing the game	FAB, CC, SRS	Medium term effects

3.4   Sample

In sum, 46 persons participated in the study, and 44 complete data sets are available. 18 persons used the VR game (one incomplete data set), 19 persons used the urban game, and 9 persons used the hybrid card game (one incomplete dataset). On average, participants were 31.09 years old ($SD = 8.88$) and ranged in age from 15 to 55. 21 persons identified as female, 24 as male, and one as non-binary. The mean value of the subjective social status is 6.98 ($SD = 1.33$) on a 10-point scale, indicating higher social class affiliations. In line with this, most individuals have a high level of education: 55.5% reached ISCED level 6 or higher, 15.2% level 5, 26.1% level 3, and only 2.2% level 2 and below.

Slightly more than half of the participants (54,3%) affiliate with an Austrian identity, i.e., the majority of the population at the study site. For the other participants, this affiliation is on average at 3.14 ($SD = 1.24$) on a 5-point scale.

Further, the mean experience with harmful discrimination is 3.22 ($SD = 1.11$) ranging from 1 = "Have never experienced this" to 7 = "often experience this" and for facilitatory behavior, the mean experience is 6.33 ($SD = 4.38$) ranging from me 3 to 6.3. Thus, the sample represents different levels of experiences with situations of discrimination.

4   Results

To analyze the relationship between game experience dimensions and the effects on moral courage and altruistic behavior, we applied partial correlations controlling the respective outcome variable before playing the game. Based on the results of Shapiro-Wilk tests for normal distributions, we calculated Pearson or Spearman partial correlations. To ensure comparability across the games and exclude the influence of the game mode, we performed ANOVAs or Kruskal-Wallis tests for pre and all post-surveys. The tests showed no significant differences between the game modes (all p-values $> .05$).

All UPEQ scales were rated as fair and at a comparable level. On the 5-point scale, the *relatedness* was rated with $M = 3.2$ ($SD = 0.89$), *autonomy* with $M = 3.69$ ($SD = 0.74$) and *competences* with $M = 3.26$ ($SD = 0.65$).

Table 3 presents the mean values and standard deviations of all points of measurement for the moral courage-related measurements. Repeated measures ANOVAs and Friedman tests reveal no significant difference over time for all variables (all p-values $> .05$).

Table 3. Mean values (standard deviations) of FAB, FAB subscales, CC, and KSV per point of measure

Scale	Pre	Short-term	Medium-term
FAB	4.32 (0.71)	4.34 (0.72)	4.41 (0.74)
FAB: MC	4.66 (1.19)	4.64 (1.3)	4.76 (1.12)
FAB: PP	3.62 (1.16)	3.7 (1.19)	3.65 (1.21)
FAB: GG	4.69 (0.93)	4.67 (1.07)	4.83 (0.93)
CC	4.83 (1.17)	4.78 (1.23)	4.72 (1.21)
SRS	5.16 (0.5)	5.16 (0.5)	5.08 (0.44)

The analysis with the pre values as control variables reveals several significant correlations: the perceived *relatedness* shows a large effect size with the overall altruistic behavior, operationalized with the FAB questionnaire, right after the gameplay ($r(42) = .504$, $p < .001$) and a moderate relationship with the FAB one week after the gameplay ($r(42) = .301$, $p = .047$). Further, the *autonomy* shows a moderate relationship to the FAB immediately after the gameplay ($r(42) = .347$, $p = .021$).

To examine which types of altruistic behavior are affected, we repeated the analysis for each subscale of the FAB. The partial correlation analysis yields a significant relationship between the *relatedness* and *moral courage* with $r(42) = .478$ ($p = .001$) after playing and an increased $r(42) = .555$ ($p < .001$) one week later. Further, participants who reported higher *autonomy* also reported higher *moral courage* immediately after the gameplay ($r(42) = .41$, $p = .006$) as well as a further increased *moral courage* one week later ($r(42) = .445$, $p = .002$).

Additionally, also the SRS correlates significantly with player *autonomy* ($r(43) = 0.348$, $p = 0.019$).

We observe a significant partial correlation with *civil courage*. In detail, *civil courage* measured right after the gameplay correlates with *relatedness* ($r(42) = .511$, $p < .001$) and *autonomy*, ($r(42) = .316$, $p = .037$)

Applying Holm's Sequential Bonferroni Procedure [15] to deal with family-wise error rates of the individual, pair-wise short-term and medium-term correlations, all results remain significant with one exception, namely the correlation between *civil courage* and *autonomy*.

No significant relationships were found for the experience dimension of *competencies*. In addition, no significant effects on *peer pressure, help-giving*, and medium-term *social responsibility* were found (all p-values $> .05$).

5 Discussion

Our results show a significant effect of the game experience on altruistic behavior with a strong effect size of relatedness in the short term, i.e. immediately after the gameplay, and a medium effect size in the medium term, i.e. after one week. Further, autonomy has a medium effect in the short term. Hence, the game experience indeed influences if social impact games foster altruistic behavior.

The in-depth analysis shows that only courageous behavior is affected. Moral and civil courage share the characteristic of defending social norms based on moral values despite the risk of high costs and even contrary to the values of the reference group [37]. In other words, subjects can not rely on support for their behavior or immediate benefits, including social rewards, but have to expect risks, such as social exclusion or being attacked, and have to fight for these values even within the peer social group.

One possible explanation that only courageous behavior is affected could be that this characteristic of moral courage leads to the higher requirements for players to get involved in the situation and relate to other actors: First, moral courage leads to higher risks for interveners. Therefore, more involvement, enabled by relatedness, may be needed as a motivational factor for this courage to be taken within the game but also to enable the persuasive effect beyond the gameplay. Second, in contrast to other altruistic behavior, especially help-giving, moral courage is a social control behavior aiming for a norm negotiation with others [17] and thus, might need the relatedness to other real and fictitious actors to come to bear. Again, the in-game experience then enables the persuasive effect afterward. The result that influential factors for moral courage and other forms of altruistic behavior differ is in line with the research on general factors for moral courage in comparison with help-giving [14,20].

We observe a medium relationship between autonomy and social responsibility. This result is in line with previous work stating that social responsibility is a key factor for moral courage [34], and thus, overlapping correlations are highly probable. However, social responsibility only correlates with autonomy, while the experience of relatedness shows a higher effect size for moral courage than autonomy. One reason could be that responsibility is closely related to the affirmation of *personal* responsibility, which, in turn, is related to the examination of one's competence to act [32] or, in a game experience wording, one's autonomy.

Since we collected post variables not only immediately after the game but also one week later, we provide insights into the persistence of the relationships. While for the overall FAB, the correlation decreases from a high effect size to a medium one, and for civil courage, only a medium short-term effect is observable, the effect size for moral courage even increases from a medium to a high effect size. Based on the fact that participants only encountered once with the moral courage games, we did not expect this increase. We assume that relatedness goes beyond a situational relationship and fosters engagement with the topic also after the game leading to an increasing or rising effect. This result indicates the relevance of relatedness, especially for achieving persisting effects.

6   Conclusion and Future Work

To analyze the relationship between game experience dimensions and moral courage, we conducted an experimental study with three game modes: a VR game, an urban game, and a hybrid card game. With our games, we did not influence behavior or attitudes, which is not surprising given the one-time intervention and the fact that moral courage as a behavioral trait requires time and effort to evolve. However, this study aims to identify relevant strategies that enable such effects.

Applying the UPEQ, we showed the relationship of relatedness and autonomy with courageous altruistic behavior but not with other forms of altruism. We conclude that persuasion for moral courage has distinct requirements. In other words, our results show that moral courage games require different persuasive design strategies, even on a user experience level, than other social impact games that target altruistic behavior. We conclude that autonomy and, foremost, relatedness should be included as explicit persuasive strategies. Thus, relatedness and autonomy are not only seen as a design aspect to enable positive game experiences but have a central position in the design process of persuasive games, ranging from the creation of narratives to game mechanisms and contexts of gameplay, and are also central in the evaluation of persuasive games for moral courage behavior change. The overtime increasing effect size promises effective fostering of moral courage by addressing these dimensions when combined with other persuasive strategies, such as those identified by [34]. With our findings, we show that especially enabling relatedness might be vital to achieving effective persuasion toward moral courage.

Additionally, enabling relatedness as a persuasive strategy in behavior-change situations beyond moral courage could be of interest. Future research should investigate why the effect size is even increasing over time. Additionally, exploring the relevance of relatedness for other domains of persuasive technology complementary to other socially oriented strategies, such as social comparison or cooperation (e.g., [29,30]), could reveal new directions for persuasive games addressing game-related aspects as a persuasive strategy.

Moreover, the importance of relatedness for enabling effects on moral courage helps to understand how fostering moral courage behavior works. Moral courage is deeply connected to our values [26]. Only through the relatedness and, thus, relationship with the fictional characters and the fellow players a reciprocal relationship develops in which the support of the change of behavior can be realized. This finding underlines that persuasive games do not follow a unidirectional stimulus-response model (see, e.g., the critique of [1]) but occur in reciprocal negotiation with technology. Designers and researchers of persuasive systems should keep this notion of users in mind, take it as an epistemological basis, and enable or explore this relationship. For instance, future investigations could refer to the actor-network theory (e.g., [23–25]) to apply a conceptual understanding of relatedness as relationship and a *network* to negotiate moral values related behavior as well as how autonomy or agency of human and non-human actors is realized and contribute to the outcome of this negotiation.

Further, future research should expand the experimental setting of investigating persuasive moral courage games. For instance, longer field phases beyond one-time play experience would enhance the ecological validity and allow the investigation of the actual persuasive effects of games. Additionally, several strategies should be included, especially incorporating and controlling moral courage factors as proposed by [34]. Further, the relevance of relatedness suggests emphasizing concrete narratives in stories on the one hand and subjectivity, social identities, and identification potentials on the other side.

With an understanding of moral courage, social issues can be reconsidered to work on a contribution to face these challenges. Until now, moral courage has been underrepresented in persuasive technology design and research efforts. We want our study to be an impetus to promote moral courage with and without the use of persuasive technology through further research to contribute to social justice in the long term.

Acknowledgements. This research was conducted as part of the project CATRINA, partly funded by the Austrian Research Promotion Agency and Federal Ministry for Climate Action, Environment, Energy, Mobility, Innovation and Technology within the program "Talente" under contract number 872969. We want to thank our partners in the project consortium for their continuous commitment to fostering moral courage behavior. Special thanks go to Christina Hochleitner for initiating the project and Isabel Wendel for her support while conducting the study.

References

1. Abdullahi, A.M., Oyibo, K., Orji, R., Kawu, A.A.: The influence of age, gender, and cognitive ability on the susceptibility to persuasive strategies. Information 10, 352 (2019). https://doi.org/10.3390/info10110352
2. Adler, N.E., Epel, E.S., Castellazzo, G., Ickovics, J.R.: Relationship of subjective and objective social status with psychological and physiological functioning: Preliminary data in healthy, white women. Health Psychol. 19, 586–592 (2000). https://doi.org/10.1037/0278-6133.19.6.586
3. Aldenaini, N., Alqahtani, F., Orji, R., Sampalli, S.: Trends in persuasive technologies for physical activity and sedentary behavior: a systematic review. Front. Artif. Intell. 3 (2020). https://doi.org/10.3389/frai.2020.00007
4. Azadvar, A., Canossa, A.: UPEQ: Ubisoft perceived experience questionnaire: a self-determination evaluation tool for video games. In: Proceedings of the 13th International Conference on the Foundations of Digital Games. FDG 2018, New York, NY, USA. Association for Computing Machinery (2018). https://doi.org/10.1145/3235765.3235780
5. Berkowitz, L., Daniels, L.R.: Affecting the salience of the social responsibility norm: effects of past help on the response to dependency relationships. Psychol. Sci. Public Interest 68(3), 275–281 (1964)
6. Berkowitz, L., Lutterman, K.G.: The traditional socially responsible personality. Public Opin. Q. 32(2), 169–185 (1968). https://doi.org/10.1086/267597
7. Bierhoff, H.W.: Skala der sozialen Verantwortung nach Berkowitz und Daniels: Entwicklung und Validierung. Diagnostica 46(1), 18–28 (2000). https://doi.org/10.1026//0012-1924.46.1.18
8. Bierhoff, H.W., Klein, R., Kramp, P.: Evidence for the altruistic personality from data on accident research. J. Pers. 59(2), 263–280 (1991). https://doi.org/10.1111/j.1467-6494.1991.tb00776.x
9. Bradley, M.M., Lang, P.J.: Measuring emotion: the self-assessment manikin and the semantic differential. J. Behav. Ther. Exp. Psychiatry 25(1), 49–59 (1994). https://doi.org/10.1016/0005-7916(94)90063-9
10. Brandstätter, V., Jonas, K.J.: Moral Courage Training Programs as a Means of Overcoming Societal Crises, chap. 16, pp. 265–283. Wiley (2012). https://doi.org/10.1002/9781118347683.ch16
11. Cozzarelli, C., Wilkinson, A.V., Tagler, M.J.: Attitudes toward the poor and attributions for poverty. J. Soc. Issues 57(2), 207–227 (2001). https://doi.org/10.1111/0022-4537.00209
12. Darley, J.M., Latané, B.: Bystander intervention in emergencies: diffusion of responsibility. J. Person. Soc. Psychol. 8(4, Pt. 1), 377–383 (1968). https://doi.org/10.1037/h0025589
13. Greitemeyer, T., Osswald, S.: Effects of prosocial video games on prosocial behavior. J. Pers. Soc. Psychol. 98(2), 211–221 (2010). https://doi.org/10.1037/a0016997
14. Halmburger, A., Baumert, A., Schmitt, M.: Anger as driving factor of moral courage in comparison with guilt and global mood: a multimethod approach. Eur. J. Soc. Psychol. 45(1), 39–51 (2015). https://doi.org/10.1002/ejsp.2071

15. Holm, S.: A simple sequentially rejective multiple test procedure. Scand. J. Stat. **6**, 65–70 (1979)
16. Johnson, D., Deterding, S., Kuhn, K.A., Staneva, A., Stoyanov, S., Hides, L.: Gamification for health and wellbeing: a systematic review of the literature. Internet Interv. **6**, 89–106 (2016). https://doi.org/10.1016/j.invent.2016.10.002
17. Jonas, K.J., Brandstätter, V.: Zivilcourage. Zeitschrift für Sozialpsychologie **35**(4), 185–200 (2004). https://doi.org/10.1024/0044-3514.35.4.185
18. Kachel, S., Steffens, M.C., Niedlich, C.: Traditional masculinity and femininity: validation of a new scale assessing gender roles. Front. Psychol. **7**, 1–19 (2016). https://doi.org/10.3389/fpsyg.2016.00956
19. Kasurinen, J., Knutas, A.: Publication trends in gamification: a systematic mapping study. Comput. Sci. Rev. **27**, 33–44 (2018). https://doi.org/10.1016/j.cosrev.2017.10.003
20. Kayser, D.N., Greitemeyer, T., Fischer, P., Frey, D.: Why mood affects help giving, but not moral courage: comparing two types of prosocial behavior. Eur. J. Soc. Psychol. **40**, 1136–1157 (2010). https://doi.org/10.1002/ejsp
21. Kinnunen, S.P., Lindeman, M., Verkasalo, M.: Help-giving and moral courage on the internet. Cyberpsychology **10**(4) (2016). https://doi.org/10.5817/CP2016-4-6
22. Kolek, L., Ropovik, I., Sisler, V., van Oostendorp, H., Brom, C.: Video games and attitude change: a meta-analysis, January 2022. https://doi.org/10.31234/osf.io/8y7jn, preprint
23. Latour, B.: On actor-network theory: a few clarifications. Soziale Welt **47**(4), 369–381 (1996)
24. Latour, B.: On recalling ant. Sociol. Revi. **47**(1_suppl), 15–25 (1999). https://doi.org/10.1111/j.1467-954X.1999.tb03480.x
25. Latour, B.: Reassembling the Social. An Introduction to Actor-Network-Theory. Oxford University Press, New York (2005)
26. Lopez, S.J., O'Byrne, K.K., Petersen, S.: Profiling courage. In: Positive Psychological Assessment: A Handbook of Models and Measures, pp. 185–197. American Psychological Association, Washington (2003). https://doi.org/10.1037/10612-012
27. Midlarsky, E., Kahana, E., Corley, R., Nemeroff, R., Schonbar, R.A.: Altruistic moral judgment among older adults. Int. J. Aging Hum. Dev. **49**(1), 27–41 (1999). https://doi.org/10.2190/GLN2-G9NF-HHU7-KNJ4
28. Ndulue, C., Orji, R.: Games for change - a comparative systematic review of persuasive strategies in games for behaviour change. IEEE Trans. Games 1–15 (2022). https://doi.org/10.1109/TG.2022.3159090, preprint
29. Oinas-Kukkonen, H., Harjumaa, M.: A systematic framework for designing and evaluating persuasive systems. In: Oinas-Kukkonen, H., Hasle, P., Harjumaa, M., Segerståhl, K., Øhrstrøm, P. (eds.) PERSUASIVE 2008. LNCS, vol. 5033, pp. 164–176. Springer, Heidelberg (2008). https://doi.org/10.1007/978-3-540-68504-3_15
30. Orji, R.: Why are persuasive strategies effective? exploring the strengths and weaknesses of socially-oriented persuasive strategies. In: de Vries, P.W., Oinas-Kukkonen, H., Siemons, L., Beerlage-de Jong, N., van Gemert-Pijnen, L. (eds.) PERSUASIVE 2017. LNCS, vol. 10171, pp. 253–266. Springer, Cham (2017). https://doi.org/10.1007/978-3-319-55134-0_20
31. Orji, R., Moffatt, K.: Persuasive technology for health and wellness: state-of-the-art and emerging trends. Health Informatics J. **24**(1), 66–91 (2018)
32. Osswald, S., Frey, D., Streicher, B.: Moral courage. In: Kals, E., Maes, J. (eds.) Justice and Conflicts: Theoretical and Empirical Contributions, pp. 391–405. Springer, Heidelberg (2011). https://doi.org/10.1007/978-3-642-19035-3_24

33. van't Riet, J., Meeuwes, A.C., van der Voorden, L., Jansz, J.: Investigating the effects of a persuasive digital game on immersion, identification, and willingness to help. Basic Appl. Soc. Psychol. **40**(4), 180–194 (2018). https://doi.org/10.1080/01973533.2018.1459301

34. Röderer, K., Himmelsbach, J., Schwarz, S., Tscheligi, M.: Engaging bystanders using persuasive technology: a meta-analysis of influencing factors on moral courage. In: Oinas-Kukkonen, H., Win, K.T., Karapanos, E., Karppinen, P., Kyza, E. (eds.) PERSUASIVE 2019. LNCS, vol. 11433, pp. 202–209. Springer, Cham (2019). https://doi.org/10.1007/978-3-030-17287-9_17

35. Ruggiero, D.: The effect of a persuasive social impact game on affective learning and attitude. Comput. Hum. Behav. **45**, 213–221 (2015). https://doi.org/10.1016/j.chb.2014.11.062

36. Sibley, C.G.: The bias-treatment scale (bias-ts): a measure of the subjective experience of active and passive harm and facilitation. J. Pers. Assess. **93**(3), 300–315 (2011). https://doi.org/10.1080/00223891.2011.559389

37. Windmann, S., Binder, L., Schultze, M.: Constructing the facets of altruistic behaviors (fab) scale. Soc. Psychol. **52**(5), 299–313 (2021). https://doi.org/10.1027/1864-9335/a000460

GardenQuest: Using Hexad Player Types to Design a Step-Based Multiplayer Persuasive Game for Motivating Physical Activity

Gerry Chan[✉] [ID], Alaa Alslaity[ID], Jaisheen Kour Reen[ID], Sussan Anukem[ID], and Rita Orji[ID]

Faculty of Computer Science, Dalhousie University, Halifax, NS, Canada
gerry.chan@dal.ca

Abstract. Exergames have the potential to reduce sedentary behavior and motivate physical activity. However, they suffer from retention problems mainly because the level of interest declines over time. In this paper, we report on the results of a social exergame prototype called Garden Quest. The game implements gamification elements based on the Hexad player type framework that have been shown to motivate players. Before the development of a full game, we designed wireframes of the game interface, followed by an interactive prototype, and conducted a usability test and heuristic evaluation with six experts. We present initial results showing that the user interface is usable and simple, and the overall system is persuasive. Based on the collected results, we plan to revise the prototype and perform a second round of evaluation before moving on to the development and field evaluation of the game with a large sample.

Keywords: exergames · gamification · persuasive design · personalization · player type

1 Introduction

Due to the COVID-19 pandemic, a sedentary lifestyle has become a concern more than ever as obesity rates continue to rise [1]. One way to address the problem is to keep an active lifestyle and participate in physical activity. Living an active lifestyle by engaging in regular exercise is associated with many health benefits [2]. However common complaints associated with physical activity are lack of time, lack of motivation and perceived feelings of exhaustion [3]. Since the release of Nintendo Wii and Microsoft Kinect, video games that require players' active body motions are considered effective tools for participating in physical activity. These video games are commonly referred to as *active video games* or *exergames* [4]. Exergames can induce behavior change by encouraging physical activity by playing games [5]. Research shows that playing exergames can enhance social wellbeing by reducing loneliness and has the potential to affect players' attitudes toward other groups of people [6].

Exergames motivate exercise by making it a more enjoyable activity [7]. In general, there are two forms of exergames: asynchronous (players exercise at different times and

© The Author(s), under exclusive license to Springer Nature Switzerland AG 2023
J. Ham et al. (Eds.): PERSUASIVE 2023, LNCS 13832, pp. 337–356, 2023.
https://doi.org/10.1007/978-3-031-30933-5_22

collect reward) or synchronous (players exercise while in-game), which may also separate physical activity from gameplay elements (e.g., collecting points through exercise to use later in the game). Although studies show that exergames are successful at capturing initial interest, the level of interest drops over time [8–10]. Existing research suggests that meaningful social interactions can increase the level of motivation [11, 12]. As such, we designed an exergame prototype as a testbed to evaluate the plausibility of matching players using personal characteristics for promoting physical activity. This is based on theory in the interpersonal relations domain from the similarity-attraction perspective [13, 14]. We believe that the better players are grouped (e.g., compatible interests and personal characteristics) the more likely they would enjoy their interactions and increase the likelihood of exercise adherence.

Many researchers have investigated the value of games for promoting exercise [7, 15, 16], and have identified guidelines for designing exergames [17–19]. Different methods have also been proposed and studied on how to increase the level of motivation and maintain exercise interest. These methods include personalizing the game experience using player-type models [20], tailoring game elements to the players' personalities [21, 22], and offering a variety of game elements [23, 24]. Gamification, the application of game mechanics in non-game contexts [25], has been heavily researched as a way to motivate exercise [23, 26, 27]. Previous studies suggest that a combination of gamification elements such as badges, social interaction, points, and leaderboards can increase feelings of intrinsic motivation [28], which has been shown as one of the strongest predictors of exercise adherence because of inherent satisfaction and enjoyment [29]. Although there is some research comparing the effectiveness of single player vs. multiplayer exergames for motivating physical activity [30], there is very little research that has explored the effects of cultivating social connectedness, the number of quality interactions shared between players [31], for increasing exergame adherence.

Social exergames are gaining research attention because players can motivate each other to keep playing and provide a platform for engaging in meaningful social interactions [32, 33] satisfying people's need to feel a sense of belongingness [34]. In the present research, we build on previous works that have studied social exergames for motivating continued play [35–37] and the idea of player matching using personal characteristics for increasing physical activity [38]. We aim to examine how well social gamification elements affect users in a realistic game environment. Our target audience are gamer designers who can implement social elements and persuasive strategies into a game for anyone interested in starting an exercise routine. The personal characteristic of interest in this research is player type as defined in the Hexad model [39].

Our contribution to the field of persuasive technology, HCI, and gamification, is twofold: (1) we designed a social persuasive game prototype to promote physical activity by applying elements that have been shown to increase enjoyment in player groups, and (2) based on the evaluation, we offer insights for designing multiplayer experiences that can strengthen the relationship (enhance social connectedness) between players interactions by tailoring persuasive game elements based on player type.

2   Theoretical Background and Related Work

2.1   The Benefits of Social Play and Group Exercise

Exergames can encourage social play in computer-mediated environments, which is vital for experiencing enjoyment [40, 41] and is made possible through social interactions. Research shows that social presence [42], social benefits [32], and the experience of social relatedness [43, 44] are common motivations for video game play. Playing in multiplayer mode can also elicit higher levels of energy expenditure compared to single-player mode [45] and playing with friends is more enjoyable than with strangers [46]. However, there is some research suggesting that even pre-existing social relationships and a variety of gameplay actions are insufficient for sustaining long-term motivation for physical activity beyond four weeks [10]. In two recent reviews on existing gamified fitness tracker apps, the authors reported that social elements were paramount in nearly every app they reviewed, particularly plot-based collaborative games, and proposed that a potential direction for future research is to perform a qualitative examination of collaborative games [47, 48]. We aim to address this gap by using the findings of this present study as a basis for the development of a fully functional exergame.

Exercising in a group can be motivating as supportive peer relationships can encourage adherence [49]. From a social psychology perspective, people are drawn to the exercise habits of those around them [50]. Research shows that social support can motivate individuals to adopt healthier habits, such as better medication compliance and a higher propensity to seek out medical care [51]. Exercising with others can help people keep an exercise program and enhance mood, and psychological functioning because social support promotes healthy behaviors. The Social Comparison Theory (SCT) [52] is a useful framework for comprehending the outcomes of group exercise. The theory argues that "humans have the drive to assess how they are doing and to assess how they are doing; they seek standards against which to compare themselves. When objective standards are not available, people look to their social environments and engage in comparison with available others" [53]. Our design applies SCT by displaying the performance of all players in the game using a leaderboard as a source of motivation.

2.2   Player Matching and Player Modeling

Despite the many benefits of social (multiplayer) exergames for helping people achieve a variety of positive physiological and psychosocial outcomes [36], existing studies show that current player-matching services are ineffective at fostering social connectedness [54]. Numerous academics and game designers are also customizing the exergame experience to improve retention [55, 56]. To create games that can accommodate a variety of playing styles, game designers can use player modelling, which is defined as "the study of computational means for the modelling of player cognitive, behavioral, and affective states which are based on data (or theories) derived from the interaction of a human player with a game" [57]. This involves identifying players' playing patterns and modifying the game content and elements generated in real-time.

Research on personalized gamification is gaining much research attention [58–61], and one of the most promising methods for personalizing gamified systems is the use of the Hexad player type model [62]. The model has been developed for understanding and explaining player preferences and behaviors in gamified systems [63, 64]. The model suggests six different types of players: (1) Philanthropists are altruistic, wanting to give to other people and enrich the lives of others in some way with no expectation of reward, (2) Socialisers want to interact with others and create social connections, (3) Free Spirits strive for exploration and act independently, (4) Achievers seek to advance within a system, (5) Disruptors are driven by the need to bring about change, and (6) Players are motivated by extrinsic rewards and winning. Individual preferences for various design elements are connected with their player types [65].

To date, the influence of groups composed of similar player types on exergame play experience and adherence has only received limited investigation. Previous research in multiplayer online games [66, 67] and exergames [68] has demonstrated the potential of matching players to promote physical activity. This research is part of larger ongoing work on player matching using personal characteristics. In this study, we examine player type as the personal characteristic [69] and preferred social behavioral elements as the motivational affordance [70] for increasing exercise motivation.

3   Game Prototype Design: GardenQuest

To investigate the effects of matching players using player type for promoting physical activity, we applied social behavioral principles based on existing work [71–73] that appeal to specific player types. This section explains the rationale for the inclusion of gamification and principles in our design and components in the game interface.

3.1   Game Concept

For this research, we needed a multiplayer group experience that allows players to make choices based on their player type and induces light to moderate levels of exercise intensity. Thus, we devised the following six requirements for our design: (1) asynchronous exergame to elicit light- to moderate-intensity exercise that is not confined to a game console or indoors, (2) exercise points as the main score item to earn in-game tokens, (3) multiplayer design to offer competitive and cooperative playing options, (4) social behavioral game elements that have been shown to be persuasive, engaging and motivating future exercise intention, (5) small individual incentives and large group rewards to encourage joint effort, and (6) a choice board for player groups to decide on the element they would like to engage in and progress in the game.

3.2   Gamification Elements

The main elements include a points system, a selection of different challenges to progress in the game and building a garden. Our proposed design is grounded in the Hexad player type model which discusses gamification elements that appeal to player types. Our study offers a new application of the Hexad Model in general group functions with the aim of better understanding how an asynchronous multiplayer exergame can motivate continued play and exercise adherence. The Hexad model has been used repeatedly as a popular tool for capturing player preferences and perceptions of gameful design aspects in various contexts [58, 74, 75] and is a reliable measure of player preferences [76]. To achieve our goal, we designed an exergame prototype called "GardenQuest", that promotes group-based physical activity. The prototype implements social gamification elements that are tailored to player types defined by the Hexad model. These elements were selected based on the results of prior studies showing that elements such as leaderboard, supporting different roles, customization, knowledge sharing and exchanging supportive updates are correlated with each Hexad type [72]. We selected five gamification elements (Table 1). We used five Persuasive Strategies, one of them is customization which is commonly employed in persuasive health applications [77, 78] and the other four were from the Persuasive System Design model adapted from Oinas-Kukkonen et al. [79]. Principles that encourage social behaviors [80] were considered such that there is at least one element that appeals to each player type.

Table 1. Gamification elements, persuasive strategies, and supporting literature.

Gamification elements	Persuasive strategies	Description	Justification and supporting literature	Target type
Customization	Customization	Set the next goal of the team	Interventions suggest health goals that are tailored based on end users' current and desired capabilities are more engaging than interventions with generic goals [81]	Philanthropist and Socialiser
Rewards	Reward/ Incentives	Collect special elements and prizes	Displaying virtual trophies or medals are common ways of implementing a reward strategy in many game user studies such as GeoFit [82] and GoalPost [83]	Achiever and Player

(continued)

Table 1. (*continued*)

Gamification elements	Persuasive strategies	Description	Justification and supporting literature	Target type
Different Roles	Cooperation and Social comparison	Intra-subgroup interaction design. Players can take turns to be the leader	In group cycling, cyclists often take turns to be the leader of a paceline to distribute the burden imposed on the leader due to air resistance [84]	All
Leaderboard	Competition	Change team order on the leaderboard and see rankings	Many mobile games that aim to persuade people to participate in physical activity use leaderboards as a source of motivation such as PhoneRow [85] and iGO [86]. Leaderboards display the performance of other players and allow them to compare against each other [52] can be motivational	All
Lottery	Reward/ Incentives	Random reward	Highly agreeable individuals are motivated by lottery elements [87]	All

3.3 Prototype Design

First, we sketched wireframes using Miro[1] (Fig. 1) to design the layout of the game interface elements. Once the basic foundations of all the screens were drawn, we created an interactive prototype using Figma[2] (Fig. 2).

---

[1] https://miro.com/
[2] https://www.figma.com/

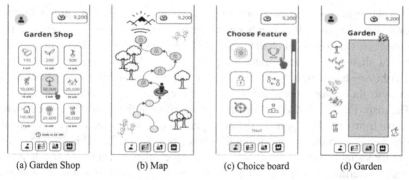

(a) Garden Shop   (b) Map   (c) Choice board   (d) Garden

Fig. 1. Initial wireframe sketches of GardenQuest game interface elements

(a) Individual   (b) Map   (c) Choice board   (d) Lottery wheel
challenges   (Group challenges)

(e) Garden shop   (f) Garden   (g) Performance   (h) Leaderboard

Fig. 2. Interactive medium-fidelity prototype of GardenQuest

3.4 GardenQuest Gameplay

GardenQuest is a step-based multiplayer exergame where players form groups and participate in step challenges. Physical activity and gameplay occur separately but are connected via a points system. As players are performing physical activity (steps are tracked by their smartphone using GoogleFit [88]) in the real world, they are collecting points to use in the game to build a garden.

The player begins by creating a new group or joining an existing group. Once the player is part of a group, they can begin taking on step challenges. There are two types of challenges: (1) individual challenges and (2) group challenges. To participate in an individual challenge, players select the prize (e.g., 100 plants require 3,500 steps – Fig. 2a) they wish to achieve and clicks "start" to begin the challenge. When the challenge is complete, the player is rewarded with a prize they can use to decorate the garden.

The map (Fig. 2b) is used to facilitate group effort in the game. To make progress, and move from one checkpoint to the next, players can participate in group challenges by engaging in a voting process using the choice board (Fig. 2c). This aims to connect players for social interaction to decide on a group challenge. There are six choices for players to determine a step challenge for the group: (1) a "lottery wheel" where the number of steps is determined by chance, (2) "win a trophy" where the number of steps is determined by the trophy they wish to win, (3) "unlock a prize" where the number of steps is determined by the prize the group wishes to unlock, (4) "rotating leadership" where the group decides on who the leader is in the next challenge, (5) "custom goal" where the group decides to set a custom step goal, and (6) "leaderboard" where the group decides to climb up the leaderboard and overtake the current group in the lead. The six choices were selected from previous literature showing positive correlations between gamification elements and player type [72]. The group can decide on spinning the lottery wheel (Fig. 2d) to determine the number of steps to be pursued by the group in the current challenge. The challenge ends when the group reaches the number of steps dictated by the wheel. The end of a challenge is followed by rewarding the group by converting steps to points. Player groups can then use the points earned to purchase items from the garden shop (Fig. 2e) to decorate the garden (Fig. 2f). Players can also view their group performance (Fig. 2g) and ranking on the leaderboard (Fig. 2h). As we are interested in evaluating the long-term effectiveness of the game for promoting physical activity, we did not define an end to the game. Players can continue to participate in challenges and grow their gardens for as long as they wish.

Based on the similarity-attraction perspective [89, 90], we expect that groups composed of similar player types are more likely to select the same choices. For example, a group composed of mostly Player-oriented traits is more likely to prefer spinning the lottery wheel and climbing up the leaderboard.

4   Study Design

To evaluate the prototype, we used a mixed-methods (qualitative and quantitative) user study approach. The evaluation was divided into three separate parts: (1) a usability test, (2) a heuristic evaluation, and (3) completing a post-study questionnaire.

4.1   Participants

Participants were recruited by email. Six (6) experts agreed and completed the evaluation. This number is informed by previous research that recommends using three to five evaluators because the amount of new problems found does not increase significantly by using larger numbers [91]. Experts were all males and ranged in age from 18–35 years old. Two experts hold Bachelor's degrees and four hold Master's degrees in Computer Science specializing in Human-Computer Interaction and Game Design.

4.2 Recruitment and Procedures

After receiving approval from our university ethics, we began recruiting participants. To participate in the study, participants had to be over 18, understand English, and have extensive experience in HCI, game design and technology. Participants who pass the inclusion criteria were asked to proceed with the following three-part procedure:

- **Part 1**: After reading the consent form and accepting it, experts completed 7 tasks (Table 3) using the prototype. After each task, experts were asked to rate the level of the task's difficulty on a 5-point Likert scale (1 = very hard to 5 = very easy) via a "Single-Ease Question" (SEQ) [92] and explain why they provided that rating. Experts were also asked to think aloud [93]. The think-aloud technique is widely used in HCI research and usability studies to better understand the choices and motivations that invite users to perform specific actions.
- **Part 2**: After completing part 1, experts were invited to evaluate *GardenQuest* using the 10 usability heuristics developed by Nielsen [94]. Experts identified the heuristic violated along with their severity ranking (0 = not a problem, 1 = cosmetic issue, 2 = minor usability problem, 3 = major usability problem, and 4 = usability catastrophe), a description of the problem, and proposed a solution.
- **Part 3**: Experts completed a questionnaire about their experience with the app. The questionnaire statements were composed of measurement instruments commonly used in HCI research to evaluate user preferences. In particular, usability [95], perceived persuasiveness [96], and simplicity [97] were all evaluated using a 5-point Likert scale (1 = strongly disagree to 5 = strongly agree).

4.3 Data Analysis

Results were analyzed using both quantitative and qualitative data analysis techniques. Quantitative data collected in the questionnaire were analyzed using descriptive statistics to first explore the data, followed by a one-sample t-test to determine whether the subjective ratings are above the mid-point (neutral score), and significant.

5 Results

5.1 Usability Test Results

The results of the usability test are summarized in Table 2. The SEQ scores revealed that the average easiness for each of the tasks that experts were asked to perform was above 3.00 except for Task 4 (Vote on an element) with an average score of 2.50 (*SD* = 0.55) and Task 8 (Move to the next checkpoint) with an average score of 3.00 (*SD* = 0.63). Looking more closely at the think-aloud comments, we observed that experts provided a low rating for two main reasons: (1) there was confusion about the meaning of some of the icons as one expert said, *"What do these icons mean? I don't understand them!"*, particularly in the choice board (Fig. 2c) and (2) they expected more direction as this was a novel game when one expert said, *"I think a tutorial at the beginning would help"*. Overall, these results show that the prototype offers decent usability, as most tasks were highly rated. Nevertheless, we found some minor issues through the think-aloud approach that some experts expected to find some functions in certain areas of the app but were not offered (e.g., a back button was missing), some labels/terminologies were misinterpreted (e.g., choose a "feature"), and some of the navigations were slightly confusing (e.g., moving from the garden to the garden shop).

Table 2. Summary of usability test results.

Tasks	M	SD	Key Comments and Issues from think-aloud data
1. Register and sign in	5.00	0.00	All experts were able to accomplish this task with ease
2. Join a group	4.50	0.55	All experts were able to accomplish this task with ease
3. Create a new group	4.67	0.52	All experts were able to accomplish this task with ease
4. Vote on an element	2.50	0.55	*"There is a lack of instruction and I feel like there needs to be more direction on what these icons mean."* *"What do these icons mean? I don't understand them!"* *"This page is not intuitive, and I don't know what I should do."*
5. Purchase an item in the garden shop	3.83	0.75	*"What is the currency here? Do I use coins or steps?"* *"I think there needs to be a price tag attached to the item"*
6. Add purchased items to the garden	3.83	0.75	*"This is hard, I am not sure if the items on the side are purchased or unpurchased."*
7. View progress/performance	4.50	0.55	*"Is the performance my coins or can I see my activity performance? I'm not sure."*
8. Move to the next checkpoint	3.00	0.63	*"I think the colours should be the opposite – completed should be a dark colour, and uncompleted should be a light colour."* *"I think a tutorial at the beginning would help."*

5.2 Heuristic Evaluation Results

The heuristic evaluation identified a total of eight problem areas. Table 3 summarizes the identified issues and proposed solutions. In general, the issues that were rated as a "major usability problem" (score = 3) related to help and documentation, visibility and system status, and user control and freedom. Suggestions to rectify these issues include offering help, tooltips and tutorials, better labels, and identification of icons, as well as allowing the user to revert their actions. Other issues that were rated as a "minor usability problem" (score = 2) were associated with helping users recover from errors, and recognition rather than recall. To address these problems, experts recommended adding tooltips and animated popups to help users understand and recover from errors. "Cosmetics issues" (score = 1) included problems with the aesthetics and minimalist design and the match between the system and the real world. Experts recommended the use of a simpler color pallet and more appropriate terminology.

Table 3. Summary of heuristic evaluation results.

Issue/Problem	Severity Ranking	Heuristic Violated	Potential Solution
Some screens lack descriptions to help the player understand the actions they need to take	3	Visibility of system status	Use animated texts/icons or pop-ups where necessary (e.g., the foot of the monkey could be placed at the level number the player is currently at)
Very few terminologies can be rephrased to make more sense to the player	1	Match between system and real world	Use "Accept" and not "Claim" for the wheel challenge
Some screens have no clear point of exit or revert a player action	3	User control and freedom	Make the point of exit clear and ensure that there is a revert functionality for every action. If the feature is not reversible, inform the player that their next action will be irreversible
I felt lost in some screens and don't know how to recover	2	Help users with errors	Animate pop-ups or text

(continued)

Table 3. (*continued*)

Issue/Problem	Severity Ranking	Heuristic Violated	Potential Solution
There is no help page	3	Help and documentation	A help page is critical in such an app to guide players when they are lost
There is no help page	3	Help and documentation	A help page is critical in such an app to guide players when they are lost
Need to remember features	2	Recognition rather than recall	Offer tooltip or hint text should be implemented
Too many color gradients	1	Aesthetic and minimalist design	Blend colors more
No tutorial and no tooltips	3	Help and documentation	Add tutorial and tool tips

5.3 Questionnaire Results

The System Usability Scale (SUS) scores and item means were reported to provide a high-level view of *GardenQuest's* usability. The SUS revealed an average score of 70.00 ($SD = 11.62$), which indicates that the overall usability of the app is "above average" [98]. One sample t-tests were conducted to compare perceived persuasiveness [96] and simplicity [97] scores to the mid-point of 3. Results showed that the game was perceived to be persuasive ($t(5) = 2.549$, $p = .026$) and the interface was simple ($t(5) = 3.722$, $p = .014$). Furthermore, 100% stacked bar charts were generated to visualize each item in the perceived persuasiveness scale (Fig. 3) and the different facets in the simplicity scale (Fig. 4). Figure 3 shows that the scores leaned toward the positive end of the scale in which 83% of experts selected agree/strongly agree for items that evaluated the relevance of the game and the degree to which the game would persuade them to reconsider their exercise habits. Figure 4 shows that the game interface was simple as over 70% of experts rated agree/strongly agree across all facets of simplicity, except for Reduction and Dynamic Complexity suggesting that the number of steps to achieve a task and the complexity of interface elements still needs more work.

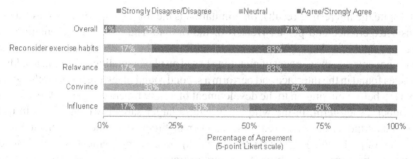

Fig. 3. Perceived persuasiveness ratings ($N = 6$).

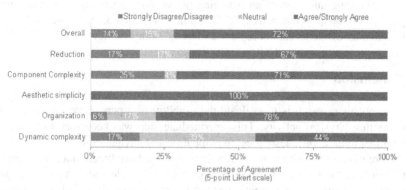

Fig. 4. Facets of simplicity ratings ($N = 6$).

6 Discussion and Future Work

Our results show that the overall game interface is usable, persuasive, and simple. Yet the game experience is still unknown and thus, the next step is to evaluate the game experience. In this study, we found that the game elements presented in the prototype were perceived to be persuasive which suggests that the game (soon-to-be developed) is likely to provoke users to reconsider their current exercise habits and promote physical activity. Experts also rated the organization and aesthetics of the interface to be rather simple, which suggests that the content and functions are consistent and systematic, and the screen design is neat and modern. Yet components related to "dynamic complexity" were rated rather poorly suggesting that the interface can be improved on the predictability of subsequent screens and taking the user to the expected desired action. This is further supported by the results in the think-aloud and heuristic evaluation sessions where experts noted that some actions were irreversible (Fig. 2b, 2g, and 2h – no back button) and there was a lack of instructions making them feel lost, particularly on the choice board (Fig. 2c). As suggested, we plan to add labels and tooltips to better guide the user with the navigation and understanding of the icons. Also, a participant suggested adding a time limit to complete group challenges and if a group is unable to complete the challenge within that time frame, the reward will not be granted, and points collected will be used towards the next challenge.

Despite the interesting results, one limitation is the use of a prototype for evaluating the user experience and persuasiveness of the design. Thus, the implementation of a game that can be evaluated in a real-world setting will be necessary to further validate the components and the concept of matching based on player qualities. We plan to address the issues found in the interface and perform a second round of testing with another group of experts before moving on to the development of a fully functional game. We also plan to conduct a long-term, in-the-wild study with a larger sample which will help us to gather quantitative, objective (e.g., the number of times an element is selected as an indication of preference) and subjective (e.g., enjoyment, engagement, social presence, intrinsic motivation, and intention for future exercise) measures, as well as qualitative interviews to gain further insights on how the game can be improved to answer our future overarching question: "Can matching players using personal characteristics in exergames promote physical activity?" The sample will include our target audience as expert-based assessments cannot replace end users' points of view.

7 Conclusion

The goal of this research is to evaluate the usability of a persuasive game prototype for promoting physical activity. This intermediate step was necessary to verify that the proposed interactions, aesthetics, functionality, and navigation flow are clear to the user before moving forward with the development of a fully functional game. Overall, participants rated the game interface to be usable and simple and perceived the game concept to be persuasive for promoting physical activity, as well as motivating repeated use (retention). An evaluation of the long-term effectiveness of the game is on the research agenda.

References

1. Kwok, S., et al.: Obesity: a critical risk factor in the COVID-19 pandemic. Clin. Obes. **10**, (2020). https://doi.org/10.1111/cob.12403
2. Alpert, P.T.: Exercise works. Home Health Care Manag. Pract. **21**, 371–374 (2009). https://doi.org/10.1177/1084822309334032
3. Myers, R.S., Roth, D.L.: Perceived benefits of and barriers to exercise and stage of exercise adoption in young adults. Heal. Psychol. **16**, 277–283 (1997). https://doi.org/10.1037/0278-6133.16.3.277
4. Peng, W., Crouse, J.C., Lin, J.H.: Using active video games for physical activity promotion: a systematic review of the current state of research. Heal. Educ. Behav. **40**, 171–192 (2013). https://doi.org/10.1177/1090198112444956
5. Adams, M.A., et al.: A theory-based framework for evaluating exergames as persuasive technology, 1 (2009). https://doi.org/10.1145/1541948.1542006
6. Theng, Y.-L., Li, J., Chen, L., Erdt, M., Cao, Y., Lee, S.-Q.: The social effects of exergames on older adults: systematic review and metric analysis. J. Med. Internet Res. **20**, e10486 (2018). https://doi.org/10.2196/10486
7. Yim, J., Graham, T.C.N.: Using games to increase exercise motivation. In: Proceedings of the 2007 Conference on Future Play - Future Play '07, p. 166. ACM Press, New York, New York, USA (2007). https://doi.org/10.1145/1328202.1328232

8. Sun, H.: Impact of exergames on physical activity and motivation in elementary school students: a follow-up study. J. Sport Heal. Sci. **2**, 138–145 (2013). https://doi.org/10.1016/j.jshs. 2013.02.003

9. Keeney, J., Schneider, K.L., Moller, A.C.: Lessons learned during formative phase development of an asynchronous, active video game intervention: Making sedentary fantasy sports active. Psychol. Sport Exerc. **41**, 200–210 (2019). https://doi.org/10.1016/j.psychsport.2018. 12.003

10. Caro, K., Feng, Y., Day, T., Freed, E., Fox, B., Zhu, J.: Understanding the effect of existing positive relationships on a social motion-based game for health, pp. 77–87 (2018). https:// doi.org/10.1145/3240925.3240942

11. Rooksby, J., Rost, M., Morrison, A., Chalmers, M.: Pass the ball: Enforced turn-taking in activity tracking. In: Conference on Human Factors in Computing Systems – Proceedings 2015-April, pp. 2417–2426 (2015). https://doi.org/10.1145/2702123.2702577

12. Depping, A.E., Mandryk, R.L.: Cooperation and interdependence: how multiplayer games increase social closeness. In: CHI Play 2017 – Proceedings of the Annual Symposium on Computer-Human Interaction in Play, pp. 449–461 (2017). https://doi.org/10.1145/3116595. 3116639

13. Montoya, R.M., Horton, R.S., Kirchner, J.: Is actual similarity necessary for attraction? A meta-analysis of actual and perceived similarity. J. Soc. Pers. Relat. **25**, 889–922 (2008). https://doi.org/10.1177/0265407508096700

14. Condon, J.W., Crano, W.D.: Inferred evaluation and the relation between attitude similarity and interpersonal attraction. J. Pers. Soc. Psychol. **54**, 789–797 (1988). https://doi.org/10. 1037/0022-3514.54.5.789

15. Lin, J.J., Mamykina, L., Lindtner, S., Delajoux, G., Strub, H.B.: Fish'n'Steps: encouraging physical activity with an interactive computer game. In: Lecture Notes in Computer Science (including subseries Lecture Notes in Artificial Intelligence and Lecture Notes in Bioinformatics) 4206 LNCS, 261–278 (2006)

16. Altamimi, R., Skinner, G.: A survey of active video game literature: from theory to technilogical application. Int. J. Comput. Inf. Technol. **01**, 20–35 (2012)

17. Mueller, F. 'Floyd,' Gibbs, M.R., Vetere, F., Edge, D.: Designing for Bodily Interplay in Social Exertion Games. ACM Trans. Comput. Interact. 24, 1–41 (2017). https://doi.org/10. 1145/3064938

18. Sinclair, J., Hingston, P., Masek, M.: Considerations for the design of exergames. 289 (2007). https://doi.org/10.1145/1321261.1321313

19. Mandryk, R.L., Gerling, K.M., Stanley, K.G.: Designing Games to Discourage Sedentary Behaviour. In: Nijholt, A. (ed.) Playful User Interfaces. GMSE, pp. 253–274. Springer, Singapore (2014). https://doi.org/10.1007/978-981-4560-96-2_12

20. Busch, M., et al.: Using player type models for personalized game design - an empirical investigation. Int. J. Interact. Des. Archit. **28**, 145–163 (2016)

21. Shaw, L.A., Tourrel, R., Wunsche, B.C., Lutteroth, C., Marks, S., Buckley, J.: Design of a virtual trainer for exergaming. In: Proceedings of the Australasian Computer Science Week Multiconference - ACSW '16, pp. 1–9 (2016). https://doi.org/10.1145/2843043.2843384

22. Mattheiss, E., Hochleitner, C., Busch, M., Orji, R., Tscheligi, M.: Deconstructing pokémon go – an empirical study on player personality characteristics BT - persuasive technology: development and implementation of personalized technologies to change attitudes and behaviors. Presented at the (2017)

23. Zhao, Z., Arya, A., Whitehead, A., Chan, G., Etemad, S.A.: Keeping users engaged through feature updates: a long-term study of using wearable-based exergames. In: Proceedings of the 2017 CHI Conference on Human Factors in Computing Systems - CHI '17. 1053–1064 (2017). https://doi.org/10.1145/3025453.3025982

24. Lin, J.-H., Winn, B., Peng, W., Pfeiffer, K.A.: Need satisfaction supportive game features as motivational determinants: an experimental study of a self-determination theory guided exergame. Media Psychol. **15**, 175–196 (2012). https://doi.org/10.1080/15213269.2012.673850

25. Deterding, S., Dixon, D., Khaled, R., Nacke, L.: From game design elements to gamefulness: defining gamification. In: Proceedings of the 15th International Academic MindTrek Conference: Envisioning Future Media Environments, MindTrek 2011 (2011). https://doi.org/10.1145/2181037.2181040

26. Matallaoui, A., Koivisto, J., Hamari, J., Zarnekow, R.: How effective is exergamification? A systematic review on the effectiveness of gamification features in exergames. In: Proceedings of the 50th Hawaii International Conference on System Sciences (2017). https://doi.org/10.24251/hicss.2017.402

27. Boulos, M.N.K., Yang, S.P.: Exergames for health and fitness: the roles of GPS and geosocial apps. Int. J. Health Geogr. **12**, (2013). https://doi.org/10.1186/1476-072X-12-18

28. Xu, J., et al.: Psychological interventions of virtual gamification within academic intrinsic motivation: a systematic review. J. Affect. Disord. **293**, 444–465 (2021). https://doi.org/10.1016/j.jad.2021.06.070

29. Teixeira, P.J., Carraça, E.V., Markland, D., Silva, M.N., Ryan, R.M.: Exercise, physical activity, and self-determination theory: a systematic review. Int. J. Behav. Nutr. Phys. Act. **9**, 78 (2012). https://doi.org/10.1186/1479-5868-9-78

30. Kaos, M.D., et al.: Efficacy of online multi-player versus single-player exergames on adherence behaviors among children: a nonrandomized control trial. Ann. Behav. Med. **52**, 878–889 (2018). https://doi.org/10.1093/abm/kax061

31. Vella, K., Klarkowski, M., Turkay, S., Johnson, D.: Making friends in online games: gender differences and designing for greater social connectedness. Behav. Inf. Technol. **39**, 917–934 (2020). https://doi.org/10.1080/0144929X.2019.1625442

32. Rüth, M., Kaspar, K.: Educational and social exergaming: a perspective on physical, social, and educational benefits and pitfalls of exergaming at home during the COVID-19 pandemic and afterwards. Front. Psychol. **12**, (2021). https://doi.org/10.3389/fpsyg.2021.644036

33. Kalaitzidou, A., Senechal, N., Dimitriou, P., Chandran, K., Mcginity, M.: "E-WAFE" - A full body embodied social exergame, pp. 286–290 (2022). https://doi.org/10.1145/3505270.3558375

34. Kaos, M.D., Rhodes, R.E., Hämäläinen, P., Graham, T.C.N.: Social play in an exergame: how the need to belong predicts adherence. In: BT - Proceedings of the 2019 CHI Conference on Human Factors in Computing Systems, CHI 2019, Glasgow, Scotland, UK, May 04–09, (2019). https://doi.org/10.1145/3290605.3300660

35. Park, T., Yoo, C., Choe, S.P., Park, B., Song, J.: Transforming solitary exercises into social exergames, pp. 863–866 (2012). https://doi.org/10.1145/2145204.2145332

36. Marker, A.M., Staiano, A.E.: Better together: outcomes of cooperation versus competition in social exergaming. Games Health J. **4**, 25–30 (2015). https://doi.org/10.1089/g4h.2014.0066

37. Altmeyer, M., Lessel, P., Sander, T., Krüger, A.: Extending a gamified mobile app with a public display to encourage walking. In: ACM International Conference Proceedings Series, pp. 20–29 (2018). https://doi.org/10.1145/3275116.3275135

38. Chan, G., Arya, A., Orji, R., Zhao, Z., Stojmenovic, M., Whitehead, A.: Player matching for social exergame retention. In: Extended Abstracts of the 2020 Annual Symposium on Computer-Human Interaction in Play, pp. 198–203. ACM, New York, NY, USA (2020). https://doi.org/10.1145/3383668.3419879

39. Marczewski, A.: Gamification Mechanics and Elements (2015)

40. Lyons, E.J., Tate, D.F., Ward, D.S., Ribisl, K.M., Michael Bowling, J., Kalyanaraman, S.: Engagement, enjoyment, and energy expenditure during active video game play. Health Psychol. **33**(2), 174–181 (2014). https://doi.org/10.1037/a0031947

41. Lyons, E.J.: Cultivating engagement and enjoyment in exergames using feedback, challenge, and rewards. Games Health J. **4**, 12–18 (2014). https://doi.org/10.1089/g4h.2014.0072
42. Tseng, F.C., Huang, H.C., Teng, C.I.: How do online game communities retain gamers? Social presence and social capital perspectives. J. Comput. Commun. **20**, 601–614 (2015). https://doi.org/10.1111/jcc4.12141
43. Kooiman, B.J., Sheehan, D.P.: The efficacy of exergames for social relatedness in online physical education. Cogent Educ. **2**(1), 1045808 (2015). https://doi.org/10.1080/2331186X.2015.1045808
44. Saksono, H., et al.: Spaceship launch: designing a collaborative exergame for families. In: CSCW 2015 - Proceedings of the 2015 ACM International Conference on Computing Cooperative Work and Social Computing, pp. 1776–1787 (2015). https://doi.org/10.1145/2675133.2675159
45. Barkman, J., Pfeiffer, K., Diltz, A., Peng, W.: Examining energy expenditure in youth using XBOX kinect: differences by player mode. J. Phys. Act. Heal. **13**, S41–S43 (2016). https://doi.org/10.1123/jpah.2016-0016
46. Chan, G., Whitehead, A., Parush, A.: Dynamic player pairing: quantifying the effects of competitive versus cooperative attitudes. In: Korn, O., Lee, N. (eds.) Game Dynamics, pp. 71–93. Springer, Cham (2017). https://doi.org/10.1007/978-3-319-53088-8_5
47. Neupane, A., Hansen, D., Sharma, A., Fails, J.A., Neupane, B., Beutler, J.: A review of gamified fitness tracker apps and future directions. In: CHI Play 2020 – Proceedings of the Annual Symposium on Computer-Human Interaction in Play, pp. 522–533 (2020). https://doi.org/10.1145/3410404.3414258
48. Neupane, A., Hansen, D., Fails, J.A., Sharma, A.: The role of steps and game elements in gamified fitness tracker apps: a systematic review. Multimodal Technol. Interact. **5**, 5 (2021). https://doi.org/10.3390/mti5020005
49. Moreno Murcia, J.A., López De San Román, M., Martínez Galindo, C., Alonso, N., González-Cutre, D.: Peers' influence on exercise enjoyment: a self-determination theory approach. J. Sport. Sci. Med. **7**, 23–31 (2008)
50. Plante: Effects of perceived fitness level of exercise partner on intensity of exertion. J. Soc. Sci. **6**, 50–54 (2010). https://doi.org/10.3844/jssp.2010.50.54
51. Kulik, J.A., Mahler, H.I.: Social support and recovery from surgery. Health Psychol. **8**, 221–238 (1989). https://doi.org/10.1037/0278-6133.8.2.221
52. Gerber, J.P., Wheeler, L., Suls, J.: A social comparison theory meta-analysis 60+ years on. Psychol. Bull. **144**, 177–197 (2018). https://doi.org/10.1037/bul0000127
53. Corning, A.F., Krumm, A.J., Smitham, L.A.: Differential social comparison processes in women with and without eating disorder symptoms. J. Couns. Psychol. **53**, 338–349 (2006). https://doi.org/10.1037/0022-0167.53.3.338
54. Horton, E., Johnson, D., Mitchell, J.: Finding and building connections: moving beyond skill- based matchmaking in videogames. In: Proceedings of the 28th Australian Conference on Computer-Human Interaction - OzCHI '16 (2016). https://doi.org/10.1145/3010915.3011857
55. Zhao, Z., Arya, A., Orji, R., Chan, G.: Physical activity recommendation for exergame player modeling using machine learning approach. In: 2020 *IEEE 8th International Conference* on *Serious Games* and Applications for *Health* (*SeGAH*) 2020. (2020). https://doi.org/10.1109/SeGAH49190.2020.9201820
56. Göbel, S., Hardy, S., Wendel, V.: Serious games for health - personalized exergames. In: MM: Proceedings of the International Conference Multimedia, pp. 1663–1666 (2010). https://doi.org/10.1145/1873951.1874316
57. Yannakakis, G.N., Spronck, P., Loiacono, D., André, E.: Player Modeling. Dagstuhl Follow. (2013). https://doi.org/10.4230/DFU.Vol6.12191.45

58. Altmeyer, M., Lessel, P., Jantwal, S., Muller, L., Daiber, F., Krüger, A.: Potential and effects of personalizing gameful fitness applications using behavior change intentions and Hexad user types. User Model. User-Adap. Inter. **31**(4), 675–712 (2021). https://doi.org/10.1007/s11257-021-09288-6

59. Busch, M., et al.: Personalization in serious and persuasive games and gamified interactions. In: Proceedings of the *2015 Annual Symposium* on *Computer*-Human *Interaction in* Play - CHI Play '15, pp. 811–816 (2015). https://doi.org/10.1145/2793107.2810260

60. Zhao, Z., Arya, A., Orji, R., Chan, G.: Effects of a personalized fitness recommender system using gamification and continuous player modeling: system design and long-term validation study. JMIR Serious Games. 8, (2020). https://doi.org/10.2196/19968

61. Rodrigues, L., Toda, A.M., Palomino, P.T., Oliveira, W., Isotani, S.: Personalized gamification: a literature review of outcomes, experiments, and approaches. In: *ACM International Conference Proceeding* Series, pp. 699–706 (2020). https://doi.org/10.1145/3434780.3436665

62. Tondello, G.F., Wehbe, R.R., Diamond, L., Busch, M., Marczewski, A., Nacke, L.E.: The gamification user types hexad scale, pp. 229–243 (2016). https://doi.org/10.1145/2967934.2968082

63. Tondello, G.F., Mora, A., Nacke, L.E.: Elements of gameful design emerging from user preferences. 129–142 (2017). https://doi.org/10.1145/3116595.3116627

64. Orji, R., Tondello, G.F., Nacke, L.E.: Personalizing persuasive strategies in gameful systems to gamification user types. In: Proceedings of the 2018 Conference Human Factors in Computer Systems –April, (2018). https://doi.org/10.1145/3173574.3174009

65. Xi, N., Hamari, J.: Does gamification satisfy needs? A study on the relationship between gamification features and intrinsic need satisfaction. Int. J. Inf. Manage. **46**, 210–221 (2019). https://doi.org/10.1016/j.ijinfomgt.2018.12.002

66. Campbell, T., Ngo, B., Fogarty, J.: Game design principles in everyday fitness applications. In: Proceedings of the ACM Conference on Computer Supported Cooperative Work, CSCW (2008). https://doi.org/10.1145/1460563.1460603

67. Xu, Y., et al.: This is not a one-horse race: understanding player types in multiplayer pervasive health games for youth. In: Proceedings of the *ACM Conference on Computer Supported Cooperative Work* (CSCW), pp. 843–852 (2012). https://doi.org/10.1145/2145204.2145330

68. Chan, G., Arya, A., Whitehead, A.: Keeping players engaged in exergames: a personality matchmaking approach Gerry. Extended Abstracts of the 2018 CHI Conference on Human Factors in Computing Systems - CHI '18. (2018). https://doi.org/10.1145/3170427.3188455

69. Barrick, M.R., Mount, M.K.: Yes, personality matters: moving on to more important matters. Hum. Perform. **18**, 359–372 (2005). https://doi.org/10.1207/s15327043hup1804_3

70. Weiser, P., Bucher, D., Cellina, F., De Luca, V.: A taxonomy of motivational affordances for meaningful gamified and persuasive technologies. In: Proceedings of the EnviroInfo ICT Sustainable 2015. 22, (2015). https://doi.org/10.2991/ict4s-env-15.2015.31

71. Villareale, J., Gray, R.C., Furqan, A., Fox, T., Zhu, J.: *Enhancing social exergames through idle game designACM International Conference Proceeding* Series (2019). https://doi.org/10.1145/3337722.3341827

72. Chan, G., Arya, A., Orji, R., Zhao, Z., Whitehead, A.: Personalizing gameful elements in social exergames: an exploratory study. In: *ACM International Conference Proceeding* Series (2021).https://doi.org/10.1145/3472538.3472578

73. Meske, C., Brockmann, T., Wilms, K., Stieglitz, S.: Social Collaboration and Gamification. In: Stieglitz, S., Lattemann, C., Robra-Bissantz, S., Zarnekow, R., Brockmann, T. (eds.) Gamification. PI, pp. 93–109. Springer, Cham (2017). https://doi.org/10.1007/978-3-319-45557-0_7

74. Altmeyer, M., Schubhan, M., Lessel, P., Muller, L., Krüger, A.: Using hexad user types to select suitable gamification elements to encourage healthy eating. In: Conference on Human Factors in Computing Systems - Proceedings (2020). https://doi.org/10.1145/3334480.338 3011

75. Amado, C.M., Roleda, L.S.: Game element preferences and engagement of different hexad player types in a gamified physics course. In: *ACM International Conference Proceeding Series*, pp. 261–267 (2020). https://doi.org/10.1145/3377571.3377610

76. Krath, J., von Korflesch, H.F.O.: Player Types and Game Element Preferences: Investigating the Relationship with the Gamification User Types HEXAD Scale. In: Fang, X. (ed.) HCII 2021. LNCS, vol. 12789, pp. 219–238. Springer, Cham (2021). https://doi.org/10.1007/978-3-030-77277-2_18

77. Orji, R., Vassileva, J., Mandryk, R.L.: Modeling the efficacy of persuasive strategies for different gamer types in serious games for health. User Model. User-Adap. Inter. **24**(5), 453–498 (2014). https://doi.org/10.1007/s11257-014-9149-8

78. Orji, R., Nacke, L.E., Di Marco, C.: Towards personality-driven persuasive health games and gamified systems. In: Proceedings of the *2017 CHI* Conference on Human *Factors* in Computing Systems - CHI '17. 1015–1027 (2017). https://doi.org/10.1145/3025453.3025577

79. Oinas-Kukkonen, H., Harjumaa, M.: Persuasive systems design: key issues, process model, and system features. Commun. Assoc. Inf. Syst. **24**, (2009)

80. Krath, J., Von Korflesch, H.F.O.: Designing gamification and persuasive systems: a systematic literature review. CEUR Workshop Proc. **2883**, 100–109 (2021)

81. Nuijten, R., Van Gorp, P., Khanshan, A., Le Blanc, P., van den Berg, P., Kemperman, A., Simons, M.: Evaluating the impact of adaptive personalized goal setting on engagement levels of government staff with a gamified mHealth tool: results from a 2-month randomized controlled trial. JMIR mHealth uHealth **10**(3), e28801 (2022). https://doi.org/10.2196/28801

82. Terry, I.M., et al.: GeoFit: verifiable fitness challenges. In: Proceedings of the 11th IEEE International Conference on Mobile Ad Hoc and Sensor Systems, MASS 2014. 720–724 (2015). https://doi.org/10.1109/MASS.2014.133

83. Munson, S.A., Consolvo, S.: Exploring goal-setting, rewards, self-monitoring, and sharing to motivate physical activity. In: 2012 6th International Conference on Pervasive Computing Technologies for Healthcare and Workshops, PervasiveHealth 2012 (2012). https://doi.org/10.4108/icst.pervasivehealth.2012.248691

84. Choi, W., Oh, J., Edge, D., Kim, J., Lee, U.: SwimTrain: Exploring Exergame Design for Group Fitness Swimming. In: Proceedings of the 2016 CHI Conference on Human Factors in Computing Systems (CHI '16), pp. 1692–1704 (2016). https://doi.org/10.1145/2858036.2858579

85. Zwinderman, M.J., Shirzad, A., Ma, X., Bajracharya, P., Sandberg, H., Kaptein, M.C.: Phone row: a smartphone game designed to persuade people to engage in moderate-intensity physical activity. In: Lecture Notes in Computer Science (*including* subseries *Lecture Notes in Artificial Intelligence* and *Lecture Notes* in *Bioinformatics*). 7284 LNCS, 55–66 (2012). https://doi.org/10.1007/978-3-642-31037-9_5/COVER/

86. Haque, M.S., Abdullah, W.M., Rahaman, S., Kangas, M., Jämsä, T.: Persuasive health and wellbeing application: a theory-driven design in promoting physical activity. In: 2016 International Conference on Medical Engineering, Health Informatics and Technology (MediTec) (2017). https://doi.org/10.1109/MEDITEC.2016.7835369

87. Nasirzadeh, E., Fathian, M.: Investigating the effect of gamification elements on bank customers to personalize gamified systems. Int. J. Hum.-Comput. Stud. **143**, 102469 (2020). https://doi.org/10.1016/j.ijhcs.2020.102469

88. Menaspà, P.: Effortless activity tracking with Google Fit. Br. J. Sports Med. **49**, 1598 (2015). https://doi.org/10.1136/bjsports-2015-094925

356   G. Chan et al.

89. Ruijten, P.A.M.: The similarity-attraction paradigm in persuasive technology: effects of system and user personality on evaluations and persuasiveness of an interactive system. Behav. Inf. Technol. (2020). https://doi.org/10.1080/0144929X.2020.1723701

90. Tenney, E.R., Turkheimer, E., Oltmanns, T.F.: Being liked is more than having a good personality: the role of matching. J. Res. Pers. **43**, 579–585 (2009). https://doi.org/10.1016/j.jrp.2009.03.004

91. Nielsen, J., Molich, R.: Heuristic evaluation of user interfaces. International Conference on Human Factors in Computing Systems, pp. 249–256 (1990). https://doi.org/10.1145/97243.97281

92. Sauro, J., Dumas, J.S.: Comparison of three one-question, post-task usability questionnaires. In: Proceedings of the SIGCHI Conference on Human Factors in Computing Systems, pp. 1599–1608 (2009). https://doi.org/10.1145/1518701.1518946

93. Nielsen, J.: Evaluating the Thinking-Aloud Technique for use by Computer Scientists. Adv. human-computer Interact. 69–82 (1992)

94. Nielsen, J.: Enhancing the explanatory power of usability heuristics. 210 (1994). https://doi.org/10.1145/259963.260333

95. Brooke, J.: SUS - A quick and dirty usability scale (1996). https://doi.org/10.1002/hbm.20701

96. Drozd, F., Lehto, T., Oinas-Kukkonen, H.: Exploring Perceived Persuasiveness of a Behavior Change Support System: A Structural Model. In: Bang, M., Ragnemalm, E.L. (eds.) PERSUASIVE 2012. LNCS, vol. 7284, pp. 157–168. Springer, Heidelberg (2012). https://doi.org/10.1007/978-3-642-31037-9_14

97. Choi, J.H., Lee, H.J.: Facets of simplicity for the smartphone interface: a structural model. Int. J. Hum. Comput. Stud. **70**, 129–142 (2012). https://doi.org/10.1016/j.ijhcs.2011.09.002

98. Bangor, A., Kortum, P., Miller, J.: Determining what individual SUS scores mean: adding an adjective rating scale. J. usability Stud. **4**, 114–123 (2009). https://doi.org/10.5555/2835587.2835589

Personal Factors in Persuasion

Does the Association Between Persuasive Strategies and Personality Types Vary Across Regions

Wenzhen Xu$^{(\boxtimes)}$ ⓘ, Roberto Legaspi ⓘ, and Yuichi Ishikawa ⓘ

AI Division, KDDI Research, Inc., Fujimino, Japan
{we-xu,xre-roberuto,yi-ishikawa}@kddi.com

Abstract. To investigate how the interaction effects of dispositional and regional factors affect the susceptibility to persuasive strategies, we conducted a large-scale online survey (n = 3,116 in eight major cities in Japan). Our results indicate that (1) the association between the persuasiveness of persuasive strategies and personality types varies across regions, but (2) the different distributions of personality types among regions could not completely account for the regional variations. Based on our findings, as well as insights from previous studies, we propose a framework demonstrating how regional factors affect personality and the susceptibility to persuasive strategies.

Keywords: Personalized persuasion · regional differences · susceptibility to persuasive strategies

1 Introduction

To date, the effects of personalized persuasive technologies for supporting volitional changes in individual attitudes and behaviors have been widely investigated and applied in e-commerce and e-marketing [1–3], health care [4–6], and public management [7, 8]. Numerous existing studies on personalized persuasion covered individual factors (e.g., personality, gender, age, value) and national-level cultural factors (e.g., individualism and collectivism). However, to our best knowledge, few of the existing investigations examined the interaction effects that exist between individual and regional factors on the susceptibility to persuasive strategies. In other words, less evidence could directly answer an intuitive inquiry such as whether the strategy of *reciprocity*[1] equally affects the decisions of people who have the same degree of *agreeableness*[2] from urban area in

---

At the time of publication, W. Xu serves as Assistant Prof. at the School of Business Administration of Hitotsubashi University in Japan (njuxwz@gmail.com), and Y. Ishikawa has moved to Mitsubishi Research Institute, Inc.

[1] *Reciprocity* is one of the six persuasive strategies of Cialdini that describes people tend to pay back favors done to them.

[2] *Agreeableness* is a personality trait of the Big Five manifested as a person's kind, sympathetic and cooperative characteristics.

J. Ham et al. (Eds.): PERSUASIVE 2023, LNCS 13832, pp. 359–368, 2023.
https://doi.org/10.1007/978-3-031-30933-5_23

Northern Europe and rural area in East Asia. Our paper aims to examine the interaction effect between region (i.e., eight major regions in Japan) and personality (i.e., four personality types proposed by [9] and replicated in the Japanese population by [3]) on susceptibility to Cialdini's persuasive strategies through a large-scale online survey. Our results indicate that region moderates the association between persuasive strategies and personality types, but the regional differences cannot be entirely attributed to the different distributions of personality types. We propose a framework to demonstrate the possible pathways through which regional factors shape personality and influence susceptibility to persuasive strategies. The rest of the paper is organized as follows. Section 2 discusses the related work and our research questions. Section 3 details the experimental method, while Sect. 4 presents the results. Finally, Sect. 5 discusses the main findings and concludes the paper.

2   Related Works and Research Questions

2.1   Within-Nation and Between Nation Variations in Susceptibility to Persuasive Strategies

In the field of persuasive technology (PT), the importance of individual-level factors on personalized persuasion have been frequently discussed and well examined (e.g., personality traits [14–17] and types [3, 18], gender [19–22], age [23], value [2], sense of agency [24, 37]), but the impact of regional or cultural-level factors are rarely investigated. Among the few works, Khaled and colleagues pioneered the investigation of within-national variations in the effectiveness of persuasive strategy [10]. In their qualitative study of a cessation game reflecting individualistic and collective cultural cues, they investigated how culture shapes immediate reactions to and interpretations of smoking. The result indicated that New Zealand Europeans (individualism orientation) and New Zealand Māori (collectivism orientation) participants' positive responses to the game reflect their cultural backgrounds. Subsequent quantitative studies on personalized persuasions investigated cultural differences in their susceptibility to persuasive strategies [11–13]. For instance, Orji investigated the between-national differences in the likelihood of being influenced by Cialdini's persuasive strategies by comparing the response of Asian and North American participants. The results showed that collectivists are more likely persuaded by *authority, reciprocity, consensus* and *liking* strategies than individualists. On the other hand, individualists perceived more persuasiveness from the *scarcity* strategy than collectivists [11, 12]. Oyibo provided indirect evidence supporting the importance of cultural factors in the selection of persuasive strategies. He compared the mechanisms through which Canadians and Nigerians can be persuaded. He found the factors of *self-efficacy* and *self-regulation* significantly affect only the Canadians' behavior, while *social support* and *body image* influence the Nigerian's behavior much more [13]. These works provided solid evidence from multiple perspectives that culture is a reliable basis for tailoring persuasive technologies. However, convincing as they are, we reckon that further investigation on this topic is still warranted due to several issues that have yet to be addressed.

   First, the impact of national-level cultural factors and individual-level factors have been investigated separately, and to the best of our knowledge, there is much to explore when it comes to the interaction effects of cultural and individual factors. To fill this gap, we investigated the interaction effects between regions and personality types (i.e., *role-model, reserved, self-centered, average*) on the susceptibility to persuasive strategies. We selected the variables of personality types rather than traits because the former contains information on the interactions among several personality traits[3] [9] and performed better when adding interactions between personality and other moderators into the prediction models [3].

Second, although the national and racial variations in susceptibility to persuasive strategies have been well examined, the more fine-grained level variations are worthy of investigation. Cultural psychologists claim that human behavior (including behavioral intention) is influenced by different levels of cultural and geographic factors ranging from regional, ethnic, religious, and linguistic levels [25–27]. There is possibility that people from different regions within the same nation have different thought and behavioral patterns. Hence, we hypothesize that the region where an individual lives will also be a potential factor affecting how likely a person can be persuaded. To examine this, we compared the susceptibility to persuasive strategies of participants from eight major regions in Japan.

2.2 Research Questions

Based on the issues we raised above, we state our primary research question (PRQ), as.

PRQ: *"Do people with the same personality types from different regions in the same nation prefer different persuasive strategies?"*.

Existing studies on susceptibility to persuasive strategy focuses on examining the impact of personality trail, while personality type is left uninvestigated. To answer the PRQ, however, the following prerequisite research question should be answered:

Pre-PRQ: *"Do people with different (similar) personality types prefer different (similar) persuasive strategies?"*.

To investigate a possible underlying mechanism for why such answer to PRQ exists, we explored a follow-up sub-research question:

Post-RQ: *"Is the conclusion to PRQ due to the different distributions of personality types across regions?"*.

3   Method

We used a dataset, which we call here as *Persuasion in Multi-Contexts* (PMC), that was collected from 3,116 Japanese participants (female: 1,559, male: 1,557; ages ranging

[3] The types are determined by the combination of all the Big Five traits (i.e., OCEAN). Role model is characterized by low N scores and high scores in the other traits. Average is characterized by the average of the five trait scores. Self-centered has low O, A and C scores. Reserved has low O and N scores.

from 20 to 60 years old; Mean = 44.7, SD = 13.6) from the representative cities of eight major regions in Japan, namely, Sapporo, Sendai, Tokyo, Nagoya, Kanazawa, Osaka, Hiroshima, and Fukuoka (see Fig. 1). PMC consists of information on demography, the Big Five (60 items) [28], and personality types [9]. It also includes behavioral intention on interventional materials representing Cialdini's six persuasive strategies in the following contexts: take-out promotion in the pandemic, take-out promotion after the pandemic, and detour behavior promotion in a heavy traffic jam (Fig. 2). All the participants reported that they have experience and willingness to order take-out food and every household utilizes at least one vehicle. Since ethically conducting our experiments was paramount, we followed fundamental ethical principles [38] to purposely preserve all participants' privacy and dignity. We obtained permission on using the data even before collecting it and removed all the personally identifiable information prior to data analysis. The percentages of participants in PMC were equally assigned by gender, age, and city, e.g., the number of females who are in their 40s and resides in Tokyo is equal to the 40s-males from Tokyo and 40s-females from other cities.

The persuasive strategies were represented by 18 (three for each strategy) web banners. These banners were created by three PT scholars and a visual designer, based on Cialdini's definition, and were then evaluated by three other PT scholars. The consistency among the three evaluators was notably high (in-class correlation coefficient of 0.967). The persuasiveness of each banner was measured with a 5-point Likert scale, in which "*1) I will never do that*" (e.g., order a take-out dish) and "*5) I will do that*". The sum of the scores of the three banners for the same strategy is the persuasiveness score of that strategy.

To answer the RQs, we applied a two-way ANOVA and multiple comparison analyses. Specifically, to answer the Pre-RQ, we conducted a set of two-way ANOVAs on the dataset with all 3,116 participants. If the significance of the interaction effect between persuasive strategies and personality types on persuasiveness is evident, we can conclude that different personality types prefer different persuasive strategies. For the PRQ, we repeated the same procedure with a two-way ANOVA on per city datasets. Thus, if the patterns that emerged vary across regions, we can conclude that region moderates the association between persuasive strategies and personality types. Finally, to resolve Post-RQ, we compared the results of a two-way ANOVA across regions with similar distribution of personality types. If the resulting patterns differ, then we can conclude that the distribution of personality is not the only cause of regional variations when it comes to the susceptibility to persuasive strategies.

Fig. 1. Locations of the eight cities

Fig. 2. Examples of interventional materials (*Authority*)

4 Results

Pre-RQ. The result of two-way ANOVAs showed significant interaction between persuasive strategies and personalities on the persuasiveness of the strategy, F (15, 9330) = 2.002, p < .001. The significant interaction effect indicates that the persuasiveness of each strategy varies across different personality types. To further investigate the details of the differences, we conducted simple main effect analyses (see Fig. 3(a)). The result showed that people with a Role-model personality type are more likely to be persuaded than those with other personality types by all six strategies. In contrast, people with Reserved personality type are less likely to be persuaded by *Scarcity* (Sca), *Authority* (Aut), and *Consensus* (Con) than all the other personality types. But the difference between people with Reserved and Self-centered personality types in *Liking* (Lik) and *Reciprocity* (Rec) strategies was insignificant. Similarly, the differences between people with Reserved and Average personality types in *Commitment* (Com) and *Reciprocity* were also insignificant.

PRQ. We conducted eight sets of two-way ANOVA analyses that followed the same procedures as the Pre-RQ for each city. The significant interaction effects between persuasive strategies and personality types on the persuasiveness of the strategy was only confirmed in the datasets of Nagoya (F (15, 1152) = 1.858, p < .05) and Fukuoka (F (15, 1152) = 2.015, p < .05). The results of simple main effect analyses showed regional variations even between these two cities (see Figs. 3(b) and (c)). We reported the statistically significant differences in the following paragraph.

For the Nagoya residents, those with the Role-model personality type are more likely to be persuaded than Reserved ones by *Scarcity* and *Commitment* strategies. Those with the self-centered personality type are more likely to be persuaded than Reserved ones by *Consensus* and *Scarcity* strategies. The Average ones are more likely to be persuaded than the Reserved ones by *Authority* strategy. For the Fukuoka residents, those with the Role-model personality type are more likely to be persuaded by *Consensus* than others, than Self-centered ones by *Liking* strategies, than the Reserved ones by *Authority* strategies. The results prove that the association between persuasive strategies and personality types vary across regions.

Post-RQ. To further investigate whether the regional differences in the association between persuasive strategies and personality types are caused by variations in personality types distribution, we compared the regions with the same distribution of personality types. Figure 4 shows the distributions of personality types of the representative cities of different regions. Interestingly, the eight cities' personality type distributions can be divided into four pairs, which are Hiroshima-Sendai (HS), Kanazawa-Nagoya (KN), Fukuoka-Sapporo (FS), and Tokyo-Osaka (TS). We presented the persuasiveness rank of KN pair by the Strategy × Personality type contingency table (Table 1).

The result indicates that amid the same distribution of personality types, the ranks of each strategy's persuasiveness for the same personality type vary across regions. "1" represents the most persuasive strategy and "6" represents the least persuasive one. " = 1" means multiple strategies ranked first place while no significant differences

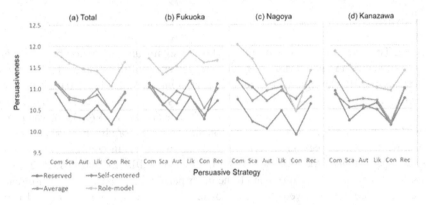

Fig. 3. a-d. The association between personality types and persuasive strategies.

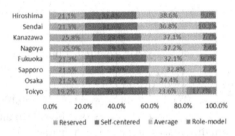

Fig. 4. The distributions of personality types in eight cities

were confirmed among those strategies. For instance, for the Role-model people in Kanazawa, the persuasiveness of the *Consensus* strategy has no significant difference from *Reciprocity, Liking, Scarcity,* and *Authority* (Fig. 3(d)). Still, for people in Nagoya who have the same personality type, *Consensus* is the least effective strategy (Fig. 3(c)).

Table 1. The rank of each strategy's persuasiveness for each personality type (KN pair).

	Commitment	*Scarcity*	*Authority*	*Liking*	*Consensus*	*Reciprocity*
Reserved	=1/=1	=4/=3	=4/5	=1/=3	=4/6	=1/=1
Self-centered	1/=1	=2/=3	=2/=3	=2/=3	6/6	=2/=1
Average	1/1	5/=3	=2/=3	=2/=3	6/6	4/2
Role-model	1/=1	2/=2	=3/=2	=3/=1	6/=2	=3/=1

5   Discussion

In this study, we found that the association between the effectiveness of persuasive strategies and personality types varies across regions, but the different distributions of

personality types among regions could not completely account for the regional variations. This should motivate PT experts, and the PT community at large, to examine the
cross-cultural validity of existing personalized PT when being applied to a new regional
or cultural group. Based on our findings, as well as insights from previous studies, we
propose a framework demonstrating how regional factors affect personality and susceptibility to persuasive strategy. By visualizing this, we provide suggestions on future
works on persuasive strategy tailoring (see Fig. 5).

Previous studies have examined two valid pathways through which region affects
susceptibility. The first is region being a factor that formulates variations in personality
[29] via selective migration [30, 31], social influence [32–34], and environmental influence [35, 36]. Subsequently, geographical differences in personality lead to variations
in susceptibility [3, 14–18]. The other pathway demonstrates that region directly affects
susceptibility [11, 12]. Our contribution is that we found a possible third pathway, i.e.,
region moderates the impact of personality on susceptibility. In other words, it is possible
that people with the same personality are likely to be persuaded by different strategies
due to their different regional orientations. However, the follow-up question remains
to be which aspect of culture or region imposes the moderating effect. For instance,
the social acceptance or preference of an individual's personality may vary across geographic or cultural groups. In a conservative and closed community, even a Role-model
figures may behave relatively introverted than their counterparts in an open and liberal
region. Our first possible future work would be to figure out this underlying mechanism
(① in Fig. 5). Another future work is to validate the framework using a more sophis-
ticated and elaborate experiment that is comprised of richer dispositional and cultural
information as moderators and behavioral data for evaluating their effects. The effect
of other individual-level and group-level independent factors (②) and moderators(③)
affecting susceptibility also need to be further explored.

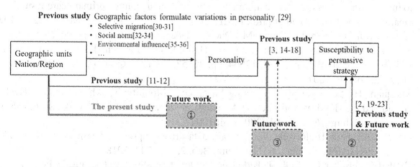

Fig. 5. Factors affecting susceptibility to persuasive strategy.

In addition, some methodological limitations should also be addressed to validate
the conclusions. First, the susceptibility to persuasive strategies was measured by a
questionnaire. Although the questionnaire was designed by three PT scholars and a
visual designer, and strictly evaluated by other three PT scholars, we still believe it
is necessary to validate our findings by assessing susceptibility through other types of
measurements, for example, gamification or using real purchase data. Second, we could

also double check the finding obtained from multiple two-way ANOVA by conducting alternative statistical analyses, for instance, a linear multiple regression analysis with a three-way interaction effect.

To conclude, our results indicate that (1) the association between the persuasiveness of strategies and personality types varies across regions, but (2) the different distributions of personality types among regions could not completely account for the regional variations. Compelled by our findings and knowledge from earlier studies, we put forward for consideration our framework that highlights how regional variables influence personality and the susceptibility to persuasive strategies.

References

1. Alslaity, A., Tran, T.: On the impact of the application domain on users' susceptibility to the six weapons of influence. In: Gram-Hansen, S.B., Jonasen, T.S., Midden, C. (eds.) PERSUASIVE 2020. LNCS, vol. 12064, pp. 3–15. Springer, Cham (2020). https://doi.org/10.1007/978-3-030-45712-9_1
2. Ishikawa, Y., Kobayashi, A., Kamisaka, D.: Modelling and predicting an individual's perception of advertising appeal. User Model. User-Adap. Inter. **31**(2), 323–369 (2021). https://doi.org/10.1007/s11257-020-09287-z
3. Xu, W., Ishikawa, Y., Legaspi, R.: The Utility of Personality Types for Personalizing Persuasion. In: Baghaei, N., Vassileva, J., Ali, R., Oyibo, K. (eds.) PERSUASIVE 2022. LNCS, vol. 13213, pp. 240–254. Springer, Cham (2022). https://doi.org/10.1007/978-3-030-98438-0_19
4. Bidargaddi, N., Schrader, G., Klasnja, P.: Designing m-Health interventions for precision mental health support. Transl Psychiatry **10**, 222 (2020)
5. Bidargaddi, N., et al.: To prompt or not to prompt? A microrandomized trial of time-varying push notifications to increase proximal engagement with a mobile health App JMIR Mhealth Uhealth, e10123 6(11) (2018)
6. Patel MS, et al.: A randomized trial of behavioral Nudges delivered through Text messages to increase influenza vaccination among patients with an upcoming primary care visit. Am J. Health Promot. Epub ahead of print. PMID: 361959822022 4 Oct 2022 8901171221131021
7. Xu, W., Kuriki, Y., Sato, T., Taya, M., Ono, C.: Does traffic information provided by smart phones increase detour behavior? In: Gram-Hansen, S.B., Jonasen, T.S., Midden, C. (eds.) PERSUASIVE 2020. LNCS, vol. 12064, pp. 45–57. Springer, Cham (2020). https://doi.org/https://doi.org/10.1007/978-3-030-45712-9_4
8. Marquart, H., Schuppan, J.: Promoting Sustainable Mobility: To what extent is "Health" considered by Mobility App studies? A review and a conceptual framework" Sustainability 14, no. 1: 47. https://doi.org/10.3390/su14010047
9. Gerlach, M., Farb, B., Revelle, W.: A robust data-driven approach identifies four personality types across four large data sets. Nat. Hum. Beh. **2**, 735–742 (2018)
10. Khaled, R., Fischer, R., Noble, J., Biddle, R.: A Qualitative Study of Culture and Persuasion in a Smoking Cessation Game. In: Oinas-Kukkonen, H., Hasle, P., Harjumaa, M., Segerståhl, K., Øhrstrøm, P. (eds.) PERSUASIVE 2008. LNCS, vol. 5033, pp. 224–236. Springer, Heidelberg (2008). https://doi.org/10.1007/978-3-540-68504-3_20
11. Orji, R.: Persuasion and culture: Individualism – Collectivism and susceptibility to influence strategies. In: Proceedings of the Personalization in Persuasive Technology Workshop, Persuasive Technology, 30–39 (2016)
12. Orji, R.: The impact of cultural differences on the persuasiveness of influence strategies. In: Proceedings of the 11th International Conference 2016 on Persuasive Technology, 38–41(2016)

13. Oyibo, K.: Designing culture-based persuasive technology to promote physical activity among university students. In: Proceedings of the 2016 Conference on User Modeling Adaptation and Personalization, pp. 321–324 (2016)
14. Alkıs, N., Temizel, T.T.: The impact of individual differences on influence strategies. Person. Individ. Diff. **87**, 147–152 (2015)
15. Oyibo, K., Orji, R., Vassileva, J.: Investigation of the influence of personality traits on Cialdini's persuasive strategies. PPT@PERSUASIVE (2017)
16. Hirsh, J.B., Kang, S.K., Bodenhausen, G.V.: Personalized Persuasion: Tailoring Persuasive Appeals to Recipients' Personality Traits. Psychological Science. 23, 6 (Jun. 2012), 578–581(2012). https ://doi.org/https://doi.org/10.1177/0956797611436349
17. Smith, K., Dennis, M., Masthoff, J.: Personalizing reminders to personality for melanoma self-checking. Proceedings of the 2016 Conference on User Modeling Adaptation and Personalization, 85–93 (2016)
18. Wall, H.J., Campbell, C.C., Kaye, L.K., Levy, A., Bhullar, N.: Personality profiles and persuasion: an exploratory study investigating the role of the Big-5, Type D personality and the Dark Triad on susceptibility to persuasion. Person. Individ. Differ. **139**, 69–76 (2019)
19. Ciocarlan, A., Masthoff, J., Oren, N.: Actual Persuasiveness: Impact of Personality, Age and Gender on Message Type Susceptibility. In: Oinas-Kukkonen, H., Win, K.T., Karapanos, E., Karppinen, P., Kyza, E. (eds.) PERSUASIVE 2019. LNCS, vol. 11433, pp. 283–294. Springer, Cham (2019). https://doi.org/10.1007/978-3-030-17287-9_23
20. Busch, M., Mattheiss, E., Reisinger, M., Orji, R., Fröhlich, P., Tscheligi, M.: More than Sex: The role of femininity and masculinity in the design of personalized persuasive games. 219–229 (2016)
21. Orji, R., Mandryk, R., Vassileva, J.: Gender and persuasive technology: Examining the persuasiveness of persuasive strategies by gender groups. International Conference on Persuasive Technology, 48–52(2014)
22. de Vries, R.A.J., Truong, K.P., Zaga, C., Li, J., Evers, V.: A word of advice: how to tailor motivational text messages based on behavior change theory to personality and gender. Pers. Ubiquit. Comput. **21**(4), 675–687 (2017). https://doi.org/10.1007/s00779-017-1025-1
23. Phillips, D.M. and Stanton, J.L.: Age-related differences in advertising: Recall and persuasion. Journal of Targeting, Measurement and Analysis for Marketing. 13, 1 (Sep. 2004), 7–20 (2004). https ://doi.org/https://doi.org/10.1057/palgrave.jt.5740128
24. Legaspi, R., Xu, W., Konishi, T., Wada, S.: Positing a Sense of Agency-Aware Persuasive AI: Its Theoretical and Computational Frameworks. In: Ali, R., Lugrin, B., Charles, F. (eds.) PERSUASIVE 2021. LNCS, vol. 12684, pp. 3–18. Springer, Cham (2021). https://doi.org/10.1007/978-3-030-79460-6_1
25. Yuki M, Sato K, Takemura K, Oishi S.: Social ecology moderates the association between self-esteem and happiness. J. Exp. Soc. Psyc. 49(4): (2013). https://doi.org/10.1016/j.jesp.2013.02.006
26. Green, E.G.T., Deschamps, J.-C., Páez, D.: Variation of Individualism and Collectivism within and between 20 Countries: A Typological Analysis. J. Cross-Cult. Psyc. **36**(3), 321–339 (2005). https://doi.org/10.1177/0022022104273654
27. Karahanna, E., Roberto E., Mark S.: Levels of Culture and Individual Behavior.: An Investigative Perspective, J. Glob. Inf. Manage. (JGIM) 13(2) 1–20 (2005). http://doi.org/https://doi.org/10.4018/jgim.2005040101
28. Murakami, Y., Murakami, C.: Scale construction of a "Big Five" personality inventory. Jpn. J. Pers. **6**(1), 29–39 (1997)
29. Rentfrow, P.J., Gosling, S.D., Potter, J.: A theory of the emergence, persistence, and expression of geographic variation in psychological characteristics. Perspect. Psychol. Sci. 3(5), 339–369 (2008)

30. Swann, W.B., JR Rentfrow, P.J., Guinn, J.S.: Self-verification: The search for coherence. In: Leary, M., J. Tagney (Eds.), Handbook of self and identity (pp. 367–383). New York: Guilford Press (2002)

31. Florida, R.: The rise of the creative class. Basic Books, New York (2002)

32. Kitayama, S., Ishii, K., Imada, T., Takemura, K., Ramaswamy, J.: Voluntary settlement and the spirit of independence: Evidence from Japan's '"Northern Frontier".' J. Pers. Soc. Psychol. **91**, 369–384 (2006)

33. Nisbett, R.E.: The geography of thought: How Asians and Westerners think differently. . . and why. New York: Free Press (2003)

34. Hofstede, G.: Culture's consequences: Comparing values, behaviors, institutions, and organizations across nations, 2nd edn. Sage, Thousand Oaks, CA (2001)

35. Magnusson, A.: An overview of epidemiological studies on seasonal affective disorder. Acta Psychiatr. Scand. **101**, 176–184 (2000)

36. Okawa, M., Shirakawa, S., Uchiyama, M., Oguri, M., Kohsaka, M., Mishima, K.: Seasonal variation of mood and behaviour in a healthy middle-aged population in Japan. Acta Psychiatr. Scand. **94**, 211–216 (1996)

37. Legaspi, R., Xu, W., Konishi, T., Wada, S., Ishikawa, Y.: Multidimensional analysis of sense of agency during goal pursuit. In: Proceedings of the 30th ACM Conference on User Modeling, Adaptation and Personalization, 34–47 (2022)

38. Bryman, A., Bell, E.: Business Research Methods. Oxford University Press, USA (2007)

Me Versus Them: Exploring the Perception of Susceptibility to Persuasion in Oneself and Others in Online Gambling

Deniz Cemiloglu[1]([✉]), Emily Arden-Close[1], Sarah E. Hodge[1], Nan Jiang[1], and Raian Ali[2]

[1] Faculty of Science and Technology, Bournemouth University, Poole, UK
{dcemiloglu,eardenclose,shodge,njiang}@bournemouth.ac.uk
[2] College of Science and Engineering, Hamad Bin Khalifa University, Ar-Rayyan, Qatar
raali2@hbku.edu.qa

Abstract. Perceived persuasiveness, an individual's acknowledgement of the system's influence on the self, may affect users' response to persuasion attempts. Existing research mainly focused on systems where persuasion supports a desired behaviour, e.g., a healthy lifestyle. Studies have also considered how people perceive persuasion in themselves but not in others. In this paper, we conducted an online survey and explored users' perception of susceptibility to persuasion in themselves and in others, taking online gambling as an example domain. We further examined how player attributes may influence their perception of susceptibility. A total of 250 participants (age range 18–75, 127 female) completed the online survey. Findings showed that susceptibility to the different persuasive design techniques differed significantly, with participants reporting the highest susceptibility to in-game rewards. Females were significantly more likely than males to report higher susceptibility to all of the persuasive design categories, and problem gamblers had higher susceptibility scores for all the persuasive design categories compared to other groups. There was a discrepancy between self-reported susceptibility scores and susceptibility scores that participants assigned to others. For each persuasive design category, participants assigned higher susceptibility scores to others compared to themselves. Moreover, the difference between self-reported susceptibility and susceptibility scores assigned to others was significantly higher for males and for all the persuasive design categories, non-problem gamblers exhibited a much greater discrepancy between the two compared to other groups. More research is required to determine whether the perception of susceptibility to persuasive design techniques is related to other individual or domain-specific factors.

Keywords: Perceived Persuasiveness · Persuasive Design Techniques · Online Gambling

1 Introduction

Persuasive systems are defined as "computerised software or information systems designed to reinforce, change or shape attitudes or behaviours or both without using

J. Ham et al. (Eds.): PERSUASIVE 2023, LNCS 13832, pp. 369–388, 2023.
https://doi.org/10.1007/978-3-031-30933-5_24

coercion or deception" [1, p.486]. Persuasive systems are typically grouped into two categories: behavioural change support systems (BCSS), in which users utilise technology to modify their behaviour or attitude to attain a pre-defined goal [2], and systems that utilise technology to persuade users [3]. Typical examples of BCSS applications are those that promote positive behaviours such as physical activity, personal well-being, and energy savings [4–6]. The second category includes online platforms that utilise persuasive interfaces to boost user engagement, such as social networks, gaming, and online gambling platforms.

Typically, the effectiveness of persuasive systems is measured in terms of their persuasiveness, which refers to a system's persuasive capacity to induce behaviour change [7]. Perceived persuasiveness, "the individual's subjective evaluation of the system and its impact on the self" [8, p.5], was suggested to be a significant factor in determining users' engagement with persuasive systems [8, 9]. Various studies have been conducted to evaluate users' self-reported susceptibility to persuasive design techniques and how culture, age, and gender may influence their susceptibility levels [9–13]. Current research, however, mostly centres on behavioural change support systems, in which users employ technology intentionally to alter their behaviour to achieve a pre-defined objective. To our knowledge, little to no research has been conducted on perceived susceptibility to persuasive design techniques in which persuasive design is not administered by the users but rather employed by the technology provider to persuade users to engage with online platforms, whether for legitimate or for questionable reasons.

Persuasive interfaces intended to maximise user engagement may induce or accelerate psychological and cognitive mechanisms related to addictive behaviour [14]. Thus, users' perception of susceptibility to persuasive design techniques may influence how they interact with potentially addictive platforms. Those who engage in addictive behaviours have the tendency to resort to denial (i.e., being assured that there is no problem to be fixed) [15] or to illusory superiority cognitive bias (i.e., having an inflated sense of own skills relative to others) to resolve discomfort they experience from having conflicting beliefs and actions [16]. Moreover, according to protection motivation theory [17], an individual's self-protective behaviours in the face of a threat are shaped by their threat appraisal (i.e., the perceived severity of the threat, the perceived probability of the threat harming the individual, the perceived reward linked to threat) and their coping appraisal (i.e., response efficacy, self-efficacy, and the response costs). Accordingly, the development and maintenance of addiction or addiction-type behaviour for the user may relate to incorrect beliefs about the dangers associated with the behaviour or underestimating the probability of dangers happening to them even when they know about the related risks [18]. Individuals who engage with online platforms in an addictive manner may be more prone to underestimating their susceptibility to persuasive design techniques compared to others, and player characteristics may also influence this. It is argued that those who attempt to quit an undesired behaviour would strive to mentally separate themselves from that behaviour's stereotypical characterisation [19]. However, when individuals engage in downward social comparison to defend their self-esteem and mood (i.e., comparing themselves to others who they perceive are doing worse than them) [20], such distancing may be hindered. This can, in return, further reinforce the undesired behaviour [21].

With the growth of the online gambling industry, persuasive interfaces have become a crucial component of the gambling experience. For example, online gambling platforms reward players with casino bonuses, offer rehearsal options with demo games and ease gambling with auto-spin functions. While debates exist on whether social networks or online gaming platforms may cause addiction, gambling disorder is recognised by DSM-5 [22] as a disorder. People with gambling disorder may face serious consequences that can compromise their health, relationships, and finances [23]. Studies show that erroneous beliefs (i.e., perceived skill, biased recall, superstition, incorrect perceptions of randomness) are a risk factor in online gambling and may contribute to the increased prevalence of gambling disorder [24, 25]. Prior research has indicated that people with gambling disorder tend to have more erroneous beliefs regarding gambling than social gamblers. Also, it was reported that males have more cognitive distortions than females when assessed by Gambling Related Cognitions Scale (GRCS) [26], and higher levels of cognitive distortion was observed to be a strong predictor of gambling disorder [27].

In this paper, we explore users' perception of susceptibility to persuasive design techniques in themselves and in others through an online survey. We take online gambling as an example domain where persuasion might lead users to the undesired behaviour of problem gambling. We restrict the scope of the research to persuasive design techniques used in games of pure chance, such as roulette, and exclude games, such as sports betting and poker in which player engagement can be influenced by knowledge and experience [28]. We further analyse how factors such as gender and addiction level may influence the perception of susceptibility to persuasive design techniques in oneself and in others.

In this study, we address the following research questions within the context of online gambling platforms.

RQ1: How susceptible do players believe they are to persuasive design techniques?

RQ2: What are the effects of gender and gambling addiction level on players' self-reported susceptibility to persuasive design techniques?

RQ3: Is there a difference between how susceptible people think they are to persuasive design techniques and how susceptible they think others are?

RQ4: What are the effects of gender and addiction level on the mismatch between self-reported susceptibility to persuasive design techniques and susceptibility assigned to others?

The remainder of the paper is organised as follows. In Sect. 2, we summarise the research methodology, and in Sect. 3, we report the study results. In Sect. 4, we discuss the findings and the limitations of our study.

2 Method

2.1 Participants

A total of 250 participants (age range 18–75, 123 male) were recruited to the online survey through Prolific™ (www.prolific.co), an established online research participant recruitment platform. Participants who regularly bet online on slot or roulette games in the past 12 months were recruited. Additional eligibility requirements were being aged over 18 years, fluency in English, and residing in the U.K.

2.2 Questionnaire Design

The questionnaire was designed using Qualtrics™ (https://www.qualtrics.com), a web-based survey platform. The data was collected as part of a larger study. Full details of the survey and procedure are reported in [29].

In the first part of the questionnaire, participants were asked about their gambling experience (e.g., the number of online gambling accounts and time spent on gambling sites per week). The 9-item Problem Gambling Severity Index (PGSI) was used to assess problem gambling severity [30, 31]. The scale includes items related to gambling behaviour and experienced adverse consequences due to gambling on a 4-point scale: 0 never; 1 = sometimes; 2 = most of the time; 3 = almost always. The standard cut-points are 0 = non-problem gambler; 1–2 = low-risk gambler; 3–7 = moderate-risk gambler; and 8 and more = problem gambler. The PGSI has high internal consistency and test-retest reliability rate and is widely employed in gambling research [32–34]. For our sample, Cronbach's Alpha was 0.93, indicating excellent internal consistency.

The second part of the questionnaire presented participants with 13 persuasive design techniques used in online gambling platforms through explanation cards. Before developing the explanation cards, we conducted a literature review to identify the persuasive design techniques utilised in online platforms. The analysis was guided by criteria set by the Persuasive Systems Design model (PSD) [1] and informed by Cialdini's work on principles of persuasion [35] and McCormack and Griffiths's work on structural and situational characteristics of internet gambling [36]. The main persuasive design techniques employed in online gambling platforms were identified by analysing seven gambling websites from six different operators with the biggest market share in the U.K. online gambling and betting market [37]. Freely accessible information on the website's homepage, casino page, slot page, roulette page, game information sections and promotion page were analysed. Due to membership limitations, we examined the game interface of one of seven online gambling platforms. We note here that most gambling operator sites rely on similar techniques developed and offered by the same major online gambling service providers. This analysis also guided the development of the illustrative material for the study. The 13 persuasive design techniques included in the study are categorised in Table 1.

Table 1. Persuasive design techniques presented in the study.

Persuasive Design Technique	Definition in The Context of Online Gambling
Primary Task Support	
Reduction	Persuades players to have continuous/uninterrupted interaction with the game by reducing the effort and actions needed to gamble
Self-Monitoring	Persuades players to interact with the game by providing the ability to track and evaluate gambling performance

(continued)

Table 1. (*continued*)

Persuasive Design Technique	Definition in The Context of Online Gambling
Rehearsal	Persuades players to interact with games by providing the ability to gamble without having to experience it in a real-world setting (i.e., without betting real money)
Dialogue Support	
Praise	Persuades players to interact with games by expressing approval or admiration via words, images, symbols, and sounds
In-game Rewards	Persuades players to gamble by giving something in return when the players perform a target behaviour set by the gambling platform
Reminders	Persuades players to interact with the gambling platform by reminding them about gambling
Social Support	
Social Norms	Persuades players to interact with the gambling platform by showing how the majority acts
Social Facilitation	Persuades players to interact with the gambling platform by showing how other players are engaging in the same activity simultaneously
Competition	Persuades players to gamble by stimulating players to compete against themselves or each other
System Credibility Support	
Authority	Persuades players to interact with the gambling platform by promoting statements or norms of authority figures
Other	
Scarcity	Persuades players to interact with the gambling platform by emphasising rarity and exclusivity or by underlining possible losses of missing such an advantage
In-game Control Elements	Persuade players to gamble by stimulating their perceived control over betting outcomes
Near Misses	Persuade people to gamble by implying that the win is missed marginally by just a symbol and is around the corner

The Persuasion Knowledge Model [38] was utilised as the primary reference model for determining the content of the explanation cards to demonstrate each technique. The explanation cards contained information about the persuader's intention, tactic and the psychological mediators associated with the persuasive technique (i.e., information on why the technique is persuasive). The cards also provided information on the risks of interacting with the persuasive technique, which was adopted from the informed consent theory [39]. Prior research was utilised to derive conclusions about how persuasive design techniques may encourage problem gambling [14]. One example of a persuasive design technique explanation card is shown in the Appendix. In the study, the face validity of the explanation cards was considered. The explanation cards' completeness, validity, and clarity were evaluated by two responsible gambling officials, four academics, and one ex-problem gambler.

2.3 Data Collection

Bournemouth University Research Ethics Committee approved the study, and the data was collected during the first two weeks of December 2021. Participants were invited to participate in an online survey that explored the impact of persuasive design techniques used in online gambling platforms on player engagement. The link to the anonymous survey was provided to those who met the inclusion criteria. Before commencing the questionnaire, participants were required to read the participant information sheet and provide informed consent. Participants were informed that they could opt out of the study at any time. After answering questions about their gambling experience, participants were instructed to read each explanation card carefully and answer questions for each persuasive design technique. On a 5-point Likert scale (1 = extremely unlikely, and 5 = extremely likely), participants were asked how much they thought they could be influenced by the persuasive design technique and how much they thought the same persuasive design technique could influence others. To lessen the effects of fatigue and habituation, the 13 persuasive design technique explanation cards were shown in a random order [40]. Eligible participants were compensated for their participation.

2.4 Data Analysis

Data was analysed using SPSS version 28. Non-parametric tests were used as the data was not normally distributed. Friedman test was used to explore the differences in susceptibility to different persuasive design techniques. Pairwise comparisons were performed with a Bonferroni correction for multiple comparisons. Mann-Whitney's U, Kruskal-Wallis H and Wilcoxon signed-rank tests were used on ordinal data to analyse group differences [41].

3   Results

3.1 Participant Demographics

Table 2 summarises participant characteristics.

Table 2. Participant characteristics.

N	250	Education (%)	
Age: M(SD)	36 (10.4)	Compulsory school education completed	14.8
Age: Range	18 – 75	Vocational training	6
Gender: Males (%)	123 (49.2)	College	23.6
Females (%)	125 (50)	University degree	40.4
Gambling Days Per Week: M(SD)	2.8 (1.9)	Postgraduate qualification (e.g., MSc, PhD)	15.2
Number of Online Gambling Accounts (%)		Employment (%)	
1 account	9.6	Full-time employment	62.4
2 accounts	23.6	Part-time employment	14.4
3 accounts	23.2	Self-employed	6
4 accounts	7.2	Unemployed	2.8
5 accounts	5.6	On sick leave	1.6
6 or more accounts	30.8	Student	5.6
Problem Gambling Severity Index (%)		Retired	0.4
Non-problem gambler	17.6	Homemaker	6
Low-risk gambler	25.6	Other	0.8
Moderate-risk gambler	29.2		
Problem gambler	27.6		

3.2 RQ1: Players' Self-reported Susceptibility to Persuasive Design Categories and Techniques

Participants were asked how much they thought they could be influenced by persuasive design techniques with a 5-point Likert scale (1 = extremely unlikely, and 5 = extremely likely). The overall self-reported mean susceptibility scores for the persuasive design categories and standard deviations are displayed in Fig. 1. A Friedman test showed that susceptibility to persuasive design categories differed significantly between categories, $\chi2(4) = 305$, $p < .001$. Significance was set at $p = 0.005$ using a Bonferroni correction as we conducted multiple tests. Post hoc analysis revealed that susceptibility to the dialogue support category (M:3.8, SD:0.8) was significantly higher than susceptibility to the other persuasive design categories, and susceptibility to system credibility support (M:2.6, SD:1.2) was significantly lower than susceptibility to the other persuasive design categories.

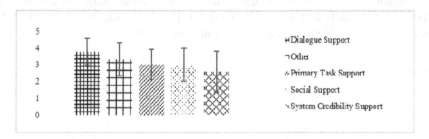

Fig. 1. Mean score for susceptibility to each persuasive design category

As shown in Fig. 2, when examined individually, out of the 13 persuasive design techniques presented in the study, participants mainly reported susceptibility to in-game rewards (M:4.2, SD:0.9), reminders (M:3.9, SD:1.0) and near misses (M:3.4, SD:1.3). In contrast, participants reported the lowest susceptibility to social norms (M:2.9, SD:1.2), competition (M:2.9, SD:1.3) and authority (M:2.6, SD:1.2). A Friedman test revealed that susceptibility to persuasive design techniques differed significantly by technique, $\chi 2(12)$ = 528, p < .001. Significance was set at $p = 0.0009$ using a Bonferroni correction as we conducted multiple tests. Susceptibility to in-game rewards was significantly higher than other persuasive design techniques except reminders. Susceptibility to authority was significantly lower than other persuasive design techniques except self-monitoring, social norms, and competition.

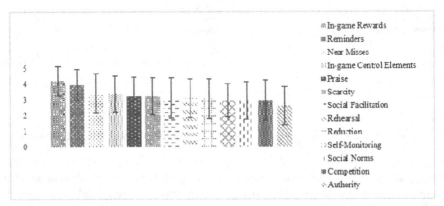

Fig. 2. Mean score for susceptibility to each persuasive design technique

3.3 RQ2: Effect of Gender and Addiction Level on Players' Self-reported Susceptibility

3.3.1 Gender Effect

Mann-Whitney U-test was used to determine gender differences in self-reported player susceptibility to persuasive design categories presented in the study. The comparison between females and males is shown in Table 3. Females were significantly more likely than males to report higher susceptibility to all of the persuasive design categories.

Table 3. Gender differences concerning susceptibility to each persuasive design category.

Gender Females Mean Rank	Sum of Ranks	Males Mean Rank	Sum of Ranks	Mann-Whitney's U	Z	P
Primary Task Support	138.0	17245.5	110.8	13630.5	6004.5	−3.0	0.003
Dialogue Support	136.4	17048.5	112.4	13827.5	6201.5	−2.7	0.008
Social Support	140.7	17584.0	108.1	13292.0	5666.0	−3.6	< .001
System Credibility Support	135.1	16891.5	113.7	13984.5	6358.5	−2.4	0.015
Other	139.6	17452.0	109.1	13424.0	5798.0	−3.4	< .001

When examined individually, Mann-Whitney U-test revealed that females were significantly more likely than males to report susceptibility to self-monitoring (p = < .001), praise (p = < .001), social norms (p = < .001), social facilitation (p = 0.004), competition (p = 0.01), authority (p = 0.01), scarcity (p = 0.006), in-game control elements (p = 0.01), and near miss technique (p = < .001).

3.3.2 Problem Gambling Severity Effect

The Kruskal-Wallis H test was used to determine differences in self-reported player susceptibility to persuasive design categories by problem gambling severity. Pairwise comparisons were performed using Dunn's procedure [42]. Significance was set at $p = 0.008$ using the Bonferroni correction for multiple tests. As indicated in Table 4, post hoc analyses revealed statistically significant differences between PGSI groups with regard to susceptibility to persuasive design categories. Problem gamblers had higher susceptibility mean ranks for all the persuasive design categories.

Table 4. Problem gambling severity difference concerning susceptibility to each persuasive design technique.

Persuasive Design Category	Mean Ranks	Dunn's Pairwise Comparison	(adj. p-value)
Primary Task Support			
A. Non-problem gambler	115.3		

(continued)

Table 4. (*continued*)

Persuasive Design Category	Mean Ranks	Dunn's Pairwise Comparison	(adj. p-value)
B. Low-risk gambler	103.2	B-D	0.004
C. Moderate-risk gambler	131.7		
D. Problem gambler	146.1		
Kruskal-Wallis H Test		χ^2 (3) = 13.3, p = 0.004	
Dialogue Support			
A. Non-problem gambler	104.4	A-D	0.005
B. Low-risk gambler	103.1	B-D	<0.001
C. Moderate-risk gambler	136.3		
D. Problem gambler	148.3		
Kruskal-Wallis H Test		χ^2 (3) = 18.8, p = < 0.001	
Social Support			
A. Non-problem gambler	112.8	A-D	0.005
B. Low-risk gambler	93.9	B-D	<0.001
C. Moderate-risk gambler	128.9		
D. Problem gambler	159.3		
Kruskal-Wallis H Test		χ^2 (3) = 29.2, p = < 0.001	
System Credibility Support			
A. Non-problem gambler	98.7	A-D	<0.001
B. Low-risk gambler	98.8	B-D	<0.001
C. Moderate-risk gambler	134.1		
D. Problem gambler	158.2		
Kruskal-Wallis H Test		χ^2 (3) = 31.8, p = < 0.001	
Other			
A. Non-problem gambler	102.6	A-D	0.001
B. Low-risk gambler	108.5	B-D	0.001
C. Moderate-risk gambler	124.6		
D. Problem gambler	156.8		
Kruskal-Wallis H Test		χ^2 (3) = 21.2, p = < 0.001	

Non-problem gambler (n:44), Low-risk gambler (n:64), Moderate-risk gambler (n:73), Problem gambler (69)

The test statistic is adjusted for ties

When examined individually, problem gamblers had the highest susceptibility mean ranks across all persuasive design techniques except rehearsal and reminder. Moderate-risk gamblers had the highest susceptibility mean ranks for rehearsal and reminder techniques.

3.4 RQ3: Self-reported Susceptibility vs Susceptibility Assigned to Others

Participants were asked how much they thought they could be influenced by the persuasive design technique and how much they thought the same persuasive design technique could influence others with a 5-point Likert scale (1 = extremely unlikely, and 5 = extremely likely). A Wilcoxon signed-rank test was conducted to compare participants' self-reported susceptibility to persuasive design categories and how they perceive susceptibility in other players. As shown in Table 5, for all persuasive design categories, there was a statistically significant difference between the self-reported susceptibility scores and the susceptibility scores they assigned to others. For each persuasive design category, most participants assigned higher susceptibility scores to others compared to themselves. Thus, participants assigned greater susceptibility to persuasive design categories in other players.

Table 5. Self-reported susceptibility versus perceived susceptibility of others to persuasive design categories.

Persuasive Design Category	N	Mean Ranks	Sum of Ranks	Z	P
Primary Task Support					
Negative Ranks	12[a]	28	336.5	−10.614[x]	<.001
Positive Ranks	152[b]	86.8	13193.5		
Ties	86[c]				
Total	250				
Dialogue Support					
Negative Ranks	44[d]	48.6	2140.5	−10.366[x]	<.001
Positive Ranks	170[e]	122.7	20864.5		
Ties	36[f]				
Total	250				
Social Support					
Negative Ranks	19[g]	41.3	785	−11.125[x]	<.001
Positive Ranks	175[h]	103.6	18130		
Ties	56[i]				
Total	250				

(continued)

Table 5. (*continued*)

Persuasive Design Category	N	Mean Ranks	Sum of Ranks	Z	P
System Credibility Support					
Negative Ranks	6[j]	42	252	−10.409[x]	<.001
Positive Ranks	144[k]	76.9	11073		
Ties	100[l]				
Total	250				
Other					
Negative Ranks	29[m]	53.4	1549	−10.334[x]	<.001
Positive Ranks	169[n]	107.4	18152		
Ties	52[o]				
Total	250				

a. Primary Task_Others < Primary_Task_Me

b. Primary_Task_Others > Primary_Task_Me

c. Primary_Task_Others = Primary_Task_Me

d. Dialogue_Support_Others < Dialogue_Support_Me

e. Dialogue_Support_Others > Dialogue_Support_Me

f. Dialogue_Support_Others = Dialogue_Support_Me

g. Social_Support_Others < Social_Support_Me

h. Social_Support_Others > Social_Support_Me

i. Social_Support_Others = Social_Support_Me

j. System Credibility_Support_Other < Credibility_Support_Me

k.System Credibility_Support_Other > Credibility_Support_Me

l. System Credibility_Support_Other = Credibility_Support_Me

m. Other_Others < Others_Me

n. Other_Others > Others_Me

o. Other_Others = Others_Me
x. Based on negative ranks

3.5 RQ4: Effect of Gender and Addiction Level on the Mismatch Between Self-reported Susceptibility and Susceptibility Assigned to Others

3.5.1 Gender Effect

Mann-Whitney U-test was used to determine the gender effect concerning the difference between the self-reported susceptibility scores and susceptibility scores assigned to others. As shown in Table 6, the difference between self-reported susceptibility and susceptibility scores assigned to others was significantly different between males and females for three of the categories.

Table 6. Gender differences regarding the mismatch between susceptibility scores (me versus others).

	Mann-Whitney U	Wilcoxon W	Z	Asymp. Sig. (2-tailed)
Primary Task Support	7203.0	14829.0	−0.9	0.379
Dialogue Support*	6201.5	13827.5	−2.7	0.008
Social Support	6942.0	14568.0	−1.3	0.182
System Credibility Support*	6396.0	14022.0	−2.4	0.016
Other*	6092.5	13718.5	−2.9	0.004

Table 7 shows the difference between the self-reported susceptibility scores and susceptibility scores assigned to others. For dialogue support, system credibility support, and the other category, males had a significantly higher mismatch in their perception than females.

Table 7. Gender differences regarding self-reported susceptibility versus susceptibility assigned to others (Mean score).

	Gender Male Self	Others	Difference	Female Self	Others	Difference
Primary Task Support	2.9	3.5	0.7	3.2	3.8	0.5
Dialogue Support*	3.6	4.3	0.6	4	4.3	0.4
Social Support	2.8	3.6	0.9	3.3	4	0.7
System Credibility Support*	2.4	3.5	1.1	2.8	3.6	0.8
Other*	3.1	4	0.9	3.6	4.1	0.5

*Significant at the 0.05 level

Female (n:125), Male (n:123)

When examined individually, out of the 13 persuasive design techniques presented in the study, the difference between self-reported susceptibility and susceptibility scores assigned to others was significantly higher for males for praise ($p = < .01$), social norms ($p = 0.003$), authority ($p = 0.01$), scarcity ($p = < 0.001$), and near misses ($p = 0.001$).

3.5.2 Problem Gambling Severity Effect

Kruskal-Wallis H test was used to determine differences between the self-reported susceptibility scores and susceptibility scores assigned to others by problem gambling severity. Pairwise comparisons were performed using Dunn's procedure [42]. Significance was set at $p = 0.008$ using Bonferroni correction for multiple tests. As shown in Table 8, the difference between self-reported susceptibility and susceptibility scores assigned to others was significantly different between PGSI groups for all persuasive design categories.

Table 8. Problem gambling severity difference regarding the mismatch between susceptibility scores (me versus others).

	Kruskal-Wallis H	df	Asymp. Sig
Primary Task Support*	17.6	3	0.001 lePara>
Dialogue Support*	20.5	3	<0.001
Social Support*	27.7	3	<0.001
System Credibility Support*	14.6	3	0.002
Other*	22.8	3	<0.001

Table 9 shows the difference between self-reported and susceptibility scores assigned to others. For all the persuasive design categories, the difference between self-reported susceptibility and susceptibility scores assigned to others was higher for non-problem gamblers and low-risk gamblers compared to other groups.

Table 9. Problem gambling severity difference regarding self-reported susceptibility versus susceptibility assigned to others (Mean score).

| | PGSI | | | | | | | | | | | |
| | Non-problem gambler | | | Low-risk gambler | | | Moderate-risk gambler | | | Problem gambler | | |
	Self	Others	Difference	Self	Others	Difference	Self	Others	Difference	Self	Others	Difference
Primary Task Support*	2.9	3.8	0.9	2.8	3.5	0.7	3.1	3.7	0.6	3.3	3.6	0.3
Dialogue Support*	3.5	4.3	0.8	3.5	4.3	0.7	3.9	4.3	0.4	4.1	4.3	0.3
Social Support*	2.8	3.8	1.0	2.6	3.8	1.2	3.1	3.8	0.7	3.5	3.9	0.4
System Credibility Support*	2.1	3.5	1.3	2.1	3.3	1.1	2.8	3.6	0.9	3.2	3.7	0.5
Other*	3.0	4.0	1.0	3.1	3.9	0.8	3.4	4.1	0.7	3.8	4.1	0.4

Non-problem gambler (n:44), Low-risk gambler (n:64), Moderate-risk gambler (n:73), Problem gambler (69).

When examined individually, the difference between self-reported susceptibility and susceptibility scores assigned to others was higher for non-problem gamblers for all 13 persuasive design techniques presented in the study compared to other groups.

4 Discussion

In the present study, we explored players' perception of susceptibility to persuasive design techniques in oneself and others by taking online gambling as an example domain.

With respect to self-reported susceptibility to persuasive design techniques, our findings showed that susceptibility to the dialogue support category was significantly higher, with players reporting the highest susceptibility to in-game rewards. This finding contradicts earlier research suggesting that reward is the least effective persuasive design technique in the health domain after customisation [43]. Such a difference in the findings may be attributable to domain differences since extrinsic motivation could be more associated with gambling [44], whereas intrinsic motivation could be more associated with having a healthy lifestyle [45]. Also, people who gamble online may be more exposed to in-game rewards such as cash bonuses and free spins. Regarding gender effect, the findings suggested that females were significantly more likely than males to demonstrate higher susceptibility to all persuasive design categories. Previous studies also reported that males and females varied greatly in their persuadability, with females being more susceptible to the majority of persuasive design techniques [43, 46]. In line with previous research, the difference between genders may be owing to the effect of conventional gender norms, in which women think they must adopt a more submissive role (i.e., adaptive, receptive to influence) and men think they must adopt a more dominant role (i.e., rigid, resistance to change) [47, 48].

Concerning the influence of problem gambling severity, problem gamblers reported higher susceptibility to all the persuasive design categories compared to other PGSI groups. It has been suggested that people are more susceptible to influence when they have conflicting goals, are under stress, cannot resist their urges and lack self-control [49]. Because people with high problem gambling severity show the aforementioned characteristics, their high susceptibility scores could be related to these constructs. Also, people who are forthcoming about the problematic nature of their gambling behaviour may also be more honest about their persuasion vulnerability, resulting in high susceptibility scores. Another interpretation could be problem gamblers emphasising their high persuadability as a means of justifying their problematic relationship with gambling.

In terms of the mismatch between self-reported susceptibility and susceptibility assigned to others, participants assigned higher susceptibility scores to others than to themselves for each persuasive design category. Individuals' underestimation of their own vulnerability to online phishing attempts is comparable with the findings of this study [50, 51]. People may have this mismatch in perception as a result of denial and self-deception since they may denigrate others in order to maintain their self-image [11, 52]. Regarding gender effect, males had a significantly higher mismatch than females for dialogue support, system credibility support, and the other category. One explanation for this difference could be *the confidence gap* [53]. Research shows that although there is no discernible qualitative difference between male and female performances, males tend to exaggerate their abilities and performance, while women tend to underestimate them [54, 55]. Lastly, findings showed that for all the persuasive design categories, non-problem gamblers had a significantly higher mismatch between the self-reported susceptibility scores and susceptibility scores assigned to others compared to other PGSI groups. This finding contradicted previous studies which claimed that misperception of chance and probability are predictors of problem gambling [24, 25, 27].

We identified issues that may affect the validity of the study and must be considered when evaluating the findings. The study measured the perception of susceptibility to persuasive design techniques in oneself and others by self-report. As mentioned in [56], perceived persuasiveness may not always predict actual engagement with persuasive design techniques. Also, due to the use of a Likert scale to measure perceived persuasiveness in the current study, participants did not have the option to pick "zero influence" when reporting susceptibility. Therefore, the study does not report an exact score of persuasiveness. Future research could employ perceived persuasiveness scales such as the four-item scale for measuring persuasiveness [57] or the 15 items Persuasive Potential Questionnaire (PPQ) [58]. In addition, future studies might examine the relationship between perceived and actual susceptibility to persuasive design techniques utilised in potentially addictive technologies. The generalisability of the findings may have been affected as only participants from the United Kingdom were recruited. Future research needs to explore how the player's perception of susceptibility to persuasive design techniques may vary by cultural context. For example, it has been suggested that people from collectivist cultures may be more prone to social support techniques than those from individualist cultures because the former places a higher importance on group membership [59]. In exploring the perception of susceptibility to persuasive design techniques, online gambling was selected as an example domain. The gambler profile may not be indicative of the broader user susceptibility to persuasive systems in other domains. Future research should examine susceptibility to persuasive design techniques in other domains that utilise persuasive interfaces, such as social networks or online gaming.

5 Conclusion

The findings of this study increase awareness about the perception of susceptibility to persuasive interfaces, how player attributes may influence this, and what can be done to mitigate this impact. It is currently unknown if erroneous beliefs regarding addiction contribute to the onset of addictive behaviour or is a by-product of such activity [55, 60]. Thus, applying social-norms interventions and correcting the perception regarding the influence of persuasive design techniques may serve as both a preventive and corrective approach in the domain of addictive technologies. Moreover, by taking a different approach, persuasion profiling [61] might be utilised to identify vulnerable user groups that show high susceptibility to certain persuasive design techniques. By such profiling, vulnerable users could be given the opportunity to opt out of persuasive design techniques. More research is required to investigate if the perception of susceptibility to persuasive design techniques may be associated with factors other than gender and addiction level, such as cognitive capacity [9] or personality qualities [50, 62].

Acknowledgment. This work has been partly supported by Kindred Group – Division of Responsible Gaming and Research, through a match-funded PhD project titled "Explainable Persuasion for Persuasive Interfaces: The Case of Online Gambling".

Appendix

(See Fig. 3).

REDUCTION

People are naturally wired to choose the path of least "effort".
The reduction technique persuades players to have continuous
/uninterrupted interaction with the game by reducing the effort to
gamble. Therefore, requiring less behaviour affordances by the player.

EXAMPLE

Auto-play enables a repetitive play by spinning the reels consecutively
and automatically without requiring the player to press any buttons.

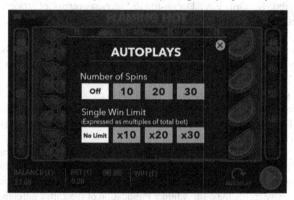

POTENTIAL IMPACT ON
PROBLEM GAMBLING

Reducing steps to gamble, in certain cases may,

- **speed up the decision-making process making
  it hard to reflect on behavior.**

- **make it difficult to resist impulses.**

Fig. 3. Example persuasive design technique explanation card

References

1. Oinas-Kukkonen, H., Harjumaa, M.: Persuasive systems design: key issues, process model, and system features. Commun. Assoc. Inf. Syst. **24**(1), 28 (2009)
2. Oinas-Kukkonen, H.: A foundation for the study of behavior change support systems. Pers. Ubiquit. Comput. **17**(6), 1223–1235 (2013)
3. Spahn, A.: And lead us (not) into persuasion…? Persuasive technology and the ethics of communication. Sci. Eng. Ethics **18**(4), 633–650 (2012)
4. Langrial, S., Lehto, T., Oinas-Kukkonen, H., Harjumaa, M., Karppinen, P.: Native mobile applications for personal well-being: a persuasive systems design evaluation. In: PACIS 2012 Proceeding (2012)
5. Oyebode, O., Ndulue, C., Alhasani, M., Orji, R.: Persuasive mobile apps for health and wellness: a comparative systematic review. In: Gram-Hansen, S., Jonasen, T., Midden, C. (eds.) Persuasive Technology. Designing for Future Change. PERSUASIVE 2020. LNCS, vol. 12064. Springer, Cham (2020). https://doi.org/10.1007/978-3-030-45712-9_13
6. Graml, T., Loock, C.-M., Baeriswyl, M., Staake, T.: Improving residential energy consumption at large using persuasive systems. In: Proceedings of the 19th European Conference on Information Systems Elektronische Ressource 2011. Helsinki, Finland (2011)
7. Orji, R., Reilly, D., Oyibo, K., Orji, F.A.: Deconstructing persuasiveness of strategies in behaviour change systems using the ARCS model of motivation. Behav. Inf. Technol. **38**(4), 319–335 (2019)
8. Lehto, T., Oinas-Kukkonen, H., Drozd, F.: Factors affecting perceived persuasiveness of a behavior change support system. In: Thirty Third International Conference on Information Systems. Orlando (2012)
9. Shevchuk, N., Degirmenci, K., Oinas-Kukkonen, H.: Adoption of gamified persuasive systems to encourage sustainable behaviors: interplay between perceived persuasiveness and cognitive absorption. In: Proceedings of the 40th International Conference on Information Systems, ICIS 2019. Association for Information Systems (2019)
10. Oyibo, K., Vassileva, J.: Investigation of the moderating effect of culture on users' susceptibility to persuasive features in fitness applications. Information **10**(11), 344 (2019)
11. Oyibo, K., Orji, R., Vassileva, J.: The influence of culture in the effect of age and gender on social influence in persuasive technology. In: Adjunct Publication of the 25th Conference on User Modeling, Adaptation and Personalization (2017)
12. Orji, R., R.L. Mandryk, and J. Vassileva. *Gender, age, and responsiveness to Cialdini's persuasion strategies.* in *International Conference on Persuasive Technology.* 2015. Springer
13. Oyibo, K., Adaji, I., Orji, R., Olabenjo, B., Vassileva, J.: Susceptibility to persuasive strategies: a comparative analysis of Nigerians vs. Canadians. In Proceedings of the 26th Conference on User Modeling, Adaptation and Personalization (2018)
14. Cemiloglu, D., Naiseh, M., Catania, M., Oinas-Kukkonen, H., Ali, R.: The fine line between persuasion and digital addiction. In: Ali, R., Lugrin, B., Charles, F. (eds.) Persuasive Technology. PERSUASIVE 2021. LNCS, vol. 12684, pp. 289–307. Springer, Cham (2021). https://doi.org/10.1007/978-3-030-79460-6_23
15. Gorski, T.T.: Denial Management Counseling Professional Guide: Advanced Clinical Skills for Motivating Substance Abusers to Recover. Herald House/Independence Press, Independence (2000)
16. Festinger, L.: A Theory of Cognitive Dissonance, vol. 2. Stanford University Press, Redwood (1957)
17. Rogers, R.W.: A protection motivation theory of fear appeals and attitude change. J. Psychol. **91**(1), 93–114 (1975)

18. Orphanides, A., Zervos, D.: Rational addiction with learning and regret. J. Polit. Econ. **103**(4), 739–758 (1995)
19. Gibbons, F.X., Gerrard, M.: Predicting young adults' health risk behavior. J. Pers. Soc. Psychol. **69**(3), 505 (1995)
20. Wills, T.A.: Downward comparison principles in social psychology. Psychol. Bull. **90**(2), 245 (1981)
21. Gerrard, M., Gibbons, F.X., Lane, D.J., Stock, M.L.: Smoking cessation: social comparison level predicts success for adult smokers. Health Psychol. **24**(6), 623 (2005)
22. American Psychiatric Association, Diagnostic and statistical manual of mental disorders: DSM-5. Arlington, VA, 2013
23. Raylu, N., Oei, T.P.S.: Pathological gambling: a comprehensive review. Clin. Psychol. Rev. **22**(7), 1009–1061 (2002)
24. MacKay, T.-L., Hodgins, D.C.: Cognitive distortions as a problem gambling risk factor in Internet gambling. Int. Gambl. Stud. **12**(2), 163–175 (2012)
25. Jacobsen, L.H., Knudsen, A.K., Krogh, E., Pallesen, S., Molde, H.: An overview of cognitive mechanisms in pathological gambling. Nordic Psychol. **59**(4), 347–361 (2007)
26. Raylu, N., Oei, T.P.: The gambling related cognitions scale (GRCS): development, confirmatory factor validation and psychometric properties. Addiction **99**(6), 757–769 (2004)
27. Donati, M.A., Ancona, F., Chiesi, F., Primi, C.: Psychometric properties of the gambling related cognitions scale (GRCS) in young Italian gamblers. Addict. Behav. **45**, 1–7 (2015)
28. Bjerg, O.: Problem gambling in poker: money, rationality and control in a skill-based social game. Int. Gambl. Stud. **10**(3), 239–254 (2010)
29. Cemiloglu, D., Arden-Close, E., Hodge, S.E., Ali, R.: Explainable persuasion for interactive design: the case of online gambling. J. Syst. Softw. 111517 (2022)
30. Ferris, J.A., Wynne, H.J.: The Canadian problem gambling index. Canadian Centre on Substance Abuse Ottawa, ON (2001)
31. Ferris, J.A., Wynne, H.J. The Canadian problem gambling index: user manual. Canadian Centre on Substance Abuse (2001)
32. Currie, S.R., Hodgins, D.C., Casey, D.M.: Validity of the problem gambling severity index interpretive categories. J. Gambl. Stud. **29**(2), 311–327 (2013)
33. Holtgraves, T.: Evaluating the problem gambling severity index. J. Gambl. Stud. **25**(1), 105–120 (2009)
34. Calado, F., Griffiths, M.D.: Problem gambling worldwide: an update and systematic review of empirical research (2000–2015). J. Behav. Addict. **5**(4), 592–613 (2016)
35. Cialdini, R.B.: The science of persuasion. Sci. Am. **284**(2), 76–81 (2001)
36. McCormack, A., Griffiths, M.D.: A scoping study of the structural and situational characteristics of internet gambling. Int. J. Cyber Behav. Psychol. Learn. (IJCBPL) **3**(1), 29–49 (2013)
37. Mintel Report, Online Gambling and Betting-UK-December 2019. Mintel Group Ltd, 2019
38. Friestad, M., Wright, P.: The persuasion knowledge model: how people cope with persuasion attempts. J. Consum. Res. **21**(1), 1–31 (1994)
39. Faden, R.R., Beauchamp, T.L.: A History and Theory of Informed Consent. Oxford University Press, Oxford (1986)
40. Porter, S.R., Whitcomb, M.E., Weitzer, W.H.: Multiple surveys of students and survey fatigue. New Dir. Inst. Res. **2004**(121), 63–73 (2004)
41. Sheskin, D.J.: Handbook of Parametric and Nonparametric Statistical Procedures. Chapman and Hall/CRC, Boca Raton (2003)
42. Dunn, O.J.: Multiple comparisons using rank sums. Technometrics **6**(3), 241–252 (1964)
43. Orji, R.: Exploring the Persuasiveness of Behavior Change Support Strategies and Possible Gender Differences. BCSS@ PERSUASIVE, 2014, vol. 1153, pp. 41–57 (2014)

44. Back, K.-J., Lee, C.-K., Stinchfield, R.: Gambling motivation and passion: a comparison study of recreational and pathological gamblers. J. Gambl. Stud. **27**(3), 355–370 (2011)
45. Papacharisis, V., Simou, K., Goudas, M.: The relationship between intrinsic motivation and intention towards exercise. J. Hum. Mov. Stud. **45**(4), 377 (2003)
46. Orji, R., Mandryk, R.L., Vassileva, J.: Gender and persuasive technology: examining the persuasiveness of persuasive strategies by gender groups. Persuas. Technol. 48–52 (2014)
47. Eagly, A.H.: Sex differences in influenceability. Psychol. Bull. **85**(1), 86 (1978)
48. Broverman, I.K., Vogel, S.R., Broverman, D.M., Clarkson, F.E., Rosenkrantz, P.S.: Sex-Role Stereotypes: a current appraisal 1. J. Soc. Issues **28**(2), 59–78 (1972)
49. Roberts, J.A., Manolis, C.: Cooking up a recipe for self-control: the three ingredients of self-control and its impact on impulse buying. J. Mark. Theory Pract. **20**(2), 173–188 (2012)
50. Halevi, T., Lewis, J., Memon, N.: A pilot study of cyber security and privacy related behavior and personality traits. In: Proceedings of the 22nd International Conference on World Wide Web 2013 (2013)
51. Williams, E.J., Beardmore, A., Joinson, A.N.: Individual differences in susceptibility to online influence: a theoretical review. Comput. Hum. Behav. **72**, 412–421 (2017)
52. Fein, S., Spencer, S.J.: Prejudice as self-image maintenance: affirming the self through derogating others. J. Pers. Soc. Psychol. **73**(1), 31 (1997)
53. Kay, K., Shipman, C.: The confidence gap. The Atlantic **14**(1), 1–18 (2014)
54. Beyer, S.: Gender differences in the accuracy of self-evaluations of performance. J. Pers. Soc. Psychol. **59**(5), 960 (1990)
55. Garnett, C., Crane, D., West, R., Michie, S., Brown, J., Winstock, A.: Normative misperceptions about alcohol use in the general population of drinkers: a cross-sectional survey. Addict. Behav. **42**, 203–206 (2015)
56. Ciocarlan, A., Masthoff, J., Oren, N.: Actual persuasiveness: impact of personality, age and gender on message type susceptibility. In: Oinas-Kukkonen, H., Win, K., Karapanos, E., Karppinen, P., Kyza, E. (eds.) Persuasive Technology: Development of Persuasive and Behavior Change Support Systems. PERSUASIVE 2019. LNCS, vol. 11433. Springer, Cham (2019). https://doi.org/10.1007/978-3-030-17287-9_23
57. Drozd, F., Lehto, T., Oinas-Kukkonen, H.: Exploring perceived persuasiveness of a behavior change support system: a structural model. In: Bang, M., Ragnemalm, E.L. (eds.) Persuasive Technology. Design for Health and Safety. PERSUASIVE 2012. LNCS, vol. 7284. Springer, Berlin, Heidelberg (2012). https://doi.org/10.1007/978-3-642-31037-9_14
58. Meschtscherjakov, A., Gärtner, M., Mirnig, A., Rödel, C., Tscheligi, M.: The persuasive potential questionnaire (PPQ): challenges, drawbacks, and lessons learned. In: Meschtscherjakov, A., De Ruyter, B., Fuchsberger, V., Murer, M., Tscheligi, M. (eds.) Persuasive Technology. PERSUASIVE 2016. LNCS, vol. 9638. Springer, Cham (2016). https://doi.org/10.1007/978-3-319-31510-2_14
59. Orji, R.: Persuasion and Culture: Individualism-Collectivism and Susceptibility to Influence Strategies. PPT@ PERSUASIVE, vol. 1582, pp. 30–39 (2016)
60. Joukhador, J., Blaszczynski, A., Maccallum, F.: Superstitious beliefs in gambling among problem and non-problem gamblers: preliminary data. J. Gambl. Stud. **20**(2), 171–180 (2004)
61. Kaptein, M., Markopoulos, P., De Ruyter, B., Aarts, E.: Personalizing persuasive technologies: explicit and implicit personalization using persuasion profiles. Int. J. Hum. Comput. Stud. **77**, 38–51 (2015)
62. Halko, S., Kientz, J.A.: Personality and persuasive technology: an exploratory study on health-promoting mobile applications. In: Ploug, T., Hasle, P., Oinas-Kukkonen, H. (eds.) Persuasive Technology. PERSUASIVE 2010. LNCS, vol. 6137. Springer, Berlin, Heidelberg (2010). https://doi.org/10.1007/978-3-642-13226-1_16

Credibility in Persuasive Systems: A Systematic Review

Felix N. Koranteng[1,2](✉), Uwe Matzat[1], Isaac Wiafe[3], and Jaap Ham[1]

[1] Department of Industrial Engineering and Innovation Sciences, Eindhoven University of Technology, Eindhoven, The Netherlands
f.n.k.m.koranteng@tue.nl
[2] Accra Institute of Technology, Accra, Ghana
[3] Department of Computer Science, University of Ghana, Legon-Accra, Ghana

Abstract. Credibility of systems is important in Human-Computer Interaction (HCI) and when designing persuasive systems. Still, the role of credibility in the design of persuasive systems remains unclear. To date, there has not been a systematic review examining the concept of credibility in persuasive systems. Therefore, this study presents a systematic literature review of primary empirical studies published from 2011 to 2020 that examined credibility within the context of persuasive systems. A total of 41 publications were reviewed. Overall, the results highlight the trends of credibility research, the theoretical frameworks that have been used to examine credibility, the research methods used in credibility studies, as well as the antecedents, and consequents of credibility in persuasive systems' context. Majority of the reviewed studies pursued a correlational research approach as opposed to testing theories through experimental studies. While giving little attention to user characteristics and how they influence the relationship between credibility and its antecedents, existing studies have also barely examined the influence of system features as antecedents. Based on these findings, we argue that existing theoretical frameworks do not provide adequate directions for implementing credibility features in system design. Future research should therefore conduct more experimental studies and provide directions for how credibility features can be implemented in system design.

Keywords: Credibility · Persuasive Systems Design · Human-Computer Interaction

1 Introduction

Credibility perceptions and persuasion have long been closely tied together. Many theories and empirical studies that attempt to determine how to effectively persuade people have either mentioned or referenced credibility [1, 2]. Both classical (e.g., [3]) and recent studies (e.g., [4]) have demonstrated the need for credibility in persuasion. In the past two decades, researchers have investigated how various persuasive design principles and concepts affect the effectiveness of persuasive systems.

© The Author(s), under exclusive license to Springer Nature Switzerland AG 2023
J. Ham et al. (Eds.): PERSUASIVE 2023, LNCS 13832, pp. 389–409, 2023.
https://doi.org/10.1007/978-3-031-30933-5_25

Particularly, scholars have investigated whether persuasive systems that are perceived to be highly credible (i.e., have increased credibility features) will be more effective in changing attitudes and behaviors or vice versa. However, to the best of our knowledge, no study attempts to analyze and summarize existing credibility studies to enlighten the relevant readership on the effectiveness of credibility as a persuasive concept. Therefore, this study seeks to review primarily published empirical findings from 2011 to 2020 inclusive, in persuasive systems (including behavior change support systems and transformational systems) research. This study attempts to answer the following specific research questions (RQ):

i.   RQ1: What are the current trends in credibility research?
ii.   RQ2: Which theoretical frameworks have been employed in existing studies?
iii. RQ3: Which research methods have been employed to study credibility?
iv.   RQ4: What factors have been identified as antecedents (determinants) and/or consequents of (determined by) credibility?

The findings from the analysis showed an inconsistent yearly trend in the number of credibility studies published per year and existing credibility-related studies are predominantly (32% of the total number of studies reviewed) conducted in the Health and Wellbeing domain. Many (83%) of the studies were published as conference proceedings and mostly in the International Conference of Persuasive Technology. This review also uncovered that many of the theoretical frameworks that have been employed to study credibility in persuasive systems context are limited and do not provide detailed theoretical and practical design directions for implementing system credibility features. The analysis further revealed that the correlational research and/or survey approach dominated the research methods/design used by existing studies to examine credibility. Relatedly, many of the antecedents and consequents of credibility were found to be perceptual variables with little causal relationships.

1.1 Background

Technology is not neutral, and it influences user behaviors [4]. Likewise, some computer systems are designed to intentionally induce attitudinal and behavioral changes in users. That is, persuasive systems are systems that are designed to shape, reinforce, or change behaviors or attitudes without deception or coercion [4]. This includes Behavior Change Support Systems (BCSS) and transformational systems. A crucial factor that affects the persuasiveness of a persuasive system is its credibility.

Credibility has been defined differently in many research areas with dozens of concepts such as reliability, fairness, accuracy, objectivity, and believability [5]. Studies have also assessed credibility in terms of the characteristics of the persuasive source, the message structure, and the medium through which the message is conveyed [6]. In other studies, three levels of credibility assessment have emerged: construct, heuristics, and interaction [7]. The construct level denotes an individual's conceptualization of credibility. The heuristics level pertains the general rules of thumb used to make credibility judgments. The interaction level signifies specific object attributes that form the bases for credibility judgment. Despite the relatively differently conceptualization of credibility, many persuasive systems researchers agree that there are at least two key dimensions of credibility: trustworthy and expertise [4, 8]. Similarly, Oinas-Kukkonen and Harjumaa [4] outlined seven design principles (including trustworthiness, expertise, surface credibility, real world feel, authority, third party endorsement and verifiability) for credibility support.

Generally, credible sources are believable when compared with sources lacking credible properties [9]. People attribute less risk to believable people [10], and thus, perceive them favorably, which may lead to a continuous association. Aside from favorable judgments, believability is a cue that induces or catalyzes persuasive effects [11]. In persuasive systems, credibility judgments have been found to influence users' positive evaluations of persuasive systems [12]. Also, users' positive evaluation of a system is an important determinant of user adoption and usage of the system [13]. And only when a system is adopted and used, can the system influence and change user behavior. Thereby, the effectiveness of persuasive systems for behavior change depends on users' perceived credibility [14]. In sum, credibility and persuasion are intimately tied [15]. As such, credibility should be prioritized in persuasive systems design.

However, there is a lack of a detailed understanding of the concept of credibility as a persuasive concept [13, 14]. Worst of all, no study has collated and analyzed studies within persuasive systems' research that prioritizes credibility to enlighten readers on its role. Rather, existing reviews have focused on persuasive systems in general and their effectiveness in application domains such as education [18], health and wellbeing [19], physical activity [13, 17], mobile e-commerce [21], green information systems [22], and sustainability [20, 21]. Others that have attempted to analyze specific persuasive design principles overlooked credibility. For example, Almutari and Orji [25] performed a systematic literature review on the effectiveness of social influence principles for promoting physical activity. Ghanvatkar, Kankanhalli, and Rajan [26] and Ghanvatkar, Kankanhalli, and Rajan [27] reviewed the effectiveness of the personalization principle in reducing sedentary behavior.

Meanwhile, current scholarly investigations and findings of credibility studies in persuasive systems research are fragmented. Thus, evidence from existing studies does not provide adequate direction for designing and evaluating credible persuasive systems. It is important that the trends and current issues in credibility research are summarized. This will enable researchers to make impactful contributions. Specifically, this review sets a research agenda, by answering specific questions that will enlighten credibility researchers on the research areas that require attention.

2 Method

This study employed Kitchenham and Charters' [28] guidelines for performing systematic reviews to systematically identify and review empirical studies that discussed credibility in persuasive systems. Kitchenham and Charters' [28] guidelines provide well-defined and adequate methods for performing systematic reviews in information systems and have been applied successfully to conduct systematic reviews in persuasive systems [26, 27] and other domains such as artificial intelligence [31] and transportation [32]. The guidelines consist of the planning phase, conducting (implementation) phase, and documenting (results/findings) phase. The following subsections describe how the guidelines were implemented at each phase.

2.1 Planning Phase

2.1.1 Search and Inclusion Criteria

A preliminary search was performed to select the most appropriate databases, search terms, and search period before the main literature search commenced. The preliminary search was performed on Google Scholar due to the ease and simplicity of performing quick searches across a broad number of databases. Five databases were selected based on their reoccurrence in the search results.

These included ScienceDirect, ACM Digital Library, SpringerLink, IEEE Xplore, and Wiley Online Library. With a similar approach, six key search terms were derived; (i) "Credibility AND Persuasive Technology", (ii) "Credibility AND Persuasive Technologies", (iii) "Credibility AND Persuasive Systems", (iv) "Credibility AND Behavior Change Support Systems", (v) "Credibility AND Behavior Change Systems", and (vi) "Credibility AND Transformational Systems"[1]. The search was conducted to reveal papers that had any of the search terms in their content, abstract, or title. Ideally, it would have been more appropriate to review all credibility studies in persuasive systems context, however, this is impossible due to the volume of information received from the preliminary search. Therefore, the search period was limited to 2011 to 2020 inclusive.

For the inclusion criteria, papers with titles that suggested that they were within the domain of persuasive systems were included. Moreover, only empirical publications from peer-reviewed journals and conferences were considered. Additionally, papers with abstracts that suggested a relationship with any of the search terms were included. Lastly, papers with contents that discuss credibility in the context of persuasive systems were selected.

2.2 Conducting (Implementation) Phase

2.2.1 Study Selection and Data Extraction

Based on the search criteria, a search was performed by searching for the aforementioned six search terms on all five databases. The search period limited results to studies published from 2011 to 2020 inclusive. A total of 953 studies were retrieved after the search. The inclusion criteria were then applied to select the appropriate studies. Figure 1 summarizes the processes involve in the planning and conducting phases.

---

[1] *Notes: Articles that spelt behavior as "behaviour" and did not include any of the other search terms may not have been included in the search results.*

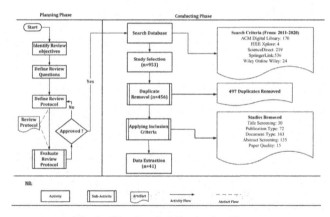

Fig. 1. Planning and Conducting Phases

A total of forty-one (41) publications (see Appendix Two) were selected based on the study selection processes. The selected publications (n = 41) were then read thoroughly by two (2) of the reviewers and the relevant information for answering the review questions were documented. The review team met to discuss the findings and resolve disparities in the analysis. In resolving contradictory findings, two (2) other reviewers assessed the relevant articles and the majority's view were accepted. The results are presented next.

3   Results

The results of this review are categorized based on the review questions as follows: (i) trends in credibility research, (ii) the theoretical frameworks (iii) research methods used in credibility research, and (iv) the antecedents and consequents of credibility.

3.1   Trends in Credibility Research

3.1.1   Publication Trends by Year

Figure 2 shows the yearly trends of credibility studies. From the results, it is observed that a relatively large proportion of credibility studies (n = 26) were published after 2015 compared to before 2015 (n = 15). After 2015, there was a decline in the number of studies from eight (8) publications in 2016 to three (3) publications in 2017, followed by an increase to nine (9) publications in 2018. The number of credibility studies has since been relatively low (i.e., three (3) publications each in 2019 and 2020).

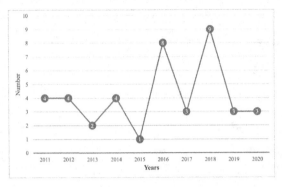

Fig. 2. Publication Trends by Year

3.1.2 Publication Trends by Research Domain

Further, the results showed that credibility studies in the context of persuasive systems spanned thirteen (13) different domains. These domains were categorized based on (1) the stated context of the study and/or (2) the characteristics of the respondents used to conduct the study. From the results, one (1) of the studies was unclassified (i.e., the reviewers were unable to place the study into a particular domain). The majority (13) of the studies were from the Health and Wellbeing domain, followed by the E-Commerce (6) and Education (6) domains. The other research application domain identified by the review are summarized in Fig. 3.

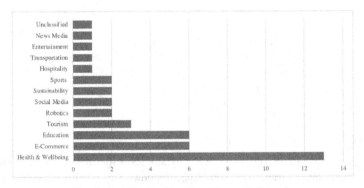

Fig. 3. Publication Trends by Research Domain

3.1.3 Publication Trends by Publication Outlet

The publication houses or outlets that publish credibility studies were also reviewed. The reviewed studies (n = 41) were published across three (3) publication outlets: ACM Digital Library, Elsevier, and Springer. None of the reviewed studies were from either IEEE or Wiley Online Library. This may suggest that the opportunities provided by IEEE and Wiley Online Library for publishing credibility-related research in persuasive systems are not recognized by researchers, or perhaps researchers perceived these outlets as not suitable for credibility research. The majority (23 of 41) of the papers were published in Springer, followed by ACM Digital Library (12) and ScienceDirect (6). Again, majority (34 of 41) of the publications were published as conference papers in twenty (20) different conference proceedings whereas seven (7) different journals published seven (7) journal articles. Out of the thirty-four (34) conference papers, 32% were published in the International Conference on Persuasive Technologies. The summary of the publication types of credibility studies is shown in Table 2 in Appendix One.

3.2 Research Methods Used in Credibility Research

From the analysis, three (3) main research methods prevailed: quantitative studies (22) ranked first, followed by qualitative studies (14), and then the mixed methods (5) approach. Figure 4 presents a summary of the results. Further, the specific research design approaches adopted in examining credibility were also analyzed. The analysis revealed that majority (73%, n = 41) of the reviewed studies adopted a correlational research design approach whereas the remaining studies (27%, n = 41) adopted an experimental research design approach.

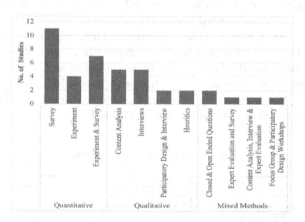

Fig. 4. Credibility Studies Publication Trends by Research Methods

3.3 Theoretical Framework Used in Credibility Research

This review discovered that many credibility studies in the domain of persuasive systems (49%, n = 41) did not report or discuss any well-substantiated theoretical perspective or guideline that explains the relationships among the proposed constructs (see Fig. 5). For the remaining studies, nine (9) theoretical foundations were discussed. These were the Persuasive Systems Design (PSD), Prominence Interpretation Theory (PIT), Elaboration Likelihood Model (ELM), Signaling Theory (ST), Cialdini's Principles (CP), Fogg's Credibility Guidelines (FCG), Unified Theory of Acceptance and Use of Technology and Technology Acceptance Model (UTAUT), Technology Acceptance Model (TAM), Perceived Persuasiveness Questionnaire (PPQ).

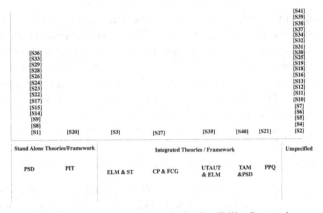

Fig. 5. Theoretical Frameworks in Credibility Research

3.4 Antecedents and Consequents of Credibility

The review identified several factors that have been studied to promote or determine credibility. First, the proposed antecedents of credibility were identified and grouped based on how they are defined, described, and/or explained in the reviewed studies. Based on the analysis and results, a three-tier level of credibility antecedents emerged: constructs, design principles, and system features. The construct level is the most abstract. The constructs are fundamental assumptions, notions, or phenomena [7] that influence credibility judgments. A total of seven (7) constructs were proposed as credibility antecedents but one (1) (i.e., Perceived Anonymity) was found to be insignificant. The significant antecedents and the related studies are shown in Table 1.

Table 1. Antecedents of Credibility

ANTECEDENT	STUDY
Constructs	
Dialogue Support	S8,S9,S17,S26
Review Credibility	S26
Product Credibility	S26
Perceived Sense of Achievement	S40
Perceived Ease of Use	S40
Perceived Social Presence	S3
Design Principles	
Trustworthiness	S2,S11,S13,S14,S23,S25,S27,S29,S30,S33,S34,S36,S37,S39
Surface Credibility	S7,S14,S18,S20,S25,S27,S29,S30,S36
Real World Feel	S20,S23,S25,S27,S29,S30,S36
Expertise	S11,S14,S16,S25,S27,S33,S36
Authority	S14,S21,S25,S29,S31,S36
Third-Party Endorsement	S23,S29,S30,S31,S36
Vefiability	S14,S25,S29,S36
Context Appropraiteness	S2,S13,S27
Tailoring	S6,S33,S38
Personalization	S6,S33,S38
Novelty	S2
Gazing with Emotions	S19
System Features	
History Page	S40
Privacy Policy Page	S5

Also, design principles are general rules of thumb or system requirements that imply how a system can be designed to influence user perceptions [4, 31]. Overall, twelve (12) design principles were reported by the studies to affect participants' credibility perceptions (see Table 1). Almost half (48%) of the studies that evaluated which design principles influence credibility (n = 32), examined the trustworthiness design principle. Lastly, the system feature level refers to the constituent components of a system [33] that may affect user perceptions. That is, how specific system features incite credibility judgements were also analyzed in some studies. A total of five (5) system features were proposed (i.e., About Us, Contact, History, Financial Information, and Privacy Policy features) but only two (2) (i.e., History and Privacy Policy) were identified as significant antecedents.

With regards to the analysis of the consequents of credibility, 49% (n = 41) of the reviewed studies proposed and evaluated factors determined by credibility. Perceived Persuasiveness (8) ranked as the most often predicted consequent of credibility. Studies that proposed Perceived Persuasiveness, Perceived Effectiveness, Continuous Engagement, Purchase Intention, Perceived Entertainment, and Engagement found evidence indicating that credibility had an effect. For brevity, the summary of the significant and non-significant consequents is shown in Fig. 6.

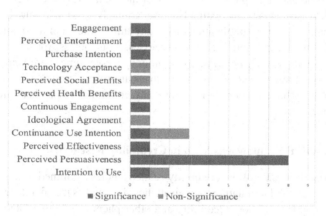

Fig. 6. Consequents of Credibility

4 Discussion

This current paper aimed to review published empirical credibility studies in the context of persuasive systems from 2011 to 2020 inclusive. The paper sort to analyze trends in credibility research, the theoretical frameworks, and research methods used in credibility research, and the antecedents and consequents of credibility. This section will discuss the results of the review with reference to the review questions.

4.1   RQ1: Trends of Credibility Research

The credibility research trends that were analyzed in this review focused mainly on yearly publications, the domain of application, and the nature (i.e., type) of publication. The results showed fluctuations in the yearly publication trends of credibility studies with some years recording higher numbers and others recording low numbers. Generally, compared to findings from other systematic reviews that focused on specific persuasive principles/concepts (e.g., [25]), the number of credibility-related studies published per year is relatively low. This may suggest a lower interest in credibility as a persuasive concept in persuasive systems design.

Consistent with Wiafe et., al. [34], majority of the studies reviewed were from the health and wellbeing domain. This confirms that likewise many persuasive systems studies, credibility-related studies target healthy behavior and the general wellbeing of people. Although many studies focused on health and wellbeing, the findings of this review uncovered a growing interest in the application of persuasive techniques in e-commerce. Indeed, studies have shown that persuasive techniques (e.g., personalization and social influence) are influential in increasing customer satisfaction [35] and loyalty [36]. Hence, with the increased competition among e-commerce vendors, persuasive techniques provide valid means for satisfying and retaining customers.

In the case of the nature of publication, many of the studies reviewed were conference paper publications. This is interesting because, arguably, journal articles are often ranked higher than conference publications by many universities and academic institutions during tenure and promotion review processes. Nonetheless, for the scientific community (such as the persuasive systems community), conferences are vehicles for faster dissemination of research ideas, getting feedback and recognition as well as socialization [37]. This may have accounted for why many credibility researchers preferred conference publications.

4.2   RQ2: Theoretical Frameworks Used in Credibility Research

The results showed that many of the credibility-related studies examined in this review did not provide a theoretical foundation for their studies. This makes it difficult for readers to understand and appreciate how credibility and other phenomena are related. Theories connect the credibility concept to existing knowledge [38] and therefore form the basis for hypothesis development. Thus, theories enable readers to interpret why certain hypotheses are proposed. This increases their understanding of the findings. It is therefore imperative for future studies to outline the underlining theoretical argumentation to broaden the existing knowledge scope.

The analysis of the studies that reported the use of theoretical foundations indicated a very uneven distribution of the frequency of theory use. A possible explanation may be that those that are frequently used are perceived as better theories or meet certain quality criteria. For example, many of the identified theories in this review such as Fogg's Behavioral Model and Prominence Interpretation Theory do not directly provide information on how to build credible persuasive systems. And others (e.g., ELM, ST, UTAUT) are borrowed theories from other domains, and may not always be appropriate for examining persuasive systems. On the other hand, the most frequently appearing theory in this review, the Persuasive Systems Design (PSD), attempts to provide a holistic approach that is directly applicable when designing and evaluating persuasive systems [4].

However, the PSD framework has been criticized on several grounds, and its ability to explain some relationships has been questioned by some studies [14, 37]. To be precise, the PSD does not describe how to implement its design principles and strategies in particular use contexts [40]. It is unclear how certain persuasive principles can be implemented in different contexts to achieve optimal results. Most important, some studies have also pointed out the difficulty in identifying specific system features for implementing certain PSD design principles (e.g., rehearsal) [41]. This makes it difficult to implement suitable design possibilities. In sum, the PSD provides a fundamental theoretical foundation but does not fulfill the current credibility research requirements in persuasive systems. In response to this, researchers must adapt and extend the existing theories to address the identified limitations. Possibly, an extension of the PSD framework that provides a catalog of how design principles can be implemented with systems features and their effectiveness in different contexts could be proposed.

4.3 RQ3: Research Methods Used in Credibility Research

The predominant use of correlational research design was observed from the results. These findings suggest the need for credibility researchers to focus their attention on conducting more experimental studies. This is because, with an appropriate theory, experimental studies provide stronger evidence to explain cause and effect in relationships as compared to correlational studies [42]. Many potential alternative explanations of associations between phenomena are ruled out in experimental studies such as randomized controlled trials.

Moreover, apart from the general research design, many studies in this area relied on self-reported measurements and depended on validated question items from other empirical studies for measuring credibility. However, this approach may result in divergent measurement items that foster the misconception surrounding credibility. Moreover, relying exclusively on self-reported data has limitations. That is, although the self-report technique is fast and less expensive, the reliability of the responses is challenged by respondents' potential memory biases, dishonesty, and misinterpretation of the question items [43].

Some studies have shown a possible relationship between physiological reactivity and persuasive concepts [44]. More crucially, physiological reactions can be used to reveal behaviors that users may not be consciously aware of, that they may want to divulge (such as perceived socially undesirable behavior), or that they may not be able to verbalize [45]. Yet, our understanding of users' physiological reactions to credibility cues is still infant. Future studies could examine users' physiological reactions (e.g., cardiovascular, and facial muscle) to specific credibility cues and their effectiveness in explaining credibility.

4.4   RQ4: Antecedents and Consequents of Credibility

Based on the results, this review proposed a three-tier level of credibility antecedents comprising: constructs, design principles, and system features. This review further postulates that the identified levels of credibility antecedents are interdependent. Precisely, the current review argues that system features are implemented to project design principles, and design principles originate from constructs. As indicated earlier, construct are fundamental assumptions, notions, or phenomena. In line with this description, dialogue support which is defined as the degree to which a persuasive system provides feedback to its users [4], for example, was categorized as a construct antecedent of credibility. Oinas-Kukkonen and Harjumaa [4] outlined seven (7) design principles (e.g., rewards, praise, and reminders) under dialogue support. Relatedly, reward, praise, and reminder design principles can be implemented in system design by integrating virtual trophies, pop-up messages, and e-mail respectively as system features (see [46]).

This implies that without system features the practical implementation of credibility antecedents in a system is impossible. However, this study's findings show that system features are the least studied. Many credibility antecedents that have been examined in the reviewed literature (i.e., constructs and design principles) are thus theoretical rather than practical. It appears there is a lack of clear examples of system features that implement the constructs and design principles. Perhaps, that is why many persuasive systems designers direct less attention to credibility in their designs. Indeed, Merz and Ackermann [17] concluded that many studies do not consider surface credibility in their system design because of the lack of practical examples.

This current study as an initial step proposes a mapping of the identified system feature antecedents (i.e., history page and privacy policy) to their corresponding design principles (i.e., expertise and trustworthiness). In reference to Oinas-Kukkonen and Harjumaa [4], the expertise design principle outlines that the system should provide information that shows knowledge, experience, and competence. Trustworthiness is concerned with providing information that is fair, truthful, and unbiased [4]. In this study's view, the expertise requirement can be fulfilled through a history feature and trustworthiness with a privacy policy. Through a history feature accessible to a user, a company can provide information about its existence, core operations, and specialties. The privacy policy feature may in turn outline how a company handles personal data and privacy issues of the client, thus, highlighting the company's trustworthiness [47]. Because this proposal is just an initial step, future studies could direct more attention to how certain credibility-related system features align with associated design principles.

Additionally, the results showed that credibility had both significant and insignificant effects on the proposed consequents. Many of these studies that explored the credibility effect employed correlational research design, therefore, it is difficult to interpret the causation of these results. Future studies could investigate these findings further. Meanwhile, there is stronger evidence in support of the recorded significant effect of credibility on Engagement and Perceived Persuasiveness since experimental research design was employed in some of these investigations. More importantly, the results strengthen the existing argument of the relevance of credibility in improving persuasiveness. As indicated earlier, highly credible sources induce more persuasion than low-credible ones. This is because credible systems are perceived as dependable and reliable [48] and this reduces perceptions of risky and biases [7, 8]. In other words, systems with increased credibility cues influence people's behavior positively. Hence, the effectiveness of persuasive systems can be increased with increased credibility cues.

Moreover, the effect of credibility on certain constructs is characterized by some inconsistent findings. Particularly, whiles some studies reported a significant effect of credibility on Intention to Use and Continuance Use intention, other studies that measured these same constructs observed either no significant or negative non-significant effect of credibility. For instance, whereas S1 found a significant effect of credibility on Intention to Use, S15 did not find any supporting evidence. Similarly, S26 found a positive effect of credibility on Continuous Use Intention, however, S8 and S9 reported a negative, yet insignificant effect.

This could be due to the differences in how credibility or the proposed consequents (i.e., Intention to Use and Continuance Use Intention) were measured in the studies. Unfortunately, none of the studies reported how the concepts were measured. Also, the differences in the findings could be attributed to the differences in users' characteristics and the context within which the studies were conducted. For example, S26 was conducted in the E-Commerce domain whereas S8 and S9 were conducted in the Education and Health & Wellbeing domains respectively. Perhaps, credibility is perceived differently in these domains. Nonetheless, the findings reveal that the effects of credibility (e.g., on Intention to Use and Continuous Use Intentions) are far from understood. This requires future studies to examine these concepts in detail with particular emphasis on users and context. Investigations into how credibility could be effectively implemented for different users and contexts would be worthwhile.

5 Conclusion

This study provides a systematic summary and analysis of published empirical literature on credibility in persuasive systems' context from 2011 to 2020 inclusive. As research on the design of persuasive systems continues to expand, the findings from this current study will support researchers and designers in the design of credible persuasive systems. A key limitation of existing studies which was identified by this study is the overreliance on correlational research and self-reported measurements. For a rigorous impact assessment of the relationship between credibility and other phenomena, experimental research is preferable. Hence, future studies that examine credibility should focus on experimental research design. Likewise, alternate measurement techniques such as physiological reactivity could be implemented to augment self-reported measurement.

The specific impact of system feature antecedents of credibility was found to be the least examined. Perhaps, this is because of the inadequate appropriate theories that provide directions as to how credibility design features should be implemented in system design. Future studies could develop a catalog, that explains how credibility design principles can be implemented with system features. More importantly, futures could assess how users of different characteristics respond to different credibility antecedents and in different contexts. To summarize, this study is one of the first to systematically review the trends and current issues in credibility research. It directs attention to the role of credibility in persuasive systems design. This is important because users form positive attitudes and will continuously use a persuasive system when they perceived it to be credible.

Appendix One: Relevant Tables

Table 2. Publication Types in Credibility Research

Publication Type	Study	No.
Journal		
Communication Design Quarterly	[S20]	1
Electronic Commerce Research	[S5]	1
International Journal of Medical Informatics	[S5]	1
Information and Management	[S3]	1
Journal of Air Transport Management	[S4]	1
Journal of Medical systems	[S23]	1
Education and Information Technologies	[S25]	1
Conferences		
International Conference on Persuasive Technologies	[S2][S8][S9][S10][S13][S17][S19][S22][S24][S26][36][S39][S41]	13
Conference on User Modeling, Adaptation, and Personalization	[S6][31]	2
Conference on Human Factors in Computing Systems	[S37][S38]	2
African Human-Computer Interaction Conference	[S29]	1
IEEE International Conference on Human-Robot Interaction	[S16]	1
Australian Computer-Human Interaction Conference	[S32]	1
International Conference on Intelligent Virtual Agents	[S21]	1
International Conference on Computers in Management and Business	[S34]	1
International Language for Specific Purposes	[S27]	1
International Conference on Pervasive Computing Advances and Applications	[S28]	1
International Conference on Enterprise Information Systems	[S18]	1
Information and Communication Technologies in Tourism	[S11]	1
International Conference on HCI in Business	[S30]	1
International Working Conference on Transfer and Diffusion of IT	[S35]	1
ICT for a Better Life and a Better World	[S15]	1
International Conference on Computing and Information Technology	[S1]	1
International Conference on Human-Computer Interaction	[S40]	1
International Conference on Interactive Collaborative Learning	[S33]	1
Advances in Ergonomics in Design	[S12]	1
FIP TC13 Conference on Human-Computer Interaction	[S7]	1

Appendix Two: List of Reviewed Studies:

[S1] Boontarig, W., & Srisawatsakul, C. (2020, May). A Framework for Designing and Evaluating Persuasive Technology in Education. In International Conference on Computing and Information Technology (pp. 93-103). Springer, Cham.

[S2] Gamberini, L., Spagnolli, A., Nucci, M., DeGiuli, G., Villa, C., Monarca, V., & Leclerq, S. (2016, April). A gamified solution to brief interventions for nightlife well-being. In International Conference on Persuasive Technology (pp. 230-241). Springer, Cham.

[S3] Wagenknecht, T., Teubner, T., & Weinhardt, C. (2018). A Janus-faced matter—The role of user anonymity for communication persuasiveness in online discussions. Information & Management, 55(8), 1024-1037.

[S4] Díaz, E., & Martín-Consuegra, D. (2016). A latent class segmentation analysis of airlines based on website evaluation. Journal of Air Transport Management, 55, 20-40.

[S5] Díaz, E., Martín-Consuegra, D., & Estelami, H. (2016). A persuasive-based latent class segmentation analysis of luxury brand websites. Electronic Commerce Research, 16(3), 401-424.

[S6] Orji, R., Oyibo, K., & Tondello, G. F. (2017, July). A comparison of system-controlled and user-controlled personalization approaches. In Adjunct publication of the 25th conference on user modeling, adaptation and personalization (pp. 413-418).

[S7] Papachristos, E., & Avouris, N. (2011, September). Are first impressions about websites only related to visual appeal?. In IFIP Conference on Human-Computer Interaction (pp. 489-496). Springer, Berlin, Heidelberg.

[S8] Dabi, J., Wiafe, I., Stibe, A., & Abdulai, J. D. (2018, April). Can an enterprise system persuade? The role of perceived effectiveness and social influence. In International conference on persuasive technology (pp. 45-55). Springer, Cham.

[S9] Oduor, M., & Oinas-Kukkonen, H. (2017, April). Commitment devices as behavior change support systems: a study of users' perceived competence and continuance intention. In International Conference on Persuasive Technology (pp. 201-213). Springer, Cham.

[S10] Johnson, G., Taylor, W. D., Ness, A. M., Ault, M. K., Dunbar, N. E., Jensen, M. L., & Connelly, S. (2014, May). Credibility and interactivity: Persuasive components of ideological group websites. In International Conference on Persuasive Technology (pp. 143-154). Springer, Cham.

[S11] Tan, W. K., & Chang, Y. C. (2011). Credibility assessment model of travel information sources: An exploratory study on travel blogs. In Information and Communication Technologies in Tourism 2011 (pp. 457-469). Springer, Vienna.

[S12] Duczman, M., Brangier, E., & Thévenin, A. (2016). Criteria based approach to assess the user experience of driving information proactive system: integration of guidelines, heuristic mapping and case study. In Advances in Ergonomics in Design (pp. 79-90). Springer, Cham.

[S13] Gamberini, L., Nucci, M., Zamboni, L., DeGiuli, G., Cipolletta, S., Villa, C., ... & Spagnolli, A. (2018, April). Designing and testing credibility: the case of a serious game on nightlife risks. In International Conference on Persuasive Technology (pp. 213-226). Springer, Cham.

[S14] Neubeck, L., Coorey, G., Peiris, D., Mulley, J., Heeley, E., Hersch, F., & Redfern, J. (2016). Development of an integrated e-health tool for people with, or at high risk of, cardiovascular disease: The Consumer Navigation of Electronic Cardiovascular Tools (CONNECT) web application. International journal of medical informatics, 96, 24-37.

[S15] Hamid, N. A., Cheun, C. H., Abdullah, N. H., Ahmad, M. F., & Ngadiman, Y. (2019). Does persuasive E-commerce website influence users' acceptance and online buying behaviour? The findings of the largest E-commerce website in Malaysia. In ICT for a Better Life and a Better World (pp. 263-279). Springer, Cham.

[S16] Andrist, S., Ziadee, M., Boukaram, H., Mutlu, B., & Sakr, M. (2015, March). Effects of culture on the credibility of robot speech: A comparison between english and arabic. In Proceedings of the Tenth Annual ACM/IEEE International Conference on Human-Robot Interaction (pp. 157-164).

[S17] Drozd, F., Lehto, T., & Oinas-Kukkonen, H. (2012, June). Exploring perceived persuasiveness of a behavior change support system: a structural model. In International Conference on Persuasive Technology (pp. 157-168). Springer, Berlin, Heidelberg.

[S18] de Sousa, A. P., & Almeida, A. M. (2016). Habits and behaviors of e-health users: a study on the influence of the interface in the perception of trust and credibility. Procedia Computer Science, 100, 602-610.

[S19] Ruijten, P. A., Midden, C. J., & Ham, J. (2013, April). I didn't know that virtual agent was angry at me: Investigating effects of gaze direction on emotion recognition and evaluation. In International Conference on Persuasive Technology (pp. 192-197). Springer, Berlin, Heidelberg.

[S20] Everett, H. L. (2018). Is good enough good enough? negotiating web user value judgments of small businesses based on poorly designed websites. Communication Design Quarterly Review, 6(2), 41-56.

[S21] Kantharaju, R. B., De Franco, D., Pease, A., & Pelachaud, C. (2018, November). Is two better than one? Effects of multiple agents on user persuasion. In Proceedings of the 18th International Conference on Intelligent Virtual Agents (pp. 255-262).

[S22] Stibe, A., Oinas-Kukkonen, H., Bērziņa, I., & Pahnila, S. (2011, June). Incremental persuasion through microblogging: a survey of Twitter users in Latvia. In Proceedings of the 6th International Conference on Persuasive Technology: Persuasive Technology and Design: Enhancing Sustainability and Health (pp. 1-8).

[S23] Win, K. T., Hassan, N. M., Oinas-Kukkonen, H., & Probst, Y. (2016). Online patient education for chronic disease management: consumer perspectives. Journal of medical systems, 40(4), 88.

[S24] Kekkonen, M., Oinas-Kukkonen, H., Tikka, P., Jaako, J., Simunaniemi, A. M., & Muhos, M. (2018, April). Participatory Design of a Persuasive Mobile Application for Helping Entrepreneurs to Recover from Work. In International Conference on Persuasive Technology (pp. 172-183). Springer, Cham.

[S25] Engelbertink, M. M., Kelders, S. M., Woudt-Mittendorff, K. M., & Westerhof, G. J. (2020). Participatory design of persuasive technology in a blended learning course: A qualitative study. Education and information technologies, 1-24.

[S26] Adaji, I., & Vassileva, J. (2017, April). Perceived effectiveness, credibility and continuance intention in e-commerce: a study of Amazon. In International Conference on Persuasive Technology (pp. 293-306). Springer, Cham.

[S27] Mustafa, F. Y., Kahar, R., Bunari, G., Zakaria, M. H., & Habil, H. (2012). Persuasive elements in online direct response sales letters. Procedia-Social and Behavioral Sciences, 66, 391-401.

[S28] Faisal, S., Nor, A. A., & Abdullah, N. H. (2019). Persuasive System Design for Global Acceptance of Smartphone Apps. Procedia Computer Science, 152, 44-50.

[S29] Nkwo, M., & Orji, R. (2018, December). Persuasive technology in African context: deconstructing persuasive techniques in an African online marketplace. In Proceedings of the Second African Conference for Human Computer Interaction: Thriving Communities (pp. 1-10).

[S30] Chu, H. L., Deng, Y. S., & Chuang, M. C. (2014, June). Persuasive web design in e-Commerce. In International Conference on HCI in Business (pp. 482-491). Springer, Cham.

[S31] Nkwo, M., & Orji, R. (2019, June). Socially responsive ecommerce platforms: Design implications for online marketplaces in developing African nation. In Adjunct Publication of the 27th Conference on User Modeling, Adaptation and Personalization (pp. 57-62).

[S32] Pathmanathan, R., Pearce, J., Kjeldskov, J., & Smith, W. (2011, November). Using mobile phones for promoting water conservation. In Proceedings of the 23rd Australian Computer-Human Interaction Conference (pp. 243-252).

[S33] Cheong, C., Filippou, J., Cheong, F., Pirker, J., & Gütl, C. (2016, September). Using persuasive system design principles to evaluate two next generation digital learning environments. In International Conference on Interactive Collaborative Learning (pp. 255-268). Springer, Cham.

[S34] Elden, M., Cakir, S. Y., & Bakir, U. (2018, May). Website Persuasiveness in Sports Marketing: A Content Analysis of Websites of Turkish Sports Clubs. In Proceedings of the 2018 International Conference on Computers in Management and Business (pp. 92-96).

[S35] Yoganathan, D., & Kajanan, S. (2014, June). What drives fitness apps usage? An empirical evaluation. In International Working Conference on Transfer and Diffusion of IT (pp. 179-196). Springer, Berlin, Heidelberg.

[S36] Gram-Hansen, S. B., Rabjerg, M. F., & Hovedskou, E. K. B. (2018, April). What makes it persuasive?. In International conference on persuasive technology (pp. 16-27). Springer, Cham.

[S37] Choi, W. (2013). What makes online health information credible for older adults? An exploratory study. In CHI'13 Extended Abstracts on Human Factors in Computing Systems (pp. 2671-2676).

[S38] Kjeldskov, J., Skov, M. B., Paay, J., & Pathmanathan, R. (2012, May). Using mobile phones to support sustainability: a field study of residential electricity consumption. In Proceedings of the SIGCHI Conference on Human Factors in Computing Systems (pp. 2347-2356).

[S39] DiMuzio, E., & Sundar, S. S. (2012, June). Does a hyperlink function as an endorsement?. In International Conference on Persuasive Technology (pp. 268-273). Springer, Berlin, Heidelberg.

[S40] Guo, Y. (2020, July). Persuasive Design Strategy of Online Health Education for Elderly Adults Based on TAM Model. In International Conference on Human-Computer Interaction (pp. 269-281). Springer, Cham.

[S41] Colbert, M., Oliver, A., & Oikonomou, E. (2014, May). The effect of credibility of host site upon click rate through sponsored content. In International Conference on Persuasive Technology (pp. 56-67). Springer, Cham.

References

1. Petty, R.E., Cacioppo, J.T.: The elaboration likelihood model of persuasion. In: Communication and Persuasion, pp. 1–24. Springer, New York (1986). https://doi.org/10.1007/978-1-4612-4964-1_1

2. Tseng, S., Fogg, B.J.: Credibility and computing technology. Commun. ACM **42**(5), 39–44 (1999)

3. Hovland, C.I., Weiss, W.: The influence of source credibility on communication effectiveness. Public Opin. Q. **15**(4), 635–650 (1951). https://doi.org/10.1086/266350

4. Oinas-Kukkonen, H., Harjumaa, M.: Persuasive systems design: key issues, process model, and system features. Commun. Assoc. Inf. Syst. **24**(1), 28 (2009)

5. Self, C.: Credibility. In: Stacks, D.W., Salwen, M.B., Eds. An Integrated Approach to Communication Theory and Research, Routledge, pp. 449–470 (2014). https://doi.org/10.4324/9780203887011-37

6. Metzger, M.J., Flanagin, A.J., Eyal, K., Lemus, D.R., Mccann, R.M.: Credibility for the 21st century: integrating perspectives on source, message, and media credibility in the contemporary media environment. In: Kalbfleisch, P.J., Ed. Communication Yearbook, vol. 27, no. 1, Routledge, pp. 293–335 (2016). https://doi.org/10.1080/23808985.2003.11679029

7. Hilligoss, B., Rieh, S.Y.: Developing a unifying framework of credibility assessment: construct, heuristics, and interaction in context. Inf. Process. Manag. **44**(4), 1467–1484 (2008). https://doi.org/10.1016/J.IPM.2007.10.001

8. Fogg, B.J., Tseng, H.: The elements of computer credibility. In: Conference on Human Factors in Computing Systems - Proceedings, pp. 80–87 (1999). https://doi.org/10.1145/302979.303001

9. Pornpitakpan, C.: The persuasiveness of source credibility: a critical review of five decades. Evidence', J. Appl. Soc. Psychol. **34**(2), 243–281 (2004). https://doi.org/10.1111/J.1559-1816.2004.TB02547.X

10. Deshbhag, R.R., Mohan, B.C.: Study on influential role of celebrity credibility on consumer risk perceptions. J. Indian Bus. Res. **12**(1), 79–92 (2020). https://doi.org/10.1108/JIBR-09-2019-0264/FULL/XML

11. O'keefe, D.J.: Persuasion: theory and research. Sage Publications. Sage Publications., (2015)

12. Lehto, T., Oinas-Kukkonen, H.: Explaining and predicting perceived effectiveness and use continuance intention of a behaviour change support system for weight loss. Behav. Inf. Technol. **34**(2), 176–189 (2015)

13. Oyibo, K., Vassileva, J.: HOMEX: persuasive technology acceptance model and the moderating effect of culture. Front. Comput. Sci. **2**, 10 (2020). https://doi.org/10.3389/fcomp.2020.00010

14. Spagnolli, A., Chittaro, L., Gamberini, L.: Interactive persuasive systems: a perspective on theory and evaluation. Int. J. Hum. Comput. Interact. **32**(3), 177–189 (2016). https://doi.org/10.1080/10447318.2016.1142798

15. Rieh, S.Y., Danielson, D.R.: Credibility: a multidisciplinary framework. Ann. Rev. Inf. Sci. Technol. **41**(1), 307–364 (2007). https://doi.org/10.1002/ARIS.2007.1440410114

16. Matthews, J., Win, K.T., Oinas-Kukkonen, H., Freeman, M.: Persuasive technology in mobile applications promoting physical activity: a systematic review. J. Med. Syst. **40**(3), 1–13 (2016). https://doi.org/10.1007/s10916-015-0425-x

17. Merz, M., Ackermann, L.: Design principles of persuasive systems – review and discussion of the persuasive systems design model. In: AMCIS 2021 Proceedings, Aug. (2021). Accessed: 15 Feb 2022. https://aisel.aisnet.org/amcis2021/sig_hci/sig_hci/3

18. Murillo-Muñoz, F., et al.: Characteristics of a persuasive educational system: a systematic literature review. Appl. Sci. 2021, **11**(21), 10089 Oct. (2021). https://doi.org/10.3390/APP112110089

19. Oyebode, O., Ndulue, C., Alhasani, M., Orji, R.: Persuasive mobile apps for health and wellness: a comparative systematic review. In: Gram-Hansen, S.B., Jonasen, T.S., Midden, C. (eds.) PERSUASIVE 2020. LNCS, vol. 12064, pp. 163–181. Springer, Cham (2020). https://doi.org/10.1007/978-3-030-45712-9_13

20. Aldenaini, N., Oyebode, O., Orji, R., Sampalli, S.: Mobile phone-based persuasive technology for physical activity and sedentary behavior: a systematic review. Front. Comput. Sci. **2**, 19 (2020). https://doi.org/10.3389/FCOMP.2020.00019/BIBTEX

21. Adib, A., Orji, R.: A systematic review of persuasive strategies in mobile e-commerce applications and their implementations. In: Ali, R., Lugrin, B., Charles, F. (eds.) PERSUASIVE 2021. LNCS, vol. 12684, pp. 217–230. Springer, Cham (2021). https://doi.org/10.1007/978-3-030-79460-6_18

22. Shevchuk, N., Oinas-Kukkonen, H.: Exploring green information systems and technologies as persuasive systems: a systematic review of applications in published research. In: ICIS 2016 Proceedings, Dec. (2016). Accessed: 10 Feb 2022. https://aisel.aisnet.org/icis2016/Sustainability/Presentations/11

23. Schiefelbein, U.H., Pereira, W.B., de Souza, R.L., Lima, J.C.D., da Rocha, C.C.: The use of persuasive strategies in systems to achieve sustainability in the fields of energy and water: a systematic review. In: ICEIS 2019 - Proceedings of the 21st International Conference on Enterprise Information Systems, vol. 1, pp. 246–253, (2019). https://doi.org/10.5220/0007800202580265

24. Suruliraj, B., Nkwo, M., Orji, R.: Persuasive mobile apps for sustainable waste management: a systematic review. In: Gram-Hansen, S.B., Jonasen, T.S., Midden, C. (eds.) PERSUASIVE 2020. LNCS, vol. 12064, pp. 182–194. Springer, Cham (2020). https://doi.org/10.1007/978-3-030-45712-9_14

25. Almutari, N., Orji, R.: How effective are social influence strategies in persuasive apps for promoting physical activity? A systematic review. In: ACM UMAP 2019 Adjunct - Adjunct Publication of the 27th Conference on User Modeling, Adaptation and Personalization, Jun., pp. 167–172 (2019). https://doi.org/10.1145/3314183.3323855

26. Ghanvatkar, S., Kankanhalli, A., Rajan, V.: User models for personalized physical activity interventions: scoping review. JMIR mHealth and uHealth, vol. 7, no. 1. JMIR Publications Inc., p. e11098, Jan. 16, (2019). https://doi.org/10.2196/11098

27. Aldenaini, N., Orji, R., Sampalli, S.: How effective is personalization in persuasive interventions for reducing sedentary behavior and promoting physical activity: a systematic review. Undefined (2020)

28. Kitchenham, B., Charters, S.: Guidelines for performing systematic literature reviews in software engineering (2007)

29. Anagnostopoulou, E., Magoutas, B., Bothos, E., Schrammel, J., Orji, R., Mentzas, G.: Exploring the links between persuasion, personality and mobility types in personalized mobility applications. Lecture Notes in Computer Science (including subseries Lecture Notes in Artificial Intelligence and Lecture Notes in Bioinformatics), vol. 10171 LNCS, pp. 107–118 (2017). https://doi.org/10.1007/978-3-319-55134-0_9/TABLES/8

30. Qasim, M.M., Ahmad, M., Omar, M.: Persuasive strategies in mobile healthcare: a systematic literature review teamwork and its impact on productivity in Agile software development (ASD) view project. Article J. Eng. Appl. Sci. (2017). https://doi.org/10.3923/jeasci.2017.8706.8713

31. Wiafe, I., Koranteng, F.N., Obeng, E.N., Assyne, N., Wiafe, A., Gulliver, S.R.: Artificial intelligence for cybersecurity: a systematic mapping of literature. IEEE Access 8, 146598–146612 (2020). https://doi.org/10.1109/ACCESS.2020.3013145

32. Armah, Z.A., Wiafe, I., Koranteng, F.N., Owusu, E.: Speed monitoring and controlling systems for road vehicle safety: a systematic review. Adv. Transp. Stud. 56, 3–22 (2022)

33. Möller, F., Guggenberger, T.M., Otto, B.: Towards a method for design principle development in information systems. In: Hofmann, S., Müller, O., Rossi, M. (eds.) DESRIST 2020. LNCS, vol. 12388, pp. 208–220. Springer, Cham (2020). https://doi.org/10.1007/978-3-030-64823-7_20

34. Wiafe, I., Nakata, K.: Bibliographic analysis of persuasive systems: techniques; methods and domains of application, no. 068. Linköping University Electronic Press, pp. 61–64, Jun. 06 (2012)

35. Alhammad, M.M., Wiafe, I., Gulliver, S.R.: Exploring the impact of persuasive features on customer satisfaction levels of e-commerce websites based on the kano model. In: Ali, R., Lugrin, B., Charles, F. (eds.) PERSUASIVE 2021. LNCS, vol. 12684, pp. 178–192. Springer, Cham (2021). https://doi.org/10.1007/978-3-030-79460-6_14

36. Adaji, I., Vassileva, J.: Perceived effectiveness, credibility and continuance intention in e-commerce: a study of Amazon. In: International Conference on Persuasive Technology, pp. 293–306 (2017)

37. Fortnow, L.: ViewpointTime for computer science to grow up. Commun. ACM 52(8), 33–35 (2009). https://doi.org/10.1145/1536616.1536631

38. Udo-Akang, D.: Theoretical constructs, concepts, and applications. Am. Int. J. Contemp. Res. 2(9) (2012). Accessed: 31 Aug 2021. www.aijcrnet.com

39. Wiafe, I.: A unified approach to persuasive systems development. Int. J. Conc. Struct. Smart Appl. 1(2), 6–16 (2013). https://doi.org/10.4018/ijcssa.2013070102

40. Harjumaa, M., Muuraiskangas, S.: Building persuasiveness into information systems. Electron. J. Inf. Syst. Eval. 17(1), 23–35 (2014). Accessed: 05 Oct 2021. https://academic-publishing.org/index.php/ejise/article/view/193

41. Langrial, S., Oinas-Kukkonen, H., Lappalainen, P., Lappalainen, R.: Influence of persuasive reminders and virtual rehearsal on information systems for sleep deprivation. In: PACIS 2014 Proceedings, Jan. 2014, Accessed: 05 Oct 2021. https://aisel.aisnet.org/pacis2014/228

42. Davies, R.: From cross-sectional to longitudinal analysis. Anal. Soc. Polit. Change, 20–40 (2014). https://doi.org/10.4135/9781849208611.N2

43. Paulhus, D.L., Vazire, S.: The self-report method. In: Robins, R.W., Fraley, R.C., Krueger, R.F., (Eds) Handbook of Research Methods in Personality Psychology. The Guilford Press, pp. 224–239 (2007)

44. Spelt, H.A.A., Westerink, J.H.D.M., Ham, J., Ijsselsteijn, W.: Psychophysiological reactions to persuasive messages deploying persuasion principles. IEEE Trans. Affect. Comput. (2019). https://doi.org/10.1109/TAFFC.2019.2931689

45. Bell, L., Vogt, J., Willemse, C., Routledge, T., Butler, L.T., Sakaki, M.: Beyond self-report: a review of physiological and neuroscientific methods to investigate consumer behaviour. Front. Psychol., 1655 (2018). https://doi.org/10.3389/FPSYG.2018.01655

46. Lehto, T., Oinas-Kukkonen, H.: Persuasive features in web-based alcohol and smoking interventions: a systematic review of the literature. J. Med. Internet Res. **13**(3), e46 (2011). https://www.jmir.org/2011/3/e46, vol. 13, no. 3, p. e1559 (2011). https://doi.org/10.2196/JMIR.1559

47. Langrial, S., Lehto, T., Oinas-Kukkonen, H., Harjumaa, M., Karppinen, P.: Native mobile applications for personal wellbeing: a persuasive systems design evaluation, p. 93, (2012). https://doi.org/10.2/JQUERY.MIN.JS

48. van Esterik-Plasmeijer, P.W.J., van Raaij, W.F.: Banking system trust, bank trust, and bank loyalty. Int. J. Bank Market. **35**(1), 97–111 (2017). https://doi.org/10.1108/IJBM-12-2015-0195

Notifying Users: Customisation Preferences for Notifications in Health and Well-being Applications

Daniele Pretolesi[(✉)] [iD], Lenart Motnikar[iD], Bieg Till[iD], and Jakob Uhl[iD]

AIT - Austrian Institute of Technology, Vienna, Austria
daniele.pretolesi@ait.ac.at

Abstract. In mobile technologies for health and well-being (mHealth), push notifications are a widely used tool to implement persuasive strategies. However, little research has been carried out to investigate the impact of notifications in such technologies and users' attitudes towards them. In this study, we address this gap by exploring the role of notifications and their customisation in the context of mobile applications that promote social and mental well-being. Based on observational data collected from 152 participants, we investigate users' attitudes and preferences towards notifications. Moreover, we explore how users' attitudes towards notifications differ along demographic dimensions. Our findings show that customisation of notifications is a desired feature that can be used to improve the persuasive aspect of mHealth applications.

Implications derived from our study can provide guidance for researchers and practitioners alike when designing app notifications to create better motivating, meaningful, and persuasive experiences.

1 Introduction

Mobile technology solutions for health and well-being (mHealth) often implement persuasive strategies in their design to keep the users engaged and motivated, and induce behaviour change efforts [31]. These strategies are integrated into the various interface elements of the respective applications and include diverse approaches, such as personalisation, self-monitoring, commitment, and reminders.

With the ubiquity of smartphones, push notifications present a convenient and commonly utilised vehicle for implementing such strategies, as they can help engage users in everyday contexts, evoke immediate action through reminders, motivators and nudges, and support sustained behaviour change and habit formation.

Despite a large amount of research on behaviour change strategies in persuasive technology, little is known about the role notifications play in such systems, how users perceive them, or how they should best be delivered.

In the persuasive technology domain, notifications have primarily been explored in terms of content personalisation and delivery optimisation [17,26],

The original version of this chapter was revised: an acknowledgement was added. The correction to this chapter is available at https://doi.org/10.1007/978-3-031-30933-5_27

J. Ham et al. (Eds.): PERSUASIVE 2023, LNCS 13832, pp. 410–424, 2023.
https://doi.org/10.1007/978-3-031-30933-5_26

while information on attitudes, customisation preferences and best design practices are limited. In these areas, insights mostly come from research that tends to be either general or about specific domains, such as marketing and advertisement [41]. Arguably, these insights do not necessarily transfer to solutions that aim to increase users' health and well-being, as they are guided by different purposes and motivations.

In this study, we aim to address the mentioned gap by exploring the role of notifications and their customisation by mapping the insights to support healthy activities and well-being support. To achieve this, we have formulated four research questions.

RQ1: What are users' attitudes and practices regarding notifications?

RQ2: What are users' attitudes and practices regarding notifications in health and well-being apps?

RQ3: Which customisation features do users deem most useful?

RQ4: To what extent do the aforementioned attitudes and practices differ between user groups?

The contributions of this paper are threefold. First, this work will contribute to persuasive research by examining the role of notifications in mHealth applications and how different user groups respond to them. Second, our study will provide insights into the users' attitudes toward notifications. We will examine how users' attitudes impact the perceived usefulness of notifications and the role of customisation in increasing their acceptance. Third, the results of this work will inform the discussion on future designs of notifications for mHealth and persuasive technologies.

2   Related Work

2.1   Push Notifications

Estimates of the average number of push notifications that smartphone users encounter range within a few dozen per day [1,6]. However, the number significantly varies between users, as they interact with different apps, use different settings, and exhibit different interaction patterns.

Notifications also vary in their purpose and content. While some notifications might only passively provide the user with certain information, others intend to elicit a response, commonly by encouraging the user to engage with the sending application. The user's reaction to the notification depends on various factors, ranging from contextual considerations, such as timing and location, to the user's relationship and attitudes towards the sender or source application [27,39].

Attitudes towards push notifications are often negative, as they can be regarded as annoying or distracting, especially when triggered too often and in inopportune situations [10,16,26,42]. In general, notifications are perceived to be most useful and elicit the most frequent and fastest responses if they pertain to communication with real people (e.g., from messaging apps) [27,33,39]. The perceived usefulness of some notifications is also what offsets some of the negative attitudes in general, as users do not wish to miss important information [9].

Regarding setting preferences, research has shown that, in most cases, users tend to accept default options, or if they don't, they usually do not implement further changes once they have been initially set [33,40]. It should be noted, however, that this does not necessarily entail satisfaction with the settings, as users might not wish to put in the effort needed to find the optimal solution [39].

To provide the best experience and outcomes for the users, guidelines for designing notifications suggest that they should provide explanations on their nature, as well as customisation features, such as opt-out and opt-in options and preference settings [39].

2.2 Notifications in Applications for Health and Well-Being

In the context of applications for health and well-being, several works have illustrated how notifications can positively impact users' adherence and commitment to the intervention programs [2,12,15].

Whether notifications could be intended for any purpose that aims to bring the users' attention to the solution, a comprehensive review of persuasive strategies in mHealth applications primarily identified their role in delivering reminders, for example, to exercise, meditate, or track food, drink, and medicine intake [31]. Reminders help keep the users engaged [2], which is particularly important in regard to the formation of habits, as for most behaviour change interventions, sustained engagement is required for positive outcomes.

In the field of persuasive technology, notifications are also often utilised as a vector for delivering motivational messages. This topic is of particular interest in the research of personalising persuasive strategies and represents a valuable effort, as motivation is an essential prerequisite for change in behaviour [8,29].

Another stream of research in the field regards optimizing the delivery of notifications, be it in terms of timing, frequency, or context [27,28]. Such research aims to automatize the detection of opportune situations for engagement and personalise the interaction patterns to best fit individual users. This too, is an important cause, as sub-optimal notification strategies can lead to dismissal and disengagement.

2.3 The Role of Customisation

The role of customisation (user-controlled adaptation) in persuasive technologies has been a topic of the research field since its inception [18,19,24,25,34], often proposed as a way to increase the persuasive aims of the system [21–23]. At the same time, customisation is said to offer a more ethical alternative to inferred personalisation (system-controlled adaptation), which may be burdened by ethical considerations, such as privacy and the facilitation of biases [30,36,37].

The common argument for implementing customisation features in designing applications states that enabling the user more agency over system parameters will allow them to better tailor the experience to their needs. Additionally, it has been proposed that in the context of motivational technology, customisation can bring about secondary benefits, as it imbues the user with a sense of personal agency, autonomy, and self-determination [35]. Such theoretical benefits considered, empirical inquiries have not been as supportive and showed that enabling elaborate customisation options might only benefit a specific type of user - namely those that already possess a high need for autonomy [4]. Indeed, excessive customisation might even be regarded as inconveniencing, as it requires additional engagement and effort from the users [25], going against the common design principle of simplicity.

This was found to be especially relevant in the design of technologies for mental health, where users might struggle with low cognitive and motivational capacity [43]. For such users, greater automatic input might be desired from the system, however, the promotion of engagement should not be neglected. Regardless of the users' mental state, the relationship between user autonomy and the amount of burden should be at the forefront of designers' considerations when implementing customisation options.

When it comes to specific customisation features, studies in the domain of persuasive technology for health and wellness have primarily explored their role in intervention programs, for example, through planning physical activity, setting goals, and tracking progress [38,43]. Other domains include the customisation of aesthetic characteristics, such as the setting of theme and sound, or in a specific case where persuasive messages were delivered through an animated character, the avatar's appearance [20].

Customising Notifications. To our knowledge, no study on applications for health and well-being has explicitly explored the role of customisation in regard to push notifications. While some studies utilise applications with such features [2,28], for example, for setting the timing or frequency of notifications, they are not the primary focus of evaluation and minimal information is provided concerning their contribution to performance metrics or about users' attitudes and preferences.

Nevertheless, the limited observations from the existing literature suggest that such features might be desired [29]. The option to set the time range of notifications can, for example, help users limit their use only to opportune times (e.g., when they are not at work) while setting the desired number can limit unnecessary disturbances. Such features might also be beneficial concerning habituation, as users might only find notifications practical when they first interact with the application, but not after they have become accustomed to it [28]. Furthermore, if the notifications regard different types of content or senders, the user might only wish to opt-in for some but not others.

3   Methods

To answer our research questions, we set out to survey a diverse population of users on their attitudes and practices concerning notifications, specifically in regard to notifications in health and well-being applications. The survey and analysis methods are described in detail in the following sections.

3.1   Materials

To understand participants' attitudes towards notifications and their customisation aspects, we designed a questionnaire partially inspired by the existing literature [27,43]. The survey had three main sections concerning attitudes and practices regarding (i) notifications in general, (ii) notifications in applications for health and well-being, and (iii) customisation settings for notifications. For the third section, we designed six mockups visualising different customisation options and participants received questions on their attitudes towards the different options. Additionally, participants were requested to complete the affinity for technology interaction (ATI) scale [11] and provide demographic information. The complete questionnaire, dataset, and analysis results are available in a GitHub repository for public access[1].

3.2   Sample

The participants were recruited using the Bilendi platform [3] (Bilendi Technology S.A.R.L., Paris, France). Bilendi is an online crowdsourcing service specialising in market research. The platform was chosen due to its focus on users residing in European countries and its high ethical and quality standards. The subjects received compensation for their participation.

The sample was constructed to reflect the general population by being gender-balanced and equally sampling from three age groups (<25, 25–60, >60). The final sample contained 152 respondents (77 male, 73 female, one non-binary, and one not specified) with an average age of 42 ($SD = 20.9$). Fifty-eight respondents had vocational, 52 had upper secondary, 37 had a university, and 5 had compulsory primary education.

3.3   Data Processing and Analysis

The data were processed and analysed using R 4.1.2 [32]. For descriptive analysis, response frequencies were calculated for the individual items. For the assessment of participants' preferences regarding the customisation options, cumulative link models were computed using the *ordinal* package [7]. Separate models were defined for each questionnaire item about the customisation options (i.e., three models). The models were specified with the respective preference item (i.e., five categories from 'strongly disagree' to 'strongly agree') as a response

---

[1] https://github.com/DanielePretolesi.

variable, the customisation options (i.e., options a to f) as a categorical fixed effect and subject as a random effect.

To assess relationships between response variables and demographic dimensions, two groups for gender (female, male) three groups for age (<25, 25–60, >60), and three groups for technological affinity (low, mid, high) were considered. Participants that identified as non-binary or did not specify their gender were excluded from demographic analysis due to insufficient sample size in these groups. For inferential assessment of group differences, cumulative link models were computed for ordinal response variables and χ^2 tests for outcomes on a nominal scale. p-values were adjusted for all analyses using Holm's method [14].

For open-ended questions, responses were analysed by inductively creating groupings of the answers inspired by thematic analysis [5].

4   Results

In this section, we present the results of our analysis. Due to limited space in the publication format, we report our findings in a condensed form. More detailed results including comprehensive descriptive statistics and regression coefficients are available in the repository referenced above.

4.1   Attitude Towards Notifications

Regarding general attitudes toward notification, 42.8% of respondents find notifications useful, 41.5% disruptive, while 28.3% reported feeling neutral towards them.

When asked whether they feel in control of the number and type of notifications they receive, 50% reported feeling in control, while 20.3% did not. The rest (29.6%) were neutral toward the matter.

Regarding the type of applications that participants deem the most useful to receive notifications from, Messaging (45.4%), News (37.5%), and Social Networks (32.9%) are considered the most useful. Concerning applications for health and well-being, 19.1% of respondents considered them a useful source of notifications.

When asked whether they manage notifications on their smartphones, the majority of the respondents answered that they do (61.2%), while the rest do not (25.7%), do not know how to do it (4.6%), or are not aware of the possibility (8.6%).

When asked what the most useful aspects of notifications are, most respondents considered the ability to receive important news and information at a glance to be the most valuable. Regarding the disruptiveness of notifications, the respondents mostly cited advertisements, non-relevant notifications, and high frequency as the primary sources of annoyance. Lastly, we asked participants how notifications could be made less disruptive. Reducing the number of notifications sent, increasing control over notifications settings, and importance filtering were identified as the most important aspects to improve notification acceptance.

4.2 Attitude Towards Notifications in Apps for Health and Well-Being

Approximately a third (35%) of the participants reported using applications for health and well-being. Among those, physical activity and fitness were most common (79.2%), followed by nutrition (47.2%), health assessment and healthcare (24.5%), and emotional and mental health (11.3%). Out of the 53 participants who reported regularly using such applications, 34 reported receiving notifications, with all but one finding them useful. According to these respondents, they find notifications useful to stay informed (51.5%) followed by getting motivated (48.5%), and keeping engaged with the application (48%). Only 12.1% finds them useful to stay connected with other people.

When respondents were asked for feedback about the optimum notification frequency in such applications, 39.5% responded with less than once a week, followed by one per day (27%), and once a week (23%). Should the frequency be too high, respondents mostly agreed (selected "agree" or "highly agree" on a 5-point Likert scale) that they would ignore the notifications (66.5%), followed by disabling them in the settings (63.1%) and deleting the app (33%).

Finally, we asked the participants about their preferences regarding notification types, with reminders and alerts being the most favoured. The rest of the distribution of the preferences is available in Fig. 1.

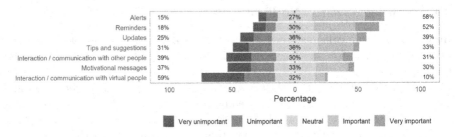

Fig. 1. Answer distributions for the question *"In terms of apps for health and well-being, how important do you find the following types of notifications?"*.

4.3 Customisation Preferences

Regarding customisation preferences, most participants (81.6%) think it is important to be able to adjust the number of notifications they receive and to determine when they should receive them (60.5%). Similarly, most respondents (79%) deem it very important to set what type of notifications they receive.

Regarding mock-ups showing different customisation options, their presentation and ratings of agreement with related questionnaire items for evaluation are available in Fig. 2. It can be observed that option *d* received most favourable ratings across all items. There, 65.5% of respondents agreed that the features gives them a sense of control, 59.2% answered that they would it to tailor notifications to their needs, and only 30% reported that they would turn off notifications completely when presented with the option.

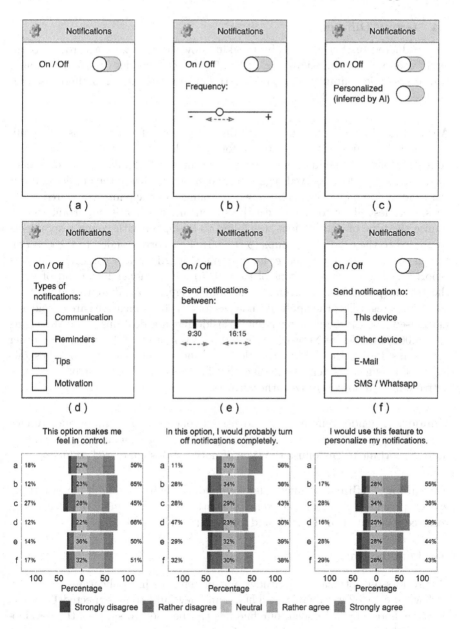

Fig. 2. The customisation options presented in the survey and the respondents' attitudes towards them.

4.4   Group Differences

We conducted further analysis by breaking down the answers according to different user groups, namely by age (<25, 25–60, >60), gender (male and female), and technological affinity (low, mid, high). For more details on methods used for analysis refer to Sect. 3.3.

Age. Regarding the usefulness and disruptiveness of notifications, a significant age difference with $p < 0.001$ for both conditions was identified with young participants having more positive sentiments. A significant age difference ($p < 0.001$) was also observed regarding the option to delete the application if it was sending too many notifications, where younger participants, compared to old ones, were less likely to agree with the statement. Finding it important to customise the type of notifications was found to be higher with young respondents compared to the other two groups ($p < 0.05$). This corresponded to the observation in customisation preferences for option d (Fig. 2d), where young respondents reported a higher sense of control ($p < 0.05$) and a higher likelihood of using the option ($p < 0.01$). Additionally, we found significant differences among the age groups regarding the application types for which notifications are considered most useful, with young participants considering notifications from Messaging ($p < 0.001$) and Social Networks ($p < 0.01$) apps more useful compared to other age groups. Lastly, the analysis revealed a significant difference ($p < 0.001$) showing that young users tend to manage notifications on their smartphones more actively in comparison to the other groups.

Gender. A gender difference was identified concerning the importance to customise the type of notifications received ($p < 0.01$), with females considering it more important to customise the type of notifications compared to males.

Technology Affinity. Concerning technology affinity, the high affinity group was observed to report a higher sense of control over the number of notifications received, compared to the mid- and low-affinity groups ($p < 0.05$).

5   Discussion

Our results on notification attitudes and preferences in applications for health and well-being offer valuable insights, some new and some expected based on previous knowledge. As such, our findings can be used to support the development of the research field and inform further application design. This is particularly important for the persuasive technology community, as such applications are a popular subject in the field and commonly use notifications as vectors to implement persuasive strategies. However, in the research context, notification strategies are often implemented naively of user preferences and tested in experimental conditions which might not necessarily translate to everyday use.

In the following, we summarise our findings according to the research questions and conclude by describing their key implications.

5.1   RQ1: What Are Users' Attitudes and Practices Regarding Notifications?

Overall, our results align with the attitudes towards notifications already known in the literature, showing that users view push notifications as useful but disruptive while revealing significant variability in attitudes. As expected, notifications are deemed the most useful when they come from messaging apps, followed by news and social media. Most respondents use notification settings, whereas the feedback received in the open-ended question suggested that having options to control notifications is generally desired.

5.2   RQ2: What Are Users' Attitudes and Practices Regarding Notifications in Health and Well-Being Apps?

About a third of the respondents answered that they use applications for health and well-being, with physical activity and fitness apps being the most common. These respondents overwhelmingly perceived notifications from these apps as useful, primarily for keeping themselves informed, motivated and engaged.

We further asked the respondents about their preferences in an arbitrary health and well-being application. Regarding notification content, reminders and alarms were rated as the most valuable features, whereas motivational messages and notifications regarding social interaction, particularly with virtual people, were deemed relatively unimportant. This offers practical information for the research field, as motivational messaging and virtual coaching are often utilised as strategies to support behaviour change. However, in terms of general acceptance, our results question their employment should they use notifications to engage end users.

Furthermore, concerning the optimum notification frequency, most respondents preferred once per week or less and about a third favoured once per day. Only a handful of respondents would like multiple notifications per day. This is an important observation, as the mHealth apps used in the academic community often utilise strategies where persuasive notifications are sent multiple times per day [17, 28]. This is a notable discrepancy, as it points out that the solutions proposed by researchers are not necessarily in line with user needs and preferences in everyday context. However, as previous research suggests, more frequent notifications may not necessarily deter users from engagement [27, 28], while our results imply that the most likely reaction to too many notifications would be disabling them in the settings, rather than disengaging by deleting the app.

5.3   RQ3: Which Customisation Features Do Users Deem Most Useful?

Respondents considered all the suggested components for customising notifications important, primarily frequency, followed by type, timing and source. This further suggests that there was a high desire among respondents for comprehensive customisation options, which was additionally informed by ratings of our proposed mock-ups. Although the differences between the mock-ups were minimal, Option *d* (Fig. 2d), which, in addition to an on-/off- button, offered an opt-in/out menu of notification types, was most favourably rated by the respondents. This was apparent by both the low rating of the likelihood of entirely switching off notifications and high ratings of feelings of control and supposed use. These results further strengthen the previous findings on the importance of customisation [34, 36] while contributing novel insights to the customisation of notification which could positively benefit the effectiveness of persuasive strategies in mHealth applications.

5.4 RQ4: To What Extent Do the Aforementioned Attitudes and Practices Differ Between User Groups?

Most prominent results could be observed concerning age, where older respondents (>60) were more likely to find notifications less useful and more disruptive. They were also less likely to use notification settings and more likely to delete the application if they felt the number of notifications was overwhelming. The optimum notification frequency for health and well-being apps was also observed to be decreasing with age.

Some trends could also be observed in gender differences, particularly in the types of apps from which notifications are deemed most practical (e.g., messaging and social media for women and news and finance for men). While the ratings for apps for health and well-being did not differ, there was some discrepancy in the optimum frequency of notifications, with women leaning towards more frequent options. Lastly, our results show that, compared to men, women consider it more important to customise the type of notifications.

Finally, we observed some trends regarding technology affinity. Respondents who scored higher on the ATI metrics were more likely to find notifications useful. This corresponds to the observations that they were more likely to use notification management settings and felt more in control of the type and number of notifications they received.

5.5 Implications for Health and Well-Being App Design

Overall, our results identify several aspects that previous research has not considered to improve the design of applications for health and well-being. Based on our findings, we derived five design implications:

1. Notification customisation is a desired feature and should be present in mHealth apps that utilize them in their persuasive strategies.
2. Easy access to customisation options should be provided to allow selecting which type of notifications one will receive.
3. Notifications should not be sent with a high frequency by default (preferably between one notification per day and less than one per week depending on target group and context).
4. Alerts and reminders should be prioritized over other notification types.

5. Notifications should be designed keeping in mind the differences in user groups, particularly in regard to age.

We hope that these design implications will provide more useful information for designing effective apps that rely on notifications to implement their persuasive strategies.

6   Limitations

The primary limitation of the study is that it was conducted as a survey and regarded notification use in an unspecified mHealth app. Therefore, the answers were collected devoid of real-life contexts and situations that shape users' perceptions and behaviours, limiting the generalisability of the findings.

Second, the survey was conducted only in Germany, which restricts the extrapolation of its findings outside its borders. While similar patterns could likely be observed in surrounding and other WEIRD countries [13], they are likely not as applicable to other cultural contexts.

7   Conclusion

In this work, we sought to survey user preferences and attitudes towards push notifications in general, with a more particular focus on applications for health and well-being. Our results are in line with previous research, while they also contribute novel insights particular to the design of mHealth applications. We observed that the customisation of notifications is a desired feature, which was only assumed or alluded to in previous research. We further investigated which aspects of potential customisation features are most preferable and concluded that users most desire control over notification type and frequency. Additionally, we identified significant differences in user groups, mostly related to age, which should be used to inform the design of future behaviour change approaches in mHealth applications.

Future research should further explore notifications usages in the wild by recording participants' sentiments towards notifications and different customisation approaches. Additionally, the customisation features proposed in this work should be implemented and tested to validate the current findings.

Acknowledgement. This work was conducted under the Buddy4All project. The project Buddy4All (no AAL-2021-8-77-CP) has received funding from AAL JP, co-funded by the European Commission and National Funding Authorities of country Austria, Switzerland and Portugal: FFG, Schweizer Eidgenossenschaft, Fundação para a Ciência e a Tecnologia.

References

1. Airship: Push Notifications & Mobile Engagement: 2021 Benchmarks. Technical report (2022). www.airship.com/resources/benchmark-report/push-notifications-mobile-engagement-2021-benchmarks/

2. Bentley, F., Tollmar, K.: The power of mobile notifications to increase wellbeing logging behavior. In: Proceedings of the SIGCHI Conference on Human Factors in Computing Systems, pp. 1095–1098 (2013)
3. Bilendi Technology: November 2022. https://bilendi.tech/
4. Bol, N., Høie, N.M., Nguyen, M.H., Smit, E.S.: Customization in mobile health apps: explaining effects on physical activity intentions by the need for autonomy. Digital Health **5**, 2055207619888074 (2019)
5. Braun, V., Clarke, V.: Thematic analysis. American Psychological Association (2012)
6. BusinessOfApps: Push Notifications Statistics. Technical report (2022). www.businessofapps.com/marketplace/push-notifications/research/push-notifications-statistics/
7. Christensen, R.H.B.: ordinal–regression models for ordinal data (2022), r package version 2022.11-16. https://CRAN.R-project.org/package=ordinal
8. Curtis, K.E., Lahiri, S., Brown, K.E.: Targeting parents for childhood weight management: development of a theory-driven and user-centered healthy eating app. JMIR Mhealth Uhealth **3**(2), e3857 (2015)
9. Fischer, J.E., Greenhalgh, C., Benford, S.: Investigating episodes of mobile phone activity as indicators of opportune moments to deliver notifications. In: Proceedings of the 13th International Conference on Human Computer Interaction with Mobile Devices and Services, pp. 181–190 (2011)
10. Fischer, J.E., Yee, N., Bellotti, V., Good, N., Benford, S., Greenhalgh, C.: Effects of content and time of delivery on receptivity to mobile interruptions. In: Proceedings of the 12th International Conference on Human Computer Interaction with Mobile Devices and Services, pp. 103–112 (2010)
11. Franke, T., Attig, C., Wessel, D.: A personal resource for technology interaction: development and validation of the affinity for technology interaction (ati) scale. Int. J. Hum.-Comput. Inter. **35**(6), 456–467 (2019)
12. Gravenhorst, F., et al.: Mobile phones as medical devices in mental disorder treatment: an overview. Pers. Ubiquit. Comput. **19**(2), 335–353 (2015)
13. Henrich, J., Heine, S.J., Norenzayan, A.: The weirdest people in the world? Behav. Brain Sci. **33**(2–3), 61–83 (2010)
14. Holm, S.: A simple sequentially rejective multiple test procedure. Scandinavian J. Statist., 65–70 (1979)
15. Horsch, C., Spruit, S., Lancee, J., van Eijk, R., Beun, R.J., Neerincx, M., Brinkman, W.P.: Reminders make people adhere better to a self-help sleep intervention. Heal. Technol. **7**(2), 173–188 (2017)
16. Iqbal, S.T., Horvitz, E.: Notifications and awareness: a field study of alert usage and preferences. In: Proceedings of the 2010 ACM Conference on Computer Supported Cooperative Work, pp. 27–30 (2010)
17. Jankovič, A., Kolenik, T., Pejović, V.: Can personalization persuade? study of notification adaptation in mobile behavior change intervention application. Behav. Sci. **12**(5), 116 (2022). https://doi.org/10.3390/bs12050116
18. Kalyanaraman, S., Sundar, S.S.: The psychological appeal of personalized content in web portals: does customization affect attitudes and behavior? J. Commun. **56**(1), 110–132 (2006)
19. Kalyanaraman, S.S., Wojdynski, B.W.: Affording control: How customization, interactivity, and navigability affect psychological responses to technology. The handbook of the psychology of communication technology, pp. 425–444 (2015)
20. Kang, H., Kim, H.K.: My avatar and the affirmed self: psychological and persuasive implications of avatar customization. Comput. Hum. Behav. **112**, 106446 (2020)

21. Kang, H., Sundar, S.S.: When self is the source: effects of media customization on message processing. Media Psychol. **19**(4), 561–588 (2016)
22. Kaptein, M.: Persuasion profiling: How the internet knows what makes you tick. Business Contact (2015)
23. Kaptein, M., Markopoulos, P., De Ruyter, B., Aarts, E.: Personalizing persuasive technologies: explicit and implicit personalization using persuasion profiles. Int. J. Hum. Comput. Stud. **77**, 38–51 (2015)
24. Mackay, W.E.: Triggers and barriers to customizing software. In: Proceedings of the SIGCHI Conference on Human Factors in Computing Systems, pp. 153–160 (1991)
25. Marathe, S., Sundar, S.S.: What drives customization? control or identity? In: Proceedings of the SIGCHI Conference on Human Factors in Computing Systems, pp. 781–790 (2011)
26. Mehrotra, A., Hendley, R., Musolesi, M.: Prefminer: Mining user's preferences for intelligent mobile notification management. In: Proceedings of the 2016 ACM International Joint Conference on Pervasive and Ubiquitous Computing, pp. 1223–1234 (2016)
27. Mehrotra, A., Pejovic, V., Vermeulen, J., Hendley, R., Musolesi, M.: My phone and me: understanding people's receptivity to mobile notifications. In: Proceedings of the 2016 CHI Conference on Human Factors in Computing Systems, pp. 1021–1032 (2016)
28. Morrison, L.G., et al.: The effect of timing and frequency of push notifications on usage of a smartphone-based stress management intervention: an exploratory trial. PLoS ONE **12**(1), e0169162 (2017)
29. Nour, M.M., Rouf, A.S., Allman-Farinelli, M.: Exploring young adult perspectives on the use of gamification and social media in a smartphone platform for improving vegetable intake. Appetite **120**, 547–556 (2018)
30. Orji, R., Oyibo, K., Tondello, G.F.: A comparison of system-controlled and user-controlled personalization approaches. In: Adjunct publication of the 25th Conference on User Modeling, Adaptation and Personalization, pp. 413–418 (2017)
31. Oyebode, O., Ndulue, C., Alhasani, M., Orji, R.: Persuasive mobile apps for health and wellness: a comparative systematic review. In: International Conference on Persuasive Technology, pp. 163–181. Springer (2020)
32. R Core Team: R: A Language and Environment for Statistical Computing. R Foundation for Statistical Computing, Vienna, Austria (2021). http://www.R-project.org/
33. Sahami Shirazi, A., Henze, N., Dingler, T., Pielot, M., Weber, D., Schmidt, A.: Large-scale assessment of mobile notifications. In: Proceedings of the SIGCHI Conference on Human Factors in Computing Systems, pp. 3055–3064 (2014)
34. Sundar, S.S.: Self as source: agency and customization in interactive media. In: Mediated Interpersonal Communication, pp. 72–88. Routledge (2008)
35. Sundar, S.S., Bellur, S., Jia, H.: Motivational technologies: a theoretical framework for designing preventive health applications. In: Bang, M., Ragnemalm, E.L. (eds.) PERSUASIVE 2012. LNCS, vol. 7284, pp. 112–122. Springer, Heidelberg (2012). https://doi.org/10.1007/978-3-642-31037-9_10
36. Sundar, S.S., Marathe, S.S.: Personalization versus customization: the importance of agency, privacy, and power usage. Hum. Commun. Res. **36**(3), 298–322 (2010)
37. Treiblmaier, H., Madlberger, M., Knotzer, N., Pollach, I.: Evaluating personalization and customization from an ethical point of view: an empirical study. In: Proceedings of the 37th Annual Hawaii International Conference on System Sciences, 2004, pp. 10 pp. IEEE (2004)

38. Wais-Zechmann, B., Gattol, V., Neureiter, K., Orji, R., Tscheligi, M.: Persuasive technology to support chronic health conditions: investigating the optimal persuasive strategies for persons with COPD. In: Ham, J., Karapanos, E., Morita, P.P., Burns, C.M. (eds.) PERSUASIVE 2018. LNCS, vol. 10809, pp. 255–266. Springer, Cham (2018). https://doi.org/10.1007/978-3-319-78978-1_21
39. Westermann, T.: User acceptance of mobile notifications. Springer (2017)
40. Westermann, T., Möller, S., Wechsung, I.: Assessing the relationship between technical affinity, stress and notifications on smartphones. In: Proceedings of the 17th International Conference on Human-Computer Interaction with Mobile Devices and Services Adjunct, pp. 652–659 (2015)
41. Wohllebe, A.: Consumer acceptance of app push notifications: systematic review on the influence of frequency. Int. J. Interact. Mob. Technol. (2020)
42. Xu, K., Zhu, M., Zhang, D., Gu, T.: Context-aware content filtering and presentation for pervasive and mobile information systems. In: 1st International ICST Conference on Ambient Media and Systems (2010)
43. Zhang, R., E. Ringland, K., Paan, M., C. Mohr, D., Reddy, M.: Designing for emotional well-being: integrating persuasion and customization into mental health technologies. In: Proceedings of the 2021 CHI Conference on Human Factors in Computing Systems, pp. 1–13 (2021)

Correction to: Notifying Users: Customisation Preferences for Notifications in Health and Well-being Applications

Daniele Pretolesi⬤, Lenart Motnikar⬤, Bieg Till⬤,
and Jakob Uhl⬤

Correction to:
**Chapter "Notifying Users: Customisation Preferences
for Notifications in Health and Well-being Applications" in:
J. Ham et al. (Eds.): *Persuasive Technology*, LNCS 13832,
https://doi.org/10.1007/978-3-031-30933-5_26**

The original version of the chapter was inadvertently published without acknowledgement in chapter 26. The acknowledgement has been added.

The updated original version of this chapter can be found at
https://doi.org/10.1007/978-3-031-30933-5_26

Author Index

J. Ham et al. (Eds.): PERSUASIVE 2023, LNCS 13832, pp. 425–426, 2023.
https://doi.org/10.1007/978-3-031-30933-5

Printed in the United States
by Baker & Taylor Publisher Services